Crossing Confessional Boundaries

Crossing Confessional Boundaries

The Patronage of Italian Sacred Music in Seventeenth-Century Dresden

MARY E. FRANDSEN

OXFORD

UNIVERSITY PRESS

2006

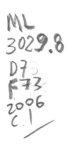

OXFORD
UNIVERSITY PRESS

Oxford University Press, Inc., publishes works that further
Oxford University's objective of excellence
in research, scholarship, and education.

Oxford   New York
Auckland   Cape Town   Dar es Salaam   Hong Kong   Karachi
Kuala Lumpur   Madrid   Melbourne   Mexico City   Nairobi
New Delhi   Shanghai   Taipei   Toronto

With offices in
Argentina   Austria   Brazil   Chile   Czech Republic   France   Greece
Guatemala   Hungary   Italy   Japan   Poland   Portugal   Singapore
South Korea   Switzerland   Thailand   Turkey   Ukraine   Vietnam

Copyright © 2006 by Oxford University Press, Inc.

Published by Oxford University Press, Inc.
198 Madison Avenue, New York, New York 10016

www.oup.com

Oxford is a registered trademark of Oxford University Press

Library of Congress Cataloging-in-Publication Data
Frandsen, Mary E., 1957–
Crossing confessional boundaries : the patronage of Italian sacred music
in seventeenth-century Dresden / Mary E. Frandsen.
     p. cm.
Includes bibliographical references and index.
ISBN-13 978-0-19-517831-9
ISBN 0-19-517831-9
1. Church music—Germany—Dresden—17th century. 2. Chapels royal—Germany—
Dresden. 3. Johann Georg II, Elector of Saxony, 1613–1680. 4. Dresden (Germany)—
Court and courtiers. I. Title.
ML3029.8.D7F73 2006
781.87'00943'214209032—dc22   2005010665

9 8 7 6 5 4 3 2 1

Printed in the United States of America
on acid-free paper

To my family

Acknowledgments

The research, writing, and publication of this book were made possible by the generosity of several philanthropic entities and institutions. I am grateful for the financial support that I received in the form of a National Endowment for the Humanities Summer Stipend, an American Council of Learned Societies Fellowship, and the research funds and leave year made possible by the Office of the Dean of the College of Arts and Letters at the University of Notre Dame. In addition, a Theodore Presser Award supported some of the research completed when I was a doctoral candidate. Most recently, generous publication subventions from the Manfred Bukofzer Publication Endowment Fund of the American Musicological Society and the Institute for Scholarship in the Liberal Arts at the University of Notre Dame helped to defray publication costs.

A number of institutions provided access to the materials in their music and manuscript collections, and also supplied microfilms, photocopies, and information. For this I am particularly indebted to the following institutions and their staffs: the Sächsisches Hauptstaatsarchiv Dresden, the Sächsische Landesbibliothek—Staats- und Universitätsbibliothek Dresden, the Uppsala Universitetsbibliotek, the Staatsbibliothek zu Berlin—Preußischer Kulturbesitz, Musikabteilung mit Mendelssohn Archiv, the Österreichische Nationalbibliothek, and the Hauptstaatsarchiv Stuttgart. Four libraries, the Sächsische Landesbibliothek—Staats- und Universitätsbibliothek Dresden, the Uppsala Universitetsbibliotek, the Staatsbibliothek zu Berlin, and the Bibliothèque royale de Belgique/Koninklijke Bibliotheek van België graciously granted permission to publish excerpts of musical works prepared from manuscripts and prints in their collections. Closer to home, I was aided tremendously in my research by the staff of the Interlibrary Loan office at the Theodore M. Hesburgh Library at the University of Notre Dame.

I also owe a great debt of gratitude to the many scholars who assisted me with translations: David Bachrach, Lars Berglund, Calvin Bower, Reinmar Emans and Monika Schmitz-Emans, Frederick K. Gable, Margaret E. Garnett, John Walter Hill, Gregory Johnston, Jeffrey Kite-Powell, Julia Marvin, Robert Norton, Ibo Ortgies,

Susan Parisi, and Edward Swenson. In addition, special thanks are due to Andrew H. Weaver, who prepared the electronic copy of the musical examples, as well to my students Haruhito Miyagi, who created the EPS files, and Jeremiah Heilman, who prepared several examples from the Albrici Mass.

Many scholars engaged with me in profitable exchanges of ideas and also provided me with scholarly help, information, and advice; others provided moral support. For their kind generosity, I would like to express my thanks and appreciation to Alexander Blachly, Lars Berglund, Laura Buch, Karen Buranskas, Veronica Buckley, Craig Cramer, Victor Crowther, Ken Dye, Jan Enberg, Dr. Karl-Wilhelm Geck, Walter Ginter, Beth Glixon, Edmund Goehring, Pastor Denise Grant and Ken Grant, Paula Higgins, Gregory Johnston, Andrew V. Jones, Robert Kendrick, Jeffrey Kurtzman, Peter Leech, Howard Louthan, Arnaldo Morelli, Mary Paquette-Abt, Paul Ranzini, Rev. Peter D. Rocca, CSC, Anne Schnoebelen, David Schulenberg, Daniel Stowe, Sigrid T'Hooft, Andreas Waczkat, Paul Walker, and Frau Christine Weisbach.

Finally, I must single out a number of individuals without whom this project could never have come to fruition. Prof. Kerala Johnson Snyder, my dissertation advisor at the Eastman School of Music, first steered me in the direction of these marvelous and undeservedly neglected Italian composers, and has lent unflagging support to me and my work for well over a decade now. Prof. Dr. Wolfram Steude took me under his wing during my first visit to Dresden in 1991, and has provided help and advice in innumerable ways since that time. Also in Dresden, Sieglinde and Helmut Petzold showed me extraordinarily generous hospitality during my many visits there. And finally, the members of my family have shown their great love, support, and belief in me throughout this long process. It is to them that this book is dedicated.

13 February 2005

Contents

Abbreviations

ASV	Archivio di Stato Veneto
BBKL	*Biographisch-Bibliographisches Kirchenlexikon*, electronic version [followed by volume:column(s)]
EQL	Robert Eitner, ed., *Biographisch-bibliographisches Quellen-Lexikon*
d	*denarii*
D-B	Staatsbibliothek zu Berlin – Preußischer Kulturbesitz, Musikabteilung mit Mendelssohn-Archiv
fl	*floren (gulden)*
gr	*groschen*
LU	*Liber usualis*
N. S.	New Style
GMO	*Grove Music Online*
PL	*Patrologia Latina*, electronic version [followed by volume: column(s)]
O. S.	Old Style
S-Uu	Uppsala University Library
Sächs HStA	Sächsisches Hauptstaatsarchiv Dresden
SLUB	Sächsische Landesbibliothek – Staats- und Universitätsbibliothek Dresden
tl	*taler*

NOTE ON THE CITATION FORMAT

An abbreviated citation format (Author_Publication Date:Page) has been used for secondary sources. Multi-volume works are cited as Author_Date-Volume:Page. Works by authors with multiple contributions from the same year are cited as Author_Date/Contribution Number:Page; the contribution numbers are given in the bibliography. Dates of first and second (or modern) editions are indicated with a slash (e. g. "1740/1994").

List of Musical Examples

Crossing Confessional Boundaries

Elector Johann Georg II (1656–1680), c. 1678, by Samuel Bottschildt (1641–1706). Oil on wood, Dresden: Historical Museum, G. G. 49. Original was destroyed in World War II; reproduction provided by the Deutsche Fotothek of the Sächsische Landesbibliothek—Staats- und Universitätsbibliothek Dresden. Used by permission of the Rüstkammer of the Staatliche Kunstsammlungen Dresden.

Prologue

The Forgotten *Mäzen* Johann Georg II

Staying in Venice amongst old friends, I discovered a method of
composition which has been considerably altered and has in part
put aside ancient styles, and will play with fresh enchantment on
today's ears; so that I might bring forth something adapted to the
modes of this school from the resources of my efforts in accordance with my purpose, I have devoted my spirit and strength to it.

— *Schütz, Symphoniae Sacrae I, xxix*

SO WROTE Schütz from Venice in 1629, in the preface to his collection of Latin
"sacred symphonies," published there that same year and dedicated to Prince
Johann Georg II of Saxony (1613–80), the son of his patron, Elector Johann Georg
I (r. 1611–56). Long regarded as an important statement from Schütz regarding his
engagement with the new Venetian style of the 1620s, the preface also stands as an
early testament to the musical inclinations of this young prince, who would in time
gather together one of the most expansive and cosmopolitan court musical ensembles in northern Europe. In his dedication, Schütz reveals that the young man was
already a formidable arbiter of musical taste, one who would "principally approve"
if the Kapellmeister could offer him "something from [his] studies which is not of
the common sort."[1] But for as much as it reveals of the prince's appreciation of music
at the advanced age of sixteen, this preface also holds a great irony, for nearly thirty
years later, as elector, this same Johann Georg II would introduce in his chapel yet
another "method of composition" that had been "considerably altered," and had "in
part put aside ancient styles," one that had also originated in an Italian musical center—Rome. But rather than serve to enrich and inform the musical style then current at the court, this new "method of composition" would usurp completely the
place of the works of the famous author of this encomium, in the very chapel in
which he had served for decades.

---

1. Schütz, *Symphoniae Sacrae I,* xxix.

In treatments of the political, social, and cultural history of Saxony, Elector Johann Georg II (r. 1656–80) generally receives only scant mention.[2] Scholars of musical life in Dresden during the Baroque era have focused their attention on the reigns of Johann Georg I, Friedrich August I (r. 1694–1733), and Friedrich August II (r. 1733–63), and have left the decades of the later seventeenth century largely unexplored. Historians have traditionally dismissed Johann Georg II as a rather insignificant sovereign, one equally famous for his profligate spending on events designed to project an image of wealth and power as for his mastery of the politics of vacillation in both the confessional and geopolitical arenas. His long-term impact as a politician may perhaps be characterized as minimal, particularly when compared to the contributions of such contemporaries as King Louis XIV (r. 1661–1715), Emperor Leopold I (r. 1658–1705), and "the Great Elector," Friedrich Wilhelm of Brandenburg (r. 1640–88). Undoubtedly his absence from the circle of major political players during this era has fostered a general view of his court as insignificant. But the resulting lack of attention to musical activity during his reign is unjustified, for here Johann Georg II stands as a bold and venturesome spirit, one who crossed confessional boundaries in order to introduce the most recent Italian sacred music into this Lutheran area of northern Europe. As elector of Saxony, he could easily have filled the post of Kapellmeister with any number of Lutheran composers—men such as Christoph Bernhard, Andreas Hammerschmidt, and Sebastian Knüpfer, whose compositional styles would have allowed him to forge a link with the musical past as defined by the music of Schütz. Yet rather than continue in the path of his father, Johann Georg II opted to break with tradition entirely. Thus he brought castrati to Dresden, appointed Roman composers as his Kapellmeisters, and advanced a new musical idiom in his court chapel, one whose influence would be felt in courts and cities as far away as Stockholm. With its large, Italian-dominated *Hofkapelle*, his court stood with those of the Holy Roman Emperor and the elector of Bavaria as one of the most important centers of musical patronage in the German-speaking lands.

As elector, Johann Georg II cultivated music in all three of the traditional spheres of court musical activity—the church, the chamber, and the theater. While not a center of opera, his court did mount performances of two Italian operas during his reign, as well as a number of German operas. Court documents also testify to the importance of music in the chamber, which usually took the form of *Tafelmusik* performed by a variety of ensembles, including the *Hofkapelle*, during extravagant meals held both in the castle and out-of-doors. But such performances hardly require an expensive troupe of Italian virtuosi. Johann Georg, however, seems to have developed a preference for Italian music early in life, likely as a result of

2. In the area of culture, however, a recent study forms an exception; see Watanabe-O'Kelly 2002.

Schütz's influence, and established his musical ensemble chiefly as a vehicle for the performance of Italianate sacred music during court worship services. He also left behind a record of musico-liturgical life at a mid-century Lutheran court that is as remarkable as it is rare, for it includes numerous orders of worship in which are recorded the musical works performed during weekly church services over a twenty-year period. The mere existence of such evidence testifies to Johann Georg's dedication to and determined cultivation of sacred music in the Italian style, but his desire to preserve a chronicle of his musical and liturgical achievements strongly suggests that he regarded both as important aspects of his legacy.

Undoubtedly a constellation of motivating factors, among them musical taste, an obsession with courtly representation and image creation, a desire to keep pace with developments in Vienna and Munich, and quite possibly Catholic leanings on his part, lay behind Johann Georg's decision to depart from the musical path forged by his father and to privilege things Italian in his chapel. But regardless of the particular configuration of impulses that fostered its genesis, an Italianate musical enterprise flourished in Dresden between 1650 and 1680, and behind this enterprise stood the person of Johann Georg II. Although the importance of the contributions of musicians to this venture cannot be understated, it is Johann Georg who ultimately must be credited with its success; given the number of elements—confessional, economic, and nationalistic—that conspired against it, such an ambitious undertaking undoubtedly would have failed in the absence of his vision, dogged determination, and willingness to take risks. Thus he stands at the center of this study, which in its broadest outlines is an examination of one seventeenth-century patron's realization of a musical ideal. It represents an attempt to remedy the lack of musicological attention to his court, and to shine a bright light on the period of tremendous musical growth and creativity that was the middle Baroque in Dresden, so that those musicians who made such developments possible—Vincenzo Albrici, Giuseppe Peranda, Carlo Pallavicino, and Sebastiano Cherici—might no longer languish in obscurity, but might take their places alongside those who have come to define the early and late Baroque eras in Dresden—Schütz on the one hand, and Heinichen, Hasse, and Zelenka on the other.

1
_____

The Advent of the Italians, 1651–56

D ESPITE HIS oft-bemoaned status as a cash-strapped monarch-in-waiting, at some point in 1650 Prince Johann Georg decided to take the radical step of enhancing his own musical ensemble with Italians.[1] His decision represents a fundamental change in his approach, for until this time the prince had either collaborated or consulted with Schütz in his various efforts to influence personnel decisions in his father's ensemble.[2] Now, with the war at an end and his father in his mid-sixties, the prince clearly began to think as a man who would soon inherit a throne and all of the rights and responsibilities attendant upon it–including the cultivation and maintenance of a powerful and glorious image–and thus began to prepare for his own future reign. Significantly, in the fall of 1649 the prince received a report extolling music in Venice from Henrich Hermann von Oeÿnhausen. An advisor to the prince's brother-in-law, Landgrave Georg II of Hessen-Darmstadt (r. 1626–61), Oeÿnhausen was traveling in Italy with the landgrave's son (and the prince's nephew), Ludwig VI (r. 1661–78).[3] Oeÿnhausen visited several of the major musical establishments in the Lagoon City and spoke with wonderment of what he heard:

> Otherwise music flourishes here most excellently. The Doge's Kapelle consists of 40 very good musicians, and the Kapellmeister is so excellent that His Imperial Majesty sought to gain his service, and offered him 4,000 *Reichsthaler;* after the Kapellmeister, the organist in the Kapelle is considered masterful and without peer. In sum, Parnassus is to be sought in Italy, which has no comparison anywhere. Not only are all of the discantists in the *cappella* here castrati, but even the altos as well, and they each possess a constant, unchangeable voice. We cannot easily have such voices in Germany,

1. For a discussion of the prince's musical ensemble in the 1630s and 1640s, see Frandsen 1997-1:1–25.
2. See Frandsen 2000.
3. In 1646, Henrich Hermann von Oeÿnhausen served as "Fürstl. Hessen Darmst. Raht und Junger Herrschafft Hoffmeister"; see Lenz 1985:258.

and must make due with those voices liable to change. There is a cloister here called *La Pietà*,[4] in which the orphans are girls; these make such music together that there is nothing that surpasses it; they excel in both vocal and instrumental music, and one of the older girls sings with such perfection that she is heard with astonishment; I have often wished that such music might resound in the electoral court chapel in Dresden.[5]

Oeÿnhausen was privileged to hear the cappella of Giovanni Rovetta, whom Emperor Ferdinand III did indeed attempt to lure to Vienna, and also enjoyed the keyboard virtuosity of Massimiliano Neri, who served as first organist at St. Mark's from 1644 to 1664.[6] Oeÿnhausen's enthusiastic description of the castrati at St. Mark's seems to have whetted the prince's musical appetite, for one of Johann Georg's next hires was the Venetian soprano castrato, Giovanni Andrea Angelini Bontempi (ca. 1624–1705). Oeÿnhausen may have heard Bontempi in the basilica that day and approached the singer concerning his possible relocation to Dresden.[7]

Not long after receiving Oeÿnhausen's letter, Prince Johann Georg embarked on an Italian musical adventure that would last for thirty years, and would alter the course of sacred music in Dresden as well as in middle Germany. By the spring of 1651, the prince had managed to expand his own musical ensemble (separate from that of his father) to include thirteen adults and five youths, and to hire six new musicians, among them three Germans (Ferdinand Francke, Balthasar Sedenig, and Johann Friedrich Volprecht) and three Italians (Bontempi, Stefano Sauli, and Giovanni Severo). Not only did this expansion in personnel open up new repertorial possibilities, it also marked the beginning of the era of the hegemony of the castrato in Dresden. Johann Georg II was by no means the first Saxon prince or elector to hire Italians; already in the sixteenth century, Antonio Scandello and Giovanni Battista Pinelli had served as Kapellmeister at the Dresden court, several Italian instrumentalists had served in the *Hofkapelle* of Elector Christian II, and violinists Carlo Farina and Francesco Castelli had briefly served in the *Hofkapelle* of Johann Georg I.[8] And Johann Georg II was certainly not the first Lutheran poten-

---

4. Serving as *maestro di coro* at the Ospedale La Pietà in 1649 was Antonio Gualtieri; see Baldauf-Berdes 1993:188.

5. Sächs HStA Loc. 8562/1, fols. 44v–45r, Henrich Herrmann von Oeÿnhausen to Johann Georg II, 21 September 1649. The German text appears in Appendix I (no. 1).

6. On the offer to Rovetta, see Saunders 1995:7; on Neri's career in Venice, see Sadie 1990:34.

7. Fürstenau suggested that Bernhard brought Bontempi back from Italy in ca. 1649–50 (*Zur Geschichte der Musik und des Theaters*, Fürstenau 1861/1971:40–41, unnumbered note); as Bernhard spent these years in Dresden and northern Germany, however, Oeÿnhausen appears the more likely candidate (see Frandsen 2000:23–25, 35).

8. See Landmann 1994:50–51, and Steude 2001/1:28–31.

tate to enhance his musical establishment with castrati; such singers had appeared in Copenhagen already in the 1630s, for example, and even earlier in Stuttgart.[9] However, in maintaining an Italian-dominated musical ensemble for three decades, and in entrusting Catholics exclusively with the musical leadership in his chapel, he stands alone among his co-religionists.

Surprisingly, given the wealth of archival evidence concerning music in Dresden during this era, documents that relate explicitly to the recruitment and hiring of musicians, whether Italian or German, have not survived, and all but one or two of the contracts of the Italian musicians hired between 1650 and 1680 have disappeared as well.[10] As a result, the dates of these three Italians' arrivals and appointments remain approximate. According to a financial document discovered by Beth Glixon, Bontempi was still in Venice in September 1650.[11] Neither Bontempi nor Sauli took part in a *Singballet* performed during a court wedding on 2 December 1650, which may suggest that neither had arrived in Dresden by that time, but the language of that libretto might also have hindered their participation in the performance. The possibility also exists that future court architect Wolf Caspar [von] Klengel, whom Prince Johann Georg sent to Italy in January 1651, played a role in the recruitment of any one or all three of the Italians.[12] The loss of the documentation, however, renders it impossible to determine either their arrival dates or the exact amounts of the presumably high salaries that the prince offered them. In letters of 17 and 22 February 1651 to his father's privy secretary, Christian Reichbrodt, the prince expressed an urgent need for money, as he had on numerous occasions during the previous decade, and stressed the considerable growth of his *Hofstaat* as one of the main reasons behind his appeal.[13] Surely the salaries of six new musicians, especially the large

9. In 1605, the Stuttgart court ensemble included one "Franciscus Franchini, Musicus"; the designation "musicus" often indicates a castrato (see Sittard 1890/1970:34). On castrati at the Danish court of Christian IV, see Hammerich 1892:114, 126–28.

10. Due to the loss of the contracts, one of the most significant surviving documents is a roster, drawn up in 1717, that lists nearly all of the musicians that served Johann Georg II when he was both prince and elector. This list, probably compiled from the contracts, provides the salary and departure date of each musician listed. See Sächs HStA Loc. 32751, Rep. LII. Gen. no. 849, fols. 145r–148v, reproduced in Spagnoli 1990:90–95.

11. ASV, Notarile atti, b. 11050, Piccini 1652, no. 1, 83v, 27 April 1652. I would like to thank Prof. Glixon for informing me of the existence of this and other Venetian archival documents concerning Bontempi, as well as for references to secondary materials. Discussions of several of the Italians who served in Dresden appear in Beth L. Glixon and Jonathan E. Glixon, *Inventing the Business of Opera: The Impresario and His World in Seventeenth-Century Venice*, AMS Studies in Music (New York: Oxford University Press, 2006).

12. Sächs HStA Loc. 8297/2, fol. 95r–v.

13. Sächs HStA Loc. 8563/2, fols. 187–88.

amounts paid to the Italians, would have exacerbated his financial duress.[14] Irrespective of their exact dates of arrival, all six musicians had joined the prince's ensemble by April 1651, for they appear on a roster drawn up in anticipation of a journey that the elector and prince would take to Lichtenburg later that same month.[15] The placement of Bontempi's name at the top of the list of eighteen musicians indicates that he had assumed the leadership of the prince's ensemble upon his arrival in Dresden. The roster also reveals the prince's priorities with respect to the disposition of higher vocal parts, as all of the eight singers are adult males[16]; the five choirboys listed are instrumentalists. But this Lichtenburg roster and related documents also attest to the growing musical strength of the prince's ensemble *vis a vis* that of the elector, and to the prince's willingness to assert some authority in matters musical, particularly when the court's reputation was at stake, for the records also include a list of the court musicians selected to make the trip to Lichtenburg. This group was dominated by the prince's musicians and apparently stood under the direction of Bontempi, for Schütz did not travel with the ensemble.[17]

Together with the rosters that he prepared for his father in April 1651, Prince Johann Georg also included an explanatory letter (given below). Apparently his father had asked him to supply a list of all of his musicians, including the recent arrivals, presumably to constitute a musical ensemble for the journey. Somehow Prince Johann Georg had "misunderstood" his father's request and had failed to mention two additional Italian musicians, both of whom had suddenly appeared at court two days earlier and had immediately ingratiated themselves with him:

> Herewith do I most obediently and humbly report to Your Grace that I reported the very same incorrectly today with respect to the musicians; I thought that Your Grace meant the Germans who have been with me and also those who have recently arrived from elsewhere; [of] the latter are two who came from elsewhere the day before yesterday, by the names of Bandino Bandini, contralto, and Gioseppe Amadei, tenor, which the late Kapellmeister in Denmark, Agostino Fontana, who so earnestly wanted to remain here, engaged for service with the present King in Denmark, where they are now going.[18]

14. According to Robert Eitner, Severo was appointed an instrumentalist in Prince Johann Georg's private cappella in 1651, at a salary of 600 tl—twice that received by Stolle and Werner; see *EQL* 9:149.

15. Sächs HStA Loc. 8687/1, fols. 247v–248r; reproduced in Spagnoli 1990:4.

16. The roster indicates that a number of the adults doubled as both singers and instrumentalists.

17. Sächs HStA Loc. 8687/1, fol. 248r. A list of the elector's musicians precedes the rosters of the prince's ensemble and the group selected to travel to Lichtenburg (ibid., fol. 247r; reproduced in Spagnoli 1990:3–4).

18. Sächs HStA Loc. 8563/2, fol. 191r. The German text appears in Appendix I (no. 2).

Neither singer remained in Dresden for long; both soon joined the musical ensemble of Danish King Frederik III.[19] But their appearance had significant musical consequences for the prince's cappella, for Bandini seems to have used his brief stay to engage in some significant musical politicking.

It seems that when faced with the problem of how a German Lutheran prince, with few if any contacts in Italy, might go about recruiting musicians there, Johann Georg first settled upon a rather unethical solution: the purloining of musicians from other northern courts. Thus, in the winter of 1651–52, the prince created something of a brouhaha when he attempted, through the agency of the castrati Bandini and Bontempi, to lure Italian musicians away from the Bavarian *Hofkapelle*. On 31 December 1651,[20] Electress Maria Anna of Bavaria (1609–1665), daughter of Emperor Ferdinand II, wrote to Elector Johann Georg I complaining that four of her Italian musicians had gone missing, having been lured away by Bandino Bandini.[21] According to the electress, Bandini had spent some time at the Bavarian court in 1650–51, and had left early in the spring of 1651 for Dresden, from whence he had promised "all manner of appeasement, such as a high salary, support, and gifts" to four of her musicians, Balthasar Pistorini, Pietro Zambonini, Francesco Santi, and Bartolomeo Sorlisi; as a result, the four had surreptitiously decided to leave Munich and enter the service of the Saxon prince.[22]

In his response of 5 January 1652, Elector Johann Georg I shared in the electress's indignation and assured her that the four were not presently in his son's ensemble.[23] He also indicated that the prince had allowed that Bandini had told him that Maria Anna's musicians had approached him about securing other positions. Still dissatisfied, however, Maria Anna wrote again to Johann Georg I on 9 February 1652 and now asserted that "Buntempi" (rather than Bandini) had sought positions for himself and others in Dresden, on his way to Denmark.[24] To demonstrate the validity of her assertion, she included evidence that Bontempi had negotiated in

19. Pirro 1913/1976:23.

20. Bavaria adopted the Gregorian reform of the calendar in 1583; see Cappelli 1969:30. In the discussion that follows, dates of the correspondence of the electress of Bavaria are N. S., those of the elector and prince of Saxony are O. S.

21. Sächs HStA Loc. 8561/5, no. 15, fols. 236r–237r.

22. "allerhandt vertrösten stattlicher besoldung, vnderhalt vnnd *Donativen*, welche er ihnen mit Vmbständen, vnnd einen ieden Acht hundert Thaller, iährliche *pension* hundert Duceten *di Donativo*, vnnd den raiß costen biß nach Treßen verspricht, dahin zuvermögen sich bemühet, das Sÿ hinderruckhs von hier ab: vnnd in E. L. Herrn Sohns diensten zue tretten sich entschlossen haben sollen" (Sächs HStA Loc. 8561/5, no. 15, fol. 236r-v).

23. Sächs HStA Loc. 8560/5, no. 21, fols. 55r–56r, Johann Georg I to Maria Anna of Bavaria, 5 January 1652.

24. Sächs HStA Loc. 8560/5, no. 21, fol. 57.

Augsburg with one of the four musicians, Pistorini, in an attempt to lure him away, and included a copy of the musician's statement of 10 January 1652 testifying to that fact.[25] In his statement, Pistorini revealed that Bontempi had negotiated with him in Augsburg regarding a position in Dresden, had offered him 300 tl for the trip to the Saxon capitol, and had insisted upon strict secrecy until such time that Pistorini had departed the Bavarian court. According to Pistorini's statement, Bontempi had sent the funds for Pistorini's travel to an Augsburg merchant on 18 January 1652 but had rescinded the order a few days later.[26] Upon receipt of this second letter from the electress, Elector Johann Georg I then questioned his son again about the matter and requested a list of the prince's musicians that included the details of their places of origin.[27] The prince dutifully provided such a list (reproduced below), which included none of the four Italians from Munich. In an accompanying letter he protested his innocence and attempted to explain away the situation as the simple result of the Bavarian electress's confusion of the names Bandini and Bontempi.[28] He also reassured his father that he would not hire any of the four musicians, should any of them show up looking for employment.

The true extent of Prince Johann Georg's involvement in this intrigue remains impossible to adduce with certainty, but Pistorini's statement implicates him to a considerable extent, for it suggests that he had dispatched Bontempi to Bavaria to negotiate for him.[29] Not surprisingly, no travel pass for Bontempi's secret journey to Bavaria has surfaced. A recently discovered Venetian notarial document, however, puts the castrato in Augsburg in December 1651—precisely when Pistorini was approached. Very conveniently for the prince, the death in Augsburg of one of Bontempi's relatives, Paulina Zonca, had necessitated that his music director travel to Bavaria to make arrangements for the funeral.[30] The prince's rather cheap attempt to blame the situation on an older woman's confusion suggests that he was trying to cover up Bontempi's activity, which he had doubtless authorized. Never did he allow

25. Sächs HStA Loc. 8560/5, no. 21, fol. 58.

26. Sächs HStA Loc. 8560/5, no. 21, fol. 58. Bontempi had established Munich connections already a decade before this incident occurred; see Sandberger 1901:xx. Sandberger (lxxxiv–lxxxv) includes a document that demonstrates that "ainen welschen Singer Khnaben von Perus, Namens Andre Bontempo" was in Munich in 1641 as a discantist at 30 fl per month, and indicates (xii) that Bontempi studied with Porro in Munich.

27. Sächs HStA Loc. 8560/5, no. 21, fol. 60r.

28. Ibid.

29. Karl August Müller briefly discussed this situation and concluded that the prince was not innocent of all charges; see Müller 1838:169–70; Fürstenau also made brief references to the episode (see 1849:74 and 1861/1971:10).

30. A Venetian notarial document dated 20 March 1653 makes reference to a debt incurred by Bontempi in Augsburg in December 1651 (ASV, Notarile atti 3471 Paulini).

that Bontempi had traveled to Bavaria during the period in question. All of the extant documentation, however, suggests that Prince Johann Georg's efforts were in vain, for none of the names of these Bavarian musicians appear on rosters from this period. Nevertheless, the contacts that the prince had established with these musicians did yield dividends in the future, for both Sorlisi and Santi joined his musical ensemble in the late 1650s.

The Bavarian correspondence also preserves a previously unknown roster (see below)[31] of the prince's musicians from January or February 1652, written in the prince's own hand, which reveals that his ensemble had grown by two members since April 1651: the prince had added a new violinist, Samuel Skahn (or Span), who had been a monk in Poland, and Christoph Magnus Naumann, a trombonist who hailed from Brussels.[32]

ROSTER OF PRINCE JOHANN GEORG'S MUSICIANS, JANUARY/FEBRUARY 1652

1. Giovanni Andrea Bontempi from Perugia, director, composer and discantist
2. Heinrich Groh, discantist
3. Friedrich Werner, alto and cornettist
4. Francisco Ferdinand Francke, tenor from Beuren
5. Philipp Stolle, tenor and theorbist
6. Stephano Sauli from Rome, bass
7. Christian Kittel, bass and viola da gamba
8. Michael Schmidt, bass and violinist from Bohemia
9. Giovanni Severo, violinist from Verona
10. Balthasar Sedenig, violinist from Rabe in Hungary
11. The new one [Samuel Skahn (or Span)], a violinist from Berlin "in the Mark" who was a monk in Poland[33]
12. Johann Friedrich Volprecht, violist and lutenist
13. Friedrich Westhoff, lutenist

---

31. Sächs HStA Loc. 8560/5, fol. 59r; the German original appears in Appendix I (no. 3). Here the spelling of most names has been regularized.

32. In the undated letter that accompanies this roster (in which the prince posits the "name confusion" theory), he explains to his father that he had left two names incomplete on the roster, which he had submitted the previous day. He identifies "the new one, a violinist from Berlin 'in the Mark'" as Samuel "Span" (Sächs HStA Loc. 8560/5, fol. 60r). On the 1717 roster, Samuel *Skahn* is listed as a violinist who remained at court until 1654 (see Spagnoli 1990:93). As the latter was likely drawn up from the actual contracts, it is probably a closer approximation of the spelling of the musician's name. In the same letter, the prince also supplies trombonist Nauman's full name.

33. See note 32 above.

14. Gottfriede Pasche, lutenist (is still a youth)
15. [Christoph Magnus] Nauman the sackbut player, who comes from Brussels
16. Matthias Weckmann, organist
17. and 18. Two youths who play the trumpet, and who can also play the sackbut and the "viol"
19. Yet another choirboy who studies the violin and sackbut[34]
20. Yet another choirboy who studies the organ and will be employed to copy music.

Recruitment Successes and Problems with Schütz

In the wake of the Bavarian debacle, Prince Johann Georg clearly recognized the need to develop a network of connections in Italy that would allow him to seek Italian musicians there. The first assistance that he received in this endeavor may have come from Bontempi's brother, Vincenzo Angelini.[35] According to a travel pass dated 9 March 1653, the prince sent one "Vincentium Angelini" to Italy to "undertake certain tasks" on his behalf, tasks which were to include some sort of procurement.[36] Angelini is likely the unnamed "agent" referred to by Müller and Fürstenau, both of whom indicated that the prince retained an agent in Venice for the purpose of engaging musicians; this agent also assumed responsibility for the prince's affairs in other Italian cities.[37] Bontempi himself also traveled to Italy early in the spring of 1653, for notarial documents place him in Venice on 20 March and 27 April[38]; his

---

34. Here again a number of instrumentalists are designated simply "Violist." Schmidt (no. 8), Severo (no. 9), Sedenig (no. 10), and Skahn (Span, no. 11) appear on the 1717 composite roster among the violinists; on the other hand, Johann Georg refers to Volprecht (no. 12) as a "Violist," and the 1717 roster lists him among the violists (*Bracisten*) (see Spagnoli 1990:93). The prince also specifies that the choirboy listed as no. 19 studies the violin ("*Geigen*").

35. In his monograph on Bontempi, Francesco Briganti quotes from a document that registers the death in Brufa (Torgiano) of one Giovanni Andrea Angelini on 28 March 1682 and identifies the deceased as the "son of the late Vincenzo Angelini of Perugia and carnal nephew of Signor Giovanni Andrea Angelini, musician"; see Briganti 1956:39: "A dì 28 Marzo 1682 Sig. Giovanni Andrea figlio del quondam Vincenzo Angelini da Perugia, nepote carnale del Sig. Giovanni Andrea Angelini musico, morì quì a Brufa a quattro ore di notte in circa."

36. Sächs HStA Loc. 8298/7, fol. 43r: "in Italiam se conferre, praesentem Vincentium Angelini ad expedienda quaedam negotia nostra."

37. Müller 1838:80, and Fürstenau 1861/1971:10.

38. As indicated in the notarial documents discussed above and ASV, Notarile atti, b. 1085, fol. 8, 23 March 1656.

Dresden travel pass, however, does not survive. Perhaps Angelini had traveled to Dresden to visit his brother, or had accompanied him to Saxony back in 1650/51; Johann Georg could easily have engaged him to look for musicians in Italy before his departure.

Assuming that they went in search of musicians, the trip of Bontempi and Angelini paid a dividend, for a comparison of the 1652 roster (above) with the composite roster of 1717 reveals that four Italian musicians arrived sometime after January/February 1652: the castrato Giuseppe Maria Donati, the tenor Stefano Boni, the bass Angelo Maria Donati,[39] and the organist Baldassare Manganoni, who served as Konzertmeister.[40] Although the evidence remains circumstantial at best, it is possible that Bontempi and/or his brother recruited any one or all of these musicians; a Venetian notarial document mentions the castrato with respect to the disposal of Manganoni's estate after his death, which may indicate a longstanding acquaintance with the organist.[41] The four likely represent those new musicians "recently arrived from Italy" that Prince Johann Georg asked Schütz to audition for him in June 1653.[42] The two Donati, who may have been related, may have come from Italy at this time; no information on their pre-Dresden careers has yet surfaced to suggest that they arrived from another northern court. The careers of Giuseppe Maria Donati (later known as *il Baviera*—"the Bavarian") and Stefano Boni testify to the quality of musician that Prince Johann Georg was able to lure to Dresden, if only for a short period of time. After his departure from Dresden in 1654, the castrato Donati enjoyed a career as a highly sought-after singer of opera and oratorio in Innsbruck, Venice, Bologna, Florence, and Rome.[43] Boni (d. 1688), who also joined the prince's ensemble during this period, served Archbishop Leopold Wilhelm in Brussels in the late 1640s and early 1650s; he traveled back to Venice from Brussels in 1649, but

---

39. It is possible that Donati's voice part was entered incorrectly on the 1717 roster, for a tenor by the same name served the emperor in Vienna from 1 October 1669 until 1670; see Köchel 1869/1976:63.

40. According to Fürstenau, court documents from 1652 on mention Manganoni as the prince's Konzertmeister (1861/1971:32; this evidence has not resurfaced). Manganoni's appointment to the position of Konzertmeister represents the inception of that title at the Dresden court.

41. ASV, Notarile atti, b. 6058, Federici 1655, fol. 80, 25 May 1655. According to Fürstenau (1861/1971:32), Manganoni died in Dresden in November 1654 and was buried in Kloster Marienstern (formerly Morgenstern) on 22 November. Kloster St. Marienstern lies about 40 kilometers northwest of Dresden in the region of Upper Lusatia (Oberlausitz), just outside of the small village of Panschwitz-Kuckau.

42. Schütz to Heinrich II of Reuss-Gera, 16 June 1653, in Jung 1972:233. See also the discussion of the events in 1653 in Frandsen 2000:5–7.

43. Both Donati left Dresden in 1654 (Spagnoli 1990:91–92). On Giuseppe Maria's later career, see Rostirolla 1982:722–25 and Monaldini 2000:248–55, 280, *et passim*.

was in Brussels again in 1650 and 1651.[44] Boni may have traveled to Dresden from Venice, or may have simply stopped in Dresden on his way to Vienna from Brussels, for he left the service of Prince Johann Georg for a position with the emperor, which he had assumed by 1 July 1654. Boni later broke his service to the imperial court for four years (1665–69), during which he returned to Venice, and sang both at St. Mark's and in operatic productions.[45]

Rather than further expand his own ensemble with these newly arrived Italians, however, Prince Johann Georg apparently placed them in his father's *Hofkapelle*, in an effort to revive that moribund ensemble.[46] In addition, in July or August 1653, the prince directed that his own ensemble, under Bontempi, serve in the court worship services on a regular basis, in alternation with his father's ensemble, under Schütz's direction.[47] These events stand in striking contrast to the prince's earlier cautious attempts to convince his father to hire Agostino Fontana and Christoph Werner[48]; now, as he had finally acquired the musical muscle to do so, the prince attempted to throw his weight around in the court chapel. In a letter of protest dated 21 August and addressed to three of the elector's chief advisors, Schütz took great umbrage at the prince's proposal that the two groups alternate, for he felt that "it would be demeaning and painful . . . to alternate regularly with a man three times younger than [himself] and castrated to boot, and to compete with him for favor, *pro loco*, as it were, before biased and for the most part injudicious audiences and judges."[49] In stark contrast to the prince's ensemble, the elector's *Hofkapelle* had regained only a small portion of its original strength by this time, and the embattled Kapellmeister clearly felt that his small group of musicians would suffer from comparison with the prince's ensemble of highly trained Italian virtuosi.[50] Two days later, he wrote directly to the prince, and, without stating so expressly, nevertheless lay the blame for the situation squarely at the prince's feet. He complained that he had been unfairly blamed

44. Algemeen Rijksarchief / Archives Génerales du Royaume, Manuscrits Divers no. 1374, fols. 6r–167r, *passim*; the references to Boni's trip to Italy appear on fols. 63v and 103v (this information was most kindly supplied by Sigrid T'Hooft).

45. See Köchel 1869/1976:59, 63, 67, Senn 1954:266, Emans 1981:66, and Termini 1981:71.

46. See also the discussion of the events of 1653 in Rifkin and Timms 1985:54–56, Rifkin 1985:655–56, and Moser 1959:208–9.

47. Schütz to [Senior Court Marshal] Heinrich Taube, [Senior Court Preacher] Jacob Weller, and [Privy Secretary] Christian Reichbrodt, 21 August 1653 (Spagnoli 1990:135).

48. See Frandsen 2000:15–22, 26–33.

49. Spagnoli 1990:135.

50. In February 1653, the roster of the *Hofkapelle* included two altos, a tenor, two basses, two organists, and five instrumentalists, as well as a timpanist and nonperforming personnel (Sächs HStA Loc. 8687/1, fol. 325v). The roster does not mention choirboys, but the prince's letter of September 1653 (discussed below) indicates that there were four.

for the presence of the Italians among the elector's musicians, which had apparently caused much displeasure to court officials.[51] With some urgency, Schütz implored the prince to intervene on his behalf and to set the record straight with these officials; his comments, and the tenor of the letter in general, reveal the sort of prejudiced resistance that the Italians encountered upon their arrival.

As a result of Schütz's protests, Prince Johann Georg seems to have pulled the Italians out of his father's ensemble and, on 30 September, offered instead a detailed plan for the improvement of that institution.[52] Here the rationale for the prince's actions of the previous two months becomes clearer, for he cannot quite disguise either his discomfiture over the pitiful condition in which the *Hofkapelle* still languished, or his fear that this threatened to damage his father's reputation in the eyes of his peers. But while the prince's latest plan for rejuvenating the electoral musical ensemble did not involve the participation of any Italians, it was nevertheless bound for failure, for not only did he recommend that his father pay his own musicians, he suggested that the elector expand the ensemble by ten or eleven members. In the prince's view, a "perfect ensemble in the eyes of all potentates" would include twenty vocalists, eight instrumentalists (among them violinists, a curtal player,[53] and a bombardist), and two organists, as well as "two good zink players and six sackbut players."[54] Some of these musicians, he pointed out, were already in the elector's service. So that the elector might have two singers in each of the three lower vocal ranges, Prince Johann Georg offered to transfer his own tenor and theorbist, Philipp Stolle, to the *Hofkapelle*. Lest his father think otherwise, however, the prince quickly pointed out that he himself could not compensate these additional musicians. Notwithstanding their futility, his suggestions do shed light on the prince's notion of an ensemble suitable for a potentate of his father's rank and position.

Despite his attempt to cloak his suggestions in a veil of altruism, however, the prince's ultimate design in offering this expansion plan emerges later in the letter: he still desired that the two ensembles alternate "both in church and at table."[55] Once constituted according to the prescription outlined by the prince, the elector's ensemble could alternate with that of his son in any venue, without putting either one at a disadvantage, and thus allaying Schütz's fears. Given the dismal state of his own finances, however, the elector almost certainly declared the prince's plan dead on arrival. After this, Prince Johann Georg never again attempted to interfere with the power structure at court as represented by the musical ensembles. Despite his genu-

---

51. Schütz to Prince Johann Georg II, 23 August 1653 (Spagnoli 1990:137–42).
52. Johann Georg II to Johann Georg I, 30 September 1653 (Spagnoli 1990:143–46).
53. The curtal, the direct antecedent of the bassoon, is also referred to as the dulcian; see Meyers 1997:84–85, 88.
54. Spagnoli 1990:146.
55. Ibid.

ine desire to improve the state of church music in the court chapel, the heir apparent would not be permitted to upstage his father. Pride, if nothing else, prevented Johann Georg I from welcoming his son's musicians into the chapel, for with such a move he would have declared his own impotence "in the eyes of all potentates."

ITALIAN ARRIVALS AND GERMAN DEPARTURES

The prince's own pursuit of the "perfect ensemble," however, soon received a boost (if temporary) from a wave of Italian musicians who made their way south from the Swedish court of Queen Christina. In November 1652, the queen famous both for her celebrated abdication and conversion to Catholicism as well as for her patronage of the arts, hired a band of Italian musicians, seven of whom would eventually make their way to Dresden.[56] Two of the queen's castrati, the soprano Domenico Melani (1634–93) and the alto Niccolo Milani, left Sweden in the summer of 1653, and the castrato Antonio Piermarini and the bass Vincenzo Cenni either accompanied them or followed shortly thereafter.[57] All may have come having heard that the Saxon prince, like Queen Christina, was rumored to to have "Catholic inclinations," but they may also have heard that Dresden had once again become a place of musical opportunity. Melani was hired by Prince Johann Georg on 1 November 1653, with a salary of 480 tl, and Milani may have received the same offer.[58] The starting salaries of Piermarini and Cenni remain unknown, but at the time of their departure from Dresden in 1654, both received 600 tl annually; Milani's salary, however, remained at 480 tl.[59] Of the four who had departed Stockholm for Dresden, however, all but Melani left for good during 1654. Piermarini went on to Innsbruck early in 1654, while Milani and Melani left for Italy in September; only Melani returned to Dresden.[60] Melani's salary history suggests that he was given additional, non-

56. See Sundström 1961.

57. Sundström 1961:301; Sundström only gives the departure date of Melani and Milani. The 1717 roster gives 1654 as the departure date of both Piermarini and Cenni (Spagnoli 1990:91–92). The two singers were apparently not related; Melani hailed from Florence, Milani from Livorno, and the Dresden documents consistently reflect the difference in spelling of the two names.

58. While Melani's first contract does not survive, a later document provides a history of his salary from the time of his hiring until 1680 (Sächs HStA Loc. 8687/6, fol. 8r).

59. The 1654 salaries of Milani, Piermarini, and Cenni appear on the 1717 composite roster in Spagnoli 1990:91.

60. Sächs HStA Loc. 8298/7, fol. 45r, travel pass dated 1 September 1654; the Latin text appears in Appendix I (no. 4). No travel passes survive for Cenni and Piermarini, but the latter probably left sometime in March; he shows up as a *Musikant* in Innsbruck court records and had lodgings with innkeeper Martin Wieser from 25 March to 27 April 1654 (Senn 1954:266). Cenni's post-Dresden musical activities remain unknown.

musical duties early in his Dresden career, for already on 1 January 1654, just two months after his arrival, Prince Johann Georg awarded him a new contract, more than doubling his salary to 1000 tl annually.[61] Unlike other musicians' contracts, Melani's does not specify his duties. During this first trip back to Italy, Melani may have recruited future Kapellmeister Peranda and/or the castrato Antonio Protogagi, but he may also have come back empty-handed, having established contacts in Italy (primarily in Florence); perhaps he extracted promises from musicians to come to Dresden at some point in the future.[62]

Unfortunately, court documents yield little information concerning the musical activities of Prince Johann Georg's Italo-German ensemble during the early years of its existence. Scattered entries in the court diaries reveal, however, that the prince's musicians were active at court, despite their exclusion from the court chapel. The earliest reference to a musical performance by the prince's ensemble appears in the records of the 1651 Lichtenburg visit. The first reference to the group's musical performance in Dresden, however, dates from Sunday, 30 October 1653, and refers to the "vocal and instrumental musical entertainment" performed by the prince's "own entire Italian and German musical ensemble" during their patron's midday meal.[63] A few months later, in February 1654, four "chamber musicians"—Melani, Milani, Georg [Giorgio] Berthold[i],[64] and Sauli—accompanied Prince Johann Georg to Wittenberg for the investiture of Abraham Calov as Gen-

61. Sächs HStA Loc. 8687/6, fol. 8r; the German translation of the Italian original appears in Appendix I (no. 5). Melani's salary remained unchanged until Easter 1662, when it was raised to 1200 tl. A document drawn up in 1680 indicates that Melani's salary was divided into two parts, 600 tl for salary and 400 tl as a *Zulage* (an additional allowance), and that he did not receive the *Zulage* for a number of years.

62. A comparison of the rosters of 1656 (below) and 1717 reveals that these two musicians were the only possibilities for recruitment by Melani at this time.

63. "bey solcher gehaltener Tafel wurde biß halbweg 4. uhr *vocaliter* und *instrumentaliter* von Ihrer Chur: Printzl. Durchl. eigener gesambter Italiänischer unnd teutzscher *Musica* musicirt" (SLUB Msc. Dresd. K 113, fol. 5v).

64. Georg [Giorgio] Berthold[i] was appointed in 1649 as a "Cammerdiener, Tenorist id Musicus" (valet, tenor and musician) (Sächs HStA Loc. 4520/2, fol. 6r), but appears here for the first time on a list of musicians. The establishment of the correct form of his name remains problematic: while the first names of the Italians were often given in their German equivalent in court documents (e.g., "Joseph Peranda"), their surnames were never altered. This tenor's name, however, appears variously as "Giorgio Bertholdi," "Giorgio Berthold," "Georg Bertholdi," and "Georg Berthold," with the latter two forms appearing often enough that a clear determination of his national origin is not possible. Berthold[i] may have hailed from a German/Italian region in southern Austria or northern Italy; for purposes of calculating the number of Italians in the Dresden ensembles, he will be counted among the Germans rather than the Italians.

eral Superintendent there.[65] During the first course of the celebratory banquet held on 13 February, Johann Georg flaunted his newly found musical ecumenism before the eminent Lutheran theologian, and had this four-part ensemble, which included two castrati, perform before Calov and the entire assembly.[66] In June of that same year, the prince again selected a group of Italians—Melani, Milani, Sauli, Severo, and Konzertmeister Manganoni—to travel as chamber musicians in the large retinue that accompanied him and his father to Altenburg for a baptism.[67] On this occasion, the prince's small ensemble (soprano, alto, bass, violin, and organ) may have performed only in private for the prince, for the records make no mention of performances of *Tafelmusik* by this ensemble. In addition, the record specifies that the Altenburg court musicians "performed beautiful music" before and after the consecration ceremony.[68]

Despite his increasing success in recruiting Italians, however, Prince Johann Georg still faced a serious retention problem—many of his early Italian musical acquisitions seem to have regarded his cappella merely as an attractive place to earn an income temporarily while they contemplated their next career moves. Although the years 1653 and 1654 saw a significant influx of Italians into the ensemble, most of these musicians left soon after their arrival: of those who received appointments in these years, only Melani remained in the prince's service (Manganoni died in November).[69] A number of factors may have contributed to this exodus. First, the newcomers may have heard rumors that their employer lacked the means to pay them. After all, the prince had expressed an urgent need for funds on several occasions in 1653, and a letter of Philipp Stolle to the prince on 30 October of that year (discussed below) indicates that at least one musician had not received his salary. In addition, Schütz's resistance, coupled with the elector's intransigence, probably denied performance opportunities in the court chapel to the prince's musicians. Third, unlike the courts of Vienna and Munich, the Dresden court lacked even a fledgling opera program, which may also have proved a disincentive to remain in the Saxon capital for young singers who entertained hopes of operatic careers. And

65. SLUB K 113, fol. 14r, entry for 13 February 1654. Calov (1612–1686), an ardent proponent of Lutheran Orthodoxy, was appointed Professor of Theology at the University of Wittenberg in 1650, where he taught until his death; he also held a similar position at the University of Königsberg (1639–43) and served as pastor and director of the Gymnasium in Danzig from 1643 until 1650; see Schüssler 1957:99–100.

66. SLUB K 113, fol. 18r.

67. Sächs HStA OHMA I Nr. 8, fol. 467r.

68. "vor und nach gehaltener Einsegnung wurde von Altenburgischen Musicanten gar schön musiciret" (Sächs HStA OHMA I Nr. 8, fol. 475v).

69. A hypothetical roster of the prince's musicians in 1654 appears in Frandsen 1997-1:32–33.

finally, the anomalous confessional situation may also have contributed to their respective decisions to leave. As a result of the departures of so many musicians around this time, the prince seems to have regarded the recruitment of singers, particularly castrati, as his main priority after 1654.

But the prince's proactive recruitment of Italians seems to have caused retention problems among the German musicians, for between the years 1653 and 1655, a number of Germans in the prince's ensemble left his employ for significant positions elsewhere. In 1653, one of the founding members of the prince's ensemble, the tenor and theorbist Stolle, wrote to the prince to ask for dismissal. Stolle had clearly heard of the prince's offer to transfer him to his father's ensemble and now feared that, "with the current constitution of the musical ensemble," the prince intended to "dispense with [his] person," despite his twenty-one years of service.[70] Stolle went on to complain that he could not support his wife and three young children on his salary of 300 tl, and that he had fallen into debt. In this respect, his letter represents an early protest vote against the salary inequities that now characterized the prince's payroll—in 1654, for example, tenor Stefano Boni (who may have replaced Stolle as a tenor) received 840 thaler.[71] In the end, the prince lost Stolle to his brother in Halle, Duke August; in 1654, Stolle assumed the position of director of music left vacant by the death of Samuel Scheidt.[72] German musicians in the prince's ensemble continued to depart in 1654 and 1655, and, with no surviving letters such as that from Stolle to provide their rationale, salary inequities and a general lack of pay stand out as the most credible explanations. While most of the Germans received the sum of 300 tl per annum at this time, salaries for the Italians began at 480 tl and reached as high as 1000 tl or more. For example, in 1654, the falsettist Heinrich Groh left Dresden for the court ensemble of Johann Georg's brother Christian in Merseburg; as one of Prince Johann Georg's altos, his salary of 300 tl stood at just half that received by soprano castrato Antonio Piermarini, and far less than half of the 744 tl paid to soprano castrato Giuseppe Maria Donati.[73] Two other Germans, lutenist Gottfried

70. Philipp Stolle to Johann Georg II, 30 October 1653 (Sächs HStA Loc. 4520/1, fol. 189r): "das beÿ itziger beschaffenheit der *Music* meiner persohn wohl zu enthra-then, . . ."

71. Spagnoli 1990:91.

72. See *EQL* 9:299.

73. Spagnoli 1990:91. Groh is listed among the altos on the 1717 composite roster, with a departure date of 1654; his service in Merseburg is noted in *EQL* 4:382. The 1717 roster reports all salaries in *Reichsthaler* (tl); however, at the time of their appointments in the 1630s and 1640s, musicians such as Stolle and Groh received their salaries in *Gulden* (fl). It remains possible that Barkstroh, who compiled the 1717 roster, did not convert the older salary figures to tl; if so, the difference between the German and Italian salaries was even greater.

Pasch and violinist Samuel Skahn (Span), also departed in 1654; Pasch, it seems, had run into trouble by stabbing a calcant in Freiberg.[74]

But even more significant was the departure of Matthias Weckmann in the mid-1650s. Weckmann, another founding member of the prince's musical ensemble back in the 1630s, had seen his chances for advancement in Dresden diminish with the arrival of the Italians; his salary remained at 300 tl (or fl), and after the November 1654 death of Manganoni, the Italian organist who served as Konzertmeister at a salary of 1000 tl, Weckmann was not promoted to that position.[75] Thus, at some point in 1655, Weckmann traveled to Hamburg to audition for the post of organist at the Jakobikirche, which had been vacated by the death on 31 December 1654 of organist Ulrich Cernitz.[76] Weckmann won the Hamburg position and received a letter of dismissal from the prince on 12 October 1655; his Hamburg contract dates from 27 November.[77] Even allowing for a possible nationalistic slant lent by Germans such as Kortkamp and Mattheson to their reports concerning Italian musicians in Dresden, it is not difficult to imagine that relations between the two nationalities had begun to deteriorate.[78] Upon the arrival of these Italian virtuosi, Prince Johann Georg seems to have become a star-struck Italophile who quickly lost his sense of perspective with respect to the contributions made by his German musicians, some of whom—such as Weckmann—were virtuosi in their own right. And the difficulties inherent in retaining the Italians forced the prince to pay the newcomers at least twice the "going rate" for Germans, which only compounded the problem—even *Oberhofkapellmeister* Schütz's salary of 400 fl could not compare

---

74. Pasch seems to have attacked the calcant in November 1653. Prince Johann Georg reported to his father that Pasch "the lutenist youth" had returned to Dresden, and that as soon as he had learned of his return, he had begun the legal process to put him in jail (Sächs HStA Loc. 8563/2, fol. 217, Johann Georg II to Johann Georg I [undated, probably November 1653]). A ballet cartel from 25 August 1653 indicates that Pasch was still in Dresden at that time (ibid., fol. 211r). See also Spagnoli 1990:93–94 (here Pasch's name is misspelled as "Rasch").

75. Spagnoli 1990:91; the post of Konzertmeister remained vacant until the appointment of Constantin Christian Dedekind to the post ca. 1666.

76. Ortgies 1993:15.

77. On Weckmann's Hamburg contract, see Ilgner 1939:38–39. Weckmann's letter of dismissal from the prince, the existence of which was previously unknown, was drafted from a similar document drawn up for Christoph Naumann; Weckmann's name and the particulars of his situation appear in pencil in the left margin of the draft document (Sächs HStA 8297/2, fol. 101r–v).

78. See Krüger 1933 and the entries for Bernhard and Weckmann in Mattheson 1740/1994:17–22, 394–98.

to that of the prince's own music director, Bontempi, who likely earned about three times that amount in 1654.[79]

At some point between January 1652 and September 1656, during these years of German departures, one of the musicians who would define sacred music in Dresden for many years joined the prince's musical ensemble. Giuseppe Peranda (ca. 1625–75), an alto, served Johann Georg II for at least nineteen years, and spent his last twelve years in Dresden as Kapellmeister.[80] He stands with Vincenzo Albrici as a purveyor of the musical style of mid-century Rome, the arrival of which marked the end of the Schütz era in Dresden. Despite his importance, however, little is known of his pre-Dresden biography. According to Agostino Rossi, he was born in Macerata,[81] but his birth date remains approximate; nothing is known of his musical training, or whether or not he was a castrato. Recent scholarship, however, suggests that he may have sung as a contralto at the Chiesa del Gesù in Rome during the years 1647, 1649, and 1650, under *maestro di cappella* Bonifatio Gratiani, a composer

---

79. Though not reported in court documents, Bontempi's salary at this time can be estimated: as of 1 January 1654, Domenico Melani received 1000 tl, as did Baldassare Manganoni, in positions of singer and Konzertmeister, both of which ranked beneath that of Bontempi, who served as the prince's director of music. Thus Bontempi probably received at least 1200 tl already in 1654. Schütz's salary had remained unchanged for years; it is reported as 100 fl per quarter on a roster of the elector's musicians drawn up between 15 March 1654 and 19 July 1655; Sächs HStA Loc. 7287/3, fol. 191r.

80. Peranda's name has long been given as "Marco Giuseppe" (or "Marco Gioseppe," or "Marco Gioseffo"). However, there is no surviving evidence in the composer's hand, in Dresden court documents of various types (including rosters, letters, court diaries, pay records, and travel passes), on seventeenth-century musical manuscripts, or in seventeenth-century publications, that his name was other than "Giuseppe (Gioseppe) Peranda." In October 1656, he witnessed Bontempi's will and signed himself "Joseph Peranda" (Briganti 1956:34), and in 1670, he signed his name "Giuseppe Peranda" in a letter to Johann Georg II (discussed below); in 1681, Albrici referred to him as "Joseph Peranda" in a 1681 inventory of music (Spagnoli 1990:224). His name is given as "Gioseppe Peranda" in the 1675 libretto of his oratorio, *Il sacrificio di Iephte* (Sartori 1990-5:86), as "Josephus Peranda" by Printz (1690/1964:146), and as "Giuseppe Peranda" by Rossi (1694/1980:137). In addition, his first name appears only as "Gioseppe," "Gios:," or "Giuseppe" in seventeenth-century music inventories (listed in Appendix II), and on the musical sources preserved in the Düben, Grimma, and Bokemeyer collections. His name first appears as "Marco Gioseffo" in Mattheson's *Grundlage einer Ehren-Pforte* (1740/1994:18–19). It now seems likely that one of Mattheson's sources mistook an abbreviation for "Maestro" as that for "Marco." As the composer himself used the Italian form "Giuseppe," that spelling will be retained here. I thank Paula Higgins and Wolfram Steude for profitable discussions of this matter.

81. Rossi 1694/1980:137.

whose influence is strongly felt in the Dresden repertoire.[82] But Peranda's where-abouts after 1650 remain shrouded in mystery; he first appears in Dresden court documents in 1656, when he is listed as an alto on a roster of the prince's musicians from September of that year (reproduced below). According to Mattheson, Peranda was a Roman musician who arrived in Dresden via the agency of Bernhard. On his first trip to Italy, according to Mattheson, Bernhard brought two castrati back to Dresden, "but as [the elector] still desired three more persons, specifically an Ital-ian Kapellmeister, an alto, and a tenor, [Bernhard] had to travel there once again, and brought back the famous 'mover of the emotions'—the Kapellmeister Marco Gioseffo Peranda—together with the two singers."[83] Wolfram Steude has suggested that these three musicians are those who arrived in 1653 and were auditioned by Schütz.[84] This date would seem too early, however. Although both Mattheson and Johann Kortkamp report that Bernhard undertook two separate journeys to Italy,[85] only a trip in 1657 can be documented.[86] Whether his second trip took place before or after this time remains open to question—no evidence survives to suggest that he traveled to Italy in 1653.

Given Peranda's absence from both lists of musicians who traveled with Prince Johann Georg in 1654, it is more likely that he arrived in Dresden sometime in 1655 or early 1656; he may have been recruited by Melani, who traveled to Italy in Sep-tember 1654 (although his sphere of activity seems to have been Florence), or by

82. Lars Berglund recently examined the account books of the Gesù and found references to payments made to one "Giuseppe contralto" on 30 September 1647 (for July–August), 3 and 30 September 1649 (for July–September), 30 December 1649 (for October–December), and possibly on 1 May 1650 ("per copie di Musica"); Archivum Romanum Societatis Iesu (ARSI), Chiesa del Gesù 2009, Libro dell'entrata e uscita per la Sagrestia della Chiesa del Gesù (anni 1637–1654). Peranda, who was hired in Dresden as an alto, was likely in Rome during these years; his musical style and textual borrowings from Gratiani suggest that the latter was highly influential upon the younger musician. I thank Dr. Berglund for allowing me to include this unpublished information.

83. "Der Churfürst war mit dieser Verrichtung überaus wohl zufrieden; weil er aber noch 3. Personen, nehmlich einen italienischen Capellmeister, einen Altisten, und Tenoristen, mehr verlangte, so muste Bernhard abermahl hin, und holen den berüh-mten Affecten-Zwinger, den Capellmeister Marco Gioseffo Peranda, samt den beiden Sängern, auch heraus, nach Dresden" (Mattheson 1740/1994:18; the reference to Peranda as a Roman musician appears on p. 19).

84. Steude 1999:68; see also Jung 1972:233.

85. According to Kortkamp, Bernhard had reported that the elector (Johann Georg II) had sent him twice to Italy, and paid his expenses; see Krüger 1933:210 and Frandsen 2000:25.

86. Bernhard was in Rome on "3./13. Septembris 1657," when he dated a dedicatory poem for his brother-in-law Constantin Christian Dedekind's *Aelbianische Musenlust*. See Fiebig 1980:34 n.1.

the Roman bass Stefano Sauli, who received a Latin travel pass on 26 June 1655, in which the destination is not indicated, but Italy remains the most likely.[87] It is also possible, however, that Peranda arrived in Dresden via the agency of Cardinal Friedrich of Hessen-Darmstadt (1616–82), the younger brother of Prince Johann Georg's brother-in-law, Landgrave Georg II of Hessen-Darmstadt (1605–61), and a man with well-established Roman musical connections.[88] Friedrich's musical interests are quite well known; he studied with Carissimi in the mid-1630s and remained in contact with the composer for many years.[89] Letters survive from Friedrich to the composer from 1642 and 1647. In those written in the latter year, Friedrich attempts to coax Carissimi into leaving Rome for Brussels in order to enter the service of Archduke Leopold; he also asks him to bring specific singers from the German College, as well as compositions:

> Try again to bring Giuseppe Scorbista with you, and a good contralto. And if it would be possible to have Odoardo [Ceccarelli], [Giuseppe] Bianchi and Giovannino, let me know about their terms, which His Highness will arrange with them. Meanwhile, send me some motet [sic], a Vespers, and a Mass with some *sinfonia* [sic], so that His Highness, while he cannot for the present enjoy your person, may at least console himself in the meantime with your beautiful compositions.[90]

At the request of Emperor Ferdinand III, the yet-to-be-ordained Friedrich was elevated to the ecclesiastical rank of cardinal on 19 February 1652, and his membership in that elite Roman circle would have only enhanced his access to Italian musicians. Most of Friedrich's sojourns in Rome between 1637 and 1666 were quite brief, but he did spend over three years there between January 1655 to late summer 1658, where he may well have hired musicians for his own household.[91] In a letter of 14 April 1655 to Prince Johann Georg, Landgrave Georg, the cardinal's older brother, mentions a request that the Saxon prince had made during Georg's most recent visit to Dres-

---

87. Sächs HStA Loc. 4520/2, fol. 184r.

88. The young Friedrich officially converted to Catholicism in Rome on 11 January 1637 and received Holy Communion at St. Peter's; Pope Urban VIII celebrated the conversion of this scion of one of the Lutheran ruling houses of Germany with a performance of the opera *Chi soffre speri* in February 1637; see Kast 1969:129–30. For a biographical sketch of Friedrich, see Noack 1928.

89. Culley 1970:180, 188–93, 330–31, 333–35.

90. Culley 1970:191.

91. Brück 1960. In December 1655, Friedrich was one of two cardinal legates that formed part of the large company that conducted Christina, the former queen of Sweden, to the pope for her official welcoming on 23 December; see Bjurström 1966:10–11 and Noack 1928:366.

den[92]; it seems that Johann Georg had asked the landgrave to communicate with his brother the cardinal about Italian musicians.[93] Georg requested that the prince send him a short description of his "intention"—presumably the specifics of what Johann Georg was seeking with respect to musicians—upon receipt of which he would gladly "discharge his duty " (i.e., communicate the same to his brother). This episode demonstrates once again that Prince Johann Georg availed himself of each and every possible opportunity and connection to acquire Italian musicians. The possibility that Peranda arrived in Dresden as a result of some association with the cardinal is further suggested by a letter dated 11 March 1670 from Johann Georg II to Cardinal Friedrich, then residing in Rome: "We have been approached most humbly by our Kapellmeister, Gioseppe Peranda, about a recommendation to Your Eminence for his brother-in-law, Doctor Gio[vanni] Batt[ist]a Gasparini of Macerata, and the same has the most obedient confidence that You will take the aforementioned, his brother-in-law, under your protection."[94] Although the text of the letter makes no reference to any previous service of Peranda with the cardinal, both the very fact that Peranda asked Johann Georg to write to Friedrich in particular and the elector's use of the phrase "has the most obedient confidence" are strongly suggestive of some previous association.

Johann Georg's family connections seem to have played no role in the recruitment of another Roman musician, the future Kapellmeister Vincenzo Albrici (1631–1690/96), whose Roman roots were both hereditary and acquired. Albrici was the grandson of the Roman composer and anthologist Fabio Costantini (ca. 1579–1644), under whom he sang as a young boy at the *Duomo* in Orvieto.[95] He continued his musical education in Rome, where from 1641 to 1645 he sang as a *putto soprano* under Carissimi at the Jesuit German College. Throughout most of 1646 he received pay-

92. According to Weck, the visit took place in January 1653 (Weck 1680:396).

93. Sächs HStA Loc. 8561/1, fols. 167–68 (here fol. 167v), Landgrave Georg II of Hessen-Darmstadt to Johann Georg II, 14 April 1655.

94. "Wir seÿn umb recommendation an E. Lbd. von unserm Capellmeister Gioseppe Peranda vor seinen Schwager Dottore Gio: Batt:a Gasparini da Macerada unterthänigst angelanget worden, und hat derselbe die gehorsamste Zuversicht, daß vom E. Lbd. gedachten seinen Schwager unter Dero Protection nehmen wolten" (Sächs HStA Loc. 8753/6, fol. 39r). Peranda's letter to Johann Georg appears on fol. 40 of the same volume.

95. The recent research of Mary Paquette-Abt has added significantly to Albrici's early biography and has revealed that Albrici's father Domenico was married to Fabio Costantini's daughter and sang as a contralto at the *Duomo* in Orvieto from 1636 to 1642, when Costantini served there as *maestro di cappella*. From 1638 to early 1641, young Vincenzo was paid one *scudo* per month to sing in the cathedral along with his father, a testament to his precocious talent. See Paquette-Abt 2003:89–91.

ments as an organist there.[96] Between December 1649 and March (or possibly June) 1651, he likely served under Gratiani as organist at the Chiesa del Gesù in Rome, where he also may have worked with Peranda.[97] In November 1652, together with his father Domenico and his brother Bartolomeo, he entered the service of Swedish Queen Christina, remaining there until at least 1 March 1653. While in Stockholm, Vincenzo served as *Organista e Compositore*, and his brother as a *Soprano non Castrato*; both were identified in the payment records as *Romani*.[98] Upon departing Sweden, the two briefly held positions at the court of Stuttgart.[99] The brothers Albrici arrived in Dresden sometime during the spring or summer of 1656; both had likely heard about the opportunities to be found in Dresden from some of the Italian musicians with whom they had served in Stockholm, such as Melani. A roster from September 1656 (reproduced below) reveals that soon after Vincenzo's arrival in Dresden, if not immediately thereupon, the prince appointed him Kapellmeister, probably in recognition of his responsibilities in Sweden; thus Vincenzo shared the rank of Kapellmeister with Bontempi. His brother Bartolomeo received an appointment as an organist.[100] Like that of Peranda, the arrival of Albrici marked a significant moment in musical life under Johann Georg II, for the Roman-trained Albrici would promulgate a new type of sacred concerto in Dresden, one that would result from his assimilation of certain style characteristics from the Roman motet and the German sacred concerto.

96. Culley 1970:216–17.

97. In his examination of the account books of the Gesù, Lars Berglund found references to salary paid to one "Vincenzo Organista" from December 1649 through March (or possibly June) of 1651; Archivum Romanum Societatis Iesu (ARSI), Chiesa del Gesù 2009, Libro dell'entrata e uscita per la Sagrestia della Chiesa del Gesù (anni 1637–1654). The musician's family name does not appear in the records. However, Albrici worked as an organist in the Jesuit circuit and was probably still in Rome at this time. Arnaldo Morelli, who has done extensive work on musicians in Rome during this period, believes that the musician in question is most likely Albrici (private correspondence, 7 March 2005). I again thank Dr. Berglund for this new information and for the permission to include it here.

98. Sundström 1961:301, 308.

99. Vincenzo's service in Stuttgart began in the Bartholomew term (24 August) 1655 and lasted until around 1 February 1656; his brother Bartolomeo may have left after the end of September (Hauptstaatsarchiv Stuttgart, A282, Ba 1391, *Kirchen Castens Verwalltung Jahr Rechnung* 1655–56 [unfoliated]). Many thanks to Paul Ranzini for informing me of the references to the brothers Albrici in these materials.

100. Albrici's appointment as Kapellmeister may suggest that Bontempi had already begun to move on to other interests. In the spring of 1655, for example, the latter seems to have designed a new *Lustbau* for the electoral princess's garden (SLUB K 113, fol. 45v, entry for 6 April 1655).

PREPARATIONS FOR MUSICAL REGIME CHANGE

In June 1655, Elector Johann Georg I established the practice of holding two morning worship services on Sundays and most feast days; apparently for health reasons,
he no longer desired to attend worship in the chapel. Thus from Pentecost Sunday (3 June) 1655, services were held first in the chapel and then in the *Steinerne
Gemach.*[101] In the spring of 1656, due to his increasingly poor health, the elector
ceased attending worship services altogether in "public" spaces in the castle and
apparently ordered that the second morning worship service be celebrated for him
privately, in his antechamber. Diary entries for 1656 record fifteen such services,
celebrated between Palm Sunday (30 March) and the Feast of Mary Magdalene (22
July); unlike the entries recording services in the *Steinerne Gemach*, most of these
entries provide details on the musical accommodations made for these double services.[102] Although the simplest solution would have been to give the morning service
in the chapel over to the prince's Italian *Director musices* and his ensemble, and to
require Schütz and his musicians to perform in the elector's antechamber, the diary
indicates that the same music director and musical ensemble usually performed in
both services, which did not occur simultaneously. For example, on Easter Sunday
(6 April) 1656, "Doctor Weller preached the sermon both in the church as well as
in the [elector's] antechamber, and the electoral Kapellmeister directed the musical ensemble at both [services]."[103] On most occasions, the septuagenarian Schütz
either conducted the music at both services, or turned responsibility for the chapel service over to Bernhard, his vice-Kapellmeister; only Schütz conducted in the
elector's antechamber. This curious arrangement suggests that the elector still held
strong feelings on the subject of the participation of the prince's musicians in worship services, and that he attempted to retain hegemony over the chapel even when
it was becoming increasingly clear that his reign would soon come to an end. Prince
Johann Georg nevertheless managed to turn the situation to his own advantage
and may have either been given or simply taken the opportunity to hear his musicians perform in the castle chapel. On Pentecost Sunday, for example, "Dr. Weller
preached the sermon both in the church and in the antechamber; however, His
Electoral Princely Highness's Kapellmeister directed the music in the church, and
the electoral Kapellmeister directed in the antechamber . . . M. Laurentius preached

---

101. SLUB K 113, fols. 49r, 51v.

102. SLUB K 113, fols. 75v–84r.

103. "Die Predigt so wol in der Kirchen, als im vorgemach, verrichtete Herr D.
Weller, vnd bey beyden Predigten die *Musica* der Churfürstl. Cappellmeister" (SLUB
Msc. Dresd. K 113, fol. 76r). The court diarists commonly refer to church services as
"sermons" (*Predigten*).

the sermon at Vespers, and the Electoral Prince's Kapellmeister directed the music in the service."[104] It remains possible that this reference indicates that Bontempi conducted the electoral *Hofkapelle* in Bernhard's stead, but it more likely documents the inaugural performance of the prince's musicians in the chapel.[105] In the case of the latter, the occasion may well have marked the first time that the court congregation heard the voices of castrati in the chapel, although they had certainly heard them in performances of *Tafelmusik*.

By September 1656, the health of Elector Johann Georg I had deteriorated to such an extent that preparations commenced for the transferral of power to his son upon his imminent death. At the beginning of the Michaelis term (29 September) 1656, a list of the members of the prince's household, including the musicians, was drawn up and submitted to the elector on the following day.[106] This September 1656 roster represents the last record of the princely musical ensemble before it was merged with the *Hofkapelle*:

MUSICA

Kapellmeisters

Giovanni Andrea Bontempi	(soprano castrato)
Vincenzo Albrici	(organist)

Discantist

Domenico Melani	(soprano castrato)

104. "Pfingstag ⊙ den 25 Maÿ . . . Die Predigt sowol in der Kirchen, als im Vorgemach verrichtete Herr D. Weller, die *Musica* aber in der Kirchen Sr. ChurPrinzl. Durchl.: und im Vorgemach der Churfürstl. Cappellmeister . . . Die Vesper Predigt thate *M. Laurentius*, und die *Musica* darbey verrrichtete der ChurPrinzl. Cappellmeister" (SLUB K 113, fol. 80r). The colon that follows "ChurPrinzl. Durchl." indicates the genitive, "Your Electoral Highness's [Kapellmeister]." While the references to the prince's Kapellmeister likely refer to Bontempi, there is some possibility that they refer to Albrici, who had arrived in Dresden sometime after early February 1656.

105. Bernhard's August 1655 contract as vice-Kapellmeister suggests that the prince's musicians did perform in the chapel (Spagnoli 1990:163–64), while a letter of court preacher Jacob Weller from 1654 suggests that they did not (Sächs HStA Loc. 8563/1, fol. 858r–v). SLUB K 113 chronicles the prince's activities from October 1653 to October 1656, and while it records his attendance at worship services, it makes no mention of his musicians performing in the chapel until the spring of 1656. Steude has suggested that the prince's musical ensemble took over for the elector's ensemble in the chapel "from time to time" beginning around 1651 (1999:66). Although not definitive, the surviving evidence suggests that this is unlikely to have been the case.

106. Sächs HStA Loc. 8681/2, fol. 237r: "Des Durchleüchtigsten Chur-Printzens und Hertzogens zu Sachßen, Jülich, Cleve und Berg, *Estat, Michaelis Anno* 1656" ("The Estate of the Most Serene Electoral Prince and Duke of Saxony, Jülich, Cleve, and Berg, Feast of St. Michael, 1656"). On the top right-hand corner of the same folio appears the following

Alto

Giuseppe Peranda   (falsettist or castrato?)

Tenors

Georg [Giorgio] Berthold[i]
Adam Merckel

Basses

Stefano Sauli
Christian Kittel

Organists

Bartolomeo Albrici   (also soprano falsettist)
Georg Rumpf

Instrumentalists

Giovanni Severo   (violin)
Friedrich Werner   (cornetto and alto)
Michael Schmidt   (violin and bass)
Balthasar Sedenig   (violin)
Johann Friedrich Volprecht   (viola and lute)
Friedrich Westhoff   (lute)
Andreas Winckler   (sackbut)

Jeremiah Seyffert   "Instrument Maker"
Hanns Christoph Schrieker   Calcant

Musical Trumpeters

Simon Leonhard
Daniel Philomathes
Wolff Voigt
Christoph Richter
Christian Rockstroh[107]

In the weeks just prior to his ascent to the throne, Prince Johann Georg could boast of a musical ensemble of twenty-two adult performing members, and prob-

note: "Den 30. Septemb. 1656. Ihrer Churfürstl. Durchl. also überreichet ward" ("Submitted to His Electoral Highness on 30 September 1656"). Fürstenau referred to this roster and indicated that Peranda appeared on it as an alto, but he did not publish the list or provide a citation (Fürstenau 1849:73); Spagnoli indicated that the roster "appears to be lost" (Spagnoli 1990:359 n. 61).

107. Sächs HStA Loc. 8681/2, fol. 239r–v. The spelling of names has been regularized, and vocal and instrumental designations added in parentheses; the names of five additional trumpeters, who are not designated as "musical trumpeters" (those who played with the musical ensemble) have been omitted here.

ably another three to five choirboys whose names do not appear on this list, as well as several nonperformers who maintained the instruments and provided wind for the organ (calcants). One new German name appears, that of tenor Adam Merckel; in addition, two former *Instrumentisten Knaben*, Georg Rumpf and Andreas Winckler, have now been graduated from those ranks to become adult members of the ensemble.[108] Georg [Giorgio] Berthold[i], who was appointed in 1649 as a valet and musician, appears here for the first time on a full roster of the prince's musicians. The roster demonstrates that while the prince was quite well supplied with vocalists and instrumentalists at this point, his ensemble had not yet attained the standing of a "perfect ensemble in the eyes of all potentates," for it still lacked some of the singers and instrumentalists included in the prince's 1653 description of such a group.

The roster does demonstrate, however, that by the fall of 1656, an endeavor that Prince Johann Georg may have begun as an experiment—the recruitment and appointment of Italian musicians—had solidified into a well-established practice. At the time of his father's death in 1656, the prince's ensemble not only exceeded the *Hofkapelle* in size, but also differed quite radically from that ensemble in its ethnic and confessional composition. Despite the constant pressure of debt, Prince Johann Georg managed to establish the musical agenda of his future electorate in the years between 1651 and 1656. During this period, he laid the groundwork for the future in several key ways, first by making at least four strategic hires—Bontempi, Melani, Peranda, and Albrici—and then by determining the stylistic direction of the ensemble by installing Italian composers at its helm, and furnishing them with Italian singers, including castrati, to perform their musical contributions. From the outset, however, doubtless due to both financial and confessional considerations, the prince found it difficult to retain Italian musicians, whose transience produced instability in his cappella membership. Thus he soon realized that establishing a network of contacts in Italy was vital to the success of his musical enterprise, and he developed a strategy for recruitment there that would lend him access to a ready supply of musicians. In this he was aided by the cessation of hostilities in German-speaking lands and the slow improvement in economic conditions there that resulted. After the war ended, a number of northern European courts enjoyed a steady influx of Italian musicians, a phenomenon first instantiated in Dresden by the groundswell in the number of Italians appointed, if only briefly, in the early 1650s. These appointments were costly, however, and although Prince Johann Georg managed to establish policies during these years that ensured the future musical success of his initiative, he did not simultaneously discover the

108. See the 1651 list above.

means to provide his musicians with financial security. Still, with his Italian composers and singers now in place, the prince found himself well positioned to introduce sweeping musical changes in the court chapel, a task that he undertook with relish soon after the guardianship of the electoral sword and habit devolved to him on 8 October 1656.

2

The Italianate Hofkapelle
of Johann Georg II, 1656–80

A New Era Begins

After his death on 8 October 1656, Elector Johann Georg I lay in state in the castle in Dresden until February of the next year, during which time his son's staff prepared for the elaborate state funeral services that took place on 2–4 February 1657.[1] The elector actually received four funeral services, the first of which took place on 16 October 1656 in the castle chapel. In February 1657, after a period sufficient to allow various invited dignitaries the time needed to travel to Saxony, three additional funerals were held over a three-day period, in three different locations—a *triduum* doubtless intended to evoke the theological symbolism of Christ's Passion, Death, and Resurrection. The first funeral took place on the morning of 2 February 1657 in the castle chapel, followed by another in the Dresden Kreuzkirche that afternoon; on 3 February the body was transported to Freiberg, and on 4 February 1657, Johann Georg I was finally laid to rest in the cathedral there, in the Italianate burial chapel designed in the late sixteenth century by Giovanni Maria Nosseni (1544–1620).[2] Although Johann Georg II's reign as elector had commenced immediately upon the death of his father, the public presentation of the symbol of his accession to the throne was delayed until the conclusion of his father's funeral, when the electoral sword was finally removed from its sheath and carried before him in the procession out of the cathedral.[3]

While the court musicians were not required to travel to Freiberg (with the exception of the bass Jonas Kittel, who carried the crucifix), they did lead the singing of hymns during the October and February funeral services held in the castle

---

1. See Spagnoli 1998 and 1990:7–16.
2. See Meine-Schawe 1992 and Fürstenau 1861/1971:83–84.
3. See Spagnoli 1990:8–9, 12–13. According to the funeral documents examined by Spagnoli, the electoral seal, crown, and sheathed sword were carried in each funeral procession; the sword was not unsheathed until the final procession.

chapel, and formed part of the official court retinue that accompanied the body into the Kreuzkirche on the afternoon of 2 February, and as far as the Dresden city gate on the morning of 3 February.[4] In order that they might participate, all of the cappella members received attire appropriate to such ceremonies, in the form of a mourning robe made either of *Leibtuch* or *Landtuch*. The list of the musicians who received robes provides the first extant roster of the new elector's musical ensemble (see below)[5] and reveals that he had merged his princely cappella with that of his late father, which at the time of his death included Schütz and Bernhard, three organists, five vocalists, and seven instrumentalists, as well as an organ builder, the court sexton (*Hofküster*), and a calcant.[6]

MUSICIANS

Heinrich Schütz*	Kapellmeister
Giovanni Andrea Bontempi	Kapellmeister and soprano
Vincenzo Albrici	Kapellmeister[7]
Christoph Bernhard*	Vice-Kapellmeister and alto
Giuseppe Peranda	?Vice-Kapellmeister and alto
Domenico Melani	Soprano
Tobias Tille*	Alto
Christian Weber*	Alto and harp
Matthias Erlemann*	Cantor, bass, and alto?
Georg [Giorgio] Berthold[i]	Tenor
Adam Merckel	Tenor
Stefano Sauli	Bass
Christian Kittel	Bass
Constantin Christian Dedekind*	Bass
Bartolomeo Albrici	Organ

4. Spagnoli 1990:8–13. The performance of figural music was prohibited during the entire period of mourning; see Müller 1838:151–52.

5. The 1657 roster, which was first published by Spagnoli (1990:13–15), appears in Sächs HStA OHMA C Nr. 8, fols. 407r–408r. The titles and voice and instrument designations for all but Schütz, Melani, Weller, Mildner, and the four choirboys have been added by the author from various rosters; the spelling of names has also been regularized. Asterisks indicate musicians of former elector Johann Georg I; of these, the third organist, sexton, and calcant do not appear here, and may have been pensioners.

6. So listed (without names) in Sächs HStA Loc. 12030, "Lit. A" (see the description of this document in n. 26 below).

7. Albrici's rank is given as Kapellmeister (together with Bontempi) in the roster of September 1656 (see chapter 1). Curiously, the 1657 funeral documents mention only Schütz and Bontempi as "the two Kapellmeisters" ("die beÿden Capellmeistere"); Sächs HStA OHMA C Nr. 8, fol. 211v.

Christoph Kittel*	Organ
Georg Rumpf	Organ
Johann Klemm*	Organ
Antonio [de Blasi], Italian[8]	Soprano
Johann Bartholomäus Buhler	??
Vicoratorius, Italian	??
Jonas Kittel*	Bass and violone
Pietro Finati	Tenor?

Instrumentalists	
Giovanni Severo	Violin
Friedrich Werner	Cornetto and alto
Michael Schmidt	Violin and bass
Balthasar Sedenig	Violin
Johann Friedrich Volprecht	Viola and lute
Friedrich Westhoff	Lute
Wilhelm Burrowes*	Viola da gamba
Friedrich Sulz*	(Instrument)
Jacob Sulz*	Sackbut
Johann Friedrich Sulz*	Sackbut
Clemens Thieme*	Curtal
Andreas Winckler	Sackbut
Johann Wilhelm Forchheim	Violin and organ
Johann Dixon*	Sackbut
Daniel Kreße	??
Tobias Weller*	Organ builder
Jeremiah Seiffert	Organ builder/tuner
Christian Mildner	Choirboy
Johann Thorian	??
Sebastian Ludwig Sulz*	Violin

Four Choirboys	
Gottfried Böhme	??
George Fritzsche	??
Johann Gottfried Behr [Ursinus]	Tenor
Gottfried Janetzky	Alto and cornetto

Given the disappearance of all but a few of the Italian musicians' contracts, the organization of lists such as this can provide important clues to the rank and specialization of various musicians at particular periods of the ensemble's history. Most important, the positioning of Peranda's name on this roster directly after that of

---

8. Spagnoli rightly suggests that this "Anthoni Italiener" is Antonio de Blasi (1990:14).

Bernhard, who was named vice-Kapellmeister in 1655, and before that of Melani, a soprano, rather than with the altos, suggests that Johann Georg II had already elevated Peranda to the rank of vice-Kapellmeister by February 1657, although the first document to associate him with that post dates from 1661.[9] The addition of the descriptor "Soprano" after Melani's name may well indicate that the singers' names commence from this point, for, from Melani on, the singers are grouped together by voice part, with the exception of the bass Erlemann, the Hofcantor. Among the organists, the position of Bartolomeo Albrici's name demonstrates once again the quick ascendance of the Italians within the cappella of Johann Georg II; although he had only recently arrived, Albrici already received the highest salary of the four, and his name appears at the head of the group, which suggests that he was regarded as the "senior" or "first" organist.[10]

In the simple act of integrating the two court musical ensembles, Johann Georg II had more than doubled the size of his cappella and produced a group capable of mounting performances of anything found in the contemporary sacred repertoire, from intimate sacred concertos to *concertato* motets for five-part double choir and a host of instruments. All but two of the forty-seven individuals listed above functioned as performers in this ensemble, thirty-eight of them adults, with seven choirboys.[11] By February 1657, the Italian presence in Johann Georg's ensemble had increased by three since September 1656; the merged ensemble included ten Italians among its ranks, three or four of whom were castrati.[12] Although the personalities would change frequently over the years, the number of Italians would remain relatively stable. While it appears to be complete, this roster actually does not represent the entire ensemble, for it omits as many as five musical trumpeters and several calcants. The September 1656 roster of the prince's musicians had included five musical trumpeters, but these musicians probably marched with the field trumpeters in the 1657 funeral processions, dressed in that livery, and thus did not require robes.[13] Thus the full ensemble numbered about fifty-four members, fifty of whom were performers. Surely this expansive group, with its fourteen or more adult singers, five

9. Peranda is listed as a vice-Kapellmeister on a 1661 roster of musicians slated to travel to Hirschberg with the elector (discussed below).

10. See the 1717 roster in Spagnoli 1990:92. The actual rank of "senior" or "first" organist did not exist in Dresden.

11. The choirboys begin with Mildner; the first three are probably older boys who now served as instrumentalists, while those listed as "Cappella Youths" are probably younger musicians who served as singers.

12. The elusive "Vicoratorius" may also have been a castrato.

13. In all, twenty-four trumpeters participated in the processions; see Spagnoli, 1990:11.

violinists, four sackbut players, four organists, and other performers, now constituted a "perfect ensemble in the eyes of all potentates."

The realities of the time, however, delayed the assumption of chapel duties by this "perfect ensemble" until late 1657 or early 1658, for the musical ramifications of the lengthy *Hoftrauer*, the period of mourning for the late elector, included the silencing of the organ and a moratorium on the performance of figural music. Thus the court diary for 1657 includes no references to church music or musicians,[14] and the first mention of an Italian, Bontempi, directing the service music in the court chapel during the electorate of Johann Georg II does not appear in a diary until January 1658:

> Friday, 1 January . . . then the worship service began, and Senior Court Preacher Dr. Weller delivered the sermon, but Kapellmeister [Giovanni] Andrea Bontempi directed the musical ensemble. . . . and after the meal Vespers was celebrated by Magister Geisthoff Laurentius, at which the aforementioned Bontempi again led the musical ensemble.[15]

Johann Georg II spent a good part of 1658 (February–August) in Frankfurt, however, where he attended the electoral diet that elected Habsburg Emperor Leopold I (r. 1658–1705). Thus the 1658 court diary chronicles his daily activities there and offers little information on life back at court. The next surviving reference to Bontempi's activity in the chapel dates from 19 December 1658, well after the elector's return.[16] Entries in a diary for January 1659, however, indicate that Bontempi and Albrici shared in the directing of the service music, and one can presume that each of them, especially Albrici, presented a number of his own compositions.[17] Musical information is lacking for the following months of 1659, however, which likely reflects another silencing of the music in the chapel due to the death on 12 February of the dowager Electress Magdalena Sibylla, Johann Georg's mother.[18] This *Hoftrauer*

14. SLUB Msc. Dresd. Q 238.

15. "[symbol for Friday] den 1. [Januar] . . . dann gienge den Gottesdienst an, und verrichtete der Oberhoffprediger D. Weller die Predigt, die *Musica* aber der Cappellmeister Andreas *Bontempi* . . . und nach derselben [i.e. Tafel] wart eine Vesper Predigt von M. Geisthoff Laurentio gehalten beÿ welcher abermals obberürter *Bontempi* die *Musica* verrichtete" (Sächs HStA Loc. 12026, fol. 494r, entry for 1 January 1658). Bontempi also directed the musical ensemble on 6 January 1658 (ibid., fol. 494v). The term *Vesperpredigt* refers to a vesper service that included a sermon (*Predigt*); "die *Musica*" (which is always italicized in the diaries) refers to the performing ensemble.

16. Sächs HStA OHMA N I Nr. 8, fol. 36r, entry for 19 December.

17. SLUB Msc. Dresd. Q 238, entries for 1 January (Bontempi), 2 January (vice-Kapellmeister, no name given), 6 January (Albrici), 9 January (Albrici).

18. Fürstenau 1861/1971:205.

seems to have lasted for a year, for a diary entry for Sunday, 19 February 1660 indicates that instrumental music was heard again for the first time on this day.[19] One wonders how the musicians, particularly the Italians, occupied themselves during these long periods of enforced inactivity. Some of them clearly used this opportunity to attend to personal matters; six travel passes for musicians survive from 1659, all of which date from the period of the *Hoftrauer*.[20]

Once the restrictions on the performance of music during worship services had been lifted, the elector's musicians resumed their weekly responsibilities in the chapel. On 13 May 1660, the Dresden court commemorated the ten-year anniversary of the 1650 *Friedensfest* (festival of peace), which had celebrated the final departure of Swedish troops from Saxony after the signing of the Peace of Westphalia, with an elaborate Sunday morning worship service.[21] The surviving documentation for this celebration includes the order of worship for the service. This, the earliest of such documents to survive from the reign of Johann Georg II, demonstrates the extent to which sacred music in the modern Italian style had already come to dominate the chapel liturgies.[22] As a court Kapellmeister typically showcased his own works during the worship services, particularly in those services in which he served as the conductor, the attributions to composers found in these orders of worship also serve as a chronicle of the musical activities of various individuals during particular periods of time. On this particular Sunday, Albrici composed all of the music sung by the members of the cappella; his compositions included large-scale settings of the Kyrie, Gloria, and a motet (now lost), *Reboent aethera*, as well a small-scale sacred concerto, *Hymnum jucunditatis*, which survives in several collections.[23]

Financial Challenges

The cost—just over 1530 tl—of the forty-seven robes provided to the musical ensemble for the 1657 funeral represented but a minute amount when measured against the 100,000 tl required to outfit the entire court in appropriate funeral garments,

19. SLUB Q 239, entry for Sunday, 19 February 1660.

20. Michael Schmidt to Bohemia, 6 May (Sächs HStA 8297/2, fol. 108r); Vincenzo Albrici to Frankfurt, 14 June (Sächs HStA Loc. 8299/1, fol. 15v); Antonio de Blasi to Italy, 15 July (Sächs HStA 8298/7, fol. 57r); Friedrich Westhoff to Lübeck, 12 August (Sächs HStA Loc. 8297/3, fol. 26v); Domenico Melani to Italy, 23 September (Sächs HStA Loc. 8298/7, fol. 57r); Angelo Maria Marchesini to Italy, 5 December (Sächs HStA Loc. 8298/7, fol. 57r). These Latin and German passes give the reasons for the musician's travel as "negotiorum suorum causa" or "seiner Angelegenheiten."

21. On the peace festivals held in Saxony between 1648 and 1650 see Keller 1998.

22. Sächs HStA OHMA N IV Nr. 1, fols. 12r–15r.

23. See the list of works in Appendix II.

and the latter figure itself comprised well over half of the total amount of 178,000 tl spent on the funeral ceremonies.[24] Now, of course, Johann Georg II could no longer depend upon his father to provide the funds to cover such expenses, but would have to assume responsibility for all costs himself. His ability to create an image as a wealthy, powerful, and cultured European ruler would depend on his ability to maintain not only a large retinue of court officers and servants, but also those "departments" most closely associated with courtly representation—the *Hofkapelle*, the stables (*Stall*), and the game and gamekeepers for the hunt (the *Jagdamt*). Thus, almost immediately after his father's death, he launched an investigation designed to reveal the true size of the household (*Hofstaat*) that he had inherited from his father, and on 31 October 1656, instructed his *Cammer Räthe*—those aristocratic court officers charged with oversight of the court treasury, who enjoyed the rank of "advisor" or "counselor"—to prepare a complete list of all of his father's employees and their salaries.[25] This daunting task required over two months to perform, and when the counselors finally responded on 19 January 1657, they reported to Johann Georg II that his father's household comprised a staggering 1036 individuals, some 600 to 750 of whom performed their duties in the Dresden castle complex, and whose salaries and perquisites (allowances for food and clothing, and at times heating materials, wine, and beer) cost the court 192,443 fl annually.[26] The advisors' gloomy report continued with the news that, although the contribution from the provincial diet (*Landschafts Bewilligung*) could be estimated at 400,000 fl annually, the elector should probably expect to receive only two-thirds of this amount, given the current economic conditions in the land.[27] They also pointed out that, when the salary total was added to the estimated cost of feeding these individuals at court, the costs climbed to about 390,000 fl per annum, and exceeded the amount of income upon which Johann Georg could depend. Finally, the counselors informed the elector that their calculations did not include the expenses related to his own musical ensemble, his annual court festivities, and other departments (such as the stables and gamekeepers) and events, and that the addition of those amounts would produce a total far higher than that given. Thus, resuming their role as counselors, they stressed the need to balance receipts with expenditures and to put something away for unexpected expenses.[28]

24. See Müller 1838:152.
25. Sächs HStA Loc. 12030, fol. 1, Johann Georg II to the Cammer Räthe.
26. Sächs HStA Loc. 12030, fols. 3r–18r, and Lit. A, a large chart (unfoliated) that lists all of the late elector's employees by department (*Amt*), together with their salaries and perquisites. The author totaled the number of employees from the figures given in Lit. A; the salary total (including a breakdown by salary and perquisites) appears on p. 2 of Lit. A.
27. Sächs HStA Loc. 12030, fols. 10r, 11r.
28. Sächs HStA Loc. 12030, fols. 6r–8r.

After meeting with his brothers in April 1657 to discuss the terms of the late elector's will, Johann Georg asked his financial counselors on 3 June 1657 to provide him with a detailed report of his financial status, as he now understood more precisely the amount of income that he would lose as a result of the will and the *freund-brüderlicher Hauptvergleich*, as the agreement between the four brothers is known.[29] The report, which the counselors delivered to the elector on 27 June 1657, included little in the way of good news: Elector Johann Georg I had bequeathed to his son a legacy of indebtedness in the amount of 11,867,720 fl, an amount which included 1,000,000 fl in back salary owed to officers and other members of the electoral household.[30] In light of the enormity of this debt, the elector's advisors appended a list of twelve of suggestions aimed at reducing the debt and reinvigorating the Saxon economy over the long term, and again urged Johann Georg II to reduce the size of his household and the costs associated with it and to suspend "excessive expenditures, costly trips, and grand hunts."[31]

But from the outset of his reign, Johann Georg II demonstrated a clear recalcitrance toward any and all reductions in spending, particularly in areas that he deemed fundamental to the cultivation of his image as elector. Rather than tighten his belt, in 1658 he asked for an increase in his allowance of 40,000 tl, in order to bring it to 100,000 tl.[32] His advisors discouraged this plan and stressed that all revenues had been exhausted; currently they were forced to buy food for the animals on credit.[33] But their pleas fell on deaf ears. By the time the provincial diet met in November 1660, the Saxon court was nearly bankrupt.[34] According to Carl Wilhelm Böttiger, "the members of the provincial diet insisted on the complete separation of the court treasury (*Kammer*) from the general tax receipts (*Steuer*), the end of the perpetual payment orders (*Anweisungen*) issued by the court treasury against the

29. Sächs HStA Loc. 12030, fols. 61r–68v, Cammer Räthe to Johann Georg II, 27 June 1657; the draft of Johann Georg's letter of 3 June 1657 does not survive, but the advisors refer to it by date in their response. On the terms of the will of Johann Georg I and the *Hauptvergleich*, see Kretzschmar 1925 and 1927.

30. Sächs HStA Loc. 12030, fols. 64v, 65v. Of the amounts listed, about a third (4,212,562 fl) comprised unpaid interest on loans.

31. "Überflüßige Außgaben, kostbahre Reisen, und Haubt Jagdten einzustellen, Ihr gefallen ließen" (Sächs HStA Loc. 12030, fols. 65v–67v; fol. 65v).

32. Sächs HStA Loc. 12030, fol. 232r. In 1662, after several years of stalling by his advisors, Johann Georg announced to them that he had raised his own allowance to 100,000 tl, out of which he would pay for a number of "line items" in the budget, including the *Hofkapelle* (Sächs HStA Loc. 10380/21, Bl. 17r–18v).

33. Sächs HStA Loc. 12030, fol. 234v, Cammer Räthe to Johann Georg II, 11 September 1658.

34. Böttiger 1831:167.

tax receipts, and a revision of the high tax rates."³⁵ In addition, Böttiger states that the diet also assumed an enormous debt, one that "still amounted to 5,200,000 fl in 1666, after four barrels of gold had been paid."³⁶ Although Böttiger does not say so explicitly, it seems clear that the provincial diet assumed the elector's debt of nearly twelve million fl, thus relieving him of this onerous burden. Court financial documents make no mention of this crippling debt after 1660, which also suggests that it became the responsibility of the diet.

Such financial exigencies sometimes forced Johann Georg to develop creative solutions in order to satisfy his obligations to those entrusted with the leadership of his musical ensemble. In 1659, for example, Bontempi appears to have acquired a property in Dölzschen, a southeastern suburb of Dresden, in exchange for a portion of his back salary, which clearly had gone unpaid for some time:

> [The sum of] 1280 fl 5 gr [is] paid to Johann Schrötel, the excise-tax collector in Dresden, according to the gracious decree of 4 November 1659 of His Electoral Highness of Saxony, for the complete satisfaction of the 3000 tl purchase price for [Schrötel's] property in Dölzschen, made over to Andrea Bontempi, and deducted from the [amount of] the aforementioned Kapellmeister's back salary.³⁷

Additional documents, which record payments to individual musicians, help to expand upon the general impression left by the financial materials discussed above, and demonstrate that Johann Georg fell behind in payments both to his Kapellmeisters and to other performers. For example, although Johann Georg raised Melani's salary in January 1654 to 1000 tl, the castrato received only a portion of his salary each year and was owed 5,800 tl by 1675; by December 1680, the total amount in

---

35. "Aber auf dem Landtage Nov. 1660 drang man auf völlige Ausscheidung der Steuer von der Kammer, die Abstellung der ewigen Anweisungen der letztern auf die erste und auf Revision der Steuerschocke" (Böttiger 1831:168).

36. "und übernahme endlich eine ungeheure Schuldenmasse, die noch 1666, nachdem vier Tonnen Goldes schon abgetragen waren, auf 5,200,000 Gülden sich belief" (Böttiger 1831:168).

37. "1280 fl. 5 gr. seind Sr. Churf. Durchl. zu Sachßen *sub dato* am 4.ten *Novembris Ao.* 1659 ergangenen gndsten Verordnung, Johann Schröteln Acciss-Einnähmern in Dreßden, zu völliger Vergnügung der 3000 thl Kauffgelder, vor sein an *Andreae de bon Tempo*, Cappelmeister überlaßenes Guth, zu Dölzschen, zahlt und uf iztgedachten Cappelmeisters hinterstelligen Besoldung *decurbir*et worden" (Sächs HStA, Rentkammer-Rechnungen Nr. 191, Debits [*Außgaben*], *Trinitatis* 1661, fol. 72r). In these treasury records, the court fiscal year began in September and comprised four terms: *Crucis* (from Holy Cross Day, September 14), *Luciae* (from the Feast of St. Lucy, December 13), *Reminiscere* (from the second Sunday in Lent), and *Trinitatis* (from Trinity Sunday, late May to early June).

arrears had climbed to over 8,600 tl.[38] When Antonio Blasi sought a pass to Italy in June 1667, he apparently had not received any of his salary for an entire year. The castrato seems to have petitioned for his back salary at that time, but did not receive payment until 1670.[39] And although the salaries of musicians were to be paid from the elector's discretionary funds, this payment to Blasi was made from the general court treasury and billed back to the elector's account. In general, the high salaries that he offered to his Italian musicians seem to have added to Johann Georg's financial problems, and their salaries often fell into arrears, sometimes for several years at a time.

Enhancement of the Worship Space

In the summer of 1661, despite these financial difficulties, Johann Georg and his "Chief State Architect" (*Ober Landbaumeister*), Wolf Caspar von Klengel, turned their attention to the creation of a worship environment suitable to the elector's expansive ensemble and its new repertoire, an endeavor that took Klengel a little over a year to complete.[40] During the many months of construction, court worship services were moved to various locations: the *Riesengemach* in the castle itself, the nearby Sophienkirche, and, from February 1662, in the recently built chapel in the home of the late dowager electress Magdalena Sibylla (d. 12 February 1659).[41] The most significant renovation for the musical aspect of worship, of course, was the erection of two new balconies for the musicians and the installation of two new positive organs, one in each balcony.[42] Although the castle chapel lost its identity as a worship space in the eighteenth century, several decades after August the Strong's 1697 conversion to Catholicism had rendered it superfluous, Klengel's balconies can be seen in the two depictions of the seventeenth-century interior that do survive— the frequently reproduced engraving of David Conrad, which appeared in 1676 as

38. Sächs HStA, Rentkammer-Rechnungen Nr. 191, fols. 8r–11r.

39. Sächs HStA, Rentkammer-Rechnungen Nr. 191/2, Debits (*Außgaben*), *Crucis* 1670, fol. 5r.

40. Klengel was ennobled by the emperor in 1664. See the biographical sketch by May 1980:40–42.

41. SLUB Msc. Dresd. Q 238, entries for 27 October, 24 November and 1 December 1661; Sächs HStA Loc. 12026, fol. 113v, entries for 10 November and 1 December 1661; SLUB Msc. Dresd. Q 240 [unfoliated], entry for 9 February 1662.

42. The new balconies were apparently accessed from the organ gallery, which in turn was accessible from the music library, known as the *Jüngste Gericht* (Last Judgement) for the painting that hung there, which was on the second floor of the castle, behind the organ gallery. See Doering 1901:210.

the frontispiece to the hymnal edited by Christoph Bernhard,[43] and an engraving published in the eighteenth century by Johann Andreas Gleich.[44] The engravings demonstrate Klengel's success in bringing to fruition his plans for the chapel, developed in collaboration with the elector.[45] Clearly visible over the altar are the two new balconies, each equipped with a positive,[46] and in the case of Conrad's depiction, filled with instrumentalists. New confessionals appear on either side of the altar, the reredos of which is framed by four small columns; in addition, all of the visible windows (including those of the sacristy, to the right of the pulpit) have been fitted with small round window panes.

No information has yet come to light regarding the style or builder(s) of the new positives, which the elector (most likely through consultations with his musicians) clearly saw as essential equipment in the new balconies. Although Gleich suggested that both organs were installed in 1662, on 28 October 1666 a court diarist reported that the "newly-built positive on the right side of the altar was played for the first time."[47] The actual date of installation of its twin in the left balcony remains unknown, but the ubiquity of the organ as a continuo instrument in this era suggests it was installed in 1662 or shortly thereafter. The location of the electoral box in the rear balcony of the chapel necessitated the placement of the main organ, and hence the musicians, in the front of the church; as a result, the singers and instrumentalists faced the elector during performances (as protocol would dictate). As represented by Conrad, the dimensions of the balconies appear to be of sufficient girth to accommodate the three to six musicians (singers and instrumentalists) typically employed in the small-scale sacred concertos of the Italians Albrici and Peranda. With an organ in each balcony, it was possible to place differently constituted ensembles on either side, each with a different role during worship. One wonders, however, if these balconies could also accommodate the expansive ensembles, which often numbered twenty-five or more musicians, that were frequently required to perform large-scale sacred concertos and mass movements during the liturgies. If the new balconies could not hold this many musicians, Conrad's depic-

43. The engraving first appeared in Bernhard 1676. The engraving postdates the installation of the red-and-white marble floor around the altar in 1669 (Sächs HStA OHMA O IV Nr. 24, entry for 19 September 1669).

44. Gleich 1730; the engraving is laid in between pages 38 and 39.

45. The correspondence between Johann Georg II, Klengel, and Johann Siegmund von Liebenau (the elector's "project manager") regarding the renovations to the chapel appears in Sächs HStA Loc. 4452/2, fols. 11r–19r.

46. By the time of Gleich, the positives had been removed from the balconies.

47. "Am 20. Sonntag nach Trinitatis. . . ward beÿ angehenden Gottesdienst zum erstenmahl das Naüe erbaute Positiv zur rechten handt des Altares geschlagen" (SLUB Msc. Dresd. Q 243, entry for 28 October 1666; see also Gleich 1730:44–45).

tion of additional instrumentalists in the side balconies and the organ gallery may
have some basis in local performance practice.

After over a year of work, the newly renovated and redecorated chapel was
rededicated on Sunday, 28 September 1662 in elaborate church services celebrated
in the morning and the afternoon. The music, all of which was newly composed
for the occasion, included a setting of Psalm 100 by Schütz (now lost) as the morning Introit, as well as Mass movements and concertos by Albrici, who directed the
service music. Although the court diary does not say as much, the court musicians
undoubtedly also inaugurated the new balconies that same Sunday morning. The
court diarist's detailed description of the elaborately embroidered clerical vestments, silver altar furnishings, and solid gold, enameled communion vessels provides a sense of the opulence of the celebration of these services. Both these visible
symbols and the elaborate music that was performed contributed to an atmosphere
of splendor.[48]

In the years following, Johann Georg periodically made additional improvements
to the chapel, each of which required the temporary relocation of worship services.
In August and September 1666, worship services were celebrated in Dowager Electress's house across from the castle; the elector and his retinue returned to the court
chapel on Feast of St. Michael, 29 September.[49] While the reason for the move is
not given, it was likely necessitated by the building of the new positive organ in the
right-hand side of the balcony; the new instrument was first heard in a service on
28 October of that year.[50] In May 1667, services were again held in the Sophienkirche
while the pews in the chapel were painted, and the altar was enhanced with marble
pedestals that were installed beneath the four framing columns.[51] Likewise, in the
fall of 1669, the court again removed to the Sophienkirche while the four wooden
columns that supported the "lowest musical balcony" (i.e., Klengel's balconies) were
replaced with columns of red polished marble, and the floor of the old choir area
around the altar was laid with marble tile, in a tricolor pattern that is discernible in
Conrad's engraving.[52] Finally, during the first two weeks of September 1677, addi-

48. A description of the chapel and the orders of worship appear in Fürstenau 1871;
the orders of worship (without the description of the chapel) also appears in SLUB
Q 240, entry for 28 September 1662. Fürstenau's source has not been located.

49. See SLUB Q 243, entries for 26 August and 2, 9, 16, 23, and 29 September 1666,
and Sächs HStA Loc. 8681 Nr. 6, fols. 257r–259r.

50. See n. 47 above.

51. Sächs HStA OHMA O IV Nr. 21, entry for 29 May.

52. Sächs HStA OHMA O IV Nr. 24, entry for 19 September. Subsequent entries
indicate that the court worshiped in the Sophienkirche on the following three Sundays
and returned to the castle chapel on 17 October. According to Gleich, the columns were
of red marble (1730:48).

tional work of an unspecified nature was carried out in the chapel, which once again required the court musicians to perform in the Sophienkirche and the chapel in the home of the late dowager electress.[53]

THE CHALLENGES OF RECRUITMENT

That Johann Georg managed to maintain an Italian-dominated musical ensemble for thirty years is evident from the names that appear on the rosters of musicians and other documents that survive from the court during this period. A comparative study of these documentary materials, however, reveals the rosters to be quite unstable, with musicians frequently arriving and departing, and this instability necessitated the constant recruitment of new musicians, both in Italy and in northern Europe. Yet the corresponding documentary evidence concerning recruitment does not survive.[54] As a result, many central questions regarding recruitment still await answers. For example, to what degree was Johann Georg required to engage in recruitment in Italy? Many of his Italian musicians seem to have arrived in Dresden directly from other northern courts, and may have learned of opportunities at the Saxon court through other musicians. Additionally, what sorts of enticements did Johann Georg offer to Italian musicians to persuade them to leave behind the splendors of Venice, Florence, Rome, and other Italian cities for a position at his northern court? Was he prepared to make any concessions to allow these Catholics to fulfill their own religious obligations? What were his tastes in voices, and his expectations for their training? How successful was his recruitment program? And finally, how did the financial package that he offered compare to those offered by his major northern competitors, particularly the courts of Munich and Vienna?

Given the general scarcity of documents directly related to the recruitment and hiring of Italian musicians in Dresden, the process can only be partially reconstructed. Helpful in this regard are rosters of musicians, correspondence that includes passing references to musicians, and ancillary materials such as travel passes and payment records. Unfortunately, all of the correspondence relating directly to recruitment seems to have disappeared—nothing survives in Dresden of the nature of the enlightening correspondence between Pfalzgraf Philipp Wilhelm of Pfalz-Neuburg and his Kapellmeister-*cum*-agent in Italy, Giovanni Battista

---

53. Sächs HStA Loc. 8682 Nr. 11, fols. 106v, 107v, and 111r (entries for 2, 9, and 15 September).

54. Two exceptions remain: the 1661 correspondence of Klengel regarding a musician recruited by Melani in Italy (discussed below), and letters from 1666 regarding Bontempi's attempts to recruit Alessandro Contili, a musician at the imperial court (Sächs HStA Loc. 7330/4, fols. 162r–164v).

Mocchi, in which, for example, Philipp Wilhelm stressed that Mocchi should seek singers that were young, inexpensive, malleable, and obedient.[55] In contrast, Johann Georg's specific attitudes, priorities, and desires remain unknown and can only be inferred from the abilities of those he is known to have hired. This missing correspondence would also reveal whether he developed a systematic hiring process, taking into account voice type or instrument, or whether he simply took any Italian musician willing to come to Dresden. The lost correspondence could also reveal the names of those who acted as recruiters and negotiators. The prince's correspondence with Commander Detloff Wedelbusch in Danzig reveals that even military officers might also perform tours of duty as musical middlemen,[56] and letters such as that from Oeÿnhausen suggest that various correspondents may also have facilitated the connections between musicians and potential patrons. In addition, Johann Georg also sent musicians on recruitment trips to Italy (discussed below). Without correspondence relating to recruitment, however, it is impossible to ascertain the amount of authority Johann Georg delegated to any particular negotiator, although this probably depended upon that individual's level of expertise. While an interested courtier such as the music-loving Oeÿnhausen might simply make contact with the musician on his own accord, and subsequently recommend him to the elector, the musicians who served as agents in Italy likely possessed the authority to audition musicians, outline the terms of employment (salary, duties, etc.), and bring (or send) qualified and interested individuals back to Dresden for an audition there, following which the successful candidates would receive contracts from Johann Georg.[57]

During this era, many German princes engaged agents in Italy, and the duties of at least some of these intermediaries included negotiating with musicians. According to Rudhart, Bavarian elector Ferdinand Maria employed agents in at least four Italian cities—Rome, Venice, Milan, and Parma—who "were instructed to send good singers to Munich"; he also noted that "the numerous entries in the lists of court expenditures 'for various Italian musicians and other masters [sent] here from Italy' furnish proof that the traffic with Italy in this area was an extremely brisk

---

55. See Einstein 1907–08:386–87.

56. See Frandsen 2000:32–33.

57. Whether Johann Georg always required a Dresden audition remains unknown, as only two pieces of evidence attest to such auditions. In 1653, Prince Johann Georg asked Schütz to return to Dresden to audition musicians recently arrived from Italy (discussed in chapter 1), and a court diary from 1667 mentions the audition of a castrato that took place after the midday meal (Sächs HStA OHMA O IV Nr. 21 [unfoliated], entry for 2 June 1667).

one."[58] Another Italophile, Philipp Wilhelm of Pfalz-Neuburg, also had Italian agents in Rome and Naples who were directly involved in the recruitment and hiring of musicians; Giacomo Fantuzzi, the Roman agent, frequently consulted Carissimi for advice on singers.[59] In addition, the Italian Kapellmeister in Neuburg, Giovanni Battista Mocchi (1620–88), made two recruitment trips to Italy, in 1662 and 1675–76.[60] The correspondence between Philipp Wilhelm, Fantuzzi, and Mocchi demonstrates the effort that such recruitment involved, and sheds light on various aspects of the negotiation process, such as the offers made by the court and the demands made by musicians; it also attests to the stiff competition between northern courts for good musicians:

> Since the bass singer Isidoro is determined not to leave Rome, I am zealously cultivating a certain Giovanni Carlo [Ferucci], who serves in St. Peter's, and whose praises Carissimi has sung to me; I fear, however, that he has already entered into service with the Lord Duke [i.e., Elector] of Bavaria . . . I have also written to Bologna, where good virtuosi usually thrive.[61]

When he entered the race to acquire Italian musicians, Johann Georg must have encountered these same challenges, and likely often lost musicians to Catholic courts with whom he stood in direct competition, as his recruitment situation was compounded by confessional complexities that did not trouble his Catholic peers. In contrast to the Munich and Neuburg courts, however, most of the surviving evidence of his recruitment efforts remains circumstantial. Johann Georg is known to have employed three agents based in Italy, Bontempi's brother Vincenzo Angelini, engaged for service in 1653, Peter Cresser, who received a contract as the elector's *factor* in Venice in 1665, and Domenico Melani, who is identified as

---

58. "[die] waren beauftragt, gute Sänger nach München zu schicken und die in den Ausgabenverzeichnissen zahlreich vorkommenden Posten 'für unterschiedliche wälsche Musikanten und andere aus Italien hieher beschriebenen Maister' liefern den Beleg, daß der Verkehr mit Italien in dieser Beziehung ein äußerst lebhafter gewesen" (Rudhart 1865:66). The Bavarian elector's Roman agent was Giovanni Battista Maccioni (Sandberger 1901:xvi).

59. Einstein 1907–08:354–69.

60. Einstein 1907–08:364, 368.

61. "Da der Baßsänger Isidoro entschloßen ist, Rom nicht zu verlaßen, bearbeite ich eifrig einen gewißen Giovanni Carlo [Ferruci], der in St. Peter dient und mir von dem Herrn Carissimi gelobt wird; ich fürchte aber, daß er sich schon mit dem Herrn Herzog von Bayern eingelaßen hat . . . auch nach Bologna hab ich geschrieben, wo gewöhnlich gute Virtuosen wachsen" (Einstein 1907–08:359; Fantuzzi to Philipp Wilhelm, 30 January 1655). According to Einstein, the bass in question is probably Isidoro Cerruti (ibid.).

the elector's agent in travel passes from 1666 and 1668, and who received a contract as *"Cammerjunker* and Agent in Italy" on 7 April 1676.[62] As he had with his brother, Bontempi seems also to have facilitated the arrangements with Cresser and set his patron up with one of his trusted acquaintances in Venice, for Cresser is named in two Venetian notarial documents from 1656 and 1657 that concern Bontempi's financial transactions.[63] Unfortunately, nothing survives to detail the activities of either Angelini or Cresser on the elector's behalf. The appointment of Cresser may have paid as rich a musical dividend as did that of Angelini, however, for in November 1669, soprano castrati Gabriel Angelo de Battistini and Giovanni Antonio Divido left San Marco in Venice for the Dresden *Hofkapelle.*[64] Melani, who had made himself indispensable to the elector soon after his arrival in 1654, traveled frequently to Italy on his patron's behalf and received at least nine travel passes between 1654 and 1674. During these frequent trips to his homeland, Melani used Florence as his home base, where he acted on behalf of the elector in a number of areas, one of which was certainly the recruitment of musicians for Dresden. Unfortunately, only one instance of his musical agency can be documented. In the winter of 1660–61, Melani traveled to Italy with Klengel, the court architect, and a *Hofcornet* by the name of Friedrich Albrecht von Götz.[65] Once in Venice, the three separated; Klengel remained in Venice, while Melani continued on to Florence, and Götz to Rome. While in Florence, Melani successfully recruited a "discantist" (a castrato), as revealed by a letter of Johann Georg to Klengel of 22 February 1661.[66] After receiving a request for funds from Klengel, then in Venice, Johann Georg

62. Cresser's Latin contract dates from April 1665; Sächs HStA Loc. 8792/5, fol. 195r–v. In the contract, his name appears as "Petrus Cresserus"; in the Venetian notarial documents (cited in the following note) it appears as "Pietro Cresser." Melani is identified as an agent in passes dated 8 February 1666 and 8 October 1668 (Sächs HStA Loc. 8298/7, fols. 63r and 69v); his 1676 contract appears in Sächs HStA Loc. 7168 Nr. 1, fol. 162r.

63. ASV, Notarile atti, b. 1085, fol. 8 (23 March 1656), and Notarile atti, b. 11060, Piccini 1656, no. 1, fol. 45v (4 April 1657). The former document further attests to Bontempi's musical connections in Venice, as it also mentions the opera composer Pietro Andrea Ziani.

64. See Emans 1981:55, 69. According to Sandberger, both castrati sang in Kerll's *Erinto* in Munich in 1661 (1901:xxx). Divido left Dresden in 1672 (travel pass to Italy, 22 April 1672; Sächs HStA Loc. 8298/7, fol. 15v), while Battistini remained until 1680 (see Spagnoli 1990:91; here Divido's name is given as "Pivido").

65. Travel passes for Klengel, Götz, and Melani were issued on 13 October 1660 (Sächs HStA Loc. 8298/7, fol. 69r).

66. Sächs HStA Loc. 10293/1, fol. 10r–v (Johann Georg II to Klengel, Dresden, 22 February 1661). The castrato in question may have been Francesco Perozzi (see below).

authorized a transfer of 3000 tl and specified that 200 tl were intended to cover the travel expenses of the singer that Melani was bringing along.[67]

In addition, Melani's vast network of musical relatives may also have helped him to recruit musicians. The castrato traveled to Italy again in the spring of 1663,[68] and on this trip may have attempted to recruit the tenor Vincenzo Leoni, as a recently published letter of Filippo (Francesco Maria) Melani to Ippolito Bentivoglio in Ferrara reveals:

> There will be an opportunity to have a good tenor by the name of Vincenzo Leoni, who is located in Orvieto, a virtuoso who is capable of everything, as much in the church as in the chamber and theater. At present he is without employment, and because of some persecution or other he cannot leave the Papal States, since some time ago, having appealed to the pope to be allowed to go to serve the Elector of Saxony, he was relegated to Orvieto, and, luckily, afterward, he was allowed to stay in the Papal States. Thus I propose him to Your Excellency, and when you want him, tell me, please, at once, so that he does not go anywhere else. And on this score, my brother Alessandro tells me that this virtuoso will accommodate himself to that which Your Excellency wishes. Thus I will await your orders, as much for my brother's business as for that which concerns Leoni.[69]

Leoni's thwarted efforts to join the Dresden *Hofkapelle* have been unknown until this time, but this new document helps to explain the contents of an undated note in Peranda's hand, headed "Names of musicians who are in prison in Macerata." Peranda's list comprises just two names, "Vincenzo Leoni, tenor," and "Giuseppino of San Pietro, soprano," and suggests that the Kapellmeister kept careful track of

67. Sächs HStA Loc. 10293/1, fol. 10r–v. Klengel requested the money for a second time in a letter of 10 April 1661 (ibid., fol. 20r–v), in which he also mentions the discantist; his first request (dated 11/21 January 1661, according to the elector's February letter) does not survive.

68. Melani's travel pass to Italy is dated 30 March 1663 (Sächs HStA Loc. 8298/7, fol. 69v).

69. Monaldini 2000:193, Filippo Melani of Florence to Marquis Ippolito Bentivoglio, 10 June 1664; the Italian text appears in Appendix I (no. 6). The author thanks John Walter Hill for providing a translation of the excerpt. Both Padre Filippo (Francesco Maria) Melani (1628–ca. 1703) and Alessandro were among the seven sons of Domenico di Sante Melani of Pistoia. The Domenico Melani who served in Dresden was also born in Pistoia, but belonged to another branch of the Melani family; see Weaver, "Melani," in *GMO*.

musicians who had been targeted for hiring.[70] Perhaps not coincidentally, Macerata was Peranda's hometown in Italy.

Like Melani, other members of Johann Georg's musical ensemble also traveled frequently to Italy, and even though personal business was given as the official reason for most of these trips, they may well have kept their eyes and ears open for potential cappella members while visiting their homeland. Kapellmeisters Albrici, Bontempi, and Peranda all received at least two travel passes to Italy, as did singers Amaducci, Battistini, de Blasi, Fidi, Marchesini, Perozzi, and Santi. Clearly a "brisk traffic" in musicians took place between Dresden and various Italian cities, but exactly how and by whose agency these musicians became contractually affiliated with the Saxon elector's court remains largely shrouded in darkness.

THE MUSICAL PERSONNEL OF THE DRESDEN *HOFKAPELLE*, 1657–80

The sort of detailed records of payments made to musicians that have allowed scholars to ascertain not only the composition of various musical ensembles, but also the whereabouts and thus activities of musicians in many courts and churches, do not survive in Dresden. The only pay records that survive from the court of Johann Georg II reflect lump-sum payments made on an irregular basis to an individual who functioned as the musicians' paymaster; records of the amounts dispersed to individuals do not survive.[71] Thus, rosters of musicians represent the main source of information concerning the personnel of Johann Georg's *Hofkapelle*. Only three complete rosters of the ensemble survive, however, dating from 1657, 1662, and 1680. While these provide a snapshot of the ensemble at particular times during this elec-

70. "Nomi delli musici che sono prigioni in Macerata / Vincenzo Leoni Tenore / Giuseppino di S. Pietro. Soprano" (Sächs HStA Loc. 8753/6, fol. 74r). The identity of "Giuseppino di S Pietro" remains undetermined. The letters published by Monaldini regarding Leoni date solely from 1664 and make no mention of his imprisonment (2000:195, 206–7, 209–14).

71. Financial records for the general court treasury (*Rentkammer*) survive only from the years 1660–62, 1670–71, and 1680–81, and those for the Privy Exchequer (*Geheime Rentkammer*), the records of the elector's discretionary funds, survive only from November 1660 to January 1664. These documents record only three payments to the entire ensemble: 1) 18,316 tl 15 gr (between 1 November 1660 and 31 January 1662), 2) 6,498 tl 22 gr 9 d (between 1 February 1662 and 31 January 1663), both in Sächs HStA Rentkammer-Rechnungen No. 410, Debits (*Außgaben*), 1 November 1660–31 January 1662, fol. 8v; and 3) 6,000 tl (14 September 1667), in Sächs HStA Rentkammer-Rechnungen No. 191/2, Debits (*Außgaben*), *Crucis* 1670, fol. 5r.

tor's reign, the names of a number of musicians do not appear on any of the three; in addition, an interval of eighteen years, during which time the membership experienced significant changes, separates the second roster from the third. Thus a true sense of the size and composition of the ensemble throughout the era of the Italians can only be developed by studying these rosters in conjunction with a number of other sources: partial rosters from 1661, 1671, and 1672, the composite roster of 1717, travel and dismissal passes,[72] letters and other court documents, and studies of musical ensembles in northern Europe and in Italy. The result of such study reveals an ensemble whose overall size remained remarkably steady over a twenty-three-year period, and in which Italians constantly represented about one quarter of the performing membership.

The *Hofkapelle* from February 1657 to October 1662

In the period between February 1657 and October 1662, a number of musicians, both Italian and German, arrived at the Dresden court. Some would remain there for many years, while others would disappear after a brief period of service. As mentioned above, some of these musicians were likely recruited by members of the *Hofkapelle*. Extant travel passes indicate that travel between Dresden and Italy was frequent during these years; Melani traveled there in 1659 and 1660,[73] Antonio de Blasi did so in the summer of 1659,[74] and Bontempi in 1660.[75] These trips quickly began to bear musical fruit, particularly in the form of castrati. Soprano Angelo Maria Marchesini probably arrived in Dresden at some point in 1659, having left the service of either the emperor in Vienna or a Hungarian nobleman;[76] he received a pass to Italy from Johann Georg on 5 December of that same year, and his exact date of return is unknown.[77] According to the 1717 roster, he served in Dresden until 1667; his tenure was interrupted, however, by service at the Neuburg court from at

---

72. But for a few references in *EQL*, the over ninety surviving travel passes have never been considered in studies of the Dresden court.

73. Sächs HStA Loc. 8298/7, fol. 57r, Latin pass to Italy dated 23 September 1659; the 1660 trip is discussed above.

74. Sächs HStA Loc. 8298/7, fols. 52r, 57r, Latin passes to Italy dated 15 and 18 July 1659.

75. Sächs HStA Loc. 8298/7, fol. 60r, Latin pass to Italy dated 1 May 1660. Bontempi also received a German pass in March 1660, with an open destination (Loc. 8297/3, fol. 27r, pass dated 15 March 1660). Travel passes written in German suggest that the travel was limited to German-speaking regions, while passes to Italy were nearly always written in Latin.

76. See Knaus 1967:23–24, 63, 65, 117, 128.

77. Sächs HStA Loc. 8298/7, fol. 57r, Latin pass to Italy dated 5 December 1659.

least December 1662 to February 1664.[78] Alto castrato Sefarino Jacobuti (or Jacobanti) also joined the Dresden ensemble during this time; both his date of arrival and previous place of employment are unknown. Jacobuti received a pass to Italy on 30 July 1660,[79] but seems to have traveled only as far as Munich, where he received an appointment in August of that year and sang in Johann Kaspar Kerll's *Erinto* in 1661.[80] The Roman castrato Francesco Perozzi (Pierozzi) first appears in Dresden court records in the summer of 1661, when he received a pass to travel to Hamburg with Vincenzo Albrici "in great haste";[81] he may be the discantist recruited by Melani (or perhaps by *Hofcornet* Götz, who traveled to Rome) in 1661. In the early 1650s, both Perozzi and Albrici had served in Queen Christina's troupe of Italian musicians.[82] As the former queen was in Hamburg from May 1661 to April 1662, this expedited visit may have been connected with her presence there; as the musicians were accompanied by a herald trumpeter, the mission may have been diplomatic in nature.[83] While in Hamburg, Albrici may have spent time with Weckmann, for he seems to have returned to Dresden with new ideas regarding scoring and contrapuntal artifice, both of which he displayed in *Omnis caro foenum*, performed in the court chapel in the summer of 1662.[84]

In July 1661, Johann Georg spent several weeks at the warm baths in Hirschberg, accompanied by an enormous retinue of 667 persons, including fourteen musicians:[85]

> Vincenzo Albrici, Kapellmeister
> Giuseppe Peranda, Vice-Kapellmeister
> Antonio de Blasi, Soprano
> Bartolomeo Sorlisi, Soprano
> Francesco Santi, Alto
> Giovanni Novelli, Tenor
> Stefano Sauli, Bass
> Bartolomeo Albrici, Organ

78. Einstein 1907–08:364–65.

79. Sächs HStA Loc. 8298/7, fol. 52v, Latin pass to Italy dated 30 July 1660. The language of the pass does not indicate that it is a dismissal pass.

80. Sandberger 1901:xxix.

81. Sächs HStA Loc. 8299/1, fol. 16r, pass dated 24 August 1661. Perozzi's name occasionally appears as "Pierozzi," but the singer used the former spelling (Sächs HStA Loc. 7166/4, fol. 25r–v, Francesco Perozzi to Johann Georg II, 19 July 1666).

82. Sundström 1966:301, 303, 308.

83. See Kellenbenz 1966:190.

84. See the discussion in chapter 6.

85. Sächs HStA OHMA I Nr. 9, fols. 60, 71r, 81r. Here the names of the musicians and instruments have been regularized.

Balthasar Sedenig, Violin
Sebastian Ludwig Sulz, Violin
Simon Leonhardt, Trumpet
Daniel Philomathes, Trumpet
Clemens Thieme, Curtal
Johann Christoph Schricker, Calcant

This document is the first to name Peranda specifically as vice-Kapellmeister, and it also introduces the names of three new Italian singers, the castrati Sorlisi and Santi, and the tenor Novelli. All three arrived from service at other northern European courts: Novelli, who soon rose to the rank of vice-Kapellmeister, left the cappella of Dowager Empress Eleonora II in November 1660 and seems to have come directly to Dresden.[86] The two castrati, however, came from Munich, and numbered among the four musicians that the electress of Bavaria had reported missing back in 1651. Their appearance suggests that Johann Georg's earlier "investment" in the Bavarian court ensemble, facilitated by Bandini and Bontempi, paid its dividends years later—Sorlisi arrived in Dresden in September 1658, and Santi appears to have followed him in 1659 or 1660.[87]

Between 18 October and 13 November 1662, the Dresden court celebrated the marriage of Johann Georg's daughter Erdmuth Sophia to Margrave Christian Ernst of Brandenburg-Bayreuth. The court musicians performed in the Sunday morning worship service on the wedding day, 19 October, as well as during the marriage ceremony (*Trauung*) itself later that day, and at the service of consecration (*Einsegnung*) the following day.[88] For the wedding, the elector's officers, advisors, and other members of his retinue received a robe to wear during the ceremonies, as did the members of the musical ensemble; as a result, each musician who participated in the wedding is listed on a roster drawn up at this time.[89]

86. Seifert 1982:546.

87. Sächs HStA Loc. 8687/6, fol. 7r. Rudhart gives Sorlisi's dates of service in Munich as 1640–57, and Santi's as 1654–59 (1865:189); as Sorlisi was only eight years old in 1640, the first date should probably be 1650. According to Sandberger, Sorlisi's Munich contract was dated 27 July 1652 (1901:xix). The Bavarian episode discussed in chapter 1, however, reveals that Sorlisi was already in Munich in 1651.

88. SLUB Q 240, entries for 19 and 20 October 1662. Before the marriage ceremony, the musicians performed a setting of Ps 127 (*Beati omnes*) by Albrici; after the ceremony they performed Bernhard's *Mulieris bona*. The next day, the ensemble opened and closed the service of consecration with Bernhard's setting of the *Te Deum* and his *Deus Benedicat*. None of these compositions survives.

89. Sächs HStA OHMA B Nr. 13/b, fol. 750v–752r (fol. 750v: "Zur Churfl. Hoff Capella gehörige Persohnen"). The roster appears in its original order in Spagnoli 1990:85–86.

"PERSONS BELONGING TO THE ELECTORAL *HOFKAPELLE*"

Kapellmeisters

Heinrich Schütz

Vincenzo Albrici

Giovanni Andrea Bontempi

Vice-Kapellmeisters

Giuseppe Peranda

Christoph Bernhard

Sopranos

Domenico Melani

Bartholomeo Sorlisi

Francesco Perozzi

Antonio de Blasi

Contralto

Francesco Santi

Tenors

Giovanni Novelli

Georg [Giorgio] Berthold[i]

Basses

Stefano Sauli

Christian Kittel

Organists

Bartolomeo Albrici

Adam Krieger

[Instrumentalists]

Giovanni Severo, violinist

Michael Schmidt, violin, bass singer

Sebastian Ludwig Sulz, violin

Johann Wilhelm Forchheim, violin and organ

Balthasar Sedenig, violin, viola da gamba, cornetto

Here the missing instrument and/or voice designations have been supplied from various other sources, the order has been somewhat changed to reflect the vocal and instrumental groups, and the spelling of names has been regularized. Fürstenau also published this roster, but inexplicably dated it 1663 (1861/1971:136).

Johann Friedrich Volprecht, lute, viola
Friedrich Westhoff, lute
Sebastian Andreas Volprecht, violone/bass viol
Clemens Thieme, curtal
Friedrich Werner, cornetto
Johann Dixon, sackbut
Andreas Winckler, sackbut
Johann Jäger, sackbut? and bass singer[90]
Jacob Sulz, sackbut

Musical trumpeters
Simon Leonhardt
Daniel Philomathes

Organ and Instrument Makers
Tobias Weller
Jeremias Seyfert

Hanß Georg Feistel, Copyist
Gottfried Leschke, *Hofküster* (court sexton)

Calcants
Hanß Kaschwicz
Johann Christoph Schricker

Choralisten
Altos
Christian Weber (and harp)
Gottfried Janetzky (and cornetto)
Ephraim Buchner, "whose voice has changed" ("so mutiret")

Tenors
Adam Merckel
Hanß Gottfried Bähr (Ursinus)

Basses
Matthias Erlemann, Court Cantor
Constantin Christian Dedekind

Christoph Kittel, Organ

90. In later rosters, Jäger is listed as a bass singer; the fact that he may also have served as a sackbut player is suggested by the position of his name in the list.

When compared with the roster from 1657, the wedding roster of 1662 reveals few changes in the essential configuration or overall numbers of the ensemble, although some of the names have changed. The 1662 ensemble is only slightly more Italianate in composition (twelve as opposed to eleven) than the earlier group, and still includes one Englishman (Dixon). But although the two rosters were generated for similar reasons (as apparel lists for official court events), the 1662 roster provides more detailed information concerning the duties of the singers, for here they are divided into two separate groups, an Italian-dominated *primo coro* (not so designated) of nine singers, and a group of seven German choristers. This latter group, with its organist, no doubt included choirboys that sang soprano, and was likely relegated to the less musically involved services in the chapel—the daily worship services and German vespers.[91]

The language found in two of the few contracts that survive from this period serves to confirm this new implied division into two choirs. While both contracts employ the language of servitude (both men were appointed to "wait on" the elector), the Italian musician's contract gives evidence of the privileged positions that the Italians enjoyed in the *Hofkapelle*. Given that the salary reported in the contract of Antonio Fidi, an alto castrato who joined the ensemble in June 1674, is identical to that of many of the Italian musicians on the 1717 roster, his contract likely typifies the agreements concluded between the elector and his foreign musicians:

> He shall especially, however, be duly bound to remain essentially at Our residence, and not to leave without Our, or Our true Kapellmeister's permission, [and] also to wait on Us most obediently, both in the church and during meals, according to the command of Our Kapellmeister (concerning which he will be advised herewith), [and also] always to be duly present at the *Exercitio* as we ordain it; in sum, to demonstrate in such a manner what befits and is proper in a true, diligent servant toward his Elector and Lord.[92]

In return for a salary of 744 tl, Fidi was expected to serve in the chapel and at the elector's table during meals, and wherever else he might be commanded, and to be present at every rehearsal (*Exercitio*). With respect to his chapel service, however, Fidi's contract remains rather vague. But the contract of a German court musician, Johann Jacob Lindner, sheds additional light on the responsibilities of the members of the *primo coro*, as it leaves no question as to the services in which Lindner, a member of the second choir, was expected to perform:

91. See chapter 7.
92. Sächs HStA OHMA K IV Nr. 3, fol. 110r. The complete German text appears in Appendix I (no. 7).

> By the Grace of God We, Johann Georg II, . . . attest and acknowledge herewith, that we have appointed and accepted Johann Jacob Lindner as our court musician and copyist, . . . He shall especially, however, be duly bound . . . to wait on Us most obediently and diligently at all times, according to the command of Our Kapellmeister (concerning which he will be advised herewith), both in the church, on Sundays and feast days as well as whenever there is preaching during the week, and including all Vespers and Prayer Hours, and early Communion, and during meals, or wherever else he might be commanded, [and] always to be duly present at the *Exercitio*, as we would order it; also to make clear copies of whatever [is given] to him by Our Kapellmeister, and vice-Kapellmeister of one thing and another of church and Tafelmusik, as well as theatrical compositions.[93]

While Fidi is identified as a "chamber musician," Lindner is designated a "court musician." And in contrast to Fidi's contract, that for Lindner is very specific concerning his duties. The German musician was not only expected to copy parts for the court composers, but, as a member of Choir 2, to sing in all of the various chapel services throughout the week, as well as on Sundays (including the early communion service) and feast days. In return for his service, Johann Georg awarded Lindner the vast sum of 250 tl—about one third of Fidi's salary for three times the work.[94]

The *Hofkapelle* from 1663 to 1672

In 1663, after more than seven years of service, the brothers Albrici decided to seek their musical fortunes in England and apparently asked to be dismissed from service in Dresden. Johann Georg granted their wish, and on 31 August the brothers received dismissal documents that allowed them to accept new positions, as well as Latin travel passes with an open destination.[95] Court diaries suggest that by this time, Bontempi was no longer actively serving as Kapellmeister in the chapel; already by 1656, Johann Georg had appointed him to the position of architect (*Baumeister*), although he retained the title of Kapellmeister as well.[96] Thus Vincenzo's

93. Sächs HStA OHMA K IV, 3, fol. 114r. The text of the German original appears in Appendix I (no. 8). Lindner, who served as a tenor from at least 1672 (see below), received this contract as a "court musician and copyist" in 1677.
94. The 1680 roster reports Lindner's annual salary as 150 tl, and the 1717 roster reports it as 200 tl (Spagnoli 1990:88, 94). Neither figure would appear to be correct.
95. Sächs HStA Loc. 7166/4, fols. 19r–v, 20r. On both documents, Vincenzo's title is given as *Capellae Magistro*, Bartolomeo's as *camerae organista*.
96. Bontempi's 1656 will names him as Johann Georg's "chori Musici Praefectus superior, ac Architectus primarius"; see Briganti 1956:105–6. Thus his appointment as

departure necessitated the appointment of a new Kapellmeister. Often when the position of court Kapellmeister fell vacant, the patron sought an outside candidate to fill the post, but in this case Johann Georg elected to promote from within the ranks of vice-Kapellmeister. There he had two options, the Italian Peranda and the German Bernhard, both of whose compositional styles were known to him, as both had supplied compositions for worship services. Despite Bernhard's seniority in the position, his ability to compose in the Italian style, and his long history at the court, Johann Georg appointed Peranda as his new Kapellmeister, presumably in the fall of 1663. With the appointment of Peranda to the top post, Johann Georg issued yet another unequivocal statement of his preference for the modern Italian musical idiom and revealed his continued determination to maintain stylistic continuity in the chapel repertoire.

Bernhard, no doubt disappointed, soon began to cast about for another position and was appointed cantor in Hamburg in December of the same year.[97] Unlike the Albrici, however, he apparently left Dresden without obtaining a dismissal. Rather than compel him to return, however, as he had Albrici in 1658,[98] Johann Georg simply demanded on 30 September 1664 that Bernhard return his letter of appointment.[99] Bernhard's departure created a vacancy in the post of vice-Kapellmeister, which Johann Georg may have filled with the Italian tenor Giovanni Novelli; the tenor is first listed as vice-Kapellmeister, however, on the roster from 22 June 1672 (below). The departure of Bartolomeo Albrici also created an opening for an organist, which was filled briefly by Carlo Capellini, who arrived in Dresden from the Viennese court of Dowager Empress Eleanor II at some point in either 1663 or 1664; according to the 1717 composite roster, he remained in Dresden until 1665.[100] Capellini was the last Italian organist appointed in Dresden, however; after his departure, German organists served both national cohorts in the ensemble.

architect to the court occurred well before 1664, the date given by Brumana and Timms in their article on Bontempi in *GMO*. The first known court document to name him "Capel- und Baumeister" is a German travel pass issued 14 January 1664 (Sächs HStA Loc. 8299/1, fol. 27v).

97. See Fiebig 1980:39 n. 4.

98. In August 1658, upon returning from Frankfurt to find that Albrici had departed without permission, Johann Georg sent Melani off to find him (Fürstenau 1861/1971:143). Melani's German pass of 31 August 1658 (Sächs HStA Loc. 8297/3, fol. 15r) makes no reference to the purpose of his journey, but Fürstenau (ibid.) quotes a document of the same date in which Melani is charged with discovering the whereabouts of Albrici.

99. Sächs HStA Loc. 4520/2, fol. 228r, Johann Georg II to Christoph Bernhard, 30 September 1664; quoted in Fürstenau 1861/1971:149–50.

100. Seifert 1982:535–36; Spagnoli 1990:92.

In 1667, the Venetian opera composer Carlo Pallavicino (ca. 1640–88) arrived on the scene in Dresden. How Johann Georg learned of Pallavicino is unknown; it may be that Bontempi, with his Venetian connections, facilitated Pallavicino's hire. The involvement of Melani, however, cannot be discounted, as he received a pass to Italy on 8 February 1666 to travel as the elector's agent. While there, he may have spent time in Venice, attended a performance of Pallavicino's *Aureliano* at S Moise during Carnival, and sent a positive report back to Johann Georg.[101] Pallavicino, who had already composed two operas for the Teatro S Moise in Venice, arrived in Dresden at some point after June 1667; in a letter dated 8 August 1667, Marco Faustini indicates that Pallavicino has gone to Dresden to produce "an opera for the duke" (Johann Georg's hereditary rank).[102] Johann Georg had likely invited Pallavicino to Dresden to compose and produce a new opera for the 1668 Carnival season in his new Komödienhaus (inaugurated in January 1667 with Ziani's *Il Teseo*), but the death on 6 January 1668 of the elector's sister, Duchess Magdalena Sibylla of Altenburg, forced the cancellation of all theatrical performances that winter.[103] Why Pallavicino, who had established a budding opera career in Venice, then remained in Dresden is a mystery—perhaps he regarded the city as fertile ground for Italian opera, with its abundance of castrati, its sympathetic patron, and the absence of censors and competing houses. Although Fürstenau states that Pallavicino served as vice-Kapellmeister from 1667, a travel pass to Italy dated 22 June 1669 gives his title as *camerae nostrae ac theatralis musicae praefectus*.[104] By this time, Pallavicino may have been absent from Dresden for some time, as the pass indicates that he was traveling with his family and his belongings, and he does not reappear in court records until June 1672.

Between 1669 and 1672, Johann Georg's Kapellmeisters were often away from court. After a six-year absence, the peripatetic Vincenzo Albrici returned to Dresden from England, and, in April 1669, directed the Tafelmusik at the banquet following the investiture of Johann Georg II into the English Order of the Garter (*der englische*

101. Sächs HStA Loc. 8298/7, fol. 63r. The dedication of the libretto of *Aureliano* is dated 25 February 1666; see Saunders, "Pallavicino," in *GMO*.

102. ASV, Scuola grande di San Marco, busta 188, fol. 168, Marco Faustini to Nicola Coresi, Venice, 6 August 1667: "Ma il Signor Pallavicino ha convenuto andare in Sassonia per un opera di quel Duca, ne' sara' di qua se non il novembre venturo." According to Beth Glixon, who has studied the Faustini papers in Venice, in June 1667 Pallavicino signed receipts related to the December 1667 production of his opera *Il tiranno humiliato d'amore*, but had someone else sign for him in January 1668 (private correspondence, 15 August 2000).

103. Fürstenau 1861/1971:227.

104. Sächs HStA Loc. 8298/7, fol. 15r. See also Fürstenau 1861/1971:147.

Hosenbandorden).[105] Albrici may have traveled to Dresden with the two Englishmen dispatched to Dresden to conduct the ceremony, Thomas Higgins and Thomas St. George, both of whom arrived on 5 April.[106] On 12 May 1670, Albrici received a payment of 300 tl in Dresden, and in January 1671, during Peranda's absence, he made a request for 685 fl in back salary; one month later, he traveled to Cologne to bring his wife and children back to Dresden.[107] Their presence in Cologne cannot yet be explained; perhaps illness or pregnancy had prevented his wife from accompanying him from England to Dresden in 1669. Albrici was in Frankfurt in March 1671, where he requested another 300 tl, perhaps for travel expenses.[108] On 26 July 1669, shortly after Albrici's reappearance, Bontempi received permission for an extended visit to his home in Perugia and did not return to Dresden until 1671.[109] In 1672 he received a new contract as *Capellmeister und Inspector der Comödienhäuser*.[110]

On 12 June 1670, Johann Georg's only daughter, Erdmuth Sophia, Margravine of Brandenburg-Bayreuth, died in Bayreuth, and once again the court was cloaked in a shroud of silence. As he was not called upon to compose and perform any elaborate music during the obligatory *Hoftrauer*, Peranda traveled to Italy in November; significantly, the travel document names him "first Kapellmeister" (*primarium Capellae nostrae Magistrum*).[111] The presence of two complete Masses (copied in 1671 and 1672) as well as a sacred concerto for a female saint, *Rorate cherubim*, in the Liechtenstein Collection suggests that Peranda may have spent time in Kroměříž on this trip.[112] It is unknown how long Peranda remained in Italy at this time. He had apparently not yet returned to Dresden in April 1671, for the instructions concerning the "Festivität des Ritter-Ordens von St. Georgen" (26 April) make provisions for the

105. Sächs HStA OHMA N I Nr. 1, fol. 16v; and OHMA O IV Nr. 24, entry for 13 April 1669.
106. OHMA O IV Nr. 24, entry for 5 April 1669. See also Watanabe-O'Kelly 2002:140–51.
107. The record of the 1670 payment appears in Sächs HStA Loc. 8687/6, fol. 21r; Albrici's 1671 request appears in Sächs HStA Rentkammer-Rechnungen, Nr. 191/2 [1670–71], fol. 63v; his travel pass, dated 2 February 1671, appears in Sächs HStA Loc. 8297/3, fol. 61r. The several works of Albrici that survive in Trier, which include settings of two Marian antiphons, may be somehow associated with this visit to Cologne (see Appendix II).
108. Sächs HStA Loc. 8687/6, fol. 21r (this document dates from the time of the dismissal of the Italians in 1681).
109. Sächs HStA Loc. 8299/1, fol. 28r. His name next appears on a roster of those who traveled with the elector to Torgau in May 1671; Fürstenau 1861/1971:168.
110. Sächs HStA, 10036 Finanzarchiv, Loc. 32967, Nr. 1918w, fol. 127.
111. Peranda's travel pass to Italy, dated 3 November 1670, appears in Sächs HStA Loc. 7166/4, fols. 22r–23r.
112. See the works list in Appendix II.

"absence of the Kapellmeister."[113] Peranda also does not appear on any of the rosters from 1671, nor on that from May 1672 (below), and is not mentioned as a Kapell-meister, together with Albrici and Pallavicino, in Bontempi's preface to his *Historia della Ribellione d'Ungheria* of 1672.[114] Only a few of his compositions appear in orders of worship that survive from December 1672 through June 1673[115]; the majority of works are those of Albrici and Pallavicino. These lacunae remain difficult to explain: it would seem likely that he had returned to Dresden by the summer of 1671 for the planned (but ultimately postponed) September premiere of the opera *Apollo und Daphne*, a collaborative effort between himself and Bontempi.[116] The next document to attest positively to his presence at court dates from 30 November 1673, when he directed the music on the first Sunday of Advent.[117] However, on 16 January and 6 February 1673, "in the evening, the Italian musical opera about Jupiter and Io was presented in the Komödienhaus."[118] According to Fürstenau, this score also resulted from a collaborative effort between Bontempi and Peranda; if so, it suggests that Peranda had spent at least part of the previous year in Dresden.[119] The presence in Ferrara and Bologna of copies of the libretto for his oratorio *Il sacrificio di Iephte* raises interesting questions about his involvement in Italy with a genre foreign to the Lutheran court repertoire.[120]

In 1672, Klengel completed the new chapel in the electoral *Jagdschloß* (hunting castle) in Moritzburg, which he had undertaken back in 1661. In June of that year, once again accompanied by a grand entourage, Johann Georg traveled the short

113. Sächs HStA OHMA N I Nr. I, fol. 112r: "In the absence of the electoral Kapell-meister, [the following] is to be observed by the director of the cappella" ("In abwesen-heit des Churfürstl. Capellmeisters, ist von dem *Directore* der Capella zu beobachten").

114. Bontempi 1672:7.

115. SLUB K 117.

116. Although Fürstenau gave 3 September 1670 as the date of the premiere of *Apollo und Daphne* (1861/1971:231), Susanne Wilsdorf has established that the premiere was delayed until 9 February 1672, due to the death of the Landgravine of Hesse; see Giovanni Andrea Bontempi and Marco Gioseppe Peranda, *Drama oder Musicalisches Schauspiel von der Dafne*, ed. Susanne Wilsdorf (Leipzig: Hofmeister, 1998), xiii.

117. Sächs HStA Loc. 8681 Nr. 8, fol. 202r.

118. "Abends wurde im Comoedien-Hause die Italiänische Musicalische Opera von Jupiter und Io praesentirt" (SLUB K 117, fols. 20v [16 January] and 27v [6 February]).

119. Fürstenau 1861/1971:243 (unnumbered note), citing Karl Gebhard, *Beiträge zur Geschichte der Cultur der Wissenschaften, Künste und Gewerbe in Sachsen vom 6ten bis zum Ende des 17ten Jahrhunderts* (Dresden: Hofbuchhandlung, 1823), 122.

120. The libretto of an oratorio composed by Peranda, *Il sacrificio di Iephte* (copies in *I-Bc, Rvat (Chigi), FEc;* on the latter, see n. 153 below) was printed in Bologna in 1675 and indicates that the work was performed on Easter Sunday (14 April) 1675 "nella capella del

distance to Moritzburg for the dedication ceremony, which took place on 22 June.[121] The roster of musicians drawn up in advance of the journey reveals that the majority of the cappella members (forty-two of fifty-four) traveled with the elector. The roster also indicates that Johann Georg seems purposely to have left most of his Italian singers, including his beloved castrati, at home in Dresden.[122] The addition of the names of other musicians known to have been in service at this time results in a relatively complete picture of the elector's *Hofkapelle* at this time:

THE DRESDEN *HOFKAPELLE* IN 1672

Vincenzo Albrici	Kapellmeister
Giovanni Andrea Bontempi	Kapellmeister
Carlo Pallavicino	Kapellmeister
Giuseppe Peranda	Kapellmeister
Gioseppe Novelli	Vice-Kapellmeister (and tenor)
Gabriel Angelo de Battistini	Soprano
Antonio de Blasi	Soprano
Domenico Melani	Soprano
Johann Müller	Alto
Johann Gottfried Ursinus	Alto
Giovanni Baptista Ruggieri	Alto
Christian Weber	Alto (and cantor, also harp)
Donato de Amaducci	Tenor
Adam Merckel	Tenor

Castello" for the Cardinal Legate of Ferrara, Sigismondo Chigi. It describes Peranda as "former *maestro di capella* to His Serene Highness of Saxony" ("già maestro di capella del sereniss. di Sassonia"); see Sartori 1990-5:86. According to Victor Crowther, the "Castello" in which the oratorio was performed was in Ferrara, not Bologna (private correspondence, 24 January 2002; the author thanks Dr. Crowther for this information). The circumstances surrounding Peranda's composition of this work have not come to light, and the performance apparently took place after his death in January 1675.

121. Sächs HStA OHMA N I Nr. 6, fol. 54v.

122. Sächs HStA OHMA N I Nr. 6, fols. 53v–55r. Names in italics, as well as the vocal and instrumental designations, have been added by the author. On the roster itself, Albrici and Pallavicino are listed as Kapellmeister, and Novelli as vice-Kapellmeister; the performers appear undifferentiated under the headings "Vocalists" and "Instrumentalists," with the exception of the musical trumpeters and timpanists, who are listed as such. It is possible that as many as five other musicians, all of whom served until 1680, formed part of the *Hofkapelle* at this time: the Italians Ludovico Marziani (violin), Pietro Paolo Morelli (violone), and Galeazzo Pesenti (tenor), and the Germans Georg Cleÿer (tenor) and Ephraim Limner (bass) (Spagnoli 1990:92–93).

Constantin Christian Dedekind	Bass (and Konzertmeister)
Johann Jäger	Bass
Georg Kaiser	Bass?[123]
Christian Kittel	Bass
Pietro Paolo Scandalibeni	Bass
Michael Schmidt	Bass (and violin)
Donat Rößler	Bass
David Töpfer	cantor (voice part?)
Two unnamed choirboys	
Christoph Kittel	Organist
Johann Heinrich Kittel	Organist
Johann Wilhelm Forchheim	Violin (and organ)
Balthasar Sedenig	Violin (and viola da gamba)
Johann Friedrich Volprecht	Viola
Sebastian Andreas Volprecht	Bass viol/violone
Paul Kaiser	Curtal (and tenor)
Gottfried Janetzky	Cornetto
Salomon Krügner [Kriegner]	Cornetto
Ephraim Biehner	Sackbut?
Andreas Winckler	Sackbut
[Johann] Friedrich Westhoff	Sackbut
Johann Moritz Roscher	"ChurPrintzl. Cammer Junge" (sackbut?)
Caspar Koch	Shawm
Heinrich Koch	Shawm
Johann Georg Koch	Shawm
(fourth player)	Shawm[124]
Christian Krausche	Musical trumpeter (and viola)
Simon Leonhardt	Musical trumpeter
Johann Heinrich Lizsche	Musical trumpeter
Daniel Philomathes	Musical trumpeter

123. It is unknown whether this Georg Kaiser is the bass who sang for Schütz; according to the 1717 roster, that singer left in 1659 (Spagnoli 1990:92).

124. While only three shawm players accompanied the elector to Moritzburg, both a court diary entry from 1665 (discussed below) and the 1680 roster indicate that there were four altogether.

Christoph Richter	Musical trumpeter (and violone)
Friedrich Sulz	Musical trumpeter
Johann David Janetzky	Musical timpanist
Georg Taschenberg	Musical timpanist (and sackbut)
Jeremias Seyffert	Organ builder
Andreas Tamitius	Organ builder
Johann Christoph Schricker	Calcant
Johann Jacob Lindner	Copyist (and tenor)[125]
Johann George Feistel	Copyist[126]

The 1672 roster (with additions) confirms that Johann Georg retained an ensemble of a certain size and configuration for many years. By 1672, however, a few aspects of the ensemble had changed. At some point during the preceding decade, the elector had added four more "musical trumpeters" to the ensemble, no doubt for the further aggrandizement of those compositions accompanied by trumpets and timpani on feast days. In addition, a new cohort of instrumentalists appeared among the members of the court ensemble: four players of the shawm, or more likely the *deutsche Schalmei*. These forerunners of the oboe first appear in Dresden attached to military units, but by 1665 seem to have migrated into the musical ensemble.[127] They are first mentioned in the court diaries in 1664, when they played Tafelmusik for the elector, together with the trumpeters and timpanists, "Turkish Timpanists," drummers, and bagpipers.[128] They not only entertained the elector during meals, but also made periodic appearances in the sacred music performed in the chapel. On Christmas morning in 1665, for example, the cappella performed Peranda's *Gaudete pastores* with four trumpets and timpani, four shawms, five instruments (either string or brass), two SSATB vocal ensembles, and continuo.[129] Given the title of the piece, Peranda likely included the shawms as literal reminders of the shepherds' pipes.

125. Lindner's vocal designation appears in the cast list from a performance of the Bontempi–Peranda *Drama oder Musicalisches Schauspiel von der Dafne*, where he is listed as having sung the part of Mars, a tenor role. See Bontempi and Peranda, *Drama oder Musicalisches Schauspiel von der Dafne*, xxi, 2.

126. According to the 1717 roster, Feistel left the ensemble in 1667 (Spagnoli 1990:94).

127. See Fürstenau 1861/1971:200–1.

128. Sächs HStA Loc. 12026, fol. 414v, entry for 22 September 1664.

129. SLUB Q 243, entry for Christmas Day, 1665.

The Death of Schütz and Geier's Ire

On 6 November 1672, elder Kapellmeister Heinrich Schütz died at his home in Dresden, at the age of 87.[130] The last recorded performance of any of his compositions by the court musical ensemble during his lifetime took place in the new chapel in Moritzburg the previous summer, where at Vespers on 23 June, the court musicians performed his settings of Ps 136 and Ps 150.[131] Schütz's funeral took place in the old Frauenkirche on Sunday, 17 November, and was described in some detail by one of the court diarists:

> [On this day] was held the funeral procession of the eldest electoral Kapellmeister, Heinrich Schütz, into the Church of our Blessed Lady, where His Electoral Highness's representative, the Privy Councillor von Wolfframsdorf was in attendance, and the Senior Court Preacher Dr. Geier preached the funeral sermon. In addition, before and after the sermon, the Electoral German Musicians performed four pieces, the first of which was composed by the former vice-Kapellmeister, Christoph Bernhard; the other three, however, were composed for voices and instruments by the departed Kapellmeister himself; another piece was sung by the Kantorei at the elevation of the body before the *Solmisch* House on Moritz Street.[132]

The court diarist does not indicate who directed the ensemble on this occasion, but given that he specifies that only the German musicians performed, it seems most likely that either Konzertmeister Dedekind or Cantor Töpfer led the group in performance. As the diarists rarely use the term "Kantorei" to refer to the electoral musical ensemble, it may be that the *Stadtkantorei* (city musical ensemble) performed the work of Schütz heard during the elevation of the body before the "Solmisch House." According to Mattheson, several years before his death, Schütz

---

130. SLUB Msc. Dresd. Q 255 [unfoliated], entry for Wednesday, 6 November: "Ist der Churfürstl. Älteste Cappellmeister Heinrich Schütz nachmittag um 4. uhr allhier in Dreßden selig verstorben, seines alters 87. Jahre, 4. Wochen, 19 3/4 Stunden" ("[Wednesday, 6 November], the eldest electoral Kapellmeister, Heinrich Schütz, died peacefully here in Dresden at 4:00 in the afternoon, at the age of 87 years, 4 weeks, and 19 3/4 hours").

131. Schütz's settings of Ps 136 and 150 are presumed lost; see the list of lost works in Rifkin and Linfield et al., "Schütz," in *GMO*. See also Steude 1982-83:18, and the discussion of this Moritzburg service in chapter 8.

132. "Wurde des Churfürstl. Älteste Capelmeisters Heinrich Schützens Leich Proceß in die Kirche zu unser Lieben Frauen gehalten, darbeÿ Churfürstl. Durchl. Abgesandter Dero geheime Rath von Wolfframsdorf ware, und die Leich-Predigt der Hl. Ober Hof Prediger Dr. Geyer ablegete, auch vor- und nach der Predigt die Churfürstl. Deütsche *Musica* Vier Stück *Musicir*te, worvon das Erste der gewesene Vice Cappellmeister Chris-

had requested that Bernhard set Ps 119:54, "Your statutes have been my songs in the house of my pilgrimage," in the "Palestrina style" for his funeral.[133]

Although the elector was in Dresden at the time of Schütz's death, having returned from another trip to Moritzburg on 29 October, court protocol apparently prevented his attendance at the funeral of a commoner—even that of a man who had served his family for over fifty years. Instead, Johann Georg sent Privy Councillor von Wolfframsdorf to represent the court, and thus did not himself hear the musical diatribe *cum* sermon delivered by court preacher Martin Geier (1614–80). At Schütz's request, Geier based his remarks–at least in part–on the same psalm verse heard in Bernhard's composition. But by November 1672, Geier had suffered the humiliation of finding himself publicly overruled by Johann Georg II on the question of the castrato Sorlisi's marriage, and for at least five years had been waging a losing battle to stamp out the celebration of Catholic Mass in the Saxon capital.[134] As a result, whatever indulgence he may have displayed in his attitudes toward Catholics upon his arrival at court in 1665 had been replaced by blind intolerance. Thus, rather than use the occasion to eulogize a musical giant who had contributed so significantly to the repertoire of the Lutheran church, Geier elected to deliver a public condemnation of the Italian music that now dominated the chapel, and to criticize its purveyors—some of whom, having been acquainted with Schütz for many years, were very likely in attendance.[135] At the appointed time in the service, Geier mounted the "bully pulpit" and began to condemn the musical idiom so highly prized by his own patron.[136] In his lengthy prolegomenon, Geier defended the Lutheran stance toward congregational singing vis a vis the Catholic position as both scriptural and historical, and criticized the Calvinists with references to the destruction of instruments, and with the comment that "those who opposed vocal and instrumental music, whether in olden times or in our own, were not quite right in the head."[137] Most important, however, he used carefully selected quotations from the scriptures and the church fathers (among them Jerome, Ambrose, and Augus-

---

toph *Bernhardi*, die übrigen dreÿ aber der Sel. Cappellmeister selbst *vocaliter* und *Instrumentaliter componire*t, wie auch noch ein Stück so bey Aufhebung der Leiche vor dem Solmischen Hause in der Moritz Straße von der Cantoreÿ gesungen worden" (SLUB Msc. Dresd. Q 255, entry for 17 November 1672). The report also appears in Sächs HStA Loc. 8681 no. 8, fol. 106v, and in Fürstenau 1861/1971:238. The author thanks Gregory Johnston for help with the translation of this passage.

133. Mattheson 1740/1994: 323, cited in Spagnoli 1990:27–28.

134. See chapter 3. On the Sorlisi marriage, see Frandsen 2005.

135. See also the discussion (with quotations from the sermon) in Fürstenau 1861/1971: 239–41.

136. See Leaver 1984.

137. Leaver 1984:37–40; the quotation appears on p. 40.

tine) to set himself up as a staunch advocate of church music, so that his criticisms of the contemporary Italian repertoire would be received as those of a man not opposed to church music, but concerned about its style. Once he had accomplished this, he launched into his objections to modern music, which seem to stem from his perception of a theatrical style in the music of the Italians:

> Here there should be mentioned what so many old and new teachers of the church have complained of, that is, the unspiritual, dancelike, yes, even ridiculous, modes of song and music one often gets to hear in the churches. If a man were to be brought there blindfolded, he would be quite of the opinion that he was in a theater where a ballet was to be danced or a comedy to be performed.[138]

While he mentioned no musicians by name, and kept his remarks general, Geier clearly intended his criticisms to be heard as direct attacks on the music of Albrici, Pallavicino, and Peranda, whose compositions he had heard each Sunday and feast day since his arrival in January 1665.[139] Geier's strategy seems to have been to "beat the Catholics with their own sticks," for he drew upon the writings of a number of Catholic theologians, including Jeremias Drexel (1581–1638), St. Robert Bellarmine (1552–1621), and Giovanni Battista Casali (d. 1648) in order to make his points:

> As a favor to the papists, we cite here the words of their man, Drexelius (*rhetor. coel. 1. 1. c. 5. para. 4.f.m.78*): "By your leave, *Herren Musici*, a brand-new manner of singing now prevails in the church, exorbitant, broken, dancelike, and by no means reverent. It is more suitable for the theater and the ballroom than for the church. We look for art and in the process lose our old zeal for prayer, and so on. We serve our curiosity and in truth lose our reverent fear of God. For what is this new skipping manner of singing but a comedy in which singers are actors? Now one, now two, now all together step forward and speak together with modulated voices. Now one man speaks alone, then the others follow and shout him down, etc."[140]

Heard in Dresden in 1672, the Jesuit Drexel's criticisms would seem directly related to various features typical of the Roman style that had become so well established in the Dresden court chapel, particularly its imitative concertos and triple-meter arias. But there is great irony in Geier's selection of Drexel as his spokesman, for the latter

---

138. Leaver 1984:42.

139. Geier's official service in the chapel pulpit began on 1 January 1665 (SLUB K 80, fol. 4r).

140. Leaver 1984:43. According to Leaver (1984:52 n. 63), the citation is drawn from Drexel's *Rhetorica caelestis seu attente precandi scientia* (Antwerp, 1636); this devotional manual was also published in Munich by Leysser in 1636.

served as court preacher in Munich from 1615 until his death, at a time when small-scale sacred concertos and *concertato* motets—two genres cultivated extensively by Schütz—held sway there, cultivated by composers such as Giovanni Battista Crivelli (d. 1652) and Rudolph di Lasso (ca. 1563–1625).[141] In the act of using the Catholics' own words against them, Geier was unwittingly condemning much of the deceased composer's output.

Geier found much fault with virtuosic, florid music as providing "bodily pleasure for the ears by all manner of modulations and contortions of the voice," in the words of another Jesuit, Bellarmine.[142] And neither did the castrati engaged at the Dresden court escape Geier's censure. Once again, however, he hid strategically behind the words of a Catholic theologian, rather than utter his own criticisms, and borrowed the words of Casali, "who in his book on the ancient usages of the church . . . also inveighs mightily against such an unspiritual, dancerlike way of singing, particularly against those who for their voice's sake have been emasculated. The church still has to suffer much evil because of this shameful ill usage."[143] But Geier's use of these writers was purely strategic, and motivated by a virulent confessionalism. In his celebration of the Lutheran adoption of the vernacular, for example, he simultaneously condemned as "unintelligible" the Latin figural psalms composed by the Dresden Kapellmeisters for the chapel vesper services, and cloaked his criticisms in anti-Catholic language:

> Oh, what a great blessedness our gracious God has granted us in the bright light of the Gospel, beyond that of our ancestors and beyond that of those who are now still sitting in the darkness of the papacy! Who in that darkness understands rightly and thoroughly a whole psalm, or even one verse of a psalm? How unintelligible the Latin psalter is! On the other hand, what noble and spirited songs we evangelicals have! Johann Weisse, an old learned man, often used to say, as Spangenberg recalls . . . "If Luther had done nothing more than put the Our Father into song as we now sing it, he would have done a better and more profitable work than all the learned men in the papacy with all their great books, for which the world cannot thank him enough."[144]

Throughout the sermon, Geier makes very calculated use of Catholic writings to criticize the contributions of local Catholic musicians, as if to suggest, "if you will

141. On Drexel's career in Munich, see Pörnbacher 1965:21–31.

142. Leaver 1984:43; here Geier is quoting Cardinal Bellarmine's *Explicationes in Psalmos* (Leiden, 1612) (ibid., p. 53 n. 64).

143. Leaver 1984:43–44; here Geier is quoting Johann Baptista Casalius, *De veteribus christianorum ritibus* (Rome, 1645) (ibid., p. 53 n. 65).

144. Leaver 1984:44–45.

not accept the views of a Lutheran, listen to the words of your own churchmen." But strangely, given the occasion for the sermon, he does not hold up the works of the recently deceased Schütz as the *summa* of church music, as one might reasonably expect him to do. While these sentiments might be presumed to be implicit in his criticisms, their nonarticulation here gives rise to the question of how much of Schütz's music Geier had actually heard. The only compositions to which he makes specific reference are the Becker Psalms—homophonic, strophic settings that were regularly sung in the weekday liturgies in the chapel.[145] By the time Geier assumed his post, Schütz had been retired for nine years, and his music was only performed on rare occasions. In one respect, Geier's sermon stands as an important defense of music in worship by a prominent Lutheran theologian, and gains in currency due to the fact that, unlike the criticisms of many other theologians, the repertoire of which he speaks can be easily identified.[146] But his criticisms are severely compromised by his active prejudices towards Catholics. Despite that fact that Peranda and Albrici presented many concertos of a meditational nature during court worship services— works that defy the descriptions "theatrical" and "dancelike"—Geier could neither see nor hear beyond his prejudices, and unfairly cast all of their compositions into the dustbin. In his eyes, these musicians were papists first and foremost, and thus any products of their artistry were suspect if not automatically condemnable.

Leadership Changes in the 1670s

Despite his fulminations, Geier seems to have had no success in altering the musical landscape in the court chapel. A court diary for 21 December 1672 to 3 June 1673 includes numerous orders of worship that chronicle the chapel activity of Peranda, Albrici, and Pallavicino, and demonstrates that works of the latter two dominated the chapel repertoire during this period.[147] The conspicuous paucity of titles by Peranda suggests that he was now less active in the chapel; by contrast, in the diaries for 1665–67, virtually all of the music performed came from his pen.[148] But changes soon came to the chapel: Pallavicino left for Italy in April 1673, and Albrici and Bontempi followed him in July of the same year, at which point the responsibility for music in the chapel likely fell to vice-Kapellmeister Novelli.[149] Bontempi trav-

145. Leaver 1984:25.
146. For comparison, see the music criticisms of seventeenth-century theologians such as Dannhauer, Lütkemann, Müller, Mithobius and Großgebauer as discussed in Irwin 1993:59–98.
147. SLUB K 117.
148. SLUB K 80 [1665], Q 241 [1665], Q 243 [1666], and Q 245 [1667].
149. Sächs HStA Loc. 8698/7, fol. 16r (pass to Italy for Pallavicino, dated 21 April 1673), fol. 70r (pass to Italy for Bontempi, dated 15 July 1673), and fol. 81r (pass to Italy for

eled to Venice, and perhaps beyond, while Albrici went to Rome, where he served as maestro di cappella at the Oratorio dei Filippini until October 1675.[150] Some nine months after their departures, following Weckmann's death in Hamburg on 24 February 1674, Johann Georg apparently requested that Bernhard return to Dresden in order to serve both as vice-Kapellmeister and as teacher (*Informator*) to his two grandsons, Johann Georg IV and Friedrich August.[151]

The final chapter in the history of the *Hofkapelle* begins with the death of Peranda in January 1675. Peranda directed the music in the chapel for the last time on New Year's Day 1675, and died on 12 January; on 15 January his body was transported to Kloster St. Marienstern for burial in the crypt there, presumably following a Requiem Mass.[152] After Peranda's death, however, Johann Georg promoted neither Novelli nor Bernhard to the vacant post, but after some nine months, finally brought in Sebastiano Cherici (1647–1704), the maestro di cappella of the Accademia dello Spirito Santo and the Duomo in Ferrara, to fill Peranda's position. Cherici's appointment may have been facilitated by Antonio Cottini, the Ferrarese bass who had returned to Italy from Dresden in 1674, and who was in his native city at Easter 1675.[153] In addition, Domenico Melani spent some time in Florence in 1675, and may well have received instructions from the elector to add a visit to Ferrara during his junket, in order to negotiate terms with Cherici.[154] Cherici led the musical ensemble for the first time on 12 September 1675, in the chapel at Moritzburg.[155] He remained

Albrici, dated 15 July 1673). All three may have left in response to a ban on celebrations of the Catholic Mass published by Johann Georg in February 1673 (see the discussion in chapter 3).

150. A Venetian notarial document places Bontempi in Venice in September 1673 (ASV, Notarile atti, Piccini 11092, fol. 288, 5 September 1673). Albrici's activities at the Oratorio dei Filippini are reported in Morelli 1991:46, 50, 129, 130, 191.

151. Fürstenau quotes a document dated 31 March 1674 in which Bernhard is appointed vice-Kapellmeister and *Informator* to the elector's two grandsons; for the two positions he received a combined salary of 1100 tl, 700 as vice-Kapellmeister and 400 as *Informator* (1861/1971:245). See also Krüger 1933:209–10, and Mattheson 1740/1994:19–20.

152. Fürstenau 1861/1971:244; Sächs HStA Loc. 8682 Nr. 9, fol. 80r (entry for 15 January).

153. Cottini was hired in Dresden in September 1672, and received a dismissal on 30 April 1674 (Sächs HStA Loc. 7166/4, fols. 26r–v, 27r). According to Walker and Bianconi, he signed the dedication to Peranda's lost oratorio *Il sacrificio di Iephte* (libretto in *I-FEc*) in Ferrara at Easter 1675 (1984:280).

154. Melani received a pass to Italy on 25 Sept 1674 (Sächs HStA Loc. 8298/7, fol. 81r). Late in the nineteenth century, Theodor Distel reported that Melani had written to the electress from Florence in 1675 (no month given) concerning a lute-playing dwarf (1896:54–55).

155. Sächs HStA Loc. 8682 Nr. 9, fol. 140v, entry for 12 September 1675.

in Dresden for a mere seven months, then left in early April 1676;[156] it is possible that Johann Georg invited Cherici to Dresden on an interim basis only, to fill the post while he arranged for Albrici's return. Four of the compositions that he presented during his brief tenure in Dresden later appeared in his 1681 *Harmonia di divoti concerti*, published in Bologna.[157] After Cherici's departure, Bernhard and Novelli shared the duties in the chapel, but once again, neither vice-Kapellmeister received a promotion; in September 1676, Albrici returned to Dresden, perhaps at the request of Johann Georg, and as the "new Kapellmeister," directed the music in the chapel for the first time on 3 September 1676.[158] From that point on, until the elector's death in August 1680, Albrici, Novelli, Bernhard, and occasionally Konzertmeister Forchheim shared the responsibilities in the chapel, each conducting and providing compositions to enhance the elector's worship experience.[159] The vice-Kapellmeisters presented music of their own composition as well as that composed by the Kapellmeisters; at Christmas in 1677, for example, Novelli led the *Hofkapelle* on December 24 and 25, and presented compositions of Albrici, but presented his own compositions on December 26, the Feast of St. Stephen.[160]

The End of an Era

On 22 August 1680, thirty years after launching his "Italian project," Johann Georg died in Freiberg, having left Dresden due to an outbreak of the plague. Soon thereafter, in an effort to reduce expenditures, his son and successor, Johann Georg III, dismissed a number of the late elector's musicians, including all of the Italians, and, the following year, installed Christoph Bernhard as his Kapellmeister and director

---

156. According to Eitner, Cherici received a dismissal pass to Italy on 31 March 1676 (*EQL* 2:416); he directed the music in the chapel for the last time on Sunday, April 2 (Sächs HStA Loc. 8682 Nr. 10, fol. 31v).

157. See the discussions of the texts in chapter 4, and the music in chapter 6.

158. Entries in a court diary for 1676 (Sächs HStA Loc. 8682 Nr. 10, fols. 36r–108r) indicate that Bernhard and Novelli alternated weekly in the direction of music in the chapel between April and August; Albrici's first appearance in September appears in ibid., fol. 121r.

159. Court diary entries for 3 September 1676 through 23 May 1680 demonstrate that the three musicians alternated on a regular basis (Sächs HStA Loc. 8682, Nr. 10 [1676], Nr. 11 [1677], Nr. 12 [1678], and Nr.13 [1679–80].

160. Sächs HStA Loc. 8682 Nr. 12, fols. 3v–5r. Forchheim seems to have been named to the position of Konzertmeister sometime after April 1677; an entry for 15 April 1677 (Easter Sunday) refers to him as *Cammer Organist* (Sächs HStA Loc. 8682 Nr. 11, fol. 47r), while entries from January and April 1678 refer to him as *Concert Meister* (Sächs HStA Loc. 8682 Nr. 12, fols. 14v, 24v).

of a smaller ensemble of German musicians.[161] In December 1680, the new elector directed Christian Kittel to determine the salary amounts owed to each of his father's Italian musicians, in order that they might be paid what they were due. In order to carry out the elector's directive, Kittel drew up a roster of the current cappella members as well as the pensioners; the resulting list includes all those musicians in service to Johann Georg II at the end of his reign, as well as the dancing master and *Kunstkämmerer*, with their annual salaries:[162]

ROSTER OF THE COURT MUSICIANS, 1680

Choir 1

1000 tl	Vincenzo Albrici, *Maestro di Capella*
700 tl	Gioseppe de Novelli, *Vice Maestro di Capella*
800 tl	Gabriele Angelo de Battistini, soprano
700 tl	Antonio Fidi, alto
600 tl	Paul Sepp, alto
700 tl	Donato de Amaducci, tenor
700 tl	Galeazzo Pesenti, tenor
700 tl	Antonio Cottini, bass
700 tl	Johann Jäger, bass
400 tl	Johann Heinrich Kittel, organist
500 tl	Pietro Paolo Morelli, "musician" and copyist (also bass viol)
1000 tl	Domenico de Melani (soprano)
700 tl	Christian Kittel (bass and "paymaster")

Choir 2

700 tl	Christoph Bernhard, vice-Kapellmeister
500 tl	Johann Wilhelm Forchheim, Konzertmeister
300 tl	David Töpfer, court cantor
150 tl	Johann Müller, alto
100 tl	Gottfried Siegmund Engert, alto
200 tl	Johann Füssel, tenor, d. 25 October 1680
200 tl	Johann Georg Krause, tenor
350 tl	Ephraim Biener, bass
120 tl	Johann Christian Böhme, organist
150 tl	Johann Jacob Lindner, copyist and tenor

161. See Fürstenau 1861/1971:260–63.

162. Sächs HStA Loc. 8687/6, fols. 31r–34v (fol. 31v: "Verzeichnüs. Derer Churfl: Sächßl: sämbtl: Capell=Bedienten *Anno* 1680." The roster also appears in Sächs HStA Loc. 8687/1, fols. 355r–357v. The entire roster, which includes pensioners and the "Court and Field Trumpeters and Timpanists," with salaries, appears in Spagnoli 1990:86–90. The list of seventeen pensioners includes Bontempi (1000 tl) and Pallavicino (100 tl,

400 tl	Johann Friedrich Wolprecht (lute, viola, and viola)
100 tl	Tobias Beutel, "Kunst Cämmerer"
600 tl	Georg Bentle[y], dance master, "for back salary"[163]

Instrumentalists

700 tl	Johann Jacob Walther, violin
700 tl	Ludovico Martiani, violin
150 tl	Johann Paul Westhoff, violin
250 tl	Simon Leonhardt, "musical trumpeter"
250 tl	Christoph Richter, "musical trumpeter"
250 tl	Johann Heinrich Lizsche, "musical trumpeter"
300 tl	Friedrich Sulze, "musical trumpeter"
300 tl	Christian Kreusche, "musical trumpeter"
250 tl	Johann David Janetzky, "musical timpanist"
200 tl	Salomon Krügner, cornetto
200 tl	Johann Merckel, cornetto
200 tl	Paul Keÿser, curtal
200 tl	Andreas Winckler, sackbut
200 tl	[Johann] Friedrich Westhoff, sackbut
200 tl	George Taschenberg, sackbut and "musical timpanist"
50 tl	Caspar Koch, "musical shawm player"
50 tl	Heinrich Koch, "musical shawm player"
50 tl	Gottfried Hering, "musical shawm player"
50 tl	Christian Elste, "musical shawm player"
200 tl	Jeremias Seÿfert, organ builder
60 tl	Andreas Tamitius, organ builder
130 tl	Johann Gräbe, court sexton
50 tl	Rudolph Weit, *Haußmann*, "plays the lute"[164]
40 tl	Johann Wilhelm Billich, calcant
40 tl	Wenzel Klemzschkÿ, calcant
	TOTAL: 18,140 tl[165]

Kittel's roster confirms that the division of the vocalists into two hierarchically ranked groups, already implicit in the 1662 roster, had become fixed. Not only does Kittel label the vocal ensembles "Choir 1" and "Choir 2," he further distinguishes

probably just a retainer), as well as a number of deceased musicians, including Schütz and Friedrich Werner, whose heirs apparently still received their salaries; see ibid., 87, 90, 93 (where Werner's first name is given erroneously as "Georg"). Designations not given in the original are provided in parentheses.

163. Sächs HStA Loc. 8687/1, fol. 356v: "auf ruckständige besoldung."

164. Sächs HStA Loc. 8687/1, fol. 32r: "verricht d. lauten."

165. With the salaries of the field trumpeters and timpanists, the total comes to 22,545 tl 6 gr (Sächs HStA Loc. 8687/1, fol. 33r).

between them by describing the members of the former (even the Germans) with Italian terminology, and the latter with German.[166] While Kittel's roster demonstrates that the overall size of the *Hofkapelle* had changed little since 1672, it also reveals that the vocal configuration within the *primo coro* had changed, and that the number of castrati had diminished significantly by the end of Johann Georg's reign. Although the elector had maintained a cohort of five or six castrati from the early 1650s through the 1660s, the numbers began to dwindle in the 1670s, and by 1680 included only three—Battistini, Fidi, and Melani; furthermore, the positioning of Melani's name near the bottom of the Choir 1 list without any vocal designation suggests that at forty-six, he was no longer singing regularly with the *Hofkapelle*. With this configuration of singers, the *primo coro* alone could no longer mount pieces requiring two SSATB vocal ensembles, and without the aid of a choirboy or falsettist from Choir 2, could not perform small-scale concertos scored for two sopranos and one to three other voices.

In conjunction with his efforts to settle all of his father's debts with the Italian musicians so that they might be dismissed, Elector Johann Georg III first asked the Dresden city council to report to him any outstanding financial obligations the musicians had with townspeople. The council responded on 20 October 1680, and their report reveals that Albrici owed 537 tl to six individuals for various goods and services:[167]

224 tl. 8 gr. 1 d.	to Hannß Thomas Friedel, tradesman, and wife, for wares received, including 30 tl in cash,
214 tl. –. –.	to Ephraim Biener, shopkeeper, musician, for wine,
18 tl. 18 gr. –.	to George Schmeltzel, shoemaker, for work done and delivered,
10 tl. 5 gr. –.	to Mitreüther, shoemaker, for work delivered,
30 tl. –. –.	to Johann Tamme, tailor, for house-rent in arrears,

166. For example, the German singers in Choir 1, Paul Sepp and Johann Jäger, are listed among the *Contralti* and *Bassi*, respectively, while the singers in Choir 2 are designated as *Altisten*, *Tenoristen*, and *Bassist* (there is only one of the latter; Sächs HStA Loc. 8687/6, fol. 31r–v).
167. Sächs HStA Loc. 8687/6, fol. 16r–v ("*Specification. Der Italiäner*, von der Churfürstl. Capelle, waß dieselbe denen Bürgern und Inwohnern an Hauß Zinß, Wahren, *Victualien*, Arbeit, oder sonsten schuldig sein, Vnd wie Dieselben ihre forderung angegeben"). This document is undated, but accompanies (and is referenced in) the letter from the Dresden city council to Elector Johann Georg III dated 20 September 1680 (ibid., fol. 13r–v).

| 40 tl. | to Johann Firschel, court musician, for a loan of cash.[168] |
| 537 tl. 7 gr. 1 d.[169] | |

Albrici's debts dwarfed those of the others listed by the council—Melani owed 166 tl to a butcher, Battistini owed 50 tl to three merchants for various wares, including two pair of shoes, Cottini owed a merchant 21 tl, and Morelli owed 20 tl for half a year's rent.[170] Johann Georg III also asked Kittel to provide him with the amount of back salary owed to the court musicians, and Kittel presented him with this information in March 1681. His report not only reveals the extent of the elector's indebtedness to these musicians, but also the measures they were forced to take to remain solvent. For example, although Albrici was owed only 88 tl from the elector's treasury, he himself owed 330 tl to four individuals, including musicians Jäger and Fidi, presumably for cash loans he had received from them; when added to his debts in the city, the total represented nearly nine-tenths of his annual salary of 1000 tl.[171] Kittel's report also reveals that several of the Italians were still owed significant amounts of back salary: Vice-Kapellmeister Novelli could claim 703 tl, a full year's salary, copyist Pietro Paolo Morelli was owed 831 tl, his salary for a year and nine months, tenor Galeazzo Pesenti was still owed 289 tl, and bass Antonio Cottini was still owed 247 tl.[172] The same document indicates that two musicians had received payment in full just days earlier; on 6 March, violinist Ludovico Martiani received 1033 tl, his salary for about one and one-half years, and alto castrato Antonio Fidi received 991 tl, compensation for nearly a year and a half.[173] Such large payments suggest that Johann Georg II, although undoubtedly well-intentioned, often fell into arrears with his musicians' salaries, due in particular to his propensity for living beyond his means. Although the non-payment of salary was not a phenomenon unique to the Dresden court, it was doubtless a factor in the decision of a number of musicians to leave Dresden for more fertile fields.

---

168. Johann Firschel's name does not appear on any rosters of court musicians.

169. Sächs HStA Loc. 8687/6, fol. 16r-v; the German original appears in Appendix I (no. 9).

170. Sächs HStA Loc. 8687/6, fol. 16v.

171. Sächs HStA Loc. 8687/6, fols. 20r-23v (Kittel and Tobias Berger to Johann Georg III, 11 March 1681), here fol. 21r; the four individuals are listed simply as "Bühler" (250 tl), "Köster" (50 tl), "Jäger" (10 tl), and "Fidÿ" (20 tl).

172. Sächs HStA Loc. 8687/6, fols. 21v, 22v, 23r. According to Kittel's records, Morelli owed 106 tl to a doctor; the latter was paid by the court and the amount deducted from Morelli's claim (ibid., fol. 23r).

173. Sächs HStA Loc. 8687/6, fols. 22r, 23r.

Throughout his reign, Johann Georg remained steadfast in his dedication to the cause of modern Italian sacred music. Despite the crushing burden of debt bequeathed to him by his father and a treasury perpetually characterized by a dearth of funds, he managed to maintain a musical ensemble that nearly matched those of Vienna and Munich in size, and that was similarly dominated by Italian musicians. The remarkable stability of the size of the Italianate component in the *Hofkapelle* throughout his reign testifies to the fact that, although his recruitment policies and procedures cannot easily be reconstructed today, Johann Georg was able to develop a successful (if somewhat unsystematic) strategy for attracting Italian musicians to Dresden. As a result, his court stood with those of Vienna, Munich, Innsbruck, and Warsaw as a major haven for Italian musicians in northern Europe. All of these courts, however, cultivated opera programs in which Italian singers and composers figured prominently. Herein resides a fundamental difference that distinguishes the Saxon elector's musical agenda from that of his peers: rather than attempt to produce annual operatic festivals, he focused on music for the liturgy, and developed his international ensemble primarily to provide Italianate sacred music in the chapel on a weekly basis. But in contradistinction to the patrons at the four courts mentioned above, Johann Georg II was a Lutheran, and thus his hiring of Catholics and castrati raised confessional issues that remained moot at Catholic courts, and introduced cultural issues that, if they had ever been of concern at those institutions, had long ago been resolved. These issues and the elector's attempts to resolve them are the subject of the next chapter.

3

Johann Georg II and the Problem
of Catholicism

IN THE COMPLEX religious history of Germany, Saxony stands as the "urevangelisches Land" and the birthplace of the Reformation. From the time of his protection of the Reformer himself following the 1521 Diet of Worms, the Elector of Saxony had played a pivotal role in the development of the new church; Ernestinian Saxony became Lutheran in 1525, and Albertinian Saxony followed suit in 1539–40.[1] But after over 120 years of nearly unflagging stewardship of the new church by the incumbents of the office of Saxon elector,[2] strong suspicions began to arise concerning Prince Johann Georg's fidelity to the "true religion," and it was widely rumored that he would convert to Catholicism. The grounds for these suspicions, however, remain elusive. Several scholars have cited Prince Johann Georg's 1647 invitation to Emperor Ferdinand III (r. 1637–57) to stand as a godparent to his son, Johann Georg III, as the earliest evidence of the prince's flirtation with Catholicism, despite that invitation's outward appearance as a seemingly innocent political gesture, particularly given the continuing peace talks in Westphalia and his father's support for the emperor.[3] In 1650, of course, Johann Georg began to assemble—and soon to

1. In 1525, Johann der Beständige (brother and successor of Friedrich der Weise, the protector of Luther) brought about the Reformation in Ernestinian Saxony; in 1539–40, Duke (later Elector) Heinrich introduced the Reformation into Albertinian Saxony; see Holborn 1982:124–40, 154–67.
2. Elector Christian I (1586–91), Johann Georg II's grandfather, had strong inclinations toward Calvinism; only his premature death prevented his imposition of the Reformed doctrine throughout Saxony; see Parker 1988:21 and Klein 1962.
3. Apparently the invitation was discussed before it was issued—could one invite the emperor to be a godparent? As Senior Court Preacher Weller raised no objection, but pointed out that the Lutherans and the Catholics were united "*quoad substantialia Baptismi*," the invitation was issued; the emperor accepted and sent Julius Heinrich von Lauenburg as his representative (Müller 1838:144–45; see also Vehse 1854:16). According to Weck, "Die Röm. Keyserl. Majest. Ferdinandum den III." appeared as the first of fifteen *Tauff-Zeugen* (baptismal witnesses) at the baptism (1680:335). Joachim Hahn points

flaunt—his Italianate musical ensemble, which doubtless added much fuel to the fire. As Bertrand Auerbach has pointed out, the prince's employment of Italians and Frenchmen, his building of a theater, and his establishment of a "miniature Sistine chapel" were viewed as "incompatible with the rigors of Lutheranism."[4] In 1652, just two years after his son had embarked upon his "Italian campaign," Johann Georg I published his last will and testament and established three semi-autonomous duchies for his younger sons upon his death. One wonders if the old elector feared that his heir would forsake the church of his fathers, and thus sought to afford his three younger sons some religious and financial protection.[5] Rumors of the prince's reported inclinations quickly reached other courts, where preparations were made for either eventuality. In July 1653, for example, a minister from the Brandenburg court authored a dispatch treating the possible scenario, "if the electoral prince does not become Catholic after his father's death, but remains Lutheran."[6] It seems that Johann Georg II had already begun to feel the heat. Undoubtedly familiar with these rumors, in February 1654 he seized the opportunity of Calov's investiture in Wittenberg as General Superintendent to reassure his future subjects of his fidelity to the faith:

> Doctor Weller, today you have entrusted the new Superintendent with the care of the souls of the listeners; hear now that I also entrust you with the soul of my young prince, and, because my Lord Father, by the grace of God, has now reached an advanced age, [and because] I also cannot know when God will call me home, [I ask] that after my death, you will allow the young man to be educated in no other doctrine than that into which I was born, now live, and in which I will constantly abide until my blessed end, with the support and help of God, and in which I will live and die, namely the only true Lutheran religion of the unaltered Augsburg Confession.[7]

out that this should not be given too much weight, given close political relationship in the Empire between Dresden and Vienna (1990:161). Still, it should be noted that the question was treated as a confessional, rather than a political issue.

4. "On le voyait s'entourer d'Italiens et de Français, favoriser des nouveautés profanes, se monter un théâtre, s'organiser une petite chapelle sixtine, toutes choses incompatibles avec le rigorisme luthérien" (Auerbach 1887:74).

5. Parker attributes the partitioning of Saxony by Johann Georg I to the elector's desire to "ensure that none of [his sons] would face the agonizing decisions that had overwhelmed him" during the war (1988:225).

6. "Wenn der Kurprinz nicht nach seines Vaters Tod katholisch wird, sondern evangelisch bleibt" (dated 18 July 1653; Auerbach 1887:75 n. 3).

7. "Herr D. Weller, ihr habt heute auf des neuen Superintendenten Seele die Seelen der Zuhörer gebunden, höret nun, ich binde auch die Seele meines jungen Prinzen auf euere Seele, und weil der Herr Vater nunmehro durch göttliche Gnade ein hohes Alter

Despite the prince's lofty protestations to the contrary, however, rumors of his Catholic inclinations continued to circulate in various quarters. At the imperial diet in Regensburg that same month, the French diplomat Vautort reported that "many believe that he will become Catholic. The father rector of the Jesuits in this city told me this, as if knowing it on good authority, and the French Recollects [Franciscans] who have lately passed through Dresden on their journey back to Poland have told me that his chamberlain, who is French, has given them much hope."[8]

In 1654, the death of the emperor's son and elected successor, King Ferdinand IV of Bohemia and Hungary, created a future vacancy on the imperial throne.[9] Given the long-standing power struggle between the French king and the emperor, the former continually sought ways in which to shift the balance of power in Europe, and here detected an opportunity to bring Saxony into France's sphere of influence, while simultaneously seating a pro-French, non-Habsburg emperor. Thus King Louis XIV, or better Cardinal Mazarin, his prime minister, conceived the unlikely scenario in which Johann Georg II, with the help of France, would be crowned the next Holy Roman Emperor. What better way to lure Saxony into the French circle than to dangle this large carrot before the future elector, who was known (or at least rumored) to have Catholic inclinations?[10] In 1656, Mazarin dispatched a French envoy to Dresden with the instruction that, should the prince show an inclination to convert, he was to inform him that the French king would spare nothing in his effort to transfer the imperial orb and scepter to the guardianship of the House of Wettin.[11] Despite the long-standing rumors of his "crypto-Catholicism," however, Johann Georg managed to resist the dual enticements of imperial crown and rosary, for he

---

erlebet, ich auch nicht wissen kann, wenn mich Gott abfordern wird, daß ihr nach meinem Tode den jungen Herrn in keiner andern Lehre wollt erziehen lassen, als darinnen ich geboren, itzo lebe, auch durch göttlichen Beistand und Hülfe bis an mein seliges Ende beständig verharren, darauf leben und sterben will, nemlich in der allein wahren Lutherischen Religion der ungeänderten Augsburgischen Confession" (Müller 1838:198). The excerpt is also partially quoted in Auerbach 1887:75. Johann Georg gave this speech at the dinner that followed Calov's investiture service, to which he had brought a quartet of Italian singers (see chapter 2). Senior Court Preacher Jacob Weller preached the investiture sermon.

8. "Plusieurs croient qu'il se fera catholique. Le père Recteur des jésuites de cette ville me l'a dit comme le sachant de bonne part, et des Récollets français qui ont passé depuis peu à Dresden, au retour de Pologne, m'ont dit que son valet de chambre, qui est Français, leur en avait donné beaucoup d'ésperance" (Auerbach 1887:75).

9. Hassel 1890:123. Ferdinand IV was elected future emperor in 1653 (Auerbach 1887:77).

10. Auerbach 1887:74.

11. Auerbach 1887:75–76; Auerbach wonders if Mazarin was serious, and if he really believed that the prospect of wearing the imperial crown would cause Johann Georg to

must have realized that the acceptance of both would have instantly thrust him into the center of a politico-confessional firestorm. His situation here adumbrates that of his grandson, August the Strong, who, through an opportunistic conversion in 1697, placed himself in contention for the throne of Poland.

In late 1656 or early 1657, Johann Georg II apparently tried to seek help from both Emperor Ferdinand III and Pope Alexander VII to overturn the provisions of his father's will.[12] Count Martinitz, the imperial governor in Bohemia, reported to the papal nuncio in Vienna that Johann Georg desired to send Johann Friedrich von Burkersroda, his ambassador to the imperial court, to Rome to discuss the matter with the pope. According to Martinitz, he had sent some "controversial writings" to Johann Georg, which the elector had read, and had subsequently discussed the veneration of the saints with the count in a manner that "astonished him." Learning of these strong Catholic inclinations on the part of the new Saxon elector, the nuncio assigned the Abbot of Neuzelle, Bernhard von Schrattenbach, to the task of bringing about Johann Georg's conversion. But suddenly the hopes of all involved were dimmed by the signing on 20 April 1657 of the treaty known as the "freundbrüderlicher Hauptvergleich," which ended the strife between Johann Georg II and his brothers with respect to their father's will, for the agreement seems to have caused Johann Georg to suspend his conversion plans for the time being.[13]

If indeed Johann Georg was inclined to convert—and his intentions are by no means clear—the one thing that likely kept him in the fold of the Lutheran church was the prospect of financial dispossession. Like his forebears, Johann Georg enjoyed no private monetary wealth, but lived on the annual contribution (*Bewilligung*) of the citizenry, allotted to him every few years by the provincial diet. But that citizenry enjoyed no confidence in his commitment to Lutheranism: so greatly did the Saxon estates fear his conversion that in 1657, at their first meeting during Johann Georg's reign, the members of the diet tied their homage and financial support to the condition that the new elector remain faithful to his religious heritage.[14] In fact, the diet even granted itself the right of insurrection, should he attempt to force another religion on the land:

> If the elector or his heirs should, through the destiny of God, allow them
> selves to be led astray from the recognized Evangelical religion to the Papist,

leap at conversion. He also suggests that Mazarin may have been trying to compensate Johann Georg for a past insult concerning an unpaid subsidy.

12. Seifert 1964:107; Seifert draws much of his information from the reports sent by the papal nuncio in Vienna back to his superiors in Rome.

13. Seifert 1964:109.

14. Böttiger 1831:161–62, 168, and Vehse 1854:16.

15. The "right to order the religious affairs of a territory." See Holborn 1982:243–46.

Calvinist, or another false religion, they shall forfeit the *ius reformandi*.[15] If in spite of this the attempt should be made to force another religion upon the land, the estates shall be authorized to oppose it, if an amicable settlement cannot be reached, and in so doing shall not have acted against their duty and conscience.[16]

At this same time, the papal nuncio in Vienna communicated to Rome that a letter from Schrattenbach had strengthened his belief that the elector would convert. In addition, the nuncio reported, during a visit of Electress Magdalena Sibylla to the warm baths in Bohemia, four members of her retinue converted upon hearing a sermon by a Capuchin. The news of this event delighted the pope, who wrote to the nuncio to express his support for the ongoing "conversations" concerning the conversion of Johann Georg.[17] But despite such evidence of his Catholic predilections, other contemporary reports portray Johann Georg as a staunch, if somewhat bibulous, adherent of the Augsburg Confession: "He showed an uncommon zeal for the Lutheran doctrine, and on days when he took communion, he showed so much respect for the sacrament that he did not get drunk in the morning; in the evening, however, he recovered lost time and drank all night, until he fell under the table, like all of his guests."[18]

Another sign of Johann Georg's comfort level with Catholicism, or at least of his ability to look beyond confession in matters of state, was his eagerness to betroth his daughter Erdmuth Sophia (1644–70) to future Emperor Leopold I. Various constituencies expressed support for the proposed match, including the papal curia, who instructed the Viennese nuncio to recommend a match with the Saxon princess; her

16. "Wenn der Kurfürst oder seine Erben durch Gottes Verhängnis von der erkannten evangelischen Religion zu den papistischen, calvini[sti]schen oder anderen Irrtümern sich verleiten ließen, sollten sie des *Ius reformandi* verlustig gehen. Würde trotzdem der Versuch gemacht, dem Lande eine andere Religion aufzudrängen, so sollten die Stände sich dem, in Entstehung gütlicher Mittel, zuwiderzusetzen befugt sein und hierdurch wider ihre Pflicht und Gewissen nicht gehandelt haben" (Seifert 1964:107).

17. Seifert 1964:108.

18. "Er zeigte ungemeinen Eifer für die lutherische Lehre und an dem Tage, wo er communizirte, bewies er so viel Respect fürs Sacrament, daß er sich nicht am Morgen betrank; am Abend aber holte er zum Ersatz das Versäumte nach und trank die ganze Nacht, bis er unter den Tisch fiel, wie alle seine Gäste" (Vehse 1854:89). This information derives from the memoirs of Anton von Grammont, a French envoy in Frankfurt, who must have met Johann Georg during the 1658 electoral diet. In 1665, the French minister Gravel also reported to Louis XIV that Johann Georg's greatest fault was his propensity to drink too much (Auerbach 1887:191).

19. Seifert 1964:109–10.

inevitable conversion and Catholic baptism would likely encourage her father to follow in her footsteps.[19] Some Protestants also supported the match; although the marriage would require Erdmuth Sophia to abjure her Lutheran faith and convert to Catholicism, it was felt that she would continue to support the Lutheran cause, given that she would "retain in her heart the precepts of the religion in which she was raised."[20] Not all remained so sanguine about this prospect, however; Johann Georg's mother wrote to him in Frankfurt in May 1658 and beseeched him not to marry his daughter to a Catholic.[21] The marriage negotiations between the ruling houses of Saxony and Austria continued intermittently until 1660, when Leopold was finally dissuaded by his Jesuit advisors from marrying a "heretic."[22]

THE CELEBRATION OF MASS IN DRESDEN

In 1661, Johann Georg's "Catholic problem" suddenly intensified, when the first known celebrations of Mass in Dresden coincided with the meeting of the Saxon provincial diet. Now, apparently for the first time, the religious activities of his Italian musicians and other Catholic court appointees threatened to complicate the elector's life considerably, for the "problem" had moved beyond suspicions generated by the international rumor mill to actual developments in his own backyard.[23] While Johann Georg could counter rumors with public statements, such as the one he had made in Wittenberg, he could not continue to fall back on mere words, for to issue public condemnations while failing to act to prevent the "vexation" would be to lend his tacit approval to the enterprise. Thus, on 27 March 1661, the Dresden city council (*Stadtrat*)[24] was ordered to be on the alert: "Because, according to reports, the papist sacrifice of the Mass (*Meßopfer*) is being held in the city, [the council] should take steps against such a vexatious activity in better diligence, and should it be at all suspicious of any unknown person entering [the city], it should immediately report any such suspicions to the authorities."[25] Eight days later, the estates

20. "les Protestants surtout y applaudissaient, car malgré son abjuration, l'impératrice eût gardé au coeur l'amour et les préceptes de la religion où elle avait été nourrie" (Auerbach 1887:110).

21. Auerbach 1887:110–11.

22. Auerbach 1887:133.

23. Other Catholics associated with the court included members of the Croatian Guard and their families.

24. On the structure of the Dresden city council at this time, see Nickel 198:83–92, 100.

25. "weil dem Vernehmen nach in der Stadt das papistische Meßopfer sollte sein gehalten worden, solchem ärgerlichen Beginnen in besserer Sorgfalt entgegen zu treten und wo er bei einer oder der anderen ankommenden fremden Person etwas zu argwoh-

thanked Johann Georg for his prompt attention to the problem of Mass celebrations in private homes in Dresden, which they asserted to have been the first example of such in their institutional memory. While the estates went on to assure Johann Georg of their confidence in his fidelity to the faith, they also took the opportunity to point out the conflicts generated by his hiring practices:

> Yet it cannot be denied that the appointment of many servants [who are] unknown foreigners, as well as adherents to a hostile religion, in well-appointed regiments, who consequently effect great change, not only in politics, but also in religious matters (in spite of the close oversight that those upon whom the care of the common good devolves have shown in this case), nevertheless gradually causes one and another vexation that subsequently will be difficult to remove again. . . . We have no doubt that Your Electoral Highness will be able to find equally qualified persons in the considerable land with which the Almighty has blessed You.[26]

The diet also reminded Johann Georg of his 1657 assurance that all of his appointees—school and church employees, counselors, officers, and ministers—would be required to take the usual religious vow (a promise that he had immediately abandoned in the case of his musicians).[27] By this time, it should be noted, Johann Georg had been employing Catholic musicians for a decade. Yet their presence seems to have provoked no complaints from the diet until they and others began to exercise a still nonexistent "freedom of worship." Until the point at which it became a public problem, the religious affiliation of Johann Georg's musicians was simply overlooked.

------

nen finden würde, solches ungesäumt zur Regierung zu berichten" (Lindau 1885:492). Through the continual reference to the Mass as the "sacrifice of the Mass" (*Messopfer*), Lutheran theologians of this era criticized the Catholic view of the sacrificial nature of the Mass. As explained in Article 24 of the Augsburg Confession, "At the same time the abominable error was condemned according to which it was taught that our Lord Christ had by his death made satisfaction only for original sin, and had instituted the Mass as a sacrifice for other sins. This transformed the Mass into a sacrifice for the living and the dead, a sacrifice by means of which sin was taken away and God was reconciled. . . . In the third place, the holy sacrament was not instituted to make provision for a sacrifice for sin—for the sacrifice has already taken place—but to awaken our faith and comfort our consciences when we perceive that through the sacrament grace and forgiveness of sin are promised us by Christ" (*The Book of Concord*, 58–59).

26. Sächs HStA Loc. 10331/8, fols. 1–2, Saxon Estates to Johann Georg II, 4 April 1661; the German text appears in Appendix I (no. 10).

27. Sächs HStA Loc. 10331/1, fol. 1r. Under Johann Georg I, contractual agreements between the elector and an appointee were sealed "with a bodily oath" ("mit einem Cörperlichen Eide") as well as in a written declaration ("in einem schrieftlichenn Reverße"),

Rather than simply express concern over the threat to the "true doctrine" posed by the Catholics in Johann Georg's employ, the diet could well have turned to church authorities for support. Back in 1597, the theology faculty at the University of Wittenberg had rendered opinions on several questions entirely relevant to the current elector's musical agenda, in response to two questions submitted to it for consideration: "whether a Christian Prince might retain Papist Musicians" and "whether the pastor should tolerate them *facti species* in the church."[28] In their response, the theologians differentiated between two types of people who stand in error: those who are entirely "blind, obdurate, and malicious" and those who are "irresolute" and, like wandering sheep, are easily led astray by false teaching. But rather than require the local prince to deal with the confessional consequences of his hiring practices, the faculty instead placed the burden upon the court preacher, whom it instructed to have patience with the latter type, since they do not "maliciously resist the truth," and urged him to work to "bring them out of their darkness into the clear light of the Gospel." As long as the singer in question and other Catholic courtiers demonstrate docility, leave reason to hope that they will come around in their own time, do not "slander the truth," and do not attempt to convert others, the court preacher should content himself with pointing out the error of their ways through the Scriptures. If the preacher's efforts over time came to nothing, however, and the Catholics in question should become obdurate in their error, the faculty declared that, since there was no short supply of Lutheran musicians, "Christian authorities" should not tolerate such obstinate people, when all hope had vanished that they could be "swayed by the heavenly truth."

Given his status as the "supreme bishop" (*summus episcopus* or *Oberst Bischoff*) of the Lutheran church in Saxony,[29] Johann Georg had a duty at least to pay lip service to established Lutheran church policies on confessional matters, including those that involved musicians.[30] But as he well knew, the university theologians were in

and the oath involved swearing allegiance to the Lutheran Augsburg Confession and *Book of Concord*; see Sächs HStA Loc. 8681/3, fol. 63r–v. Albrici's contract with Johann Georg II, however, indicates that the new Kapellmeister sealed his agreement with the elector simply "with a handshake in lieu of an oath" ("durch einen Handschlag an Eÿdesstadt") and a written declaration; see Spagnoli 1990:156.

28. As found in: *Consilia theologica Witebergensia*, part 4:60–61. The relevant excerpts appear in Appendix I (no. 11).

29. As a result of the introduction of the Reformation in Saxony, the elector of Saxony assumed the role of head of both church and state; secular and ecclesiastical power were unified in him. See Naumann 1991:94 and Honecker 1968:105–10.

30. In one area—the hiring of castrati—he was given a pass, however, for the Saxon theologicans never adopted an official stance on either the "creation" or the employment of these singers.

no position to issue instructions to the sovereign, who was both a member of the aristocracy (and thus their superior in social class) and the patron and protector of their institution.[31] Such realities forced them to navigate carefully between the two positions and to avoid any direct statement regarding the sovereign's duty to follow the recommendations of his court preacher. Thus the clause that expresses their thoughts on the action to be taken with recalcitrant Catholics essentially gave Johann Georg the "green light" to proceed with his plans, for what irrefutable evidence could any long-suffering court preacher garner to convince his prince, who had a vested interest in retaining the musicians, that he had reached the point of no return with these "obstinate servants" who had "turned to Papal darkness"? Given the formulation of the decision, any prince and patron could request that his court preacher continue in his efforts *ad infinitum*.

In 1664, one of Johann Georg's political decisions contributed publicly to the growing suspicions concerning his confessional loyalties. In the so-called "Reduction of Erfurt," Johann Georg gave up all hereditary claims to the Thuringian city in favor of the Archbishop-Elector of Mainz, thus handing this historically Lutheran city over to a Catholic sovereign.[32] In the complex negotiations that brought about the agreement, ministers for Johann Georg built up hopes of his potential conversion in both Vienna and Paris.[33] According to the papal nuncio in Vienna, these ministers (likely Burkersroda and Reiffenberg) told Count Martinitz in the fall of 1664 that Johann Georg would soon convert; so convinced of the possibility was Martinitz that he pushed the nuncio to meet secretly in Prague with Johann Georg. Although the cautious nuncio felt that Johann Georg's true intentions should be determined before such a step was taken, he did send the count's comments on to Rome and requested an "Instruction" for the potential negotiations with the Saxon elector.[34]

Throughout the 1660s, the movement to allow Catholics the opportunity to worship freely in Dresden gained constant momentum, and Johann Georg found himself beleaguered by forces both within and without his territory. In March 1665, a letter arrived from Elector Friedrich Wilhelm of Brandenburg, in which the Great Elector relayed the details of a strikingly ecumenical proposal from the Elector of Mainz: if both Friedrich Wilhelm and Johann Georg would permit a Catholic church

31. Wittenberg University was founded in 1502 by Elector Friedrich der Weise, one of Johann Georg's ancestors. In 1525, Friedrich's brother and successor, Johann der Beständige, established Wittenberg University as his state university (*Landesuniversität*); see Naumann 1991:87, 93.

32. As hereditary Landgrave of Thuringia, Johann Georg enjoyed a certain feudal jurisdiction over the city. See Helbig 1865 and Auerbach 1887:149–99.

33. Helbig 1865:422.

34. Seifert 1964:110.

in their land or city of residence, the Elector of Mainz would build both a Lutheran and a Reformed church, either in Mainz or nearby, and would allow the free exercise of religion in each house of worship.[35] Recognizing the importance of the proposal, if perhaps not the long-range implications, Friedrich Wilhelm asked Johann Georg for his opinion on the matter. In his response, which saw a delay of over two months, Johann Georg neither accepted nor rejected the proposal from Mainz, but, instead, expressed concern about the future implications of such a decision (among other things) and deftly bounced the ball right back into the Great Elector's court, leaving it up to him to do whatever he thought best.[36] Given the stand taken in 1661 by the provincial diet, and the general reaction to the Reduction of Erfurt, it is not surprising that Johann Georg could not see his way clear to grant freedom of worship to Catholics in Dresden. But the Saxon elector seems to have found an alternate way to accommodate the proposition of his colleague in Mainz, for at this same time he permitted Catholics in Leipzig to use the former Franciscan Barfüsser Kirche (later the Neue Kirche), a decision for which he was roundly criticized in early 1666 by his brother, Duke August of Halle-Weißenfels. In his response to his brother's censure, Johann Georg reproached August for casting aspersions on his relationships with Catholics, and presented himself as an enlightened, modern statesman who had renounced confessional politics:

> I hope that no one who is unaffected by prejudices shall suspect me, if I enter into relationships with my allied electors and others, after our blessed forefathers' example and without any consideration of religion. If Elector Moritz and his successors had not been on a friendly footing with the Catholics, our line would scarcely have been granted electoral dignity over other considerable countries or peoples.[37]

35. Sächs HStA Loc. 10299/1 [unfoliated], Friedrich Wilhelm to Johann Georg, 23 March 1665.
36. Sächs HStA 10299/1 [unfoliated], Johann Georg II to Friedrich Wilhelm, 9 June 1665.
37. "I detta upptager kurfursten äfven en fråga, som af admistratorn i hans bref af 5 jan. vidröres, frågan om förhållandet till katolikerna. För [Karl Gustaf] Wrangel hade nämligen bl. a. berättats, att kurfursten upplåtit för katolikerna 'die Barfusse Kirche' i Leipzig. Om sin ställning till katolikerna yttrar nu Johan Georg: Jag hoppas, att ingen, som ej är intagen af fördomar, skall misstänka mig, om jag efter våra saliga förfäders exempel utan hänsyn till religionen träder i förbindelse med mina medkurfurstar och andra. Hade ej kurfurst Moritz och hans efterföljare stått på vänskaplig fot med katolikerna, hade svårligen vår linje erhållit kurfurstlig värdighet och andra ansenliga länder och folk" (Lundqvist 1908:356 n.3). Here "electoral dignity" refers to the *Kurwürde*, the privilege of holding the rank of elector. The author thanks Jan Enberg and Lars Berglund for help with the translation.

During these same years, however, rumors of Johann Georg's impending defection from the state church continued to circulate, with apparent good reason. Reports of the papal nuncio to Vienna to the home office, although not free of a certain amount of wishful thinking on the part of the author, reveal "not only the great initiatives on the Roman Catholic side, particularly in 1657, 1666, and 1668, which were supposed to lead to the conversion of Johann Georg II, but also the initiatives of the elector himself in 1666, in which he attempted to secure a possible conversion by military means."[38] In 1666, the year of the conversion of his close advisor, Burkersroda, Johann Georg began to pursue the idea of his own conversion with greater purpose.[39] Early in 1666, Johann Georg sent Count Lutzan, a former advisor to the emperor and a convert to Catholicism, to the imperial court to discuss the matter of his conversion, and through Lutzan, delivered letters to both the emperor and the papal nuncio. Lutzan described the elector's strong inclination toward the Catholic faith, and stressed the need for the emperor's support in the endeavor, given the potential political problems. Rome apparently shared this view, and in April, the nuncio discussed the matter of support with Leopold, and encouraged him to work to influence Johann Georg through his ambassadors at the Dresden court.[40] In letters to the nuncio early that summer, Burkersroda repeatedly stressed how favorable were the conditions for the elector's conversion, and finally convinced Johann Georg to send him to Vienna, along with Reiffenberg, to inquire of the emperor just how much money and how many troops Johann Georg could expect to receive in support of his conversion. This request, however, seems to have quashed any inclination the emperor may have had to support the elector, for Leopold would commit to send neither troops nor funds. In a failed effort to pressure the emperor to reconsider, the Saxon ministers indicated that without Leopold's support, Johann Georg would have no choice but to form an alliance with Sweden and France. The elector made good on his threat that same July, and Burkersroda soon reported to the nuncio that this new alliance had dealt a serious blow to his conversion efforts.[41] Although glimmers of hope surfaced on several other occasions in 1666 and 1668,

38. "Sie enthüllen nicht nur die großen Initiativen von römisch-katholischer Seite aus, die besonders in den Jahren 1657, 1666, und 1668 eine Konversion Johann Georg II. herbeiführen sollten, sondern auch Eigeninitiativen des Kurfürsten im Jahre 1666, wobei er einen möglichen Übertritt militärisch versuchte" (Hahn 1990:162; Hahn's comments are based on Seifert 1964:111–15).

39. According to Seifert, Burkersroda was the animating force behind the conversion plans at the Saxon court (1964:112). It seems that the minister's conversion had been rumored already in 1665, for in October of that year, the nuncio reported to Rome that a highly placed Saxon official would soon become Catholic (ibid., 111).

40. Seifert 1964:112–13.

41. Seifert 1964:113.

any real chance for the return of the Saxon elector to the Catholic church seems to have been lost at this time.[42] Yet stories of Johann Georg's "Catholicity" continued to circulate. According to Vehse,[43] Urbano Cerri, the "propaganda minister" to Pope Innocent XI (1676–89), also reported Johann Georg's great inclination toward the Catholic religion, and quoted a report (given in Seifert) that a German Jesuit who had spent many years in Dresden had sent to the Pope:

> The Saxon elector prays every day for the true faith, often confesses to a priest, eats no meat on Fridays, invokes the Blessed Virgin, allows Mass to be said in private homes, enjoined a Catholic captain not to leave his soldiers without spiritual support, allowed a Turk in his service to be secretly baptized a Catholic, erases the insults to the pope in his own Lutheran prayer books with his own hand, tolerates no Catholic apostates at his court, undertakes many laudable practices that are actually forbidden by the heretics, and also, in order not to hear anything spoken against Catholicism, does not listen to the sermons of the preachers. He has expressed his bewilderment that no pope has yet taken the reunification of Germany in his hand; [in his view], if [the pope] would just allow Communion in both species, all princes would easily return to the Catholic Church.[44]

Much of this "report," which attributes a veritable litany of Catholic virtues to Johann Georg, can be dismissed as a propagandistic effort by its author to rally curial support for the Catholic cause in Saxony. Like the reports of the nuncio discussed above, however, it likely holds at least a grain of truth. But Johann Georg's true confessional intentions remain as inscrutable to the modern observer as to his contemporaries: in 1660, if not earlier, this same "crypto-Catholic" sovereign instituted at his court the annual observance of the signal event of the Reformation, Luther's nailing of the

---

42. Seifert 1964:114–16.

43. Vehse 1854:19–20.

44. "Der sächsische Kurfürst bete alle Tage um den wahren Glauben, beichte oft einem Priester, äße Freitag kein Fleisch, rufe die heilige Jungfrau an, erlaube in Privathäusern die Messe zu lesen, habe einem katholischen Hauptmann eingeschärft, seine Soldaten nicht ohne geistlichen Beistand zu lassen, habe gestattet, daß ein Türke, der in seinem Dienst ist, heimlich katholisch getauft würde, habe aus seinen lutherischen Gebetbüchern eigenhändig die Verwünschungen gegen den Papst ausradiert, dulde an seinem Hofe keinen katholischen Apostaten, nehme viele löbliche Übungen vor, die von den Ketzern eigentlich verboten sind, so wie er auch, um nichts gegen den Katholizismus Gesprochenes zu vernehmen, den Predigten der Prädikanten nicht zuhöre. Er habe seine Verwunderung geäußert, daß noch kein Papst die Wiedervereinigung Deutschlands mit der Kirche in seine Hand genommen hätte, gestatte er nur das Abendmahl unter beiderlei Gestalt, so würden alle Fürsten leicht zur katholischen Kirche zurückkehren" (Seifert 1964:115).

95 Theses to the castle door in Wittenberg, with an annual commemorative service in the chapel, complete with its own liturgy. In 1667, the year of the sesquicentennial of the Reformation, he declared 31 October an official *Gedächtniß-Tag* to be observed annually throughout Saxony, as well as in the court chapel:[45]

> Thursday the 31st [of October]. In the morning, in the presence of the entire assembled Most Gracious Electoral and Princely Royal Family, an annual sermon of thanksgiving and commemoration was delivered by the senior court preacher, Dr. Martin Geier, on a text drawn from the prophet Isaiah, chapter 6, verse 23, in which God's great blessing and goodness, which He began to allow to shine forth in this land in the year 1517, on this very day, with the blessed Dr. Martin Luther's nailing of the theses in opposition to the papist indulgence peddler, Tetzel, to the castle church in Wittenberg, through which the Christian act of reformation was accomplished, was recalled and reflected upon in an elegant and detailed account and sermon, and at the conclusion, the German *Te Deum laudamus* was sung.[46]

While Johann Georg's establishment of the Feast of the Reformation in Saxony could easily be cast as a shameless attempt to appease a citizenry long *in dubio* about his Lutheran convictions, the solemn annual observance behind the castle walls suggests that, despite his flirtations with Catholicism, his most deeply felt loyalties lay with Luther.

Johann Georg's "Catholic problem" took on a new meaning in 1667, however, with the February arrival of the French diplomat, Henri de Chassan, under whose aegis the Catholic Mass became a growth industry in Dresden.[47] Somewhat ironically, the resulting confessional brouhaha, which continued nearly unabated until the elector's death, was a direct consequence of Johann Georg's own foreign policy. For years, Johann Georg had entertained the advances of both Louis XIV and Emperor Leopold I, and from at least 1664 onward, played Paris and Vienna off one another and employed a "vacillating foreign policy" (*schwankende Außenpolitik*) for both political and financial gain.[48] Both the French king and the emperor saw fit to install permanent resident ambassadors in Dresden, all of whom, of course, were Catholic. The provisions of the Peace of Westphalia granted members of the minor-

---

45. Discussed in chapter 8.

46. Sächs HStA OHMA O IV Nr. 21, entry for 31 October 1667; the German text appears in Appendix I (no. 12).

47. Chassan arrived in Dresden on 30 January 1667 and had his first audience with Johann Georg on 8 February; see Auerbach 1887:221, 239–40, and Sächs HStA OHMA O IV Nr. 20 [unfoliated], entry for 8 February.

48. The term is that of Blaschke (1974:526–27). On the elector's relationships with France and the Empire, see Auerbach 1887 and Hassel 1890.

ity religion (Lutheran or Catholic) in a particular territory the right to hold their own religious exercises privately, "behind closed doors," even in territories where the practice of that religion had been prohibited. This accorded foreign ambassadors a certain degree of "diplomatic immunity" with respect to the exercise of religion, but only they themselves and the members of their households might attend these private services.[49] Once in Dresden, however, Chassan moved quickly to provide for his own worship needs as well as for those of other Catholics, and in a letter dated 22 April 1667, proudly informed Louis XIV of the celebrations of Mass in his home, "which one has scarcely seen in Dresden since they embraced Lutheranism."[50] Chassan and the imperial ambassadors stretched the provisions of the peace treaty to their breaking point, however, and opened their doors to large numbers of Catholics, among them court musicians.[51] Frustrated, the Lutheran clergy in Dresden complained to Johann Georg II, who in turn implored the ambassadors to forbear; in response, both diplomats demanded a written order, which the elector "dared not to draft."[52] Chassan's religious activities also incensed his landlord, Dr. Leuber. Already in June 1667, Leuber had added a surcharge of fifty tl per month to Chassan's rent of 120 tl as an indemnity, and claimed that Chassan had opened his home to more than twenty-four people per day, including foreigners—Italians, Hungarians, Croatians, and Bohemians—which strongly suggests that some of Johann Georg's singers attended daily Mass in Chassan's residence.[53] Two years later, having trumped up charges that Chassan had damaged his property and housed servants in the master bedroom, Leuber set out to evict the diplomat. Despite Leuber's efforts, however, Chassan both refused to leave and to close his doors to his co-religionists.[54]

In August 1667, Geier wrote to the elector and strongly urged him to take action against Roman Catholic worship in the city. Geier pointed out that celebrations of the Mass were taking place in two locations, and that those in attendance included the elector's own court appointees, of both high and low rank. He also expressed his fear that the continued toleration of the Mass would lend the impression to all concerned that they in Dresden no longer considered Article 24 of the Augsburg Confession ("On the Mass") to be of any great importance. Geier thus implored Johann Georg to crack down on the problem and derided Catholicism in his usual manner:

49. See Auerbach 1887:403, Hahn 1990:162, and Holborn 1982:368–71.
50. "ce qu'on n'avait guère vu à Dresde depuis qu'ils ont embrassé le luthéranisme" (Auerbach 1887:403).
51. See below.
52. "Tous deux exigèrent une note écrite que l'Electeur n'osa pas rédiger" (Auerbach 1887:404).
53. Auerbach 1887:405.
54. Auerbach 1887:405–6.

Therefore, my most melancholy entreaty and supplication once again comes to Your Electoral Highness, through Christ, that You will, in accordance with Your Electoral renown and Christian vigilance, most graciously intervene in the matter, so that this Papist abomination, to which our most praiseworthy Christian forefathers did not willingly come too closely, even those in imperial service (despite of the fact that they knowingly and willingly allowed it in their own lands), be vigorously restrained.[55]

Geier's plea, however, apparently failed to prod the elector into action. On 27 November 1667, the Dresden city council reported to Johann Georg that Chassan had held public Masses on the third floor of his residence on the Töpfergasse— where he had set up a chapel and erected an altar—and that the imperial residents on the Seegasse and Webergasse had followed suit.[56] Throughout that year, however, Chassan had enjoyed regular audiences with Johann Georg, and had occasionally dined with him—apparently neither allowed these confessional tensions to hinder their political discussions.[57]

Yet the problem continued to fester, and the High Consistory finally confronted Johann Georg with it in a letter of 8 March 1668. Apparently the members of the consistory had alerted the elector in the previous month of the need for vigilance, as the celebration of Mass was making inroads in Dresden, particularly in the home of the French ambassador.[58] Shortly thereafter, they discovered (to their great displeasure) that Mass was also being celebrated in the imperial ambassador's residence. Now, despite the repeated admonitions of Johann Georg II, the situation had grown

55. "Also gelanget hierauf nochmahls an Eure Churf. Durchl. dies mein wehmühtigstes flehen, v. bitten durch Christum, Sie wollen nach Ihrem Churfürstlichen rhume v. Christlicher wachsamkeit, gnädigstes dahin vermitteln laßen, das diesem Päbstischen greuel, deme die Christ-rhümlichsten Vorfahren nie gerne zu nahe kommen wollen, auch in keiserlicher bedienung (geschweige, das sie in ihren eignen landen wißend- vnd williglich es solten verstattet haben,) nachdrücklich möge gesteuert werden" (Sächs HStA Loc. 10299/1 [unfoliated], Martin Geier to Johann Georg II, 20 August 1667). According to Susan Karant-Nunn, "Luther and other Reformers in German-speaking lands so often applied the phrase, *abomination of the Mass* (*greuel der Messe*) to the papist ritual that it became a kind of antipapal stock in trade" (1997:114). The phrase, which is still common parlance in the writings of Geier and his generation, also appears in the Smalcald Articles (1537); see *The Book of Concord*, 293.
56. Lindau 1885:492.
57. Sächs HStA OHMA O IV Nr. 20 [unfoliated], entries for 8 February, 8 March, 8 April, and 23 September 1667; OHMA O IV Nr. 21 [unfoliated], entries for 8 April, 2 June, 12 July, and 25 August 1667.
58. Sächs HStA Loc. 30115 [unfoliated], Dresden High Consistory to Johann Georg II, 8 March 1668; see the excerpt in Appendix I (no. 13).

entirely out of hand, and people were literally flocking to Mass: "Now scores of people drive, ride, and walk to the Mass unabashedly, as if to a pilgrimage, and daily still the room is filled indiscriminately with foreigners and locals, such that, according to rumor, many who would like to go in are forced to remain outside because of the crowd."[59] The members of the consistory were clearly incensed by the brazen manner in which the ambassadors opened their private religious celebrations to members of the local Catholic community; they reminded Johann Georg that those among his co-religionists who served as ambassadors at Catholic courts were granted no such religious liberty—if they were allowed to exercise their religion at all, the time was set by the local authorities, and guards were placed at the door to ensure that no one but the ambassador and his immediate family attended the ceremonies.[60] After listing the many potential dangers of inaction on this issue to both present and future generations, Geier and the other members of the consistory urged the elector to deal forcefully with the situation, "so that such a great scandal might finally be remedied once and for all, and God's servants might no longer have to suffer this abomination either publicly or privately."[61]

A month or two later, the Dresden city council wrote to Johann Georg to inform him of the continuing Mass activity at the ambassadors' residences.[62] On 9 May 1668, Johann Georg responded to the council, instructing them to "keep a watchful eye" over the Mass celebrations at the homes of the two ambassadors and to sternly remind any of those who were in attendance at these Masses, and who fell under their jurisdiction, of the elector's decree of 27 March 1661.[63] Here the crucial phrase is "who fall under your jurisdiction" ("so eüerer Bothmäßigkeit unterworffen"); through the inclusion of this language, Johann Georg could exempt members of a foreign ambassador's retinue as well as his own employees from punishment and overlook their transgressions of his own directives. The council took its charge very seriously and immediately began to dispatch "Mass police" to keep track of Catholic activity in Dresden. On 13 May 1668, the council reported back to the elector the results of surveillance undertaken throughout the three-day feast of Pentecost, which fell on 10 May:[64]

59. Sächs HStA Loc. 30115; the German text appears in Appendix I (no. 13).
60. Sächs HStA Loc. 30115.
61. "damit so großen ärgernüß endlich einmahl in der that abgeholffen werden möge, und Gottes diener nicht länger, so öffentlich alß heimlich, über solche Greuel seuffzen dürffen"(Sächs HStA Loc. 30115).
62. The letter does not survive, but is referenced in the elector's response of 9 May 1668 (see below).
63. Sächs HStA Loc. 30115 [unfoliated], and Loc. 10299/1 [unfoliated], Johann Georg II to the Council of Dresden. See also Lindau 1885:492.
64. In 1668, Easter (and hence Pentecost) fell on the same date in the Julian and Gregorian calendars: 22 March (O. S.) / 1 April (N. S.) (Cappelli 1969:56, 106).

As Your Electoral Highness most graciously commanded us on the 9th of May, Because the Most Gracious Opinion on the sacrifice of the Mass, which will have been held here until now, has been privately communicated to the Imperial and Royal [i.e. French] Residents, we should, if the aforementioned *cultus* is further celebrated at the homes of those residents, keep a vigilant eye on it, and after discovery most obediently make report, we have taken this Most Gracious Command as our bounden duty. By means of a few sworn quartermasters, we kept watch throughout these holidays to see whether the Mass-sacrifice would again be celebrated at the imperial resident's home, as before, and if any unauthorized persons would be found there. Today these quartermasters reported that the sacrifice of the Mass was celebrated at the home of the aforementioned resident in the Golden Eagle here over the course of these three days, as happened before. The doors were open between 8:00 and 9:00, as usual. They saw the Croatian riding-master's wife enter, and the wife of General Keplier, as well as the Italian court musicians and other Italians, such as lemon sellers, and the same various Croatians; in addition, a few women and workmen whom they did not recognize were also at Mass throughout these feast days.[65]

Although Johann Georg now possessed concrete evidence that his Italian musicians were attending Mass (if he had entertained any doubts), no evidence survives to suggest that they suffered any negative consequences at the hands of the elector for their religious activity. Such reports do, however, vividly illustrate the types of sacrifices made by Italian musicians who elected to cross confessional boundaries and enter the service of a Lutheran patron. Whether or not Johann Georg winked at their attendance at these worship services, the musicians still found themselves the subjects of surveillance, and attended Mass in the full knowledge that such activity was *verboten* and would be reported. In addition, they doubtless were forced to listen to the fulminations of various local theologians on the "abomination" of the Mass itself and may well have been harassed by townspeople.

No communications between Johann Georg and the imperial ambassador on this matter have survived, but that same month (May 1668), Johann Georg granted

65. Sächs HStA Loc. 10299/1 [unfoliated], "Der Rath zu Dreßden" to Johann Georg II, 13 May 1668; the German text appears in Appendix I (no. 14). One wonders, however, about the time of day that these Masses were celebrated: if they took place during the morning hours, with Italian musicians in attendance, who was minding the store back in the court chapel, where the Lutheran *Gottesdienst* was being celebrated concurrently? For reasons of secrecy, as well as scheduling conflicts such as those encountered by the musicians, the Mass may well have been celebrated at night. One also wonders whether Johann Georg's musicians ever "moonlighted" and provided music during these Masses.

Chassan's petition to allow a priest and six Discalced Carmelite monks to enter Dresden to serve in his home.[66] Chassan used the elector's magnanimity to his advantage, however, and further aggravated the situation in the city by proselytizing for his faith: in December 1668, he effected the conversion of one of the Lutheran secretaries in his employ.[67] One year later, on 7 April 1669, Chassan received another notice from the elector, who ordered him, politely but firmly, to keep his religious celebrations private.[68] But in spite of these efforts, the Mass activity continued unabated. On 20 June 1669, Johann Georg put the imperial ambassador on notice that he was not to have Mass celebrated in his home on the Feast of Corpus Christi.[69] Chassan viewed this most recent affront as a consequence of the current struggle between Saxony and Vienna concerning the church in nearby Lusatia, and the fact that the imperial ambassador's priest was a Jesuit; in Chassan's estimation, "the [Lutheran] preachers have a particular aversion to the Jesuits, of whom they are extremely fearful."[70] On 5 December 1669, Johann Georg issued yet another decree, this time addressed to his privy council. It seems that the ever-vigilant Geier had complained that celebrations of the Mass were taking place at the residences of both ambassadors even in their absence, which was a clear violation of the provisions of Westphalia. Although he expressed "extreme regret" at having to do so, Johann Georg strictly forbade such celebrations, as he had warned the ambassadors to cease and desist from such practices, and encouraged them to worship in Upper Lusatia.[71] At some point in 1670, Johann Georg finally promulgated a public decree against the "exercise of Catholicism," but, in the words of Auerbach, it remained a "dead letter."[72]

By 1673, the religious atmosphere in Dresden and beyond had disintegrated to such an extent that it can only be described as contentious confessionalism of the worst variety. On 1 February, the theological faculties in Wittenberg and Leipzig

66. Sächs HStA Loc. 10331/8, fol. 3r, Johann Georg to Henri de Chassan.

67. Auerbach 1887:404.

68. Sächs HStA Loc. 10331/8, fol. 4r–v.

69. Auerbach 1887:404. Lutherans did not celebrate the feast of Corpus Christi, which commemorates the Eucharist; given the utter "Catholicity" of this particular feast, its observation in Dresden could only have further inflamed the tempers of Lutheran clerics.

70. "les prédicants ayant une aversion particulière pour les jésuites qu'ils appréhendent extrêmement" (Auerbach 1887:404). On the religious controversy in Lusatia, see Seifert 1964:91–104, and Thomas 1998.

71. Sächs HStA Loc. 10331/8, fol. 5r–v, Johann Georg to his Privy Council, 5 December 1669.

72. "En 1670, un décret contre l'exercice du catholicisme fut enfin publié. Mais il resta lettre morte" (Auerbach 1887:404). No copies of the 1670 decree have surfaced, but the order is referenced in a letter from the provincial diet to Johann Georg II of 12 February 1680 (Sächs HStA Loc. 30115 [unfoliated]).

requested that Johann Georg issue an ordinance prohibiting celebrations of the Mass. According to Auerbach, the document stands as a "monument of theological intolerance" in which basic dogmas of Catholicism are "refuted with magisterial hauteur," and the "doctrine of the Mass is discussed and characterized as [an] execrable idolatry which turns Christians into Jews," and derided as nothing other than "the abominable idol Maosim."[73] Apparently the provincial diet had voiced renewed objections as well. Thus, on 27 February 1673, Johann Georg yielded to pressure, and issued a sternly worded public decree forbidding attendance at Mass at the ambassadorial residences in Dresden, enjoining individuals from privately seeking out the ministrations of priests, and threatening all offenders with "fines, imprisonment, eviction from the city, or even harsher punishments."[74] Johann Georg empowered the commanders, district magistrate, and inspector of the city to carry out the decree and punish the guilty, but restricted their authority in particular cases: "as far as it concerns Our employees, [the officials] are to await Our further instruction in humility, after most obediently making a report."[75] According to the decree, Catholics should content themselves with worshiping on the Bohemian border or in Upper Lusatia.[76] Johann Georg also threatened with detention those "priests who sneak into people's homes, either to make innocent people err in their beliefs, or to exercise their Papist worship, in whatever form," as well as those found aiding

73. Auerbach 1887:405, "La doctrine de la messe y est discutée, qualifiée d'idolâtrie exécrable et qui rend les chrétiens juifs; la messe n'est autre chose 'que l'abominable idole Maosim'. Les principaux dogmes papistes, le culte de la Vierge et des Saints, sans compter le syncrétisme qui n'est qu'un samarétisme (?), y sont réfutés avec cette même hauteur magistrale." Auerbach examined Chassan's translation of the document, which the diplomat sent back to France on 2 March 1673. *Mausim* (or *Mäusim*) is a pejorative term used by contemporary Lutheran theologians in reference to the Catholic "Mass-sacrifice."

74. "Befehlen demnach allen und ieden/ wie obgemelt/ hiermit außdrücklich und ernstlich/ Sich hinfüro bey dem Päbstischen Meßhalten und Kirchenwesen in angeregter Ministrorum Behausungen weiter nicht einzufinden/ noch die Päbstischen Priester in geheimb zu sich zuziehen, aufzuenthalten/ . . ./ mit außdrücklicher Verwarnung/ daß die Verbrecher/ nach ereigenden Umbständen/ mit unnachläßlichen/ als Geld/ Gefängnüs/ Außschaffung aus der Stadt/ auch wol härteren Straffen/ angesehen und beleget werden sollen" (Sächs HStA Loc. 10331/8, fol. 14). See also Lindau 1885:493.

75. "Wie Wir dann Unsern *Commandan*ten/ Ambtmann/ und Rath der Stadt alhier/ hiermit zugleich gnädigst anbefohlen haben wollen/ fleissige Auffsicht und genaue Nachforschung darauf zu legen/ die Widerspänstigen mit Gewalt abzuhalten/ sich auch wohl derselben zu versichern/ und so viel Unsere Bediente betrifft/ nach geschehenen gehorsambsten Anmelden/ Unserer fernern Verordnung in Unterthänigkeit zuerwarten" (Sächs HStA Loc. 10331/8, fol. 14).

76. Sächs HStA Loc. 10331/8, fol. 14.

and abetting the Catholic cause.[77] Despite the ruling's seemingly comprehensive language, however, it stopped just short of contravening Westphalia, for Johann Georg had clearly refused to submit to those around him who had pressed for an outright ban on all celebrations of the Mass.

Johann Georg's 1673 decree threatened to bring ecumenical relations in Dresden to a new low. Its oppressive and persecutory tone conceals any and all traces of the elector's widely-reported "inclination" toward Catholicism. While he carefully protected his court employees, he left the fate of the "average Catholic" in the hands of the overseers. Despite the unequivocal language of the decree, however, neither ambassador succumbed to the pressure to close his doors to his co-religionists, and the celebrations of Mass continued without pause in both residences, with as many as two hundred souls in attendance. Furthermore, the elector's musicians continued to attend—after all, the elector had essentially blown the "all clear" in his decree. Just two months after the promulgation of the decree, for example, over one hundred people attended Mass at Chassan's residence, among them Albrici, Pallavicino, Melani, Battistini, and a number of other Italian singers.[78] But despite the protections incorporated in the decree, the elector's actions may still have had deleterious effects on music in the court chapel. Pallavicino and the singer Ruggieri left Dresden in April of that year, and Albrici and Bontempi departed the court in July; while the reasons are unknown, their departures may have been votes of protest against the sheer effrontery of the decree and the constant harassment by city officials charged with "Mass oversight."[79]

Louis XIV recalled Chassan to France in the spring of 1674, and the diplomat departed on 18 May, the same day the imperial diet in Regensburg declared war

---

77. "Do auch hierüber ein oder ander Meß-Priester sich in die Häüser einzuschleichen/ unschuldige Leuthe in ihren Glauben irre zu machen/ und zu verführen/ oder ihren Päbstischen Gottesdienst/ in was Stücken es sey/ außzuüben unterstehen wolte; Sollen so wohl dieselben angehalten/ als die Wirthe/ die ein solches in ihren Häüsern verstattet/ oder die jenigen/ so dazu geholffen/ unnachläßig bestrafft" (Sächs HStA Loc. 10331/8, fol. 14). That such activities took place is evidenced by Bartolomeo Sorlisi's reception of Last Rites from a priest prior to his death in March 1672, over which the Dresden consistory later raised objections; see Lindau 1885:492–93.

78. "Trotzdem fand man bei dem französischen Gesandten auf der Töpfergasse und bei dem kaiserlichen im goldnen Adler auf der Seegasse bald nachher sehr zahlreiche Versammlungen bis zu 200 Personen, so z. B. am 6. April 1673 bei dem französischen 106, darunter zwei italienische geheime Kämmerlinge (Milano und Gabrieli), die Kapellmeister Vincenz und Pallavicini, mehrere italienische Kapellsänger, u.s.w." (Lindau 1885:493–94). The exact numbers suggest that the inspector continued to provide surveillance reports. See also Vehse 1854:19 and Auerbach 1887:405.

79. See chapter 2.

on France.[80] Whatever its implications for foreign policy, Chassan's departure had little effect on Catholic worship life in Dresden, apart from reducing the number of Catholic "houses of worship" by one. By this time, due in large part to Chassan's efforts and his unshakable belief in his right to worship as he saw fit, Mass celebrations themselves had become *de rigeur* in Dresden. In December 1674, an observer from the city council counted ninety-four in attendance at a Mass during Advent, and even more at Christmas.[81] In February 1676, during their regular meeting in Dresden, the members of the provincial diet once again raised the issue with Johann Georg, who in response issued another, even more sharply worded decree. This time, even court employees might well find themselves in custody as a consequence of attending Mass:

> Furthermore, however, we will have ordered herewith not only our chief district magistrate and the council here to apply scrupulous oversight and diligent inquiry each time, and, when they ascertain something, promptly to report the same to Us, but we also will have particularly ordered the commander to make preparations in that street and near the house in which the Mass is held, at the established hours, with an officer and an appointed squad of men, so that those coming to such a Mass, whether it be on foot, by coach, or on horseback, are prevented from attending it; those, however, who are met when coming out, or who dare to resist when they are prevented from entering, shall be taken into custody when the occasion arises, or their names shall be reported to Our provincial government for emphatic censure. Similarly, those taken into custody, if they are in court or military service, or belong to the district magistracy, are to be taken immediately to our chief district magistrate; the others, however, are to be taken immediately to the council for further inquisition and punishment.[82]

Once again, Johann Georg focused his attention on unauthorized attendance at religious ceremonies and did not criminalize the celebration of the Mass itself. In stark contrast to his 1673 decree, however, this one makes no allowance for court employees. While the elector does grant the officers some discretion in determining whether to make arrests or simply to turn in the names of offenders, he seems insis-

---

80. Auerbach 1887:396–97; Chassan's travel pass was issued on 10 April 1674 (Sächs HStA Loc. 8299/5, fol. 37r).

81. Seifert 1964:117. The report of the council to the elector is dated 28 December 1674.

82. Sächs HStA Loc. 10331/8, fol. 16, printed decree dated 10 February 1676; a manuscript copy of the decree appears on fols. 6r–7v, 9r–v. The German text appears in Appendix I (no. 15).

tent that they deal severely with all *Verbrecher*. But the coincidence of both decrees with the triennial meeting of the provincial diet strongly suggests that the estates pressured the elector to act, and that the latter felt obligated to create at least the appearance that he took this religious matter seriously. Like previous edicts, however, this too seems to have been hopelessly ineffective. A December 1679 report of the city council indicated that Mass was held not only on Sundays, but also during the week, with as many as two hundred in attendance.[83] And although the elector's charge to the city officers would suggest that the Dresden jails were filled to capacity on Sunday evenings, no evidence survives to indicate that they ever detained and punished anyone. In addition, the extant travel passes for the years 1676–80 give no hint of an exodus of musicians. And Albrici, who had attended Mass at Chassan's residence in 1673, returned to Dresden in September 1676 and remained at court until the elector's death in 1680: if religious persecution had indeed motivated his earlier departure, it would seem that it no longer represented a major concern.

All of this raises a number of questions about Johann Georg's understanding of Catholics and Catholicism and his expectations when he embarked on his Italian musical adventure—did he ever pause to consider the potential difficulties of a *Hofkapelle* dominated by those of a "hostile religion?" Viewed in one light, Johann Georg might be seen as a champion of ecumenism, in that he happily hired Catholics, and, unlike at least one of his peers, did not impose a conversion requirement upon them. But it is a peculiar brand of confessional enlightenment that does not require conversion, but fails to provide alternative worship opportunities. Perhaps clandestine Catholic worship had already appeared in Dresden in the 1650s. If not, one wonders if Johann Georg rather naively expected that musicians such as Bontempi, Severo, Sauli, and Melani would simply forsake their church. One wonders also if Johann Georg's knowledge of Catholicism extended to an understanding of the Catholic's obligation to attend Mass and receive the Eucharist. Did he simply assume that his musicians would forgo the sacraments for months or years at a time? Or did he expect that they would commune in the court chapel?[84] As is made clear in the various decrees issued by the elector, Catholics were expected to take advantage of worship opportunities in Bohemia and Upper Lusatia. Simple logistics, however, dictated that the Italian musicians obligated to sing in the Dresden court

---

83. Seifert 1964:117.
84. Although forbidden to do so by their own church, Catholic musicians serving in Lutheran establishments did at times take communion there without first converting; see, for example, Sittard 1890/1970:42.

chapel on Sunday morning could not easily travel to Mass in one of these areas.[85] However, Johann Georg's exemption of the *primo coro* from service at vespers on Saturdays and all holy eves except those of the three high feasts may suggest that he incorporated a quiet concession to the Catholic musicians into his *Kirchen-Ordnung*, one that allowed allow them to attend a vigil Mass on most Saturdays.[86] Of course, these musicians were well aware of the confessional reality in Saxony when they accepted their positions. And given his own inclinations, it would seem that Johann Georg did not interpret the acceptance of his offer by a Catholic musician as an automatic renunciation of the Catholic faith. While many of these questions cannot easily be answered, their examination provides at least some sense of the challenges faced by these musicians in Dresden, even though they enjoyed the favor of their patron.

Given the conflicts between the contemporary reports and Johann Georg's statements on the subject, as well as his actions, it remains difficult to characterize the exact nature of the elector's own religious beliefs and confessional attitudes. Did he yearn to cross these confessional boundaries himself? And if so, were his reasons grounded in genuine religious sentiment or political aspirations? Perhaps the points of theological disagreement between the two confessions, which had hardened into firm positions after a century of dispute, had somehow lost relevance for him. As the discussion above reveals, contemporary assessments portray Johann Georg alternately as a staunch Lutheran and as a closet Catholic; doubtless his own actions gave rise to such starkly contrasting assessments. Yet the contradictions render it nearly impossible to separate plain facts from those embroidered with confessional hyperbole. In the late 1660s, for example, at the time that the elector had authorized espionage to gather information on those Catholics who attended Mass, Chassan reported that Johann Georg's doctors had "obliged him to observe a regime of sobri-

---

85. The closest Catholic church lay in the town of Zinnwald (Cinovec), just over the Bohemian border and about 22.5 miles south of Dresden. Two larger towns, Teplitz (Teplice) and Tetschen (Děčín), each lay about 30 miles from Dresden. The closest Mass opportunity in Saxony was offered by the convent St. Marienstern near Panschwitz-Kuckau in Upper Lusatia, about 24 miles northeast of Dresden, and the closest cathedral (and bishop) lay in Bautzen (Budissin), about 31 miles to the northeast. However, Emil Trolda discovered that between the years 1706 and 1733 some twenty works of Albrici formed part of the music collection at Kloster Ossegg (Osek) in Bohemia (Trolda 1938; the author thanks Jan Enberg for alerting her to the existence of this article). Kloster Ossegg was also Sorlisi's final resting place; taken together, these two bits of information begin to suggest that Dresden musicians made pilgrimages to this abbey in Bohemia and perhaps performed there as well. It is also possible, however, that these works of Albrici were acquired from sources in Prague.

86. See chapter 8.

ety," and that, "to complete his hygienic penitence, he observed Ember Days and Vigils, as a result of which one conjectured that he inclined toward Catholicism."[87] At first glance, this statement would seem to reveal a fundamental conflict between the private and the public man—a private Catholic by inclination and a public Lutheran by necessity. But here Chassan, like so many of the "reporters" discussed above, may simply have "spun" the facts to impress his superiors, for ever since the reign of Johann Georg I, the court had held preaching services on Wednesday, Friday, and Saturday mornings (the traditional ember days), and Johann Georg II had instituted vigil vespers on Saturday afternoon.[88] And in the locus of worship life in the castle, the chapel, Johann Georg's liturgical praxis remained solidly rooted in Lutheran traditions throughout his reign. But his apparent intoxication with Italianate sacred music and texts derived from Jesuit circles may betray an inner fascination with the contemporary Roman rite—or at least with its musical accouterments.

Although some of the documentation related to the Catholic Mass issue likely does not survive, the extant materials do portray Johann Georg as a man extremely reluctant to lend his name to undisguised attacks on Catholics, for only direct and repeated appeals from the provincial diet and church officials could prod him into action. In religious matters, Johann Georg seems to have developed his own brand of *Realpolitik,* one mixed with a healthy dose of opportunism. Given the dearth of self-revelatory statements from the elector himself on the question of his religious beliefs, any understanding of his actions and policies toward Catholics between ca. 1661 and 1680 depends chiefly upon an understanding of his own personal agenda and the many constituencies that he desired to please—or to appease, or, at the very least, to avoid provoking—constituencies whose agendas conflicted directly with one another, yet were intricately interwoven with his own. As elector, Johann Georg desired to create and maintain an image of a highly cultured potentate and patron of the arts, one who possessed the means to fill his halls with elaborate Italian music and to mount extravagant court festivals. All of this presumed a certain financial status, however, and the provincial diet, which held the purse strings, tied its ongoing financial support of the elector and his enterprise to his religious fidelity, a cause for which it found support among the court and city clergymen in Dresden. Like so many rulers of smaller states, however, Johann Georg also yearned for recognition in the international political arena, and thus sought to curry favor with the two major continental powers of the day, both of whom alternately promised him financial rewards for his political support.[89] For help in this endeavor, he

87. "ses médecins l'avaient astreint à un régime de sobriété: pour comble de pénitence hygiénique, il observait Quatre-Temps et Vigiles, d'où l'on augurait qu'il penchait vers le catholicisme" (Auerbach 1887:335).

88. See chapter 7.

89. See Auerbach 1887:76, 136, 256, 334, and Helbig 1865:433.

sought the most experienced advisors he could find, regardless of their confession. Thus, when large numbers of court appointees flocked to Mass in Dresden, Johann Georg found himself in somewhat of a bind. An outright crackdown on the situation risked the wholesale exodus of Italians from his chapel, and the effective end of his Italianate musical enterprise. Clearly the prevention of such an artistic catastrophe required that he display religious tolerance toward his musicians. But neither could he risk losing the support of the Saxon provincial diet, whose financial largesse enabled him to pursue his cultural and political goals. And in his relationships with Emperor Leopold I and Louis XIV, Johann Georg could neither afford to lend the impression of being an ineffectual ruler in matters domestic, nor to jeopardize the carefully crafted alliances into which he had entered with these potentates—alliances that had proven financially advantageous to him. Given the potential domino effect of a single flawed decision, Johann Georg was forced to engage in a lively and sustained juggling act to keep each constituency at least somewhat satisfied. In the grand scheme of things, then, the celebration of Mass in Dresden represented more of an annoyance than a real crisis for Johann Georg, particularly when weighed against the financial, cultural, and foreign policy disasters that might have resulted from any number of so-called "solutions" to the "Catholic problem."

4

Piety, Penitence, and Praise:
The Dresden Textual Repertoire

T HE PREVIOUS discussion of Johann Georg's strongly suspected leanings toward Rome leads quite naturally into an examination of the texts of the musical repertoire presented in the court chapel under his watch, for the musical settings of the sacred concertos and motets that he established as part of his liturgies offered the greatest potential for the introduction of Catholic dogma into the Lutheran *Gottesdienst*. Most of the extra-liturgical compositions of Johann Georg's Catholic Kapellmeisters involved free (nonscriptural, nonliturgical) Latin texts that displayed striking differences from the texts of the *Spruchmotetten* and scripture-based sacred concertos composed by Schütz and other Lutheran composers of his generation.[1] Instead, these texts were now very similar in style and content to those regularly performed during Masses in Italy. Indeed, the simple fact that Catholics now inhabited the office of Dresden court Kapellmeister would seem to challenge the very notion that "Lutheran church music" continued to be cultivated at the Dresden court during the reign of Johann Georg II. Yet, as the discussion below reveals, the introduction of these texts did not result in a musical repertoire that stood in contravention of Lutheran doctrine. On the contrary: the vast majority of the texts set by these Catholics posed no challenges to that doctrine, and, perhaps more important, were fully consonant with the body of devotional literature developed by and for Lutherans from the middle of the previous century. Thus, regardless of their origins, many of the ideas expressed in these texts can be located securely within seventeenth-century Lutheran thought.

The facts surrounding the survival of this musical repertoire would in themselves seem to confirm the suitability of these works for Lutheran worship, and render moot any questions of confessional soundness, for all of the works that survive today were copied for use by various Lutheran cantors and Kapellmeisters: Gustav Düben, Kapellmeister at the court of Stockholm; Samuel Jacobi, cantor of the *Fürstenschule* (electoral school) in Grimma (near Leipzig); and Georg Österreich and Heinrich

---

1. Craig Westendorf defines the *Spruchmotette* as "a polyphonic setting of any portion of the German translation of Scripture" (Westendorf 1987:1).

Bokemeyer, Kapellmeisters at the north German court of Gottorf.[2] Without these copies, the repertoire would be unknown today, for the manuscripts that formed part of the court music collection disappeared long ago. In 1861, Fürstenau reported that the Dresden court music collection of the sixteenth and seventeenth centuries had been destroyed in 1760 in a fire that resulted from the Prussian bombardment of the city.[3] More recently, however, Eberhard Möller discovered a document that suggests that already in 1683, a large part of the court collection—including hundreds of sacred concertos and other sacred compositions—had been given to the city music ensemble in the Saxon town of Schneeberg.[4] No trace of these works survives today. As a result of both events, of the several hundred works composed for Johann Georg's chapel by Albrici and Peranda, today fewer than eighty sacred concertos survive, together with a few Masses, psalm settings, and other works.[5] Another 196 titles of lost works (99 by Albrici and 97 by Peranda) appear in the court diaries and in inventories of lost music collections. But as some of the Dresden diaries do not survive, and others include either few or no orders of worship, the total number of known extant and lost sacred concertos can only represent a small portion of the works in that genre composed in Dresden by Albrici and Peranda. The total number of compositions remains impossible to estimate; in 1662 alone, for example, Albrici presented fifty-five different sacred concertos from his own pen, as well many more by other composers. Of the works of the other Italian Kapellmeisters, very few sacred compositions by Bontempi and Pallavicino have survived, and none by Novelli. Rather than providing a complete picture of the Dresden repertoire, then, the surviving works instead reflect the repertorial needs, stylistic tastes, and textual preferences of their collectors.

THE TEXTUAL REPERTOIRE OF MID-CENTURY ROME

Albrici and Peranda spent their musically formative years, the 1640s and early 1650s, primarily in Rome, at a time when many Italian Catholic composers had begun to move toward more affective, freely composed texts of a composite nature, in which

---

2. Over the past forty years, a number of studies of the three collections have been undertaken. These include Krummacher 1963 and 1965, Grusnick 1964 and 1966, Rudén 1968, Kümmerling 1970, Webber 1996, and Wollny 1998.
   3. Fürstenau 1862/1971:360.
   4. Möller 1991:73.
   5. See the list of works of both composers in Appendix II. The total number of concertos composed for (or performed in) Dresden does not include works that survive (or may survive) in Kroměříž, Prague, and Trier, which were presumably composed for Catholic venues. For a discussion of the sources, including the watermarks, see Frandsen 1997-1:100–25.

isometric verse increasingly appeared in various combinations with prose.[6] Albrici and Peranda experienced these developments firsthand; not surprisingly, the textual and musical idioms that they transported to Dresden remained firmly grounded in Roman traditions. Rome was home to a host of composers, many of whom were affiliated with Jesuit churches and institutions. Foremost among these composers was Giacomo Carissimi, *maestro di cappella* at San Apollinare and the Jesuit German College. But Carissimi had a number of colleagues in the papal city whose names are less familiar today, including Bonifatio Gratiani (1604/5–64), Francesco Foggia (1604–88), Giovanni Bicilli (1623–1705), Carlo Cecchelli (fl. 1626–64) and Giovanni Marciani (ca. 1605–ca. 1663). Albrici worked directly under Carissimi as a choirboy at the German College, and probably under Gratiani as well, as organist at the Chiesa del Gesù, the Jesuit mother church. Peranda may also have served there under Gratiani (see chapter 1); this and the textual borrowings from Gratiani in his Dresden compositions strengthen the argument that he too had ties to the composer. He may also have known Cecchelli, who preceded Gratiani as *maestro di cappella* at the Gesù and the Jesuit Roman Seminary. And both Peranda and Albrici may have known Bicilli, who served as *maestro di cappella* at another Jesuit church, the Chiesa Nuova, for many years beginning in 1648.[7] All of these composers cultivated ensemble motets with the type of composite text that would prove to be so influential upon the Dresden repertoire. Most typical of these texts is their sectional nature and combination of prose and metric verse, as seen in Gratiani's *O bone Jesu* (1649):[8]

O bone Jesu,	O gentle Jesus,
o piissime Jesu,	O Jesus most kind,
humani generis amator.	lover of the race of humanity:
Qui te gustant esuriunt,	Those who are hungry taste you,
qui bibunt ad huc sitiunt.	those who still thirst now drink.
Sitio ad te, fontem aquae vivae,	For you I thirst, O font of living water,
nec satiabor donec requiescam	and I will not be satisfied
in te,	until I find rest in you,

6. Karl Gustav Fellerer and Geoffrey Webber have also called attention to the appearance in this repertoire of settings of free Latin poetry of a religious type; see Fellerer 1976-2:98 and Webber 1996:93–96. See also the discussion of Carissimi's texts in Jones 1982-1:129–48.

7. See Smither, "Bicilli," in *GMO*.

8. *R. Floridus canonicus de Sylvestris a Barbarano . . .* (Rome, 1649 [1649²]). For additional examples of similar texts, see *R. Floridus canonicus de Sylvestris . . . Florida verba* (Rome 1648 [1648¹]), and *Floridus modulorum hortus . . .* (Rome, 1647 [1647²]).

quia de amore tuo vulnerasti me.	for with your love you have wounded me.
O mentis delectatio,	O delight of the mind,
o cordis iubilatio,	O joy of the heart,
o amoris consummatio.	O consummation of love.
Ecce, langueo pro te, amor meus,	Behold, I long for you, my love,
quia tunc prior dilexisti me,	for you first loved me,
nec habeo quid tibi praebeam,	and there is nothing that I might offer you,
nisi te dederis mihi	had you not first given yourself to me,
largitor omnium.	O generous giver of all things.
Ecce, cantabo et delectabor in te,	Behold, I will sing, and I will delight in you,
quia es omnia et ego nihil sum,	for you are everything and I am nothing,
et tamen delectaris esse cum filiis hominum	and yet you delight to be among the children of men.[9]

O bone Jesu well represents the extended, discursive texts that were in vogue in the Italian motet repertoire of this era, and stands in stark contrast to the straightforward scriptural texts still favored by Schütz and many Germans at mid-century. It is striking both for its intermingling of prose and poetry and its unrestrained display of religious devotion expressed by an individual speaker. In contemporary Roman motet collections, such lengthy articulations of personal spirituality are common; typically, the speaker addresses Christ or Mary in evocative language that resonates with mystical *topoi* and allusions to that font of much mystical thought, the Song of Songs.[10]

The expansion of the Italian motet text in the 1640s by means of poetic insertions had significant musical consequences, for the choice of literary medium

9. Translated by Julia Marvin and Calvin M. Bower.

10. Two of the more obvious Song of Songs references in *O bone Jesu* appear in the third passage (Song of Songs 4:9: "vulnerasti cor meum") and the fifth (Song of Songs 2:5, 5:8: "quia amore langueo"). In addition, the text borrows from two stanzas of the medieval devotional hymn *Jesu dulcis memoria*, st. 21/16 and 40/34 (see the discussion of the versions of the poem and the numbering of stanzas below).

played a crucial determinative role in the musical styles employed by Roman composers at mid-century.[11] In texts such as *O bone Jesu*, for example, the combination
of prose and poetry resulted in a dichotomy between "speech" and "song" that was
new to the motet—one that inheres within the text itself, and remains independent
of any musical reading. Through such manipulations of literary modes the author-
compilers of these texts captured the sense of emotional transport experienced
by the speaker—the utterance of a passionate speech, rendered in prose, moves
the speaker to erupt into song, couched in metric poetry. In the first four sections of Gratiani's *O bone Jesu*, for example, the speaker twice moves from speech
to song. Roman composers exploited this dualism in modes of language to great
musical effect—while "speech" found its musical corollary in declamatory writing
for a soloist, the speaker's subsequent "song" was often cast in exuberant tutti passages in triple meter. In ensemble motet texts that date from the 1640s and 1650s,
these poetic insertions are still limited to isolated duplets and tercets. By contrast,
in the solo motet, which enjoyed cultivation after 1650, the poetic component often
involves more extended groups of stanzas. At this point, the spoken "song" dons
the melodic garb of an aria.

Although neither Albrici nor Peranda cultivated the solo motet to any great
extent, nor, as far as can be determined, presented solo motets by other composers
in the court chapel, both seem to have been influenced by the textual and musical features of the genre, particularly the incorporation of both recitative and aria.
While Carissimi composed only a dozen solo motets, his contemporary at the Gesù
specialized in the genre and left behind some seventy-four works; his contributions began with his Op. 3 collection of 1652.[12] Both Albrici and Peranda clearly
knew Gratiani's first collections of solo motets, for at a time when composers rarely
borrowed free texts from their peers, both of the Dresden Kapellmeisters based a
number of their own compositions on texts also set by Gratiani. As the dedication of Gratiani's Op. 3 collection bears the date of 16 March 1652, the print had
likely appeared in Rome before Albrici left for Sweden that fall; if not, he may have
acquired it in northern Europe, as the collection was reissued in Antwerp that same
year.[13] Albrici's textual borrowing began during his stay in Sweden, where he set
Laboravi clamans, a text that appears in Gratiani's Op. 3 collection of solo motets.[14]

11. Susanne Shigihara sees a direct relationship between the great degree of formal
variability exhibited in Gratiani's solo motets and the organization of the texts; see Shigihara 1984:493.

12. See the works list in Jones 1982-2:3–129; see also Shigihara 1984:368. Three volumes of Gratiani's solo motets, Op. 3 (1652), Op. 6 (1655), and Op. 8 (1658), are reproduced in Schnoebelen 1988.

13. Miller, "Gratiani," in *GMO*.

14. Rudén has dated the manuscript to 1654 (Rudén 1968, vol. 2, Bilaga I, 140).

Either before leaving Sweden or after arriving in Dresden, Albrici set *O cor meum*, another text from the same collection.[15] Peranda also borrowed from Gratiani, and although the majority of the pieces involved do not survive, the titles of a number of works by Peranda suggest that he depended even more heavily upon Gratiani than did his Dresden colleague:

EXTANT WORKS (BORROWINGS FROM GRATIANI SOLO
MOTET COLLECTIONS)

Albrici, *O cor meum*	1652 (entire text)
Albrici, *Laboravi clamans*	1652 (entire text)
Peranda, *Ad cantus, ad sonos*	1652 (*Plaudite vocibus*, opening stanza, 1st prose passage)
Peranda, *Fasciculus myrrhae*	1652 (*Ardet amans*, borrows five poetic strophes)

LOST WORKS (POSSIBLE BORROWINGS)

Albrici, *Plaudite vocibus*	1652 (same title)
Peranda, *Ad caelestem Hierusalem*	1652 (same title)
Peranda, *Fremite ad arma currite*	1652 (*Fremite, currite*; opens "Fremite, currite, ad arma")
Peranda, *Plaudite vocibus*	1652 (same title)
Peranda, *Rorate nubes*	1655[16] (same title)
Peranda, *Vos qui states in hac vita*	1655 (same title)

This borrowing on the part of Albrici and Peranda may have been necessitated by their relocation to northern Europe, as a result of which both lost access to the networks that they had likely developed for procuring texts. Nevertheless, it also suggests that both composers gravitated toward Gratiani's solo motets in particular—neither seems to have borrowed from his collections of ensemble motets from 1650 and 1652, for example.[17] Surprisingly, however, Albrici and Peranda did not regard Carissimi's works as textual quarries ready for the mining, even though the court owned a number of his compositions.[18]

15. See the scorings in Appendix II and the discussion of the two versions of *O cor meum* in chapter 5.

16. *Il secondo libro de motetti a voce sola*, Op. 6 (Rome: Balmonti, 1655); reproduced in Schnoebelen 1988.

17. *Motetti a due, tre, quattro, cinque, e sei* voci (Rome: Mascardi, 1650); *Il secondo libro de motetti a due, tre, quattro, cinque e sei voci* [Op. 2] (Rome: Mascardi, 1652).

18. Albrici presented a number of motets by Carissimi in the court chapel in 1662. His only textual borrowing from Carissimi seems to have been from *Hymnum jucunditatis*, but no record of a performance of the Carissimi setting appears in the court diaries.

While the solo motet texts share several traits with those for ensemble motets, particularly their discontinuous, sectional form and their incorporation of both prose and poetry, they differ in both their internal and external proportions. As the text of Gratiani's *Laboravi clamans* (1652) demonstrates, solo motet texts are generally of greater length, include a disproportionately high ratio of strophic poetry to prose, and, like the contemporary secular cantata, display groupings of the two literary media designed for composition as recitative and aria:

Laboravi clamans,	I have labored with crying,
rauce factae sunt fauces meae,	my throat has become hoarse, (Ps 68:4)
dum oro ad te, Domine,	while I pray to you, O Lord,
dum extollo ad te manus meas,	while I lift up my hands to you, (Ps 27:2)
dum clamo per noctes et lacrymis meis	while I cry out throughout the night,
irrigo stratum meum.	and moisten my bed with tears. (Ps 6:7)
Vide quomodo factus sum vilis,	See how worthless I have become,
et in dolore vulnerum meorum	and in the anguish of my wounds
liquefacta est prae lachrymis virtus mea.	my strength has been weakened by my tears. (SS 5:6, Ps 68:27)
Peccavi, deliqui,	I have sinned, I have offended [you],
o summe regnator,	O highest ruler,
o dulcis amator,	O sweet lover,
nunc scelus reliqui;	now I have abandoned my evil deeds:
si nolo peccare,	[for] if I do not sin,
tu noli damnare.	you will not condemn [me].
Quam horres peccantem,	How harsh you seem to the sinner,
tu animam meam,	to my soul,
dolentem iam ream	already grieving [and] guilty;
nunc amat amantem.	now [my soul] loves the loving one.

Accede festina,	Swiftly, come near to me,
iam pium, nam reum,	once guilty, now godly,
absconde cor meum	shelter my heart
sub luce divina.	beneath the divine light.
O quam benignus es, o	O how kind you are, o how
quam suavis.	sweet.
Tenuisti dexteram meam,	You have held my right hand,
et de profundo lacu liberasti me,	and from the boundless deep you have freed me,
et factus est spes mea in	and you have become my
saecula sempiterna.	hope for everlasting ages.[19]
Ergo mecum coeli amantes,	Therefore, sing praises with me,
laudate, celebrate,	loving heavens; celebrate,
coeli regem exaltantes,	O heavens, exalting the king,
date illi gloriam.	give glory to him.
Vos mortales iubilantes	You mortals rejoicing
in dolore, in amore,	in sorrow, in love—
semper vivite sperantes,	always live hoping
in amante numine.	in the loving divinity.
Super uno peccatore	Resound, sing out
resonate, decantate,	over one sinner
cui rex magnus summo amore	to whom the great king in his exalted love
coelo dedit veniam.	has given pardon in heaven.
Quantum placet penitentis,	My soul teaches
quantum pudor, quantum dolor,	how much the shame, how much the sorrow,
quantum lachrymae languentis	how much the tears of the languishing penitent
mea docet anima.	praise the Lord.[20]

19. *Lit.* "and my hope has been created for everlasting ages."
20. Translated by Margaret E. Garnett.

In contrast to *O bone Jesu*, the structure of which displays a nearly regular alternation of prose and metric verse, the text of *Laboravi* includes just two passages of prose ("Laboravi" and "O quam benignus es"), each of which introduces three or four stanzas of poetry. Like many texts of this era, including those set in Dresden, *Laboravi* includes two different stanzaic types, one typical of medieval poetry and the other of more recent vintage. While the trochaic tetrameter of the final four stanzas occurs with great frequency in medieval poetry, a fact that suggests that these stanzas may derive from a medieval source, the amphibrachic meter ($\cup$–$\cup$ $\cup$–$\cup$) of the first three stanzas does not, and seems to represent a more recent poetic development (see below). In their texts, Peranda and Albrici favored the same general types of poetic stanzas as did Gratiani and his contemporaries—those with six- or eight-syllable lines, straightforward meters, and simple rhyme schemes. In his setting of *Laboravi*, Gratiani set the prose passages as florid recitative and the poetic stanzas as strophic arias. Albrici and Peranda seem to have been most attracted by the coupling of solo recitative and aria in texts such as this, for they incorporated similar solo units into their ensemble concertos, but reduced to one or two the number of poetic stanzas following any given passage of prose.

To date, no all-encompassing examination of the texts set as musical compositions in Italy during this era has been undertaken. As a result, the tremendous amount of research that remains to be done on the motet during this period of Italian music history renders problematic any attempt to generalize about its texts. This, together with the fact that most of this repertoire has not appeared in modern editions, renders difficult any assessment of developments in textual content and style. Nevertheless, even a brief inquiry quickly reveals that numerous features distinguish the texts favored by mid-century Italian Catholic composers from those preferred by their Lutheran counterparts in the north. At mid-century, one can still identify two different traditions, each of which arose out of different confessional circumstances and requirements—a simple comparison of the texts found in two collections published in 1650, Schütz's *Symphoniarum sacrarum tertia pars* and Gratiani's *Motetti a due, tre, quattro, cinque, e sei voci*, easily illustrates this point. But the type of composite motet text cultivated in Italy ca. 1650 soon began to make inroads in the north, and its appearance would have significant consequences for compositional activity there. With their respective transalpine moves, Albrici and Peranda helped to transport this new type of text to Germany, where it continued to develop, quite removed from Italian influences.

THE DRESDEN TEXTUAL REPERTOIRE

The Problem of Authorship

One of the great unsolved mysteries of the textual repertoire of both the Latin motet in Italy and the Latin sacred concerto in Germany concerns the identity of its authors or author-compilers, as none of the musical compositions bear any attributions to the authors of the texts. While texts from scripture and the liturgy were likely selected by the composers themselves, the free texts invite a number of questions regarding their origins. Scholars who have examined portions of this vast repertoire have developed several plausible hypotheses. In his discussion of the "non-scriptural, non-breviary" texts of the "new Lombard motet," which evince some commonalities with texts set in Dresden, Robert Kendrick points out that "there is no indication of authorship in any of the Milanese repertory," and the "texts did not circulate independently of their musical transmission"[21]; both observations are valid for the Dresden repertoire as well. Kendrick cites evidence that suggests that at least some of the texts originated outside the convent walls, but also observes that some of the patrician members of the community possessed the education to compose texts in Latin.[22] With respect to the texts set by Carissimi, Andrew Jones points to both musicians and clerics as potential authors, and cites one of the only known references to an author of motet texts, Odoardo Ceccarelli, "who sang in the choir of Sant' Apollinare at various times between 1622 and 1645" and who was noted as an "excellent writer of Latin words for setting to music." Jones also points out that a number of texts set by Carissimi "display a preference for scriptural subjects and images which were characteristic of (though not exclusive to) Jesuit spirituality" and adds that priests at the German College would have been "erudite enough" to have compiled texts on various themes.[23] In confronting this same problem in the texts set by Gratiani, Shigihara suggests that the authors were probably Jesuits or other clerics, and that the composer himself likely authored some texts.[24] After examining the texts set by Albrici, Carl-Allan Moberg concluded that "sometimes these poetic additions are instantaneous embellishments of the text which can only be attributed to the composer himself, in relationship with the structure of the piece."[25] Moberg added that "many of [Albrici's] sacred concertos leave little doubt that the composer of these works collected the texts himself and treated them poetically."[26] Elisabeth Schedensack suspects that the composer Isabella Leonarda (1620–1704) authored

21. Kendrick 1996:279.
22. Kendrick 1996:280.
23. Jones 1982-1:142.
24. Shigihara 1984:456–57.
25. "Manchmal stellen diese poetischen Zuschüsse innerhalb des Textes nur momentane Ausschmückungen dar und werden kaum von irgend einem anderen als dem Komponisten selbst und zwar im Zusammenhang mit der musikalischen Einrichtung herrühren können" (Moberg 1962:203).
26. "Das Aussehen manches seiner Kirchenkonzerte lässt wenig Zweifel, dass der Komponist in diesen Werken die betreffenden Texte selbst zusammengestellt und poetisch behandelt hat" (Moberg 1962:204–5).

some of the texts that she set as solo motets.[27] The implications of this evidence for Dresden are complicated by the fact that there the Italian Kapellmeisters found themselves isolated from any large community of Catholic clerics or scholars. Some Jesuit priests did reside in Dresden from at least 1667, however, and the court Kapellmeisters may have pressed them into service in the compilation of texts.[28] And some of the texts may have been composed "in house" by Albrici, Peranda, or other members of the *Hofkapelle*. Bontempi, for example, authored musical treatises, historical monographs, and the libretto of his opera *Il Paride*, and certainly possessed the erudition required to write or compile concerto texts. The fact that the successful author-compiler would by necessity have to possess an understanding of music and a sensitivity to the requirements of the composer also suggests that the composers of this school prepared their own texts

In the end, the identities of the author-compilers of the texts have no real bearing on the musical compositions. But in a cross-confessional situation such as that which obtained in Dresden, the continuing anonymity of the author-compilers hinders somewhat one's ability to accurately assess the content of the texts from a confessional perspective. Thus, lacking the identities of the creators of the texts, it is important to attempt to identify the bodies of literature upon which they drew. In the nonscriptural, nonliturgical prose that appears in these texts, one sees a striking similarity in style and tone to prose passages found in contemporary devotional manuals used by both Lutherans and Catholics. A significant portion of the poetry, on the other hand, appears to be medieval, and may lurk somewhere in the myriad volumes of *Analecta hymnica*, but an index of the first lines of all stanzas would be required to identify the various odd stanzas that appear in many concerto texts.[29] The style of poetry employed by these composers is not typical of Jesuit neo-Latin poetry, however, which was written in imitation of classical models, and exhibits much more sophisticated metric and rhyme schemes. One need only compare the poetry of Jacob Balde, one of the most celebrated Jesuit poets of the seventeenth century, to the verse found in the Dresden concerto texts to conclude that the latter

27. Schedensack 1998-1:104. Leonarda's texts share many features with those set by Gratiani, Albrici, and Peranda.

28. The retinues of both of the ambassadors resident in Dresden included Jesuit priests. Given the fact that musicians including Albrici attended Masses in their homes, it remains quite possible that these Jesuits provided some of the texts that Albrici, Peranda, and Pallavicino set as sacred concertos for the court chapel. Siegfried Seifert has identified two of these priests, Bernhard Zefferin, SJ (1620–82), who arrived in Dresden in 1667 in the service of the imperial ambassador and remained until 1673, and August Bildstein, SJ (1625–90), who arrived in 1670 and served first the imperial ambassador and later Chassan, the French ambassador (Seifert 1994:75–76).

29. Blume and Dreves 1886–1922.

was not drawn from that body of recent poetic literature.[30] But while the medieval (or perhaps neo-medieval) poetry can be associated with a body of known work, the origins of the six-syllable poetry in amphibrachic meter found here continue to elude scholars.[31] Despite its status as a staple poetic ingredient in motet and concerto texts in the latter half of the seventeenth century, it remains virtually unrecognized by literary historians. In contrast to much of the medieval verse employed in these texts, particularly neo-Latin verse, the amphibrachic poetry generally lacks figurative language, multivalence, and metaphoric complexity, and may represent verse written by and for an educated lay audience. It remains possible that this verse form arose in conjunction with music, as it seems to appear first in musical settings in the 1640s.[32] Whatever its sources or origins, its strongly rhythmic ductus seems to have made it a natural choice of composers seeking suitable aria texts. Shigihara has pointed out that a tremendous number of strophes with six-syllable lines appear in Gratiani's solo motet texts, and identifies amphibrachic meter as the most common metric pattern in those works[33]; significantly, this metric pattern also plays an important role in the Dresden textual repertoire.

Other lacunae in the literature on the Latin motet and sacred concerto of this era exist in the area of textual analysis and assessment. For the individual worshiper, the impact of the message communicated through the music performed from the balcony may have equaled or surpassed that of messages read from the lectern and delivered from the pulpit. To date, however, theologians, church historians, and literary scholars have not undertaken examinations of these texts *qua* texts; in this respect, the literary aspect of the repertoire has suffered from even more neglect than the music itself.[34] Despite the constant presence of motets and concertos within worship services, their texts have yet to be recognized by these scholars as an integral part of the nexus of devotional and exegetical messages transmitted during worship. It must be said, however, that the apparent inattention of these scholars to this textual repertoire may well be a consequence of the inaccessibility of much

---

30. See Balde 1729/1990 and Thill 1999.

31. Both Shigihara and Schedensack point out that this six-syllable verse type seems to have no model in classical poetry; see Shigihara 1984:414–17 and Schedensack 1998-1:102. (Only Shigihara identifies the meter as amphibrachic.)

32. See, for example, *Per rigidos montes* by Carlo Cecchelli (fl. 1626–64), in *R. Floridus canonicus de Sylvestris a Barbarano Florida verba a celeberrimis musices auctoribus* (Rome: Robletti, 1648) [RISM 1648¹]: [st. 1] "Per rigidos montes / per frigidos fontes / per invias valles / per asperas calles / iam Sponsa celestis / dilectum quaerebat / sic illa dicebat / et vocibus mestis." Peranda also set this text (see Appendix II).

33. Shigihara 1984:413–15.

34. In his seminal work on the relationship between meditation and seventeenth-century church reform, for example, Udo Sträter makes no mention of the texts presented in musical settings during worship (see Sträter 1995).

of the musical repertoire, only a small portion of which is available in modern editions. As a result, the texts of the liturgy, as well as sermons and devotional materials, have remained the focus of attention.

Textual Composition

Once in Dresden, to what extent did Albrici and Peranda remain true to the textual traditions of their Roman mentors, and to what extent did they move in new directions? Some answers to these questions emerge from a comparison of the Dresden textual repertoire with that of the two prominent Roman composers with whose music the Dresden Kapellmeisters were familiar, and whose texts have been evaluated by scholars: Carissimi and Gratiani. In his discussion and analysis of Carissimi's texts, Jones identifies four principal textual categories, the largest of which comprises texts in which scriptural passages, often modified, appear in combination with free material. The other three types include entirely free texts, unaltered liturgical texts, and modified scriptural texts. To these four main groups Jones adds those few texts that comprise unaltered scripture, or freely augmented portions of the liturgy, or combinations of paraphrases of both scriptural and liturgical elements.[35] In a comparison of the texts set by Carissimi with those set by Albrici and Peranda, one finds that unaltered liturgical texts represent just over twenty percent of the texts set by Carissimi, while such texts in the Dresden repertoire (which include Breviary hymns) number slightly under fifteen percent. Texts that combine scriptural and free material appear in about a third of Carissimi's motets, while such texts comprise a slightly smaller portion (about a quarter) of the extant texts set by the Dresden Kapellmeisters. But while free texts constitute only about a quarter of Carissimi's output, they represent virtually half of the extant texts set by Albrici and Peranda. In this regard the Dresden texts display more affinity with those found in Gratiani's solo motets, where nonliturgical, freely composed texts form the vast majority of the total—close to ninety percent.[36] Although freely composed, however, these texts often invoke scriptural passages through citation, paraphrase, and allusion. Texts that comprise solely modified scripture, which represent about one-seventh of Carissimi's texts, form a negligible part of the Dresden repertoire.[37] The incorporation of altered or expanded scriptural passages remains an important aspect of the texts set in Dresden, but these passages are now incorporated into texts dominated by free material (as seen in *Laboravi* above). In general, the texts examined by Jones also stand apart from those set by Albrici and Peranda in that they are often composed in prose throughout; metric verse plays a very secondary role. In this

---

35. Jones 1982-1:129–48.
36. Shigihara 1984:371–74.
37. Jones 1982-1:130.

respect, the texts set in Dresden also display a distinct commonality with the texts of Gratiani's solo motets, for metric poetry in the same few stanzaic types accounts for a significant portion of the free material in both repertoires.

While the various textual categories developed by Jones and Shigihara shed light on the composition of motet texts during this era, such categories offer little insight into the actual content of the texts. It is this content, however, that is central to an understanding of the way in which the texts are reflective of contemporary spirituality in a given cultural and confessional context, and the ways in which they may have functioned in a particular liturgical context. Questions of textual origins must also figure prominently in any examination of the Dresden repertoire; since these composers were active in a cross-confessional situation, the theological and confessional "purity" of the content cannot be presumed. Equally important to a study of the content, however, is an examination of the structure of the texts, and the various literary media employed there, for while the content directly informs the composer's decisions regarding affect in the composition, the literary medium significantly influences his stylistic choices.[38] Thus, an examination of both aspects of the text can shed valuable light on this musical repertoire. In the following two chapters, the impact of the composers' musical responses to these texts, particularly as reflected in the style, structure, and affect of their compositions, will be taken up. First, however, it is important to examine the content of these texts, in order to gain a sense of the mode of spirituality that these Italians introduced into the Dresden chapel.

Thematic Content

The *tavole* in Latin motet collections printed in Italy during the seventeenth century often served as thematic indices of the collections, as they offered liturgical designations for each composition. Of these designations, the three most common categories are *per ogni tempo* (for any time), for saints' days, and for feasts of the Blessed Virgin. These designations appear in many collections, such as Sebastiano Cherici's 1681 collection of motets, *Harmonia di devoti concerti*, which includes four works (all designated *per ogni tempo*) that received performances in Dresden in 1676, during Cherici's brief tenure there as Kapellmeister. While the prints of Gratiani's solo motets generally lack such guidelines, Shigihara has analyzed the content of his texts and broken them down by thematic and/or liturgical category. Not surprisingly, the same three major categories appear, as do two others: texts for the Elevation of the Host, and texts for feast days. Texts *per ogni tempo* constitute just under half of the repertoire, followed in number by texts dedicated to the saints, Marian texts, texts for feast days, and texts for the Elevation. Shigihara goes on to examine the content of

---

38. See Gianturco 1990 for a discussion of this interdependency with respect to the seventeenth-century secular cantata.

the texts *per ogni tempo* and provides a detailed breakdown.[39] In her discussion, she underscores the predominance in this portion of the repertoire of texts that express an "enraptured-mystical love of Jesus" ("schwärmerisch-mystische Jesusminne"); of the thirty-four texts that she has categorized as appropriate "for any time," a full two-thirds are of this devotional nature.[40] In fact, of the entire repertoire of solo motet texts, more than one quarter are expressive of such Christocentric devotion. Not insignificantly, this category also predominates in the Dresden textual repertoire.

When the works of Albrici and Peranda are filtered through Shigihara's textual categories, the resulting breakdown reflects the expected absence of Marian, Eucharistic, and sanctoral texts. And, just as in the texts set by Gratiani as solo motets, the largest part of the Dresden textual repertoire may also be designated as *per ogni tempo*. Within the category of texts *per ogni tempo*, devotional texts predominate, but several other themes, including *vanitas*, penitence, and praise, are represented by a significant number of works. Other themes also appear, albeit in fewer works: salvation through Christ; the salvific power of Christ's blood and wounds; God as a source of help, strength, and peace; and confidence in God or Christ. Outside of the texts *per ogni tempo*, texts for feast days represent the largest textual category in Dresden; such texts constitute more than a fifth of the existing repertoire. Such an essential breakdown of the Dresden repertoire by theme helps to underscore the extent to which these Italian composers' acceptance of appointments in a Lutheran court chapel affected their thematic priorities. Like Gratiani and other contemporary Catholic composers in Italy, the Dresden Kapellmeisters placed their emphasis on texts *per ogni tempo*, and displayed a similar enthusiasm for texts that appeal to Christ in language imbued with mysticism. But as one would expect, of the categories typically assigned to Italian motets, the second and third largest—those with texts addressed to the Blessed Virgin and the saints—remained almost completely unrepresented in Dresden, forbidden on theological grounds due to their invocation of the intercession of both. Neither did Lutherans have a tradition of music at the elevation of the host—if indeed the host was elevated at all during the Communion service.[41] In addition, in contrast to the themes expressed in Gratiani's solo motets, the texts of the Dresden repertoire reveal a stronger emphasis on *vanitas*, as well as on penitence and praise.

But although the thematic priorities seen in the Dresden textual repertoire differ from those of the contemporary Italian motet, neither do they line up in all

39. Shigihara 1984:375–80.
40. Shigihara 1984:377.
41. On the Lutheran practice of elevating the host during the Communion rite, see Nischan 1999. It is unknown whether the practice continued in seventeenth-century Dresden, but as regards music, it is a rather moot point, for the Communion liturgy there seems to have involved no extra-liturgical music (see the discussion in chapter 8).

respects with those of the German Lutheran textual corpus of the time. In his study of North German Lutheran church music in the later seventeenth century, Geoffrey Webber isolated three main thematic categories, *Lob, Andacht,* and *Erbauung* (praise, devotion, and edification), as those into which most of the examined texts naturally fell.[42] Texts of praise are drawn predominantly from the psalms, while devotional texts, which are often in Latin, betray a significant debt to medieval mysticism. Edifying texts include Gospel texts and Gospel dialogues, as well as centonized scriptural texts and composite texts that mingle prose with poetry.[43] These three main categories, while also relevant for Dresden, assume a slightly different order there. Devotional texts loom particularly large in the Dresden repertoire and borrow from three of the same sources or themes of Catholic mysticism that appear in the North German repertoire: the hymn *Jesu dulcis memoria,* the Song of Songs, and the theme of *vanitas.*[44] However, the Dresden devotional repertoire also draws upon additional textual sources not identified by Webber (see below). Concertos expressive of general praise and rejoicing (encomiastic texts) were also performed in Dresden, but, in contrast to the Schütz era, presentations of settings of Gospel texts, which Webber designates as edifying, were now rare occurrences in the Saxon chapel. Absent from both repertoires, however, are texts whose function is *Trost,* or comfort, a theme that dominates the Lutheran *Spruchmotette* repertoire of ca. 1525–1630.[45] Not surprisingly, given the confessional affiliation of the Italians, this quintessentially Lutheran concept, whereby the individual soul, terrified at the prospect of eternal damnation, receives comfort in the message of justification (and hence salvation), essentially disappears from the musical repertoire in Dresden after Schütz.[46] In its place, however, appeared another type of comfort, that provided by Christ to the individual Christian who sought His mystical presence in prayer.

42. Webber 1996:86.
43. Webber 1996:86–87, 92–101.
44. As Webber has pointed out, the Lutheran devotional repertoire also included settings of Marian antiphons by Italians whose texts were rewritten to address Christ (Webber 1996:87–90). None of these appear in the Dresden court diaries, but the Rudolstadt inventory attributes an *O sponsa Christi laetare* to Peranda. This may have been *Regina coeli laetare* in a Christocentric disguise, but whether Peranda or another musician altered the text cannot be determined (see Baselt 1963:117).
45. See Westendorf 1987:105–283; such texts also represent a significant portion of those found in the Lutheran sacred concerto repertoire of ca. 1620–50.
46. A few isolated examples, such as Peranda's *Herr, wenn ich nur dich habe* (Ps 73:25–26), do appear in the diaries.

Neue Frömmigkeit and the Devotional Text in Dresden

Already popular in Catholic Italy soon after 1600,[47] texts expressive of Christocentric devotion begin to appear in musical compositions in Lutheran areas in the mid-1620s, with the publication of Thomas Schattenberg's *Jubilus S. Bernardi de nomine Jesu* (1620) and Schütz's *Cantiones sacrae* (1625). As the century progressed, the popularity of devotional texts among Lutherans grew exponentially, particularly after ca. 1640. Between 1641 and 1649, for example, Andreas Profe published five volumes of Italian motets intended for the Lutheran market and included many settings of devotional texts,[48] while the Zittau organist Andreas Hammerschmidt began publishing his own settings of devotional texts in 1641. This trend continued: Johann Rosenmüller, organist at the Nikolaikirche in Leipzig, set a number of devotional texts in his *Kern-Sprüche* of 1648 and 1652–53, J. J. Weiland, vice-Kapellmeister in Wolfenbüttel, published a collection of works in 1656 based almost exclusively on Latin devotional poetry, including *Jesu dulcis memoria*[49] and Samuel Capricornus (1628–65), Kapellmeister in Stuttgart, composed numerous works on Latin and German devotional texts in the 1650s and 1660s. After their arrival in Dresden, Albrici and Peranda revived the tradition first established there by Schütz and regularly cultivated musical settings of mystically imbued expressions of love and devotion to Christ in this center of Lutheran worship—more than a quarter of their extant concertos are settings of such texts. As seen below in the text set by Albrici, the intimacy of these devotional texts, which represent the private prayers of an individual (uttered, somewhat paradoxically, in public), contrast dramatically with texts of praise or edification:

VINCENZO ALBRICI, *O BONE JESU*

O bone Jesu, charitas,	O good Jesus, love,
tu me totum transmutas,	you transfigure me totally,
tu me totum transfigis,	you transfix me totally,
o dulcis amor.	O sweet love.
In te solo respiro,	In you alone I find relief,
et semper te adoro.	and I always adore you.
Sine te, amor meus,	Except you, my love,
nil prorsus ultra quaero.	truly I ask for nothing more.
Tu es lux,	You are light,
tu es spes,	you are hope,
mi chare Jesu.	my dear Jesus.

47. For examples of Roman motets in this vein, see Dixon 1981-2. See also the discussion in Webber 1996:87–91.

48. For a discussion and analysis of these collections, see Sponheim 1995.

49. See Webber 1996:87–88.

Here the individual stands alone, entirely oblivious to the world that surrounds him, having willingly distanced himself from the community of believers. He approaches a good, sweet, accessible Christ as he might an earthly lover. But while *O bone Jesu* might first appear to be an uncomplicated expression of adoration, the speaker's recollections of having been transfigured and transfixed by Christ, and his reference to finding relief "in" Christ, serve as metaphors for that ephemeral state of full or perfect union with Christ, the attainment of spiritual ecstasy.[50]

The prominence of devotional texts in the Lutheran repertoire of the latter half of the seventeenth century, including that composed in Dresden, reflects the integration of two separate worlds, those of private, individual devotion and of public, corporate worship. While the expressive language and intimate tone of Albrici's *O bone Jesu* might seem somehow out of place in this era of Lutheran Orthodoxy, a period in church history that is often characterized as "stern" or "rigid," the work of church historians over the past four decades has revealed that the dogmatism that characterized Orthodox theology itself was accompanied by a new devotionality in the private sphere, a phenomenon that has been characterized as "new piety" (*neue Frömmigkeit*) or "early pietism" (*Frühpietismus*).[51] Personal expressions of devotion to Christ, such as that seen in *O bone Jesu*, began to appear in Lutheran prayer books soon after 1550 and remained important for at least the next century and a half. Paul Althaus has traced the individualization of the language of prayer—the shift from "we" to "I"—in Lutheran devotional literature in the sixteenth century and has demonstrated the significance of medieval devotional manuals for the Lutherans, who borrowed extensively from these sources. Not insignificantly, one of the consequences of this borrowing was the introduction of medieval mysticism into Lutheran private prayer in the latter half of the sixteenth century.[52] Thus the appearance of texts like *O bone Jesu* in sacred art music intended primarily for use in Lutheran venues is not in itself surprising; far more remarkable is the fact that such texts took so long to emerge as fodder for that vehicle.

One of the first and most important examples of mystically inspired devotional literature compiled by a Lutheran for a Lutheran audience was the work of Andreas Musculus (1514–81), a professor of theology in Frankfurt.[53] Musculus's first publi-

---

50. See Poulain 1950:237–40.

51. Given the recent explosion of scholarship on this topic, only a brief list of contributions is possible here. See, for example: Zeller 1962, 1971, and 1978, Breuer 1984, Brecht 1993, Sträter 1995, Wallmann 1995, Axmacher 1989/1, 1989/2, and 2001, Nieden and Nieden 1999, and Sommer 1999.

52. Althaus 1927/1966:59–142.

53. Musculus was educated in Leipzig and studied theology in Wittenberg at the time of Luther; later, he was a signatory to the Formula of Concord; see Lohmann, "Musculus," *BBKL* 6:380–81.

cation in this vein appeared in 1553 under the title *Precandi formulae piae et selec-tae, ex veterum Ecclesiae sanctorum doctorum scriptis*; six years later, he published a revised edition of the collection under the title *Precationes ex veteribus orthodoxis doctoribus*, in which form the collection appeared in eighteen editions between 1559 and 1624.[54] For his *Precationes*, Musculus drew the majority of his texts from three medieval devotional writings that enjoyed wide circulation in the sixteenth and seventeenth centuries, the *Meditationes, Soliloquia* (i.e., the *Soliloquiorum ani-mae ad Deum*), and *Manuale*. These three works, once commonly attributed to St. Augustine, were actually compilations of passages excerpted from the writings of a number of medieval theologians. The *Meditationes* comprise Anselm's *Orationes* in large part, but also include passages from the writings of Augustine, Gregory, Alcuin, and others.[55] The *Soliloquia* were drawn from Augustine's *Confessiones, de spiritu et litera*, Hugo de St. Victor's *De diligendo Deo*, and other works. And of the thirty-six chapters of the *Manuale*, the first nine are identical to Anselm's four-teenth *Meditatio*, while the last six are taken from the same author's *Proslogium*. The remaining twenty-one chapters include excerpts from various authors, including Hugo de St. Victor and St. Bernhard of Clairvaux.[56] These three collections, which Althaus dubbed the "'three-part braid' (*dreifältige Schnur*) of devotional writings," served as Musculus's primary sources; he also culled passages from the writings of Jerome, Origen, Cyprian, Anselm, and others.[57] In 1559, Musculus also published his *Betbüchlein*, a collection of prayers in German dependent upon the same trio of Latin writings, but rather than simply translate or paraphrase various texts, here he authored many of the texts himself, and incorporated the fund of ideas found in the Latin repertoire of the *Precationes*. As a result, Musculus was able to create something entirely new from the old, "which is missing neither the German idiom nor Lutheran content."[58] Althaus credits Musculus with having ushered in a new era in the history of Lutheran prayer literature with this collection of prayers in the

54. Althaus 1927/1966:98; Althaus examined a copy published in Leipzig in 1575, as did this author. Musculus, like a number of other sixteenth-century Lutheran theolo-gians, also used the writings of the church fathers to support various tenets of Lutheran doctrine in his theological writings; see Kolb 1998.

55. Althaus 1927/1966:26. Dom André Wilmart, OSB, has pointed to Jean de Fécamp (d. 1078) as the author-compiler of the *Meditationes* (Wilmart 1932:127–28, 173, 191). According to Kolb, although Erasmus had already expressed doubts about the attribu-tion of the *Meditationes* to St. Augustine, Musculus raised no doubts about its authentic-ity (1998:114).

56. Althaus 1927/1966:74 n. 1.

57. Althaus 1927/1966:99; see also Kolb 1998:114, 120–22.

58. "welches weder das deutsche Idiom noch den evangelischen Gehalt vermissen läßt" (Althaus 1927/1966:101).

vernacular.⁵⁹ As a source of inspiration to seventeenth-century Lutheran composers seeking devotional texts for realization in music, however, his Latin collection
stands as far more significant.

While Musculus succeeded in introducing medieval mysticism into the realm
of Lutheran prayer, the work of another Lutheran theologian, Martin Moller (1547–
1606), proved fundamental to its wider reception. In 1584 and 1591, Moller, a pastor in Görlitz (Upper Lusatia), published the two parts of his *Meditationes sanctorum Patrum*.⁶⁰ Like Musculus, Moller also borrowed heavily from the *Meditationes,
Soliloquia, and Manuale*, and included texts of Bernhard, Tauler, Cyprian, Jerome,
and Anselm, but translated them into German.⁶¹ In his translations, however,
Moller sought to bring certain aspects of medieval mysticism into conformity with
Lutheran doctrine.⁶² According to Elke Axmacher, Moller's texts were fundamental
to the development of a "theology of piety"; only Johann Arndt's *True Christianity*
(*Das Wahre Christentum*, 1606) and *Paradieß-Gärtlein* (*Little Garden of Paradise*,
1612) figure more prominently in the "Protestant reception of mysticism."⁶³

In the course of her work on Moller, Axmacher has sought to identify and define
the underlying ethos of the texts that so inspired this Lutheran theologian. Her
description of the essence of the *Meditationes, Manuale*, and *Soliloquia*, however,
could easily stand as a description of the devotional texts set by Albrici and Peranda
in Dresden:

> That which binds these texts together is the fundamental mystical theme of
> the soul in the captivity of sin and of its homelessness in this world, from
> which it longs to return to its original security and freedom with God. With-
> drawal from the world [and] contemplation of the suffering of Christ are
> the conditions under which the human being once again attains God and

59. Althaus 1927/1966:101.

60. [Part I:] *MEDITATIONES sanctorum Patrum. Schöne/ andächtige Gebet/ tröstliche Sprüche/ Gottselige Gedancken/ Trewe Bußvermanungen/ Hertzliche Dancksagungen/
vnd allerley nützliche vbungen des Glaubens. Aus den heyligen Altvätern Augustino, Bernhardo, Taulero vnd andern. . . .* Görlitz: Fritsch, 1584; [Part II:] *ALTERA PARS Meditationum ex sanctis Patribus. Ander Theyl Andechtiger schöner Gebet/ tröstlicher Gedancken/
trewer Bußvermanungen/ vnd allerley nützlicher vbungen des Glaubens. Aus den heyligen
Altvätern Cypriano, Hieronymo, Augustino, Bernhardo, Anshelmo, vnd andern. . . .* Görlitz: Fritsch, 1591.

61. Althaus summarizes Moller's borrowings as follows: the *Meditationes* (46 prayers
in Part I), the *Manuale* (in Part II: 36 prayers), the *Soliloquia* (11), and writings of Bernhard (8), Tauler (5), etc. (1927/1966:134–35). Elke Axmacher provides a more detailed
breakdown of Moller's source material in 1989/1:109–12.

62. See Axmacher 1989/2:14–26.

63. Axmacher 1989/2:16–17.

climbs ever higher to the true tranquillity of the heart and to the complete delight of God. In the human being, the dualism between the world and God is reflected through asceticism on the one hand and ecstatic love of God on the other. Love is now the main theme of these writings. In [love], everything is united that is otherwise divided: God and man, Christ and the sinner, the eternal and the temporal. The human being, who immerses himself in divine love and perceives God as He is, namely as love, can do nothing else but be inflamed with love for Him in return.[64]

Love, according to Axmacher, is the foundation upon which the religious expression of these medieval texts rests. In them expressions of love for Christ predominate, and, just as in the devotional texts set in Dresden, this love is often expressed in the language of earthly erotic passion. Passages such as the following, drawn from the third section ("Ad Filium") of Musculus' *Precationes*, reveal the tone and style of the Christocentric texts published by both Musculus and Moller, in which the speaker pours out feelings of intense love and desire for Christ, whom he longs to touch and to taste:

> Domine Jesu Christe, redemptor meus, vita et salus mea, te laudo, tibi gratias ago, . . . Domine Deus meus, creator meus, adiutor meus, te sitio, te esurio, te desidero, ad te suspiro, te concupisco benignissimum, suavissimum et serenissimum, te volo, te quaero, in te spero. . . . O dulcis Christe, bone Jesu, charitas, Deus meus, accende me toto igne tuo, amore tuo, charitate tua, ut diliga te Dominum meum dulcissimum et pulcherrimum, ex toto corde meo, per omnem vitam meam, et per omnia secula seculorum.[65]

> (Lord Jesus Christ, my redeemer, my life and salvation, I praise you, I give thanks to you, . . . Lord, my God, my creator, my aid, I thirst for you, I hunger

---

64. "Das Verbindende zwischen diesen Texten ist das mystische Grundthema von der Seele in der Gefangenschaft der Sünde und von ihrer Heimatlosigkeit in dieser Welt, aus der sie sich zurücksehnt in ihre ursprüngliche Geborgenheit und Freiheit bei Gott. Abkehr von der Welt, Betrachtungen des Leidens Christi sind die Voraussetzungen dafür, daß der Mensch wieder zu Gott gelangt und immer höher aufsteigt bis zur wahren Ruhe des Herzens und zum völligen Genuß Gottes. Dem Dualismus zwischen Welt und Gott entspricht der Mensch durch Askese einerseits, ekstatische Gottesliebe andererseits. Die Liebe nun ist das Hauptthema dieser Schriften. In ihr ist alles vereinigt, was sonst getrennt ist. Gott und der Mensch, Christus und der Sünder, das Ewige und das Zeitliche. Der Mensch, der sich in die göttliche Liebe versenkt und Gott erkennt, wie er ist, nämlich als Liebe, kann nicht anders, als wiederum in Liebe zu ihm zu entbrennen" (Axmacher 1989/2:15).

65. Excerpt from Musculus 1575:46–47, attributed by Musculus to Augustine, *De contritione*, ch. 3. The text does not appear in the latter work, however, but in the pseudo-Augustinian *Meditationes*. See *PL* 40:942, 930 (*Meditationes*) and 40:943–50 (*De contritione*).

for you, I desire you, I long for you, I covet you, most kind, most delightful, and most serene, I want you, I seek you, I place my hope in you . . . O sweet Christ, good Jesus, love, my God, set me alight with all of your fire, with your love, with your charity, that I might love you, my most sweet and beautiful Lord, with all of my heart and for all of my life, and for eternity.)

O bone Jesu, o dulcis Jesu, O Jesu fili Mariae virginis, plenus, misericordia et veritate, O dulcis Jesu miserere mei, secundum magna misericordiam tuam. O benigne Jesu, te deprecor per illum sanguinem tuum pretiosum, quem pro nobis miseris peccatoribus effundere dignatus es in ara crucis, ut abijcias omnes iniquitates meas, et ne despicias humiliter te petentem, et hoc nomen tuum sanctissimum Jesus invocantem. Hoc nomen Jesus, nomen dulce est, hoc nomen Jesus, nomen salutare est. . . . O misericordissime Jesu, miserere mei. O dulcissime Jesu, libera me. O piissime Jesu, propitius esto mihi peccatori.[66]

(O good Jesus, O sweet Jesus, O Jesus, son of the Virgin Mary, filled with compassion and truth, O sweet Jesus, have compassion for me as befits your own great compassion. O kind Jesus, I pray to you through your precious blood, which you deigned to pour out for us miserable sinners on the altar of the cross, that you cast off all of my iniquities, and that you not spurn the one humbly beseeching you and invoking this your most holy name, Jesus. This name Jesus, this name is sweet, this name Jesus, this name is salvific. . . . O merciful Jesus, have compassion for me. O most sweet Jesus, free me. O most pious Jesus, look with favor on me, a sinner.)

In these passages, the individual Christian expresses an intense, intimate, passionate love for Christ. The ever-heightening language of adulation and yearning lends the texts a quality of ecstatic abandon. The speaker constantly reaches for adjectival superlatives—it seems that no words can truly describe his Lord. The total effect is that of constant reaching, constant striving toward the emotional and experiential boundary beyond which words fail. Language itself limits and constrains the speaker, whose emotional state is ineffable.

Devotional Sources for the Dresden Repertoire

In both their essential ethos and their typical modes of expression, the large body of devotional texts addressed to Christ that were set by composers in Italy and Germany in the seventeenth century display a remarkable degree of consonance with

---

66. Excerpt from Musculus 1575:50–51, attributed to St. Bernhard (the passage is not to be found in *PL*).

the contemplative texts of these medieval mystics. Prose and poetry alike resonate with the language and sentiments of the earlier writings. Several examples from texts set by Albrici, including *O bone Jesu* (above), *O amantissime sponse*, and *O cor meum*, reveal the degree to which the author-compilers relied upon the earlier corpus of devotional material:

ALBRICI, *O AMANTISSIME SPONSE*

O amantissime sponse, Jesu cordis mei et pars meum, Jesu in
  aeternum.
Te laudem, te amem, te quaeram, te cantem.
O amor, o Deus, o vita, o salus, o bonitas infinita. O Jesu mi
  dulcissime.

Amabilissime Jesu et salvator animae meae,
O Jesu, salus mea et vita mea,
te amo, te volo, te quaero, te cupio, te desidero.

O most beloved groom, Jesus of my heart and my portion, Jesus
  in eternity.
Let me praise you, let me love you, let me seek you, let me sing
  to you.
O love, O God, O life, O infinite goodness. O Jesus most sweet.

Most beloved Jesus and savior of my soul,
O Jesus, my salvation and my life,
I love you, I want you, I seek you, I long for you, I desire you.

ALBRICI, *O COR MEUM*

O Jesu dilecte,	O beloved Jesus,
o salus amata,	O beloved salvation,
o vita beata,	O blessed life,
lux mea tu es.	you are my light.
Quid est exaltare	What use is it to exult,
et corda laetari,	what use for hearts to rejoice,
gaudere, cantare,	to be glad, to sing,
quid est sine te?	what is it without you?

PSEUDO-AUGUSTINE, *MEDITATIONES*

Defecit gaudium cordis mei, versus est in luctum risus meus: defecit caro mea et cor meum, Deus cordis mei et pars mea, Deus in aeternum.[67]
(The joy of my heart is gone and my happiness has been turned to sorrow: my body and my heart are gone, God of my heart and God, my portion in eternity.)

67. *PL* 40:942; the text includes a quotation from Ps 72: 26.

Dulcissime, benignissime, amantissime, charissime, pretiosissime, desider-
antissime, amabilissime, pulcherrime, quando te videbo?[68]
(Most sweet, most kind, most beloved, most dear, most precious, most
desired, most loved, most beautiful, when will I see you?)

Spes mea Christi Deus, hominum tu dulcis amator, lux, via, vita, et salus.[69]
(God of Christ my hope, you are the lover of men, light, path, life, and salvation.)

PSEUDO-AUGUSTINE, *DE CONTRITIONE*, CH. 3

Domine Jesu Christe, redemptor meus, vita et salus mea, te laudo, tibi gratias
ago, . . .[70]
(Lord Jesus Christ, my redeemer, you are my life and salvation, I praise you,
I give my thanks to you, . . .)

PSEUDO-AUGUSTINE, *MEDITATIONES*

Quid enim mihi est in coelo, et a te quid volui super terram? Te volo, te spero,
te quaero: tibi dixit cor meum . . . [71]
(For what is there for me in heaven, and what do I want from you on earth? I
want you, I place my hope in you, I seek you: my heart spoke to you . . .)

A comparison of these concerto texts with those drawn from devotional manuals
also begins to reveal the process by which the devotional texts set by composers
were prepared. Some represent the borrowing of large sections of contiguous material; Capricornus, for example, set lengthy passages from the *Meditationes, Manuale,*
and *Soliloquia* in a number of concertos published posthumously in his *Theatrum
musicum* (1669).[72] Similar examples appear among the works of Hammerschmidt,
Pohle, and Rosenmüller. Other texts, however, including these two set by Albrici,
reveal that the practice of centonization was often taken to the extreme, and that
author-compilers also created texts by stringing together catch-phrases culled from
a variety of disparate passages. Comparatively few of the devotional texts in the
Dresden repertoire, however, display the degree of correspondence with source
texts seen in these two Albrici texts, which may well have been drawn from Muscu-

68. *PL* 40:934.

69. Musculus 1575:37; *PL* 40:914.

70. Musculus 1575:46; *PL* 40:944; author given as "incertus," Migne suggests either
St. Augustine or St. Anselm of Canterbury.

71. Musculus 1575:37–38, 46; *PL* 40:942.

72. Timothy D. Newton has identified the texts set by Capricornus in this collection;
see Newton 2004:36–50, 149–73.

lus or a similar source. But all of the devotional texts set in Dresden are steeped in the same fervent love for the second person of the Godhead, and express this love in the same literary style.

Hymnic poetry expressive of the same sort of intense mystical devotion also served as the basis for concerto texts in Dresden. Stanzas from one of the most popular of all medieval hymns, *Jesu dulcis memoria* (the so-called *Jubilus Bernhardi*), appeared in a number of concertos by both Albrici and Peranda. The hymn is suffused with mystical images and concepts; Heinrich Lausberg has even asserted that in its entirety, the hymn represents "a logically constructed treatise on the pre-mystical and mystical steps" to mystical union.[73] If Albrici and Peranda understood the text in this manner, however, neither seems to have sought to observe the step-wise or methodical nature of the text, for neither set sequential stanzas. Instead, each gathered a few nonsequential yet thematically related stanzas from the hymn to serve as the text for a concerto. Many of the texts in the surviving Dresden repertoire owe at least some debt to this hymn; four texts include literal stanzas, while two texts include stanzas that either paraphrase or make references or allusions to the hymn; five others include stanzas that imitate the meter, rhyme scheme, and content of the famous poem. In addition, some texts include isolated phrases commonly associated with the text, particularly the phrase "Jesu mi dulcissime," which appears in five texts.[74]

LITERAL STANZAS

Albrici, *Jesu dulcis memoria* (st. 1, 3, 5, 50/–)[75]
Albrici, *Sperate in Deo* (st. 38/32, 39/33, 32/30, 15/–)
Peranda, *Laetentur coeli* (st. 13/11, 19/14, 11/10)
Peranda, *O Jesu mi dulcissime* (28/23, 23/18, 29/24, 11/10)

---

73. "Der Hymnus . . . ist geradezu ein logisch aufgebauter Traktat über die vormystischen und die mystischen Stufen" (Lausberg 1968:363).

74. Philipp Wackernagel published a version of the poem with fifty stanzas, forty-eight of which he took from the version published by Mabillon in 1667, and two that appeared in the version published by Georg Fabricius in 1564; see Wackernagel 1:117–19. In 1944, André Wilmart collated versions of the poem found in nearly ninety manuscripts and published a definitive version with forty-two stanzas; he also included a version of seventy-nine stanzas that incorporates all of the stanzaic material that he encountered; see Wilmart 1944:146–55, 183–97. As two of the stanzas set by Albrici do not appear in Wilmart's version (these are represented here by a dash), both the Wackernagel and Wilmart numberings are included here. W. Bremme also gives a version with fifty stanzas, based again on Mabillon and Fabricius; see Bremme 1899:37–43.

75. Albrici also later set this text for four voices and two instruments; the stanzas included are unknown at this time. See: http://www.enberg.nu/Prague_time/Albrici_in_Prague.htm.

REFERENCE/PARAPHRASE/ALLUSION
(OR ALTERNATE VERSIONS?)

Albrici, *Mihi autem bonum est* (st. 28/23–29/24)
Peranda, *Te solum aestuat* (st. 26/21, 20/15, 24/19)

IMITATION[76]

Albrici, *Sive vivimus*
Peranda, *O ardor, o flamma*
Peranda, *Si vivo mi Jesu* (two versions)
Peranda, *Vocibus resonent*

It remains difficult, however, to determine which version or versions of the poem provided Albrici and Peranda with source material for texts, given the number of Italian and northern prints (both Catholic and Lutheran) that include the hymn, and the number of variants within these prints. Likely sources include the popular Catholic devotional manual *Paradisus animae Christianae*, first published in 1644 by Jacob Merlo Horstius (1597–1644),[77] and the equally popular Lutheran prayer book, *Paradieß-Gärtlein*, published in 1612 by Johann Arndt (1555–1621).[78] In two cases, however, breviary hymns may have provided the inspiration. Three hymns drawn from the poem appear in the *Breviarium Romanum*,[79] but these hymns do not include the stanzas set by Albrici and Peranda. However, Albrici included stanzas 1, 3, 5, and 50/– in his *Jesu dulcis memoria*, and thus the text corresponds to the Breviary hymn of the same title in all but its omission of stanza 2, which is also found there.[80] In compiling his text for *O Jesu mi dulcissime*, Peranda seems to have taken his inspiration from the Breviary hymn *Jesu decus angelicum*, which includes five stanzas (23/18, 21/16, 28/23, 11/10, and 36/31).[81] Peranda borrowed and rearranged the order of three of the breviary hymn stanzas and also included st. 29/24 as the third stanza (Peranda's text: 28/23, 23/18, 29/24, 11/10). Not insignificantly, the opening

76. None of the Latin imitations or paraphrases listed here appear in Bremme, but he does include several others, which illustrate that such reworkings were common (1899: 52–55, 73–75, 97–102). Albrici and Peranda may well have been familiar with yet other Latin paraphrases of the hymn that do not appear in these editions.

77. Cologne: Johannes Kinchius, 1644; the author consulted an edition published in Cologne by Balthasar Egmont in 1716. Merlo's version of the hymn includes fifty stanzas; his st. 40, however, is an altered version of st. 50/–; st. 40/34 does not appear.

78. Arndt's *Paradieß-Gärtlein* was first published in 1612; the author consulted an edition of 1615 published in Magdeburg by Johan Franck. Arndt's version of the hymn includes forty-eight stanzas; he omits st. 9/– and –/12.

79. *Jesu dulcis memoria, Jesu Rex admirabilis*, and *Jesu decus angelicum*; in *Breviarium Romanum* I: 460–61, 471–72.

80. *Breviarium Romanum* I: 460, *Jesu dulcis memoria* (st. 1, 2, 3, 5, 50/–).

81. *Breviarium Romanum* I: 471–72.

line, "O Jesu mi dulcissime," agrees with the text as found in the breviary, although this line appears to be a variant of the more common line "Jesu, mi dilectissime."[82] Breviary hymns, however, do not appear to have inspired the other two texts based upon this poem, Albrici's *Sperate in Deo*, and Peranda's *Laetentur coeli*; here any number of printed sources may have supplied the stanzas that the composers incorporated in these two texts.[83]

In the hymn *Jesu dulcis memoria*, Albrici and Peranda encountered a situation similar to that discussed above concerning devotional writings, in that a text familiar to them as Catholics had decades before been absorbed into Lutheran devotional culture. Due both to its inclusion in the breviary and to the hymn's popularity with composers in Italy, which began in the latter decades of the sixteenth century, Albrici and Peranda likely knew the hymn as a source text well before setting foot in Dresden.[84] Upon their respective arrivals, however, both would have quickly learned of the hymn's similar, if more recent, attraction for Lutherans. In 1587, Martin Moller included a paraphrase of the hymn, "Ach Gott, wie manches Hertzeleydt," in his *Meditationes sanctorum Patrum*, and in 1612 Arndt published both the Latin version (mentioned above) and a German paraphrase of eighteen stanzas entitled "O Jesu süss, wer dein gedenckt" in his *Paradieß-Gärtlein*[85]; both versions enjoyed popularity throughout the century. The text's popularity is also attested to by the fact that Schütz set a portion of the paraphrase published by Arndt, as well as that of another poet, Johann Heermann, in both his *Symphoniae sacrae III* (1650) and his *Zwölf geistliche Gesänge* of 1657.[86] In addition, seventeen verses of the hymn also appeared in German translation in the local hymnal, the *Dresdnisch Gesangbuch* of 1656.[87] Surely the inclusion of both the Latin hymn and

82. See Wilmart 1944:151, 169 and Wackernagel 1964-1:118. The line also appears as "O Jesu mi dulcissime" in Merlo 1716:400.

83. See also the list of sixteenth- and seventeenth-century prints in Bremme 1899: xii–xiv.

84. Palestrina, for example, set the breviary hymn *Jesu, Rex admirabilis* in his *Hymni totius anni secundum Sanctae Romanae Ecclesiae consuetudinem* (Rome, 1589). Just after the turn of the seventeenth century, Lodovico Viadana including a setting of *Jesu dulcis memoria* in his *Cento concerti ecclesiastici* (1602).

85. Arndt 1615:674–79. The identity of the author of the German paraphrase remains uncertain, but may have been Arndt himself (Bremme 1899:367–77). Arndt's paraphrase includes the following stanzas (in the Wackernagel/Wilmart numberings): 1, 4, 13/11, 17/13, 20/15, 23/18, 26/21, 27/22, 28/23, 29/24, 31/26, 32/30, 36/31, 40/34, 45/–, 46/39, 47/40, 48/41.

86. SWV 405, 406, and 427.

87. *Dreßdenisch Gesangbuch . . . wie sie in der Churfürstl. Sächß. Schloß-Kirchen zu Dresden gesungen worden* (Dresden: Bergen, 1656); the hymn *O Jesu süß, wer dein gedenkt* appears on pp. 144–45, under the heading "Der Jubilus S. Bernhardi von dem Namen Jesu. Im Thon Erschienen ist der Herzlich Tag."

these German paraphrases in numerous Lutheran devotional materials and hymnals served as an invitation to Albrici and Peranda to present settings of various Latin stanzas in the court chapel.

CONTENT, NARRATIVE, AND AFFECT IN INDIVIDUAL TEXTS

Introduction

Throughout the seventeenth century, word and music enjoyed an intimate, symbiotic relationship. Composers privileged the musical effectuation of the text's emotional content and strove to move the listener to experience vicariously that same emotion. This focus upon the affects, or the emotions of the speaker, soon became concretized as the concept of musical affect, which quickly attained the status of a primary governing force in the compositional ethos of the seventeenth century. When the later seventeenth-century composer approached a prayer *cum* musical text, he or she was often confronted with a literary entity with a complex form that could not easily be overlooked in a musical setting, and with content that was colored by a particular affect, due to the manner in which the content was expressed. But as intense prayers, these texts also possessed an internal shape independent of their external form, a shape that was determined solely by the emotional narrative. While a number of these texts share an identical form and similar content, no two share the same affect or emotional shape, as the content is given voice in myriad ways, and the emotional journey undertaken by each speaker renders that particular narrative unique. The formal organization of the text, which encompasses the types and styles of textual media employed, and the order of their presentation, influences the composer's technical decisions; the overall formal disposition of the composition, for example, results from the treatment of sections of text as concertos, declamatory passages, and arias. The ways in which composers approached the formal aspects of the mid-seventeenth-century text are addressed in chapter 5. But the other elements mentioned above remain equally important to the musical realization of the text: the content and particularly the affect influence the composer's decisions regarding the establishment of a governing musical affect, and the emotional shape of the text affects the "emotional trajectory" of the composition and determines the placement of any climactic musical event. Many of the questions taken up in the analyses in chapter 6 have their roots in these aspects of the texts. Only by examining the text itself, for example, is one able to determine if a relationship exists (or what relationships exist) between the textual and musical structure; in what manner the textual affect and content influence or condition the composers' musical response; how many aspects of the text the composer took into account, or was able to take into account, and what elements remain unacknowledged in his setting; what aspects of the text he privileged; and whether the shape of the text with respect to its emotional narrative exists in a state of tension with the resulting musical form. In order to understand the musical realizations of these texts, it is essential to examine them from the multiple perspectives afforded by their multiple properties, as each of these exerted some degree of influence upon the composer during the creative process.

Christocentric Devotion

For his concerto *O Jesu mi dulcissime*, one of the most compelling musical treatments of the text from this era, Peranda selected four stanzas of the hymn *Jesu dulcis memoria*.[88] Two of these stanzas, 28/23 and 29/24, appear successively in the hymn, but Peranda interpolates st. 23/18 between them, and concludes with st. 11/10. Rather than illustrate an emotional progression, Peranda seems more intent on developing one of the hymn's most prominent themes. Thus he fashions a text that is suffused with the mystical topos of Christ's sweetness, a theme that permeates the writings collected in the *Mediationes, Manuale,* and *Soliloquia,* as well as those of many other mystics,[89] and that is introduced in the opening stanza of the source poem:

PERANDA, *O JESU MI DULCISSIME*

O Jesu mi dulcissime,	O my sweetest Jesus,
spes suspirantis animae,	hope of the sighing soul,
te quaerunt piae lacrimae,	my pious tears
te clamor mentis intimae.	and the cry of my innermost soul
	seek thee.
Jesu, decus angelicum,	Jesus, glory of the angels,
in aure dulce canticum,	a sweet song in the ear,
in ore mel purificum,	purifying honey in the mouth,
in corde nectar caelicum.	heavenly nectar in the heart.
Quod cunque loco fuero,	In whatever place I may be,
mecum Jesu desidero:	I desire Jesus with me:
quod laetus cum invenero,	how happy when I find him,
quam felix, cum tenuero.	how blessed, when I hold him.
Mane nobiscum, Domine,	Remain with us, Lord,
et non illumen lumine,	with light so far from darkness,
pulsa mentis caligine,	drive out the darkness of the mind,
corda reple dulcedine.	fill our hearts with sweetness.[90]

88. See the discussion of the composition in chapter 6.
89. See Lausberg's discussion of *dulcedo* as a theme in the hymn (1968:363).
90. Translated by Patrick Macey and Calvin Bower.

Peranda establishes the primary affect of his text through his choice of st. 28/23 as the opening stanza. Coming as it does well into the speaker's prayer, the stanza reflects the heightened emotional state that the speaker has attained. As a result, the listener is plunged instantly into the world of the languishing soul, who seeks Christ with sighs, through a veil of tears. In its content, the stanza recalls the words of St. Bernhard, who counseled that such intense prayer would bring the presence of Christ, if but for a moment:

> For when the Lord has been sought in watching and prayers, with strenuous effort, with showers of tears, He will at length present Himself to the soul; but suddenly when it has gained His presence He will glide away. Again, He comes to the soul that follows after Him with tears; He allows Himself to be regained, but not to be retained, and, anon, He passes away out of its very hands. . . . He will not return unless He be sought again with the whole desire of the heart. [91]

In the following stanza (st. 23/18), emotion subsides temporarily as the speaker meditates on Christ's sweetness and spins out comparisons with honey and nectar. Here the mystical concept of the "spiritual senses" enters the text, particularly spiritual taste and perhaps that of smell.[92] In the mystical event, the individual who has experienced Christ's mystical presence often later strains to communicate the essence of the unfamiliar by turning to familiar sensory experiences—seeing, hearing, touching, and tasting Christ. This concept of the mystical senses, so important to the medieval mystical writings repopularized in the sixteenth century, remained very much a part of the Lutheran *Gedankengut* of the seventeenth century, as illustrated in an excerpt from the devotional writings of Heinrich Müller (1631–75), a contemporary of Peranda and Albrici whose works were likely read by many in the court circles:

> HEINRICH MÜLLER, *GEISTLICHE ERQUICKSTUNDEN* (1666)
>
> Faith is the eye with which we regard Jesus. A blind eye is still an eye, a weeping eye is still an eye. . . . Faith is the hand with which we touch Jesus. A trembling hand is still a hand. Ah, he believes, in whom the heart trembles in the body when he lays hold of and grasps Jesus. . . . Faith is the tongue, with which we taste how pleasant the Lord is. A tongue little able to taste is still a tongue. Then we still believe, even when we do not taste a little drop of comfort. . . . Faith is the foot that carries us to Jesus. A diseased foot is still a foot; he who comes slowly, still comes.[93]

---

91. Poulain 1950:467–68, from St. Bernhard, Sermon 32 on the Song of Songs.
92. Poulain 1950:88–90.
93. In Zeller 1962:296–97; the German text appears in Appendix I (no. 16).

After this moment of contemplation, the topos of seeking Christ introduced in the first stanza returns in the third stanza (st. 29/24), but is now intensified by the desire to be with Christ—the desire for mystical union. In the final stanza, the darkness/light dichotomy and reference to the "darkness of the mind" recall St. John Chrysostom's "two nights of the soul," which represent the "borderland of the mystic state."[94] Although in its original position in the hymn, st. 11/10 ("Mane nobiscum, Domine") forms part of the pre-mystical experience in Lausberg's analysis, here it confirms the culmination of the soul's search; in "remain with us, Lord," the search has ended, and she has found Christ.[95] Although it comprises nonsequential stanzas, Peranda's text nevertheless displays a certain logic and unity; the topos of sweetness resonates nearly throughout the text, save in the third stanza, but here the thread of seeking Christ introduced in str. 1 is picked up again. When Christ is found in the final stanza, the speaker's plea to "fill us with sweetness" ties both thematic threads together.

Other mystically informed texts reveal a greater debt to scripture than to pseudo-Augustine or Latin hymns, and are particularly indebted to those books traditionally associated with mysticism, the Psalms and the Song of Songs. In such texts the intensity of the emotions expressed sometimes surpasses that of the texts derived solely from the writings of medieval mystics. In Peranda's *Jesu dulcis, Jesu pie*, for example, the emotional level is ratcheted up to a still higher degree than in the texts examined above, primarily through the use of allusion to familiar passages from the Song of Songs. Due in part to its forays into the language of erotic desire, this text set by Peranda portrays a speaker much closer to the attainment of full union than in *O Jesu mi dulcissime*:[96]

Jesu dulcis, Jesu pie,	Sweet Jesus, kind Jesus,
Jesu chare, mea spes,	dear Jesus, my hope,
pro me, Jesu, cruci amare,	for me, Jesus, my life,
mea vita affixus es.	you were affixed to the bitter cross.[97]
Sequar te, bone Domine,	Let me follow you, good Lord,
per aspera et adversa	even through rough places and misfortunes
usque dum te obtineam.	until I attain you.
Te, fontem vivum, sitit	For you, living fountain, my soul
anima mea;	thirsts;

94. Poulain 1950:200–19.
95. Lausberg 1967:483.
96. See also the musical discussion in chapter 6.
97. Scriptural references: Philippians 2:8, Colossians 2:14.

quando satiabor de	when will I be filled with the
ubertate,	abundance
vulnerum tuorum	of your wounds,
o dulcissime Domine	o most sweet Lord
Jesu Christe?	Jesus Christ?[98]
Cor meum te desiderat,	My heart desires you,
anima mea in te deficit,	my spirit becomes weak in you,
te suspirat,	sighs for you,
et totus amore tui langueo.	and I languish completely from
	love of you.[99]
Euge, anima mea,	Well done, my soul,
ne sis ingrata,	so that you should not be
	ungrateful,
tanto amori disce mori.	learn to die with so much love.

Peranda's text runs a different emotional course than that of *O Jesu mi dulcissime*. While the latter text opens with the speaker in the heat of spiritual passion, manifested in his tears, *Jesu dulcis* opens with a speaker who is at the beginning of his spiritual journey, but who quite suddenly ascends to a higher state of mystical contemplation. While the text in its entirety is an expression of intense devotion, the speaker's invocation of Christ's death on the cross in the opening section locates that devotion within the broader context of Christocentric soteriology. While love,

98. Scriptural references: John 4:10: "Respondit Iesus et dixit ei si scires donum Dei et quis est qui dicit tibi da mihi bibere tu forsitan petisses ab eo et dedisset tibi aquam vivam"; Ps 41:2: "quemadmodum desiderat cervus ad fontes aquarum ita desiderat anima mea ad te Deus"; references or allusions to the *Meditationes* of pseudo-Augustine: ch. 37: "quando satiabor de pulchritudine tua?" ch. 41: "Sitivit anima mea ad Deum fontem vivum, quando veniam et apparebo ante faciem Dei mei" (Ps 51:3); *PL* 40:934, 942. This passage also bears a clear resemblance to the third section of Gratiani's *O bone Jesu*: "Sitio ad te, fontem aquae vivae, nec satiabor donec requiescam in te, quia de amore tuo vulnerasti me," which in turn includes an allusion to the Song of Songs 4:9: "vulnerasti cor meum soror mea sponsa, vulnerasti cor meum in uno oculorum tuorum et in uno crine colli tui."

99. Scriptural references: Song of Songs [SS] 2:5: "fulcite me floribus stipate me malis quia amore langueo"; SS 5:8: "adiuro vos filiae Hierusalem si inveneritis dilectum meum ut nuntietis ei quia amore langueo"; Ps 41:2: "quemadmodum desiderat cervus ad fontes aquarum ita desiderat anima mea ad te Deus"; Ps 72:26: "defecit caro mea et cor meum Deus cordis mei et pars mea Deus in aeternum"; Ps 83:3: "Concupiscit et deficit anima mea in atria Domini cor meum et caro mea exultavit in Deum vivum"; reference to the *Meditationes*: "Defecit gaudium cordis mei, versus est in luctum risus meus: defecit caro mea et cor meum" (*PL* 40:942).

both that of Christ and of the speaker, serves as the binding core of the text, this love is specifically associated with the events at Calvary. Very quickly, however, the speaker moves beyond the recollection of the crucifixion to an articulation of desire for mystical union, which he introduces with the familiar "seeking/finding" topos; here, however, his search culminates in attainment ("Sequar te"). At the mere mention of attainment ("Te, fontem vivum"), in itself a metaphor for mystical union, the speaker's ardor intensifies exponentially, and he expresses a seemingly insatiable thirst for Christ. Again the speaker falls back on sensory experience to express his desire for union, to "sense God's penetration into the soul."[100] With the invocation of the image of Christ as a "living fountain," this portion of the text introduces the topos of Christ as refreshment, and seems to allude to the biblical account of Christ's meeting with the Samaritan woman at the well, in which he refers to himself as "living water" (*aquam vivam*).[101] Such expressions of spiritual thirst also appear frequently in the writings of mystics:

> With what a thirst is this thirst [for the mystic union] desired! . . . it is a thirst very painful; it afflicts yet carries with it a satisfaction, wherewith our former thirst is allayed; so that it is a thirst which only extinguishes thirst in respect of earthly things; else it satiates so, that when God satisfies it, one of the greatest favours that He can do the soul is, to leave her in this necessity, which continues always greater to drink again of this water.[102]

Still unsatiated, the speaker again longs for union, which he now expresses as an expectant yearning to be filled with the "abundance of Christ's wounds." In the context of *Jesu dulcis*, the speaker's invocation of the wounds of Christ neatly recalls the soteriological event referenced at the opening of the text. But the concept of taking refuge in both the wounds inflicted during the crucifixion event as well as in the blood that flowed abundantly from those wounds also resonates with one of the themes common to contemporary Lutheran spirituality, particularly as expressed in the popular writings of two seventeenth-century Lutheran theologians, Johann Arndt and Johann Gerhard (1582–1637). Both Arndt and Gerhard published books of prayers or meditations that enjoyed enormous popularity throughout the century; Gerhard's *Meditationes sacrae ad veram pietatem excitandam*, which drew upon works of Augustine, Bernhard, Anselm, and Tauler, appeared in 1606, and Arndt's *Paradieß-Gärtlein* in 1612.[103] Not surprisingly, coming as they do after both

---

100. Poulain 1950:88.
101. John 4:7–15.
102. Poulain 1950:458, from St. Theresa of Avila, *The Way of Perfection*, ch. xix.
103. Althaus 1927/1966:152–53. The first German edition of Gerhard's meditations was published in Magdeburg by Franck in 1607. On the content of Gerhard's volume, see Bautz, "Gerhard," *BBKL* 2:215–16.

Musculus and Moller, both of these publications offer evidence of their respective authors' mystical inclinations.[104] Both devote attention to the mystical healing properties of Christ's blood and wounds; two passages in particular display a remarkable similarity in their conceptual framework with the text of *Jesu dulcis*:[105]

Arndt, *Paradiess-Gärtlein*

Ah, my love! you were wounded for the sake of my love, wound my soul with your love. Ah! your precious blood, shed out of great love, is so fine, so penetrating, that it might soften a heart of stone: ah, let it penetrate my heart, so that your love might also penetrate my heart, for your love is in your blood. Ah! that my heart might open up, to receive and to drink in your fragile and fine little drops of blood, which fell on the ground during your struggle with death.[106]

Gerhard, *Meditationes Sacrae*

Thou didst give Thy life, O Lord Jesus, as a ransom for many (Matt. xx. 28); let that come to my succor in my distress. Thy most holy body Thou didst give to be scourged, to be spit upon, to be buffeted, to be lacerated with thorns, and to be crucified, and all for me; O let that come to my help in distress. Let Thy most precious blood, which Thou didst so freely shed in Thy bitter sufferings and cruel death upon the cross, and which cleanseth us from all sin (I John i. 7), be my help. . . .In Thy bleeding wounds is my only remedy; let them succor me. Let Thy most holy passion be my defense.[107]

As the text of *Jesu dulcis* continues to unfold, the speaker's ardor steadily intensifies in the quest for mystical union. In the section that follows ("Cor meum"), the speaker leaves behind the familiar metaphors of seeking and thirsting to speak

---

104. See Althaus 1927/1966:152–53; Brecht 1993, and Wallmann 1995.

105. See the discussion of the emphasis placed on meditation on Christ's wounds by various seventeenth-century reform theologians in Sträter 1995:48, 58–60.

106. "Ach mein Liebhaber du bist vmb meiner liebe willen verwundet/ verwunde meine Seele mit deiner Liebe. Ach dein köstliches Blut aus grosser liebe vergossen/ ist so edel/ so durchdringend/ daß es ein steinern Hertz wohl erweichen mag/ Ach laß dasselbe durch mein Hertz dringen/ auf daß auch deine liebe mein Hertz durchdringe/ denn deine Liebe ist in deinem Blut. Ach daß mein Hertz sich aufthete/ zu empfahen vnd in sich zu trincken/ deine zarte vnd edle Blutströpfflein/ die in deinem Todeskampff auff die Erden gefallen seyn" (Arndt 1615:225–26). Arndt's words also recall the famous passage from the Song of Songs 4:9, an allusion to which appears in Gratiani's *O bone Jesu* ("vulnerasti cor meum, soror mea, sponsa, vulnerasti cor meum in uno oculorum tuorum et in uno crine colli tui").

107. Gerhard 1896:61.

directly of desire, and borrows the language of the Psalms and the Song of Songs. As is so common in mystical texts, here the speaker resorts to the language of erotic love in an attempt to express the sublime and ineffable spiritual love that dwells in a realm beyond words. At this point, the emotional trajectory of the text reaches its peak, for the speaker's passion has increased to the point that it has rendered him powerless. At this point, the mystical experience as recounted in the text comes to an abrupt end. At the outset of the text, the speaker stood at the threshold of the mystical experience, upon which he soon embarked. As the text concludes, the speaker has left the experience behind, and has assumed a more distanced stance. Now he addresses himself in the second person, and adopts a tone of self-congratu-latory exhortation. In these last lines, however, the speaker looks forward expec-tantly to the next experience, and speaks figuratively of dying, an idea that recurs with frequency in the writings of mystics such as St. Theresa as a metaphor for the experience of full union: "The soul is asleep, fast asleep, as regards the world and itself . . . being unable to think on any subject [save God] even if it would. . . . In fact, it has died entirely to this world, to live more truly than ever to God. This is a deli-cious death to suffer."[108]

In both its structure and its use of source material, the text of *Te solum aestuat* offers some contrast with those discussed above. Here the author-compiler has care-fully organized the text so that each passage of prose, save the first, is paired with a stanza of poetry. Albrici in particular seems to have favored texts disposed in this manner, for five compositions with similarly organized texts survive from his pen.[109] Both he and Peranda took a similar musical approach to such texts, and set each grouping of prose and poetry as an often florid declamatory passage followed by an aria strophe. In some of these texts, all of the prose derives from a single source, while in others the origins are more diverse. As discussed above, the prose passages in *O amantissime sponse* derive from a pseudo-Augustinian work, while those found in *O Jesu Alpha et Omega* were extracted from various of the *Quindecim orationes sanctae Brigittae de passione Domini* once ascribed to St. Birgitta of Sweden (ca. 1303–73).[110] In *Ubi est charitas*, by contrast, the author-compiler drew the analogous prose passages from I Corinthians 13, but added free extensions in the style of the author of the *Meditationes*:

108. Poulain 1950:241, from the *Interior Castle*, Fifth Mansion, ch. 1, 3.

109. *O amantissime sponse, O Jesu Alpha et Omega, Quid est mundus, Ubi est charitas*, and *Tu es cor meum*; see also Peranda's *Spirate suaves* (discussed below), which opens with poetry, but then continues with prose-poetry pairs.

110. Jan Enberg discovered this textual relationship between Albrici's text and the *Orationes* and has pointed out that one of the poetic stanzas also tropes the Latin text (private correspondence, 7 August 2001). The text appears in Merlo 1716:378–82.

ALBRICI, *UBI EST CHARITAS*

Charitas patiens est, benigna est, *mi dulcis Jesu, amor cordis mei.*	Love is patient and kind, *my sweet Jesus, love of my heart.* (I Cor 13:4 and free extension)
Nunc autem mansi fides, spes, charitas, tria haec; major autem horum est charitas, *quia tu Jesu charitas est.*	So faith, hope, love abide, these three; but the greatest of these is love, *because you, Jesus, are love.* (I Cor 13:13 and free extension)
Et si habuero omnem fidem ita ut montes transferam charitatem autem non habuero, nihil sum; *qui manet in charitate manet in Christo.*	And if I have all faith, so as to remove mountains, but have not love, I am nothing; *for he who remains in love remains in Christ.* (I Cor 13:2b and free extension)

In *Tu es cor meum*, the author-compiler crafted two passages of prose from scriptural quotations (Psalms, I Timothy, and Job), and either derived the other two from an unknown devotional source or composed them himself (see the discussion of the text below). In *Te solum aestuat*, the author-compiler drew upon three somewhat diverse textual sources: the Psalms, the *Transfige* (Prayer of St. Bonaventure), and stanzas from *Jesu dulcis memoria* that had been reworked.

All of the devotional texts considered thus far represent the prayers of individuals in various stages of transport to spiritual ecstasy. While the speaker in *Jesu dulcis* attained that desired state over the course of the text, the speaker in *O Jesu mi dulcissime* had already ascended to a higher level of mystical prayer as the text began. In a similar manner, the speaker in *Te solum aestuat* languishes at the brink of the mystical experience as he begins his prayer. Like *Jesu dulcis*, *Te solum aestuat* traces the speaker's mystical journey, but here the journey takes a somewhat different emotional path: the text opens with the speaker in a state of intense desire for Christ (sections 1–3 below), moves on to the experience of mystical presence itself (sections 4–5), and closes with the postmystical experience (sections 6–7). Like other devotional texts, *Te solum aestuat* relies upon several basic mystical *topoi*, such as Christ's sweetness and Christ as the soul's true refreshment, but it lacks literal references to the spiritual "senses" of seeing, tasting, and touching encountered in the texts above.[111]

---

111. See also the musical discussion in chapter 6.

TEXT AND SOURCES OF PERANDA, *TE SOLUM AESTUAT*

1. Te solum aestuat,

valde desiderat anima mea,

suavissime Domine Jesu Christe.

(My soul intensely desires,
burns with love for you alone,
most sweet Lord Jesus Christ.)

Quemadmodum desiderat
cervus ad fontes aquarum,
ita *desiderat anima mea* ad
te, Deus.[112] (Ps 41:2)

2. O Jesu, cordis mei,

unice dilectissime,
transfige, quaeso,

medullas et viscera animae meae

suavissimo ac saluberrimo
amans tui jaculo.

Deus *cordis mei*, et pars mea,
. . . (Ps 72:26b)

Transfige, dulcissime
Domine Jesu,
*medullas et viscera animae
meae,*
suavissimo et *saluberrimo
amoris tui* vulnere, . . .
(Prayer of St. Bonaventure)

(O Jesus of my heart,
singly most beloved,
transfix, I beseech you,
the center and inmost part of my soul
by the sweetest and most healthy
dart of your love.)

3. Jesu, mira suavitas,
cordi placens benignitas,
o quae mentis felicitas
quas stringit tua charitas.

Jesu, summa *benignitas*,
mira cordis iocunditas,
incomprehensa bonitas,
tua me *stringit caritas*. (*Jesu
dulcis memoria* st. 26/21)

(Jesus, wonderful pleasantness,
kindness pleasing to the heart,
o what happiness enjoys the mind
which your love binds.)

(Jesus, greatest kindness,
wonderful joy of the heart,
unfathomable goodness,
your love binds me.)
(II Cor 5:14)

112. Another possible source: Isaiah 26:9 "Anima mea desiderat te in nocte."

4. Hospes animae meae,
dulcissime Jesu, mi praeclarissime,
o Deus vitae meae.
Te solum amat,
in te deficit anima mea.

*Concupiscit et deficit anima
mea in atria.* (Ps 83:3)

(Guest of my soul,
sweetest Jesus, most excellent to me,
O God my life.
My soul loves you,
faints in you alone.)

5. Tua, Jesu, dilectio,
et mentium refectio,
amantis aestuatio,
omni carens fastidio.

*Tua, Jesu, dilectio,
grata mentis refectio,
replens sine fastidio,
dans famem desiderio.* (*Jesu
dulcis memoria* st. 20/15)

(Yours, Jesus, is pleasure
and spiritual refreshment,

the burning desire of a lover,

free from all satiety.)

(Your love, o Jesus,
is the pleasing nourishment
of the mind,
your love satisfies without
satiety,
causes hunger through longing.)

6. O quam magna multitudo
dulcedinis tuae Domine;

quid mihi est in coelo aut ad te,
quid volui super terram?

*Quam magna multitudo
dulcedinis tuae, Domine,
quam abscondisti.* (Ps 30:20)
*Quis enim mihi est in coelo?
Et tecum nihil volui super
terram.* (Ps 72:25)

Deus cordis mei et pars mea,

Deus in aeternum.

*. . . Deus cordis mei, et pars
mea,
Deus in aeternum.* (Ps
72:26)[113]

---

113. This section also resembles a passage in the *Meditationes* of pseudo-Augustine, ch. 41, which utilizes the same psalm verses: "Deus cordis mei et pars mea Deus in aeternum. Renuit consolari anima mea, nisi de te, dulcedo mea. Quid enim mihi est in coelo, et a te quid volui super terram?" (*PL* 40:942).

(O how great is the multitude
of your sweetness, Lord,
what is there for me in heaven beside you,
and what do I desire on earth?
God of my heart and my portion,
God into eternity.)

7. Rex perpotens, rex gloriae,	*Rex* virtutum, *rex gloriae,*
rex maximae victoriae,	*rex* insignis *victoriae,*
largitor almae gloriae,	Jesu, *largitor* gratiae,
honor polaris curiae.	*honor* coelestis *curiae.*[114]
	(*Jesu dulcis memoria* st. 44/38)

(Very mighty king, king of glory,	(King of valor, king of glory,
king of greatest victory,	distinguished king of victory,
liberal giver of bountiful glory,	Jesus, dispenser of grace,
honor of the celestial court.)	honor of the heavenly court.)

The text opens with the speaker in a liminal state, poised on the threshold of the "mystical presence-experience."[115] The opening expression (section 1) seems to derive from the well-known Psalm verse, "like as an hart desireth still waters" (Ps 41:2), but the author-compiler has changed the addressee of the sentiment from God to Christ and has significantly intensified the nature of the speaker's love through the use of the verb *aestuo* and the adverb *valde*.[116] Most crucial to the understanding of the text as a narrative of the mystical experience, however, is section 2, the only "active" portion of the text. Here the speaker petitions Christ to enter his heart and to transfix him with that dart of His love that is both sweet and salubrious. Here one sees once again the speaker's desire to be transfixed by Christ, expressed by the same reference to *Amor*'s arrow seen in Albrici's *O bone Jesu*.[117] The speaker's opening address ("O Jesu, cordis mei") alludes to Ps 72:26, but the speaker's request itself derives from an altered quotation from the opening portion of the Prayer of St. Bonaventure (1218–74), the "Seraphic Doctor":[118]

114. Possible scriptural reference: Ps 23:8–9 "Quis est iste rex gloriae? Dominus fortis et potens, Dominus potens in proelio."
115. The phrase "mystische Präsens-Erlebnis" is borrowed from Lausberg 1967.
116. Isaiah 26:9 represents another possible source: "Anima mea desiderat te in nocte, sed in spiritu meo in prae cordiis meis te quaero."
117. On the mystical "wounds of love," see Poulain 1950:144.
118. The text of Peranda's *Quis dabit* also makes allusion to the same passage.

Pierce, o most sweet Lord Jesus, my inmost soul with the most joyous and healthful wound of Thy love, with true, serene, and most holy apostolic charity, that my soul may ever languish and melt with love and longing for Thee, that it may yearn for Thee and faint for Thy courts, and long to be dissolved and to be with Thee.[119]

While the thoughts and sentiments of the *Transfige* echo those of the other medieval devotional writings discussed above, the eucharistic devotion expressed in a subsequent section of this mystical prayer would seem to make it an unlikely candidate for inclusion in Lutheran devotional literature of the time. But Schütz's incorporation of this same opening portion of the prayer into his own *O bone Jesu* (SWV 471) suggests that the *Transfige* may well have been accepted into Lutheran prayer literature, although perhaps in an altered form.

As the fore-mystical portion of the text continues in section 3, the speaker moves into expressions of praise of Christ. In this case, by revising the stanza from *Jesu dulcis memoria*, particularly the last two lines, the author-compiler helps to forge a somewhat closer relationship with the previous passage (see section 3 in the text above). Then, at the midpoint of the text (sections 4 and 5), the speaker experiences mystical union. Yet Christ does not enter the speaker's soul permanently, but as a guest, which underscores the ephemeral nature of the mystical presence. The speaker's subsequent expressions of love for Christ ("my soul loves you, faints in you alone") help to unify the text by recalling the very opening lines, but his admission here of spiritual weakness also resonates with the continuation of that portion of the Prayer of St. Bonaventure quoted in the concerto text (see above). In the accompanying poetic stanza (section 5), the speaker's fainting soul experiences revivification in Christ, whose abundant refreshment never produces surfeit, but by its very nature causes the soul to continue to hunger after it.[120] Both the original stanza and the revision focus on this common mystical theme of "satisfaction without satiety," but in the revision, the author-compiler has recast the desire or longing (*desiderio*) of the original as the "burning desire of a lover," which focuses attention on the quality of the love, rather than the love itself (see section 5 in the text above).

At this point (section 6) the mystical experience has come to an end, and the speaker now praises God with words of thanks in the afterglow of His presence.

---

119. "Transfige, dulcissime Domine Iesu, medullas et viscera animae meae suavissimo ac saluberrimo amoris tui vulnere, vera serenaque et apostolica sanctissima caritate, ut langueat et liquefiat anima mea solo semper amore et desiderio tui, te concupiscat et deficiat in atria tua, cupiat dissolvi et esse tecum." Merlo 1716, "Manuale pietatis," 51. (The "Manuale" appears at the end of most editions of the *Paradisus animae Christianae* and is paginated separately.)

120. See Lausberg 1967:484–85.

In contrast to the earlier passages of prose (sections 1, 2, and 4), section 6 draws exclusively upon psalm verses and frames the question "[Lord,] what more could I want in heaven or on earth but you?" with phrases of praise and assurance. But this particular psalm verse, one of the quintessential scriptural expressions of the Lutheran concept of *Trost* (comfort), rests a bit uneasily in the midst of this predominantly mystical text, despite its references to "sweetness" and "desire."[121] One wonders if this turnabout in the text's essential tone and focus resulted from textual revisions demanded by the court preacher. In addition, as the author-compiler has made no attempt to recontextualize these Old Testament quotations through the simple substitution of "Jesu" for "Domini" and "Deus," the Christocentricity of the text also disappears at this point. And while the stanza that follows quickly reintroduces Christ as the addressee of the text, his portrayal there as the victorious King of Heaven introduces a martial element that distances the subject of the text even further from the sweet Christ encountered earlier.

As mentioned above, all three of the three stanzas of poetry (sections 3, 5, and 7) that stand interposed between the passages of prose in *Te solum aestuat* either derive from an alternate version of the hymn *Jesu dulcis memoria,* or represent reworkings of the three stanzas by the author-compiler himself. Each of the three stanzas replicates the poetic meter of the earlier poem, and each shares the end-rhyme and a significant amount of vocabulary with the stanza that served as the exemplar. The resulting degree of correspondence between the new stanzas and their models would have called *Jesu dulcis memoria* readily to the listener's mind. All three may well derive from an as-yet-unidentified alternate Latin version of the hymn; over a century ago, Bremme demonstrated the existence of such alternate Latin versions and included several in his publication.[122] Curiously, however, only the revisions to "Tua, Jesu, dilectio" (section 5) result in a closer thematic relationship between the stanza and the preceding passage of prose.

Vanitas and the Rejection of the World

Let us consider for a moment how short life is, what a slippery path it is, how certain is death, and how uncertain the hour of death. Let us consider how much bitterness is mixed in, and that whatever sweetness or joy there might be along the path of life makes sport of us in passing. Let us consider that whatever one's love for this world might bring forth, and whatever temporal

121. On the Lutheran concept of *Trost*, see the discussion and secondary materials in Westendorf 1987:105–59 *et passim.*

122. See Bremme 1899:97–102 (*Jesu beata memoria*).

beauty or mien it might promise, it is false, suspect, instable, and transitory. (Augustine, *On Contrition*, Book 1)[123]

Like the devotional writings discussed above, another group of texts also found resonance with both Catholic and Lutheran audiences—those that explored the topic of *vanitas*.[124] These form a subset within the larger category of devotional texts but are radically different in nature from the intimate expressions of devotion seen, for example, in *O Jesu mi dulcissime* and *Jesu dulcis*. In their often derisive and contemptuous tone, these texts appear to have only the most tenuous connection with devotion. The theme with which they are concerned, however—*Weltabsagung*, or the rejection of the world and all its hollow pleasures—springs from the concept of complete devotion to Christ expressed in texts such as *Te solum aestuat*: when measured against the assurance of salvation in Christ, the world and its attractions offer but empty promises. This foundational dichotomy of Christian thought gives rise here to several closely related *topoi*, including the transitory nature of earthly existence (compared to eternal life), which cannot be depended upon (as can Christ), and the spiritual poverty of worldly beauty, glory, and wealth, all of which are merely empty vanity.[125]

The closely related themes of *vanitas* and *Weltabsagung* did not appear in Lutheran repertoires as a result of the musical agency of Italian composers, however, but were introduced by Lutherans themselves; as Craig Westendorf has demonstrated, many of the *Spruchmotetten* composed by Lutherans between 1601 and 1630 explore this same theme.[126] The frequency with which these themes were encountered may have actually increased in the second half of the century, however, for at that time, settings of free (rather than scriptural) *vanitas* texts by Italians significantly expanded this portion of the repertoire, as demonstrated by the texts of many works that survive in the Düben and Bokemeyer collections.[127] Both Albrici and Peranda cultivated this theme musically in Dresden; ten of the extant works from the repertoire fall into this category. In the area of *vanitas* texts, as in that of personal devotion, Albrici and

---

123. Augustine, *De contritione cordis*, Bk. 1 (*PL* 40:943): "Cogitemus ergo quam brevis sit vita nostra, quam via lubrica, quam mors certa et hora mortis incerta. Cogitemus quantis amaritudinibus admixtum sit, si quid dulce aut jucundum in via hujus vitae occursu suo nobis alludit; quam fallax et suspectum, quam instabile et transitorium est, quidquid hujus mundi amor parturit, quidquid species aut pulchritudo temporalis promittit."

124. For a discussion of the role of music in art devoted to the *vanitas* themes, see Austern 2003.

125. For some of the scriptural roots of the *vanitas* theme, see I John 2:17, I Corinthians 7:31, 2 Peter 3:10, Romans 8:20, John 5:44, and Galatians 1:10.

126. Westendorf 1987:246–48.

127. See Webber 1996:86–89.

Peranda once again encountered the phenomenon of cross-confessionality, for they quickly discovered that concepts inculcated in them in their catechetical training as young Catholics were perfectly acceptable to the adherents of the Augsburg Confession. In fact, their settings of *vanitas* texts were among their most popular works among Lutherans, as judged from their appearance in collections and inventories outside of Dresden: Albrici's *Omnis caro foenum* found its way into either seven or eight collections, and his *Cogita o homo* into at least five, while Peranda's *Quo tendimus* formed part of six other collections.[128] The widespread acceptance of these works around Germany and in Scandinavia helps to underscore the centrality of the theme of *vanitas* in Lutheran self-examination and devotion.

The thematic complex represented by the term *vanitas* constituted an important aspect of Lutheran mystical and pietistic devotionality from at least the latter half of the sixteenth century until well into the eighteenth, and runs through the writings of many of the theologians of the era. In her study of Moller's mystically influenced publications, for example, Axmacher has identified the "tendency of the contemplative life toward withdrawal from the world" and points to the centrality of *Weltabsagung* in the thematic nexus of mystical devotion—the soul, made captive to sin, longs to return to her original security and freedom with God. This desire for reunion with God, however, represents a perpetual struggle:

> According to the Reformation understanding, the Christian lives in a contradiction that originates in his participation in two realities: the reality of God, in which evil is already conquered, but which fact is not yet evident, and the reality of Satan, who to the end will not abandon the effort to bring human beings to ruin, although his power is already broken. In this struggle, whose deadly gravity is not changed by the fact that the end result has already been determined, the Christian is a co-combatant on one side, but a powerless onlooker on the other. The idea of struggle, which informs all of Luther's historical thinking, will now be taken up . . . in the ascetic tendencies of post-Reformation piety. The rejection of the world, Satan, and one's own flesh and blood, as the powers of the world are generally called in [Moller's] *Meditationes sanctorum Patrum*, does not originate in a weak-willed need for peace and lack of conflict, but represents the expression of this struggle.[129]

---

128. Culled from the inventories listed in Appendix II.

129. "Der Christ lebt nach reformatorischer Auffassung in einem Widerspruch, der aus seiner Anteilhabe an zwei Wirklichkeiten entsteht: der Wirklichkeit Gottes, in der das Böse schon besiegt, die aber noch nicht offenbar ist, und der Wirklichkeit des Satans, der bis zum Ende den Versuch nicht aufgeben wird, den Menschen ins Verderben zu stürzen, obgleich seine Macht schon gebrochen ist. In diesem Kampf, an dessen tödlichem Ernst der schon entschiedene Ausgang nichts ändert, ist der Christ einerseits

In Book I of Johann Arndt's *Vier Bücher vom wahren Christenthum* ("Four Books on True Christianity"), published in 1606 and arguably the most important edifying work by a seventeenth-century Lutheran theologian before Spener, this struggle against the world is accorded the status of a central principle. In Arndt's soteriology, to reject the world for Christ is to take the first step on the path to salvation; as stated in the title of Book I, ch. 14: "a true Christian must hate his own life in this world and learn to despise the world according to the example of Christ."[130] Throughout the text, Arndt relentlessly hammers away at this theme and constantly admonishes his reader to turn away from the world and to recognize the transience of earthly existence. In Arndt's view, only by spurning both the world and the flesh can the Christian hope to inherit eternal life:

> It follows that a man must deny himself (Lk. 9:23); that is, break his own self-will; give himself completely to God's will; not love himself but hold himself as the most unworthy, miserable man; deny all that he has (Lk. 14:26); that is, reject the world and its honor and glory; consider his own wisdom and power as nothing; not depend on himself or on any creature but only and simply on God; hate his own life, that is, the fleshly lusts and desires such as pride, covetousness, lust, wrath, and envy; have no pleasure in himself, and consider all his acts as nothing; praise himself for nothing; ascribe no power to himself; attempt to attribute nothing to himself but mistrust of himself; die to the world, that is, the lust of the eyes, the lust of the flesh, and the pride of life; be crucified to the world (Gal. 6:4). This is the true repentance and mortification of the flesh without which no one can be a disciple of Christ.[131]

Arndt's *True Christianity*, while not free from controversy, nevertheless quickly became a classic text of Lutheran spirituality, one "more important than all the dogmatic systems of Orthodoxy."[132] The devotional treatise was frequently reprinted well into the eighteenth century, and his ideas greatly influenced developments in spirituality long after his death. As a result of his influence, later seventeenth-century

---

Mitstreiter, andererseits aber ohnmächtiger Zuschauer. Der Gedanke des Kampfes, der Luthers gesamtes Geschichtsdenken prägt, wird nun . . . in den asketischen Tendenzen der nachreformatorischen Frömmigkeit aufgenommen. Die Absage an die Welt, den Satan und das eigene Fleisch und Blut, wie die Weltmächte in den [*Meditationes Sanctorum Patrum*] meist genannt werden, entspringt durchaus nicht einem schwächlichen Bedürfnis nach Ruhe und Konfliktlosigkeit, sondern ist Ausdruck jenes Kampfes" (Axmacher 1989/2:25).

130. Arndt 1979:78.

131. Arndt 1979:42.

132. "Das Wahre Christentum, . . . ist auf die Dauer wirksamer geworden als alle dogmatischen Systeme der Orthodoxie" (Brecht 1993:139).

Lutheran devotional writings continued to resonate with the Arndtian themes of *vanitas* and *Weltabsagung*, as demonstrated in this passage by Joachim Lütkemann:

> We live here in the world as in a well-built city, in which there are many things to see, but in which one thing surpasses everything else: the goodness of God. If there is anyone (and unfortunately the entire world is full of the same) who boasts, saying, "this and that happiness have I experienced," so one may ask, "have you also tasted God's goodness? If he says "no," then I answer, "then what interest do I have in all of your experience? You have certainly missed the best thing."[133]

The writings of Moller, Arndt, and Lütkemann help to establish the Lutheran context in which the *vanitas* texts of the Dresden repertoire were heard and received, and also illustrate the degree to which those texts resonate with ideas then circulating in contemporary Lutheran thought. But although the fundamental precepts presented by Arndt in *True Christianity* recur throughout the *vanitas* texts set by both Albrici and Peranda, they are at times recast in language that seeks to coax rather than reprove. In Albrici's *Quid est mundus*, for example, the listener is confronted with the same fundamental choice that Arndt lays before his readers, but Arndt's admonishing tone has been replaced by one of gentle urging:

[. . .]

Qui cogitat de mundo	He who thinks of the world
de mundo est;	is of the world;
qui cogitat de Deo	he who thinks of God
filius haereditatis Dei est.	is a son of the inheritance of God.
Nomen suum haud meretur	The world, that unclean sea,
mundus pelagus immundus,	by no means deserves its name,
immo baratrum profundum	call it rather a deep abyss
in quo haerens absorbetur.	in which the one who clings to it is swallowed.
Jesus est fons puritatis,	Jesus is the fountain of purity,
limpidus et inexhaustus,	clear and unexhausted,

133. "Wir leben hier in der Welt als in einer wohlerbauten Stadt, darin vielerlei zu sehen, eins aber übertrifft alles: die Güte Gottes. Ist jemand (wie leider die ganze Welt derselben voll), der sich rühmt: Dies und jenes Glück habe ich erlebt, so mag man fragen: Hast du auch wohl Gottes Güte geschmeckt? Spricht er: Nein, antworte ich: Was frage ich denn nach aller deiner Erfahrung, das Beste hast du gewiß versäumt" (Lütkemann, *Der Vorschmack göttliche Güte* [1653], in Zeller 1962:267).

hunc qui sitit bibit faustus	lucky is the one who thirsts and drinks of this
et mundatur a peccatis.	and is made clean from sins.
[. . .]	
Manu regit et exemplo	He guides every motion, every step
omnem motum, omnem gressum,	by hand and by example,
quin et bajulat defessum	nay, he even carries the weary one,
donec coeli fistat templo.	till he presents himself at the temple of heaven.
Mundus contra blandimentis	On the other hand, the cruel, faithless world
quos inebriat crudelis	intoxicates with flatteries
spe frustratos infidelis,	those who, deceived by the hope of the unfaithful,
tandem angit in tormentis.	it torments on the rack.[134]

Often, however, the author-compilers of *vanitas* texts do not seek constantly to remind the listener that Christ is the only alternative, as in *Quid est mundus*, but instead dwell primarily on the dark side of the topic, particularly the emptiness and transience of this worldly life, in order to convince the listener of the need for repentance and change. Many of these texts move reluctantly from "darkness to light," and only exhort the listener to abandon the world in the concluding lines, after having painted a very grim picture throughout. Although the theme of *vanitas* falls under the general heading of devotion, these texts do not represent the prayers of individuals who seek intimacy with Christ, but instead are the castigations of an omniscient judge directed at those who linger in the grip of the world's entice-ments. Thus they consciously cultivate an atmosphere of distance and alienation, and employ language intended to brand the addressee as "other" and as a stranger to the community of Christ.

In many of the Dresden *vanitas* texts, the author-compilers borrowed a style of direct address from homiletics and wrote (or compiled) a "sermon" for an anony-mous speaker to "preach" to his audience. At times these homilies take the form of an extended trope, in which homiletics are brought into service in the thematic elaboration of a maxim. Such is the case in Albrici's *Omnis caro foenum*:

---

134. The nonscriptural sources of this text have yet to be identified.

Omnis caro foenum, et gloriae eius sicut flos, sicut umbra praetereunt, evanescunt.	All flesh is grass, and its glories pass away, vanish like a flower, like a shadow.

Quam breve festum est haec mundi gloria, ut umbra transiens sunt eius gaudia quae semper subtrahunt aeterna praemia et ducunt miseros ad dura devia.	What a brief feast is this glory of the world; like a passing shadow are its delights which always steal away eternal rewards and lead the wretched to difficult paths.

Haec carnis gloria quae tanti perditur, sacris in literis flos foeni dicitur, vel leve folium quod vento rapitur; sic vita hominis ex mundo tollitur.	This glory of the flesh which is lost at such price in sacred books is called the flower of grass, or the trifling leaf that is carried away by the wind; thus the life of man is stolen from the world.

O esca vermium, o massa pulveris, o nox, o vanitas, cur sic extolleris? Ignoras penitus utrum cras vixeris. Fac bonum sedulo quam diu poteris.	O food of worms, o mass of dust,[135] O ignorance, O vanity, why are you thus exalted? You are wholly ignorant if you will be alive tomorrow. Do good zealously as long as you are able.

Nil tam amaveris quam potes perdere; Quod mundus tribuit, intendit rapere. Superna cogita, cor sit in aethere.	Love nothing so much that you cannot bear to lose it; that which the world granted it intends to snatch away. Think on heavenly things, let the mind be in heaven:

135. This passage seems to recall the ideas expressed in Ecclesiasticus 10:9–11: "What has a man to be so proud of? He is only dust and ashes, subject even in life to bodily decay. A long illness mocks the doctor's skill; today's kind is tomorrow's corpse. When a man dies, he comes into an inheritance of maggots and vermin and worms" (*New English Bible*).

> Felix, qui didicit mundum
> contemnere.

> Happy is the one who learns
> to despise the world.

To open the text, the author-compiler begins with the famous maxim on the fleeting nature of earthly existence, drawn from Isaiah 40:6.

> Vox dicentis, clama, et dixi, quid clamabo? Omnis caro faenum, et omnis gloria eius quasi flos agri. Exsiccatum est faenum, et cecidit flos, quia spiritus Domini sufflavit in eo vere faenum est populus. Exsiccatum est faenum, cecidit flos, verbum autem Dei nostri stabit in aeternum. (Vulgate, Isaiah 40:6–8)
> (A voice says, "Cry!" And I said, "What shall I cry?" All flesh is grass, and all its glory is like the flower of the field. The grass withers, the flower fades, when the breath of the Lord blows upon it; surely the people is grass. The grass withers, the flower fades, but the word of our God will stand forever.) (RSV)

Rather than quote the text exactly, however, the author-compiler removes the references to the Lord that appear at the beginning and end of the Vulgate text, and expands the simile with the addition of "sicut umbra" ("like a shadow"). Then, through the substitution of "vanish" and "pass away" for "withers" and "fades," he creates more abstract images, all of which contribute to the ominous tone of the text. In addition, his removal of the passage from its original context and associations with the spirit of God further helps to underscore its bleak nature.

The text then continues with stanzas from a well-known medieval poem on the contempt of the world, *De vanitate mundi cantio*.[136] In a perfect marriage of texts, the poem expounds upon the nihilistic lesson taught by Isaiah and even alludes to the opening passage itself ("the glory of the flesh . . . in sacred books is called the flower of grass").[137] As the poetic text opens, the author seems to view the transience

---

136. Although the poem was long attributed to the thirteenth-century mystic Jacopone da Todi (1230/6–1306), recent scholarship has cast doubt on Jacopone's authorship; see Donnini 2001:300–1. The poem, which begins "Cur mundus militat sub vana gloria," appears in Spitzmuller 1971:968–71, where it is attributed to "Iacobus de Benedictis / Jacopone de Todi." Here it has thirteen stanzas; the four set by Albrici (with some variants) are found as 10, 12, 11, and 13. According to Spitzmuller, the first "complete edition" of Jacopone's works was published in 1617 by Tresati in Venice (ibid.,1774); thus Albrici may have found the poem in a relatively recent publication.

137. The remarkably close semantic relationship between the two texts suggests that the poetry may have appeared in a contemporary devotional manual as a trope or gloss on this particular verse from Isaiah.

of the world with some degree of melancholy, but then, in stanza 3, leaves Isaiah's evanescent flora behind for more disturbing images culled from Sirach 10:10–11. In contrast to *Quid est mundus*, where the author-compiler seeks to provide comfort and hope to his listeners by ever holding up Christ's goodness against the world's evils, here the poet impresses a wholly dark and hopeless vision of life upon his reader. Only in the penultimate line does the poet finally redirect his gaze upward, and shine a dim light on the way out of the abyss.[138]

Given its didactic nature, the topic of *vanitas* also lends itself to more dynamic rhetorical approaches, particularly the dialogue. Albrici's *Quid est mundus*, for example, opens with a query from one speaker, "what is the world?," and the response of another, who borrows the famous words from Ecclesiastes: "vanity of vanities, and all is vanity."[139] Peranda's *Quo tendimus mortales*, one of the most striking works in the entire Dresden repertoire, explores the *vanitas* theme through a more extended dialogue, in which an anonymous speaker poses a series of existential questions, each of which drips with nihilism, and again hears the equally nihilistic words from Ecclesiastes in response—all is vanity.[140] In each of these texts, the finality of physical or earthly death is a central theme, explored through various imagery; here, in a passage derived from 2 Samuel 14:14, the text likens death to the irretrievability of spilled water. Just as in *Omnis caro foenum*, however, the nihilism of the speaker is not complete, but is tempered by the promise of eternal life: since all is vanity, let us learn to despise the world and its ephemera.

Quo tendimus mortales?	Whither do we strive, mortals that we are?
Quo progredimur miseri?	Whither do we proceed, we wretched ones?
Quo properamus infelices?	Whither do we hasten, we unhappy beings?
Ecce omnes morimur,	Behold, we all die,
et quasi aquae quae non revertuntur	and we, like water that cannot be recovered,
terram dilabimur.	are spilled upon the ground. (2 Samuel 14:14)

138. See also the discussions of *Omnis caro foenum* in chapters 6 and 8.

139. Ecclesiastes 1:2: "Vanitas vanitatum, dixit Ecclesiastes, vanitas vanitatum omnia vanitas."

140. Carissimi employs a similar dialogic approach in his *Audite sancti*; there the series of questions and answers are derived from St. Paul's question, "who shall separate us from the love of Christ?" Carissimi's *Audite* was likely familiar to Peranda, as it was performed in the court chapel under Albrici on Trinity 25 in 1662 (SLUB Q 240, entry for 16 November 1662).

Quid vita nostra?	To what purpose our life?
Vanitas vanitatum, et omnia vanitas.	Vanity of vanities, and all is vanity. (Ecclesiastes 1:2)
Quid seculi pompa?	To what purpose the pretension of our age?
Vanitas vanitatum, et omnia vanitas.	Vanity of vanities, and all is vanity. (Ecclesiastes 1:2)
Quid avorum iactantia?	To what purpose the boasting of our fathers?
Vanitas vanitatum, et omnia vanitas.	Vanity of vanities, and all is vanity. (Ecclesiastes 1:2)
Quid mundanus usus?	To what purpose worldly profit?
Currit, fluit, labitur et evanescit.	It runs, it flows, it slips away and disappears.
Eia ergo, o mortales, si omnia vanitas, despiciamus ergo quae pereunt, ut in osculo Domini morientes aeterna praemia consequamur.	Therefore, O fellow mortals, if all is vanity, let us then despise the things that perish, so that we, dying in the embrace of the Lord,[141] may pursue prizes eternal.

The centrality of the theme of *Weltabsagung* in the writings of Johann Arndt, one of the most widely read seventeenth-century Lutheran theologians, helps to contextualize it as a topic for sacred art music performed in Lutheran chapels and churches of the era, whether composed by Catholics or Lutherans. Another prominent Lutheran theologian, Johann Gerhard, addressed the topics of *vanitas* and *Weltabsagung* in his *Sacred Meditations*, which was also widely read throughout the century. Once in Dresden, both Albrici and Peranda could have easily acquired a copy of the Latin edition of Gerhard's meditations. Neither composer seems to have borrowed any text directly from Gerhard, but all three of the concerto texts dis-

---

141. Literally "in the Lord's kiss." Translation by Calvin Bower.

cussed above present the same ideas explored by Gerhard in two of his meditations: "The Transitoriness of Life" (no. 38) and "The Vanity of the World" (no. 39). In the former, Gerhard employs the same rhetorical question-answer strategy seen in Peranda's *Quo tendimus*; in fact, one passage from this meditation may have served as Peranda's inspiration:

> What is man?
> Well, he is death's purchased possession, a transient traveler; his life is lighter than a bubble, briefer than a moment, more worthless than an image, more empty than a sound, more fragile than glass, more changeable than the wind, more fleeting than a shadow, more deceptive than a dream.
> What is this life?
> Why, it is a constant looking forward to death, a stage upon which a farce is enacted; a vast sea of miseries, a single little measure of blood, which a slight accident may spill, or a little fever corrupt. The course of life is a labyrinth which we enter at birth, and from which we withdraw by the portals of death. We are but as dust, and dust is nothing but smoke, and smoke is nothing at all, and so we are nothing. . . . Do not, therefore, O beloved soul, devote thy highest thoughts to this life, but rather, in mind, aspire to the joys of that life which is to come. [142]

Penitence and Forgiveness

Confession and absolution remained an integral part of the spiritual lives of seventeenth-century Lutherans, even though penance had not retained its sacramental status in Lutheran doctrine.[143] Luther exhorted his co-religionists to avail themselves of the comfort provided by confession and absolution, and his followers heeded his advice. Until the end of the eighteenth century, Lutherans regularly visited the confessional and received absolution from their *Beichtväter* before participating in the sacrament of Holy Communion.[144] At the mid-seventeenth-century Dresden court, the practice was alive and well: the court diaries indicate that Johann Georg II regularly made his confession before receiving communion.[145] Not surprisingly, then, penitence represents yet another facet of contemporary devotional life that is reflected in the German Lutheran textual repertoire, as well as that of the Dresden court chapel. Of the surviving works, seven texts set by Albrici

---

142. Gerhard 1896:219; here the text has been arranged by the author to emphasize the rhetorical structure.

143. See Vercruysse 1983:164.

144. See Roth 1952 and Uhsadel 1961.

145. On Johann Georg's communion practices, see chapter 8.

and Peranda are penitential in nature, as are two of the surviving four presented by Cherici in the chapel.

Some of these penitential texts, such as Albrici's *Tu es cor meum*, take the form of hope-filled entreaties in which the sinner freely acknowledges his sinful state.[146] Despite its rather discursive nature, the text of *Tu es cor meum* drives home a coherent message: between Christ's ineffable greatness and the individual's own weakness and imperfection lies a vast zone of separation that is only bridgeable by Christ's mercy. But here, the penitent's desire to leave behind this state of sin and achieve perfection and union with Christ is very much in evidence. He begins with words of intimacy evocative of the pseudo-Augustinian writings, but then suddenly shifts to a more encomiastic mode. As the text progresses, the speaker gradually emerges from his position of reverent distance and approaches Christ. Finally, the speaker abandons his expressions of wonderment at the power and majesty of Christ, and reverts to the tone of the opening statement. Here he finally achieves physical intimacy with his Lord, and embraces a now affectionate—rather than awe-inspiring—Christ:

Tu es cor meum,	You are my heart,
tu es spes mea,	you are my hope,
mi chare Jesu.	my precious Jesus.
Quis sicut tu, Domine	Who is like you, Lord
Jesu Christe?	Jesus Christ?
Excelsus es, immensus,	You are exalted, immeasurable,
terribilis,	terrible,
et humilia respicis	and you provide for the humble
in coelo et in terra.	in heaven and on earth. (Ps 112:5–6)
Peccavi, deliqui,	I have sinned, I have failed,
o summe regnator;	O highest sovereign;
sincere amator,	sincere friend,
iam nefas reliqui.[147]	now I have left my sin behind.
Quantus es tu, Rex Regum	How great you are, King of Kings
et Dominus Dominantium,	and Lord of Lords, (I Tim 6:15)
qui imperas astris	you who rule the stars
et apponis erga hominem cor	and set your heart upon
tuum,	man, (Job 7:17)

---

146. Other examples include Peranda's *Cor mundum*, *Hac luce cunctos*, and *Plange anima*.

147. This stanza also appears in *Laboravi clamans*, where it has two additional lines (see above).

o Jesu, Deus, salutare meum.	O Jesus, God, my salvation.
Qui cuncta gubernas, tu nosti cor meum, quam multum sit reum; me servum ne spernas.	You who govern all, you know my heart, and how guilty it is; do not reject me as your servant
Amore te teneo, amantissime Jesu, nec dimittam te, quia tu es unica expectatio, salus et gloria mea.	I embrace you with love, most affectionate Jesus, and I will never renounce you, because you are my only expectation, health, and glory.
Ah, cor meum sana, o Jesu amate, plus millies grate restaura, complana.	Ah, cleanse my heart, O beloved Jesus, a thousand times dear to me, restore it and make it smooth.

In other penitential texts, however, the author-compiler seeks to remind the listeners of their utter worthlessness before God and need for forgiveness. In Peranda's *Peccavi O Domine*, the sinner speaks as one separated from God by sin and repeatedly admits his guilt in a manner reminiscent of the ancient confessional formula *mea culpa, mea culpa, mea maxima culpa*. In order to placate an angry God, the speaker engages in self-denigration and expresses a willingness to accept even physical punishment. For this speaker, Christ's mystical presence remains an incomprehensible, distant dream. Only at the end of his prayer does he presume to ask for mercy, and then but cautiously:

Peccavi, o Domine, super numerum arenae maris, et non sum dignus videre altitudinem caeli prae multitudine iniquitatis meae.	I have sinned, O Lord, more than the sands of the sea, and I am not worthy of seeing the vault of heaven because of the multitude of my sins.
Peccavi, o Domine, peccata grandia, peccata enormia, peccata innumera.	I have sinned, O Lord, great sins, enormous sins, innumerable sins.

Peccavi, mi Pater in caelo, et coram te,	I have sinned before you, my Father in heaven,
iam non sum dignus vocari filius tuus.	now I am not worthy to be called your son. (Luke 15:21)
Id circo flagellari et puniri non recuso.	Therefore I do not hold back from being beaten and punished.
Flagella me, o amantissime mi Pater, et afflige me parcus modo in aeternum.	Scourge me, my most beloved Father, and afflict me so that I might be spared in eternity.
Permitte, Domine Jesu, ut meae lacrymae misceantur tuo sanguine et misereberis.	Grant, Lord Jesus, that my tears might mingle with your blood, and you will have mercy [on me].[148]

In *Peccavi o Domine*, the author-compiler employs a technique noted by Jones in his discussion of the texts set by Carissimi, in which a brief quotation from scripture is "set in the midst of freely written material which illustrates a central theme."[149] Here, in the midst of a penitential text of unknown origin, a quotation from the Parable of the Prodigal Son (Luke 15:11–32) provides the central theme.

In Cherici's *Deplorandus et amarus* the penitential theme is explored from a slightly different angle. Whereas most of the penitential texts in this repertoire represent supplications composed in the first person, Cherici's *Deplorandus* differs in that it is written in several voices in the manner of a dialogue and largely avoids the first person. As the text opens, several speakers bewail their own sinful state and its cause, original sin. Unlike the speaker in Peranda's *Peccavi, o Domine*, however, this group seems devoid of all hope; their tone of utter desperation suggests that they languish in complete oblivion of the Christ-event. Suddenly, however, an *angelus ex machina* enters and consoles them with the promise of redemption through Christ. This message calls forth rejoicing, and an invitation for Christ to come to earth:[150]

148. Translated by David Bachrach and Margaret E. Garnett.
149. Jones 1982-1:138.
150. See the musical discussion in chapter 6.

Deplorandus et amarus

primi patris adae casus
miseram pro geniem.

The fall of the first father
Adam
is bitter, and to be deplored:
in this calamitous and toil-
some ruin,

Quam praesentem quam futuram

in funestam hanc et duram
posuit perniciem.

in the present as well as in the
future
it has put misery
in the place of joy.

Hinc sunt quae pectora

humani germinis
angunt suspiria
paterni sceleris.

From this cause arise the
souls
of human breed
who breathe sighs
for the sin of the father!

Hinc o posteritas
nostrae miseriae

dolor, calamitas,
planctus et lacrimae.

From this source, O posterity,
[arise] the pathetic misfortune,
the lament and tears
for our miserable state.

Sistite quid ploratis et
lacrimamini!
Cur lugetis

et contristamini?

Ecce, Creator caeli et terrae,

Deus aeternus,
ex occulta Trinitatis Abijsu

humana molitur Redemptionem.

Justify why you weep and
wail!
Why do you wear mourning
cloths,
why are you covered with
gloom?
Behold, the Creator of heaven
and the earth,
God Eternal,
From the unfathomable
depth of the Trinity
has set redemption in motion
with human flesh!

Vertant se in gaudia
planctus et suspiria
cessent omnes lacrimae
risus quaerant animae.

Let laments and sighs
be turned into joy,
Let every tear be dried,
and let souls find reason for
laughter!

Veni ergo Domine	Even so come! O Lord,
maestos Adae filios redime	Redeem the sorrowful sons of Adam,
et consolare.	and grant them consolation.[151]

The Encomium: Glorification of God

Praise and adoration have defined Christian worship from the inception of the church itself. Since its earliest days, encomiastic texts, in the form of hymns, psalms, and antiphons, have formed an essential, if not definitive, portion of the church's textual repertoire, as the testimony of the fourth-century Spanish nun Egeria demonstrates.[152] Such texts are naturally found in the seventeenth-century repertoire, including that composed for Dresden, but the number of extant encomia is dwarfed by the number of surviving expressions of Christocentric devotion; even given the number of pieces that have not survived, these proportions still strongly suggest that a shift in textual emphasis took place in the latter half of the seventeenth century. General texts of praise and thanksgiving in the Dresden repertoire—those that claim no affiliation with a particular feast day—figure about as prominently as do the penitential texts.[153] But although sacred art music in the latter half of the century often inclined more strongly towards quiet devotion than jubilant adoration, other elements of the liturgy that were sung every Sunday throughout the year, particularly the Latin Gloria and its German congregational counterpart, *Allein Gott in der Höh' sei Ehr*, provided opportunities for communal praise. In Dresden, for example, the court diaries attest to the inclusion of both texts throughout the year—even during Lent, when the Gloria was sung *a cappella*. In addition, the *Te Deum*, another hymn of praise, was sung on a number of occasions throughout the year.[154]

The encomiastic texts are drawn from a variety of sources, and thus display a considerable amount of variety in style, structure, and length. Some, for example, comprise brief excerpts drawn exclusively from scripture, such as Albrici's *Misericordias Domini* (Ps 88:2) and Peranda's *Cantemus Domino* (Exodus 15:1–2):

ALBRICI, *MISERICORDIAS DOMINI*

Misericordias Domini in	Of the mercies of the Lord
aeternum cantabo;	will I sing forever,

151. Translated by Calvin Bower.
152. Weiss and Taruskin 1984:21–23.
153. These also include complete settings of Vesper psalms, such as *Laudate pueri*, which are not considered here.
154. Issues of musical repertoire and liturgy are treated in detail in chapter 8.

in generationem et generationem annunciabo veritatem tuam in ore meo.	with my mouth will I make known thy faithfulness to all generations.
Alleluia.	Hallelujah.

PERANDA, *CANTEMUS DOMINO*

Cantemus Domino gloriose enim magnificatus est.	Let us sing to the Lord, for he has triumphed gloriously;
Aequm et ascensorem proiecit in mare.	the horse and his rider he has thrown into the sea.
Alleluia.	Hallelujah.
Fortitudo mea et laus mea Dominus,	The Lord is my strength and my song,
factus est mihi in salutem.	and he has become my salvation.

Others represent lengthier compilations of free prose and poetry whose style indicates a much more recent date of origin. In Peranda's *Spirate suaves*, for example, the amphibrachic verse favored by Gratiani and others predominates. The text opens with two quatrains in amphibrachic meter; these are followed by two prose-poetry groupings, each of which concludes with an amphibrachic tercet. Unlike the two previous texts, *Spirate* seems unusually worldly and almost "unsacred," a fact that clearly distinguishes it from the German Lutheran textual repertoire of the first half of the century. Here the author-compiler freely invokes nature, but his nature stands more closely allied with that of the ancient Romans than with the realm of the Christian God. Even the exhortations to "mother church" strike a strangely secular tone—one wonders if the text began life as a secular cantata:

PERANDA, *SPIRATE SUAVES*

Spirate suaves, o aurae, concentus, praedulces accentus extollite, aves.	Blow sweet harmonies, O winds, lift up sweet sounds, O birds.
Aufugite bella Neptuni frementis, procellae furentis abite flagella.	Get ye away, o battles of roaring Neptune, get ye hence, O scourges of raging storms.
Hodierna festiva dies, exultant coeli cives, congeminant cantus, extollentes magnalia Dei.	Today is a festive day, the citizens of heaven exult, they redouble songs exalting the greatness of God.

Erumpite, flores,	Burst forth, flowers,
et novos ad auras	and spread new scents
diffundite odores.	to the air.
Plaude, mater ecclesia,	Clap, mother church,
laetans, agens memoriam	rejoicing, remembering
hodiernae festivitatis;	today's festivity;
convoca coetum in laetitia	call together a meeting of your
gentis tuae.	people in gladness.
Concinnite semper	Always sing together
in laude sonora,	in sonorous praise,
ardenter, ferventer.	ardently, fervently.
Alleluia.	Hallelujah.[155]

Several sources, including the Dresden court diaries, attest to the versatility of these encomia as texts *per ogni tempo*. In 1662, Albrici's *Misericordias Domini* was performed in Dresden on *Septuagesima* Sunday (the third Sunday before Lent) as well as on Trinity 4; Peranda's *Cantemus Domino* was heard in the chapel during the Easter season in 1666, 1667, and 1676, but was performed in Grimma on the Feast of St. Michael in 1688 and again in 1698.[156] Peranda's *Spirate suaves* had an equally rich performance history, particularly in 1665, when it served for three different feast days. With its references to an unspecified "festival day," the text lent itself to any number of occasions throughout the church year. The first known performance took place on New Year's Day in 1665, which was celebrated in Dresden as a feast day. The following list of performance dates in Dresden betray no particular pattern, however, suggesting that the text held no particular *de tempore* associations for Peranda:

New Year's Day, Vespers (1665)
Purification (Feb. 2), Vespers (1665)
Quasimodogeniti, Morning Service (1665)
Christmas II, Morning Service (1665)
Quasimodogeniti, Morning Service (1667)

Some years later, however, Johann Philipp Krieger performed Peranda's *Spirate* in the court chapel in Weissenfels, on one Christmas II, one of the same feast days for which it had served in Dresden.[157]

---

155. See the discussion in Schmidt 1961:204.
156. The dates appear on the *verso* of the folded continuo part that serves as a title page and receptacle for the parts, SLUB 1738-E-511.
157. Gundlach 2001:307.

Texts *de tempore*

After the devotional texts, those texts associated with particular events in the church year (*de tempore*, or "of the time"), taken as a group, represent the largest category in the Dresden repertoire. Albrici and Peranda composed seasonal pieces for the three major feasts, Christmas, Easter, and Pentecost (each of which was celebrated for three days), for the three feasts celebrating events in the life of Mary that remained in the Lutheran calendar (Purification, Annunciation, and Visitation), and for the other feasts in the calendar (listed below); they also regularly presented works of Schütz on certain occasions. In addition to the traditional feast days of the Lutheran church, however, several other occasions were regularly marked with festive worship services in the Dresden court chapel: the birthdays and name days of Elector Johann Georg II and Electress Magdalena Sibylla, as well as those of Prince Johann Georg III.[158] Concertos composed for these events thus achieved *de tempore* status, particularly Peranda's *Sursum deorsum*, composed in 1664 on the *symbolum*, or motto, of Johann Georg II, and performed on his birthday (May 31). Albrici also composed one or two works with texts based on the elector's motto, both of which were performed in 1673 and 1679 but which do not survive.[159]

REPRESENTATIVE *DE TEMPORE* WORKS BY THE DRESDEN COMPOSERS

Christmas

Albrici: *O admirabile commercium*

Peranda: *Dies sanctificatus, Florete fragrantibus*; *Die Geburt unsers Herrn und Heilandes Jesu Christi* (lost, 1676, 1678)

Schütz: *Historia, des freuden- und gnadenreichen Geburth Gottes und Marien Sohnes, Jesu Christi* (SWV 435/a/b)[160]

Epiphany

Peranda: *Laetentur coeli*

Purification (February 2)

Albrici: *Hodie beata Virgo Maria* (lost)

Peranda: *Nunc dimittis* (lost)

Cherici: *Nunc dimittis* (lost?)

---

158. The name day of the elector and the electoral prince was St. John the Baptist (June 24), while that of Electress Magdalena Sibylla was the Feast of Mary Magdalene (July 22).

159. No compositions known to have been dedicated to the electress or to Prince Johann Georg III survive; her birthday fell on 1 November (1612), his on 20 July (1647).

160. On the dating of Schütz's Christmas History, a version of which was likely performed in the court chapel as early as 1660, see Rifkin and Linfield et al., "Schütz," in *GMO*.

Annunciation (March 25)

Albrici: *Sancta et immaculata Virginitas* (lost)

Peranda: *Missus est Angelus* (Gospel dialogue)

Judica Sunday

Bernhard: Passion according to St. John[161]

Schütz: Passion according to St. Matthew (first performance 1666)

Palm Sunday

Schütz: Passion according to St. Luke (first performance 1666)

Good Friday

Peranda: Passion according to St. Mark (first performance 1668)

Schütz: Passion according to St. Luke (first performance 1667)

Schütz: Passion according to St. John (first performance 1665, 1673)

Easter

Albrici: *Aurora lucis emicat, Jesu nostra redemptio, Surrexit Dominus Salvator* (lost)

Peranda: *Abite dolores, Accurrite gentes, Dic nobis Maria, Gaudete cantate, Surrexit pastor bonus* (lost)

Cherici: *Venite populi*

Schütz: *Historia der frölichen und siegreichen Aufferstehung unsers einigen Erlösers und Seligmachers Jesu Christi* (SWV 50) (1662, 1665–67, 1673)[162]

Ascension

Peranda: *Ascendit Deus* (lost)

Albrici: *Viri Galilei* (lost)

Pentecost

Peranda: *Ad cantus, ad sonos, Repleti sunt omnes, Veni Sancte Spiritus*

Birthday of Johann Georg II (May 31)

Peranda: *Sursum deorsum*

Albrici: *Sursum deorsum, Moveantur cuncta sursum deorsum* (lost)

Trinity

Albrici: *Te Deum*

Peranda: *Te Deum* (lost)

161. For a complete listing of the performances of passions and other like works by Schütz, Peranda, and other court composers between 1656 and 1697, see Steude 2001/2:170–71.

162. See Steude 2001/2:170, and Schmidt 1961:207–8.

St. John the Baptist (June 24), the Name Day of Johann Georg II

[Composer not identified]: *Herr Gott, wir loben dir* (German *Te Deum*)

St. Michael (September 29)

Peranda: *Dum praeliaretur; Factum est praelium*
Albrici: *Dum praeliaretur; Factum est praelium* (both lost)

All of these *de tempore* texts relate to feast days; there is no indication that these Italian Catholics made any attempt to create cycles of concertos or motets on the Sunday Gospels in the German Lutheran tradition of the *Evangelien-Jahrgang*. In the orders of worship, one detects a stronger seasonal than weekly emphasis on the themes of the liturgical year as established by the lectionary, but one also sees examples of close thematic relationships between some concerto texts from the Trinity season and the Gospel for the day.[163] Eberhard Schmidt has pointed to the Italians' use of Roman liturgical texts on the particular feast day with which they were traditionally associated, or within that festal period, but divorced from their original liturgical placement. He cites, for example, the performance of Peranda's *Dic nobis Maria*, a setting of a portion of the Easter sequence *Victimae paschali laudes*, after the *Magnificat* at Vespers on Easter Sunday, rather than at the point in the morning service where the sequence was traditionally sung.[164] Although many of the "decontextualized" performances that Schmidt cites result from the structure and content of the Lutheran liturgy at the time, particularly as it manifested itself in Dresden, his examples do underscore the continued stress on seasonal themes during festal periods. But although many concertos contributed to the thematic fabric of the various feasts, a comparison of extant pieces with the court diaries reveals that devotional texts remained important in each season; only a portion of the texts performed on feast days bore a direct (or even indirect) relation to the feast. On the Feast of St. John the Evangelist (the third day of Christmas) in 1665, for example, Peranda presented two concertos in the morning service, his *O Jesu mi dulcissime* and *Verbum caro factum est*, and presented his *Jesu dulcis, Jesu pie* and *Attendite fideles* at Vespers.[165] Two of these were settings of devotional texts that lacked any specific seasonal content. Only *Verbum caro factum est*, which does not survive, seems to have borne any clear relation to either the lections or the season in general, as it included the last verse of the Gospel for the day (John 1:1–14); in addition, *Attendite fideles*, which also does not survive, may have had a Christmas text.

The *de tempore* texts in the Dresden repertoire display the same variety in structure and style and a similar dependence on a variety of source materials as do the

163. Discussed in chapter 8.
164. Schmidt 1961:202.
165. SLUB Q 241, entry for 27 December 1665.

encomiastic texts discussed above. Given their function—the articulation of themes associated with a particular event or personality in the history of the church—these texts often include quotations from the liturgy or the scriptures. The brief text of Peranda's *Dum praeliaretur Michael*, for example, is drawn from the traditional Roman liturgy for the Feast of St. Michael, where it serves as the second antiphon for Second Vespers:

PERANDA, *DUM PRAELIARETUR MICHAEL*

Dum praeliaretur Michael	While the Archangel Michael was
Archangelus	doing battle
cum dracone,	with the dragon,
audita est vox dicentium:	a voice was heard, saying:
Salus Deo nostro, alleluja.	Victory to our God, hallelujah.[166]

While some of the liturgical items used as concerto texts in Dresden, such as *Dum praeliaretur*, seem to have been drawn directly from the Catholic liturgy, others also appeared in Lutheran chant books, such as the 1545 *Cantiones ecclesias / Kirchenge-senge Deudsch* of Johann Spangenberg, the 1553 *Psalmodia* of Lucas Lossius (2/1561), and the 1573 *KirchenGesenge Latinisch vnd Deudsch* of Johannes Keuchenthal.[167] All three may have served as textual repositories for the Dresden Kapellmeisters; with its inclusion of abbreviated Latin Matins and Vesper services, however, the Lossius collection may have been the most useful. Even though the chants published by these and other compilers no longer formed part of the Dresden liturgies, their retention by sixteenth-century Lutherans rendered them unproblematic as texts for Lutheran sacred music. One of the liturgical borrowings in Peranda's *Repleti sunt omnes*, for example, also appears in Lossius. Here the author-compiler has assembled a text that is entirely feast-specific, using elements drawn from Pentecost liturgies together with free poetry of unknown provenance that displays a typically medieval scansion. The text opens with the third antiphon for Second Vespers on Pentecost Sunday ([1] below), and continues with an altered version of the second Alleluia verse from the same festal Mass ([2] below).[168] In addition, the second passage of prose ("Qui discipulis") seems to paraphrase the antiphon at the Magnificat

166. Feast of St. Michael (Sept. 29): 2nd Antiphon for 2nd Vespers (*LU* 1659–60). The text is drawn from Revelation 12, vv. 7 and 12.

167. Both Spangenberg and Keuchenthal include a large number of hymns as well as chants for the morning service (*Hauptgottesdienst*); Lossius includes very few hymns.

168. [1] Third antiphon at Second Vespers, Pentecost Sunday (*LU* 884); also part of the Responsory at Matins, Pentecost Sunday (*LU* 875); does not appear in Lossius, who has only antiphons for the *Magnificat* at Vespers on Pentecost. [2] Second Alleluia verse at Mass on Pentecost Sunday, alt.; see *Graduale de tempore* 1614/2001, fol. 188v: "Alleluia. Veni Sancte Spiritus, reple tuorum corda fidelium: et tui amoris in eis ignem accende"; also in Lossius 1561/1996, fols. 137v, 142v (the text is as found in the 1614 *Graduale*).

at Second Vespers on Pentecost Sunday.[169] Like *Spirate suaves, Te solum aestuat, Tu es cor meum,* and a number of other works, the text features an opening portion (here in prose) followed by prose-poetry groups:

PERANDA, *REPLETI SUNT OMNES*

Repleti sunt omnes Spiritu Sancto	All were filled with the Holy Spirit
et coeperunt loqui, Alleluja. [1]	and began to speak, Hallelujah.
Veni, Sancte Spiritus,	Come, Holy Spirit,
reple corda fidelium	fill the hearts of the faithful
tuae charitatis incendio. [2]	with your fire of love.
Te docente nil obscurum,	When you teach nothing is obscure,
te praesente nil impurum,	when you are present nothing is impure,
cuncta sunt splendentia.	all things are brilliant.
Qui discipulis in igne apparuisti,	You who appeared in fire to the disciples,
fove, protege,	foster, protect,
et doce nos viam veritatis.	and teach us the way of truth.
Veritatem notam facis,	You make known the truth,
et ostendis viam pacis	and you show the way of peace
nobis hic degentibus.	to us living here.
Alleluia.	Hallelujah.

Other seasonal texts contain no discernible allusions to or quotations from scripture or liturgy, but comprise exclusively freely composed material. In some of these seasonal texts, such as Peranda's *Abite dolores*, an Easter concerto, the connection to the feast is not apparent from the title. Here the content seems much more distantly

---

169. See *LU* 886–87, Antiphon for the *Magnificat* at Second Vespers on Pentecost Sunday: "Hodie completi sunt dies Pentecostes, alleluia: hodie Spiritus Sanctus in igne discipulis apparuit, et tribuit eis charismatum dona: misit eos in universum mundum praedicare et testificari: qui crediderit, et baptizatus fuerit, salvus erit, alleluia"; this text also appears in Peranda's *Ad cantus, ad sonos.*

related to the feast and the event it commemorates than more traditional Easter texts such as "Surrexit Christus," "Surrexit Pastor bonus," and "Heut' triumphiret Gottes Sohn." Poetry predominates in *Abite dolores*; the text comprises poetic stanzas in various meters and includes but one brief prose statement ("sed quid canere dicimus"). Peranda's *Abite dolores* also stands as an example of a type of seasonal text, introduced in Dresden by the Italians, that seeks to introduce private devotion into reflections on the central events of Christian history. While the speaker does refer to Christ's death and resurrection, he seems unable to rejoice in the salvation won for him by Christ. Instead, he expresses his longing and desire to experience Christ's mystical presence and regards Christ's self-sacrifice as the source of mystical nourishment. This lends the text an interesting rhetorical shape, for the speaker gradually turns his focus inward, and completely personalizes the events referenced in the opening before turning outward again.

PERANDA, *ABITE DOLORES*

Abite, dolores	Farewell, ye sorrows
jam mundi furentis,	of the raging world,
venite, clamores	come, ye sounds
nunc coeli canentis.	of singing heaven.
Rectoris aeterni	For the eternal ruler's
nam redditur pax,	peace is given to us,
tortoris inferni	while the infernal torturer's
dum teritur fax.	torch is quenched.
Date sonos, date melos,	Offer up song, offer up music,
lyrae, plectra, organa vos,	ye lyres, plectra, organ,
resonate, reboate,	resound, cry out,
en canemus ecce nos.	come, let us sing.
Sed, quid canere dicimus,	But why do we say "sing"
si charitatis ardore nostra	if our hearts melt with the heat
corda liquescunt?	of love?
Ah, si nunc langueo,	Ah, if now I languish,
plene jam video	I see fully
quod laetus sim;	that I am happy.
Ah si nunc ardeo,	Ah, if now I burn,
recte jam sentio	I feel justly
amoris vim.	the power of love.
Nam ut languentium	For so that the breath of those who
pascatur halitus,	languish should be nourished,
se Christus dat;	Christ offers himself;

ac ut ardentium	and so that the spirit
alatur spiritus	of those who are ardent should be strengthened
nobiscum stat.	he sojourns with us.
Eia, laetamini!	Come, rejoice!
Eia, fruimini!	Come, delight!
et facti laeti	and let the voice of him who is made joyful
canat nunc vox.	sing now.
Alleluja.	Hallelujah.

Other Texts

After the five categories of texts discussed above, no other thematic category reveals itself to be as important in the Dresden textual repertoire. The remaining texts fall into a number of thematic categories, none of which includes more than four examples. Of these, the more prominent categories include soteriological texts, communal petitions for God's help and strength in times of trial, and expressions of confidence in God or Christ. Like the texts discussed above, these exhibit the same variety in structure and style, and the same dependence on a variety of sources. All of these texts might be designated *per ogni tempo*, as the number of occasions upon which several of the settings were performed makes plain. In 1662, for example, Albrici presented his *Sive vivimus, sive morimur* on five occasions, four times during the Trinity season, and once again on Christmas Eve. Peranda scheduled performances of his *Dedit abyssus*, a setting of Habakkuk 3:10b–12, on at least three different occasions: on *Quasimodogeniti* Sunday in 1665, and on the Feast of the Epiphany and Trinity 12 in 1666; Albrici presented his late colleague's composition again on Pentecost Tuesday in 1676. However, no work in the Dresden repertoire can boast of more documented performances than Peranda's petition for God's guidance, *Propitiare Domine*. The composer presented it on five occasions in the Dresden court chapel in 1665 and 1666; some years later, singers at the electoral school in Grimma under Samuel Jacobi presented it on nine occasions during the Trinity season between 1684 and 1700.[170]

PERANDA, *PROPITIARE DOMINE*

Propitiare, Domine,	Be propitiated, Lord,
supplicationibus nostris,	by our prayers,

---

170. See Appendix II for details on the Dresden performances; the Grimma performances were documented by Jacobi on the title page of the part set, SLUB 1738-E-500a.

et benignus nos protege	and benevolently protect us
coelesti auxilio,	with heavenly aid,
ac concede ut te toto corde,	and grant that we may love you with all our heart,
ore et opere ita diligamus,	in utterance and action,
ut te duce, te rectore[171]	that with you as our guide and ruler
sic transeamus per temperalia,	we may pass through temporal things,
ut non amittamus aeterna.	that we may not lose those that are eternal.

Roman Catholic Texts?

When Johann Georg II ascended the Saxon throne in 1656, Roman Catholic composers assumed musical authority in his Lutheran court chapel. Normally such a situation would call into question the confessional or doctrinal purity of the repertoire performed in a given court chapel during such an unusual tenure. In the Dresden case, however, the fact that the surviving repertoire owes its very existence to the copying efforts of Lutheran cantors and Kapellmeisters, who regarded it as eminently performable in their own Lutheran institutions, immediately puts to rest any suspicions of "creeping Catholicism" in the texts of the surviving works composed for Dresden. The previous discussion has illustrated the degree to which many of the texts set by Albrici and Peranda, although likely rooted in a Catholic perspective, were nevertheless consistent with long-standing trends in Lutheran devotional practices. Thus they may be regarded as standing in conformity with Lutheran doctrine itself, at least as it manifested itself in the praxis of piety. Of the perhaps several hundred compositions supplied by Albrici and Peranda for the elector's chapel, a core repertoire found acceptance in a number of other Lutheran schools and court chapels in the various German states as well as in Scandinavia. As significant as is the Lutheran sanction of these works, however, the reasons that underlie that approval are even more important. Clearly the sacred concertos of Albrici and Peranda not only manifested a musical style much sought after at the time, but the texts of these concertos also responded to Lutheran sensibilities, and helped to satisfy the spiritual needs of contemporary Lutherans.

In many ways, the cross-confessional situation that obtained in the Dresden court chapel in the 1660s and 1670s simply reflected a continuation of the long-standing Lutheran practice of borrowing music by Catholic composers. As far back as 1578, for example, during the service celebrated to dedicate the Dresden Annenkirche,

---

171. This line appears in Musculus (1575:37) and in the *Meditationes* (*PL* 40:907), but neither source includes the entire text.

before the sermon, three hymns were sung, and then a Latin piece, Clemens non Papa's motet *Jubilate Deo omnis terra*, with six voices and in two parts, was sung by the cantor and his students, and was accompanied by the city instrumentalists. After the sermon had been preached, another Latin motet was sung, Orlando [di Lasso]'s *Te Deum Patrem unigenitum*, with six voices and in two parts, again accompanied by the city instrumentalists.[172]

This at a time when a large "Lutheran" repertoire composed by Lutherans was widely available. Here, of course, the texts involve a psalm and a commonly used liturgical item. Potentially far more dangerous, however, were the free texts composed by advocates of a particular doctrinal point of view.

The occupancy of the office of Dresden Kapellmeister by Catholic composers would seem, at least at first glance, to raise some rather obvious questions concerning the repertoire of Lutheran church music during the Baroque era, a repertoire which has long been defined by the music of Schütz on the one hand, and Bach on the other. Just what constitutes "Lutheran church music" in the latter half of the seventeenth century? Could it be composed by Catholics as well as Lutherans? It would seem from the repertoire performed in Dresden, as well as in many other Lutheran schools and court chapels, that the "Lutheran church music" of the years between ca. 1650 and 1710 had a pronounced ecumenical nature. Given their acceptance by both confessions, many of the free texts set by Italians during this era might be better described as "culturally Catholic" rather than actually theologically or doctrinally so. But even this description reflects a modern misconception of the devotional reality in the seventeenth-century Lutheran church. If nothing else, the boundary-crossing practiced by the musical ensembles of many Lutheran schools and court chapels at this time, including Dresden, demonstrates that the appearance of a text in the Catholic liturgy or in a published collection of music by a Catholic composer did not automatically define its content as "Catholic" and thereby restrict its usage to the co-religionists of the composer. Most, if not all, of the texts sung in Dresden could easily have been presented in Catholic venues.

To be sure, Albrici and Peranda generally avoided texts that would have failed to pass confessional muster with the court preacher. These included, for example, any in which Mary was praised or venerated (outside of Luke 1:26–38), those that

---

172. "Bei der Einweihung der Kirche 1578 wurden vor der Predigt drei geistliche Lieder und darauf von dem Cantore und seinen Schülern–dem Chor der Annenschule–ein lateinischer Gesang als des Clementis Non Papae mutet mit 6 Stimmen und 2 Theilen, Jubilate Deo omnis terra gesungen, auch von den Stadtpfeifern darein musicieret. Nach geschehener Predigt wurde wiederum eine lateinische mutet Orlandi Te Deum Patrem unigenitum mit 6 Stimmen und 2 Theilen gesungen, auch ließen sich die Stadtpfeifer gleichfalls dabey hören" (Rautenstrauch 1907/1970:176, from Schramm, *Geschichte der Annenschule in Dresden*, 1860:11).

invoked the intercession of Mary or the saints, interpreted the Mass as a sacrifice, venerated the elements of the Eucharist, invoked the doctrine of transubstantiation, made reference to purgatory, and so forth. And yet, a significant degree of congruence existed between the themes that remained available to the Dresden Kapellmeisters and those of their own tradition. Like the Lutheran borrowing of devotional materials published by and for Catholics in the later sixteenth century,[173] the texts of sacred art music that became popular in the later seventeenth century reveal similarly striking commonalities in the devotional beliefs and practices of both Catholics and Lutherans a century later. Even if each confession promulgated its own particular view of the place of piety and its relation to doctrine and dogma, many of the devotional texts worked interchangeably in either context.[174] And, if the texts of Italian sacred compositions were deemed incompatible with Lutheran doctrine, they were simply brought into agreement through alteration. For example, settings of Marian antiphons by Italian composers were regularly heard in Lutheran venues in the later seventeenth century (although not in Dresden) with their texts revised to invoke the intercession of Christ rather than Mary.[175]

Still, a few lost works of Albrici, perhaps tellingly not copied for use elsewhere, suggest that Marian texts, scrupulously avoided as "papist" by contemporary Lutherans, did find their way into the Dresden liturgies, at least on occasion. In February and March of 1673, during the period of intense confessional strife in Dresden, Albrici presented two concertos in the court chapel whose titles cannot be said to reflect any aspect of contemporary Lutheran piety and devotion. At Vespers on the Feast of the Purification (2 February), members of the *Hofkapelle* performed his *Hodie beata virgo Maria*, and at Vespers on the Feast of the Visitation (25 March), they sang his *Sancta et Immaculata Virginitas*.[176] In 1681, Albrici listed both works in his inventory of compositions that he had kept at his home, presumably for rehearsal purposes, and was now returning to the court music library; the inclusion of both works in this inventory suggests that they were among pieces that were regularly performed.[177] Neither title appears in Lossius, but both represent items from the Catholic liturgy; *Hodie Beata Virgo Maria* is the antiphon for the *Magnificat* at Second Vespers on the Feast of the Purification, and *Sancta et Immaculata*

173. As documented by Althaus 1927/1966:59–142.

174. See Preus 1970-1:29.

175. For example, in one of Carissimi's settings of the *Salve Regina* that survives in the Düben collection (S-Uu VMHS 80:117), the text has been altered to begin "Salve Rex Christe, Pater misericordiae"; other passages are similarly altered. See Jones 1982-2:99–100 for a list of sources for the composition. On the Lutheran rejection of Mary as "Mater misericordiae," see Gritsch 1992:241.

176. SLUB K 117, fols. 26v, 36v; the scorings appear in Appendix II.

177. Spagnoli 1990:226.

appears as the sixth responsory at Matins on Christmas Day.[178] Due to the loss of the musical compositions, the complete texts can never be known. Both, however, may well have been entirely concordant with Luther's own views on Mary, for the Reformer rejected neither the doctrine of her immaculate nature nor that of her perpetual virginity.[179] But despite the possible conformity of each text with the views of Luther and others in his circle, neither can be described as typical of the Lutheran textual repertoire of the time.[180] In the sixteenth century, prior to both the Tridentine decrees and the Formula of Concord (1577), Lutherans seem to have been more comfortable with such references to Mary, as suggested by the marginalia provided by Lossius in 1553 for the Responsory for Purification, *Gaude Maria virgo*:

RESPONSORY TEXT	MARGINALIA
Dum virgo Deum et hominem genuisti, et post partum virgo inviolata permansisti.	Virginitas inviolata et perpetua Mariae etc.[181]
While a virgin you bore God and man; and after the birth you remained an inviolate virgin.	Inviolate and perpetual virginity of Mary etc.

At the same time, however, Lossius dealt with the "intercession problem" by presenting one of the Marian antiphons with a "corrected" text:

178. *LU* 1367: "Hodie Beata Virgo Maria puerum Jesum praesentavit in templo: et Simeon, repletus Spiritu Sancto, accepit eum in ulnas suas, et benedixit Deum in aeternum." ("Today the Blessed Virgin Mary presented the boy Jesus at the temple, and Simeon, filled with the Holy Spirit, accepted him in his arms, and blessed the Lord into eternity"); ibid., 384: "Sancta et immaculata Virginitas, quibus te laudibus efferam, nescio: Quia quem caeli capere non poterant, tuo gremio contulisti. V. Benedicta tu in mulieribus, et benedictus fructus ventris tui." ("Holy and spotless Maidenhood, I know not with what praises to exalt thee; For whom the heavens could not contain thou didst bear in thy womb. Blessed art thou among women, and blessed is the fruit of thy womb.") Translation: *Mass and Vespers* 1957:1059, 1956–57.

179. In the Smalcald Articles, Luther refers to Mary as *semper virgo*, and the 1577 Formula of Concord he praises her as the "laudatissima virgo." See Gritsch 1992:235–42.

180. In Walker and Walker 1992, no examples of Marian texts (outside of the Visitation texts) composed by Lutherans appear. Although the catalog includes only works with three or more vocal parts, it nevertheless presents a good overview of the repertoire.

181. Lossius 1561/1996, fol. 197a.

LOSSIUS, *REGINA COELI CORRECTUM PER M. HER: BONNUM.*	*LIBER USUALIS*, 275
Rex Christe, omnes in te laetamur, Halleluiah.	Regina caeli laetare, alleluia.
Quia pertulisti pro nobis mortem, Alleluia. etc.[182]	Quia quem meruisti portare, alleluia. etc.
King Christ, we all rejoice in you, hallelujah.	Rejoice, Queen of heaven, hallelujah.
Because you suffered death for us, hallelujah etc.	Because of he whom you were worthy to carry, hallelujah, etc.

Soon after the second edition of Lossius's *Psalmodia* appeared in 1561, however, the condemnatory decrees that emanated from Trent began to ring in the ears of Lutheran theologians. In the exhaustive Lutheran response of Martin Chemnitz, published between 1565 and 1573, the Braunschweig superintendent challenged the doctrine of the Immaculate Conception as lacking scriptural foundation, and concluded his argument with the following summation:

> But in this dispute I want nothing taken away from the dignity of the blessed Virgin Mary. For I embrace with the greatest reverence of mind what she herself sings: "Henceforth all generations will call me blessed, for He who is mighty has done great things for me." But I think that the Virgin Mary is rightly proclaimed blest if those things are attributed to her which are both in agreement with Scripture and can be proved from there, so that the name of the Lord may be holy. No other celebration can be pleasing to her.[183]

After this time, Lutherans seem to have gone beyond the avoidance of intercessory texts to reject even the slightest hint of Marian veneration or devotion, including any references to Mary as the "immaculate and perpetual Virgin," despite the fact that Lutheran teachings, collected in the *Book of Concord* of 1580, "affirm commemorative veneration of the saints and Mary, but reject any invocation of them."[184]

With respect to these two compositions, it is tempting to speculate that Albrici's decision to program them at this time represents one composer's response to the

---

182. Lossius's version is much longer and includes three statements of each alleluia, each with a different text, etc. (1561/1996, fol. 114a–b).

183. See "Fifth Topic. Whether the Blessed Virgin was Conceived without Original Sin," in Chemnitz 1971:383.

184. See "The Problem in the Sixteenth Century," 33, in *The One Mediator*; the point is confirmed by a survey of the titles in collections and inventories of seventeenth-century sacred music.

tensions that surrounded the celebration of Mass at the ambassadorial residences, and the elector's response to these tensions. On 27 February 1673, at the time that these two Marian concertos were performed in his chapel, Johann Georg II issued his decree on the Mass, either willingly or hesitantly. It is difficult not to impute some intentionality on Albrici's part here—at a time that confessional tensions were running high, he elected to present compositions with distinctly Catholic overtones. Perhaps these works represent Albrici's attempt to reassert his own confessional identity in response to the public pressure being placed upon him and his co-religionists by the elector and his court preacher. Or perhaps they provide a clue to the elector's own personal, secretly held beliefs concerning the Blessed Virgin. In any case, the sudden re-emergence of Marian texts in Dresden after nearly a century of disuse in Lutheran venues is notable and lends a distinct air of confessional ambiguity to the Dresden textual repertoire.

That the texts favored by Albrici and Peranda were for the most part typical of those preferred in numerous other Lutheran institutions of the era reflects a significant shift in the nature of Lutheran public worship after the Thirty Years' War. While the Schütz generation continued to reflect the Lutheran emphasis on the Word in its textual choices, and focused its attention on scriptural texts, particularly the Psalms, many of which provided that comfort sought by the terrified soul, composers writing for educated Lutherans of the later seventeenth century exchanged the more abstract comfort provided by the doctrine of justification for the more tangible and immediate comfort provided by a mystically influenced, personalized devotion to Christ. Through their activities in Dresden, Albrici and Peranda became—perhaps unwittingly—active participants in a movement that witnessed the infiltration of private devotion into public worship in the Lutheran domain, particularly through the vehicle of sacred art music. This new public devotionality, coupled with the renewed German interest in and access to Italian music after the war, helps to account for the pronounced preference among Lutherans for devotional texts. In many respects, the textual repertoire of the chapel during this era would seem rather "un-Lutheran," given the complete absence of texts on such fundamental Lutheran themes as comfort, justification, word and sacrament, and the Law/Gospel dichotomy, among others. Yet such a view fails to take into account the composers' response to the *neue Frömmigkeit* of the era. In the end, although rather anomalous in its domination by Catholic foreigners and their music, the Dresden *Hofkapelle* and its repertoire did not fall completely out of step with currents in Germany. Instead, the radical shift in textual and musical style preferences that took place there after 1656 mirrored the changes taking place, if less abruptly, in many other Lutheran institutions in Germany and in Scandinavia.

5

Roma trapiantata:

The New Sacred Concerto in Dresden

IN THE NINETEENTH century, Dresden was known throughout Europe as "Florence on the Elbe," in recognition of the architectural achievements proudly displayed on or near the river bank—the *Residenzschloß*, the Katholische Hofkirche, and particularly the Frauenkirche, whose imposing, bell-shaped dome dominated the skyline as does the *Duomo* in the city of the Medici.[1] But in the mid-seventeenth century, decades before the construction of these two churches, such a sobriquet could easily have been associated with the papal city, rather than the Tuscan capital, given the close relationship between the musical repertoire that dominated the chapel liturgies at that time with that heard in various Jesuit churches in Rome, including San Apollinare and Il Gesù. Although Albrici and Peranda did not roundly reject the musical conventions of the Schütz generation during their tenure in the Saxon *Residenzstadt*, they did take the repertoire of the Dresden court musical ensemble in a distinctly new musical direction. Johann Georg II himself was the driving force behind these musical changes; not only did he invite these young adherents of an unwelcome and suspect confession into his chapel, he granted them considerable professional latitude, and not only allowed them to replace the concertos of Schütz with music in a patently Italian style, but also to reintroduce Latin as the primary language of musical texts sung by the members of the *Hofkapelle*. During their respective tenures at court, Albrici and Peranda, calling upon their training and experience as students and church musicians in Rome, effected the complete "Italianization," or even "Romanization," of the chapel repertoire. As a result, when viewed solely through the lens of the court musical ethos as defined by the works of Schütz, the corpus of concertos by Peranda and Albrici represents a discontinuity, and marks a sharp and sudden break with time-honored practices. But when these same works are regarded as the transplanted continuation of the Italian motet tradition, they reveal many continuities with the innovative repertoire composed in Italy, particularly in the papal city, during the previous two decades.

---

1. Today the dome of the rebuilt *Frauenkirche* once again dominates the Dresden skyline.

As Graham Dixon's seminal work on Roman liturgical music has revealed, in 1603 Agostino Agazzari (1578–ca. 1640) inaugurated a new manner of motet so distinctive to Rome that it quickly acquired the toponymic epithet *concertato alla Romana*.[2] According to Dixon, the *concertato alla Romana* distinguished itself through the disposition of a text into discrete versets, or sections, and the use of a different scoring and musical treatment in each section, which resulted in constant variations in style and vocal texture.[3] Dixon has established that this "sectional type [of motet] was peculiar to Rome" and represented an approach "rarely encountered in the north," one that was "recognized in the north as a Roman innovation" after 1618.[4] As the decades wore on, however, Roman composers gradually abandoned this designation; by the 1640s, "the principle of sectionalization had become so assimilated into the general motet style that the word 'concertato' fell out of use."[5] By this time, solos and reduced scorings dominated the motet repertoire in Rome, while at the same time, the individual sections underwent development and expansion. The result was a repertoire of extended motets—Giovanni Marciani's *Quasi stella matutina*, for example, stretches to 335 measures—that required superior vocal skills on the part of the singers.[6] During this decade, the solo voice won an increasingly favored position in ensemble motets (those composed for two or more singers), due at least in part to the predominance of devotional texts written in the first person. By the end of this decade, affective solos in a florid declamatory style had secured a prominent position within the ensemble motet; these were contrasted with sections scored for several voices, usually in a contrasting meter. Formal strategies such as the use of refrains also became more prevalent, as did the use of an expansion technique that appears to have been typically Roman, in which the vocal ensemble immediately reiterated and developed material first presented by a soloist.[7]

Given that motet procedures in Italy varied considerably between Rome and Venice during the first half of the seventeenth century, any search for the stylistic antecedents of the Dresden repertoire must take the regional ties of its expatriate

---

2. Dixon 1981-1:257, 266–67. Dixon explains on p.ix that his use of the term *concertato* comports with Roman seventeenth-century usage: music in which scorings vary during the course of the work.

3. Dixon 1981-1:258–72.

4. Dixon points out that works of this type were even described as such in Venice; in Diruta's *Compieta concertata* of 1623, for example, a setting of *Miserere* is described as "a versetti concertato alla Romana" (1981-1:257, 266, 315).

5. Dixon 1981-1:272.

6. Dixon 1981-1:280. See the discussion of the Marciani motet below.

7. As Dixon's study terminates with the year 1645, these latter observations are those of the author, gleaned from examinations of various Roman motet publications of the later 1640s and 1650s.

composers into consideration. Albrici's musical link with Rome can be firmly established, and Peranda's biography, musical style, and interest in Gratiani's motet texts all indicate that he too spent a considerable period of time in the papal city. All of this suggests that the direct antecedents of the Dresden concerto style ought first to be sought in Rome. And not surprisingly, a comparison of the Roman motet repertoire of the 1640s and 1650s with the repertoire of sacred concertos produced for the Dresden court in the two succeeding decades reveals striking similarities in both style and strategy that clearly show the Dresden concertos to be a later efflorescence of the *concertato alla Romana*. A number of the musical features that predominate in the compositions of Carissimi, Gratiani, Foggia, D. Mazzocchi, Marciani, Cecchelli, and Bicilli, but which are absent from the northern motet repertoires, were adopted and developed by Albrici and Peranda. Some of the most innovative features of the later repertoire, however, appear most prominently in the motets of Gratiani; his forward-looking approach to the motet, in scorings for one or several singers, appears to have exercised a much stronger musical influence upon both of the Dresden Kapellmeisters than did the works of Albrici's former choirmaster Carissimi, seven of whose motets were heard in the court chapel in 1662.[8] Yet none of these works displays the stylistic variety or the forward-looking features evinced in Gratiani's motets, such as the incorporation of metric verse and the disposition in sections set off by metric changes. Carissimi's motets do, however, exemplify many of the stylistic and formal features of the Roman motet discussed above, and also stand as precursors of the Dresden concerto in that respect. But the attention to the aria and the focus on florid declamatory writing in the context of the ensemble motet seems to have been either an innovation or a particular interest of Gratiani, whose influence on the Dresden repertoire remains much stronger than that of Carissimi.[9] Thus the Roman musical ties of Albrici and Peranda, and particularly those to Gratiani, hold the key to a modern understanding of the post-Schützian sacred concerto in Dresden.

THE ROMAN MOTET AT MID-CENTURY

Composers in mid-century Rome celebrated both textural and stylistic variety in their motets but, at the same time, often sought to impose a certain degree of musical unity on these works, perhaps as a way of exerting some control over the texts, whose expansiveness and diversity threatened to make them unwieldy. The pri-

8. SLUB Q 240.
9. Lars Berglund has also noted the importance of Gratiani for the works of Christian Geist, who modeled two works on motets of the Roman composer; Berglund 2002:149–55, 170–71, *et passim*.

mary unification device remained the refrain, the use of which also contributed to the rhetorical shape of the composition, for through the refrain the composer lent emphasis to certain ideas, themes, or concepts presented in the text. In addition, Roman composers also lent rhetorical emphasis to portions of the text through the use of immediate tutti restatements or imitative reworkings of material originally presented by a soloist. Examples of the approaches outlined here abound in the motet publications of the 1640s. A work published in 1649, Gratiani's *O bone Jesu*, typifies a number of them,[10] and attests to the contemporary Roman preference for discursive, sectionalized texts.[11] Although it was culled from a variety of sources, it nevertheless coheres as the prayer of an individual who longs to experience Christ's mystical presence. The diversity displayed in its various literary styles, however, literally invites musical contrast and variety (Table 5.1).

From the very outset of his setting, Gratiani establishes a musical affect that corresponds to the prayerful nature of the text. Here the singer assumes the persona of the speaker and presents the opening petitions in an affective solo (Ex. 5.1). Gratiani begins his musical prayer tranquilly, and underscores Christ's goodness ("bone") with a descending leap to the leading-tone. The quietude of the opening address is immediately shattered, however, when the soprano leaps to an *e'* for the second petition. In this slowly descending line, Gratiani intensifies the speaker's longing for Jesus "the most kind" through an extended suspension figure that cadences on G. He then proceeds with his presentation of the text, but now employs the rhetorical repetition figure *epizeuxis*, and twice restates the new motive (mm. 5–10); this rhetorical ploy also allows him to move sequentially by fifths, and to close the entire section on A with a prolonged cadence on "amator." Over the course of these first ten measures, the bass has become more active, in preparation for the tutti entrance that immediately follows. At this point (m. 11), Gratiani embarks upon an intensification of the solo exordium in a suspension-filled, imitative reworking of the material, rendered by all three singers. Suddenly the emotional level is heightened considerably, first in the stereophonic exclamation "O" (m. 11) and the polyphonic conclusion of the motive, and then in the ascending, sequential entries of "o piissime Jesu" (mm. 13–15), which culminate in a cadence on E. As the passage proceeds, the three parts play with the motive "humani generis amator" until they finally come to rest again

---

10. See the translation, sources, and discussion in chapter 4. Musical examples prepared from S-Uu UVMTR 544–48.

11. Additional examples of works by Gratiani that display similar repetition schemes include *Media nocte*, in *R. Floridus canonicus de Sylvestris . . . Florida verba . . .* (Rome, 1648 [1648¹]), *O Jesu fili Mariae* and *Rex magne celitum*, in *Motetti a due, tre, quattro, cinque, e sei voci. Di D. Bonifatio Gratiani . . .* (Rome, 1650), and *Laudate celites*, in *Motetti a due, tre, e cinque voci. Di D. Bonifatio Gratiani . . . Libro Terzo, Opera Settima* (Rome, 1656).

Table 5.1 Gratiani, *O bone Jesu* (1649), Formal Overview

	Text	Meter	Scoring	Style	Bars
1	O bone Jesu, o piissime Jesu, humani generis amator.	C	S1	declamatory	1–10
	O bone Jesu, o piissime Jesu, humani generis amator.		SST	*concertato*	11–24
2	Qui te gustant esuriunt, qui bibunt ad huc sitiunt.	3/2	SST	*concertato*	25–50
3	Sitio ad te fontem aquae vivae, nec satiabor donec requiescam in te, quia de amore tuo vulnerasti me.	C	S1	declamatory	51–67
4	O mentis delectatio, o cordis iubilatio, o amoris consumatio.	3/2	SST	*concertato*	68–99
5	Ecce, langueo pro te, quia tunc prior dilexisti me, nec habeo quid tibi praebeam, nisi te dederis mihi largitor omnium.	C	S2	declamatory	100–24
6	Ecce cantabo et delectabor in te, quia es omni–	C	SST	*concertato*	125–34
	a et ego nihil sum,	3/2			
	et tamen delectaris esse cum filiis hominum.	C			
7 [4]	*O mentis delectatio, o cordis jubilatio, o amoris consumatio.*	3/2	SST	*concertato*	135–72

EXAMPLE 5.1 Gratiani, *O bone Jesu*, mm 1–16

on A (mm. 17–24). In these first twenty-four measures, Gratiani has employed rhetorical repetition as an intensification technique on three levels: in the opening solo (at "humani generis"), in the simple event of the tutti restatement itself, and in the development of the motivic material by the three soloists during the course of the restatement.

The opening affect of hopeful expectation quickly gives way to one of pure joy, however, as the speaker rejoices in the prospect of mystical union, here invoked through the metaphors of mystical hunger and thirst (Ex. 5.2). As the speaker's rising passion causes him to shift from speech to song (see sections 1 and 2 of the text), he suddenly bursts forth in a proclamatory hymn in which the quiet intensity of the opening is quickly left behind. Gratiani concomitantly shifts to triple meter and a more homophonic style that preserves a sense of the familiar text as isometric verse. Even the contrapuntal moments that do occur (mm. 29–34, 39–50) reveal the tendency to "homophonize" in the homorhythmic nature of the individual lines.

At the conclusion of this hymnic insertion, the text once again becomes contemplative. In response, Gratiani suddenly replaces the driving triple with a sustained passage in common time, whose bass line becomes more active as the passage proceeds. He casts this next portion as a declamatory solo, and in it, captures the urgency in the speaker's expression of intense longing and desire (Ex. 5.3). As in the opening portion of the motet, the harmonic foundation supports, but does not compete with, the vocal line; it functions to provide the speaker with a platform from which to address Christ. At this point in the text, the speaker has begun the ascent to mystical union, and the experience that the text relates finds its musical corollary in Gratiani's musical treatment. For while the rest in Christ for which the speaker yearns is ostensibly found in the cadence on C in m. 56, the residual affect is that of unattainable satiety, for at "requiescam in te," the vocal line ascends to the highest pitch region yet attained in the motet and then "rests" there momentarily. But rather than create a true sense of repose, the high g'' —first sustained, then ornamented—only increases the tension felt by the listener, simply by withholding the descent that is both expected and desired. In his treatment of this line, Gratiani succeeds in conveying the paradox that inheres in the text: though the speaker seeks rest in Christ, he will never find it; his thirst, even as it is being quenched by Christ's mystical presence, will be ever increased by that same presence. After this climactic display, Gratiani subjects the speaker's final line ("quia de amore . . . ") to rhetorical repetition (*epizeuxis*), thus underscoring the root cause of the speaker's desire: he has been wounded by Christ's love. Here the disjunct melodic line and the constantly shifting harmonic framework serve as musical metaphors for the pain and ecstasy felt by the speaker in his "wounded" state.

Gratiani follows this declamatory passage with a *concertato*-style setting of the rhymed verse that follows, "O mentis delectatio," an adaptation of stanza 40/34 of

EXAMPLE 5.2 Gratiani, *O bone Jesu*, mm. 25–50

EXAMPLE 5.2 (*continued*)

Jesu dulcis memoria.[12] This sharp musical contrast, so typical of the *concertato alla Romana*, projects the new tone of the text, for at this point, the speaker has been roused out of a state of deep rapture to sing forth in adulation to Christ (Ex. 5.4). In contrast to the exuberant delight expressed in "Qui te gustant," however, here the speaker's emotional state is one of a much more subdued joy. In response, Gratiani creates a somewhat quieter hymn, chiefly through the use of preponderantly descending motion.

The more restrained affect of the second hymn allows an easy transition to the mood of the following declamatory solo, in which the language turns to longing as expressed in the Song of Songs. Gratiani again pairs this solo with a *concertato*-style setting of the subsequent text; here, however, he takes a more rhetorical approach than that seen in the hymns above. He begins with a lively imitative section in duple meter (mm. 115–29), in which the speaker "sings" and "delights," and proclaims that "[Christ] is everything," but then contrasts this with the speaker's concluding admission, "and I am nothing," by shifting to a brief homophonic triple (mm. 125–29). He then restores the duple meter that opened the section and proceeds with an equally brief imitative treatment of the final line (mm. 130–34). To conclude the motet, he recalls the speaker's central paean to Christ ("O mentis delectatio").

Gratiani's *O bone Jesu*, with its two basic compositional styles, typifies the Roman motet before 1650. Around mid-century, however, the amount of metric verse in texts of ensemble motets began to increase; the poetic component now usually

---

12. St. 40/34: "Tu mentis delectatio, amoris consummatio, tu mea gloriatio, Jesu, mundi salvatio."

EXAMPLE 5.3   Gratiani, *O bone Jesu*, mm. 51–67

appeared in the form of octaves in amphibrachic meter. While the more typical treatment of isometric verse in this context remained the *concertato* style, composers began to experiment with the integration of the aria into the motet and began to fashion aria strophes for soloists from these stanzas. In Gratiani's *Rex magne* of 1650 (see Table 5.2) and *Laudate celites* of 1656, the poetic stanzas occur in alternation with other prose portions of the text, rather than consecutively.[13] This inclusion

13. *Motetti a due, tre, quattro, cinque, e sei voci* (Rome: Mascardi, 1650). *Laudate celites* appears in Gratiani's 1656 collection of ensemble motets, *Motetti a due, tre, e cinque voci* (Rome: Balmonti, 1656).

Table 5.2 Bonifatio Gratiani, *Rex magne caelitum*

Text/Style	Scoring	Meter	Form
1. prose/declamatory	B	C	a
2. prose/*concertato*	SS, SSB	C	b
3. poetry/aria (st. 1)	S1	3/2	c
4. prose/*concertato*	SSB	C, 3/2	d
5. poetry/aria (st.2)	S2	3/2	c′
6. prose/*concertato*	SSB	C	e
7. poetry/aria (st. 3)	S1	3/2	c′′
8. poetry/aria (st. 3, tutti restatement)	SSB	3/2	c′′′

of arias in the ensemble motet, while infrequent, opens up a new stylistic dimension in these works, and distances them even further from the traditional notion of a "motet."

In both its stylistic variety and musical organization, *Rex magne* adumbrates the concerto in Dresden, for in it Gratiani draws upon the three compositional styles favored by Albrici and Peranda. Perhaps most significant here is Gratiani's approach to the aria within a work for multiple singers, for it was adopted and developed by both Albrici and Peranda. As the author-compiler (Gratiani?) has intercalated the stanzas among the other portions of the text, Gratiani fashions an "interrupted aria" from the poetry—each stanza, while not consecutive, receives the same (or very similar) musical treatment. In another sense, however, the aria strophes function as a refrain with ever-varying textual content. This idea of the interpolation of a strophic aria among other, contrasting musical elements became a hallmark of the concertos of Albrici and Peranda; here, in works such as *Rex magne*, lie the seeds of the "concerto with aria" developed by Albrici in Dresden.[14] To conclude the motet, Gratiani reworks the third stanza in *concertato* style, in much the same manner as that observed in *O bone Jesu* above. This sort of tutti restatement of solo arias, however, suggests that Gratiani does not yet regard the aria as a totally independent stylistic entity, but as material that can be used as the basis for a concerto as well as a solo. Nevertheless, the aria strophes in *Rex magne* do display his typical aria form and style (see below).

Another musical event of great significance for the future Dresden repertoire was the re-emergence in Rome of the solo motet shortly after 1650, when Gratiani began

---

14. Albrici's development of the "concerto with aria" in Dresden is discussed below.

EXAMPLE 5.4 Gratiani, *O bone Jesu*, mm. 68–83

to publish works in this genre.[15] These motets are virtuosic compositions scored most often for a soprano castrato, whose "angelic" voice would spin its roulades out over those in attendance at the Gesù.[16] In his solo motets, Gratiani makes no attempt to include a quasi-*concertato* style in which the voice and continuo line engage in motivic exchange; instead, in the absence of the textural contrasts available to him in the ensemble motet, he strives for a greater contrast between declamatory and lyrical styles of writing. As a result, while the declamatory solos in ensemble motets often present the singer with vocal challenges, those in the solo motets demand a virtuoso with well-developed coloratura and the ability to negotiate florid *passaggi*. In his earlier solo motets, those most familiar to Albrici and Peranda, Gratiani regularly alternated between the two styles and produced recitative-aria pairs or sets, a feature that did not escape the notice of the two younger composers. Like the texts of the ensemble motets of the 1640s and 1650s, the texts of Gratiani's early solo motets, illustrated here by his *O cor meum* of 1652,[17] include both prose and isometric verse (here amphibrachic). Different here, however, are both the structural organization of the text and its proportions. The verse component is now often arranged in consecutive stanzas, and poetry tends to predominate over prose.

O cor meum quo vagaris,	O my heart, whither do you wander,
quo raperis?	whither are you snatched away?
Cur blandimenta sequeris?	Why do you follow flattering words?
Quare mendacium quaeris et vanitatem diligis?	Why do you seek falsehood and esteem vanity?
Terrena quae cernis	The earthly things which you perceive
dum flores arescunt,	dry up as you flourish,
et donis aeternis	and become worthless
equata vilescunt.	compared to eternal gifts.

15. See Dixon 1981-1:320, and Shigihara 1984:468–69, 479–80. Shigihara points out that chronology problems in Carissimi's works make it difficult to establish with certainty the identity of the instigator of the solo motet in Rome, whether Carissimi or his colleague at the Roman Seminary, but suggests that Gratiani assumed a leadership role here, based on the prominence of solo motets in his overall *oeuvre*. According to the works list in Jones 1982-2:3–122, solo motets comprise only about one-tenth of Carissimi's overall motet output.

16. See Shigihara 1984:29–30, on the vocal ensemble at Il Gesù during Gratiani's tenure there.

17. *Motetti a voce sola*, Op. 3 (Rome: Mascardi: 1652), 11-17; reproduced in Schnoebelen 1988.

Surge, cor meum, surge, elevare,	Arise, my heart, arise, lift up,
exaltare ad sidera,	exult to the heavens,
et meditare perennis vitae	and reflect on the joys of
gaudia vitae gaudia.	everlasting life.
Dilatare, aperire, cor meum,	Spread out, open up, my heart,
ut replearis dulcedine	so that you are filled with the
suavitatis coelicae.	charm of celestial sweetness.
O Jesu dilecte,	O beloved Jesus,
o salus amata,	O beloved salvation,
o vita beata,	O blessed life,
lux mea tu es.	you are my light.
Quid est exultare	What use is it to exult,
et corda laetari,	what use to rejoice,
gaudere, cantare,	to be glad, to sing,
quid est sine te?	what is it without you?
Possideam terrae	Let me possess the subjects
subjecta marique,	of the land and of the sea,
sim clarus ubique,	let me be renowned everywhere,
sim populi rex;	let me be ruler of the people;
iam videar palmis	indeed, let me flourish with glory
auroque vigere,	and with gold,
sed totum habere,	but what use is it to have every-thing
quid est sine te?	without you?
Exultet cor meum,	Let my heart rejoice,
det carmen canorum	let it offer a melodious song,
et coeli bonorum	and let it resound in the hope
resultet in spe.	of the goods of heaven.
Inveniat semper	Let it always find you,
te semper amatum,	always loved,
sic vivat beatum,	thus let it live blessed,
sic vivat in te.	thus let it live in you.

Gratiani's musical response to this *vanitas* text, scored for soprano and continuo, displays all of the features typical of his early solo motets. He presents the two passages of prose in a florid declamatory style and casts the poetic stanzas in aria style (Table 5.3). Thus he creates both clearly delineated sections and the pairs of declamatory passages and arias that were common to both the solo motet and the contemporary secular cantata.

Table 5.3 Gratiani, *O cor meum*, Formal Organization

Bars	Text	Musical Treatment	Meter	Form
1–17	Prose	Declamatory	C	a
18–35	Poetry	Aria (one strophe)	3/2	b
36–62	Prose	Declamatory	C	c
63–178	Poetry	Aria (three strophes)	3/2	d, d′, d′′

Gratiani opens his motet with a dramatic, rhetorically conceived passage of declamatory writing of considerable musical presence, which, although equal in length to the subsequent aria with which it is paired, far surpasses it in musical weight (Ex. 5.5).[18] Gratiani marks each semantic division of the text with a cadence[19] and establishes a new musical idea for each phrase or segment of text. He opens with a broad hortatory gesture, but then quickly shifts into a mode of some urgency, and expands the opening line through the use of the rhetorical figure *paronomasia*,[20] and twice restates "cor meum," each time set to shorter note values and set off by rests, before bringing the line to its culmination in a jagged, directionless melisma (mm. 5–7) that evokes the essence of the word "vagaris." Gratiani then capitalizes on the castrato's legendary vocal capabilities to create a musical whirlwind illustrative of the event of being "snatched away" (mm. 8–10). As the text progresses, the vocal line first attempts to coax ("cur blandimenta"), then to demand ("quare mendacium quaeris"), reflecting the varied temptations to which the speaker has succumbed. And although an abstract concept such as "vanity" does not easily call forth a musical corollary, Gratiani underscores the centrality of this concept to the text with a rhythmically agitated melisma over a prolonged phrygian cadence ornamented with a 7-6 suspension (mm. 15–17). He leaves the declamatory passage harmonically open, however, and thereby adds sense of expectation that he satisfies in the following aria, which is closed on D.

From the amphibrachic quatrain that appears between the two passages of prose Gratiani creates a brief aria as a musical foil to the dramatic exordium. The speaker here dwells on the ephemeral nature of earthly existence, and the combination of

---

18. Musical examples prepared from Schnoebelen 1988.

19. The cadence type encountered here, $vii^{7\text{-}6}$ - I (untransposed), is also common in the works of Albrici and Peranda, and is identified as a "tenor cadence" by Bernhard in his *Tractatus* (Hilse 1973:69–70). It is described by Printz as a "*[clausula] ordinata descendens*" in his *Satyrischer Componist* (1676–96); see Dahlhaus 1990:218–19.

20. "A repetition of a musical passage, with certain additions or alterations, for the sake of greater emphasis"; Barthel 1997:350.

EXAMPLE 5.5 Gratiani, *O cor meum*, mm. 1–17

the minor mode with a rhythmic pattern akin, even if by chance, to the sarabande, effectively conveys the darkness faced by the speaker. This first aria is followed by a second declamatory passage, one that is more extended and considerably more florid than the first. Here Gratiani captures the speaker's new emotional state: gone is the critical soul-searching of the opening, replaced by joyous confidence. The topos of ascent suffuses this text as well as its musical setting; Gratiani uses the exhortative verbs "elevare" and "exaltare" as opportunities for displays of vocal fireworks, the shape of which capture the speaker's upward striving. He also emphasizes the oblique references to the mystical experience through *passaggi* at "dilatare" and "suavitatis."

The concluding aria ("O Jesu dilecte") that follows the declamatory passage comprises three strophes that vary only slightly from one another (Ex. 5.6). As in the first aria ("Terrena quae cernis"), each of the concluding aria strophes displays the lyrical, *bel canto* style and extended bipartite (ABB′) form typical of the Italian aria of this period.[21] This miniature yet well-defined form, as manifested in the motets of Gratiani, includes an A section that generally comprises the setting of the first half of the poetic stanza (here mm. 63-71), and a B section that represents the initial presentation of the stanza's conclusion (here mm. 72-84). In the following B′ section, the composer transposes and restates the setting of the latter half of the stanza as a means of closing the strophe in the opening key area, and often subjects the material to motivic elaboration. In Ex. 5.6, the B′ section ensues with the anacrusis to m. 85, where Gratiani first presents the latter half of the stanza, transposed up a minor third from its first presentation, and then adds a coda-like passage, which may be either brief or quite extended (here b. 3 of m. 93 through m. 99). In strophes 1 and 2, he employs a simple rhetorical device in the extension, and repeats the interrogative "quid," followed by rests, to stress this pivotal question. While in contemporary opera, the complete form of the bipartite aria frequently involves two strophes and two ritornellos, with no intervening recitative, in the motets of Gratiani one sees no corresponding convention. Instead, individual bipartite strophes

21. The preponderance of this form in the arias of seventeenth-century secular genres has long been recognized by scholars. Gloria Rose identified ABB′ as one of the two most common aria forms in Carissimi's cantatas, together with da capo form (Rose 1962:208-09), and Ellen Rosand discusses ABB′ or extended bipartite form as the predominant type in Venetian opera, and notes that Alfred Lorenz "christened this form the 'Seicento Aria'" (Rosand 1991:288-295; the Lorenz quote appears on p. 288). But the importance of this aria form in the seventeenth-century motets of Carissimi, Gratiani, Bicilli, Albrici, Peranda, and others seems to have passed unnoticed by scholars. In *GMO*, Westrup and Walker discuss ABB′ form in the arias of this period but cite only examples from secular genres; there is no indication here that such arias are also an important stylistic element in Italian sacred music ca. 1650–1680 (see Westrup and Walker, "Aria. 2. 17th-Century Vocal Music," in *GMO*).

EXAMPLE 5.6 Gratiani, *O cor meum*, mm. 63–99

often stand between recitatives, and groups of as many as four strophes may appear in succession.

In the Roman motet repertoire of the 1640s and early 1650s, the basic ground-work for the concerto style of Peranda and Albrici was laid. All of the stylistic developments discussed above were of fundamental importance for Albrici and Peranda, and provided the essential vocabulary of their musical dialect. The similarities extend beyond the broad outlines of formal design, however, and include details of musical style that are so similar that the kinship of the two bodies of works is unde-niable. Both seem to have borrowed the idea of pairing recitative and aria from the solo motet, while also recognizing the possibilities that the ensemble motet held for solo writing within the context of a composition for a small group of singers. These latter works also provided them with the basic approach to writing for the tutti— *concertato* style—which they employed with regularity in their Dresden works, as a backdrop or framing device for the solos that dominated the idiom as they cul-tivated it in the north. In their concertos for Dresden, the majority of which they scored for a small ensemble of two to four singers, they regularly included solo arias as well as recitative-aria pairs, and employed various refrain forms and tutti restate-ments. The decision to focus upon ensemble works may well have been driven by the sheer size of the *Hofkapelle*, and particularly by the number of Italian singers present at any give time; with so many virtuosi on hand, it simply became more practical to compose works for a vocal ensemble and to provide the individual per-formers with solos within the context of an ensemble piece. Given their tendency to draw upon all three compositional styles common to the Italian motet of the era, their Dresden concertos might be characterized as "composite" works. A consider-ation of the Dresden concertos as the direct descendants of the mid-century Italian motet, however, quickly renders such a designation superfluous, for the concept of contrast and variety that the designation "composite" seeks to communicate defined the motet in mid-century Italy as they knew it.

The Emergence of the Roman-Influenced Concerto in Dresden

On the Sunday after Christmas, 30 December 1660, Albrici directed the music at the morning worship service in the court chapel. The order of worship, one of the earliest that survives, provides the only record of a performance of one of Albrici's two set-tings of *O cor meum*, which was performed by two castrati and a number of instru-mentalists in a service dominated by compositions of Palestrina ("Praenestini").[22] By this date, worshipers in the Dresden chapel must have become acclimated to the

---

22. Sächs HStA Loc. 12026, fol. 60v.

lack of stylistic uniformity that characterized music in the court chapel, a quality that had become even more pronounced when Bontempi and Albrici took over for Schütz as *Hofkapellmeister*, soon after Johann Georg II's accession in 1656. As first organist, Albrici's brother Bartolomeo would have improvised the organ interpolations in the *alternatim* performance of Palestrina's Mass Ordinary indicated in the order of worship; one can only wonder if he strove for stylistic continuity, or teased the congregants' ears with versets in a post-Frescobaldian style.[23] Discontinuity now defined the musical component of the Dresden liturgies; on this occasion, for example, the ultramodern, as exemplified by Albrici's concerto *O cor meum*,[24] was sandwiched in between Palestrina's *stile antico* Credo and Luther's rather severe Dorian creedal hymn, *Wir glauben all an einen Gott*. In any Lutheran service of the time, the figural music provided musical and textural contrast with the old modal chorales, sung in unison and without accompaniment by the congregation. In Dresden, however, this contrast gained a new dimension, when the early tonal idiom of Albrici and then Peranda replaced the modally informed harmonies of Schütz and his contemporaries.

This order of worship is also the only one to record a Dresden performance of one of Albrici's settings of a text borrowed from Gratiani's 1652 collection. Two versions of Albrici's *O cor meum* survive in the Düben collection in Uppsala, in copies made within a decade of Albrici's 1663 departure from Dresden. Gustav Düben copied sets of individual parts as well as organ tablatures for both versions, and dated one tablature "16.2.1664," the other "1671."[25] Bruno Grusnick suggested that both sets of parts originated contemporaneously with their respective tablature sources, given the close correspondence between each.[26] Only the composition copied in 1664, however, includes the entire text as set by Gratiani. In the later version, Albrici elim-

23. In the order of worship, alongside the listing of the Kyrie, Christe, and Kyrie runs the rubric "*A cappella*, with instruments; between each section the organ was played, Palestrina's composition" ("*Choraliter* mit Instrumenten, darzwischen iedesmahl die Orgel gebrauchet wurde, *Praenestini composition*"). This is the sole documented *colla parte* and *alternatim* performance of a Mass Ordinary in the corpus of service orders from Dresden and may reflect a practice normally left unrecorded by court secretaries.

24. In the order of worship, Albrici's *O cor meum* is identified as a "Concert." While the published Roman antecedents of this repertoire bear the designation "motet," the Dresden works of Albrici and Peranda generally receive the designation "concerto" in the court diaries; in those volumes, the term "motet" generally refers to a composition in *stile antico*. See also the discussion of genre designations in Frandsen 1997-1:126–45.

25. S-Uu VMHS 77:114 and 84:26, respectively (see Appendix II). Musical examples prepared from S-Uu VMHS 1:16 and 97:114.

26. Earlier parts: S-Uu VMHS 1:16, dated 1663 by Grusnick; later parts VMHS 47:11, dated 1671 by Grusnick; see Grusnick 1966:81, 140. Modern editions of both in Frandsen 1997-3:196–222 (earlier), 223–45 (later).

inated a total of sixteen lines of poetry and made numerous other musical changes, in an apparent effort to streamline the composition and reduce the amount of musical repetition. It is likely that he presented the earlier composition in December 1660 and had composed the work either in Dresden or in Stockholm.

In its exhibition of a number of distinctly Roman traits, such as the inclusion of arias within the context of an ensemble work, and tutti restatements of various types, Albrici's earlier setting of *O cor meum* attests to his experience with the Roman idiom. But the concerto also reveals his efforts to redefine that idiom somewhat, in order that it might better serve his new northern context. Thus, in response to the musical traditions of his new artistic environment, which had long shown a partiality toward the participation of instruments in the sacred concerto, Albrici abandons the sparser texture of the Roman solo motet for a much richer scoring that includes two sopranos, a complement of either two or five strings (two violins, two treble viols, and violone), and basso continuo.[27] Like his new German colleagues, he employs the instrumental ensemble as an articulative agent that also furnishes timbral and textural contrasts. He opens the concerto with an instrumental sinfonia in triple meter, and quickly establishes the affect of tranquillity that pervades the composition. His reading of this *vanitas* text, however, differs considerably from that of Gratiani; for Albrici, the serene joy in Christ's love expressed by the speaker annuls completely the harsh sentiments of the opening, and calls forth a musical response whose affective language takes its inspiration from the speaker's later serenity (Ex. 5.7).

In Albrici's opening duet, the dramatic rhetoric of Gratiani's opening has disappeared and has been replaced by a gentle invocation cast in gracefully flowing melodic lines over a steadily moving bass line. Solos and homophonic writing predominate; only at "et vanitatem" do the voices engage in the motivic exchange typical of the *concertato* style. Also absent from Albrici's setting is the sense of urgency that Gratiani creates through rhetorical devices—only in the thirty-second note ornaments of the word "raperis" (mm. 22–23) does the younger composer indulge

27. Each of the individual parts in the Uppsala source VMHS 1:16 bears the descriptive note "Aria â 2 Canti con 2 overo 5 Viole." Düben clearly labeled the parts as "Violino 1," "Violino 2:do," "Viola 3," and "Viola 4:ta." The part for Viola 5 is missing from VMHS 1:16, but the range of the part in the tablature source (VMHS 77:114) suggests that it is a violone part. Düben notated Violins 1 and 2 in treble clef (G2) and Violas 3 and 4 in soprano clef (C1), which suggests that the latter parts were to be played by treble violas da gamba. Given the inconsistent use of the terms "viol." and "viole" in the Düben collection, however, one can often only assume that the term represents a generic reference to "strings" rather than to any specific type of string instrument. As with many works copied by Düben, it is impossible to know if Albrici included all five string instruments, or if the two violas da gamba were added by Düben.

EXAMPLE 5.7 Albrici, *O cor meum*, mm. 17–30

EXAMPLE 5.7 (*continued*)

in a subtle musical reference to the text. In another contrast with Gratiani, Albrici expands the opening portion of the piece by restating nearly all of the material, with the voices exchanged, and adding a slight extension (mm. 39–41).

Albrici carries the placid mood of the opening *concertato* section over into the ensuing aria, a brief setting of the quatrain "Terrena quae cernis" in which he displays his considerable gifts as a melodist. He presents the text in a syllabic, duple-meter setting that opens and closes in the tonic A major (Ex. 5.8), and in which the only melodic expansion involves a very brief codetta (mm. 48–49). Immediately upon the cadence that concludes the strophe, however, Albrici repeats the entire strophe in a five-part harmonization for the instrumental ensemble. This passage, labeled *Sinfonia* in the parts, functions as a ritornello throughout the rest of the concerto. While Albrici regularly employs ritornelli in his concertos, such a reworking of an entire aria strophe for the instrumental complement remains unusual and recalls the tutti restatements so popular with Roman composers. In another nod to that practice, Albrici follows the ritornello with an arrangement of the same aria as a duet for the sopranos, who pass the melody between them, phrase by phrase (mm. 57–65). He follows this duet with yet another statement of the Sinfonia, and thus closes a section of music expanded from eight to thirty-one bars through the varied repetition of the original, brief aria—an artful display of the economy of means.

For the next section of text ("Surge cor meum . . . suavitatis coelicae"), Albrici returns to the *concertato* duet idiom of the opening and treats each phrase of text to a new musical idea, allowing the voices to exchange material in the traditional manner of the sacred concerto. For the three stanzas that close the text, Albrici shifts back to aria style and first assigns a solo strophe to each soprano. To conclude the concerto, however, he presents the final stanza as a duet. In his construction of these strophes, Albrici's interest in musical unity is in evidence already. As these octaves are twice the length of the earlier quatrain, "Terrena quae cernis," Gratiani

EXAMPLE 5.8 Albrici, *O cor meum*, mm. 42–49

apparently felt obliged to compose an entirely new musical setting for the concluding stanzas. Albrici, however, retains the music of the earlier aria strophe for the
first four lines of the longer stanzas and adds complimentary musical material to
accommodate the last four lines in each of the three stanzas (mm. 120–126 in Ex.
5.9). This reuse of the opening aria strophe, which is closed on the tonic, necessi-
tates an emphatic modulation to the dominant in the second half to avoid harmonic
stagnation. This Albrici achieves by immediately proceeding to the dominant in the
second half of the strophe by way of the secondary dominant (mm. 120–23, beat 1),
before returning to the tonic. Finally, he unifies the entire strophe melodically by
borrowing the closing cadential figure from the first half of the strophe (mm. 118–19,
125–26). Through his incorporation of the initial aria here, Albrici creates a musical
bridge between the two parts of the concerto (Ex. 5.9).

After an absence of fifty-three measures, the string ensemble reappears in the
second aria and again supplies ritornelli after each solo strophe, as well as between
the first and second half in the duet. Only in the final sixteen bars of the concerto
does Albrici integrate the instruments into the *concertato* texture (mm. 173–188);

EXAMPLE 5.9 Albrici, *O cor meum*, mm. 112–26

up until this point he has kept the vocal and instrumental domains carefully circumscribed. As the three statements of the ritornello during the aria comprise the ornamented first half of the aria, by the time the concerto concludes, the listener has heard this material ten times, rendered either by instruments or voices.

A number of features of the earlier version of *O cor meum*, such as the graceful melodies and well-crafted harmonies, demonstrate that by the age of twenty-nine, Albrici had become an accomplished composer, one well prepared to lead the Dresden *Hofkapelle* during these crucial years of stylistic transition. In certain respects, however, it is apparent that the work is one of his earlier compositions. In addition to the harmonic traits discussed above, the amount of sheer repetition is unusual among his works, as is the near-complete segregation of the instrumental and vocal ensembles and the paucity of metric contrast—save the opening sinfonia, only the second *concertato* section involves any writing in triple meter. Indeed, Albrici must have found these and other aspects somewhat unsatisfactory, for he later undertook a wholesale revision of the work; among other changes, he eliminated both the first quatrain, and the sinfonia based upon it, and recast the aria in triple meter.

In addition to the stylistic contrast that it affords with Gratiani's setting, however, Albrici's *O cor meum* also stands apart in another respect, for its harmonic language displays a closer affinity with the key of A major than with any modal construct.[28] From the beginning of the sinfonia to the final cadence of the concerto, Albrici establishes and maintains A major as a true tonic and explores the tonic-dominant polarity typical of tonal music; only the few brief tonicizations of IV that occur momentarily dilute the strength of the key that now enjoys tonic pretensions. The harmonic language of *O cor meum*, in which "the tonic of a major or minor key forms the point of departure and focus of a network of tonal relations,"[29] typifies that found in most of Albrici's works and in many of Peranda's. The harmonic language of both composers exhibits a number of features normally associated with tonal harmony, such as a sense of "goal-directedness," a focus on a circumscribed set of harmonic goals, a general restriction of modes to major and minor, an "emancipated" seventh chord,[30] a slower harmonic rhythm, and the absence of harmonic practices and gestures common to the music of previous decades that

28. On the appearance of a key or mode based on A (with a major triad) in late seventeenth-century treatises, see Lester 1989:80–85. The vocal parts of *O cor meum* display three sharps, which is unusual for this date. As the parts are copies made by Düben, it remains impossible to determine whether the signature stems from Albrici himself. Nonetheless, it represents a key signature that was contemporaneous with the composer.

29. Dahlhaus 1990:18, 166.

30. Dahlhaus 1990:61, 64, 143, 157.

tend to weaken the sense of a particular key area as a tonic.[31] But this harmonic idiom is still in its nascent stages—several important features of later tonal music have yet to develop, such as the modulation to and tonicization of closely related keys.[32] Although Albrici and Peranda compose in essentially the same early tonal harmonic idiom, Albrici's compositions display a clearer sense of hierarchical tonal organization and are always oriented toward major and minor keys, while some vestiges of the older modal practice live on in Peranda's surviving works, particularly those in minor keys or modes. Their harmonic practices place them in the first generation of Roman composers who consistently employ a harmonic idiom that is better described as "tonal" than "modal"—the former description fits neither the music of Carissimi, with whose musical style both were familiar, nor that of Gratiani, whose musical style both most closely emulated.[33]

STYLES IN THE DRESDEN REPERTOIRE

In their Dresden concertos, Albrici and Peranda engaged regularly with three contrasting musical styles, each of which has textural implications, in order to lend their works stylistic variety. Two of these, the *concertato* and declamatory styles, appear in the Roman motet repertoire of the 1640s; the third, aria style, first appears there in the early 1650s. *Concertato* style, the most traditional of the three, is characterized by the imitative exchange of text-bound motives, and is the direct descendant of the imitative polyphony that was normative to the *stile antico* motet.[34] While imitation continues to inform the texture of motets and concertos of this era, however, it has forfeited the hegemonic position it once enjoyed and now represents but one of several compositional approaches favored by composers. Intensely imitative passages still appear, however, and dense imitation still occasionally dominates entire

31. These include the use of the minor dominant in a major key, and the major subdominant in a minor key (Dahlhaus 1990:64–65), as well as "tonicizations" of (or arrivals on) VII and tertial shifts that occur mid-phrase.

32. Dahlhaus 1990:164–65.

33. For more extensive observations on the harmonic language of the Dresden composers, see Frandsen 1997-1:273–318.

34. According to Anne Kirwan-Mott, "The adjective *concertato* is applied both to a style of writing which exploits such contrast effects and to the characteristic type of imitation in which these early concertos abound: the interplay of short and rhythmically precise motifs which are tossed between the voices in a fashion which suggests contention between them. In its fairly consistent use of such imitation, the *concertato* style became the Baroque's version of the contrapuntal principle, which in the sixteenth century had been expressed through the motet"; Kirwan-Mott 1981-1:12–13.

compositions, as in Carissimi's *Viderunt te Domine* and Peranda's *Dedit abyssus*.[35] But as cultivated by mid-century Roman composers (including those in Dresden), *concertato* style also displays a distinct tendency to "homophonize"; in other words, the composer establishes an imitative texture at the outset of the passage, but allows it to dissolve quickly into homorhythmic writing. As a result, such sections fall only nominally within the bounds of *concertato* style, for the imitative episodes serve only to animate an otherwise essentially homophonic texture.

Albrici and Peranda also brought to Dresden the type of *bel canto* aria that pervaded the mid-century Italian motet, cantata, and opera. In these aria strophes, a poetic text is presented in a musical environment that both realizes the general affect of the text in music and underscores the metric and rhyme schemes of the verse. Poetic lines are set to regular phrases of equal or near-equal length that exhibit a consistent rhythmic pattern from phrase to phrase.[36] At times both composers set the text syllabically or nearly so, while at other times they expand their strophes with melismatic writing. Rarely, however, are these melismatic passages technically demanding; such writing is reserved for the more declamatory sections of the concerto. Like their predecessors, Albrici and Peranda typically cast their aria strophes in extended bipartite (ABB′) form. But unlike their Roman mentors, both often take advantage of the instruments at their disposal, and articulate the three sections of their more expansive strophes with brief ritornelli.

The Problem of "Arioso"

The third style employed by Albrici and Peranda, declamatory style, had by the early 1640s become a staple feature of the Roman motet. These passages, generally settings of prose in common time, are grounded firmly in the tradition of recitation over a sustained bass line, but move beyond the "static, repeated-note idiom" manifested by much recitative in contemporary operas and secular cantatas.[37] Instead, they display several features that seem to distinguish them stylistically from recitative per se, including textual repetitions that produce melodic sequences, and florid, virtuosic *passaggi* that often involve dramatic leaps and melismatic writing, as in the bass solo from Carissimi's *Militia est vita hominis* (1643), performed in the Dresden court chapel in 1662 (Ex. 5.10).[38] It is these latter features in particular that have led a number of scholars of sacred music to appropriate the term "arioso" (or "arioso

---

35. See the discussion of both compositions in chapter 6.
36. See also the discussion in Webber 1996:153–58.
37. Gianturco 1990:49.
38. *Floridus Concentus sacras* (Rome: Fei, 1643) [1643¹]. The performance is recorded in SLUB Q 240.

EXAMPLE 5.10 Carissimi, *Militia est vita hominis*, mm. 78–88

style") for such passages, in an attempt to convey the sense that this style, while similar in conception to recitative, differs in several key respects.[39] Despite its broad acceptance in musicological literature on sacred music of this era, however, the linkage of this recitational style with the term "arioso" remains problematic, for it stands

39. See, for example, Snyder 1970:183–84, Jones 1982-1:177–80; Shigihara 1984:488–92; Dixon 1986:28–29, and Frandsen 1997-1:132–45, 220–45 (the present author has reconsidered the question). In his discussion of motets and sacred concertos from the 1620s and 1630s, Roche uses the term "arioso" strictly in the sense of "aria-like"; the passages he

in direct conflict with the contemporary understanding of "arioso" as "a style that is songlike, as opposed to declamatory."[40]

In his *Breve discorso sopra la musica moderna* (Warsaw, 1649), Marco Scacchi sought to reply to those who had criticized use of the recitative style in sacred music as the improper importation of the theatrical style into the church.[41] Significantly, these critics had apparently also complained about the singing of *ariette* in church. In response, the composer-theorist argued that all recitative is not the same and distinguished between theatrical recitative, the "simple representational type (*semplice rappresentativo*), which is the one that is accompanied by acting in the theatre," and a "hybrid (*imbastardito*)" or "mixed" style, in which the recitative is suddenly "varied with *passaggi* and other melodic effects" that are not permitted in the theatrical style.[42] Scacchi goes on to explain that "what the moderns sometimes use in church, according to the demands of the occasion, the place and also the text, is a varied (*modular*) kind of vocal line as opposed to the representational recitative. Thus it is not altogether the same style as is used in theatres."[43] For Scacchi, the charge of impropriety leveled by these critics was unfounded, for they "[did] not consider that [the recitative style sung in church] is not the true representational style."[44] Significantly, in his effort to squelch these critics of musical progress, Scacchi also reveals that they perceived this musical style as recitative, or at least that this term came closest to their experience. His discussion also confirms something that is evident in the repertoire: composers took a different approach to recitative in sacred music. But it is important to note that Scacchi employs the term "recitative" in both contexts without any hesitation and regards the two styles merely as different approaches to a single idiom.

But simply to relegate such passages in the works of Albrici and Peranda to the category of recitative is not unproblematic either, for this sort of declamatory writing seems to have been perceived as somehow distinct from recitative by at least one contemporary theorist who served in the Dresden *Hofkapelle*. In his *Tractatus com-*

identifies as "arioso" are always in triple meter (Roche 1984:70, 75, 80). Kendrick employs the term "arioso" to refer to triple-time (thus "aria-like") passages in works composed in the 1640s, but describes florid recitative in duple meter found in solo motets from the 1680s as "recitative arioso"; see 1996:327–28, 357, and 398–99. Berglund employs the earlier descriptor "stile recitativo" for similar passages in the works of Geist (2002:119–23) (the author thanks Dr. Berglund for profitable e-mail exchanges on this topic).

40. See Budden et al., "Arioso," in *GMO*; unfortunately, the article does not consider the question of the use of this manner of writing in sacred music in the seventeenth century.

41. See Palisca 1972:202–3.

42. Palisca 1972:202–3. See also the discussion in Webber 1996:146–53.

43. Palisca 1972:202–3.

44. Palisca 1972:203.

positionis augmentatis of ca. 1657, Christoph Bernhard discusses two highly embellished contrapuntal styles, the *stylus luxurians communis*, found in vocal works for both church and table, as well as in instrumental pieces, and the *stylus [luxurians] theatralis*, which "derives its name from the place where it is used the most."[45]

> 9. *Contrapunctus luxurians* is the type consisting in part of rather quick notes and strange leaps—so that it is well suited for stirring the affects—and of more kinds of dissonance treatment (or more *figurae melopoeticae*, which others call *licentiae*) than the foregoing. Its melodies agree with the text as much as possible, unlike those of the preceding type [i.e., *contrapunctus gravis*].
> 10. [*Contrapunctus luxurians*] can again be subdivided into *communis* and *comicus*, the first being used everywhere, the second most of all in theatrical productions, although something recitative-like is also often employed in church or table music. No style succeeds as well in moving the heart as *theatralis*.[46]

Given his description of *contrapunctus luxurians*, and his first-hand experience with the Roman repertoire, Bernhard's observation that "something recitative-like" (*etwas recitativisches*) often occurs in sacred as well as in theatrical music undoubtedly refers to the very type of declamatory writing under discussion here. Bernhard goes on to list and illustrate the dissonance figures associated with each style, and then praises Albrici, Peranda, Bontempi, and Schütz (among others) as masters of the *stylus luxurians communis*. He also hails Albrici and Bontempi as worthy exponents of the *stylus theatralis* (or *comicus*), but here curiously omits both Schütz and Peranda, despite the latter's engagement with a number of the dissonance figures identified with this "luxuriant" style.[47] Bernhard's familiarity with the Dresden compositions of Albrici and Peranda sets him apart as the sole contemporary commentator to enjoy a knowledge of the styles evinced by the Dresden repertoire gained from performing the works under the composers themselves. But his comment both relates this declamatory style to recitative and simultaneously sets it apart as somehow distinct from that style, without offering an explanation of the subtleties that separate the two. As a musician who performed the repertoire in question, his apparent reluctance to associate this declamatory style with recitative without some degree of qualification suggests that the hesitation of modern scholars to do the same has some foundation in history. But even in his imprecision, he clearly regards this style as declamatory, rather than "aria-like."

Several features common to recitative are also common to the declamatory passages found in the works of Albrici and Peranda: duple meter, scoring for voice and

---

45. Hilse 1973:91, 110.
46. Hilse 1973:35.
47. Hilse 1973:122.

continuo alone, a slow-moving or sustained bass line, and recitational style, at least in part. But beyond these, their declamatory style is undergirded by drama and powerful rhetoric. Both composers draw upon a variety of means to breathe life into the text, including the rhetorical placement of rests, the creation of lines that leap in an angular fashion, frequently outlining chords, the use of sudden, often tertial, harmonic shifts, and the inclusion of outbursts of florid passage-work; in addition, when writing for the bass, both composers explore the extremes of the singer's range and regularly demand leaps of an octave or more. Finally, their declamatory passages are intensified through the use of many of the dissonance figures codified by Bernhard (below),[48] as well as the rhetorical repetition figures common to music of the era.

DISSONANCE FIGURES OF CHRISTOPH BERNHARD

From the *stylus luxurians communis*:

anticipatio notae: anticipation of a note, either ascending or descending

multiplicatio: division of a dissonant note into several smaller notes

passus duriusculus: a melodic progression by semitones, or one that includes diminished or augmented intervals

prolongatio: a dissonance that is longer in value than the preceding consonance

quaesitio notae: "occurs when part of a note is cut off, so that this may be placed in front of the following note in the degree immediately below"

saltus duriusculus: a harsh intervallic leap

syncopatio catachrestica: "occurs when a syncopation [suspension] is not resolved through a subsequent consonance a step below, as the rule demands"

variatio: vocal ornamentation, usually divisions or *passaggio*

From the *stylus theatralis*:

extensio: "the rather sizable lengthening of a dissonance, generally combined with *multiplicatio*"

A number of these figures appear in a declamatory passage for tenor from Peranda's *Languet cor meum*, the text of which begins with a panegyrical salutation and concludes with an entreaty:

Immensae bonitatis,	Lord of immeasurable goodness,
dulcedinis infinitae,	infinite sweetness,
consolationis aeternae,	eternal consolation,
solatii indesinentis Deus:	boundless solace:
concede mihi nil amare,	grant to me to love nothing,

48. Hilse 1973:90–110.

nil desiderare,   to long for nothing,
nil concupiscere   to desire nothing
praeter te, Deum meum.   beside you, my God.

In his setting of the opening panegyric, Peranda builds slowly, hinting at things to come with a few pungent diminished intervals (*passus duriusculae*) before breaking through the "bounds" in an uncontrolled passage of *variatio* at "indesinentis." In the latter half of the text, the author-compiler employs *anaphora* or *repetitio*, which occurs "when the beginnings of numerous subsequent phrases are formed with one and the same word" (here "nil").[49] In order to reflect this textual parallelism, but also to capture the sense of emotional metamorphosis from love to desire inherent in the text, Peranda relies on *epizeuxis*, the "immediate and emphatic repetition of a word, note, motif, or phrase,"[50] and effects a musical intensification of the passage through the presentation of each successive phrase a perfect fourth higher. Both this climactic passage and the conclusion that follows are rife with the dissonance figures catalogued by Bernhard (Ex. 5.11).[51]

The vast majority of "recitative-like" passages in the works of Albrici and Peranda, here characterized as "declamatory," share many of the musical attributes exhibited by the tenor solo from *Languet cor meum*. A few, however, display some of the melodic and formal features more closely associated with the aria, and for these the term "arioso" seems more appropriate. Perhaps not insignificantly, the instrumental ensemble accompanies each of these solos, which seems to have caused the composer to moderate the style somewhat.[52] In an example drawn from Albrici's *Mihi autem*, an arioso passage appears amid the stanzas of an aria. This solo concerto for soprano, two violins, viola da gamba (bass clef), and continuo belongs to Albrici's first group of concertos for Dresden; although the court diaries include no references to the work, it had already found its way to Düben's hands in Stockholm by 1664.[53] The text opens with an altered version of Ps 72:28 and continues with stanzas written in emulation of the *Jubilus Bernhardi*. Albrici uses the psalm text as the basis for the concerto for voice and instruments that frames the aria. In the latter, he sets stanzas 1, 2, and 4 for voice and continuo only, and fashions lilting triple-meter settings that are very similar to one another (Ex. 5.12).[54]

In stanza 3, however, Albrici alters his approach. Although the speaker made some oblique allusions to the mystical *Gedankengut* in stanza 1, he now begins to speak

---

49. Barthel 1997:186; the definition is drawn from the *Epitome* of Susenbrotus.
50. Barthel 1997:263.
51. Musical example prepared from SLUB 1738-E-508.
52. See also the discussion of Peranda's *Jesu dulcis, Jesu pie* in chapter 6.
53. The tablature source in the Düben collection, S-Uu VMHS 77:131, is dated 1664.
54. Musical examples prepared from S-Uu VMHS 1:5.

EXAMPLE 5.11 Peranda, *Languet cor meum*, mm. 207–15

explicitly of mystical union and colors his speech with the metaphor of the *Sponsa* and *Sponsus* drawn from the Song of Songs. In response to this sudden heightening of emotion, Albrici heightens the intensity musically with a shift to duple meter, a slowing of the tempo to *adagio*, and the introduction of a "halo" of strings that envelops the vocal part (Ex. 5.13). He does not abandon the melodic content of the previous strophes, however, but refashions it in the new duple-meter framework. But his rhythmic treatment of the melody here, particularly his use of rests between the phrases, does alter the way in which the listener perceives the text. The insistent, somewhat breathless quality of the previous strophes disappears, and the listener now has the opportunity to contemplate each line of the stanza. Through his rhythmic placement of the text, Albrici also lends declamational weight to individual words, particularly the adulatory superlatives with which the speaker describes Christ—"dulcissime, clementissime." In *adagio* settings such as this, the singer may well have exercised great interpretational freedom by prolonging accented syllables

Jesu Rex potentissime,   Jesus most powerful king,
amator fidelissime,   most faithful lover,
salvator benignissime,   most kind savior,
spes suspirantis animae.   hope of the sighing soul.

EXAMPLE 5.12 Albrici, *Mihi autem*, mm. 28–42

and by interpreting the brief rests as rhetorical pauses—all of which would place even more distance between the strophe and the stylistic norms of the aria. While "O sponse mi dulcissime" might be described as a slow aria in duple meter, it is much better seen as a passage in arioso style, for the former characterization would not accurately reflect its relationship to the other arias in Albrici's output, which are uniformly in moderate to fast tempi, make no rhetorical use of rests, and display rhythmic regularity.[55]

55. See, for example, the aria from *O cor meum* in Ex. 5.8. above.

O sponse mi dulcissime,   O my sweetest bridegroom,
O Deus clementissime,   O most merciful God,
tua mea est anima   my soul is your bride,
sponsa quamvis adultera.   though an unfaithful one.

EXAMPLE 5.13 Albrici, *Mihi autem*, mm. 76–86

EXAMPLE 5.13 (*continued*)

Still, a small number of the declamatory passages found in the Dresden repertoire are best described as recitative, despite Bernhard's apparent reluctance to do so, due to the straightforward recitational style employed. These include passages of accompanied recitative, several examples of which appear in Peranda's concerto, *Peccavi o Domine*, scored for soprano, alto, bass, two violins, and continuo.[56] The deeply penitential prose text falls into six sections, each of which forms a complete utterance, and Peranda sets the first three sections as highly dramatic passages of accompanied recitative for the alto, soprano, and bass, respectively. The soprano solo (mm. 57–79) well represents the style found in all three (Ex. 5.14). Unlike the declamatory passage in *Languet cor meum*, here the stiffly angular melodic line, which chiefly follows the chordal outline, is vertical in conception, and conveys no sense of forward motion. Each phrase is replete with repeated pitches, and the rhythm is derived directly from the stress pattern of the words. Coloratura is completely absent, as if the singing of *passaggi* would in itself betray a want of true penitence. In its use of textual repetition and rhetorical repetition figures it recalls the declamational style found in Carissimi's oratorios, and may well provide a glimpse of Peranda's own oratorio style, forever lost with his oratorio *Il sacrificio di Iephte*.

56. SLUB 1738-E-524a; see the text, translation, and discussion in chapter 4.

EXAMPLE 5.14 Peranda, *Peccavi o Domine*, mm. 57–72

EXAMPLE 5.14 (*continued*)

TEXTUAL AND MUSICAL FORM IN THE DRESDEN CONCERTO

With the exception of the concertos with aria, whose texts are either similar or identical in structure, the majority of concertos by Albrici, Peranda, and Cherici do not easily fall into categories defined by form. Instead, these highly combinative texts result in works that do not share their form with any other. While the textual media employed by the author-compiler do not dictate the composer's stylistic response in this repertoire, they do seem to limit his compositional choices to some extent.[57] Settings of prose texts, for example, only rarely include true arias, while settings of poetic texts tend to be dominated by aria-style writing. But both prose and poetic texts also call forth the solo with tutti restatement device so common in Rome, which clearly suggests that the composer did not feel bound or limited by the textual medium. Settings of texts that intermingle prose with poetry generally display an attendant mixture of musical styles, but even here, with the exception of the textual format associated with the concerto with aria, one cannot always predict the composer's musical response by examining the text alone. Indeed, that which lends the Dresden repertoire its individuality is precisely this celebration of variety in the approach to style and form on the part of the composers.

From its inception, the sacred concerto in both Italy and Germany generally involved a prose text exposed, at least for some portion of the work, to treatment in imitation. In the Dresden repertoire of some sixty years later, however, prose

57. In her discussion of Carissimi's cantatas, Rose expressed the opinion that "the musician viewed the text not as a determinant, but as a suggestion or merely a possibility for the direction of his own composition" (Rose 1962:207). Gianturco, however, sees textual form as determinative of musical style and form in the secular cantata repertoire; see Gianturco 1990.

texts elicited a variety of musical approaches—some traditional and others more recent—from the composers, who responded to the particulars of length, structure, and style in each text. Among those Dresden works that might be dubbed "traditional sacred concertos" is the first composition by Albrici with a documentable performance date in Dresden, his jubilant *Hymnum jucunditatis.*[58] This free, encomiastic text is formed of two extended sentences, each of which Albrici apportions into two shorter segments. He then further divides each segment into word groups (e.g., "Hymnum jucunditatis / cantemus Deo nostro") and creates a distinctive motivic identity for each (Ex. 5.15).

Like all of those who engaged with this genre before him, Albrici treats each text-bound motive in *concertato* style and employs repetition and imitation to expand each musical section. As the concerto proceeds from one section to the next, metric contrast is achieved through the simple alternation of duple and triple meter. While the entire work represents an affective treatment of the text, Albrici specifies that the setting of the final textual segment should be performed "Adagio," likely in response to the invocation of mystical themes in that portion of the text ("totus amabilis, totus delectabilis, semper desiderabilis").[59] He then restates the opening section (mm. 8–24) and closes with a highly imitative Alleluia in which he places considerable vocal demands on the two castrati in the form of extended *passaggi*.

While it includes neither declamatory writing nor arias, Albrici's *Misericordias Domini*, a sober setting of Ps 88:2 with an appended Alleluia, exemplifies nonetheless an approach that, although related, still stands quite distinctly apart from that employed in *Hymnum jucunditatis*. Here the composer relies upon one of the musical expansion techniques typical of the Roman repertoire to create a composition of some length—150 measures—from a very brief text.[60] The concerto opens with a seven-measure sinfonia, after which the vocal ensemble (alto, tenor, and bass) presents "Misericordias Domini" in an imitative passage whose extreme brevity allows no motivic development; the meter then shifts to triple for the bass's concise presentation of the phrase "in aeternum cantabo." Albrici then returns to the opening material ("Misericordias Domini"), but expands it by introducing the material heard in mm. 8–9 with a statement of the motive in the soprano part; he then pro-

---

58. Performed during the "Festival of Peace" (*Friedensfest*) held on 13 May 1660; Sächs HStA OHMA N IV Nr. 1, fols. 13r, 16r. Modern edition in Frandsen 1997-3:71–92. For the complete scorings of the works discussed in this section, see Appendix II. Musical example prepared from D-B Mus. ms. 501, no. 3.

59. This is one of very few tempo markings to appear in these manuscripts, and may derive from the copyist.

60. Modern edition in Frandsen 1997-3:171–83; text and translation in chapter 4. Musical example prepared from S-Uu VMHS 1:14.

Let us sing a hymn of pleasantness to our Lord.

EXAMPLE 5.15 Albrici, *Hymnum jucunditatis*, mm. 8–17

ceeds to "in aeternum cantabo," but now assigns this material to the vocal ensemble. Here Albrici lends rhetorical weight to the thematic material first presented by the bass through motivic development and repetition; when considered together with the following instrumental restatement of the vocal material as well as the vocal coda, the length of the section has undergone a six-fold expansion (Ex. 5.16). Albrici then shifts back to duple meter for a *concertato*-style presentation of the concluding

EXAMPLE 5.16 Albrici, *Misericordias Domini*, mm. 8–30

EXAMPLE 5.16 *(continued)*

phrases of the text ("in generationem et generationem / annunciabo veritatem tuam in ore meo"), to which he assigns two contrasting musical motives, the first of which recalls the opening motive. Upon the conclusion of the Psalm text, Albrici restates the opening portion of the concerto in its entirety (fifty measures), then closes the concerto with two iterations of an Alleluia in *concertato* style, expanded through the instrumental echoes of each vocal statement.

Other compositions based on prose texts include works that evince a more for-ward-looking style through their inclusion of both declamatory passages and *concertato*-style writing. In one such work, Peranda's *Quo tendimus mortales*, for two sopranos, bass, and continuo, the three singers present much of the text in *concer-*

tato style, but the concerto opens with a virtuosic showcase for the bass singer.[61] The bass who performed the work in the mid-1660s may well have been the German Johann Jäger, who had joined the *Hofkapelle* by 1662; the Italian bass Sauli had left in 1663, and Scandalibeni and Cottini had yet to arrive.[62] In *Quo tendimus*, the bass soloist represents the questioning Speaker of Ecclesiastes and opens the work with a technically demanding declamatory solo in which he puts forth a series of unanswerable questions. In the first of these—"Whither do we strive, mortals that we are?"— Peranda uses *catabasis* to associate the "mortals" addressed by the speaker with the base and lowly.[63] After the expansive beginning, however, he quickens the rhythmic pace of the second question ("Whither do we proceed, we wretched ones?"), and continues to build toward the cadence through the third question ("Whither do we hasten, we unhappy beings?") by employing *epizeuxis*. Peranda then employs a tertial shift (Ex. 5.17, mm. 9–10) to set off the speaker's next words, with which he cautions all who will listen about the inevitability and finality of death: "behold, we all die, and we, like water that cannot be recovered, are spilled upon the ground." Peranda's musical response to the speaker's nihilistic summation of the human condition results in the longest, most demanding passage for the bass to appear in the Dresden repertoire.[64] He takes his inspiration from "dilabimur" ("we are spilled"), which he vividly portrays in a dramatic cascade of thirty-second notes that embellish a seemingly infinite chain of descending thirds; the length of the sequence twice forces him to double the line back on itself to accommodate the singer's range. When the singer reaches low *A* for the second time, both patterns suddenly change—the melodic motion now ascends by perfect fourths, and the ornament ascends through a third, only to fall back to its starting point, but finally reaches *b*, the highest pitch yet heard. The bass scarcely has an opportunity to brush

61. Text and translation in chapter 4; modern edition in Frandsen 1997-3:709–19. Musical example prepared from SLUB 1738-E-519 and S-Uu VMHS 1:19.

62. See the discussion of the *Hofkapelle* personnel in chapter 2. Mattheson included an anecdote regarding Jäger's vocal abilities in his *Grundlage* article on Christoph Bernhard: "Jäger, the German bass, . . . lay in wait for the cadenzas of the castrati, which they greatly prolonged; when they were finished, Jäger followed and made his miraculous *passaggi* in front of them, much better than theirs" ("Jäger, der deutsche Bassist, . . . laurete auf die Cadentzen der Castraten, die sie lange ausdehnten; wenn solche nun vorbey, kam Jäger hernach, und machte, vor sich, seine wunderwürdige Passaggien, viel besser, als jene"; 1740/1994:18).

63. Barthel defines *catabasis* as "a descending musical passage which expresses descending, lowly, or negative images or affections (Barthel 1997:214).

64. Such an overt demonstration of human skill and sensual pleasure stands as an apparent (and doubtless intentional) contradiction to the *vanitas* theme; see Austern 2003:293–96, 312–13.

EXAMPLE 5.17 Peranda, *Quo tendimus mortales*, mm. 1–39

EXAMPLE 5.17 (*continued*)

the note, however, before he must plummet to low *D* for the cadence that concludes the section (Ex. 5.17, mm. 1–19).

Once he has come to the end of this emphatic pronouncement, the speaker poses a second set of searching questions: "To what purpose our life? To what purpose the pretension of our age? To what purpose the boasting of our fathers?" Each of these new questions, however, he answers with the famous words from Ecclesiastes: "vanity of vanities, and all is vanity." Here Peranda elects to enhance the dialogic nature of the text and assigns these three responses to two soprano castrati, whose voices contrast dramatically with that of the bass. He casts their pronouncements in a light passage in triple-meter that seems to mock the speaker and instantiate vanity itself. At the conclusion of their musical retort, they disappear into the ether in ascending octave scales.[65] Each of the speaker's profound questions calls forth this same taunting response, and thus the mood during these exchanges shifts constantly between gravity and superficiality (Ex. 5.17, mm. 20–39).

Several of the techniques noted above reappear in settings of texts that comprise poetry throughout, but that involve a mixture of stanzaic types. In those texts in which the stanzas are metrically identical, however, the inclusion of metric verse usually induces the composer to compose arias, and spawns some approaches not yet discussed. In Albrici's *Quam suave est*, for example, the text comprises four stanzas that alternate between tercets and quatrains; all four share the same trochaic tetrameter. Albrici treats each in the same manner: the soprano first presents the entire stanza in a metric aria style, and the tutti restates and expands upon this material. As a result, stanzas 3 and 4 are the musical equivalents of stanzas 1 and 2. In *Ecce plangendo*, Albrici confronted a text of four stanzas, the first three of which share essentially the same metric structure, whereas the final stanza differs entirely.[66] Once again the technique of tutti restatement and development dominates the composition; after the largely homophonic opening section, the three subsequent stanzas are treated as three different aria-style solos followed by tutti restatements. These two works contrast considerably with those in which the stanzaic types are identical throughout. In both Albrici's *Jesu nostra redemptio* and Peranda's *O Jesu mi dulcissime*, for example, the composers cast the texts as concertos with aria. In these works, the first stanza is set as a concerto, while the subsequent stanzas are set as an aria, the individual strophes of which are sung by the various soloists in the ensemble; following the last stanza, the opening concerto is repeated.

Different still in conception is one of the few large-scale works that survives from this era in the court's musical history, Peranda's *Veni Sancte Spiritus*.[67] Here Peranda extracted eight stanzas (1–3, 5, 7–10) from the sequence for Pentecost for a grand concerto to adorn the festal *Hauptgottesdienst*, and cast the work in a refrain form. Accompanied only by the continuo group, a solo soprano introduces the first line of the text as a motto that is echoed immediately by the full instrumental ensemble (five-part *favoriti* plus *ripieni*). The soprano then proceeds with the stanza, accompanied by the instrumental *favoriti* (strings and bassoon), in a lyrical yet vocally demanding presentation of the text that is entirely worthy of the feast. The next three stanzas (2, 3, and 5) are presented either by a bass soloist or a trio of the lower solo

---

65. One might easily associate these disappearing lines with the evanescent bubbles that formed part of the *vanitas* trope; see Austern 2003:299–309.

66. Modern edition in Frandsen 1997-3:60–69.

67. Modern edition in Frandsen 1997-3:893–929. Musical example prepared from SLUB 1738-E-526.

voices, and the soprano enters with the refrain after each stanza. But at the refrain statement that follows stanza 5, Peranda becomes more ingenious with its use: here the soprano begins as usual, but after the first phrase, the three lower voices co-opt the refrain and present it in its entirety, accompanied only by the continuo. This frees the soprano to present stanza 7, but the trio twice interrupts the stanza, singing the first line of the refrain. In stanza 8 ("Flecte quod est rigidum"), Peranda reverses the procedure—the trio presents the stanza, with interjections from the soprano (Ex. 5.18). This trope-like intercalation works to intensify the rhetorical effect of the refrain, as the six petitions heard in these two stanzas, each of which calls upon the Holy Spirit to work His renewing power, are juxtaposed with the central appeal, "Come, Holy Spirit." After these two stanzas, Peranda presents the original refrain in its entirety one last time and then abandons it altogether, at which point the full ensemble (SATB *favoriti* and *ripieni* plus instruments) enters and lends its collective weight to stanza 9, in a homophonic triple-meter setting. The final stanza is first presented in *concertato* style by the *favoriti*, both vocal and instrumental, who are then joined by the entire ensemble for a grand conclusion.

The majority of concertos in the Dresden repertoire feature texts in which prose and poetry appear in various combinations. Most of the mixed texts are unique in structure, and thus the majority of concertos are as well, but this group of texts also includes those of the concerto with aria, which form a subgroup that stands out as distinct. Texts that display various patterns of elements dominate this textual repertoire, however, and the musical responses of the Dresden Kapellmeisters to these mixed texts resulted in a body of concertos that display a multiplicity of formal designs. Once again, the stylistic and formal heterogeneity of these compositions demonstrates that while the textual medium might suggest options to the composer, it never forced predetermined choices upon him. For example, in *Spirate suaves*, a concerto for two sopranos, two violins, bassoon, and continuo,[68] Peranda set an encomiastic text that opens with two quatrains of amphibrachic verse, followed by two passages of prose, each of which is paired with a tercet of amphibrachic verse, and which concludes with Alleluia.[69] In his setting, Peranda once again eschews an introductory sinfonia, and begins immediately with a two-stanza strophic duet in aria style. Following the duet, each soprano presents a solo declamatory passage and an aria strophe; the two singers then join ranks for a concluding Alleluia in *concertato* style. Although its form and style typify pieces in this repertoire with composite texts, *Spirate* nevertheless stretches the definition of the word "concerto" considerably, for nothing resembling *concertato*-style writing appears until the very end of the work.

68. See the information regarding a performance with cornetti in Appendix II.

69. Text and translation in chapter 4; modern edition in Frandsen 1997-3:782–809. Musical examples prepared from S-Uu 30:11 and D-B Mus. ms. 17081 no. 15.

1. Veni, Sancte Spiritus.   Come, Holy Spirit.

8. Flecte quod est rigidum,   Bend that which is rigid,
   fove quod est frigidum,   warm that which is cold,
   rege quod est devium.   straighten that which is crooked

EXAMPLE 5.18 Peranda, *Veni Sancte Spiritus*, mm. 107–20

EXAMPLE 5.18 (*continued*)

Several aspects of this setting are worthy of notice. First, in addition to setting the tercets to the same music, Peranda also uses strophic variation technique to relate the two declamatory passages as well (see Ex. 5.19, where the two are presented together for purposes of comparison; the instrumental parts have been omitted). In comparison to the text of the first of these ("Hodierna"), the second ("Plaude") projects a heightened sense of emotion, due to the shift to the imperative mood, and Peranda captures this emotional heightening largely through the employment of the rhetorical repetition figure *paronomasia*, in which a phrase is transposed and restated,

EXAMPLE 5.18 (*continued*)

with new material added for emphasis. The use of this figure, however, demands some musical compromise with respect to the strophic variation. At the outset, the speaker exuberantly iterates the imperative "plaude" (mm. 129–30) before coming to the object of the directive, "mater ecclesia," and then repeats "hodiernae" in a similar manner at the outset of the third phrase (mm. 134–35). While the opening phrase of the previous passage ("Hodierna") easily accommodates its own alteration in the second through *diminutio*, Peranda's use of *paronomasia* in measures 134–35 involves the insertion of entirely new material. And in the fourth phrase, at "convoca coetum" (mm. 137–40), Peranda's deployment of the figure requires that he deviate completely

EXAMPLE 5.19 Peranda, *Spirate suaves*, mm. 76–89, 129–45

EXAMPLE 5.19 (*continued*)

from the melody and harmony of the first passage. Despite these changes, however, the two settings share enough material to stand as musical equivalents.

Paired with these declamatory passages are two melodically identical aria strophes, based on amphibrachic tercets, which together constitute another interrupted aria. While their style is quite typical of the arias of both composers—lilting triple meter, conjunct melodic lines—their form is not. In each strophe, Peranda fashions a miniature motto aria in ABA' form (Ex. 5.20). The brief motto opening, with its trill, forms the melodic and rhythmic kernel of the entire strophe. Rather than expand the individual lines with extended melismas, as he does in various arias, Peranda opts instead for three different expansion techniques in his effort to create strophes from these succinct stanzas that will be sufficient in length to balance the declamatory passages. One of these techniques is the motto opening; the second is the immediate restatement of both the second and third lines of text. The third, however, involves the use of da capo form, which here makes its sole appearance in a work by Peranda.[70] Immediately upon the completion of the restatement of line 3, Peranda repeats the opening motto and the instrumental response. To avoid a modulation, however, he quickly jettisons the opening material and segues instead into the melismatic line heard previously (mm. 103–10).

Just as interesting here is Peranda's motivic approach in the Alleluia section. In some of the Alleluia or Amen sections that conclude their concertos, Albrici and Peranda wed the text to a single theme, one that usually involves the sequential treatment of a brief sixteenth-note motive; some of these sections involve the simple iteration of this theme, while others resemble fugues, or borrow from fugal procedures. In some concertos, however, they establish two or more themes, each of which is associated with the same text. The formal procedure used in Alleluia sections with multiple themes represents a variant of that seen in most imitative or *concertato*-style sections, in which textual fragments are associated solely with one musical idea. To conclude *Spirate suaves*, Peranda fashions a lively movement built upon four different motives (Ex. 5.21); here, both his generation of the thematic material and his use of it as the movement unfolds represent striking adumbrations of procedures common to the music of the eighteenth century.

Themes A and B involve the sequential treatment of a motive followed by a cadential figure, while themes C and D are much more concise. Each of the four themes bears its own distinctive characteristics and appears at first glance to be independent of the others. Closer inspection of theme B, however, reveals that Peranda has simply borrowed the sixteenth-note figuration that first appears in the latter portion of theme A (m. 187) and subjected it to sequential treatment (see the bracketed notes labeled "x" in Example 5.20 above). Peranda is likely using the rhe-

•

70. The only example of a da capo-form aria in Albrici's concertos appears in his *O Jesu Alpha et Omega*; there the aria strophes exhibit the form ABB'A'.

EXAMPLE 5.20 Peranda, *Spirate suaves*, mm. 92–128

EXAMPLE 5.20 (*continued*)

torical figure *anadiplosis*, "the repetition of the ending of one phrase at the beginning of the following one."[71] But one also might regard this as an early manifestation
of "thematic transformation" *a la* Haydn. In his Sonata 60 in C major (Hob. XVI:
50), Haydn adopts very much the same procedure—he draws a cell from the ornamented restatement of the first theme and uses it as the basis for the transitional
theme that follows.[72] Peranda's resulting theme B, introduced by the violins, bears
all the hallmarks of a typical ritornello-like echo of the final bars of a vocal statement, rather than of autonomous material, but it soon establishes its independence.
Once all four motives have been introduced, Peranda presents them in groups, no
two of which are identical: ABCD / ABD / ABDCCB / A´ABB´B´. In a number
of respects, Peranda's treatment of his themes looks ahead to the approach Vivaldi

71. Barthel 1997:180.
72. Hob. XVI: 50; see measures 7–15.

Theme A (Soprano 1):

Theme B (Violin 1):

Themes C and D (Soprano 1):

EXAMPLE 5.21 Peranda, *Spirate suaves*, Alleluia themes A–D

will take to motivic material in many of his concerto ritornelli. Peranda rearranges the order of presentation of thematic material (in the third group), divides longer units and treats each constituent part separately (themes C and D), fuses two non-consecutive motives together (here C to B in mm. 207–208), and finally abandons some themes (C and D) in order to develop others (A and B). As a result, there is much here to tease the ears of the attentive listener.

Settings of more extended mixed texts display the same sorts of textural and stylistic variations seen above. The text of Cherici's *Deplorandus et amarus*, for example, is disposed in seven sections, five of which are stanzas of metric verse.[73] Cherici sets the two opening tercets in trochaic tetrameter as an aria of two ABB′ strophes,

---

73. Text and translation in chapter 4; see also the discussion in chapter 6.

each of which is rendered by one of the two sopranos. These tercets are followed by a quatrain in dactylic dimeter, which Cherici sets as a new, highly florid aria strophe for the bass, also in ABB′ form; each of these three strophes is followed by an instrumental ritornello that incorporates much of the vocal material. Although the following quatrain shares its meter with the previous one, Cherici here abandons solos and elects a fuller vocal texture, and sets the text for the vocal trio in a nearly homophonic style. At this point ("Sistite quid ploratis"), the author-compiler introduces an extended passage of prose, which Cherici presents as a bass recitative that breaks out into disjunct melismas at its conclusion. Another quatrain in trochaic tetrameter catalectic ($-\cup-\cup-\cup\cup$) follows, which Soprano 1 presents as a "walking-bass" aria; the violins, which have been silent for a time, now reenter with a ritornello. Only in the final section, a setting of the brief petition that closes the text, does Cherici marshal the full vocal and instrumental resources; here he involves both voices and instruments in a lively imitative conclusion. Unlike Albrici and Peranda, Cherici did not hail from Roman musical circles, but studied with Giovanni Paolo Colonna (1637–95) in Bologna.[74] The marked similarity in his style and overall approach to that of Albrici and Peranda, however, suggests that by the later decades of the seventeenth century, regional styles had surrendered to national trends to produce a "pan-Italian" style in the Italian sacred concerto and motet. Still, in the works of all three composers described here, the legacy of the early seventeenth-century *concertato alla Romana* remains very much in evidence.

The Development of the Concerto with Aria in Dresden

Among the concertos of the Dresden repertoire there exists a discrete group of compositions that distinguish themselves through their highly patterned use of the musical elements discussed above. In the most straightforward (and most common) type in this group, the "concerto with aria" *per se*, two identical statements of an imitative concerto frame an aria of three to five strophes.[75] Across the group, the use of a

---

74. See Surian, "Cherici," in *GMO*.

75. Krummacher established the nomenclature "concerto-aria cantata" for these compositions back in 1965 (Krummacher 1965:29–31, 34–36). In the years since Krummacher's work appeared, the term has been accepted by a number of scholars; see, for example, Krummacher 1965:36 (reference to acceptance of the term by Friedrich Blume and Martin Geck), Braun 1981:227, Snyder 1997:198–200, Gille 1973:106, and Märker 1995. Given the conflict of the term "cantata" with the designations found in the Dresden court diaries, however, here the revised nomenclature "concerto with aria" will be used to describe such works, in an attempt both to acknowledge the contemporary usage of the designation "concerto" for these works in the court diaries and to avoid the pitfalls of historical incongruity.

concerto as a framing device remains the unifying structural principle; one may see in this a desire for a musically rounded composition. Other works in this category, however, are more expansive and include declamatory passages and/or additional iterations of the concerto. Although the two essential styles of writing with which this genre remains most closely associated, the concerto and the aria, represented essential elements in the works of the Roman school, they did not appear there in this particular configuration; to date, this type of composition has not been identified in the Italian motet repertoire of the seventeenth century.[76] Instead, it appears to be a development in the sacred concerto that took place on northern soil and found no subsequent resonance in Italy.[77] With the development of the concerto with aria, the Saxon capitol can lay claim to yet another major contribution to the history of the sacred concerto, in addition to those of Schütz, for the Dresden Kapellmeisters, particularly Albrici, seem to have conceptualized and cultivated this form soon after their respective arrivals at court. Not long after its emergence in Dresden, the concerto with aria gained such popularity among German composers that it was long regarded as a German innovation.[78]

A number of developments that took place in the Roman motet repertoire of the 1640s and 1650s, including the use of refrains and the restatement of material, had formal as well as stylistic implications for the later concerto with aria. When Roman composers of the 1640s began to privilege declamatory solos in their sacred compositions, they frequently contrasted these with writing for the vocal ensemble. At times, however, they presented such passages in regular alternation with a *concertato*-style tutti that was either identical or slightly reworked each time, the result of which was a rondo-like refrain structure.[79] In Giovanni Marciani's *Quasi stella matutina* (1647), for example, the composer follows each declamatory solo with a statement of a triple-meter refrain, "O virum praeclarissimum," the first portion of which is musically identical each time (see Table 5.4 and Ex. 5.22).[80]

Following the third statement of the refrain *cum extensio*, Marciani concludes the motet with an Alleluia in *concertato* style. Another motet in the same collec-

76. An examination of Roman motet collections of the 1640s, and those of Gratiani from 1650, 1652, and 1656 reveals no works in this form. According to Andrew Jones, Carissimi does not appear to have composed works in this form (private correspondence, 18 July 1995).

77. To date, scholarship has revealed no examples of the concerto with aria in the Italian motet repertoire of ca. 1650–1700.

78. On Albrici's contribution to the development of the concerto with aria, and the dating of his concertos *vis a vis* those of David Pohle, the first German to compose works of this type, see Frandsen 1996 and 1997-1:246–72.

79. Rondo-like forms also appear among the secular cantatas of Carissimi as well; see Rose 1962:207–8.

80. *Floridus modulorum Hortus ab excellentissimus musices auctoribus...* (Rome, A. Fei,1647). Musical example prepared from S-Uu UVMTR 553–57.

Table 5.4 Marciani, *Quasi stella matutina*, Musical Structure

Text	Meter	Scoring and Style
Quasi stella matutina, et quasi sol refulgens in medio nebule; praeclaris virtutum et sanctitatis laudibus terrarum orbem illustravit Beatus N.	C	Alto: declamatory
O virum praeclarissimum, *o virum beatissimum,* *o virum dignissimum,* ut folium gloriae in caelis hodie teneat.	3/2	Tutti: *concertato*
Quasi scintillae in arundi neto, et quasi lampades ignis atque flammarum refulgent hodie in templo Dei praecelsa merita Beati N.	C	Tenor: declamatory
O virum praeclarissimum, *o virum beatissimum,* *o virum dignissimum,* ut mereatur hodie coronam pulchritudinis accipere a Domino.	3/2	Tutti: *concertato*
Quasi flos rosarum in diebus vernis, et quasi lilia in transitu aquae, et quasi hortus voluptatis fructificavit in conspectu Domini suavitatem odoris Beatus N.	C	Bass: declamatory
O virum praeclarissimum, *o virum beatissimum,* *o virum dignissimum,* ut gaudeat cum angelis, exultet cum Archangelis, cum summo Dei Filio	3/2	Tutti: *concertato*
triumphet in aeternum,	C	
Alleluia.	3/2	Tutti: *concertato*

tion, Virgilio Mazzocchi's *Domus mea*, follows the same general pattern as the Marciani work, although Mazzocchi's refrain statements are identical. Similar examples appear in the collections of Florido de Silvestris from 1648 and 1649.[81] In Gratiani's *Resonate, jubilate* (1648), each iteration of the refrain represents a reworking of the

---

81. *R. Floridus canonicus . . . Florida verba* (1648); *R. Floridus canonicus . . . cantiones alias sacras ab excellentissimus auctoribus* (1649). See also Jones 1982-1:280.

EXAMPLE 5.22 Marciani, *Quasi stella matutina*, mm. 18–30

original motive, while in Carissimi's *Surgamus, eamus* (1649), the statement of the refrain is identical each time. The latter work, scored for alto, tenor, bass, and continuo, was also heard in Dresden; Albrici presented it in the court chapel on three occasions in 1662.[82] As discussed above, the works in these and other collections of the 1640s exhibit a growing preoccupation with declamatory writing for the solo voice, and an increasing preference for this sort of contrast between solo declamatory passages and *concertato*-style tuttis.

Two other innovations of the Roman motet that figure prominently in the Dresden concerto repertoire in general also contributed to the development of the concerto with aria: the incorporation of poetic stanzas and their musical realization as solo arias, and the pairing of declamatory passages with arias in solo motets. In his 1652 collection of solo motets, Gratiani adopts the latter principle, seen above in *O cor meum*, in nearly every composition. In several motets in the collection, however, such as *Hodie collaetantur caeli cives*, he alternates regularly between melodically related declamatory passages and the individual strophes of an aria, the con-

82. 13 April, 21 September, and 24 December (SLUB Q 240).

sequence of which is the sort of interrupted aria seen in his *Rex magne* of 1650.[83] In *Hodie collaetantur*, he also closes each declamatory passage with the same text and music, much in the manner of a refrain; as a result, a strophic approach is found in both the declamatory and lyrical portions of the motet. Unlike *O cor meum*, however, a declamatory passage (rather than an aria) concludes the motet.

Once he had settled in Dresden, Albrici seems to have synthesized these developments in what became a new variation on the Roman motet. His settings of both *Laboravi clamans* and *O cor meum* point to his attempts to reconcile a familiar textual format with the demands of the court musical institutions in Stockholm and Dresden, but his attempts to adapt these texts as concertos for an ensemble seem to have led him to experiment with other formal solutions. In these newer compositions, Albrici writes for an ensemble of two to four vocalists and several instruments and apportions the solo material equally among the several singers. But as the typical solo motet text favored by Gratiani did not easily allow for such balanced distribution, Albrici seems to have turned to the formal principles inherent in ensemble motets such as *Rex magne* and *Quasi stella matutina* and derived a more symmetrical textual format involving the aria from these Roman models. Albrici's innovation was to frame a strophic aria with two presentations of a vocal concerto, which resulted in a rounded, balanced form—the concerto with aria. The new format allowed him to incorporate tutti sections in *concertato* style for the vocal ensemble and to assign each singer a solo aria strophe, or a solo "set" that comprised a declamatory passage followed by one or two aria strophes. By Christmas 1660 he had begun to present these new compositions in the court worship services on a regular basis, as a comparison of orders of worship from December and January of 1660–61 with his extant works reveals. Of the sixteen psalm settings and sacred concertos presented by Albrici in these liturgies, five concertos survive, four of which exhibit these new formal traits (see Table 5.5).[84]

The second concerto with aria to appear in a Dresden court diary, *Benedicte Domine*, manifests the simplest form of this new type of composition.[85] Albrici introduces the composition with an imitative instrumental sinfonia, the opening of which adumbrates the opening motive of the vocal concerto. Although brief, the

---

83. There, of course, the strophes alternated with sections in *concertato* style. Similar examples from the 1652 collection of solo motets include *Quam pretiosa meritis* and *Plaudite vocibus*.

84. The fifth work is *O cor meum* (discussed above), performed on 30 December 1660; Sächs HStA Loc. 12026, fols. 54r–65r. See Appendix II for the respective liturgical occasions.

85. Modern edition in Frandsen 1997-3:2–25. Scoring: two sopranos, bass, two cornetti, bassoon, and basso continuo. Musical examples prepared from S-Uu VMHS 1:4.

Table 5.5 Concertos with Aria Performed in December 1660 and January 1661

Date	Service	Title	Description
12/23/60	Vespers	*Tu es cor meum*	concerto with aria (expanded)
12/27/60	Vespers	*Benedicte Domine*	concerto with aria
1/1/61	Morning	*Jesu dulcis memoria*	concerto with aria
	Vespers	*Venite cantemus*	concerto with aria

following concerto displays the contrapuntal exchange of text-bound motives so typical of the form in the seventeenth century (Ex. 5.23).

Following a brief instrumental codetta, the more lyrical portion of the work ensues, in which each of the three singers presents a solo strophe (Ex. 5.24). Albrici fashions a strophic-variation aria from the poetic stanzas; while strophes 1 and 3 remain nearly identical, the central strophe, sung by the bass, includes a number of alterations, although it retains essentially the same bass line.[86] Albrici creates extended-bipartite (ABB′) strophes from the three stanzas; slightly curious here is the opening of the B′ section, which begins as an untransposed restatement of the opening of the B section, but which soon takes flight in an extended melisma that carries the harmony back to the tonic A minor. Albrici articulates the first two parts of the strophe with instrumental passages that echo the previous vocal material, then follows each strophe with an instrumental ritornello. At the conclusion of the aria, Albrici restates the opening concerto, now shed of its sinfonia and concluding codetta, and thereby lends the concerto the rounded form that is one of its most distinguishing features.

Two of the other three concertos with aria performed during the Christmas–New Year's period in 1660–61 share their form with *Benedicte Domine*. The fourth, however, exhibits a related but significantly more complex structure that betrays even more clearly the influence of its Roman antecedents. In *Tu es cor meum*, Albrici casts the speaker's introductory utterance as a concerto in triple meter, then employs this concerto as an articulative element throughout the work. Following both the textual format and the musical precedent established by Gratiani in his solo motets, Albrici creates three solo sets, each of which comprises a declamatory passage and an aria strophe, from the alternating passages of prose and metric poetry. By interpolating the opening concerto at regular intervals throughout the piece, following each solo set, Albrici produces a refrain form similar to that found in many Roman ensemble motets, but one now expanded through the addition of aria strophes. In

---

86. The most significant changes occur in bars 100–105, where Albrici omits the melisma sung by both sopranos at this point (compare mm. 51–59 and 141–152).

EXAMPLE 5.23 Albrici, *Benedicte Domine*, mm. 9–21

EXAMPLE 5.23 *(continued)*

EXAMPLE 5.24 Albrici, *Benedicte Domine*, mm. 26–63

EXAMPLE 5.24 *(continued)*

keeping with the traditions of the northern sacred concerto, Albrici incorporates two violins in the scoring; these introduce the concerto and delineate major sectional breaks with brief interludes that echo the vocal material. All in all, *Tu es cor meum* represents a considerably expanded version of the concerto with aria. But in its formal outline and stylistic content, it also clearly demonstrates that, as early as 1660, Albrici had fashioned a type of sacred concerto that shared a number of characteristics with the sacred cantata that appeared much later in the century, in the same geographic region.

A comparison of Albrici's eighteen surviving concertos with aria with the entries in the court diaries reveals his active involvement with this form during his first stay in Dresden (1656–63) and demonstrate his keen interest in both rounded and patterned refrain forms. By the end of 1662 he had already presented at least eleven such works in the court chapel (see Table 5.6 below), and his colleague Peranda had presented at least two. After Albrici's departure in 1663, Peranda continued to work with the concerto with aria; however, the loss of many compositions listed in the diaries of 1665 to 1667 prevents an accurate assessment of the full extent of his activity in this area. During Albrici's later tenures in Dresden (ca. 1669–73 and 1676–80), he continued to present by now familiar concertos with aria in the chapel; works performed during these years include *Cogita o homo* and *Venite cantemus*.[87] Again, due to lacunae in the orders of worship and the staggering loss of musical compositions, one cannot determine to what extent he continued to present new compositions organized around these same formal principles. Of the titles by Albrici that first appear in the court diaries from the 1670s, only *Quid est mundus* survives.[88] One of the surviving sources for another composition, *Mortales audite*, has been assigned a copying date between February 1675 and November 1676 by Rudén; such dates, however, only serve as *termini post quem*, and may or may not suggest an approximate date of composition.[89]

Within a fairly circumscribed formal paradigm, the concertos with aria of Albrici and Peranda display considerable variety, but the principle of an aria framed by a concerto informs nearly every composition. In a few cases, the restatement of the concerto is supplemented by a concluding Alleluia in *concertato* style, while in a few others, this Alleluia replaces the concerto. Albrici frequently restates the opening concerto only once, after the entire aria (CaaaC), but he also shows some affinity for more elaborate refrain structures. In *Cogita o homo*, for example, he breaks up the four-strophe aria with a restatement of the concerto after the first two strophes, and then rounds off the piece with a statement of the concerto at the end; Peranda's

---

87. For additional performance dates, see Appendix II.
88. Modern edition in Frandsen 1997-3:264–304.
89. Rudén 1968, Bilaga I: 25–26; source: S-Uu VMHS 85:52.

Table 5.6 Extant Concertos with Aria by Albrici and Peranda

Composer	Title	First Documented Performance or Date on Manuscript	Form
Albrici	*Tu es cor meum*	23 December 1660	CdaCdaCdaC
Albrici	*Benedicte Domine*	27 December 1660	CaaaC
Albrici	*Jesu dulcis memoria*	1 January 1661	CaaaC
Albrici	*Venite cantemus*	1 January 1661	CaaaC
Albrici	*Sperate in Deo*	22 December 1661	CaaaC
Albrici	*Cogita o homo*	2 February 1662	CaaCaaC
Albrici	*Spargite flores*	6 April 1662	Caa′aa′aa′X*
Albrici	*Ave Jesu Christe*	25 May 1662	CaCaCaC
Peranda	*Si Dominus mecum*	31 May 1662	CaaCaaC
Albrici	*Sive vivimus*	15 June 1662	CaaaC
Albrici	*Omnis caro foenum*	10 August 1662	CaaaaC
Peranda	*Fasciculus myrrhae*	12 October 1662	CaaaadaC
Albrici	*Amo te, laudo te*	30 November 1662	CaadCX
Albrici	*Mihi autem*	Tablature dated 1664**	CaaraC
Peranda	*Languet cor meum*	30 May 1664	CaadaaC†
Peranda	*Te solum aestuat*	30 May 1664	CdadadaC
Peranda	*Repleti sunt omnes*	31 May 1664	CdadaX
Peranda	*Sursum deorsum*	31 May 1664	C¹C²aC¹aC¹aC¹
Peranda	*Dic nobis Maria*	27 March 1665	CaCaCaX
Peranda	*O Jesu mi dulcissime*	9 July 1665	CaaaC
Peranda	*Laetentur coeli*	1 January 1666	CaaaadaC
Peranda	*Si vivo mi Jesu*	16 April 1666	CaaaC
Albrici	*Quid est mundus*	21 June 1678	CraaraaraaX
Albrici	*Jesu nostra redemptio*	copied after 9/28/1676††	Caaaac‡
Albrici	*Mortales audite*	copied between 2/1675 and 11/1676‡‡	CaCaCX
Albrici	*O amantissime sponse*	copied after 1690	C¹C²dadadaC¹
Albrici	*O Jesu Alpha et Omega*	copied after 1690	CdadadaX
Albrici	*Ubi est charitas*	copied after 1690#	CdaadaadaaX

Key: C, Concerto; a, aria strophe; d, declamatory passage; r, arioso; X, Alleluia in *concertato* style.

* Here each aria strophe is restated by the vocal ensemble.

** S-Uu VMHS 77:131.

† Here the declamatory passage falls between two different, unrelated arias.

†† Rudén 1968, Bilaga I: 54; source: S-Uu VMHS 86:28.

‡ In the restatement of the concerto Albrici sets a doxology, "Gloria tibi Domine," which is not part of the original hymn.

‡‡ Rudén 1968, Bilaga I: 26; source: S-Uu VMHS 85:52.

These last three works survive in the Bokemeyer collection; see Wollny 1998:60–72.

Si Dominus mecum shares its form with *Cogita*.[90] In *Ave Jesu Christe*, Albrici fashions an interrupted aria by repeating the concerto after each of the three aria strophes. He produces a different variation on the basic form in *Spargite flores*, where he hearkens back to a technique popular with Roman composers and includes tutti restatements of each solo aria; here he also replaces the concluding iteration of the concerto with a tutti Alleluia.[91] In both Peranda's *Fasciculus myrrhae* and Albrici's *Amo te, laudo te*, the author-compiler has included a passage of prose somewhere in the midst of the poetic stanzas; both composers treat this in a declamatory style. In Albrici's *Amo te*, the declamatory passage falls between the aria and the restatement of the opening concerto, which is followed by an Alleluia; in *Fasciculus myrrhae*, Peranda assigns the declamatory passage to the bass, and pairs it with the final strophe of the aria. In *Tu es cor meum*, which exhibits the most complex text in the early group, Albrici creates a refrain-form concerto with aria that includes passages of declamatory writing.[92] Each soloist sings a set that comprises a declamatory passage and an aria strophe, and each set is articulated by a restatement of the opening concerto. All that distinguishes the external form of this composition from Gratiani's *Hodie collaetantur* is Albrici's addition of a *concertato*-style refrain, the idea for which he could have drawn from any number of ensemble motets.

Peranda likely turned his attention to the concerto with aria as a result of the influence of his colleague; the court diaries reveal that he had begun to cultivate pieces of this type by 1662, if not earlier, and an examination of these works demonstrates that he adopted a number of the formal strategies employed by Albrici. For the elector's birthday in 1664, for example, he set a poetic trope on Johann Georg's own *symbolum* or motto, "sursum, deorsum" ("as above, here below").[93] Peranda presented the *symbolum* text, complete with the requisite ascending and descending musical lines, in the opening concerto, and reintroduced this material after each aria strophe, which produced the by-now-familiar interrupted aria. That same year, Peranda presented two concertos with aria, *Repleti sunt omnes* and *Te solum aestuat*, that exhibit the pairing of declamatory passages with aria strophes seen in Albrici's *Tu es cor meum*, but which lack the interior refrain; in addition, like Albrici's *Spargite*, Peranda's *Repleti* also replaces the closing concerto with an Alleluia.[94] In 1665, Peranda borrowed part of the Easter sequence *Victimae paschali laudes* for his *Dic nobis Maria*, which exhibits a refrain form with an appended Alleluia in *concertato* style. In 1665 and 1666, he presented two concertos with aria

90. Modern edition in Frandsen 1997-3:739–50.

91. Modern edition in Frandsen 1997-3:317–66; see also the discussion in chapter 6.

92. Modern edition in Frandsen 1997-3:367–99.

93. Modern edition in Frandsen 1997-3:810–32. See the note on this work in Appendix II.

94. Modern editions in Frandsen 1997-3:720–37, 833–51.

in the court chapel, *O Jesu mi dulcissime* and *Si vivo mi Jesu*, both of which exhibit the most familiar form of the subgenre.[95] While generally a more intimate composition scored for three or four voices and several instruments, the concerto with aria did admit of some textural expansion. Peranda created at least two larger-scale concertos with aria, *Fasciculus myrrhae* and *Laetentur coeli*, by supplementing the scoring of the tutti section with additional voices and instruments *in ripieno*. In the case of the latter, the court diary for 1666 confirms the enhanced scoring of the surviving part set as original to Peranda rather than the Grimma copyist, Samuel Jacobi. The parts that survive include parts for ten singers, five *favoriti* (SSATB) and five *ripieni* (SSATB), and the court secretary recorded the scoring of *Laetentur* as performed on New Year's Day in 1666 as "à 10 voc: et 10 inst: 2 Tromb et Timpagni."[96] While Peranda was clearly involved with this subgenre, his surviving works suggest that he showed somewhat less interest in these highly patterned refrain forms than did Albrici, and preferred freer, less predictable combinations of concerto, declamatory writing, and aria.

The majority of the surviving concertos by the Dresden Kapellmeisters incorporate poetic stanzas set in aria style. However, only the concerto with aria regularly features a set of equivalent stanzas that allows the composer to employ some sort of repeating strophic form, either simple or modified. While the simple strophic arias may include minor alterations in subsequent strophes to accommodate the range of the singer, the modified strophic aria here normally includes one strophe that differs significantly from the others. The contrasting strophe may appear either in the center of the aria, as in Albrici's *Spargite flores* and *Benedicte Domine*, or as its final strophe, as in Peranda's *Te solum aestuat* and *Fasciculus myrrhae*. At times, however, Albrici's modified strophic form begins to approach strophic variation, in that the contrasting strophe represents a recognizable alteration of the others, and the continuo line is essentially retained from strophe to strophe. In *Benedicte Domine*, for example, the bass strophe (mm. 76–109) closely follows the melody and continuo line of the preceding soprano strophe until bar 97, at which point Albrici composes a new section for the bass. In addition to these two strophic forms, strophic-variation arias appear in several of Albrici's concertos, and both he and Peranda composed a few through-

---

95. Modern editions in Frandsen 1997-3:639–54, 768–780.

96. SLUB Q 243, entry for 1 January 1666. The few surviving large-scale works of Albrici and Peranda display the contemporary scoring convention of five-part instrumental groups, a (primarily) string ensemble of two violins, two violas, and bassoon, and a brass ensemble, usually a supplementary group, of two cornetti and three trombones. The instruments in the two groups are identical in cleffing (see, for example, Peranda's *Veni Sancte Spiritus* above). In the case of *Laetentur coeli*, the secretary recorded the scoring as including ten instruments, as well as two trumpets and timpani, which suggests that the exemplar copied by Jacobi (SLUB 1738-E-531) was missing parts for two violas and bassoon.

composed arias. The individual strophes of these arias nearly always open and close in the tonic, even in the interrupted arias, where they are separated by declamatory passages, restatements of the opening concerto, or both. But even when the strophes are not contiguous, the degree of melodic and harmonic identity that both composers lend to the individual strophes makes the designation of "aria" fitting.

Albrici's concertos with aria, which very likely constitute the first manifestation of the form, display enough discrete characteristics to set them apart as a new and distinct subgroup within the sacred concerto genre as cultivated in Dresden. In his engagement with the concerto with aria as early as 1660, if not earlier, Albrici seems to stand alone; neither Gratiani nor Carissimi had composed similar works, nor had Albrici's German contemporaries, such as Hammerschmidt, Capricornus, Ahle, Rosenmüller, Kerll, and others.[97] Works of this type represent virtually half (17 of 35) of Albrici's total extant sacred concertos, a fact that points to a particular inclination toward patterned or balanced formal structures on his part, as well as to the reception of the form, as all of the sources are copies. Within the formal parameters outlined above, however, Albrici's response to individual texts results in distinctive compositions, all of which rely on the same few formal principles. The formal variety seen in these works demonstrates that while he valued the high degree of organization inherent in this formulaic design, he regularly sought opportunities to create variety and contrast within its rather rigid formal constraints. Clearly the concerto with aria represented an important formal vehicle for both Albrici and Peranda, one that allowed them to write for an ensemble of soloists and to distribute solo material equally between them, thereby meeting at least one of the many challenges presented by the competing egos within the Dresden *Hofkapelle*. But some intriguing questions regarding the development of the genre still remain. Was there something essentially German, or particularly Lutheran, about the concerto with aria? Did its creation require a move to the north? Or would Albrici have developed the form in Rome, had he remained there as a *maestro di cappella*? While the answers to these and other questions may rest with Albrici, their pursuit continues to uncover new intricacies in the complex relationship between the musical cultures of Germany and Italy during this era.

---

97. Krummacher examined the printed works of Hammerschmidt, Johann Rudolph Ahle, Rosenmüller, and Capricornus, and found no concertos with aria (Krummacher 1965:473–81). Although a number of concertos by Kerll, a student of Carissimi, include extended bipartite aria strophes, none displays the form of the concerto with aria; see Sandberger 1901. Neither does the concerto with aria appear in Capricornus's *Geistliche CONCERTEN, mit 2. und 3 Stimmen* . . . (Stuttgart: Endter, 1658) or his *Dritter Theil / Geistliche Harmonien / mit zwei und drei Stimmen und 2. Violinen* (Stuttgart: Rößlin, 1664; modern ed. edited by Paul Walker: Samuel Capricornus, *Geistliche Harmonien III*).

The textual and musical commonalities shared by the concertos of Peranda and Albrici and the mid-century Roman motet leave little doubt as to the roots of the idiom that these two Italians transported to the Saxon court. The Dresden works, however, stand as a later manifestation of Roman style, and as such reveal certain discontinuities, each of which was a consequence of the ongoing development of the idiom under new musical and confessional circumstances, far removed in many respects from the source of the tradition. In their works for Dresden, Albrici and Peranda adapted, refined, and synthesized various aspects of the earlier style, and these processes yielded up a repertoire that, while it clearly hearkened back to its models, could simultaneously define itself as separate and distinct from them. Each composer made his own peace with the eternal combatants, tradition and innovation, and through this struggle, left a unique stylistic imprint upon his musical output.

Despite the individual stylistic idiosyncrasies of the two composers, however, the Dresden corpus of sacred concertos can stand as a unified body of works. When viewed as such, five essential characteristics emerge that lend it stylistic unity but also distinguish it from the works of the Roman circle from whence its creators came. First, Albrici and Peranda engaged with an early tonal harmonic idiom, one that did not eschew occasional recollections of the past, but that nevertheless bestowed a fresh patina upon even traditional compositional approaches. Second, both of the Dresden Kapellmeisters regularly incorporated aria strophes into their works for a vocal ensemble and thus turned Gratiani's early experiments in this area into a distinctive element of their approach to the concerto. Third, given the large *instrumentarium* available at the Dresden court, as well as the long tradition of instrumental use under Schütz, the newcomers quickly associated themselves with this northern convention. The Italians in Dresden employed instruments much in the same manner as did their German contemporaries: in introductory sonatas and sinfonias, articulative ritornelli, postludes, and other brief interjections, and in motivic engagement with the voices in *concertato* passages. While the addition of instruments did not change the essential shape of their works, it did expand them texturally, and altered their fundamental sonic essence. Fourth, Albrici and Peranda inclined toward a relaxed approach toward *concertato* style, and viewed it as yet another vehicle for the communication of affect, one that was particularly suited to settings of poetry. And finally, during his first tenure in Dresden, Albrici developed and cultivated a distinct type of concerto that employed either two or all three of the basic stylistic elements discussed above in a highly patterned or schematized arrangement: the concerto with aria. Through these latter works in particular, he left his own indelible mark on seventeenth-century Lutheran church music.

6

Musica pathetica: *Style and Affect* in the Dresden Concerto

ALBRICI AND PERANDA lived in an era when musicians and philosophers alike displayed a fascination with the "passions" or "affects"—the various states of emotion experienced by the human being. Not only did writers seek to distinguish between and quantify the essential emotions, they also sought to explain the phenomenon by which the exposure of the individual to certain stimuli, including musical sounds, could effect emotional change, and they attempted to explain the psycho-physiological processes set in motion by such stimuli that in turn produced these emotional changes. Not surprisingly, music's ability to move the emotions of its listeners became a focus of theoretical inquiry during this era, as well as an aspect of its nature that was exploited in practical composition. In contrast to the sixteenth century, the manipulation of the listener's emotional state by means of text and music was now privileged as a primary objective of compositional activity.

One of most extensive discussions of music's power to move the emotions appeared nearly contemporaneously with the Dresden repertoire: Athanasius Kircher's *Musurgia universalis* (Rome, 1650), a magisterial compendium of musical knowledge and speculation.[1] An examination of Kircher's ideas on affect is particularly appropriate with respect to the musical developments that took place in Dresden after 1656: not only did the composers, particularly Albrici, have ties to Roman Jesuit institutions such as the Collegium Germanicum, but the famous Jesuit polymath himself also corresponded with Johann Georg II and supplied him with a number of his publications.[2] Kircher was fascinated by music's effect upon both the mind

---

1. For this study, Kircher's 1650 Latin publication was consulted in conjunction with the 1662 German edition of Andreas Hirsch, *Kircherus Jesuita Germanus Germania redonatus . . . Philosophischer Extract und Auszug*. Hirsch includes six of Kircher's original ten books, and in some cases (such as Kircher's discussion of styles) only briefly summarizes the original. In many sections, however, including those quoted below, he has been faithful to the original Latin and has rendered a literal translation.

2. On 11 December 1663, Johann Georg II wrote to Elector August of Braunschweig-Wolfenbüttel to thank him for the book by Kircher that the famous bibliophile had sent

and the body—particularly its ability to move the "passions" and to cure disease. His explanation of the physiology of the passions seems to echo the views of Descartes, published in the late 1640s, but Kircher focuses on music (harmony) as the stimulus that sets the process in motion.[3] In Book VII, Kircher asks, "if, why, and how music has a power to move the emotions (*Gemüter*) of people, and if what was written of the wonder-workings of ancient music is true."[4] After citing several examples from the ancients on the power of music, he concludes that "such a powerful moving [of the emotions] can arise in man in many ways." Kircher discusses three of these, the first two of which are either "supernatural and unnatural," or a mixture of the supernatural and the natural, and are associated with the Devil, who, by playing the cithara, can powerfully throw the *humores* of man into disorder, with disastrous consequences. But the third manner in which emotional change can be effected is entirely natural: through the harmonic *sonum*. Here Kircher goes into greater detail and explains that for music to have its effect, four conditions must be fulfilled; if any of the four remain unfulfilled, music loses its power to move the listener:

1. the harmony itself
2. the number and *proportio*
3. the power and effect of the speech or words themselves
4. the receptivity and capacity of the listener

Not insignificantly, these four conditions rest on a continuum in Kircher's view—the successive fulfillment of each condition substantially increases the affective power of music:

---

to him (Sächs HStA Loc. 8561/5 Nr. 38, fol. 34r). On 26 December 1665, August wrote to Johann Georg and indicated that Kircher had sent him a letter that he wished to have forwarded to the Saxon elector, together with exemplars of three of his publications (ibid., fol. 180r). Neither Johann Georg nor August mention the titles of Kircher's works. Kircher's 1665 letter, dated Rome, 31 October, also survives (Sächs HStA Loc. 8561/5 Nr. 64) and indicates that he had sent Johann Georg a copy of his *Mundus subterraneus*, published that year in Amsterdam by Jansson and Weyerstraet as *Mundus subterraneus in xii libros digestus*. In a letter to Johann Georg of 10 June 1671, Kircher indicates that he had sent the elector a copy of his *Latium: id est, nova & parallela Latii tum veteris tum novi descriptio: qua quaecunque vel natura, vel veterum Romanorum ingenium admiranda effecit* (which he cites as *LATINUM, sive de verum Romanorum*), which was issued in Amsterdam by the same publishers in 1671 (ibid.).

3. See, for example, Hirsch 1662/1988:138–39, and René Descartes, *Passions of the Soul*, as quoted in Weiss and Taruskin 1984:212–17.

4. "Ob/ warum/ und wie die Music eine Kraft hab/ die Gemüter der Menschen zu bewegen/ und obs wahr sei was von den Wunder=würckungen der alten Music geschrieben wird" (Hirsch 1662/1988:135). The text upon which the following discussion is based appears in Appendix I (no. 17).

And indeed, the harmony has such power over the human spirit, as much as it similarly moves and excites the inner implanted air or living spirit, according to the harmonic motion of the air, whence the delight and sweetness of the music. If determined and proportioned numbers [i.e., meter and rhythm] are added, the harmony has a doubled effect, and moves the spirit not only to inner emotions, but also to outer bodily movements, as in dancing. . . . If the power of speech is added to this, especially when it is expressively moving, and contains a beautiful story or a sad case, then the harmony possesses an exceedingly great power to excite all sorts of emotions. However, the disposition of the soul, or the capacity of the audience must first exist; otherwise one would be able to move a stone more easily than a man.

Kircher's discussion of musical styles and *genera*[5] is well-known among scholars of seventeenth-century music. In many respects, however, his stylistic categories do not hold for the music of the Dresden Kapellmeisters and their contemporaries. Although Kircher includes a discussion of recitative, and includes examples of contemporary music, such as Carissimi's *Jephte*, his is nonetheless a somewhat retrospective consideration of musical styles. But importantly, Kircher situates all of his specific style classifications, including those most relevant for the Dresden concerto—the *stylus melismaticus* and the *stylus recitativus*—within a larger and all-encompassing category, that of *musica pathetica*, which has but a single goal: to "arouse all sorts of affects in men."[6] Kircher defines *musica pathetica* as "nothing else than a harmonic *melothesi* or composition by an experienced musician, so arranged according to art that it can move the listener first to this and then to that affect."[7] Once again, however, he adds that four conditions must be fulfilled for a composition to qualify as *musica pathetica*:

1. the composer must select a theme that is well-suited to arouse the emotions;
2. he must set this theme in a suitable mode;
3. he must establish the rhythm or the measure of the words according to the harmonic rhythm;
4. he must have the composition pronounced and sung by experienced singers at a suitable time and in a suitable place.[8]

---

5. Kircher 1650-1:581–97.

6. "Der einige Zweck der Pathetischen Music ist/ allerhand *affectus* in dem Menschen zu erwecken" (Hirsch 1662/1988:149; cf. Kircher 1650-1:564).

7. Hirsch 1662/1988:153; the German texts of this and the following passage appear in Appendix I (no. 18).

8. Kircher gives these suitable places and times in detail: places (size, building materials, contents, placement of singers/audience, whether indoors or outdoors) and times (times of the day, seasons, weather conditions, etc.) (Hirsch 1662/1988:154–56).

Both Albrici and Peranda were masters of *musica pathetica* and were recognized during the Baroque era for their affective styles of composition. Writing in 1690, Printz, who had visited the Dresden court in the early 1660s, remembered Peranda as a "composer of concertos, in which he expressed the stirrings of the soul beyond all measure."[9] Fifty years later, Mattheson praised Peranda as "the famous mover of the affects."[10] While neither of these theorists similarly associates the affective style with Albrici, Bernhard hailed both Albrici and Peranda as masters of affective writing, particularly as evidenced in their evocative treatment of dissonance. In his *Tractatus*, Bernhard cited both men as exponents of the two styles of contrapuntal writing that take the text into account, the *stylus luxurians communis*, in which "language and music are both masters," and the *stylus [luxurians] theatralis*, in which "language is the absolute master of music."[11] Bernhard includes both Albrici and Peranda among those composers who worked with the former style that he deemed worthy of emulation, but curiously includes only Albrici among the masters of the *stylus [luxurians] theatralis*.[12] In his definitions of these contrapuntal styles, Bernhard makes clear that *contrapunctis luxurians* is that style most directly associated with the arousing of the listener's emotions:

> *Contrapunctis gravis* is the type consisting of notes which do not move too quickly, and few kinds of dissonance treatment. It does not consider text as much as it does harmony; and since it was the only type known to men of former ages, it is called *stylus antiquus*—as also *a cappella* and *ecclesiasticus*, since it is better suited for that place than for others, and since the Pope permits this type alone in his churches and chapel.
> *Contrapunctis luxurians* is the type consisting in part of rather quick notes and strange leaps—so that it is well suited for stirring the affects—and more kinds of dissonance treatment (or more *figurae melopoeticae*, which others call *licentiae*) than the foregoing. Its melodies agree with the text as much as possible, unlike those of the preceding type.[13]

The desire to respond musically to the text through dissonance treatment undergirds Bernhard's entire system of figures, which, as they are always text-generated,

9. "Josephus Peranda aber in Compositione der Concerten, in welchen er die Gemüths=Regungen über alle Massen wohl ausgedrucket" (Printz 1690/1964:146).

10. "der berühmten Affecten=Zwinger" (1740/1994:18). Mattheson is almost certainly engaging in a play on words here, as the famous Zwinger palace in Dresden was completed during the famous musical polymath's lifetime.

11. Hilse 1973:110.

12. Hilse 1973:122; perhaps Peranda had not yet composed many works for the chapel by the time of the writing of the *Tractatus* (ca. 1657).

13. Hilse 1974:35 (Chapter 3. Different Types of Counterpoint).

remain central to the creation of affect. Although he does not include text in most of his examples of the various musical figures, Bernhard makes plain in several passages that these figures belong to a style of writing in which the text either reigns supreme over music, or rules as a co-regent alongside it.

The treatises of Kircher and Bernhard, which appeared within a decade of one another, are vastly different in scope and underlying philosophy. With respect to the treatment of affect in particular, Bernhard's treatise contrasts with that of the Jesuit scholar and takes a much more practical approach to the subject. While Kircher provides the reader with an exhaustive examination of just how and why music moves the emotions, Bernhard leaves such questions unasked; instead, he offers his readers—students and composers—the tools necessary to produce the very "Wunder-Würckungen" that so fascinated Kircher. Yet irrespective of their significantly different priorities and approaches, both affirm the centrality of affect in the compositional thinking of this era.

But despite the number of words spilled during the seventeenth century on the topic of the "passions," an assessment of affect in sacred music still remains problematic. How does one define or identify the emotions associated with religious devotion, particularly those associated with the emotional state(s) of the individual engaged in mystical prayer? While most emotions are combinations of, or variations on, one or two fundamental emotions, the feeling or feelings of "devotion" experienced by many of the speakers of the devotional texts from this era would seem to represent far more complex amalgamations of many feelings—love, desire, joy, comfort, fear, wonder, and hope. While Descartes identifies six basic "passions" (wonder, love, hatred, desire, joy, and sadness),[14] and Kircher expands the emotional palette to include at least eight (alternately love, sorrow, joy, anger, grief, sadness, pride, and despair, or love, sorrow, joy, anger, compassion, fear, insolence, and astonishment),[15] neither author associates particular emotional states (or affects) with the religious experience, nor suggests that the quality or nature of any affect differs in the religious as opposed to the secular sphere. But Kircher does recognize the transformative role that affective music can play during the exercise of devotion,

---

14. Descartes, *Passions of the Soul*, Weiss and Taruskin 1984:214–17.

15. "Lieb/ Leid/ Freud/ Zorn/ Klagen/ Traurigkeit/ Stoltz/ Verzweifflung/ etc."; and "Lieb/ Leid/ Freud/ Zorn/ Mitleiden/ Forcht/ Frechheit/ Verwunderung" (Hirsch 1662:1988:156, 158; cf. Kircher, *Musurgia Universalis* 1650-1:580, 598). In yet another discussion, however, Kircher points out that different stimuli produce correspondingly different affects, fourteen in all, which he groups as: "anger, fury, rage, . . . love, joy, hope, . . . sadness, pain, fear, compassion, . . . measured joy, peace, security, confidence" ("Zorn/ Grim/ Rasenei/ . . . Lieb/ Freud/ Hofnung/ . . . Traurigkeit/ Schmertzen/ Forcht/ Mitleiden/ . . . Freud/ Ruhe/ Sicherheit/ Zuversicht"; Hirsch 1662/1988:138–39, cf. Kircher, *Musurgia Universalis* 1650-1:551).

and makes one of the strongest statements from this period on the role of music in the religious experience:

Consequently, when a man is engaged in his devotions, and is occupied in the contemplation of heavenly things, and one introduces the same sweet- ness and loveliness into his thoughts through beautiful music intended for that purpose, then one will see how suddenly his external emotional state will be moved and his mind carried off by the harmonic sweetness.[16]

Kircher's assertion recalls the age-old maxim of the popes on the purpose of sacred music, "to arouse the listener to devotion." Here, however, music has acquired the power to move suddenly and powerfully—to overcome, it would seem—the lis- tener who is engaged in acts of devotion, and thereby to enhance the experience. As seen in chapter 4, many of the mystical-devotional texts set by Albrici and Peranda relate a type of transfixing or transforming religious experience, which the compos- ers sought to realize in affective music. But although Kircher left unarticulated any thoughts he may have had on the existence of specifically "religious passions," he did undertake an experiment whose details suggest that he may have taken such associations as a given:

Different emotions are found in men, and *objecta* of one sort cannot move all *subjecta* to the same emotions. In order to establish the reason for this discrepancy, the author undertook something rather special. He selected eight of the main emotions, including love, sorrow, joy, anger, lamenting, sadness, pride, and despair, then selected eight passages of scripture, one to conform to each emotion, and sent the eight to the very best composers in all of Europe, and asked each to set the eight themes according to all of the rules of art, and in so doing, to keep the intended emotions in mind, and to express these in the best way possible. Through this he wanted to learn to which emotions particular individuals—first the composers themselves, then their listeners—would incline, if all nations—Italy, Germany, England, France—would agree in the same emotions, or would disagree with one another, and wherein such discrepancies would exist, and thereby he would be able to completely restore pathetic music. But since the composers took a long time, his work on music has gone forth without their compositions, which shall follow in a special print.[17]

16. "Also wann ein Mensch in seiner Devotion stehet/ in Betrachtung himlischer Ding/ und man bringt ihm deroselben Süssigkeit und Lieblichkeit in das Gedächnus/ durch ein schöne darzu erfundene Harmony/ da wird man sehen/ wie plötzlich er in äusserliche Affecten und *raptus mentis*, durch die harmonische Süssigkeit wird commo- virt werden" (Hirsch 1662/1988:137; cf. Kircher, *Musurgia Universalis* 1650-1:550).
17. Hirsch 1662/1988:156–57; the German text appears in Appendix I (no. 19).

Adopting an analytical stance from which to approach this repertoire is no easy matter. One could easily privilege harmonic language, as the early tonal harmonic idiom in which these composers worked has yet to be fully explained or explored for its relationships to earlier and later tonal systems. Yet one could just as easily focus on form and style, given the sectional nature of so many of the concertos and their dependence upon styles of writing that point clearly to the later sacred cantata. But the importance that affect assumed in theoretical and practical discussions of music during this era, and the esteem in which Albrici and Peranda were held for their ability to move the emotions of their listeners, would seem to demand an exploration of these compositions chiefly as affective musical responses to and realizations of at times complex verbal expressions. Thus the analytical perspective adopted here is that of affect and its effectuation in music. In the discussions that follow, various musical parameters are considered, including style, form, melody, harmony, counterpoint, and the use of rhetorical and dissonance figures, but all are viewed primarily as vehicles for the expression of the text—not only its voice, content, and manner of expression, but also its external form and internal narrative shape. Throughout, the attempt is made to discover the musical means by which these composers achieved their goal of moving the listener "first to this, then to that affection." In the words of Kircher, then, what follows is a study "of *musica pathetica* itself, and how it shall be accomplished."[18]

PERANDA: *O JESU MI DULCISSIME*

The rise of the Christocentric devotional text presented new and particular challenges to the composer of sacred music, who was now called upon to capture the voice of the individual at prayer. In their musical settings of devotional texts, composers sought to capture in music the emotional state of the text's speaker, and to urge the listener toward the attainment of a similar state through an emotional metamorphosis engendered by affective music. Peranda's *O Jesu mi dulcissime*, a concerto with aria, affords a prime example of one composer's achievement of this goal.[19] The composition is one of his most arresting works, one singular in its ability to capture musically the complex of emotions—love, affection, yearning, hope, confidence—that accompany the religious experience. The number of documented performances—five between 1665 and 1667, and another in 1676—suggest that this sensual and atmospheric work also found favor with the elector.[20] One measure of its

18. "Caput 4. Von der Pathetischen Music selbsten/ wie sie soll ins Werck gesetzet werden" (Hirsch 1662/1988:156).

19. Text and translation in chapter 4; modern edition in Frandsen 1997-3:640–54. Musical examples prepared from S-Uu VMHS 30:6.

20. See Appendix II.

effectiveness derives from the scoring; to the group of three vocalists (SSA) Peranda adds a five-part string ensemble dominated by violas da gamba, and capitalizes on the rich, warm timbre of these instrument throughout the composition.[21] Indeed, one of the more unusual features of the composition is the fact that each strophe of the aria is accompanied by the strings.

In the opening instrumental sinfonia, Peranda begins to develop the affect of desire that inhabits the subsequent vocal concerto. The introductory movement unfolds slowly and is filled with harmonic tension created by slow, ornamented suspensions; these were doubtless enhanced in performance with *esclamatione* in the strings. The passage begins with a contrapuntal duet between Violetta/Violin 1 and Viola da gamba 2, supported by chordal writing in the other three parts. After the cadence that marks the conclusion of the first phrase complex, Violetta/Violin 2 and Viola da gamba 1 take over the roles of duet partners. As the brief movement proceeds to the final cadence on D, Peranda's writing becomes more rhetorical in nature; here he employs several instrumental "sighs," both of which are set off by rests in all parts, that foreshadow the sighs of the speaker in the ensuing concerto. The compositional style here suggests that by 1665, Peranda had become more fluent in instrumental writing, doubtless through a familiarity acquired in Dresden with German instrumental sonatas (Ex. 6.1).

Peranda steeps the expansive opening concerto, which presents the deeply felt expressions of the soul seeking to experience Christ's mystical presence, in emotional intensity. Each line of the stanza draws forth a different response from the composer, and he uses texture as well as harmony and rhythm in his affective strategy. To open the concerto, he borrows the idea of the motto from the contemporary aria. All three singers utter the speaker's opening address, "O Jesu," as if with one voice; their words are echoed immediately by the strings, and then the entire ensemble restates the material and continues. The line culminates in an affect-laden coloring of "dulcissime"—a drawn-out 7–6 suspension over a Phrygian cadence on the dominant (Ex. 6.2).

The harmonic tension achieved with this cadence is resolved with the introduction of the next line of text, "spes suspirantis animae," where Peranda abandons the homophony of the opening for imitative counterpoint. In his depiction of the "sighing soul," Peranda reduces the scoring to voices alone and employs multiple entries

---

21. Two of the diary entries record the scoring used in the performance on that particular occasion; the first reflects the scoring for five strings, two sopranos, and alto preserved in the Uppsala parts, while the second indicates that the two inner string parts were sometimes omitted in performance (see Appendix II). In S-Uu VMHS 30:6, the instrumental parts are labeled "Violetta ó Violino I and II," "Viola da gamba I and II," and "Violone" (cleffing: G1, C1, C3, C4, F4).

EXAMPLE 6.1 Peranda, *O Jesu mi dulcissime*, mm. 1–14

EXAMPLE 6.2 Peranda, *O Jesu mi dulcissime*, mm. 15–69

of the motive to create a continuous web of suspensions that captures the sense of the soul's disquiet, for as soon as the tension is resolved in one voice, it is reintroduced in another. In order to break finally the pattern of suspensions, Peranda moves to VI⁶ (m. 33), which ushers in the extended, hemiola-informed cadence on "animae" that closes this passage. Not anxious to bring the passage to a complete close, however, Peranda moves "deceptively" to VI⁶ (m. 37) while still preserving the V–I cadential motion in the bass, and then uses an instrumental echo to close on the tonic (m. 41). Following this brief interlude, the third line of text, "te quaerunt pie lachrimae," receives his most succinct treatment—a mere five bars of homophony—but here Peranda points up the intensity of the speaker's pain with a particularly rich cadential progression (VI⁷–vii°⁶/V–V) at "lachrimae" (mm. 44–46). At the concluding line of the stanza, "et clamor mentis intimae," Peranda first returns

EXAMPLE 6.2 (*continued*)

EXAMPLE 6.2 (*continued*)

EXAMPLE 6.2 (*continued*)

EXAMPLE 6.2 (*continued*)

to imitation for three plaintive, ascending imitative entries, then quickly turns to homophonic statements of the text, rhythmically enlivened through hemiola figures. At the cadence, he effects a strident clash that stands as a metaphor for the speaker's heightened emotional state, as the $F_\sharp$ in Soprano 2 chafes against the $F_\natural$ in the uppermost string part (m. 61).[22] Similar cross-relations, in the form of juxtapositions rather than simultaneities, color the duple-meter close of the concerto.

22. The $F_\sharp$ arises from the convention of raising the third at the cadence in minor keys and modes, but the clash is clearly intentional, as it occurs at important junctures throughout the composition.

The aria that forms the centerpiece of Peranda's *O Jesu* offers an interesting look at the tension that often informs the relationship between musical form and the emotional narrative or shape of a text. While Peranda may have read this text as a narrative of the speaker's progress toward mystical union, which is attained in the third stanza and then recollected in the fourth, he could not easily duplicate the trajectory of an emotional journey in a concerto with aria. For, like the da capo aria, the concerto with aria does not allow for the emotional transformation of the speaker; in both, the speaker is bound to return to his or her original emotional state in the obligatory restatement of the opening material. In the concerto with aria, the text of the opening (and closing) concerto naturally occupies a position of prestige with respect to the remainder of the text, due to its placement, and normally inspires the affect that dominates the entire composition. Here, in the three stanzas that form the aria, Peranda might have attempted to set the third apart musically as the emotional climax of the text, but he would have had difficulty in doing so without transgressing the formal and stylistic conventions of the mid-century aria. Thus he eschews any attempt to distinguish between the aria strophes and shapes a strophic setting that confines all three to the same emotional plane. But after having heard the aria, the listener might well perceive the restatement of the concert somewhat differently.

Normally Peranda's arias, like those of Albrici, are scored for voice and continuo alone, with the instrumental ensemble entering only to supply interludes or concluding ritornelli. Peranda's strophic aria in *O Jesu* is thus unusual in that it is enriched both texturally and harmonically by the accompaniment of the four lower string instruments, none of which doubles the vocal line.[23] In contrast to a number of his arias, such as those found in *Languet cor meum* and *Te solum aestuat* (discussed below), Peranda does not expand the vocal strophes with interludes, melismatic passages, or multiple restatements of phrases, but sets these stanzas nearly syllabically. As they include only a simple reiteration of the final line, the strophes do not exhibit the full ABB′ form so typical of the arias of this period. Yet what his aria might lack in length and formal complexity it compensates for in intensity: each strophe begins "off-tonic," both melodically and harmonically, and is led to the dominant through a slightly chromaticized descending tetrachord, one of the quintessential symbols of the lament in this era. In the three subsequent phrases, Peranda

23. This scoring suggests that Peranda sought a consistent timbre such as that produced by a single family of instruments, and that the C1 part was played by a small viola da gamba (violetta), rather than a violin. All three strophes share the same bass line and harmony. The strophes for Soprano 1 and 2 are melodically identical, while that for the alto includes a few alterations to accommodate the singer's range; here also, the instrumental parts are rewritten somewhat (in mm. 98 and 100–101, Violetta/Violin 2 presents the melody as sung by the sopranos) but these changes do not alter the harmony.

moves through the relative major to bring the initial presentation of the text to a close on the dominant (m. 78). In order to effect harmonic closure, he restates line 4, set to new melodic material and dominated by sigh figures, and supports the phrase with a dominant pedal. The rich chord progression in the final vocal phrase, which includes descending parallel $^6_3$ chords over a bass pedal (m. 79), was apparently so unusual that either Peranda or the Swedish copyist felt compelled to write out the harmony in full for the continuo player. Peranda continues his play with cross-relations to the very end of the aria, for at the final vocal cadence, the F♯ in Violetta 2 is immediately followed by the F♮ in Violetta 2, which enters for the ensuing instrumental interlude (Ex. 6.3).

PERANDA: *JESU DULCIS, JESU PIE*

In contrast to *O Jesu mi dulcissime*, in which Peranda uses a poetic text as the basis for a concerto with aria, in *Jesu dulcis, Jesu pie* he opts for a through-composed form that makes use of various Roman compositional techniques.[24] By foregoing a rounded organizational plan, he is better able to project the emotional trajectory of this intensely mystical text through his musical setting. Like so many other settings of devotional texts, *Jesu dulcis* appears to have been well received in the court chapel—fully eight performances can be documented in Dresden between 1664 and 1667. The diary entry that records the performance in 1666 includes the scoring, which agrees with what is reflected in the sole surviving set of parts, with the exception that in the Dresden performance, the bass member of the instrumental ensemble was a viola da gamba rather than a bassoon. But like the other diary entries that include scorings, this one also makes clear an important aspect of the performance practice of the sacred concerto during this era, for it leaves no doubt as to the number of performers involved: "à 6. 1 Sop: 1 Alto 1 Tenore 2 Viole. et 1 Violtagamba."[25] Once again, Peranda's sonic ideal for the musical representation of an intensely devotional text involves a darker, warmer string color. The nature of the text seems also to have influenced Peranda's choice of key and tonal organization, for he contrasts sections in the tonic key of G minor with passages in iv (rather than III).

In the opening concerto, which is not prefaced by an instrumental introduction, Peranda captures the supplicatory quality of the words of the speaker, who is anxious to win Christ's ear, through the use of the minor mode, and through the insistent and unremitting nature of the musical response. Peranda sets the first half of the stanza homophonically, for the vocal ensemble, then expands his treatment with

---

24. Text and translation in chapter 4; modern edition in Frandsen 1997-3:582–98. Musical examples prepared from SLUB 1738-E-522.
    25. See Appendix II.

EXAMPLE 6.3 Peranda, *O Jesu mi dulcissime*, mm. 70–83

EXAMPLE 6.3 *(continued)*

immediate restatements of each phrase and phrase group, differentiated through dynamics.[26] No instrumental interludes intrude on the vocal writing to give the listener respite from the speaker's incessant, full-voiced entreaties. Peranda also uses the 6/4 meter to help underscore central words in the text, and fashions motives that begin on beat 2, after a rest. As a result, the first half of the bar serves as an anacrusis to the second half, where each of the speaker's characterizations of Christ—"dulcis," "pie," "chare" and "spes"—receives the heaviest rhythmic emphasis in the measure (Ex. 6.4).

   The second half of the stanza, which becomes more overtly personal and self-referential ("for me, Jesus, my life, you were affixed to the bitter cross"), is sung by the soprano alone. The suddenly transparent texture of the solo contrasts with that

26. While the dynamic markings *forte* and *piano* that appear throughout the first section may have been added by a later copyist, the repetitive structure of the setting suggest that they originated with the composer.

EXAMPLE 6.4　Peranda, *Jesu dulcis, Jesu pie*, mm. 1–16

EXAMPLE 6.4 (*continued*)

of the opening, as well as with that of the following section, in which Peranda transposes the opening material up a perfect fourth to the subdominant (the key change
is achieved through a simple quartal shift). Here he also adds the instruments, and
fashions a restatement of the speaker's supplication that is intensified through the
shift in tessitura and enrichment of the texture. In this second statement, the alto
sings the solo, as Peranda has exchanged the melodic material between the two top
parts in order to keep the parts within range. But rather than end with the solo, in
the subdominant, Peranda returns to the tonic G minor via another harmonic shift
and presents an expanded restatement of the solo material for the full ensemble.

Peranda sets the speaker's next three utterances in arioso style, and, just as in
the aria of *O Jesu mi dulcissime*, enhances each solo with a "halo" of strings. Here
he exchanges a more contemplative reading of this mystical text for the more rhetorically charged interpretations that typify many of his solo settings of compara-
ble expressions. In *Te solum aestuat*, for example, such texts are realized in angular
lines, dramatic and often awkward leaps, sudden pauses, melismatic writing, dissonance figures, and other musical and rhetorical devices. In contrast, the melodic
lines in these passages generally fall closer in style to those of the lyrical aria and

achieve their effect through more subtle means. Peranda begins quietly and achieves a gradual heightening of emotion over the course of the three arioso passages both by carefully assigning them to the three singers with careful regard for the range of each (tenor, alto, soprano), so that the vocal tessitura rises as the speaker's ardor increases, and by heightening the musical tension from one arioso to the next. Each of the three solos cadences in the subdominant, but begins elsewhere, either on the tonic, the submediant, or the mediant, and the resulting lack of tonic closure also contributes to the level of emotional tension.

The first arioso passage, sung by the tenor, numbers only seven measures (plus a two-bar instrumental close) and includes a rare example of self-borrowing by Peranda, for the setting of the final phrase, "until I attain you," also concludes each of the aria strophes in *O Jesu mi dulcissime*.[27] The second passage, sung by the alto, is heightened emotionally through the use of *epizeuxis* ("Te fontem vivum sitit anima, *anima, anima mea*"); each iteration of "anima" rises by a perfect fourth, and the line climaxes in a slight elaboration of the final and highest instantiation of the motive. Peranda then articulates the speaker's imploring question, "when will I be filled with the abundance of your wounds?" by means of musical *interrogatio*.[28] In the third arioso passage, sung by the soprano, the speaker has ascended to a higher emotional plane, one much closer to the indescribable state of mystical union, and speaks of his desire for Christ with an allusion to the familiar phrase from the Song of Songs, "quia amore langueo."[29] In response, Peranda's musical setting becomes more expansive, and he lingers over each word of the speaker's few ardent phrases. He draws the listener's attention to the focal word of the opening phrase, "desires," with a chromatic progression and lends additional emphasis to the vocal line at this point through a downward leap of a diminished fifth at "desiderat." Bernhard would characterize such an "unnatural leap" as a *saltus duriusculus*; as it stands here, the figure also constitutes the same author's *heterolepsis* (the "seizure of a second voice").[30] In the phrase that follows, Peranda represents the impassioned speaker's sigh simply, with a brief rest between "te" and "suspirat," coupled with a descending leap on the latter word, and then proceeds to a "languid" line at "langueo," where he suspends the harmony (and the listener) over a long dominant pedal (Ex. 6.5).

27. The line even includes the full chords in the continuo part (see mm. 78–81 in Ex. 6.3 above). It is difficult to determine in which piece the material originated; *Jesu dulcis* has the earlier documented performance date (1664 vs. 1665), but the records from the years 1663–64 are too incomplete to allow either piece to be dated precisely.

28. "A musical question rendered variously through pauses, a rise at the end of the phrase or melody, or through imperfect or phrygian cadences"; see Barthel 1997:312. Bernhard recognized this figure, and stated that "questions are commonly expressed by ending the phrase a second higher than the foregoing note and syllable" (ibid., 314).

29. Cf. Song of Songs 2:5 and 5:8.

30. Hilse 1973:105, 118.

EXAMPLE 6.5 Peranda, *Jesu dulcis, Jesu pie*, mm. 65–81

With the entry of the vocal ensemble at "euge, anima mea," Peranda draws the curtain on the mystical experience. In the closing text, the speaker turns his focus inward, and Peranda signals this shift through changes in meter, texture, and style. He returns to the tonic G minor (again via harmonic shift), and the homophonic texture of the opening, and contrasts the languidity and "otherworldly" quality of the solos with a motion-filled triple. In contrast with his succinct approach to the solo passages, Peranda here fashions a protracted treatment of the final line of the

EXAMPLE 6.5 (*continued*)

text, "tanto amori disce mori," in which the speaker commands himself to learn to die—to achieve full mystical union—for the love of Christ. Peranda's musical response to these few highly charged words is twofold: he begins rather urgently, and presents "tanto amori" ("with so much love") in a homophonic setting that is immediately reiterated, but at "disce mori" he shifts suddenly to the languor of the soul dying in mystical union, which he represents in staggered entries of a motive that gently snakes around the main pitch. Thus "tanto amori" acquires the sense of a

EXAMPLE 6.6 Peranda, *Jesu dulcis, Jesu pie*, mm. 115–30

EXAMPLE 6.6 (*continued*)

command, while the actual imperative, "disce mori," is transformed into a languid, dying swoon. Just as he did in the opening concerto, Peranda again restates a large block of material, but here the order of harmonies is reversed to effect a tonic close: the section begins (in m. 96) on the subdominant, then is restated on the tonic (m. 115ff), with two additional restatements of "disce mori" (Ex. 6.6).

Peranda: *Te solum aestuat*

In *Te solum aestuat*, Peranda borrowed Albrici's "expanded" concerto with aria form for his setting of an intensely devotional text.[31] This composition stands today as Peranda's most widely distributed piece, for it was owned by at least eight Lutheran institutions in the seventeenth century, a fact that helps to underscore the centrality of mystical devotion in the worship lives of contemporary Lutherans. The presence

31. Text and translation in chapter 4; modern edition in Frandsen 1997-3:834–51. Musical examples prepared from S-Uu VMHS 30:12.

of this concerto in both court and Latin school music libraries also attests to the musical abilities of seventeenth-century German musicians, including choirboys, for Peranda presents the three singers with considerable technical challenges. The title first appears in a Dresden court diary entry for Pentecost Tuesday 1664 and reappears on three dates in 1665 and 1666. According to the court secretary, the performance on *Jubilate* Sunday 1666 was "à 6," and involved "2 Sop: 1 Basso 2 Violi: et 1 Fagot"; this disposition of parts matches that of two of the three extant sources.[32] In its formal design, *Te solum aestuat* resembles a number of works by Albrici, including his *Tu es cor meum*, but here there are no internal restatements of the concerto, and the concerto serves solely as a framing device. Peranda's harmonic approach also differs from that of his colleague, for while Albrici opens and closes each of the ten sections of *Tu es cor meum* in the tonic, Peranda casts only the framing concerto in the tonic A minor.[33] The six inner sections are alternately modulatory, with cadences on the tonic, or harmonically closed on the dominant. This harmonic concept also contrasts somewhat with that of the composer's own *Jesu dulcis*; there he also establishes a harmonic dichotomy between sections, but one that involves the less tension-filled relationship between tonic and subdominant.

But Peranda's *Te solum aestuat* also reveals the tension between form and content that resides in many of these settings of devotional texts. Like the two works considered above, *Te solum aestuat* represents a musical vehicle for the communication of an intimate prayer, the culmination of which is the mystical presence experience. As the prayer progresses, the speaker's expressions of longing for Christ's mystical presence seem to lead to the experience of mystical union; at its conclusion, the experience causes the speaker to marvel at God's greatness. With the expanded concerto with aria, the genre for which the text seems to have been conceived, Peranda is able to accommodate the emotional trajectory embodied in the text to a great extent. The exigencies of the form, however, dictate a restatement of the opening concerto, which reestablishes the opening affect at the end of the composition, an affect that contrasts considerably with that of the final solo set, in which the speaker bursts forth in praise and adoration.[34] Just as in *O Jesu mi dulcissime*, then, the setting of the opening portion of the text plays a determinative role in the listener's perception of the affect of the entire composition, despite the fact that the text recounts an emotional journey. Thus all three of these devotional pieces demonstrate that in this repertoire, musical form often ultimately trumps the narrative or emotional shape of the text.

---

32. See Appendix II; the part set in the SLUB lacks a bassoon part.

33. The same is true of Albrici's *O amantissime sponse*, another expanded concerto with aria; in that work, each of the nine sections is closed on the tonic G minor.

34. In similar expanded works that may well date from the following decade, Albrici often elects to close with an "Alleluia" or "Amen," perhaps to avoid this very problem.

Peranda introduces the opening vocal concerto with a brief, duple-meter instrumental sinfonia that both establishes A minor as the key of the work and provides metric contrast with the subsequent vocal concerto.[35] In its style, this opening concerto is paradigmatic of the opening sections in settings of devotional texts by both Peranda and Albrici, in which the musical style itself is a metaphor for the emotional state of the speaker. In fashioning the opening movement, Peranda divides the opening text into two parts, and, as in *O Jesu mi dulcissime*, takes widely divergent approaches with each. The speaker's initial expression of burning desire for Christ ("te solum aestuat, valde desiderat") is heard in a largely homophonic setting for voices alone. Peranda then derives two motives from the concluding portion of the text, "suavissime Domine Jesu Christe," and treats these in a relaxed contrapuntal style. He introduces his first motive as a solo for Soprano 1 (mm. 29–33), and allows the entire lilting line to be absorbed by the listener before it is heard in another voice. To create contrapuntal interest, he adds his second motive as a "countersubject" to each subsequent entry of this first motive, or "subject." The regular series of entries of the subject and countersubject in the various voices produces invertible counterpoint, but Peranda's overall approach results in a transparent texture that is only nominally "contrapuntal" due to the rhythmic similarity of the two motives. Each motivic duo closes with an example of Bernhard's figure *extensio*, in this case a prolonged, elaborate suspension figure (either 7–6 or 2–3) between the voices that "resolves" in a pungent clash of semitones (Ex. 6.7).[36]

In the restriction of motivic material, the invertibility of the themes, and the regularity of entries of both motives in each voice, the influence of permutation techniques is readily apparent.[37] But although Peranda borrows a sophisticated contrapuntal technique, he makes it subservient to the overall affect, and does not challenge the listener with complex counterpoint. Here the object is not intellectual engagement, but emotional and spiritual transport. With writing like this, both Peranda and Albrici not only seek to capture musically the emotional state of a speaker who is on the pathway to mystical union, and thus no longer completely

---

35. The sinfonia also includes another example of Peranda's self-borrowing, for it closes with a motive (mm. 7–11) that also appears in the sinfonia to his *Quis dabit* (discussed below).

36. "*Extension* is the rather sizable lengthening of a dissonance" (Hilse 1973:111). Here the reference tone in Soprano 2 anticipates the next pitch just as the dissonant tone in Soprano 1 resolves, producing a semitone clash; Bernhard would probably label this a *cadentia duriuscula* (see Hilse 1973:109–10).

37. Albrici uses the same style and technique in the opening concerto of his *Jesu dulcis memoria*, which predates Peranda's *Te solum aestuat* by several years, and Peranda employs similar techniques in his *Languet cor meum*. See also the discussion of Albrici's *Omnis caro foenum* (below).

EXAMPLE 6.7 Peranda, *Te solum aestuat*, mm. 29–59

EXAMPLE 6.7 (*continued*)

conscious of his surroundings, but also to carry the listener off to that same place. In an effort to produce the affect of yearning and desire, both composers work within the same set of parameters, which include a slow triple meter, a relaxed imitative texture that features seemingly incessant, well-spaced entries of the same motive or motives, and the constant vacillation between two harmonic poles, most typically tonic and dominant. In its lack of actual harmonic progress, i.e., modulation away from these poles, the music thus symbolizes the psychological state of the speaker in these texts, who is transfixed by Christ and thus motionless.

Peranda concludes the opening tutti with a duple-meter cadence that is colored by another extended suspension, and then moves directly into the first solo declamatory passage, sung by Soprano 1, without interposing an instrumental interlude. Quite suddenly, the affect of trancelike reverie developed in the opening concerto is replaced by a new sense of immediacy and urgency. In this, the only truly active portion of the text, the speaker entreats Christ to transfix him with "the dart of [His] love," and Peranda garbs the speaker's supplication in virtuosic embellishments and dissonance figures that serve as musical metaphors for the adulatory language in which the speaker cloaks his plea.[38] The crux of the passage resides in the speaker's petition, "tranfix the center and innermost part of my *soul*"; as the speaker invokes the soul (*anima*), Peranda depicts the soul's transcendent flight to a higher emotional plane with a double *climax* (the repetition of a phrase one step higher) and *paronomasia* (the repetition of a phrase with new material added at the end for emphasis).[39] This leads directly into the emotional and musical apex of the passage at "suavissimo," which begins on the highest vocal pitch yet heard, g'', from which it descends by leaps through the octave. (Ex. 6.8).

Upon the conclusion of the aria strophe that follows (discussed below), Soprano 2 enters to present a similar set. Normally, given that no two passages of prose share the same structure, Albrici and Peranda fashion independent musical settings for each. But in two concertos, including *Te solum aestuat*, Peranda employs a type of "strophic variation" also seen in the solo motets of Graziani, in which declamatory passages are set to related musical material.[40] For a time, this passage borrows much of its melodic and harmonic material from the previous declamatory passage. But when the speaker reaches the threshold of mystical union ("te solum amat, in te deficit anima mea"), Peranda departs from the model and closes with a line that meanders aimlessly. In contrast with the first, this second declamatory passage has

---

38. These include the dissonance figures *variatio, multiplicatio, anticipatio notae,* and *superjectio,* catalogued by Bernhard, as well as the repetition figures *epizeuxis* and *paronomasia.*

39. See Barthel 1997:220, 350.

40. See Gratiani's *Hodie collaetantur caeli cives* (1652) and Peranda's *Spirate suaves* (discussed in chapter 5).

EXAMPLE 6.8 Peranda, *Te solum aestuat*, mm. 60–75

an overall descending melodic ductus, and lacks some of the ornamentation seen in the previous passage, as well some of the of urgency; here the speaker has slipped gently into that ineffable state and lost awareness of himself and his surroundings.

Peranda follows these first two declamatory passages with aria strophes that are virtually identical, and that are carefully designed to convey the affect of the text. Here the soul takes flight and soars ever heavenward in ecstasy. Peranda conveys this sense of ascent and ethereality by setting the aria strophes entirely in the minor dominant, so that they seem to float in suspension above the tonic, unable to descend back to it, as well as by focusing on melodic writing that is consciously expansive.[41] Throughout the aria, the phrases constantly strive upward toward new heights and then gently descend again. Although the concerto is contemporaneous with *O Jesu mi dulcissime*, these strophes exhibit none of the succinctness seen in that aria. Instead, Peranda repeats various phrases, stretching the lyrical lines with "sigh" figures and melismas at every opportunity.[42] Both strophes are cast in the full ABB′ form, in which the musical climax is delayed until the expanded B′ section, which demands a high a'' from the soprano castrato (Ex. 6.9).

In the final two sections of the text, the mystical experience lies behind the speaker, who now praises God with words of adoration. Peranda underscores the speaker's newfound confidence in a declamatory passage that exhibits the coloratura, angular lines, and extremes of range typical of writing for the bass during this era, and thus marries virtuosic display to affective textual representation. While every previous transition between sections involved a smooth transition from tonic to dominant or the reverse, here Peranda signals the change in the speaker's emotional state with a tertial shift to the relative major. As the speaker marvels at God's greatness, Peranda casts his words in a syllabic declamatory style. When the speaker mentions God, however, he bursts into a florid extension of the phrase in which the fundamental chordal outline is filled out by means of *variatio* (Ex. 6.10).[43]

The speaker then goes on to pose a rhetorical question that resonates with the theme of *vanitas*: "what is there for me in besides You, and what do I desire on earth?" For Peranda, this represents the essence of the text, and its references to heaven and hell doubtless caused him to assign this text to the bass voice, through

41. The voice range also contributes to the affect; it is not insignificant that Peranda assigns these two strophes to soprano castrati and not to the bass.

42. Peranda takes a similar approach in the first two aria strophes in *Languet cor meum*; there he further expands each strophe with a brief instrumental interlude (modern edition in Frandsen 1997-3:600–18; see esp. mm. 105–41, 151–87).

43. According to Bernhard, *variatio* is "called *passaggio* by the Italians and *coloratura* in general" and "occurs when an interval is altered through several shorter notes, so that, instead of one long note, a number of shorter ones rush to the next note through all kinds of step progressions and skips" (Hilse 1973:96).

EXAMPLE 6.9 Peranda, *Te solum aestuat*, 76–109

EXAMPLE 6.10 Peranda, *Te solum aestuat*, 185–204

which he could best realize the unfathomable distance between heaven and hell through extremes in pitch.[44] As the phrase complex begins at "quid mihi est," the bass's quick ascent to middle *c´* at "in coelo" carries the declamatory passage to a new emotional height. Here Peranda opts for dissonance figures over *passaggio* as a means of adding emphasis to the end of the line, and he fashions an ornate cadence that concludes with a *saltus duriusculus*, in this case a diminished fifth.[45] As the speaker continues, the intensity builds steadily due to Peranda's use of the rhetorical repetition figure *epizeuxis*, both at "quid volui" and at "super terram." In the latter instance, he fashions a descending motive in response to the content of the text (*catabasis*) but, somewhat paradoxically, uses ever-higher restatements of the motive to build musical tension.[46] This excitement continues to grow throughout the angular extension of the third statement, which descends rapidly through an octave and a half, and finally comes to rest solidly on low C, the aural representation of *terra firma*. To begin the penultimate phrase, "Deus cordis mei et pars mea" (mm. 197–204), Peranda requires the bass to leap up nearly two octaves in order to call out "Deus." But the bass immediately returns to the depths (*catabasis*) and reaches E at "pars mea"; although the Deity remains the subject of the speaker's statement, the extremely low range here seems to be a metaphor for the speaker's own humility and self-abasement. In the concluding phrase, "Deus in aeternum," Peranda again depends on *epizeuxis* and motivic extension, and enlivens the line with *superjectio*.[47] Not content to conclude with a single cadence on the tonic, however, Peranda reinforces the home key with a redundant cadence, and uses this as an opportunity to dip one last time into the lower reaches of the bass's range.

Just as the castrati had done moments earlier, the bass also concludes his solo offering with an aria strophe. Some features of the bass strophe, such as the triple meter, melismatic lines, and ABB´ form, recall the earlier strophes of the castrati, but Peranda does not borrow melodic material from those lyrical solos. Instead, he calls the soaring soul back to earth (and to the tonic) and imbues the strophe with the same air of confidence exuded by the declamatory passage. Here melodic leaps

---

44. In his discussion of the *stylus theatralis*, Bernhard indicates that "that which is heightened in ordinary speech should be set high, that which passes unemphasized set low." "Similar observations," he says, "should be made in connection with texts wherein Heaven, Earth, or Hell are mentioned" (see Hilse 1973:111).

45. Bernhard describes the *saltus duriusculus* as an "unnatural step progression or leap"; see Hilse 1973:105, 118–19.

46. Barthel defines *catabasis* as "a descending musical passage which expresses descending, lowly, or negative images or affections"; see Barthel 1997:214.

47. According to Bernhard, *superjectio* "occurs when a note is placed next to a consonance or dissonance, a step above. This happens most often when the notes should naturally fall a second" (Hilse 1973:92).

replace the conjunct motion of the soprano strophes. Whereas the cadences in the soprano strophes were reached by smooth, stepwise descents, those of the bass are marked by decisive leaps. In addition, Peranda closes both the B and B′ sections with hemiola figures that lend these cadences a different sort of rhythmic stress and a greater sense of finality. The harmonic shape of the strophe also differs from that seen earlier, and from most of his arias, for Peranda casts the A and B sections in the tonic, but shifts to the dominant for the B′ section, which sets up a dominant-tonic relationship between the end of aria and the restatement of concerto.

ALBRICI: *OMNIS CARO FOENUM*

Albrici's most widely distributed composition, the concerto with aria *Omnis caro foenum*, stands out among his compositions for its scoring and for its highly contrapuntal sinfonia and framing concerto.[48] It also enjoys the distinction of being the only work of Albrici's to have been published in the seventeenth century, albeit not under his name; in 1669, it appeared as a work of Samuel Capricornus in the posthumous collection *Continuatio Theatri Musici*.[49] It is also one of very few works in this repertoire for which manuscript sources survive from four different collections.[50] Two of these, which form part of the Grimma collection, transmit a different instrumental scoring from the sources found in Uppsala and Berlin: in the Grimma sources, the scoring includes four vocal parts (soprano, alto, tenor, and bass) and a diverse instrumental quartet: violin, cornettino, trombone, and bassoon. The cornettino is replaced by a violin in both the Düben and Bokemeyer sources, and, in

48. Text and translation in chapter 4; modern edition in Frandsen 1997-3:247–63. Musical examples prepared from SLUB 1821-E-501 and 502.

49. Tim Newton has sorted out a number of the problematic attributions in this collection; see Newton 2004:51–60. In the *Continuatio*, Albrici's concerto is scored for four "Viol.", SATB voices, and continuo.

50. The Grimma collection includes two independent part sets for the work, 1821-E-501 and 502; the former represents a "foreign" set of parts, one not copied by Jacobi or his students. Unfortunately, the watermark is unreadable, and the parts bear no other clues to their origin. This set, however, likely served as Jacobi's exemplar for 1821-E-502, which is in his hand throughout. In 1821-E-501, the repetition of the opening concerto is indicated with rubrics that stand at the end of the aria, written in Latin for the singers, and in German for the instrumentalists. The alto part, for example, includes the instruction "Omnis carofoenum: repete ab initio usque ad Ten solo Quam breve: et claudatur," while the continuo player's instructions read "Omnis caro foenum wirdt wied. angefangen biß zum Tenor solo. Quam breve. et claudatur." The use of the two languages suggests that this set of parts may well have derived from the Dresden court, for copyists there likely provided rubrics in Latin for the Italian singers and in German for the native instrumentalists. In Jacobi's copy, the rubric appears as "Omnis caro foenum da capo" in most parts.

the latter, a violetta replaces the trombone and the bassoon is omitted entirely; the continuo part, which doubles the bassoon throughout in the other sources, simply replaces it in the Bokemeyer source. Although the instrumental scoring found in the Grimma sources remains unique among Albrici's extant works, it was not altogether uncommon in the seventeenth century, particularly in instrumental works. A number of seventeenth-century Italian composers working in Austria and southern Germany, among them Biagio Marini (Neuburg), Giovanni Valentini (Vienna), and Marc-Antonio Ferro (Vienna), composed sonatas for this same mixed ensemble, as did Albrici's contemporary in Vienna, Johann Heinrich Schmelzer (ca. 1623–80).[51] Not insignificantly, however, eight sonatas scored for this same "broken consort" also survive from the pen of Matthias Weckmann (more on this below).

Albrici opens the sinfonia with motivic material that adumbrates the countersubject of the fugue in the subsequent concerto, and he foreshadows his contrapuntal approach to the vocal concerto with a brief instrumental fughetta in which he creates twelve bars of music from two concise motives (Ex. 6.11). In the opening concerto that follows, Albrici seeks to match the severity of this *vanitas* text with contrapuntal rigor and abandons the more typical *concertato* style for the first two-thirds of the opening in favor of a brief double fugue.[52] Here the setting of Isaiah's stark proclamation, "all flesh is grass," forms the subject, while the remaining portion of the scriptural text is consigned to the countersubject. Albrici introduces the subject in the alto voice, but rather than double the initial entry in the continuo part, as he does in the fugal close of *Spargite flores* (discussed below), he unobtrusively introduces the countersubject in the continuo part (see Ex. 6.11).

Upon the entry of the answer in the soprano on the dominant (m. 16), the alto proceeds with the countersubject. The accommodation of the balance of the scriptural text to the countersubject required that Albrici underlay this pre-existent musical material with twenty-one syllables of text, the result of which is a rhythmically active countersubject. But Albrici's goal here is not simply to supply the sustained opening motive with a contrapuntal foil. In the process of underlaying the text, he rhythmicizes the countersubject in a manner that underscores musically the content of the scriptural passage. In bars 18–19, for example, he sets off the words "umbra" (shadow), "praetereunt," (pass away), and "evanescunt" (vanish) with rests, thereby causing the countersubject to seem to dissolve. The soprano entry in bar 16 represents a real answer until bar 18, at which point Albrici lowers the first and last pitches by a half step. He also alters the countersubject by flatting the *b*, which in an exact transposition would remain natural. These melodic alterations allow him

51. Liner notes to *Matthias Weckman (1619–1674): Die X Sonaten und Lieder*, 8–9.
52. Albrici's overt use of contrapuntal artifice in a setting of a *vanitas* text may well represent another layer of textual interpretation or commentary; see Austern 2003:293 *et passim*.

EXAMPLE 6.11 Albrici, *Omnis caro foenum*, mm. 1–28

to redirect the harmony back to the tonic D minor, but they come as a bit of a surprise after the implied dominant motion in bars 16 and 17. At the conclusion of his presentation of both motives, the alto drops out of the texture for the time being, and the fugal exposition continues to unfold with tonic entrances of the subject and countersubject in the bass and soprano (m. 19). Here Albrici displays the invertibility of his themes and places the subject below the countersubject.[53] As soon as the soprano has concluded the presentation of the countersubject (m. 22), the tenor takes up the subject, accompanied now by the countersubject in the bass. When the

53. The first part of the countersubject is also transposed up an octave, to keep it within the castrato's range.

EXAMPLE 6.11 *(continued)*

tenor continues with the countersubject (m. 25), the soprano takes up the subject. The brief fugue ends in bar 28 (b. 2), at which point the soprano relinquishes the countersubject to the vocal quartet. Throughout the fugue, Albrici avoids introducing nonmotivic material and maintains a two-part texture as much as possible.[54]

54. When the motives occur in the upper voices, the continuo part becomes semi-independent, and supplies harmonic support (see mm. 16–20 and 25–27).

EXAMPLE 6.11 (*continued*)

In many respects, Albrici's handling of this motivic material resembles the permutation fugue. In the words of Paul Walker, "the term permutation fugue refers
to a fugal movement with three to six melodic units put together according to five
structural restrictions: 1) the voices enter successively, as in a fugue, 2) entries alternate between tonic (final) and dominant, possibly incorporating tonal answers, 3)
each voice always presents the melodic units in the same order, 4) melodic units
appear as in *Stimmtauch*, i.e., in invertible counterpoint, and 5) there is little or no

EXAMPLE 6.11 (*continued*)

free counterpoint, i.e., non-thematic material."[55] Albrici has scrupulously observed the first four restrictions, and done his best to observe the fifth as well; the only actual difference between his fugue and the true permutation fugue concerns the number of melodic units, which he limits to just two. Albrici's fugue is very brief

55. See Walker 2000:232. The first four restrictions are adapted from Carl Dahlhaus,

EXAMPLE 6.11 (*continued*)

"Zur Geschichte der Permutationsfuge," *Bach-Jahrbuch* 46 (1959): 95; Walker has added the fifth restriction. The author's discussion of this and other fugues in the Dresden repertoire has profited greatly from discussions with Prof. Walker on the subject.

and includes only one true "permutation," the single inverted entry of the motivic material; still, the writing shows close adherence to this set of procedures, at a rather early date.

Given the unusual instrumental scoring and the paucity of fugal writing in Albrici's extant works, one might well wonder if the motivation behind the composition of this piece can be traced to the influence of any particular musician or musicians. In this case, the facts of Albrici's biography provide ample material for speculation. The first recorded Dresden performance of *Omnis caro foenum* took place in the court chapel in August 1662. Just a year earlier, however, Albrici had undertaken a quick junket to Hamburg with the singer Perozzi, the purpose of which remains unknown.[56] During their stay in the port city, the two musicians may have visited or even boarded with former *Hofkapelle* member Weckmann, organist at the Jakobikirche. In addition, the two Italians may have met Johann Adam Reincken, organist of the Katharinenkirche, and may even have attended (or participated in) a performance or two of Weckmann's collegium musicum, founded in 1660.[57] In light of Albrici's northern excursion, Weckmann's sonatas take on new significance vis a vis *Omnis caro foenum*, for Albrici may have borrowed the scoring from these chamber works of Weckmann.[58] But even more significantly, Hamburg was at this time a hub of contrapuntal activity; as Walker has shown, both of these city musicians displayed a keen interest in invertible counterpoint and discussed various contrapuntal and fugal procedures in theoretical treatises. According to Walker, these composers "worked primarily from Sweelinck's *Compositions-Regeln* to develop a new sort of fugue based on the treatment of two or more themes in a continuous display of invertible counterpoint."[59] Albrici's fugue corresponds most closely to the principles espoused by Weckmann and Reincken, both of whom focused attention on counterpoint that was invertible at the octave.[60] All of this suggests that Albrici's interactions with the Hamburg contrapuntists spurred his interest in works of this nature. But Walker also points out that although Weckmann composed a sacred concerto using permutation techniques, and both Weckmann and Reincken discussed the combination of fugal techniques with invertible counterpoint, neither composed an actual permutation fugue.[61] This makes the date of Albrici's concerto all the more significant, for it suggests that he was one of the first musicians to compose such a piece and, once again, took the compositional techniques of other composers to a new level.

56. See chapter 2.
57. See Silbiger, "Weckmann," in *GMO*.
58. Lüneburg KN 207/14; edited in Weckmann 1942.
59. Walker 2000:203.
60. Walker 2000:206–7.
61. Walker 2000:205–17, 234.

In the fugal portion of the vocal concerto, Albrici focuses the listener's attention on Isaiah's bleak assessment of the human condition, "all flesh is grass," and relegates the remainder of the prophet's words to the contrapuntal backdrop. Upon the completion of the final tonic entry of the subject and countersubject (mm. 25–28), however, he leaves the opening dictum behind in order to highlight the equally pessimistic thoughts embodied in the continuation of the text, "and its glories, like a flower, like a shadow pass away, vanish." But in these final bars of the concerto, Albrici abandons the severe counterpoint that has dominated the writing to this point and opts for a more homophonic presentation of the countersubject that involves all four voices (mm. 28–31). He then intensifies the ending with a codetta (mm. 31–34), a new, *presto* setting of the final word, "evanescunt." Here Albrici again evokes the central theme of the text, the transience of life, this time with rapid sixteenth-note scales followed by brief, rhetorical silences in all parts. To heighten the rhetoric of the vocal conclusion, he adds an echo of the final phrase, marked *piano*. The concerto concludes with an instrumental sinfonia that restates the final four bars of the vocal concerto (mm. 35–38), then reverberates with ever more distant echoes of the word "vanish" after the speaker himself has "disappeared."

The aria portion of *Omnis caro foenum* represents one of the few through-composed arias found in Albrici's works in this genre. Each strophe stands as an independent, harmonically closed unit, and each one is articulated by a succinct instrumental ritornello, the first three of which are identical. In his musical presentation of these bleak stanzas, Albrici carefully preserves the somber affect established by the foregoing fugue. He assigns the first three stanzas to the lower three voices, sets each in common time, and gives each its own melodic identity. He lends the first three strophes a certain degree of affinity, however, through the nearly ubiquitous use of several closely related rhythmic motives, each of which is derived from the textual meter (see, for example, "Haec carnis gloria" in Ex. 6.12, m. 54). In contrast to most of Albrici's aria strophes, which are defined by graceful, fluid lines, these three strophes possess a somewhat discontinuous quality that results from his fragmentation of each line of the alexandrine verse into two distinct parts, set off by rests. The resulting musical effect, that of ephemerality, recalls once again the theme of the text. In the fourth stanza, however, when the poet allows a thin shaft of light to penetrate the darkness, Albrici permits a similar sense of hope to insinuate itself into the music. He shifts to triple meter, and drives out the darkness and uncertainty of the first three strophes with confident, flowing lines sung in the luminous range of the soprano castrato.

In their arias, the Dresden composers generally sought to project a single affect rather than engage in musical depictions of textual content. At times, however, they deviated from this path and incorporated "text-painting," or passages in which they sought to realize specific words and ideas in music. The second aria strophe of *Omnis caro foenum* represents one such case; here Albrici seeks to bring certain of the vivid textual images to life, and he calls upon one of Johann Georg's virtuoso basses for assistance. In this strophe, Albrici takes an unusually declamatory approach to a poetic text and employs motivic repetition and dramatic *passaggi*. As a result, the style of the strophe falls somewhere between that of aria and arioso (Ex. 6.12).

In the first portion of the strophe, Albrici retains the same rhythmic pattern that he had introduced in the first strophe. His representational approach to the stanza begins in the first line, where he first takes the bass up to an optimistic *a* at "gloria," then immediately plunges the vocal line into the depths when the text speaks of loss ("perditur"). He continues with this same rhythmic pattern through the next three half-lines of text and, as a result, dispenses with the first five phrases of text quickly, while taking the bass up to middle *c ʹ*, the highest pitch yet attained. At the midpoint of line 3, however, the bass suddenly abandons the familiar rhythm and launches into a flurry of sixteenth notes—a musical depiction of the wind scattering the defenseless leaf (see mm. 59–60). On a less literal level, this abrupt departure from the established norm also serves as a metaphor for the theme of unreadiness that runs through these stanzas. But it is the final line of the stanza that dominates the aria strophe. Here tonal instability also contributes to Albrici's affective concept; first, after settling on C (V/III) in m. 60, he employs a disorienting tertial shift to E (V/V) in mm. 60–61, in order to set off the central line of the stanza, which expresses the poet's fatalistic view of the quality of life on earth. As the second half of the strophe continues, even though the basic chordal progressions are straightforward, the harmony gains a sense of disquietude due to the predominance of chords in inversion. In his presentation of the final line of text (the B section of the strophe), the bass becomes a cunning orator, one who first builds a sense of expectation in his listeners by repeating "thus is the life of man . . . ," and who then startles his hearers with a barrage of sixteenth notes designed to evoke the sense of a sudden and undesired departure ("stolen from the world"). In this virtuosic passage, which covers the span of a fifteenth, the bass must swiftly fly up to the topmost reaches of his range (*e ʹ*), and negotiate runs and leaps. Following this musical climax, Albrici restates this dramatic passage (the B ʹ section), now transposed to effect closure on the tonic; as a result, the voice disappears into the abyss, on the lowest vocal pitch heard in the entire work.

Albrici: *Cogita o homo*

Another of Albrici's early concertos with aria, *Cogita o homo*, is also based on a *vanitas* text.[62] It stands out among his works in that genre particularly for its aria, which represents one of only two surviving examples of his use of strophic variation; in

---

62. Modern edition in Frandsen 1997-3:27–58. Musical example prepared from S-Uu VMHS 1:5.

EXAMPLE 6.12 Albrici, *Omnis caro foenum*, mm. 54–69

contrast, his colleague Peranda seems to have shown no interest in this approach to the strophic aria.[63] The first documented Dresden performance of *Cogita* occurred in 1662, during Vespers on the Feast of the Purification (2 February), and the work seems to have remained one of the elector's favorites, for it represents the only extant work for which performances can be documented during all three of Albrici's tenures in Dresden as Kapellmeister. It was also one of the more widely disseminated of Albrici's works; copies of *Cogita* are found in all three collections that preserve his works (Düben had acquired it by 1663), and the concerto is also listed in two inventories. The scoring includes a quartet of solo voices (soprano, alto, tenor, and bass), as well as two violins, bassoon, and continuo; here, as in most of Albrici's works scored for this combination of obbligato instruments, the bassoon plays intermittently, with the violins, and does not form part of the continuo group. In its overall form, *Cogita* hearkens back to the Roman refrain form, for the concerto recurs in the middle as well as at the conclusion of the work.

In contrast to *Omnis caro foenum*, here Albrici takes a more (but not entirely) conventional approach to the opening concerto. He opens with an instrumental sinfonia that, while extremely brief, still manages to establish the E-minor tonality, and exhibits the tonic-dominant polarity that controls the harmonic language. In contrast to many concertos, however, the instruments do not drop out at this point, but accompany the voices in the vocal concerto. For the concerto, Albrici takes the traditional "text-bound motive" approach and divides opening dictum of this *vanitas* text into three sections, each of which receives separate musical treatment: "Cogita, o homo, / omnia transitoria in hoc mundo / praeter amare Christum Dominum" ("Reflect, o man, / everything is transitory in this world / except to love Christ the Lord").[64] The speaker's opening admonition—"reflect, o man"—is delivered first by the soprano alone, but is then immediately taken up by the tutti in a short-lived imitative restatement in the Roman manner. Once the speaker has gained the listener's attention, he proceeds to warn of the danger inherent in trusting in things temporal; in response, Albrici shifts suddenly to a faster tempo (*Allegro*) and fashions

63. Albrici's other strophic-variation aria appears in his *Ave Jesu Christe*. Moberg first identified Albrici's use of strophic variation, and even reconstructed a hypothetical cantus firmus that he suggested may have served as the basis for the aria melody of *Cogita o homo*; see Moberg 1962:211–15.

64. The opening text makes reference to Ephesians 1:11 and Hebrews 9:15, and may also have been developed from the opening lines of Augustine's *De contritione*: "*Cogitemus ergo quam brevis sit vita nostra, quam via lubrica, quam mors certa et hora mortis incerta. Cogitemus quantis amaritudinibus admixtum sit, si quid dulce aut jucundum in via hujus vitae occursu suo nobis alludit; quam fallax et suspectum, quam instabile et transitorium est, quidquid hujus mundi amor parturit, quidquid species aut pulchritudo temporalis promittit*" (*PL* 40:943; emphasis added by the author).

an evocative motive dominated by a rapidly ascending scale, which he takes to an imitative climax. But here Albrici also introduces harmonic instability as a metaphor for earthly transience and allows this section to close while still suspended on the dominant. After delaying the speaker's completion of the opening text with his musical treatment of these two phrases, which succinctly present the two elements that define the concept of *Weltabsagung*, Albrici finally allows the speaker to reveal his message of confidence to the listener: only in loving Christ can one find peace and security. In his treatment of the final phrase of text, Albrici leaves behind the affect of transience for one of certitude, and moves from *concertato* style into a stricter style of imitation that approximates a fugue. Each singer in turn takes up the "subject" at two-measure intervals, on $f_\#'$ (alto), b' (soprano), and e (bass), respectively, and presents the motive that Albrici has crafted for this portion of the text in the manner of a fugal exposition. While neither as intricate nor as lengthy as the fugue in *Omnis caro foenum*, this passage nevertheless stands as another example of Albrici's interest in this compositional technique and of his appropriation of fugal procedures for affective purposes.

Albrici derived his aria text from the extended medieval poem *Homo Dei creatura*, and disposed his borrowings in four quatrains in order to provide an aria strophe for each singer.[65] In its tone, the poetry matches that of the sentiments expressed by the poet. But while the homilist in *Omnis caro foenum* concluded by allowing the listener a slight glimmer of hope, this speaker remains pessimistic to the end and never ceases in his attempt to alter the listener's behavior with threats of dire things to come:

Homo, Dei creatura,	Man, creature of God,
cur in carne moritura	why in the flesh about to die
est tam parva tibi cura	is there so little concern on your part
pro aeterna gloria?	for eternal glory?
O si poenas infernales	O if you knew what the eternal punishments are,
agnovisces, quae et quales,	and what they are like,
tuos utique carnales	you would certainly subdue
appetitus frangeres,	your carnal appetites,
Et innumera peccata,	And the innumerable sins

---

65. The poem (with forty-two quatrains) appears in Merlo 1716:160–62; Albrici includes st. 1, 3, 4, and 39. A version with eighty-nine octaves appears in *Analecta Hymnica* 33: 303, no. 262; Merlo's st. 39 does not appear there.

dicta, facta, cogitata,	said, done, and thought,
mente tota consternata	you would rightly bewail
merito deplangeres.	with a mind thrown completely
	into confusion.

Ecce, mundus evanescit,	Behold, the world disappears,
decor eius iam arescit,[66]	its beauty dries up,
et quotidie vilescit	and daily its false glory
fallax eius gloria.	becomes worthless.

Albrici, however, seeks to temper the stern rhetoric of the poet in his musical realization of the poetry; as a result, the aria lacks the severity of that in *Omnis caro foenum*. He retains the E minor of the opening concerto, but softens its effect by quickly modulating to the relative major and then to its dominant, before embarking on the return to the tonic. He casts the aria in a gently undulating triple meter and fashions a rhythmic ductus that recalls the courante; the affinity with the French court dance is strengthened by the double hemiola figure that occurs at the closing cadences of each strophe (Ex. 6.13). In addition, the flexibility offered by the strophic variation form allows him to establish a single, overarching affect, while simultaneously lending each stanza its own musical identity. In each of the first three strophes (sung by the soprano, alto, and tenor respectively), the same bass line (with a few minor changes) supports the melodic lines, which are similar but not identical. In the soprano strophe, however, Albrici illustrates the word "aeterna" (mm. 45–46) by sustaining an e'' over nearly four bars. At the analogous spot in the alto and tenor strophes, he omits two measures, as the musical illustration previously employed no longer suits the text. In these three strophes he responds musically to individual words and phrases on a few other occasions; for example, the soprano line suddenly drops an octave at "moritura," and the awkward tenor line at "deplangeres" intensifies the speaker's lament. These rather slight musical reflections of the text, however, pale in comparison to those of the fourth strophe, sung by the bass. It seems that Albrici could not resist the potential this stanza held for musical imagery; perhaps he found that even the pliable strophic variation form placed too many constraints upon his imagination. At first, his departure from the established pattern affects only the melody, which he composes anew for the bass's first presentation of stanza 4 (mm. 143–60); here he alters it only slightly by adding an extra bar (m. 159). After this presentation, however, he departs entirely from the established material at bar 161 and completely rewrites the continuo line at the restatement of the fourth line of

66. For "arescit" Merlo has "marcescit," from *marceo*: to wither, droop, be feeble.

EXAMPLE 6.13 Albrici, *Cogita o homo*, Comparison of Aria Strophes

EXAMPLE 6.13 (*continued*)

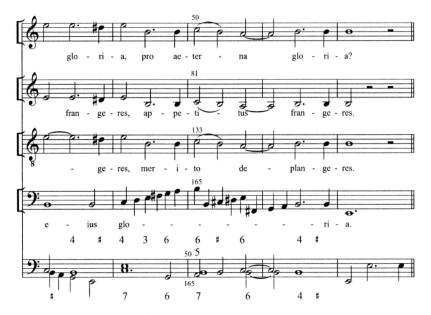

EXAMPLE 6.13 (*continued*)

text (the B′ section), as neither the rhythmic nor the melodic contours of the bass's melodic line now correspond with the pre-established bass line (see mm. 161–67).[67] In his musical response to this text, Albrici again takes full advantage of the bass's great range and vocal flexibility for purposes of affect. He depicts the central idea of the *vanitas* theme, the utter worthlessness of the world and its "false glory," with dramatic falling octaves that evoke the image of trap doors snapping open, sending sinners plummeting into the abyss, followed by tortuous melismas that mock the very idea of glory.[68]

PERANDA: *QUIS DABIT CAPITI MEO*

In its rich variety of textual and musical elements, as well as its vocal scoring, Peranda's concerto *Quis dabit capiti meo aquas* recalls many features of the Roman

67. The stemming in the continuo part in mm. 161–66 reflects the changes made in the bass line at this point; notes with upward stems correspond to the line as it appears in the first three strophes; notes with downward stems reflect the line that supports the bass singer's melodic line.
68. The change of affect in the bass strophe also suggests that Albrici sought to facilitate the transition to the sterner mode of the opening concerto, which follows this strophe.

ensemble motet of the 1640s, but also reveals Peranda's development of that idiom while in Dresden.[69] This composition, scored for three lower voices (alto, tenor, and bass) and instruments (two violins, bassoon, and basso continuo), seems to have found particular favor with Johann Georg II, for members of the *Hofkapelle* performed it for him on at least six occasions between 1662 and 1667.[70] It represents one of the earlier extant sources, as Düben had already acquired it by 1663.[71] In *Quis dabit* Peranda employs the sort of metric and stylistic contrasts observed in the works of Gratiani and others, contrasts which now represent normative features of the sacred concertos of both Dresden Kapellmeisters. Like the earlier Roman motet, *Quis dabit* unfolds as a succession of contrasting sections, all of which represent musical responses to both affective and structural aspects of the text. But in contrast to the Roman composers of the previous few decades, both Peranda and Albrici take full advantage of the timbral colors now available to them and score the majority of their concertos for voices and instruments; in *Quis dabit*, Peranda uses a small complement of instruments to bind the disparate musical strands together.

Like so many of the texts in the Dresden repertoire, that of *Quis dabit* (below) shows evidence of having been centonized from various sources, several of which remain unidentified. Despite this fact, however, the text displays a distinct thematic unity. The text opens with a well-known passage from Jeremiah's lament for Judah, altered to reference the speaker's own contrition; just as Jeremiah sought tears with which to weep for the "slain of the daughter of [his] people" (RSV), the speaker seeks tears to weep without ceasing for his sins.[72] This affective opening passage sets the emotional tone for a penitential text in which the speaker calls upon Christ for forgiveness. Unlike *Peccavi O Domine*, however, the speaker has moved beyond confession and self-flagellation; as a result, the text is undergirded by an air of confidence that remains unexpressed until it finally receives its voice at the conclusion. As the text proceeds, the speaker seems to allude to Ps. 138:7, but adds a free extension that locates the psalmist's thoughts within New Testament Christology.[73] At the center of the text appear two stanzas that share the meter of *Jesu dulcis memoria*, in which the speaker addresses his supplication to the One Intercessor (in the Lutheran view). In the final portion of the text, the speaker explicitly places his trust

69. Modern edition in Frandsen 1997-3:687–707. Musical examples prepared from S-Uu VMHS 1:18 and D-B Mus. ms. 17081 no. 18.

70. See Appendix II.

71. Düben's parts (S-Uu VMHS 1:18) are dated 1663.

72. Vulgate text: "Quis dabit capiti meo aquam et oculis meis fontem lacrimarum et plorabo die et nocte interfectos filiae populi mei?" (Jeremiah 9:1).

73. Compare "Ad quem recurram . . . " to Ps 138:7 (Vulgate): "Quo ibo ab spiritu tuo et quo a facie tua fugiam?" ("Whither shall I go from thy Spirit? Or whither shall I flee from thy presence?" Ps 139:7, RSV). Compare also Ps 17:3, 30:4, 61:8, and 90:2.

in Christ, and draws first upon the *Transfige* of St. Bonaventure, and then concludes with the final three lines of the Marian antiphon *Salve Regina*, altered to redirect the text towards Christ, as required in Lutheran use.[74] Considered without the poetic strophes, the prose portion of the text reads as a thematically and syntactically unified passage that may have originated in a contemporary prayer book or devotional manual, and may have been addressed to Mary in its original incarnation.

Quis dabit capiti meo aquas?	Who will give waters to my head?
Quis dabit oculis meis lachrymas,	Who will give tears to my eyes,
ut defleam die ac nocte	that I might night and day
omnes iniquitates meas?	bewail all of my sins? (Jeremiah 9:1)
Ad quem recurram,	To whom shall I return,
ad quem confugiam,	to whom shall I flee
nisi ad te,	except to you,
o benignissime Fili Mariae?	O most kind son of Mary? (Ps 138:7, alt.)[75]
Aures clementer aperi,	Gently open your ears,
te invocanti subveni,	relieve the one calling on you for help,
noli clientem spernere	do not spurn the suppliant
saucium gravi vulnere.	distressed by an oppressive wound.
Sed Patri tuo coelico	But zealously commit me to the care
me commendare sedulo,	of your heavenly Father,
ut iram suam mitiget	that he might sooth his anger
culpasque meas condonet.	and forgive my sin.
Quoniam tu es spes mea,	Because you are my hope,
auxiliatio mea,	my help,

74. Prayer of St. Bonaventure (excerpt from third section): "ut tu sis solus semper *spes mea*, tota fiducia mea, divitiae meae, . . . dulcedo mea, cibus meus, refectio mea, *refugium meum, auxilium meum*, sapientia mea, portio mea, [etc.]; *Salve Regina* (conclusion): "O clemens, o pie, o dulcis Virgo Maria."

75. Ps 138:7: "Quo ibo ab spiritu tuo et quo a facie tua fugiam?" ("Whither shall I go from thy Spirit, and whither shall I flee from thy presence?")

et refugium meum,	and my refuge,
o clemens, o pie,	O merciful, O compassionate,
o dulcis Fili Mariae.	O sweet son of Mary.

Peranda establishes the somber tone of the work immediately, in the instrumental sinfonia that serves as an introduction, after which the alto and tenor offer Jeremiah's poignant entreaty in an expressive contrapuntal duet (Ex. 6.14). This approach represents another Dresden modification of the Roman model, for while many Roman composers initiated their ensemble motets with a declamatory passage for solo voice, Peranda and Albrici generally open with a sinfonia followed by vocal writing in *concertato* style, regardless of whether the text begins with prose or poetry.[76] Normally they involve the full complement of voices, but at times both composers opt to open with a reduced scoring.

In this plaintive opening section, with its biting dissonances, Peranda responds musically to the sentiments of desolation expressed by the prophet.[77] The passage represents some of Peranda's most powerful and affective writing, in which he reveals his great gift for "express[ing] the stirrings of the soul beyond all measure." After the tenor and alto each present a solo line that sighs as it moves through its descent, and then ascends to reflect the question posed by the speaker, the two voices come together to spin an imitative web of suspensions that holds the listener in its grip until the final cadence (mm. 32–33). Much of the passage's effectiveness derives from Peranda's harmonic approach. First, he imbues the passage with a certain harmonic ambivalence, and writes in an idiom that references both E minor and the E/A harmonic dualism of the Phrygian mode. Perhaps the sorrowful words of Jeremiah, with their reference to tears, called forth Peranda's allusions to the Phrygian mode, the affect of which a number of theorists deemed perfectly suited to the lament.[78] Second, he twice uses a harmonic device beloved by the previous generation: the abrupt harmonic shift by major or minor third, which creates

---

76. A few exceptions include Peranda's *Ecce ego mittam piscatores* (solo declamatory passage follows the sinfonia), *Quo tendimus mortales* (Frandsen 1997-3:709–19; no instruments, begins with declamatory solo) and *Timor et tremor* (Frandsen 1997-3:854–90; declamatory solo follows the sinfonia and is accompanied by strings), and Albrici's *O amantissime sponse* (instruments silent at the beginning, opens with declamatory solo) and *Quantus amor Jesu* (solo concerto for bass and two violins, declamatory passage follows the sinfonia).

77. In this passage, readings from D-B Mus. ms. 17081 no. 18 have been incorporated.

78. Kircher, for example, lists the modal quality of Phrygian as "lachrymosus" on his table of modes; Kircher 1650-2:51; Burmeister regarded it as appropriate for *lamentosae* subjects, while Herbst relegated it to his "sad and gentle" ("traurig und gelind") modes. See Lester 1989:26, 65, and Linfield 1992:92.

EXAMPLE 6.14 Peranda, *Quis dabit capiti meo aquas*, mm. 12–33

EXAMPLE 6.14 (*continued*)

a cross-relation between parts, as well as a sense of harmonic dislocation.[79] In order to set off the final phrase of the text, "omnes iniquitates meas," Peranda employs two dramatic tertial shifts, the first from A to F (mm. 23–24), and the second from E to C (m. 27). At the close of the vocal section, Peranda briefly recaps the thematic material of the end of the sinfonia (mm. 8–12, restated in mm. 32–35). This scalar motive, which encompasses a descending fifth, now becomes a semiotic marker for the tears of the opening and recurs several times as the piece progresses (Ex. 6.15).

79. Examples abound in the Italian and German repertoires of ca. 1600–50; often the shift occurs mid-phrase, as a coloring device. See, for example, Schütz's *Wie lieblich sind deine Wohnungen* (SWV 29), from the *Psalmen Davids* of 1619 (on "lieblich"), and his *O süßer, o freundlicher* (SWV 285) from the *Kleine geistliche Konzerte* of 1636 (at "süßer" and "freundlicher"); Alessandro Grandi's *O quam tu pulchra es* (at "Quia amore langueo"); Gabrieli's *In ecclesiis*, from *Sacrae symphoniae* (1615), at "Deus, Deus," as well as many other works. Jerome Roche also discusses Gabrieli's use of these "tertial harmonic juxtapositions" (Roche 1984:115).

EXAMPLE 6.15 Peranda, *Quis dabit capiti meo aquas*, mm. 8–11

In the bass solo that follows, the speaker asks "to whom shall I flee," then confi-
dently appeals to the "most kind Son of Mary." The reference to a benevolent Christ
causes Peranda to moderate the affect of the opening in this passage, which allows
a smooth transition to the mood of the setting of the poetic stanzas that follow.
These two stanzas offer Peranda a basic compositional choice: aria or concerto? As
the Roman examples demonstrate, either option was viable. His solution, however,
represents one of the ways both he and his colleague capitalized on their Roman
inheritance, for Peranda opts to involve the vocal trio in a setting of the poetry in
concertato style. Here, however, both the homophonic opening and the subsequent
imitative portion owe a considerable stylistic debt to the aria (Ex. 6.16). Peranda
treats both strophes in the same manner; as the first strophe concludes in m. 102,
the violins enter with a ritornello based on the melismatic material heard just
moments earlier (mm. 102–112). In mm. 113–64, the entire procedure is repeated,
with the new text.

At this point, the speaker has attained a different emotional plane and has left
his despair behind; thus nothing in Peranda's setting of these two stanzas recalls
the sheer visceral power of the opening duet. As each stanza progresses, the musical setting moves gradually away from simple homophony to an imitative texture
animated by the type of melismatic writing often seen in Peranda's arias.[80] By slowing the pace of the imitative entries, and casting the poetry in a slow triple meter,
Peranda projects the "gentleness" invoked in the first line of the first strophe and
transports the listener into Christ's comforting presence. Peranda's harmonic decisions also reflect the new affective reality here: while he moves again between E and

80. Cf. *Languet cor meum*; modern edition in Frandsen 1997-3:600–18; this concerto
also features the gentle type of *concertato*-style writing seen in *Quis dabit*.

EXAMPLE 6.16 Peranda, *Quis dabit capiti meo aquas*, mm. 61–102

EXAMPLE 6.16 (*continued*)

A, he takes time to modulate smoothly to each key area through its respective dominant. Absent entirely are the disorienting tertial shifts heard in the opening.

With the speaker's confident statement, "because you are my hope, my help, and my refuge," Peranda returns to a more declamatory style, and assigns each singer a solo passage following the tutti declamation of "Quoniam." Here the bass commands the most attention, as he far outdoes the other two vocally with a long melisma on "refugium meum." In fact, one of the most distinctive features of this repertoire is the fact that, despite the abundance of castrati, the most virtuosic music is regularly assigned to the bass. As a codetta to the bass solo, however, Peranda does not borrow from the melodic material just sung by the bass, but once again invokes the brief instrumental passage drawn from the close of the sinfonia. The affect of this brief motive contrasts sharply with that created by the bass's vocal acrobatics and functions as an affective bridge to the quiet invocations of the closing; it also connects the final portion of the concerto with the very opening. For the conclusion of the concerto, Peranda returns to the slow triple meter and musical style of the poetic strophes and brings in the instruments to echo the vocal phrases. In the final seven measures, the instruments join the vocalists and, in the penultimate measure, introduce one last echo of the motive from the sinfonia.

CHERICI: *DEPLORANDUS ET AMARUS*

The Ferrarese composer Sebastiano Cherici (1647–1703) assumed the position of Kapellmeister in Dresden in September 1675, more than half a year after the death of Peranda the previous January. Cherici received his musical training in Bologna under Giovanni Paolo Colonna (1637–95), a composer of Albrici's generation who had also studied with Carissimi in Rome.[81] Sixteen years younger than Albrici (b. 1631), however, and more than twenty years younger than Peranda (b. ca. 1625), Cherici brought the music of a later generation of Italian composer to the Dresden court. While his texts closely resemble those set by Albrici and Peranda in form, style, and content, his approach to the texts differs in some respects from that seen in their works. Although no orders of worship survive from the first three months of his tenure, the court diary SLUB Q 260 includes many of the orders of worship for the 1675–76 church year, and these reveal that Cherici's works formed the major part of the repertoire performed between Advent 4 (19 December) and *Quasimodogeniti* (Easter 1). Members of the *Hofkapelle* presented his *Deplorandus et amarus*, a concerto for two sopranos and bass, two violins, "bassetto viola," and organ, at vespers on Christmas Eve in 1675, and again at vespers on the Feast of the Purification

81. See Surian, "Cherici," and Smith and Vanscheeuvijck, "Colonna," in *GMO*.

(2 February 1676).[82] Cherici casts the concerto in C minor, and opens with an aria of two strophes, each of which is sung by one of the sopranos and followed by the same ritornello (A). In this his approach differs from that of Albrici and Peranda, who prefer to fashion duos and trios from any verse that stands at the beginning of a text. In this aria, Cherici's melodic style also differs somewhat from that of his predecessors, for he concentrates on smooth scalar lines that afford the singer a multitude of opportunities for *variatio*. Although the two stanzas are disposed as tercets, rather than as quatrains (which appear with greater frequency), Cherici succeeds in designing well-proportioned strophes in ABB′ form, and also adds musical interest by varying both the phrase lengths and the rhythmic patterns. While well-constructed, however, the opening strophes do lack the degree of harmonic tension that usually informs such miniature structures, for Cherici avoids the dominant at the important structural cadence that closes the B section, and moves instead to the subdominant (Ex. 6.17). In the B′ section, he lends a bit of affective emphasis to the text through a chromatic coloring of "misery." And although the opening stanza speaks of the "bitterness that is to be deplored," Cherici does not strive to create an ominously dark affect, but instead allows the gentle lyricism of the aria to temper the severity of the text.

The text continues with two more equivalent stanzas, now disposed as quatrains in a new meter (–∪∪–∪∪, rhymed abab). Albrici and Peranda normally use musical identity to underscore such textual equivalencies, just as Cherici did in the opening aria. Here, however, the younger composer seeks to sever the structural and semantic relationship between the two stanzas by setting the first as an aria strophe for the bass, and the second as an unrelated *concertato*-style section for the vocal ensemble. In the bass aria, "Hinc quae sunt pectora," a new and far more assertive voice enters the scene. Cherici's musical response to this text seems to be governed more by a perceived need for musical contrast than by the actual content, for he uses this doleful text as an excuse for vocal fireworks executed in a brisk tempo. Normally the invocation of sighs in a text would call forth melodic gestures suggestive of yearning or emotional pain from a composer of this era. Cherici, however, avoids any and all musical suggestion of both the sighs and of the affect that they imply and creates a mood that seems best described as wrathful. Long, sequential *passaggi* dominate the writing and occur with regularity at the ends of phrases; only the "sin of the father" ("paterni sceleris") would seem to provide the textual rationale for such musical bluster. Although virtuosic, however, the aria does not exploit the lower regions of the bass's range, but stays instead in the uppermost tenth ($B\flat$ to d').

---

82. *Harmonia di devoti concerti* (Bologna: Monti, 1681). Exemplar owned by the Bibliothèque royale de Belgique/Koninklijke Bibliotheek van België, Fétis 1.737 A. In the dedication to Cardinal Nicolo Acciaioli, Papal Legate in Ferrara, Cherici makes no mention of his compositional activities in Dresden. Text and translation in chapter 4.

EXAMPLE 6.17 Cherici, *Deplorandus et amarus*, mm. 1–29

Upon the conclusion of the new ritornello (B) that follows the bass solo, the three voices join forces to present the stanza "Hinc o posteritas." At this point, Cherici returns to the affect of the opening. He opens the section on A♭, with quietly emphatic homophonic statements of the first two lines of the stanza, throughout which he descends by fourths. Upon reaching F, he shifts to the parallel minor (Ex.

EXAMPLE 6.18 Cherici, *Deplorandus et amarus*, mm. 125–41

6.18, m. 130). What follows constitutes the most striking portion of the concerto, in which Cherici sets himself apart quite decisively from his predecessors. Inspired by the text "the pathetic misfortune, the lament and tears [for our miserable state]," he borrows from the musical semiotic code of the secular lament, the descending chromatic tetrachord,[83] and presses it into service in the creation of a sacred lament. But rather than use the tetrachord as a ground, he weaves the familiar descending figure into an imitative texture in the upper parts, to the text "dolor, calamitas," set against a rising contrasting motive ("planctus et lacrimae"). Thus he invokes the idea of the ground bass through multiple sung iterations of the descending line (Ex. 6.18).

This polyphonic lament provides an affective foil for the following section, in which an authority figure, perhaps an angel, enters to address the assembled. As they listen, the speaker invites them to cease their weeping and wailing and communicates to them the message of salvation. Cherici assigns this text to the bass and shifts to a recitational mode. Like analogous passages by Albrici and Peranda, this is rhetorically conceived. But in contrast to their declamatory writing, Cherici's stands much closer to simple recitative, like that sung by a narrator, which likely reflects his work in Italy with the oratorio genre. He sets the text syllabically and only expands the final word of the passage, "redemption," with passage work. Like Peranda, he outlines chords in his *passaggi*, but rhythmically never moves beyond eighth notes—the bass is never given the opportunity to display his coloratura. Neither does Cherici exploit the singer's low range, as his predecessors regularly did in their declamatory solos for bass.

After a brief walking-bass aria for Soprano 1 and another statement of ritornello B, the full ensemble enters for the compelling final tutti, "Veni ergo Domine." For the first time, all three voices and instruments come together in service to the text. As he had done in the preceding ritornelli, Cherici bases his writing for the violins in this section on the vocal parts; there is no sign here yet of independent, idiomatic parts for the strings. Cherici's fondness for counterpoint is again on display, for after the basically homophonic treatment of the opening phrase, "Veni ergo Domine," he fashions two contrasting motives from the subsequent clause ("mestos adae filios redime / et consolare") and poses one against another in a subject/countersubject relationship (Ex. 6.19). He further enhances the contrapuntal texture with chains of suspensions that arise from the imitative treatment of the latter motive ("et consolare"). In a manner seen often in the works of the Romans, Cherici first treats all of the motivic material in one key, in this case the minor dominant, and then develops it further in a restatement in the tonic. The tonic restatement follows an instrumental interlude based on the vocal material, which Cherici uses to accomplish a modu-

---

83. Here the tetrachord is not quite fully chromatic, as it lacks a D♮.

EXAMPLE 6.19 Cherici, *Deplorandus et amarus*, mm. 190–205

EXAMPLE 6.19 (*continued*)

lation, rather than simply to shift from dominant to tonic. Although uncomplicated in its design, the restatement technique can have rhetorical as well as musical consequences, as is often seen in earlier Roman motets. In this tutti, the transposition to the tonic shifts the vocal material up a fourth; as a result, the simple act of restatement intensifies the urgency of the speakers' supplication, "come, Lord."

ALBRICI: *SPARGITE FLORES*

In *Spargite flores*, another work from the 1660s, Albrici displays yet again the formal flexibility of the early concerto with aria.[84] With a nod to his Roman heritage, he adds tutti restatements of each of the three aria strophes and further expands the composition through the interpolation of instrumental sinfonias that adumbrate the following aria strophes. He also eschews the restatement of the opening concerto at the conclusion and instead appends a fugal Alleluia. At 339 bars, *Spargite* stands as one of Albrici's lengthiest extant compositions; other concertos with aria, such as *Omnis caro foenum* and *Benedicte Domine*, are about half this length. A source for this work survives only in the Bokemeyer collection, where the scoring includes soprano, alto and tenor, two violins, violone, and continuo.[85] Albrici presented the concerto on three occasions in 1662, the only year for which performance records for the work exist; during that year, it was first heard at vespers on the Sunday after Easter (*Quasimodogeniti*), then again in the morning *Hauptgottesdienst* on 20 June, on the occasion of the fifteenth birthday of Prince Johann Georg III, and finally at vespers on Christmas Eve. The concluding Alleluia, as well as the performance on *Quasimodogeniti*, may indicate that *Spargite* was conceived as a composition for the Easter season, but any perceived allusions to the Resurrection event, such as Christ as the "blooming rose," are sufficiently ambiguous so as to render the text suitable for any joyful period in the church year.[86]

Spargite flores, fundite rosas, et date lilia dilecto Jesu Domino.	Scatter flowers, spread roses, and give lilies to the beloved Lord Jesus.
Rosa vernans miro flore	The blooming rose with the wonderful flower

84. Modern edition in Frandsen 1997-3:318–66. Musical examples prepared from D-B Mus. ms. 501 no. 8.

85. See Appendix II.

86. See the performance information in Appendix II. The sources of the prose statement and the poetic stanzas are unknown; the author-compiler may have written the opening to correspond to the poetry, or conversely, selected the poetic stanzas (particularly the first) as a sort of trope on the opening material.

es, o Jesu mi, serenus,	are you, O my Jesus, serene,
pulcher gratus et amoenus,	beautiful, delightful, and pleasing,
replens corda coeli rore.	replenishing hearts with the dew of heaven.
Nemo digne sat laudare,	No one is sufficient to worthily praise you,
sed nec ullo valet modo	nor yet is in any way able
te qui coeli sedes polo	to proclaim with worthy praise you who sit
laude digna praedicare.	in the vault of heaven.
Tamen gessit creatura	Still your creation brings forth
quantum potest preces voce;	prayers as best he can with his voice;
tu nos rege, tu nos doce,	rule us, teach us
te laudare mente pura.	to praise you with a pure mind.
Alleluia.	Hallelujah.

Albrici establishes joy as the reigning affect of the composition in the lively instrumental sinfonia that opens the work, the motives of which contains hints of the material to be introduced by the voices in the upcoming concerto. But despite the brevity of the introduction, Albrici also manages to encapsulate the essential harmonic content of the concerto here as well, by modulating from the tonic C major to the relative minor and back again. With the entry of the voices, Albrici captures the imperative mood of the text in a confident setting characterized by florid lines and driving rhythms. Here he fashions a musical motive for each of the imperatives of the text, "spargite flores / fundite rosas / et date lilia dilecto Jesu Domino," and treats each in a marginally imitative *concertato* style. Once he has addressed all three motives, he explores each a second time, and more than doubles the concerto's length in the process. Albrici also adds to the weight of the concerto by adding the instruments to the voices, save during the first two solo entries of the initial motive. The accompanying violin parts share the rhythmic gestures of the vocal parts, but do not actually double the vocal lines; instead, they function as harmonic and textural "thickening agents."

The central portion of the work, the aria, follows immediately and begins with a triple-meter instrumental ritornello in which Albrici prefigures the vocal material soon to come. While the aria melody is not actually present in the instrumental parts, much of the bass line is similar or identical to that of the aria, and the

EXAMPLE 6.20 Albrici, *Spargite flores*, mm. 70–110

melodic and rhythmic gestures of the violins adumbrate those of the vocal melody. At the conclusion of the ritornello, the instruments drop out to make way for the soprano, who presents the first aria strophe accompanied only by the continuo. In the simplicity of its melodic content, the aria strophe captures the new sense of tranquillity introduced in this joyful devotional text, but in the general upward sweep of its phrases, it also succeeds in maintaining an affective link with the preceding concerto. In the strophe, which falls into the typical ABB′ form, Albrici also demonstrates an intention to expand the work at all levels, for he stretches the A section with echoes of the first two phrases, marked *piano* (Ex. 6.20).

But rather than present three solo strophes, interrupted only by brief ritornelli, Albrici opts to create an "aria complex" that includes tutti restatements of all three solo strophes. His approach to the restatement differs somewhat from that of Gratiani, whose reworking of the material often involves imitation. In contrast, Albrici borrows the complete bass line from the strophe and shapes a three-part homophonic version of the solo over it, but alters the aria melody such that the restatement takes the form of a variation or paraphrase (Ex. 6.21).

Albrici follows this vocal tutti with another statement of the ritornello, and then abandons the material entirely in the second aria strophe, sung by the alto. As he must rework the melodic contour of the aria to accommodate the range of the alto, he elects to rewrite the strophe entirely, in duple meter. He does, however, retain the ABB′ form and pattern of repeated phrases introduced in the soprano strophe, and takes a similar approach to the tutti restatement. The middle strophe also contrasts harmonically with the first, for while it opens and closes in C, its secondary focus is E minor (iii), rather than the relative minor. Following the second tutti restatement, Albrici supplies a ritornello that limns the previous material much as did the first ritornello. With the entry of the tenor for the third strophe, Albrici returns to the melodic material presented earlier by the soprano, and closes the complex with a tutti restatement that essentially recapitulates the first, but is now amplified with the instrumental ensemble.

The fugal closing section of *Spargite* further attests to Albrici's interest in contrapuntal procedures and stands as another contribution to the development of the vocal fugue in the years following 1650. For this concluding Alleluia, Albrici designs a modulating fugue subject that falls into two parts, a series of eighth notes that fills in the octave between *c′′* and *c′*, followed by a sixteenth-note "tail." Albrici fashions two separate expositions of the subject, the first in I (mm. 311–15), and the second essentially in V (mm. 318–22), to which each vocalist contributes a single entry. In the first exposition, he uses a real answer (mm. 312–14), which raises the question of the need for a tonal answer in a fugue that appears at the end of a composition, when the tonality of the composition has already been firmly established.[87] As in

87. Suggested to the author by Paul Walker (private correspondence, July 2002).

EXAMPLE 6.21 Albrici, *Spargite flores*, mm. 111–26

the previous portions of the concerto, however, the upper instrumental parts do not double the voices; unlike his colleague Peranda, Albrici does not use the instruments to supply additional fugal entries. What sets this fugue apart most distinctly from others in the repertoire, however, is Albrici's inclusion of episodic material: he follows each exposition with sequential development of the sixteenth-note figure that concludes the motive (m. 312), first briefly in mm. 315–17, and then much more extensively in mm. 322–39 (Ex. 6.22).[88]

As seen in Example 6.22, Albrici alters the "tail" of the subject in the second exposition to facilitate a return from V to I. Here the entries appear in the order

88. Compare the fugue in Peranda's *Accurrite gentes* below.

EXAMPLE 6.22 Albrici, *Spargite flores*, mm. 311–22

EXAMPLE 6.22 (*continued*)

answer/subject/answer, which suggests the influence of Bertali's writings on fugal procedure.[89] In measures 319–20, Albrici adds a voice in parallel tenths to the subject. The resulting composition may easily be regarded as a fugue or fughetta, as it includes both fugal expositions and episodes that further develop the subject material. It must be said, however, that the fugue in *Spargite* does not display the thoroughgoing adherence to fugal procedure evidenced in Peranda's *Accurrite gentes* (discussed below). After the second exposition, the writing devolves into a *concertato*-style treatment of motives drawn from the subject, into the midst of which two additional "stray" entries of the subject are interwoven, separated by seven bars. Still, the writing remains very subject-oriented to the end, with nearly every contribution derived from that primary thematic material.

Peranda: *Dedit abyssus*

One of the stylistic hallmarks of the new sacred concerto as conceived by Viadana and his contemporaries was the rapid exchange of text-bound musical motives between the voices. This type of writing defines a significant portion of the sacred concerto repertoire composed between 1602 and 1660, particularly in Germany, and was a direct consequence of the continued reliance of composers of this new genre upon the "motet principle" as a compositional strategy. The compositional procedure grounded in this principle involved the fragmentation of a text into short semantic units, the fashioning of a distinct musical motive for each fragment, and the treatment of these text-bound motives in imitation, or later, in *concertato* style. While the motet principle still undergirds the tutti sections of the concertos of Albrici and Peranda, at least to some extent, the imitative writing that it engenders rarely predominates in their works, but normally yields place to declamatory and lyrical solos. Not surprisingly, given their interest in solo idioms, each composed relatively few concertos in which imitation is prized over other compositional techniques.[90] For this reason, Peranda's *Dedit abyssus* stands out among his works, for it adheres to the motet principle throughout and grants the listener no respite from its highly imitative texture. In contrast to other settings of scriptural texts, such as his *Cor mundum*,[91] here the composer makes no attempt to fashion the prose into arias and declamatory passages. And although the concerto is disposed in several large sections, Peranda makes no effort to create the stylistic contrast between these sections that normally helps to define his concerto style.

89. See Walker 2000:166–85.
90. Other highly imitative concertos include Albrici's *Domine Deus, Hymnum jucunditatis*, and *O admirabile commercium*, and Peranda's *Cantemus Domino, Dum proeliaretur, Plange anima suspira*, and *Propitiare Domine*.
91. Modern edition in Frandsen 1997-3:501–18.

Peranda may well have been inspired by the affective potential of this text upon hearing Carissimi's *Viderunt te, Domine,* which was presented in the court chapel on Easter Tuesday, 1662.[92] Both composers found musical stimulation in the vivid Easter imagery with which these words of the Old Testament prophet Habakkuk are imbued, and both set essentially the same excerpt from chapter 3 of that book; Peranda, however, omitted verse 10a and began with 10b, and also appended an Alleluia:

10a.	Viderunt te, Domine, et doluerunt montes;	The mountains saw thee, Lord, and writhed;
10b.	Dedit abyssus vocem suam altitudo manum suam levavit.[93]	The abyss gave forth its voice, it lifted up its hand on high.
11.	Sol et luna steterunt in habitaculo suo, in luce sagittarum ibunt,	The sun and moon stood still in their course, at the light of your arrows they went,
	in splendore fulgurantis hastae tuae;	at the brilliance of your glistening spear;
12.	in fremitu conturbabis terram,	you will throw the earth into confusion with roaring,
	in furore obstupefacies gentes.	you will trample the nations in anger.
	Alleluia.	Hallelujah.

Carissimi's motet, scored for soprano, bass, and continuo, is an example of his generally more conservative approach to the genre, particularly when compared with works of Gratiani and other of his Roman colleagues, for he fashions neither aria-like passages nor declamatory solos. Instead, he adopts the motet principle throughout: he disposes the text in smaller units, shapes motives for each of the various words and phrases that result, and treats these imitatively, in succession. In this respect, Peranda's setting is very similar. Not surprisingly, however, different aspects of the text caught the creative eye of each composer. For example, Carissimi subjects the opening line (which does not appear in Peranda's setting) to an extended treatment of twenty-two measures and captures the "writhing" of the mountains in a tortuous vocal melisma. Following this, however, he all but passes over the phrase that would so captivate Peranda's imagination, "dedit abyssus vocem suam," and

92. SLUB Q 240. The motet was first published by Florido de Silvestri, *Floridus modulorum hortus* (Rome: Fei, 1647) [1647²]; a modern edition appears in Jones 1982-2:456–63. Musical examples prepared from S-Uu UVMTR 553–57.

93. Carissimi's text reads "altitudo manus suas levavit."

EXAMPLE 6.23 Carissimi, *Viderunt te Domine*, mm. 22–36

EXAMPLE 6.23 (*continued*)

limits his treatment to a pair of entries of the motive, which displays the requisite descending leap at "abyssus" (Ex. 6.23).

Carissimi, of course, was cited by Bernhard as a master of both the *stylus luxurians communis* and the *stylus luxurians theatralis*, and *Viderunt te* helps to explain the rationale behind the theorist's designation.[94] At "altitudo manus suas *levavit*," for example, Carissimi enlivens the essentially triadic lines with a figure that Bernhard designates as "variation" or *passaggio*, the alteration of an interval "through several shorter notes, so that, instead of one long note, a number of shorter ones rush to the next note through all kinds of step progressions and skips."[95] At "in luce sagittarum," a portion of the text upon which Peranda would also dwell, Carissimi enhances the "splendor" of the "glistening spear" through the use of the figure identified by Bernhard as *superjectio* (Ex. 6.24). At times, Carissimi lines the vocal entries up in such a manner that the two lines move in parallel tenths (as seen in Ex. 6.24 in mm 61–63). But these homophonic oases are brief, and only provide brief respites from an otherwise unremittingly imitative contrapuntal texture.

The first documented Dresden performance of Peranda's treatment of this same text also took place during the Easter season, three years after the 1662 performance of Carissimi's *Viderunt te Domine*.[96] In his musical response, Peranda also observes the "motet principle," but he seems to seek to outdo Carissimi on every front. He borrows the essence of Carissimi's scoring concept, but doubles the number of voices and scores the concerto for two soprano castrati, two *bassi profundi*, and

94. Hilse 1973:122.
95. Hilse 1973:96–98.
96. See Appendix II. Modern edition in Frandsen 1997-3:520–48. Musical examples prepared from S-Uu VMHS 30:4 and SLUB 1738-E-527.

EXAMPLE 6.24 Carissimi, *Viderunt te Domine*, mm. 43–65

EXAMPLE 6.24 (*continued*)

continuo. With respect to sheer technical difficulty, he exacts longer and even more difficult *passaggi* and technically demanding lines from his singers, with the result that *Dedit abyssus* numbers among his most vocally taxing concertos. Peranda also seeks to take better advantage of this unusual scoring in his effort to realize musically the dramatic imagery of the text (*hypotyposis*). In a spectacular opening duet for the two basses, Peranda creates a striking musical image of the depths (*hypobole*) through the use of octave displacement at "abyssus," where the vocal line abruptly plunges a major seventh (*saltus duriusculus*) and completes the half-cadence literally *in profundo* (Ex. 6.25). As the abyss then issues forth its "voice," Peranda slowly takes the bass up to *d´*—a full two octaves above his first cadence (*hyperbole*)—in lines that ascend by ornamented thirds. But before Bass 1 can complete his presentation of the text, Bass 2 enters with the opening motive; at one point, the two bass voices are involved in a 7–6 suspension displaced by an octave and complete the half-cadence separated by a tenth. Here Peranda exploits the timbral and contrapuntal potential of the two-voice texture and fashions a dramatic half-cadence using two or perhaps even three of the dissonance figures catalogued by Bernhard in his *Tractatus*. In measure 5, Bass 1 abandons his role in the 7–6 suspension, which normally would demand that he resolve from d' to c' on beat 4, and leaps instead to the d below, and then up to g, where he participates in the 4–3 suspension that concludes the passage. This is Bernhard's *syncopatio catachrestica*, which "occurs when a syncopation [suspension] is not resolved through a subsequent consonance a step below, as the rule demands." Bernhard provides three variations on the figure, the third of which occurs when the "driving note" (in this case the d' of Bass 1 in m. 5) does not fall a second, but leaps to another note, as in the passage in *Dedit abyssus*.[97] As Hilse notes, this figure can also be regarded as a type of *heterolepsis*, the "seizure of a second voice," as Bass 1 here "seizes" an inner part in measures 5–6.[98] In the d'–d leap of Bass 1, one might also find a variation on Bernhard's *multiplicatio*, the "splitting of a dissonance," whether a suspension or a passing tone, into two or more parts; Bernhard's examples, however, involve conjunct motion.[99] Once the cadence has been concluded, Bass 2 continues with his presentation of the opening motive and is joined by Bass 1, who enters in measure 7 to present the same material a perfect fourth higher; Bass 2 follows suit in measure 11. Peranda's inversion of the voices lends the cadential figure a new intensity, however, for in measures 8 and 12, the octave drops result in a semitone clash. As the basses progress toward the cadence that closes the section (m. 17), they engage in a sequential exchange of a brief motive drawn from the original treatment of "vocem," and finally cadence without fanfare on G. This opening demonstrates just how different was the response of each composer to this text. After dwelling for a considerable period of time on the opening line ("viderunt te, Domine"), Carissimi dispenses with this next phrase of text in just three measures. In contrast, Peranda opens with this phrase and dwells upon it; the motivic complex itself stretches over six measures in its first manifestation. Peranda also explores a lower portion of the bass range than does Carissimi, but even more important, he renders the sopranos mute throughout the passage in order to explore the idea of the abyss through intervallic displacement as well as tessitura. Although Carissimi also acknowledged the abyss with a steep descending leap, he presented the line first in the soprano range, which did not allow the listener to make the same spatial association.

97. Hilse 1973:102–103.
98. Hilse 1973:118.
99. Hilse 1973:100–101.

EXAMPLE 6.25 Peranda, *Dedit abyssus*, mm. 1–17

EXAMPLE 6.25 (*continued*)

Just as the low bass tessitura vividly depicted "the depths" in sound, the higher range of the sopranos who now enter corresponds aurally to the "heights"; in this manner, Peranda effectively captures the idea of spatial polarity encapsulated in the opening verse. When the basses have finally completed their presentation of verse 10a, they fall silent and allow the sopranos to take up the concluding phrase of verse 10b, "it lifted up its hand on high." In this duet, Peranda steps back from the drama of the opening and allows the listener a brief respite from the intense counterpoint that dominates the concerto. Here he first employs an ascending motive at "altitudo," which he briefly treats in close imitation between the two castrati, and then shows off the castrato's technique in a more martial, trill-like figure at "manum suam *levavit*." Each soprano presents the entire motive as a solo, at different pitch levels, and then the two come together to close the section in measures 30–32.

The two opening duets represent the only time that Peranda deviates from four-voice texture in the entire concerto. He splinters the next two and one-half verses of text and the Alleluia into thirteen small fragments, some of which comprise only one word, and furnishes each fragment with its own motivic identity. As he has elected to employ imitative counterpoint throughout, he creates contrast through changes in meter and texture. At "sol et luna," he shifts to triple meter and presents the first brief motive in a transparent imitative texture in which each voice drops out after stating the motive; the effect is that of an echo. To expand the length of this section, he transposes the motivic material first heard in measures 33–52 and develops it further in a restatement in measures 53–81. Upon the close of this section, the mood immediately changes. Peranda returns to duple meter, which he retains for the remainder of the work, and embarks upon a remarkable fifty-two measure contrapuntal *tour de force* (mm. 82–136) in which the imitative writing suffers no breaks or lulls, but continues uninterrupted to the concluding cadence (Ex. 6.26). Here the vocal demands placed upon the singers are many—the rhythm is driving and relentless, and the motives are filled with fast-moving, unyielding passage

EXAMPLE 6.26 Peranda, *Dedit abyssus*, mm. 82–103

work. Motive after motive is introduced and treated in an imitative contrapuntal style that at times becomes Bachian in its density. Peranda brings the image-filled text to life with elaborate coloratura on such highly charged words as "sagittarum" (which surely must have brought a smile to Schütz's face), "fulgurantis," "hastae," "furore," and "obstupefacies," all of which enter and reenter in rapid-fire succession. All in all, this fascinating passage clearly communicates the idea of the awesome power of God inherent in the text.

EXAMPLE 6.26 (*continued*)

To conclude the concerto, Peranda presents the Alleluia in the same driving contrapuntal style. Here, however, he bases the entire section on a single musical motive; as a result, the Alleluia recalls the early fugue in several respects. But the Alleluia in *Dedit abyssus* is not as "fugue-like" as the concluding portion of *Accurrite gentes* (discussed below). First, each entry comprises several subsequent statements of the subject that occur without interruption. Second, the entries appear in *stretto* throughout; no presentation of the subject—not even the first—is ever completed

EXAMPLE 6.26 (*continued*)

before the "answer" appears in another voice. As a result, the subject doubles as a countersubject. Yet the effect is not quite that of *concertato* style, for there is never a sense that the voices are tossing a motive back and forth; instead, one perceives fugal imitation at all times. A comparison of the Alleluia with the preceding section reveals just how short is the distance between imitative writing and fugal proce-

EXAMPLE 6.26 *(continued)*

dure; in the previous section, the imitative entries came just as frequently, but the voices did not restate the material without an intervening rest. But in its dedication to complete entries of each motive (i.e., the motives are not dissected and "tossed about"), the imitative writing in measures 82–136 appears just as "fugal" as that in the Alleluia.

EXAMPLE 6.26 (*continued*)

PERANDA: *ACCURRITE GENTES*

Like several of the concertos discussed above, Peranda's *Accurrite gentes*, a *de tempore* composition for Easter, is a text-driven setting that exhibits the same sort of sectionalism and stylistic variety seen in the Roman motet.[100] The composite text opens with an exhortation that approaches poetry in its style ("Accurrite gentes, venite, properate, ad jubila volate"), and continues with two equivalent amphibrachic quatrains, a passage of prose of moderate length, a rhymed tercet, and a brief closing statement. Peranda scored his musical setting for three singers (alto, tenor, and bass), an instrumental ensemble of two cornetti and bassoon, and continuo. The first documented performance of *Accurrite* took place on Easter Tuesday, 1665; three of the four documented performances took place during the Easter season, but one occurred on the fifth Sunday after Epiphany, during the season that precedes Lent.[101] As only one line makes explicit reference to "the risen Lord," it remains possible that the text was altered slightly on this occasion. The composition itself probably dates from 1665 or a bit earlier; by 1666, Gustav Düben had already made a copy of the concerto for the Stockholm court music collection.

100. Modern edition in Frandsen 1997-3:453–75. Musical examples prepared from SLUB 1738-E-510.

101. See Appendix II.

As do a few other compositions in the Dresden repertoire, *Accurrite gentes* lacks an introductory sinfonia; instead, the voices enter after a single chord played by the continuo. Peranda sets the opening text as an expansive triple-meter concerto and betrays his fondness for the aria in the shape and lyricism of the opening motives. Although the voices enter in points of imitation, the concerto is not highly contrapuntal, but instead exhibits the same tendency to "homophonize" seen in the Roman repertoire. After the vocal opening, which presents the entire brief text ("run people, come, hasten, fly to shouts"), the instrumental ensemble takes up the motivic material in a fairly extensive interlude; following this, the ensemble restates the latter portion of the concerto. As a result, the extended bipartite aria exerts its influence on both the melodic style and the formal organization of this first section of the concerto. Rather than set the concerto off definitively as a semi-independent section, however, Peranda elides it with the following duet, thus musically underscoring the interrelationship between the opening imperative statements and the subsequent poetic stanzas:

Invitat fidelis,	He invites us, the faithful,
qui pectora emollit,	who softens our hearts,
peccata qui tollit,	who removes our sins,
nos pastor de coelis.	the pastor of the heavens.
Huic laeti, canamus,	To him let us sing, fortunate ones,
triumphum sonemus,	let us celebrate triumph,
votaque donemus,	and let us give votive offerings,
laudesque feramus.	and let us bring praises.

In the duet, however, this joy gives way to pensive reflection. Peranda seems to have taken his primary inspiration for the affect in these strophes from the second line of the first stanza, for he slows the tempo to *Adagio* and presents the first two lines of the stanza in tranquil parallel sixths and thirds. He also moves away from the major harmonies that dominate the opening concerto and for a time favors the minor side of the harmonic equation, although he eventually turns back to the major in the latter half of the strophe. But Peranda's decision to treat these two stanzas strophically actually runs somewhat counter to the text, for the same musical affect that enhances the imagery of the first stanza serves to mute somewhat the praises offered in the second. As the singers conclude the second strophe, the instrumental ensemble enters and brings the entire opening complex to a definitive conclusion with a brief cadential ritornello.

At this point, the text takes a sudden turn towards the dramatic: the speaker falls silent, and the risen Lord Himself "appears," in the manner of a *deus ex machina*, and personally extends to any who will hear Him the very invitation celebrated by the duo:

Venite omnes	Come, all you	Come to me,
qui concupiscitis me,	who eagerly desire me,	
qui laboratis et onerati estis,	you who labor and are burdened,	all who labor and are heavy laden,
et ego reficiam vos.	and I will restore you.	and I will give you rest. (Matt 11:28)
Ego enim sum pastor,	For I am the shepherd,	I am the good shepherd. (John 10:11a)
ego enim sum cibus,	for I am food,	
ego sum potus.	I am drink.	
Credite in me,	Believe in me,	Take my yoke upon you and learn of me,
et pascua invenietis	and you will discover pastures	. . . and you will find rest
animabus vestris.	for your souls.	for your souls. (Matt 11:29)

These lines, which elaborate upon familiar passages from the Gospels of Matthew and John, introduce a decidedly mystical element into the text: Christ, the Good Shepherd, nourishes the soul desirous of union with Him. In accordance with long-established tradition, Peranda casts Christ as a bass and presents His words in a declamatory solo that relies more heavily upon harmonic tension (on several levels) and rhetorical repetition figures (particularly *epizeuxis*) than pure vocal fireworks for its affective power (Ex. 6.27). The passage opens quietly, with simple triadic statements of "venite omnes," on G and C. But at the mere mention of "desire," the harmony immediately loses its stability and remains volatile throughout the presentation of this portion of the text. As Christ extends His invitation to those who desire Him (m. 105), Peranda employs a sudden tertial shift from C to A; he takes the line to D major, but then shifts by third again, and moves to B major at "qui laboratis." A sequential restatement of this motive carries the harmony to E major (m. 108) and then immediately to A major at "et onerati estis" (mm. 108–9), where it remains through the cadence in bar 110. This cadence, however, brings with it another surprise. The movement from E major to A major in bars 108–9 implies a continuation of the cycle of fifths to D major, but although Peranda does continue on to D, he substitutes the minor form of the triad in the vocal line (m. 109), and then drops precipitously to the tension-filled leading tone below (m. 110). The speaker has yet to complete his thought, however, so Peranda iterates the latter half of the "reficiam" motive twice and arrives convincingly on E major (bar 112), where he lingers for a moment. Peranda's approach to this passage well illustrates the affective options that any particular text offers the seventeenth-century composer: rather than construe Christ's words here as essentially pacific in nature and render them in a placid atmosphere created by harmonic stasis, Peranda depicts this act of restoration or refreshment as a dynamic, purgative process. In so doing, he conveys

EXAMPLE 6.27 Peranda, *Accurrite gentes*, mm. 103–24

through music the mounting emotion of the sinner as he longs ever more urgently for peace and restoration. This elusive peace finally begins to descend in the next section, where Peranda presents Christ's words, "I am the Good Shepherd," in A minor and avoids the harmonically unexpected; he does, however, heighten the tension of the vocal line somewhat with additional descending leaps to the local leading tone (see mm. 113–16).

In another abrupt harmonic maneuver, Peranda shifts back to the G/C harmonic axis of the opening at the bass's introduction of Christ's invitation, "credite in me," and once again, a more stable harmonic progression seems to stand as a musical metaphor for sublime peace. This motion finally resolves the structural dissonance introduced in the previous section, whose E/A harmonies conflicted with the overall G/C harmony of the concerto. But the final section is not without musical tension, for in the final five measures of the declamatory passage, Peranda attempts to close the entire solo with a sense of climax, and it is here that he finally affords the bass an opportunity for vocal display. Once again the singer shows off his great range and his ability to sing *passaggi* in a florid, sequential rendition of "animabus." But Peranda has already spent his emotional energy elsewhere; despite its coloratura, the closing fails to recapture the emotional fervor of the central section (mm. 105–12).

Once the bass has completed his declamatory solo, Christ vanishes just as suddenly as He did at the supper in Emmaus; as in that account, however, His departure here also causes the witnesses to express their joy in having seen the resurrected Lord:[102]

Ergo, laeti, decantemus,	Therefore, fortunate ones, let us sing repeatedly,
et triumphos celebremus,	and let us celebrate triumph
resurgenti Domino.	to the risen Lord.

Peranda returns to the *concertato* style of the opening trio and treats this tercet in triple meter. However, despite the predominance in his works (and those of Albrici) of *concertato*-style writing of this sort, in which the imitative sections frequently devolve into homophony, the finale of *Accurrite gentes* demonstrates that Peranda, like his colleague Albrici, also enjoyed the challenges presented by rigorous contrapuntal procedures. To conclude the work, he fashions an *alla breve* fugal treatment of the final lines of text, "Ut cum eo in eternum triumphemus. Alleluia" ("So that we might triumph with him into eternity. Hallelujah."). In several respects, this movement looks forward to the fugues of the later Baroque, particularly in its distinctly Handelian subject and countersubject, its use of real answers, and its motivic density. Like Albrici, and perhaps due to his influence, Peranda also became involved with invertible counterpoint and demonstrated an interest in fugues with counter-

102. See Luke 24:13–35.

EXAMPLE 6.28 Peranda, *Accurrite gentes*, mm. 166–80

EXAMPLE 6.28 *(continued)*

subjects at a time when such were virtually unknown in his (adopted) region of Germany (Ex. 6.28).[103]

Peranda opens his fugue with two entries of the subject on C before introducing the answer on G. Already in the second entry of the subject, however, his treatment of the countersubject contrasts with that of Albrici in *Omnis caro foenum*; although Peranda employs real answers throughout the fugue, he frequently transposes or otherwise alters the countersubject to accommodate local harmonic demands. In the vocal portion of the fugal exposition, the entries remain evenly spaced, and Peranda alters the rate of entry only slightly in the cornetti entrances.[104] Upon completion of its presentation of the subject and countersubject, each individual voice either immediately begins to develop the motive that identifies the latter, or does so after a brief pause, which causes the musical texture to become gradually more dense. Upon the subject entry of Cornetto 2 (m. 177), the texture becomes five-part, then remains so until the final cadence (m. 196). At the conclusion of the fugal exposition, rather than introduce an episode, Peranda increases the frequency of subject entries and creates an extended stretto in the latter half of the fugue (mm. 177–89). These stretto entries, which often jettison the countersubject entirely, typically enter at two- or three-beat intervals; on one occasion, however, Peranda affects a miniature canon by introducing subject entries (on G and C) in the cornetti, separated by a single beat (see mm. 177–78). Like many fugues of this era, Peranda's fugue lacks episodes; but for the final four or five measures, the subject is omnipresent. The absence of episodes and the reliance on the countersubject for material to fill out the texture result in a fugue that is saturated with musical ideas that are present from the outset of the section. This saturation persists until the final cadence; even in the final four measures, each voice still receives its motivic identity from the countersubject.

Peranda's *Accurrite gentes* also stands out among his works for its interestingly ambivalent harmonic language. Throughout the concerto, the harmony vacillates between G major and C major, denying the role of tonic to either key. Instead, it seems that the hypomixolydian mode, or vestiges of it, informs Peranda's harmonic thinking. This is suggested primarily by the cadential stress on G and C in the work, which correspond to the final and *repercussio* of the mode, as well as the frequent substitution of F♮ for F♯ in passages in G. But neither does the concerto recapture the harmonic flavor of the Schütz era, for Peranda cannot abandon entirely the principle of chordal hierarchy so characteristic of the early tonal harmony that his music now exhibits. Nevertheless, he does divide his harmonic attention between two key centers and first concentrates on one, then the other. In other words, the harmony

---

103. See Walker 1995:60.

104. The number of beats increases to six and then decreases to four in the entrances of the cornetti.

is not "purposefully oriented toward one center," but toward two.[105] While many features cause *Accurrite* to sound more "tonal" than "modal," the identity of the actual tonic remains elusive until the final cadence.

Peranda begins nominally in G, with a single chord in the continuo, and then proceeds to play harmonic games with the listener, alternating every two measures between perfect cadences on G and C for the first eleven measures, as if he is trying to decide which area to tonicize. Finally he decides upon C (mm. 12–21), but the ambivalence returns in the instrumental interlude, which also finally opts for C. At the restatement of "properate," however, Peranda employs a shift (rather than a modulation) to G and tonicizes it through its dominant. The harmony remains in G until the duo begins, after which point it moves into E minor and A minor, then closes in C major (mm. 52–102; the entire sequence is repeated in the second strophe of the duet). Peranda then shifts back to G for the opening of the bass solo (mm. 103–128), then explores the "dissonant" E/A (minor) complex before returning to G major, but then closes the solo solidly in C. In the tutti that follows (mm. 129–65), the harmony again swings between C major and G major, with neither key area predominating; the section opens in C and closes in G. The fugue also opens in C and closes in G, but here Peranda's firm grounding of his subject and countersubject in C major strongly suggests that this key will prevail in the end. This idea gains strength as the fugue continues, for despite the numerous entries on G, complete with the requisite F♯s, Peranda never effects a true modulation to G major. Instead, he always quickly brings the harmony back to C major and does not allow this key to relinquish its hold on the fugue until the last five measures of the concerto—the last cadence on C occurs only six bars from the end of the work. But having set up this harmonic dichotomy, Peranda cannot permit himself to close the work in C major. Despite the fact that this key area dominates the fugue, and that he only paid lip service to G at the opening of the work, he still regards it as the "tonic" of the concerto. Thus he attempts to reinforce the sense of G as the "tonic" or final by accelerating the pace of the harmonic rhythm in the last few measures and cadencing repeatedly on G. But even here, the frequent F♯s in the various lines raise the specter of a final return to C. In a true hypomixolydian composition, the composer would not concern himself with addressing this harmonic "ambiguity." Here, however, Peranda's harmonic thinking has clearly been colored by tonality: although he sets out to compose a hypomixolydian piece, he cannot ignore the exigencies of the early tonal idiom with which he now normally works.

---

105. See Linfield 1990:159: "was zu einer zielstrebig auf ein Zentrum hin orientierten Harmonik führt."

7

Johann Georg's Vision for Worship

B<small>Y THE TIME</small> he ascended the Saxon throne in 1656, Johann Georg II had experienced nearly four decades of worship at court and had developed his own ideas regarding both music and liturgy. During those decades, of course, he had also witnessed the war-induced decline and stagnation of his father's once-magnificent *Hofkapelle*. That ensemble, together with the state of music in the chapel liturgies, had reached its nadir in the 1640s, and had only begun to recover in the decade before his accession. Not surprisingly, in light of the active interest that he had displayed in matters musical since the 1630s, the new elector quickly revealed himself to be a musico-liturgical interventionist, one committed to a vision of worship life that would, by virtue of its splendor, enhance and aggrandize the image of his court and his electorate. Thus, virtually upon taking his seat at the Saxon helm, Johann Georg II initiated a program of musico-liturgical reform that would take six years to bring to full fruition, and that would culminate in his *Kirchen-Ordnung* ("church order"), the codification of both the schedule of feasts and liturgical forms that would remain in use in the chapel until his death in 1680.[1] His program of reform, which was doubtless undertaken in consultation with court preacher Jacob Weller, advanced in three basic stages: the establishment of the number and nature of services to be celebrated on feast days throughout the liturgical year, the musical enhancement of the various liturgies, and finally, the promulgation of his *Kirchen-Ordnung* and its realization in the chapel liturgies.

T<small>HE</small> S<small>AXON</small> L<small>ITURGICAL</small> H<small>ERITAGE</small>
 <small>OF THE</small> S<small>IXTEENTH</small> C<small>ENTURY</small>

In 1539, the death of the staunchly Catholic Duke of Saxony, Georg "the Bearded" (r. 1500–1539), cleared the path for the introduction of the Reformation into Albertinian Saxony by his brother and successor, Duke Heinrich "the Pious" (r. 1539–41). Despite the brevity of his reign, Duke Heinrich left a lasting imprint on Saxon litur-

---

1. For a discussion of Lutheran church orders, see Herl 2004:36–53.

gical history through his promulgation in 1539 of a *Kirchen-ordnunge*, or church order, which was reissued the following year under the title *Agenda – Das ist/ Kyrchenordnung*.[2] This essential liturgical tool, which combined aspects of various traditional types of liturgical books, remained the official liturgical authority in Saxony for more than two centuries.[3] Despite the liturgical and musical changes that accrued to these services over the decades, no attempt was made to update the liturgical forms in the *Agenda* to reflect contemporary practices. This may well reflect Luther's own de-emphasis of liturgical uniformity.[4] But it must also be said that the morning service as given in the *Agenda* remained the backbone of the *Hauptgottesdienst* in Saxony, as the various city *Kirchen-Ordnungen* from that region reveal.[5] Although dependent upon the liturgies formulated for the church by its founder, the liturgical forms promulgated by Heinrich replicated neither Luther's *Von ordenung gottis diensts in der gemeine* and *Formula missae et communionis* of 1523, nor his *Deudsche messe* of 1526.[6] In his *Kirchen-ordnunge* (*Agenda*), Heinrich established the forms of matins, vespers, and the primary Sunday communion service for all city and village churches in his territories, and provided forms for those both with and without Latin schools and choirs. He also established the texts and rubrics for baptisms and emergency baptisms, weddings and funerals, confession and absolution, and private communion, and also included numerous liturgical helps. The *Agenda* of Duke Heinrich[7] is of great significance for the liturgical life of Saxony in general as well as that of the court chapel, for it likely documents the liturgical forms first celebrated at the newly Lutheran court in the 1540s. The first known liturgical formulary for the Dresden court, the *Ordnung* of Elector August (r. 1553–86), was established in 1581; it retains the forms of the services essentially as they are found in the *Agenda*.

2. The *Kirchen-ordnunge* of 1539, with annotations reflecting the changes made in the 1540 and 1555 editions of the *Agenda*, is reproduced in Sehling 1:264–81. Duke Heinrich's younger son, Elector August (r. 1553–86), also reissued the *Agenda* in 1580 as part of his comprehensive *Kirchen-Ordnung*, which codified all aspects of church life and governance in Saxony; see Sehling 1:359–457. For this study, a copy of the *Agenda* published in 1540 by Wolrab in Leipzig was consulted.

3. Herl's research has revealed that the 1539 *Kirchen-ordnunge* was "reprinted numerous times through 1748 with only minor changes" (Herl 2004:17).

4. See Strasser 1941:211.

5. See the comparative tables in Herl 2004:215–38.

6. Schmidt 1961:96; the services appear in Sehling 1:2–26. See also the discussion in Herl 2004:3–16.

7. *Agenda* 1540, fols. 22v–23v.

SUNDAY MORNING WORSHIP SERVICES (*HAUPTGOTTESDIENSTE*)
OF DUKE HEINRICH AND ELECTOR AUGUST

Duke Heinrich's *Agenda* (1540)	Elector August's Court *Ordnung* (1581)[8]
1. Introit for Sunday or feast day	1. Introit
2. Latin Kyrie and Gloria	2. Kyrie, with German trope[9]
	3. Gloria, with German trope
3. Collect, German or Latin	4. Collect
4. Epistle, read in German facing the congregation	5. Epistle
5. Sequence or German psalm, or other sacred song	6. Hymn
6. Gospel, read in German facing the congregation	7. Gospel
7. Credo [intoned], in Latin, followed by *Wir glauben all an einen Gott* (the German creedal hymn)	8. *Wir glauben all an einen Gott*
8. Sermon on the Gospel for Sunday or feast day	9. Sermon verse on feast days[10]
10. [Communion] Paraphrase of Lord's Prayer and exhortation to the sacrament, read facing the altar; Words of Institution, sung in German; [Hymn] *Jesus Christus unser Heiland* or *Gott sei gelobet.* One may at times, particularly on feast days, omit the Paraphrase of the Lord's Prayer and the exhortation, and instead sing the Latin Preface, after which the Latin Sanctus. After the same the Lord's Prayer and the Words of Institution	10. Sermon
	11. Hymn
	12. Communion Hymns (when communion is celebrated)

8. Schmidt 1961:95.

9. For example, from Christmas Day until Holy Week the German troped Kyrie "Kyrie Magne Deus O Vater allmechtiger Gott" was sung (Schmidt 1961:98 n. 15).

10. According to Schmidt, the sermon verse (often a hymn) is a completely new liturgical element in the 1581 court liturgical formulary and does not appear in Duke Heinrich's *Agenda* (Schmidt 1961:99).

in German, which is given in notes
at the end of the book, and during the
communion in both forms, the Latin
Agnus Dei and the German *Jesus
Christus [unser Heiland]* are sung;
one may also sing Ps. 111 (*Ich dancke
dem Herrn von gantzem Hertzen*)
according to whether there are many
or few communicants. During the
hymn the people receive communion
in both species.

10. Collect	13. Collect
11. Benediction	14. Benediction

Vesper Services of Duke Heinrich and Elector August

Duke Heinrich's *Agenda* (1540)[11]	Elector August's *Ordnung* (1581)[12]
Vespers shall be held at the usual time in the afternoon, and the students shall sing one, two or three psalms, with the antiphons for that Sunday or feast day, thereupon a responsory or hymn shall be sung, where available.	1. German psalm
	2. One or two German hymns
After this one shall have a boy read a lection from the New Testament; after the reading the *Magnificat* is sung, also with the antiphon for that Sunday or feast day,	3. Reading from the Old Testament
	4. *Magnificat*
	5. German evening hymn
and [one] closes with the Collect and Benedicamus.	6. Collect
	7. Benedicamus

In the liturgies celebrated according to the codifications in the 1540 *Agenda* and the 1581 court *Ordnung*, the musical responsibilities of the Dresden *Hofkapelle* were likely the same as those of Latin school choirs around Saxony. Musical items to be sung by the choir included the Introit, Kyrie, Gloria, and Credo during the *Haupt-gottesdienst*, and the psalms, antiphons, and *Magnificat* at Vespers. Antiphons and

---

11. *Agenda* 1540, fol. 22r. The formulary for Vespers is given as a Saturday, or vigil, service; the rubrics in the *Agenda* indicate that on Sundays, Vespers are to be celebrated as on Saturday (ibid., 23v–24r).

collects were available in collections compiled for Lutheran usage by Spangenberg, Lossius, Keuchenthal, and others; the 1579 *Gottesdienstordnung* for the Saxon town of Annaberg, for example, specifies that the Vesper collects are to be drawn from Spangenberg.[13] Luther's creedal hymn *Wir glauben all an einen Gott* (1524) was widely sung by the congregation from the earliest days of the new church, the practice having been instituted by Luther in his 1526 *Deudsche messe*.[14] By 1581, if not earlier, the hymns sung in both services were likely sung by the congregation, with support from the choir. Unfortunately, neither document ordains whether or when the liturgical elements should be sung *choraliter* or *figuraliter* (as chant or as "figured music," i.e., polyphony), and thus both leave open the possibility for performances in either mode. Information from various Saxon towns and cities (including Dresden), however, indicates a variety of practices. The two idioms might alternate weekly, or the services might be sung *figuraliter* only on feast days, or polyphonic music might be heard once a month.[15] It is also important to note that nowhere do these services provide for the interpolation of extra-liturgical compositions of sacred art music. However, descriptive reports from the era reveal that motets and other polyphonic compositions (such as Passions) became standard additions to the liturgy, particularly that of the morning service, in the latter half of the sixteenth century (see below). In addition to the choir, however, the pastor also played a musical role; as the celebrant had done for centuries, the Lutheran pastor intoned the Gloria and the Credo, and sang the Proper Preface (when used).[16] And although the *Agenda* states that the pastor read the Epistle and the Gospel, in practice both were sung to separate recitation formulae, given in the *Agenda* with illustrative examples.[17] Unlike the vespers celebrated at the court in the seventeenth century, however, in these sixteenth-century liturgies there is no indication of the opening versicle, "Deus in adjutorium meum intende," which, if used, would also have been intoned by the pastor and answered by the choir. In addition, Lutheran vespers also often included a sermon; the *Agenda* makes reference to such services (called *Vesperpredigt*), but does not include a sermon in the orders of worship given for vespers.[18]

12. Schmidt 1961:95–96.

13. For the Annaberg *Gottesdienstordnung*, see Rautenstrauch 1907/1970:168.

14. Herl 2004:8, 11–13, 58–59.

15. See Rautenstrauch 1907/1970:177-88, and Sehling 2:568–69.

16. In the case of the Gloria and Credo, the 1540 *Agenda* does not state explicitly that the pastor sings the intonation, but implies such by enumerating separately the intonation and continuation of each item: "Darauff das Kyrie eleison/ Gloria in Excelsis/ Vnd/ Et in terra/ Latinisch" (fol. 22v); "Darauff das Credo in vnum Deum, vnd das Lateinische Patrem &c" (fol. 23r). The tones for the Proper Prefaces appear on fols. 47v–54v.

17. The formulae and examples appear in the 1540 *Agenda*, fols. 40r–47r.

18. *Agenda* 1540, fols. 22r, 23v–24r, 26r.

The musical amplification of the Dresden court liturgy, as codified in Johann Georg's *Kirchen-Ordnung*, has its roots in Lutheran musico-liturgical practices that developed in the sixteenth century, particularly in the custom of interpolating works of sacred art music into the morning liturgy at specific points. The musical expansion of the liturgy remains somewhat difficult to chronicle, however, as the majority of *Kirchen-Ordnungen* remain silent concerning such accretions.[19] This may be explained in part by the fact that some musical interpolations arose as accompaniments to physical movements, such as the procession of the pastor from the altar to the pulpit following the Gospel, and others as accompaniments to ritual actions, such as the distribution of communion, and thus were not considered elements of the liturgy *per se*. But evidence of this practice of interpolation survives in descriptive accounts from the sixteenth century, which, together with the astonishing number of motets composed and published by Lutheran musicians during decades following the Reformation, strongly suggests that congregations in towns and cities with Latin schools heard performances of extra-liturgical compositions far more regularly, and from a far earlier date, than a study of the various *Kirchenordnungen* would suggest.[20]

The first interpolation of sacred art music to appear in *Kirchen-Ordnungen* from Saxony and Thuringia involves the insertion of a motet following the Epistle, either in place of or in addition to a congregational hymn. The *Kirchen-Ordnung* for the St. Wenzelskirche in Naumburg from 1537/38, for example, provides that following the Epistle, one should sing

> a German psalm appropriate to the time, or which corresponds to the Gospel; on high feasts, when one sings polyphony, may the cantor sometimes sing a good Latin motet for the "Et in terra," likewise before the psalm, which one sings after the Epistle, and sometimes, when the Introit is beautiful, sing the same instead of *Komm heiliger Geist*.[21]

The 1568 *Kirchen-Ordnung* for the city of Zerbst, in the principality of Anhalt (northwest of Saxony), ordained that Sunday services should be sung alternately *choraliter* and *figuraliter*; musical interpolations on "polyphonic" Sundays could include

---

19. The comparative tables given in Herl 2004:215–38 help to illustrate this point.

20. See Westendorf 1987:159–283.

21. "ein deuzscher psalm nach der zeitgelegenheit oder der sich mit dem evangelio reimet, an den hohen festen, wenn man mensur singet, mag der cantor wol bisweilen vor das et in terra etc. item für dem psalm, so man nach der epistel singet, eine gute lateinische muteten und bisweilen, wan ein schöner introitus ist, denselben vor das Kom heiliger geist singen" (Sehling 2:71). Similar examples appear in in the *Kirchen-Ordnungen* from Meiningen (1566), Wasungen (1566), and Neuhaldensleben (1564); see Sehling 2:339, 356, 457.

motets following the Gloria, the Epistle, and the sermon.[22] Documentary evidence from Saxony from this same period reveals a similar enhancement of the liturgical forms established in the Saxon *Agenda*, particularly on feast days or special occasions. According to the 1578 *Kirchen-Ordnung* for Weißenfels, for example, a *mutetam figuraliter* (polyphonic motet) was sometimes sung between the Gospel and the German Creed in the Sunday morning service, and the performance of a motet prefaced the singing of hymns at communion when there were many communicants.[23] In the festive liturgy held in 1578 to celebrate the dedication of the Dresden Annenkirche,[24] polyphonic compositions of Lasso were performed before and after the sermon. On that occasion, the performance of the *Te Deum* that followed the sermon represented a free interpolation before the communion service in the liturgy established in Duke Heinrich's *Agenda* (see above). In a *Kirchen-Ordnung* from the Saxon town of Annaberg dating from the following year, the rubrics for Christmas, Easter, Pentecost, and Trinity Sunday indicate that during the Sunday morning worship service, the Credo was sung in Latin and German after the Gospel, while after the sermon, "when the Superintendent does not begin to sing a German hymn with the people, a motet is sung."[25] In the latter case, polyphonic music supplanted the congregational singing of a hymn, or the playing of the organ, either of which was stipulated to occur at this spot on ordinary Sundays.[26] Concerning the performance of figural music during communion, this same church order prescribes that on feast days, the Sanctus and several polyphonic motets are sung; at other times, however, verses of German communion hymns are sung in alternation with organ versets.[27] Here the "Latin option" provided in the *Agenda* concerning the Preface and Sanctus has been expanded through the addition of several motets, which must have been sung during the Distribution, following the Words of Institution. Unfortunately, descriptive evidence of this sort from the sixteenth-century Dresden court has not emerged. Nevertheless, these documents reveal that the performance of extra-liturgical music during the Sunday morning *Gottesdienst* gradually became standardized at three particular liturgical junctures: following the Gospel, following the sermon, and during the Distribution. Given the talent pool available in the Dresden *Hofkapelle*, it is likely that the liturgical forms established by Elector

22. See Sehling 2:568–69.
23. Sehling 1:693.
24. See chapter 4.
25. "Do der Herr Superintendent nach der Predigt nicht anfehet mit dem Volck ein deutzsch lied zu singen, pflegt mann eine mutet zu singen" (Rautenstrauch 1907/1970:170).
26. Rautenstrauch 1907/1970:167
27. Rautenstrauch 1907/1970:167. Herl includes this *Gottesdienstordnung* in his comparative tables but does not include this information (Herl 2004:232.)

August underwent a similar, if undocumented, musical embellishment. While this likely occurred during the later sixteenth century, the first documentary evidence of such embellishment dates from the second decade of the seventeenth century, in the liturgies celebrated for the hundredth anniversary of the Reformation.[28]

Given that the actual responsibility for these musical interpolations fell to the cantor or Kapellmeister, it is not surprising that some of the most revealing information about contemporary musico-liturgical trends appears in the writings of a composer of sacred music. In the lengthy prefaces to several of his music collections, Michael Praetorius (1571–1621), who served as Kapellmeister at the ducal court of Wolfenbüttel, reveals that by the inaugural decade of the seventeenth century, the performance of motets or sacred concertos after the Gospel and/or the sermon had become a widespread practice. In the preface to the fifth part of his *Musae Sioniae*, published in 1607, Praetorius suggests that the lengthier of the polyphonic chorale settings contained in that collection might be performed "not always simply at the very beginning of the service, where one is in the habit of singing psalms with the congregation, but also before or after the sermon, instead of Latin motets and concertos."[29] Twelve years later, in the extensive preface to his *Polyhymnia Caduceatrix* of 1619, Praetorius indicates that the more extensive works in that collection of *concertato* chorale settings might be apportioned into three parts and performed after the Epistle, after the Gospel, and after the sermon during the Sunday morning *Hauptgottesdienst*. For performances at Vespers, Praetorius suggests that such works might either replace the *Magnificat*, or might be performed before and after the sermon.[30] Of great significance here is the fact that in both publications, Praetorius is addressing his remarks to a broad audience of his co-religionists, and speaks as if these musical interpolations are not exceptional, but standard practice.[31]

Johann Georg's Proto-*Kirchen-Ordnung* of 1657

Despite the numerous changes made to the court liturgies in the decades after 1581, no evidence of an incarnation of the court *Ordnung* from the reign of Johann

28. See Schmidt 1961:119–20

29. "nicht eben allezeit im anfang der angehenden Versamblung/ do man die Psalmen mit der Gemein zu singen pfleget/ Sondern negst vor oder nach der Predigt an stadt lateinischer Muteten und Concerten musiciren könne" (Praetorius, *Musae Sioniae, Teil V*, xi).

30. See Praetorius, preface to *Polyhymnia Caduceatrix et Panegyrica*, xv.

31. Praetorius's recommendations may have particular significance for the Dresden court, for between ca. 1613 and 1616, and again in 1617, the composer-theorist served Johann Georg I temporarily as court Kapellmeister. In this capacity he presided over the music during the 1613 baptism of Prince Johann Georg II and in 1617 helped to organize

Georg I has surfaced. Instead, the 1581 formulation of Elector August seems to have retained its currency until the early 1660s, when it was replaced by the *Kirchen-Ord-nung* of Johann Georg II. It seems that the liturgical and musical accretions of the intervening decades, seen in the few liturgies that survive from the reign of Johann Georg I, were established by precedent and observed in practice, but never properly formalized.[32] Thus, already in the fall of 1657, even before embarking upon his castle renovation project, Johann Georg II sought to fill in this lacuna and began to lay out his vision of worship life in the chapel. In a brief document that comprises just eight concise points, the new elector outlined the cycle of feasts to be observed at court, and the type and number of services that would mark each festal occasion through-out the liturgical year.[33] His use of the conditional mood, and his description of his thoughts on the matter as "provisional" ("ungefehrliche"), help to define the docu-ment as a proposal, rather than a decree; most likely he planned to consult Weller before implementing any permanent changes to the court worship schedule. Unlike the later *Kirchen-Ordnung*, this document does not include actual orders of worship, and makes no mention of music. But its list of feasts, designation of services, and rubrics mark it as a prototype of the later formulary, for all of this information is also found in the *Kirchen-Ordnung*. That document, however, is much more detailed, and includes a few additional feasts as well as services of other types.

> His Electoral Highness's most gracious provisional opinion concerning the way in which, in the future, the feast days would be observed throughout the entire year, to begin in the approaching season of Advent.[34]
>
>   1. Latin Vespers would be held on the eve of all high feasts and other feasts.
>   2. On the first Sunday of Advent, as the beginning of the new church year, there would be a service with a sermon in both the morning and the afternoon.[35]
>   3. On the first day of the holy feasts of Christmas, Easter, and Pentecost, the feast would be rung in from 4:00 until 4:30 a.m., after the firing of three

the music for two major events: the emperor's visit and the festival to celebrate the cen-tennial of the Reformation. See Steude 2001/1:33, 37.

32. Several of these liturgies are discussed below.

33. Sächs HStA Loc. 12026, fol. 233r–v.

34. The German text appears in Appendix I (no. 20).

35. Rather than make specific reference to the *Hauptgottesdienst* and the vespers, Johann Georg uses the simple verb "geprediget" ("preached") to indicate both types of worship services and restricts his use of the term "vespers" to instances when the after-noon service would not involve a sermon. Here the verb has been translated as "service with a sermon."

cannons on the *Creuz* Tower, and there would be a service with a sermon in both the morning and the afternoon on these days.

4. On St. Stephen's Day, as well as on Easter and Pentecost Mondays, there would be a service with a sermon in both the morning and the afternoon.

5. On the Feast of St. John the Evangelist, Easter and Pentecost Tuesdays there would be a service with a sermon in the morning, but only vespers in the afternoon.

6. During Holy Week, there would be morning services with sermons throughout the entire week, from Palm Sunday until Good Friday; on Maundy Thursday, however, due to [the celebration of Holy] Communion, there would be a service with a sermon in both the morning and the afternoon. NB. If the Feast of the Annunciation fell during Holy Week, or on Easter Sunday, it would be celebrated on Palm Sunday.

7. On New Year's Day, as well as on the feasts of the Annunciation, Ascension, Holy Trinity, and St. Michael, there would be a service with a sermon in both the morning and the afternoon.

8. On the feasts of Epiphany, Purification, St. John the Baptist, Visitation, and Mary Magdalene, there would be a service with a sermon in the morning, and vespers in the afternoon.

This 1657 document not only establishes the annual festal calendar to be observed, but also points up Johann Georg's interest in vespers and his desire to regularize the celebration of these services. But it remains difficult to determine with certainty whether the schedule of vesper services that he put forward in this document represented major changes to the liturgical calendar at court as observed during his father's reign, or just relatively minor modifications. The 1539 Saxon *Agenda* mandates the celebration of a number of feasts with a morning *Gottesdienst*,[36] but does not ordain that vespers be celebrated as well. By contrast, the 1581 *Ordnung* of Elector August for the Dresden court chapel provides for vespers on every Sunday and feast day, but only provides for a sermon at vespers on the first day of each of the three high feasts of the church year.[37] And, with only two exceptions, diary entries for feast days celebrated between 1641 and 1656 record the celebration of vespers on

36. These include Christmas (three feast days), Circumcision, Epiphany, Purification, Annunciation, Maundy Thursday, Good Friday, Easter (three feast days), Ascension, Pentecost (here there is no mention of services on days 2 and 3), Trinity, John the Baptist, Visitation, St. Michael. Optional feasts include the Conversion of St. Paul, Mary Magdalene, the Beheading of St. John the Baptist, St. Stephen, etc.; see *Agenda* 1540, fols. 37v–39r.

37. Schmidt 1961:99.

only those occasions.[38] But it remains highly unlikely that the court of Johann Georg I did not to mark the other feast days with vespers as well, as this was typical of Lutheran practice.[39] Still, the omission is most curious. And while the entries from the diary for 1641–50 are very brief, those from the spring and summer of 1656 that record the double services held during Johann Georg I's decline contain much more detail, but even these do not mention vesper services, save on Easter, Pentecost, and the eve of the Feast of St. Michael.[40] The general silence on the part of the court secretaries with regard to vespers during these years may indicate that such services did not form part of the worship schedule, or that the afternoon service usually did not include a sermon, or perhaps that Johann Georg I did not attend these services.

Although the records from this period are somewhat incomplete, they do reveal that Johann Georg's thoughts on worship life were more than just "provisional," for many had been realized already by December 1657. According to a document from that year entitled "*Ordnung* / How the Holy Feast of Christmas shall be celebrated," the services held during the first three-day feast of the church year conformed to the elector's proposal from earlier that fall.[41] But Johann Georg departed Dresden for the electoral diet in Frankfurt on 11 February 1658 and did not return until 28 August of that year. As his diarists accompanied him, documentation is lacking for life back at court during those months, which saw the celebration of the high feasts of Easter and Pentecost. However, the services on New Year's Day and the Feast of St. Michael in 1658 also reflect the provisions given in the proposal, with the morning *Hauptgottesdienst* followed by a *Vesperpredigt* in the afternoon.[42] The records for the Christmas season of 1658, however, while they do not yet include orders of worship, do include far more detail, and document not only the realization of the elector's vision of worship on the three high feasts, but also the appropriation of worship for the purpose of representation.

38. Sächs HStA OHMA O IV Nr. 5, and SLUB K 113 (1653–56); both services included a sermon. The two exceptions involve references to vespers (apparently without a sermon) on Pentecost Monday 1641 and the Feast of St. Stephen (Christmas II) 1642, found in OHMA O IV Nr. 5 [unfoliated].

39. Letters from the 1640s of both court preacher Weller and Prince Johann Georg suggest that this was the case. Weller's letter appears in Sächs HStA Loc. 8687/1, fols. 234–36 (a portion of the letter is quoted in Schmidt 1961:121); the prince's letter is discussed in Frandsen 2000:20.

40. SLUB K 113 fols. 76r, 79v.

41. "Ordnung wie es aufs heilige Christ fest soll gehalten werden" (Sächs HStA, OHMA N I Nr. 8, fol. 18r). The document reports that the celebration of Christmas Day and the Feast of St. Stephen involved a morning service and a "Vesperpredigt," while the Feast of St. John was marked by a morning service and "Vesper ohne Predigt" (fol. 19r).

42. New Year's Day 1658: Sächs HStA OHMA N I Nr. 8, fol. 19r; Feast of St. Michael 1658: SLUB Q 238, entry for 29 September 1658.

Johann Georg's *Kirchen-Ordnung* and the
Stabilization of Liturgical Forms

Despite the many changes and accretions to the court liturgies in the decades since the promulgation of Elector August's 1581 court *Ordnung*, that document had apparently never undergone a revision—no evidence survives to suggest that either Johann Georg I or his predecessors had issued a similar document. Thus Johann Georg II seized the opportunity to fix the court liturgies as he had long envisioned them and, in so doing, contrived to use his expansive, Italian-dominated *Hofkapelle* to the greatest possible advantage. But a new and detailed liturgical formulary had also become a practical necessity, for Schütz's Italian Catholic successors could not be expected to possess even a working knowledge of Lutheran liturgical practices. In this *Kirchen-Ordnung*, however, they had a ready reference at their disposal that provided either complete liturgies or rubrics for the feasts listed by the elector in 1657, as well as for regular Sundays, apostles' days, Reformation Day, St. Martin's Day, and the various weekday services.[43] With the implementation of his *Kirchen-Ordnung*, Johann Georg thus ensured musico-liturgical uniformity throughout the church year. As the court diaries for the years 1662–80 attest, the *Kirchen-Ordnung* set the liturgical standard throughout these years of Johann Georg II's reign, for the services included in those chronicles follow the document meticulously, and confirm its use until the death of the elector.

The exemplar of the *Kirchen-Ordnung* now preserved in Dresden is undated,[44] but the formulary itself likely received its final form sometime between 1662 and 1665. A comparison of extant orders of worship from the years 1660–62 and 1665, however, demonstrates that the liturgical forms found in Johann Georg's *Kirchen-Ordnung* had largely been put in place by December 1660.[45] A diary for 1662 (SLUB Q 240) includes a complete cycle of detailed, enumerated liturgies for the Sundays and feast days of that entire calendar year, and all but four of these follow exactly the forms found in the elector's *Kirchen-Ordnung* (see below). The only deviations occur in four of the festal liturgies.[46] But as no orders of worship survive from 1663, and very few from 1664, the first surviving orders of worship for these same four feasts in which the liturgical forms follow those found in the *Kirchen-Ordnung* date

---

43. Schmidt points out that the cursus of feasts in Johann Georg's *Kirchen-Ordnung* follows that established in 1581 for the court by Elector August, save that the Conversion of St. Paul has replaced St. Laurentius Day in the schedule of apostles' days, and St. Martin Luther's Day has been added (Schmidt 1961:44–45, 91).

44. SLUB K 89, fols. 1–23; a full transcription and translation appears in Spagnoli 1990:175–209.

45. Sächs HStA Loc. 12026, fols. 55r–66v; SLUB Q 240, Q 241.

46. Purification, St. John the Baptist, Visitation, and St. Michael.

from 1665 or 1666.[47] Thus the year in which the elector finalized his liturgical formulary cannot be determined with precision.

The orders of worship for New Year's Day found in the *Kirchen-Ordnung* and given below are representative of those for Sundays and feast days throughout the entire church year in Dresden with respect to both their liturgical forms and musical content. Both the morning and afternoon service typically included elaborate figural settings of liturgical items, as well as concerted psalms and sacred concertos.[48] But within the liturgical forms established in the *Kirchen-Ordnung* one also sees the observance of the principle of "progressive solemnity,"[49] as the document carefully sets the observance of the various feasts and festal seasons of the church apart from that of ordinary Sundays, and distinguishes between the celebrations on each of the three days of the three high feasts. On most feast days, for example, a polyphonic setting of a Latin Introit was sung, whereas on a few lesser feasts and all non-feast Sundays, a German hymn served in its place. The concerted Credo replaced the sacred concerto that followed the recitation of the Gospel on nearly all feast days (Day 1 of Christmas, Easter, and Pentecost, as well as Epiphany, Purification, Annunciation, Ascension, Trinity, St. John the Baptist, Visitation, and St. Michael), but the Litany was sung at this point on the Feast of Mary Magdalene. The concerto after the sermon was replaced by concerted setting of the *Nunc dimittis* (in either German or Latin) on the Feast of the Purification, and by a figural setting of the *Te Deum* in Latin on the Feast of the Holy Trinity, and in German on the Feasts of St. John the Baptist and Mary Magdalene, the name days of the elector and electress. On the former occasion, the performance by the *Hofkapelle* was further enhanced by the participation of trumpeters and timpanists, and punctuated by the firing of cannons at three preordained junctures in the liturgy.

Similar types of substitutions appear in the vespers services. On Christmas Day, for example, the concerted psalm was followed by a musical setting of the Christmas History, and the performance of the *Magnificat* was amplified by the interpolation of three congregational hymns, whose titles are specified in the *Kirchen-Ordnung*; in this service, which also included a sermon, the usual two hymns (nos. 5 and 9 below) and the reading were omitted, presumably due to the greater length of

47. The orders of worship appear in SLUB Q 241 (Purification, Visitation, St. Michael) and Q 243 (St. John the Baptist).

48. This and the following observations on the morning and afternoon liturgies are drawn from the *Kirchen-Ordnung*, as found in Spagnoli 1990:179–89.

49. Although the concept of "progressive solemnity" was recognized for centuries by both Catholics and Lutherans, the term as such was first articulated after the Second Vatican Council; see the *Institutio generalis de liturgia horarum* (Rome: Typis Polyglottis Vaticanis, 1971), no. 273, "Principium itaque 'progressivae' solemnitatis," and subsequent publications.

the service. On Easter Sunday, Ps 114 sung *choraliter* in German replaced the concerted Latin psalm, and a performance of the Resurrection History replaced the first sacred concerto; on Pentecost Sunday, that concerto was to be a setting of *Veni Sancte Spiritus*. For most feast days, however, the *Kirchen-Ordnung* includes only a rubric that establishes the form of vespers to be celebrated, either that of vespers on a holy eve, or of the second or third day of the high feasts (the latter is identical in form to that for the eve of a high feast), and creates two classes of festal liturgies, those that include a sermon and those that do not.[50] The latter service, which did not differ from the former with respect to the number of musical elements, was often described as "musical vespers" ("musicalische Vesper") in the court diaries. The two services do differ slightly in their ordering of elements, however; if a sermon was to be preached, the order of the first hymn and reading were reversed, and the sermon then followed the hymn, which gave the minister time to move from the altar to the pulpit, located in the nave.

MORNING *GOTTESDIENST* AND AFTERNOON VESPERS
ON NEW YEAR'S DAY

Kirchen-Ordnung of 1662[51]	SLUB Msc. Dresd. Q 240 [1662][52]
1. Zum *Introitu*: Helfft mir Gottes Güte preisen	1. Helft mir Gottes güte preysen.
2. *Missa, musicaliter.*	2. *Missa, Vinc. Alb:*
3. Allein Gott in der Höh seÿ Ehr.	3. Allein Gott in der Höh.
4. *Collect* und die Epistel.	4. Collecta und die Epistel.
5. Jesu nun seÿ gepreiset.	5. Jesu nun seÿ gepreÿset.
6. Evangelium.	6. Evangelium,
7. Ein Teützsch *Concert*, das alte Jahr vergangen ist, oder ein lateinisches.	7. *Concert. Diligam te Dom. V. A.*
8. Der Glaube.	8. Der Glaube,

50. Feast days that include a sermon: day 2 of the high (three-day) feasts, New Year's Day, Annunciation, Maundy Thursday, *Quasimodogeniti*, Ascension, Holy Trinity, and St. Michael; those that do not include a sermon: vigils and day 3 of the three high feasts, Epiphany, Purification, St. John the Baptist, Visitation, Mary Magdalene; Spagnoli 1990:179–89. This division does not correspond exactly to the group of feast days that include the figural Credo in the morning.

51. Spagnoli 1990:180–82; the rubric for vespers on New Year's Day indicates that it shall be celebrated as on the second day of a high feast.

52. Translation/explanation: 1. Hymn (as Introit). 2. Mass (Kyrie and Gloria), by Vincenzo Albrici. 3. German Gloria hymn. 4. Collect and the Epistle. 5. Hymn. 6. Gospel. 7. Concerto, *Diligam te Dom[ine]*, by Albrici (lost). 8. German creedal hymn. 9. Sermon,

9. Predigt, und für dem Vater Unser, Nun lasst uns Gott dem HERREN.	9. Predigt, und für dem Vater Unser: Nun last Unß Gott dem [Herren].
10. Concert.	10. *Mot. Reboent aethera. V. A.*
11. Ein Teüzsch Lied.	11. Nun lob mein Seel den Herren.
12. *Collecta* und der Segen.	12. Collect und der Segen.
13. Ein kurz Lied zum Beschluß.	13. Ach mein herzliebster Jesulein.
Vespers on the Second Day of a High Feast	Vespers, New Year's Day, 1662[53]
1. *Deus in adjutorium meum.*	1. *Deus in adjutorium meum.*
2. Ein lateinischer Psalm, *musicaliter.*	2. *Dixit Dominus. J. Perand.*
3. Ein kurz *Concert* oder *Motetto.*	3. *Venite cantemus. V. A.*
4. Lieset der Priester vorm Altar, einen Text, oder Psalmen abe.	4. Wird abgelesen der 65. Psalm Gott man lobet dich.
5. Ein Teüzsch Lied.	5. Dancket dem Herrn heüt und.
6. Predigt, und für derselben, Ein Kindelein so löbelich.	6. Predig, und für dem Vatter V. Ein Kindelein so löbelich.
7. *Magnificat.*	7. *Magnificat.* Vinc. Alb.
8. Ein *Concert* oder *Motetto.*	8. Concert. *Lauda anima mea. V. A.*
9. Ein Teüzsch Lied.	9. Jesu nun seÿ gepreÿset.
10. *Collecta.*	10. *Collecta.*
11. *Benedicamus.*	11. *Benedicamus Domino.*

Very few descriptive liturgies survive from the long reign of Johann Georg I. A comparison of the form of his *Hauptgottesdienst* with that of a service celebrated in 1655 (see below),[54] however, reveals that in his *Kirchen-Ordnung*, Johann Georg II

and before the Lord's Prayer, a hymn. 10. Motet, *Reboent aethera*, by Albrici (lost). 11. Hymn. 12. Collect and Blessing. 13. Hymn.

53. Translation/explanation: 1. Opening versicle. 2. Concerted Psalm, *Dixit Dominus*, by Peranda. 3. Concerto, *Venite cantemus*, by Albrici. 4. Reading of Psalm 65, "Gott, man lobet dich." 5. Hymn. 6. Sermon, and before the Lord's Prayer, a hymn. 7. *Magnificat*, by Albrici (lost). 8. Concerto, *Lauda anima mea*, by Albrici (lost). 9. Hymn. 10. Collect. 11. Blessing.

54. SLUB K 113, fols. 58r–59r; the service was held in the chapel of Schloß Freudenstein in Freiberg, in commemoration of the Peace of Augsburg concluded 100 years earlier. The record makes no mention of Schütz or of the *Hofkapelle* and does not include the titles of the motets; Schütz presumably directed the music on this occasion (Rifkin and Timms 1985:57–58).

remained faithful to court tradition and retained the liturgical form of the principal service in use under his father. Here one sees the same number and placement of hymns, the performance of a concerted Latin Kyrie and Gloria and the congregational restatement of the Gloria in its traditional hymn form, as well as the interpolation of figural works after the Gospel and the sermon.[55]

Jubel- und Danckfest, 25 September 1655	1 January 1662
Hymn	Hymn
Missa	*Missa*
Allein Gott in der Höh sei Ehr	*Allein Gott in der Höh sei Ehr*
Collect and appointed text [in place of the Epistle][56]	Collect and Epistle
Hymn	Hymn
Appointed text [in place of the Gospel],	Gospel
Motet	Concerto
German creedal hymn	German creedal hymn
Sermon with hymn and Lord's Prayer	Sermon with hymn and Lord's Prayer
Motet	Motet
Hymn	Hymn
Collect and Blessing	Collect and Blessing
Hymn	Hymn

In contrast to the liturgy for the *Hauptgottesdienst*, however, the vespers liturgies reported in the 1662 diary clearly demonstrate that Johann Georg took a rather strong hand with the afternoon service and introduced significant changes to the form and musical content of the service as celebrated in the 1650s.[57] First, the new elector introduced the versicle *Deus in adjutorium meum* as the opening of the liturgy, and followed it with two musical compositions, a concerted psalm and a sacred concerto in the position of an antiphon substitute; only after these three items, performed by the *Hofkapelle* (with the assistance of the minister in the versicle) did the service proceed to a hymn and a reading. The latter half of the service, from the *Magnificat* to the end, still bore a resemblance to the service as celebrated in

55. See also Schmidt 1961:119.

56. On the occasion of this special celebration, alternate texts were chosen for the Epistle and Gospel.

57. The lack of uniformity in the liturgical form of Lutheran vespers renders problematic any discussion of "traditions" with respect to musical interpolations in these services. See the discussion in Leaver 1990.

the 1650s. But although the vesper services from 1650[58] and 1655[59] included the performance of either a motet or a concerted psalm, as well as the *Magnificat*, neither included any additional motets or sacred concertos; thus the *Hofkapelle* was responsible for only two concerted works.[60] In the service developed by Johann Georg,[61] four concerted works enhanced these services on feast days: concerted settings of a Latin psalm and the *Magnificat*, and two sacred concertos. In the space of just a few years, Johann Georg had considerably expanded both the musical and the textual content of the vesper service and had established it as the musical counterweight to the morning *Gottesdienst*.

1650 *FRIEDENSFEST*	1655 *JUBEL- UND DANCKFEST*	NEW YEAR'S DAY, 1662
Hymn as Introit	Motet	*Deus in adjutorium meum* Concerted psalm Concerto
	Hymn	
Appointed Psalm read	Appointed text read	Appointed Psalm read
Psalm concerto or motet	Hymn	Hymn
Sermon[62]	Sermon	Sermon
Magnificat (German)	*Magnificat* (Latin?)	*Magnificat* (Latin) Concerto
Hymn	Hymn	Hymn
Collect and Blessing	Collect and Blessing	Collect and Blessing
Hymn		

It is important to stress that while Johann Georg II did endeavor to strengthen the musical component of vespers, his views on the role of music in the liturgy in general cannot be considered in any way idiosyncratic; nor do they suggest the influence of Catholicism. Rather, his musico-liturgical practices reflect Lutheran customs established in the mid-to-late sixteenth century and perpetuated for at least two hundred years thereafter. Thus Schmidt's contention that the prominence of music in Johann Georg's Dresden liturgies represented the "insertion of a concert program into the *Gottesdienst*," a claim that implies that the practices of the electoral chapel deviated from those of the typical Lutheran establishment, has no

58. Sächs HStA OHMA N I Nr. 1, fols. 4r–v; the service was celebrated on 22 July 1650.

59. SLUB K 113, fols. 58r–v.

60. See Schmidt 1961:120.

61. SLUB Q 240, entry for 1 January 1662.

62. The sermon was part of a longer pulpit service, which included the singing of one or more hymns and the recitation of the Lord's Prayer.

basis in fact.[63] In actuality, this sort of "musicalization" defined the liturgical ethos of numerous Lutheran courts and cities through the time of Bach. Prescriptions for liturgical celebrations in a number of towns and courts in the region, including Bischofswerda in ca. 1620, Liegnitz (now Legnica in Poland) in 1625, Dresden in the 1660s and 1670s, Weißenfels in the 1680s, and Leipzig in 1710 and 1723, serve as examples of what was typical in Lutheran court chapels and town churches for over a century.[64] Each demonstrates that the *Hofkapelle* or choir from the local Latin school was regularly called upon to perform as many as four extra-liturgical compositions, as well as polyphonic or concerted elements of the liturgy itself, during the morning *Gottesdienst*. These documents also reveal that the use of Latin in the liturgy, and the performance of strictly monophonic music on some occasions during the church year, remained alive well into the eighteenth century. The form of vespers as established in these records differs from place to place, and once again demonstrates the flexibility in the content and design of the afternoon service that characterizes Lutheran practice.[65]

Johann Georg's *Kirchen-Ordnung* sets forth the manner in which worship was to be conducted in his court chapel throughout the liturgical year. But the document also reveals much about the musical responsibilities and the division of labor between the full *Hofkapelle*, dominated by the Italians, and the smaller group of German choristers. The elector's instructions divide the services into two broad categories—those in which the Italian Kapellmeister and the full electoral musical ensemble, *die Musica*, participated, and those for which the court cantor and his "Choralisten," or choristers, supplied the music.[66] One of the Italian Kapellmeisters conducted the music during the *Hauptgottesdienst* on Sundays and feast days, and during the vesper services on feast days, the vigil vespers on the eves of Christ-

63. "Diese Praxis, in den Gottesdienst ein Konzertprogramm einzuschalten, bleibt nicht auf die hohen Festtage beschränckt, sondern scheint sich auch an gewöhnlichen Sonntagen des Kirchenjahres in der Dresdener Schloßkirche durchgesetzt zu haben" (Schmidt 1961:203).

64. Bischofswerda ca. 1620: Sehling 2:106; Liegnitz 1625: Liliencron 1893/1970:121–31; Weißenfels 1685 and 1688: Gundlach 2001:51–75; Leipzig 1710: *Leipziger Kirchen=Staat*, 1–48; Leipzig 1723: *Bach-Dokumente* I:248-49 (Leipzig liturgy as recorded by Johann Sebastian Bach in 1723).

65. See in particular the liturgies for Bischofswerda (Sehling 2:106), which lacks the canticle, and Weißenfels (Gundlach 2001:61), in which the *Hofkapelle* performed "Music" (presumably concerted music) at three points in the service.

66. In 1662 the "Choralisten" included basses Matthias Erlemann (the court cantor) and Constantin Christian Dedekind, two tenors, two altos, and a young man whose voice had changed ("so mutiret"); presumably the choirboys sang soprano (see Spagnoli 1990:86).

mas, New Year's Day, Easter, and Pentecost, and the morning service on an apostle's day—even though the latter service featured elements of the *deutsche Messe* rather than the Latin Mass. On weekdays, and on most Sunday afternoons and festal eves, however, music in the chapel remained the domain of the German court cantor and his choristers. In his *Kirchen-Ordnung*, Johann Georg provided orders of worship for each of the three types of services celebrated during the week and on Sunday afternoons: vespers, prayer hours (*Beht Stunden*) and weekday morning services with a sermon (*Wochenpredigten*).[67] These services were far less elaborate than the Sunday morning and festal liturgies, and the choristers were only responsible for a minimal amount of concerted music. But the court cantor and choristers clearly shouldered a heavy burden in the court chapel, for they were responsible for daily service music at court, but also performed with the *Hofkapelle* on Sundays and feast days. As discussed in chapter 2, this division of labor is made manifest in the contracts for Antonio Fidi and Johann Jacob Lindner. While Fidi's duties were defined very broadly as service in the castle chapel and "at table," those of Lindner were given in detail, and included service in the chapel "both on Sundays and feast days as well as at weekday sermons, and at all vespers and prayer hours, early communion, and at table."

When viewing the court documents related to worship life, however, the importance of the court cantor and choristers is easily overlooked, for with one notable exception (the week of the chapel dedication in September 1662), the court diarists omitted virtually all of these orders of worship and recorded only those in which the Italians directed and performed, probably in accordance with the elector's instructions. Thus a reading of the diaries without reference to the *Kirchen-Ordnung* could easily lead to the erroneous conclusion that the German musicians played an insignificant musical role at court. While in the prayer hours and weekday morning services they sang only one Schütz-Becker psalm, and otherwise functioned as leaders of the congregational singing, their responsibilities at vespers included presentations of Latin- or German-texted concertos and figural settings of the *Magnificat*, in addition to psalms sung *choraliter*. The only indication of the actual concerted repertoire sung in these services, however, dates from September 1662; during this inaugural week, members of this small group performed sacred concertos by Giovanni Valentini, *Laudate pueri* and *Paratum cor meum*, during the Wednesday and Saturday vespers services.[68] The choristers likely also performed works of Schütz and his contemporaries, and may have presented less-demanding works of the Italian Kapellmeisters on occasion; it is also likely that Dedekind, a chorister himself, composed

67. The liturgies are given in Spagnoli 1990:176–77, 190.

68. SLUB Q 240, entries for 1 and 4 October 1662; for an extensive treatment of the music of Valentini, see Saunders 1995:178–222.

many of his sacred works for this ensemble.[69] Given the high salaries paid to the Italian musicians, their comparatively light duties must have rankled the German musicians, who saw chapel duty every day of the week, and who received far less compensation in return. Indeed, for many weeks during the Trinity season, the Italians were only called upon to perform at the Sunday morning *Hauptgottesdienst* and the following midday meal, and often traveled with the elector on his summer tours of his various territories.

Johann Georg II founded and developed his *Hofkapelle* primarily as an accoutrement of worship and an enrichment of daily life at court. In contrast to his colleagues in Munich and Vienna, he did not require the Italian musicians on his roster to perform Italian operas on a regular basis. Instead, performances of elaborate sacred music during the chapel liturgies, and *Tafelmusik* during meals, defined the major responsibilities of the elector's musicians. Given his firm belief that one of the marks of a sovereign of high rank was a large musical ensemble that could enhance his chapel liturgies, it is not surprising that soon after his father's death, which effectively silenced any opposition to the involvement of the Italian-dominated ensemble in the chapel, Johann Georg trained his attention on the chapel liturgies, with an eye toward affording his *Hofkapelle* multiple opportunities to perform on Sundays and feast days. Between 1657 and 1662 he not only renovated and expanded the worship space with new balconies for the musicians, and attempted to ensure the sources of funding for the ensemble, but he also undertook a program of liturgical renewal and worked to fix the liturgical forms of the morning and vesper services that would be celebrated throughout his reign. This effort resulted in a new *Kirchen-Ordnung* for the court chapel, apparently the first since that promulgated by Elector August in 1581. Even a cursory glance at the *Kirchen-Ordnung*, and at the related liturgies and narrative descriptions contained in the court diaries, reveals an ethos of worship that privileged musical splendor. By fixing the amount of musical content in each liturgy, specifying its genre, and hiring highly trained musicians to present it in the chapel, Johann Georg guaranteed that he and the court community would be treated to virtuoso performances of modern Italian music throughout the liturgical year. But at the same time that he encouraged a modern Italian repertoire of sacred art music, he allowed this to coexist with the traditional German music of the congregation, and located both within a traditionally Lutheran liturgical framework. While he essentially adhered to Lutheran traditions in the design of the morning

---

69. See, for example, the concertos in his *Sonderbahrer Seelenfreude oder kleinerer Geistlichen Concerten* (Dresden, 1672), and *Musikalischer Jahr=Gang und Vesper=Gesang* (Dresden, 1673–74).

service, he considerably expanded the musical content of vespers, with the result that the afternoon service nearly balanced the morning *Gottesdienst* in musical weight. Seen from this perspective, Johann Georg's organization of the court liturgical calendar becomes a direct effort to optimize the talents of the *Hofkapelle*. The manner in which this ensemble realized the provisions of his *Kirchen-Ordnung* on a weekly basis resulted in a liturgical year of musical splendor and magnificence.

8

Musik im Gottesdienst:
The Liturgical Year at the Dresden Court

W HILE A SIGNIFICANT amount of the sacred repertoire performed in seventeenth-century religious establishments, both Protestant and Catholic, survives in
print and manuscript sources, reconstructions of the daily or weekly use of that
musical literature in particular locales has remained largely out of the reach of
scholars. For the most part, records detailing the musico-liturgical life at religious
institutions of this era do not survive; some inventories of the holdings of now-lost
music libraries have been preserved, but these frequently provide no dates or occasions upon which the works were performed.[1] Thus the numerous orders of worship
for services celebrated in the Dresden court chapel found in Johann Georg's court
diaries represent a treasure-trove of information on the liturgical performance context of sacred music in a seventeenth-century Lutheran establishment. These stand
as a precious resource, for, among other things, they provide the scholar with a
unique tool with which to explore one of the last frontiers in the study of sacred
music: its relationship to the scriptural or theological topos of particular services
as established by the *de tempore* readings, particularly the Gospel. Not only do the
Dresden court diaries document where, when, and under what circumstances a
particular composition was performed, they also provide some clues to the exegetical role played by extra-liturgical music in the service in Dresden, and, by extension,
in other Lutheran venues.

However, the documentary materials, both archival and musical, that survive
from the Dresden court of this era present a study of this sort with two basic limitations. The first of these concerns lacunae in the orders of worship available for
study. Prior to 1660, the court secretaries did not incorporate orders of worship into
the court diaries. This prevents the examination of the stylistic nature of the music
heard in the court chapel, and its role in the worship service, during the incipient
years of the reign of Johann Georg II, just after he installed his Italian Kapellmeisters

---

1. In at least one case, that of the Weißenfels court (under the musical leadership of
Krieger and his son), performance dates are also included in the inventory; see Gundlach 2001.

in the chapel. In addition, for the twenty-year period between 1660 and 1680, only the diary for 1662 preserves a series of service orders that is virtually complete, and that includes the entire Trinity season[2]; after the diary for 1662, only those for 1665 and 1666 preserve orders of worship for a significant number of non-feast days. For six of the twenty-five calendar years of this elector's reign, the diaries either include no orders of worship, or do not survive at all (see the list below).

Surviving Orders of Worship in Court Diaries and Other Records from the Reign of Johann Georg II

Complete and Nearly Complete Years

1662: SLUB Q 240 (virtually complete)

1665: SLUB K 80, Q 241, both missing some Sundays in Trinity; New Year's Day and 29 January to 3 February also in Sächs HStA Loc. 12026, fols. 216r–227v; 24 August (St. Bartholomew's Day), Sächs HStA Loc. 12026, fol. 281r

1666: SLUB Q 243 (entries include the scorings of many sacred concertos)

Partial Years

1660: 13 May (*Friedensfest*); 23 December (Advent 4) to 30 December (Sunday after Christmas), Sächs HStA OHMA N IV Nr. 1, fols. 12r–16v; Loc. 12026, fols. 56r–61r

1661: 1–6 January (Sunday after New Year's Day), 1 November, Sächs HStA Loc. 12026, fols. 63v–66v, 112r, 257r

1664: Pentecost I–III, Trinity Sunday, Feast of Mary Magdalene, 31 December, Sächs HStA Loc. 12026, fols. 34r, 234r, 395v–404v; SLUB K 80 fol. 2v

1667: 1 January to 22 July (many services missing), SLUB Q 245; Pentecost I–III, Birthday of Johann Georg II (*Wochenpredigt*) also in Sächs HStA Loc. 12026, fols. 253r–255v, 528r–v

1668: 20 March (Good Friday) to 29 March (*Quasimodogeniti*); 31 May (Birthday of Johann Georg II), Sächs HStA Loc. 12026, fols. 244r–249v; OHMA N I Nr. 7, fol. 58r

1672: 22–24 June (Dedication of Moritzburg Chapel); 21 December (Advent 4, vigil) to 29 December (Sunday after Christmas), Sächs HStA OHMA N I Nr. 6, fols. 36r–40r; SLUB K 117, fols. 2r–11r

1673: 1 January to 31 May; 30 November, SLUB K 117, fols. 11v–59r; Sächs HStA Loc. 8681 Nr. 8, fols. 201r–202v

1675: 19 December (Advent 4) to 27 December (Feast of St. John), SLUB Q 260

2. Until the mid-1970s, Lutherans enumerated the Sundays of the long summer and fall seasons of the church year with reference to Trinity Sunday, in contrast to the contemporary Roman tradition of enumerating these as Sundays after Pentecost. Lutheran bodies today have adopted the latter practice, but the enumeration in this chapter reflects the earlier custom.

1676: 1 January to 3 December (Advent 1) (many services missing), SLUB Q 260

1677: 16 and 23 September (Trinity 14 and 15), 29 September (Feast of St. Michael), Sächs HStA Loc. 8682 Nr. 11, fols. 111r–121r

1678: 2 February (Purification); 29 September (Feast of St. Michael), Gabriel Tzschimmer, *Durchlauchtigste Zusammenkunft*, 51; Sächs HStA Loc. 8682 Nr. 12, fols. 134v–135r

1679: 31 May (Birthday of Johann Georg II), Sächs HStA Loc. 8682 Nr. 13

Periods for which No Orders of Worship Survive

8 October 1656 (death of Johann Georg I) to 16 December 1660 (Advent 3), 1663 (entire year)

1680 (January to August)

The survival of a relatively small number of compositions performed during the morning *Hauptgottesdienste* presents a second difficulty. The majority of the surviving sacred concertos by Albrici and Peranda that appear in the diaries formed part of the vesper services. This may reflect the fact that these works tended to be more modestly scored than those for the morning service, and thus more accessible to smaller court and city musical establishments.[3] The works performed during the morning service that do survive, as well as the numerous scorings included in the court calendar for 1666 (SLUB Q 243), however, indicate that these compositions were often scored for many voices and instruments. For example, on Christmas morning in 1665, the *Hofkapelle* performed Peranda's *Gaudete Pastores*, now lost, which the secretary described as "ein groß Concert" scored for a ten-part vocal ensemble (SSSSAATTBB), five unspecified instruments, four shawms, and four trumpets and timpani. The next morning, on the Feast of St. Stephen, Peranda presented his *Caeli enarrant*, also lost, which required four tenors and four basses. A few days later, the celebration on New Year's morning included a performance of Peranda's extant composition *Laetentur coeli*, which featured ten voices, ten unspecified instruments, two trumpets, and timpani.[4] Works such as these likely remained beyond the reach of most court and church musical establishments with more limited resources, which may explain their general absence from the various collections.

Still, even given the limitations presented by these lacunae, the works that do survive, as well as the title incipits of lost works, allow one to form an impression of the degree to which the music and the scripture readings were integrated in each service or festal season. The Gospel text appointed for a particular Sunday or feast

---

3. This phenomenon extends to the works of Peranda and Albrici listed in inventories of lost collections.

4. SLUB Q 243; see the discussion of these services below.

day traditionally established the topic or theme of the service and served as the basis for the sermon.[5] Thus the interpolation of a musical work after the Gospel (and before the sermon) provided composers the opportunity to relate that work to the scripture reading. If, for example, the composition included either the entire Gospel text or a few verses selected from it, the congregation heard two successive interpretations of that same text, first in the musical composition and then in the sermon, after having heard the minister recite the text itself. As the seventeenth century came to a close, the exegetical potential afforded by the structure of this part of the service was exploited by Lutheran composers to an ever greater extent, as the proliferation of *Evangelien Jahrgänge* (Gospel cycles) demonstrates. By the eighteenth century, the practice of relating the *Hauptmusik* performed after the Gospel to that central text had become *de rigeur*. But in the 1660s and 1670s in Dresden, as in many other places, church musicians did not exploit this particular aspect of the liturgical form—both the titles listed in the orders of worship as well as the extant compositions demonstrate that neither Albrici nor Peranda set the Gospel text with any degree of regularity. Both did, however, regularly strive to present musical realizations of texts appropriate to the occasion, as will be demonstrated below. During festal periods, many of these texts exhibited a direct thematic relationship to the feast, rather than to any one particular Gospel. During the long Trinity season, however, mystical-devotional texts were often selected for their allegorical relationship to the Gospel for the day.

The orders of worship in the court diaries demonstrate that from 1662 on, the form of the worship services adhered strictly to the models given in the elector's *Kirchen-Ordnung*. As a result, one sees great liturgical consistency in Dresden between 1662 and 1680. Given that the services on a particular day in the church calendar were celebrated in exactly the same manner from one year to the next, one can undertake an examination of the church year in Dresden by drawing upon liturgies celebrated in various years. Therefore, in what follows, the shape and flow of the liturgical year in Dresden as defined by music are explored through an examination of liturgical celebrations that took place throughout Johann Georg's reign. But as a combination of various aural and visual stimuli contributed to the totality of the worship experience at a seventeenth-century court, a number of other aspects of worship life are examined here as well: chapel decorations, altar furnishings, communion vessels, liturgical vestments, and ceremonies performed by the palace guards prior to some of the worship services. Throughout this examination, the centrality of music's role continually rises to the foreground.

5. Although Luther made a number of significant changes in the Mass, he retained the Catholic lectionary virtually intact, as he stated in his *Deudsche messe und ordnung gottis diensts* of 1526 (see Sehling 1:13).

SUNDAYS AND FEAST DAYS FROM ADVENT
THROUGH TRINITY SUNDAY

The opening of the new church year in Dresden was marked with festal celebrations on the first Sunday of Advent (the fourth Sunday before Christmas Day).[6] With their concerted mass movements and sacred concertos, these services contrasted markedly with those celebrated on the three subsequent Sundays of this penitential period, which were distinguished by music performed *a cappella*.[7] In their selection of sacred concertos to be performed in the morning and at vespers, both Albrici and Peranda focused to a great extent on texts related to the seasonal themes of expectation, the advent of the Lord, and the passage from darkness into light, all of which were encapsulated in the Epistle and Gospel readings for the day and echoed in the quintessential Lutheran Advent hymn, the Reformer's own *Nun komm der Heiden Heiland*, which was traditionally sung after the Epistle on that Sunday.[8] In the Epistle, Romans 13:11–14, St. Paul exhorts his readers to "cast off the works of darkness and put on the armor of light" (v. 12, RSV), and in the Gospel, Matthew 21:1–9, the evangelist relates Christ's entry into Jerusalem riding on a donkey, in fulfillment of the words of the prophet Isaiah (62:11); the passage includes the familiar verse "Tell the daughter of Zion, behold, your king is coming to you" (v. 5, RSV). Both passages find resonance in the works presented by the Italian Kapellmeisters on Advent 1. In 1666 and 1673, the assembly heard Peranda's *Veni Domine* ("Come, Lord") after the sermon in the *Hauptgottesdienst*; although the composition does not survive, the incipit strongly suggests a thematic relationship with the Gospel.[9] After the morning sermon in 1676,[10] Albrici presented a motet entitled *Ad te levavi*, which is also lost, but which was likely a setting of the traditional Introit for Advent 1.[11] At vespers in 1666, a small ensemble of singers and instrumentalists performed Peranda's *O vos*

6. The order of worship for Advent 1 in Johann Georg's *Kirchen-Ordnung* also provides the prototype for services on ordinary Sundays throughout the year, both with and without the celebration of communion (see Spagnoli 1990:177–78). The diaries reveal, however, that the main morning service on Advent 1 normally did not include communion; instead, the rite was held before the main service.

7. In contrast to today's practice, the Gloria was not suppressed during Advent (SLUB Q 241, Q 243).

8. SLUB Q 240, entries for 30 November, 7, 14, and 21 December 1662; records from 1666 also reveal that it was sung repeatedly throughout the season (Q 243, entries for 2 and 16 December 1666). See the discussion of the *Detempore*, or cycle of hymns prescribed for each Sunday of the church year, in Graff 1937:133–34.

9. SLUB Q 243, entry for 2 December 1666, and Loc. 8681 Nr. 8 [1672–73], fol. 202r.

10. SLUB Q 260, entry for 3 December 1676.

11. *LU* 318; *Ad te levavi* also appears as the Introit for Advent 1 in Lossius 1561/1996, fol. 7a.

omnes after the *Magnificat*.[12] Only the text of this concerto survives, but it reveals a close relationship with the morning Epistle, which in Lutheran practice frequently served as the sermon text in the afternoon, for Peranda's text begins "O all ye who walk in darkness and the shadow of death, arise, hasten, come to the light."[13] At vespers on Advent 1 in 1676, however, the minister selected another Old Testament exhortation to the Daughter of Zion, Zephaniah 3:14–15, as the text for his *Vesperpredigt*; on this occasion, the performance of Albrici's *Jucundare filia Sion* after the concerted psalm comprised a setting of at least a portion of the lection itself, which begins "Sing aloud, O daughter of Zion; shout, O Israel! Rejoice and exult with all your heart, O daughter of Jerusalem!" (v. 14).[14] In contrast to the order of worship for the morning service, in which the concerto follows the reading of the Gospel, the performance of Albrici's *Jucundare* anticipated the reading of the text itself, which followed directly upon it; after the hymn that followed the reading, the congregation settled in for yet another interpretation of the text, this time in the sermon. But the records also reveal that the Advent 1 repertoire also included devotional pieces. At vespers on Advent 1 in 1662, for example, Albrici presented two concertos with aria, *Amo te, laudo te*, which begins "I love you, I praise you, o my dear Lord Jesus Christ,"[15] and *Jesu dulcis memoria*, both of which represent the intimate prayers of an individual.[16]

So few of the orders of worship for the morning service communicated in the diaries include the communion rite, which was normally celebrated every Sunday in Lutheran churches during this era, that a reading of the diaries alone would suggest that Lutherans at the Dresden court had only occasional access to the Eucharist. A 1668 copy of the *Ordnung* used by the office of the senior court marshal (*Ober Hofmarschall*), however, clarifies the matter and states that "on all Sundays throughout the year a sermon [morning service] and vespers will be held, and if communicants are present, communion will be celebrated at 6:00 a.m. [on Sundays] as well

---

12. SLUB Q 243, entry for 2 December 1666.

13. "O vos omnes ambulantes in tenebris, et umbra mortis, surgite, properate, venite ad lucem"; the entire text appears in the entry for 31 May 1665 in SLUB K 80 fols. 77v–78r; the documentation of the 1666 performance appears in SLUB Q 243, entry for 2 December 1666, where the scoring is given as two sopranos and bass and two violins (the continuo is never included by the diarist). Q 243 also reports that the work was performed earlier in 1666, on *Septuagesima* Sunday (21 February); for that performance, Peranda used a five-part string ensemble (scoring given as "2 Sop: e Basso 2. Violini e 3. Viole"). See the discussion of the use of the composition at Easter below.

14. SLUB Q 260, entry for 3 December 1676.

15. "Amo te, laudo te, o mi care Domine Jesu Christe."

16. SLUB Q 240, entry for 30 November 1662.

as on high feasts."[17] Although the diarists recorded only those early communion services during which the elector himself communicated, an event that took place only four or five times each year, it seems likely that communion was offered nearly every Sunday before the main service for the benefit of the various court officers, courtiers, and staff members who lived in the castle.[18] A source that derives from late in Johann Georg's reign, the published record of the 1678 festival known as the "Durchlauchtigste Zusammenkunft," indicates that early communion services were held at 6:00 a.m. on each of the first three Sundays in February.[19] The occasions upon which Johann Georg made his confession to the senior court preacher are also recorded in the diaries, which reveal that he confessed either following the Saturday vesper service, as was typical in Lutheran practice, or early in the morning, just before the communion service. Curiously, Johann Georg's *Kirchen-Ordnung* (see below for example)[20] includes neither the form of the morning communion liturgy nor rubrics pertaining to it. In their preservation of these communion services, the diaries reveal the flexibility of this particular liturgical form, which, like the *Hauptgottesdienst* and vespers, was more or less elaborate, depending upon the day.

COMMUNION SERVICE ON ADVENT 1 (30 NOVEMBER)
[1673,] 6:30 A.M.
"and there was preluding on the organ until Your Electoral Highness had taken Your seat; at that point the Mass commenced, which was held in the German language,"[21]

1. Der. 6. Psalm D. Beckers nach der Melodeÿ des Capellmeisters Heinrich Schüzens,	Ps 6 from Schütz's *Becker Psalter*
2. *Kyrie* Gott Vater in Ewigkeit,	German Kyrie hymn

17. "Alle Sontage Durchs Jahr, Eine Predigt und Vesper, und wenn communicanten vorhanden, wird umb 6. Uhr Communion, sowohl die hohe Fest Tage gehalten" (Sächs HStA OHMA N I Nr. 8, fol. 4v).

18. A court diary for 1660, for example, indicates that Johann Georg received communion on 6 January (Epiphany), 19 April (Maundy Thursday), 10 June (Pentecost), 28 October (Simon Judas), and 23 December (Advent 4); Sächs HStA OHMA O IV Nr. 9, entries for dates given. On the separation of the sermon and communion services, see Graff 1937:176–79.

19. Tzschimmer 1680:59, 168, 225.

20. Sächs HStA Loc. 8681 Nr. 8 [1672–73], fols. 201v–202r; another such service appears in SLUB K 117, fol. 4r–v. The material in the right-hand column represents a brief description of the elements in the liturgy, rather than a literal translation.

21. "undt wardt auff der Orgel *preambuli*ret bis Churf. Durchl. in Dero Stuhl, hierauff gieng der *Missa* an, so in Deüzscher Sprache gehalten würde" (Sächs HStA Loc. 8681 Nr. 8, fol. 201v).

3. *Intonirte* der Priester das Gloria	Intonation of the Gloria, followed by
4. All Ehr und Lob soll Gottes seÿn	German Gloria hymn
5. *Collecta* und der 51. Psalm, nebst dem Gebeth *Manasse*.	Collect, Ps. 51, and the Prayer of Manasseh[22]
6. Teüzsche Litaney, von denen knaben vor dem Altar.	German Litany, sung by the choirboys kneeling before the altar.[23]
7. 1. Corinth. 11. Von 23. biß schlüßung des 32. Verses, Wortte der Einsetzung.	I Cor 11:23–32, followed by the Words of Institution
8. Allein zu dir Herr Jesu Christ.	Communion Hymn
9. *Consecration*, und *communicir*ten Churf. Durchl. alleine in Persohn.[24]	Consecration and communion of Johann Georg II, "alone, in person"
10. Worbeÿ gesungen wurde, Jesus Christus unser Heÿland.	Hymn sung during communion
11. *Collecta* und der Seegen.	Collect and Blessing
12. Gott geb unß allen seiner Gnad und Seegen.	Hymn

Notable in this communion service is the complete absence of the Latin Ordinary, save perhaps the intonation of the Gloria (but see below).[25] Instead, like the service on an apostle's day, the communion service took the form of a *deutsche Messe* in which German Kyrie and Gloria hymns replaced the Greek and Latin texts sung in the *Hauptgottesdienst* on Sundays and feast days. The musical responsibility for these early communion services lay not with the Italian Kapellmeister and his virtuoso singers, but with the cantor and choristers, whose ranks included choirboys and an organist, and whose duties apparently did not include the performance of figural

22. A penitential prayer that comprises the Apocryphal book of the same title.

23. Such entries usually read "von den Knaben kniend vor dem Altar." Luther's Litany (with which he replaced the Roman Litany of the Saints) is given in the 1540 *Agenda*, fols. 27r–29r.

24. Here the record continues to indicate the four court officers who assisted with the houseling cloth.

25. Exceptions to this did occur on occasion. In 1665, for example, Advent 4 fell on Christmas Eve, and the morning communion service included a Kyrie by Palestrina, performed without the interpolated German hymns; this was followed by an intonation of the Gloria and the hymn *Allein Gott in der Höh sei Ehr*. The service also included the Credo, again by Palestrina and presumably from the same mass setting (SLUB Q 243, entry for 24 December 1665).

music during the Distribution.[26] Although the diaries never indicate the mode of performance of these texts, Jürgen Heidrich has suggested that the musicians may have sung Schütz's polyphonic settings of *Kyrie Gott Vater in Ewigkeit* and *All Ehr und Lob soll Gottes sein*, both of which appear in his *Zwölf Geistliche Gesänge* published by court organist Christoph Kittel in 1657.[27] It is significant that Schütz set this Gloria hymn rather than the more common *Allein Gott in der Höh sei Ehr*, which was sung on every Sunday and feast day during Johann Georg's reign. If Schütz's settings were still in use, however, it remains curious that the diarists regularly failed to recognize him as the composer, or even to indicate whether the hymns were performed *figuraliter* or *choraliter*, given that they did take care always to acknowledge him as the composer of the Becker psalms, as the service from 1673 illustrates.

The logistics associated with the event of the elector's communion, which necessitated different seating arrangements as well as an entry protocol not normally required during the main services, required detailed planning before the event.[28] The physical act of receiving the consecrated elements obligated the elector and his family to sit in the nave of the chapel, rather than in the electoral loge or "Empor-Stuhle" in the rear balcony. Descriptions provided by court secretaries indicate that chairs and cushions (kneelers?) for the elector and his immediate family were set up in the choir area around the altar, in two facing rows in the manner of choir stalls. For example, in preparation for the communion service held on Advent 4 (23 December) in 1660, "in the choir, gilded chairs were set up on both sides, which, like the entire choir and floor, were decorated with tapestries."[29] After the service, before vespers in the afternoon, these chairs were removed, and, on some occasions, the hangings on the altar and pulpit were changed.[30] The elector's relocation to the altar area also necessitated that he process into the church. As the quotations above illustrate, his entry was always accompanied by "preluding" on the organ; in fact, communion records such as this hold nearly the sum total of information concerning the use of the organ in Dresden during this era. The diaries reveal no clues to the protocols associated with the elector's ingress and egress for the main services, however, except for those *Hauptgottesdienste* that included the communion rite (see below); as he likely entered his loge directly from the second floor of the castle, any

26. This information derives not from the *Kirchen-Ordnung* but from Johann Lindner's contract (see chapter 2).

27. Heidrich 2001:37.

28. As revealed in the instructions for the elector's communion on Advent 4 in December 1659 (OHMA N I Nr 8, fol. 36r–v).

29. "In den Chor waren auf beÿden seiten vergütterte Stühle aufgeschlagen, welche, wie auch der ganze Chor und Fußboden, mit Tapeten bekleidet wahren" (Loc. 12026, fol. 55r, "Diarium. Heÿlig Christ Fest Anno 1660").

30. Loc. 12026 fol. 56v, entry for Advent 4 (23 December) 1660.

processing took place in the corridors of the castle proper, unobserved by those assembled for worship.

Records of the private communion services attended by the elector and his family, as well as descriptions of the chapel at Christmas and Easter, provide a glimpse into the manner in which the chapel was decorated on these special occasions and a sense of the elaborate manner in which worship was celebrated in general. Various diary entries describing the tapestries hung around the chapel at Christmas and Easter also point to the wealth of the holdings of the sacristy, which included richly decorated paraments and vestments, as well as costly altar furnishings and communion vessels, such as candlesticks, crucifixes, chalices, patens, pyxes, and other items. While not unknown in public churches, which often owned elaborate vestments and other items, the use of such valuable worship appurtenances in the court context contributed to the establishment of an aura of wealth, prestige, and power associated with the elector himself. For example, when Johann Georg received communion on Advent 4 in 1672,

> the rite was celebrated by the middle court preacher, Valentine Herrbrandt; the chasuble was of red velvet, upon which the birth of Christ was depicted with pearls, and the ordinary chalice, paten, as well as all of the other vessels were used. On the altar stood the ordinary silver crucifix and the gilded silver candlesticks known as "the Angels,"[31] and the golden yellow embroidered houseling cloth was used.[32]

Six years later, on Advent 4, the celebrant at communion appeared in the same chasuble, but used solid gold communion vessels inlaid with gemstones.[33] The entry

31. Philipp Hainhofer described these candlesticks in 1629, in his report of his visit to the Dresden court: "More [items] are in the sacristy; along with the patens and chalices, [there are] also silver candlesticks on the altar, which angels carry in their hands" ("Mehr seind in der sacristeÿ, neben der patinae vnd calici, auch silberne leichter auf dem altar, so engel in den händen tragen"); see Doering 1901:203.

32. "Das Ambt hielte der Mitlere Hoff Prediger, Herr Valentin Herrbrandt, das Meß Gewandt war von rothen Sammet, worauff die Gebuhrt Christi mit Perlen gestückt, und wurde der ordinari Kelch, Paten, sambt aller Zugehör gebraucht. Auff dem Altar stunde das ordinar Silberne Crucifix, und die vergöldeten Silbern Leüchter, die Engel, und wurden die Gold Gelb gestickten Unterhalts Tüchlein gebrauchtet" (SLUB K 117, fol. 4r–v). These cloths were held under the elements as they were distributed to the communicant, to prevent spillage, in the manner of the long-handled paten formerly used during the Roman Catholic Eucharist for the same purpose; see Graff 1937:196 and Herl 2004:111, 128. Four court officers served at communion and were responsible for holding the houseling cloth.

33. Sächs HStA OHMA N I Nr. 8 [this portion of the manuscript is unfoliated], entry for 23 December 1678.

for New Year's Day 1665 indicates that the celebrant's chasuble was of black velvet, upon which the Nativity scene was similarly depicted in pearls.[34] On the Feast of the Annunciation (also Palm Sunday) in 1665, the diary reports that

> the communion was celebrated by the middle court preacher, whose cha-
> suble was of light-brown velvet, richly adorned with gold and pearls; on the
> altar stood the ivory crucifix, as well as the gilded silver candlesticks known
> as "the Angels," and the gold houseling cloths, as well as the solid gold chalice
> with its accompanying paten and pyx, were used.[35]

The entry for the same feast in 1673, which indicates that a chasuble of the same color was worn, suggests that the "rich" adornment of this particular vestment took the form of a crucifix.[36] New paraments, vestments, and communion vessels were occasionally added to the collection. An entry for 28 October 1660, for example, indicates that the vessels mentioned above were acquired at that time.[37] Another entry reports that in honor of the elector's birthday in 1665, "the altar and pulpit were bedecked with entirely new paraments of rich yellow in gold and white-sil-ver cloth, and the same chasuble was also used."[38] Records from the later years of Johann Georg's reign suggest that he continued to acquire similarly ornate items for the sacristy.

At Christmas and Easter, the castle chapel was hung with tapestries that depicted various events in the life of Christ. These the diarists always refer to by name and indicate their location in the chapel. One set of tapestries, hung at Christmas, depicted events that took place throughout the life of Christ, while another set, hung at Easter, was confined to the events of Holy Week and Easter Sunday.[39] Those used at Christmas are listed, with their locations, in a diary entry for the eve of Advent 4 in 1677; this account is also particularly rich in its description of the other hang-

34. SLUB K 80, fol. 3r, entry for 1 January 1665.

35. "Daß Ambt hielte der mitlere Hoffprediger, deßen Meßgewandt war von Viol braunen Sammet, reich mit goldt und Perlen gestücket, auff dem Altar stunde das holffenbeinerne Crucifix, so wohl die Silbern vergüldeten Engel Leüchter, und wurden die Goldtgelben gestückten unterhalt Tüchlein, auch der ganz goldene Kelch mit Zuge-höriger *Paten* und *Hostien* Schachtel gebrauchet" (SLUB K 80, fol. 45r–v). The paten is a small plate from which the Host is distributed; the pyx ("Hostien Schachtel") is a small container in which the Host is stored.

36. SLUB K 117, fol. 35r, entry for 23 March 1673.

37. SLUB Q 239, entry for 28 October 1660.

38. "Der Altar und Predigt Stuhl war mit einem ganz nauen Ornat von reich gelb in goldt und weiß Silbern Stück bekleidet, auch dergleichen Meßgewandt gebrauchet" (SLUB K 80, fol. 76r–v, entry for 31 May 1665).

39. See the description of Easter Eve 1665 below.

ings and worship appurtenances that met the worshiper's eye as he or she entered the castle chapel.

How the Holy Feast of Christmas in the future year of 1678 would be celebrated, if it please God.

On Saturday, the 22nd of December [O.S.] / 1st of January [N.S.], the church would be bedecked in the following manner: the parament on the pulpit would be of white satin, embroidered with silk flowers, upon which is depicted the throng listening to Christ in the temple. The altar would be bedecked with a red velvet parament, edged in gold, and embroidered with a depiction of Mary as she held Christ on her lap after he was taken down from the cross. On the altar would stand the ivory crucifix and the gilded silver embellished candlesticks with white wax candles. The choir would be decorated with tapestries, upon which the coats of arms of the electoral provinces are embroidered, and the floor covered with flowered tapestries, and prepared with red velvet chairs and cushions. The church would be decorated with gold and rich satin embroidered tapestries, which depict the following narratives: on the right side of the altar, "The Last Supper," and on the left side of the same, "The Ascension of Christ." Over the church door, the "*Ecce Homo*." Beside it, under the arch where the councillors stand, "The Judgement and Handwashing of Pilate"; under the electoral loge, "The Ascension"; over the sacristy, "Christ led out to be Crucified"; on the right side of the pulpit, "Christ on the Cross"; under the arch where the ladies-in-waiting stand, "Christ being taken down from the Cross," "The Resurrection," and "The Descent into Hell"; on the electoral balcony, "The Birth of Christ" and "The Three Kings"; on the electoral box, a red velvet hanging, embroidered with the coats of arms of Denmark, Electoral Saxony, and Brandenburg.[40] And this decoration would remain until [the following] Friday, when it would be taken down again.[41]

On the eve of the fourth Sunday of Advent, vespers were celebrated in a solemn manner, in recognition of the penitential nature of the season. Few examples of

40. The House of Wettin was allied with the houses of Denmark and Brandenburg-Bayreuth through a number of marriages; in 1634, Johann Georg's sister Magdalena Sibylla had wed Prince-Elect Christian V of Denmark, and in 1638, Johann Georg II had wed Magdalena Sibylla of Brandenburg-Bayreuth. More recently, his daughter Erdmuth Sophia had married Margrave Christian Ernst of Brandenburg-Bayreuth (1662), and his son and heir, Prince Johann Georg III, had married Anna Sophia, the daughter of King Frederik III of Denmark (1666).

41. Sächs HStA OHMA N I Nr. 8 [unfoliated portion], entry for 22 December 1677; the German text appears in Appendix I (no. 21).

this particular service survive, but the order of worship for this occasion from 1672 reveals that the *Hofkapelle* presented a setting of *Dixit Dominus* by Morales, and a *Magnificat* by Palestrina; the description of the chapel that precedes the order of worship in the diary reveals that they sang in a chapel adorned with the very tapestries described above.[42] This service was followed the next day with early communion, a solemn *Hauptgottesdienst*, and vespers, during each of which the liturgy and musical interpolations were again sung *a cappella*.[43] Finally, on Christmas Eve, the end of the penitential season was marked with "musical vespers," in which the compositions of the Italian Kapellmeisters once again dominated the service. On Christmas Eve in 1662, Albrici presented his own setting of Ps 109, *Dixit Dominus*: given the date, this may have been the setting that survives in the Düben collection, whose style suggests that it is earlier than the setting found in the Bokemeyer collection.[44] Throughout the psalm, Albrici contrasts polyphonic writing for the entire five-voice ensemble with more intimate solos and highly imitative duos, several of which allow the singers to demonstrate their virtuosity (Ex. 8.1). In true Roman style, often the material introduced by a soloist or duo is immediately restated by the full ensemble. Albrici followed the psalm with Carissimi's *Surgamus, eamus*; in the latter half of the service, he presented one of his own settings of the *Magnificat*, followed by his concerto with aria, *Spargite flores*.[45]

Ten years later, on the same occasion, Pallavicino presented his own setting of Ps 109, and followed it with his setting of Ps 112, *Laudate pueri*, as the sacred concerto that followed the concerted psalm.[46] On Christmas Eve in 1675, Cherici presented two compositions, the second of which was his *Deplorandus et amarus*, performed after the *Magnificat*. This penitential text can also be read as appropriate to Advent, given its invitation to Christ to come and fulfill his promise to redeem mankind: "Even so come! O Lord, redeem the sorrowful sons of Adam, and grant them consolation."[47]

The vesper service on Christmas Eve, with its return to the full-blown contemporary Italian musical idiom, ushered in the three-day feast of Christmas. Like the other church feast days celebrated at the Dresden court, the observation of Christmas included an elaborate pre-service protocol that took place out of doors and

42. SLUB K 117, fol. 2r–v.
43. SLUB K 117, fols. 4r–6r.
44. See Appendix II. Musical example prepared from S-Uu VMHS 82:3.
45. SLUB Q 240, entry for 24 December 1662.
46. SLUB K 117, fol. 6r; items 4–7 of the vesper service, which include the *Magnificat* and the following concerto, are missing from the order of worship as reported in the diary. Neither composition survives.
47. The entire text and translation appear in chapter 4.

EXAMPLE 8.1 Albrici, *Dixit Dominus*, mm. 95–111

EXAMPLE 8.1 (*continued*)

involved both military and musical elements.[48] Thus, while for many services only the musical and scriptural aspects can be reconstructed, for a number of feast days, descriptions survive that greatly enhance one's understanding of the interplay between worship and spectacle in a seventeenth-century court. Although very representational in nature, and designed primarily for those who dwelt in the castle complex, the protocol does reveal that Johann Georg sought to involve the surrounding community to a certain extent, as an account from Christmas Day in 1677 demonstrates:

> Tuesday the 25th of December. On Holy Christmas Day the watchman blew a signal call at 3:00 a.m. on the castle tower, upon which the chimes were played for a good half hour, and then at 4:00 a.m. on the *Creuz* Tower, three half three-pound culverins were fired with live ammunition.[49] Following this the feast was rung in until 4:30 a.m. with all of the bells of the castle, inside and outside the fortress, as well as those in Old Dresden, after which the shawm players played sacred songs in the castle courtyard and in front of the castle in the Zwinger. Afterward, at 6:30 a.m., the bells were rung for the first time, and the guards began to parade.[50] The *Trabanten* stationed themselves from the further castle gate through the further court, up through the inner castle gate. Then the company of Swiss *Trabanten* paraded in the castle, and stationed themselves between the Green Gate and the *Keller*, upon which the three companies of the *Unter-Guardie* marched through, and stationed themselves in the Zwinger in front of the castle, by the Gold House, upon which the little squad of musketeers followed, and paraded by the *Münzberg* on the High Wall, and stationed themselves on the Fireworks *Platz*. These were followed by the Free Squad, which stationed itself next to the *Unter-Guardie*. At this point three salvos were fired on the High Wall, each time three half cannons royal, and from the four companies; then the company of

48. Instructions for the dates of these parades and the firing of weaponry are given in an undated *Ordnung* contained in Sächs HStA OHMA N I Nr. 8, fols. 8r–13r, in particular fols. 11r–13r. The court diary for the years 1653–56 indicates that military protocols preceded the services on feast days under Johann Georg I, but were not nearly as elaborate as those developed under Johann Georg II (SLUB K 113, fols. 10r, 37v, 46r–v, 49r–v, 76r, 79v–80r, 82r).

49. A culverin was a long cannon common in the sixteenth and seventeenth centuries.

50. These were signals that informed the castle community of the impending worship service, and were always rung in the morning at 6:30, 7:00, and 7:30 on Sundays and feast days; at 7:30, the worship service began. The first peal also served to signal the beginning of the parading of the guards.

Swiss *Trabanten* paraded out through the Green Gate and Stables, followed by the three companies of the *Unter-Guardie* and the Free Squad. The squad of musketeers, however, paraded up the *Münzberg* over the fortress into the arsenal, the High German *Trabanten* up to the further gate, and assumed the watch. Afterward at 7:30 the bells were rung for the third time, and the worship service was held in the following manner; Kapellmeister Vincenzo Albrici directed the music in the morning as well as at vespers, and also the next day.[51]

This musico-military protocol, which represents a continuous series of events that led directly into the worship service, reflects Johann Georg's unabashed effort to combine the display of secular power with the observation of a holy day in the church calendar. Such activities contributed to the politicization of worship that took place at the court, as did the elector's exploitation of occasions for worship to enhance his own personal image and to legitimize his birthright to the Saxon throne.[52] The protocol, however, mixes the private and public spheres, and combines traditions that date back to the medieval era, such as the ringing of bells and the signal calls of the city watchman, with a display of the awe-inspiring might of modern weaponry. Into the midst of this display of pomp, Johann Georg injected a charming musical element, a consort of shawms that played sacred songs of the season, first in the castle courtyard, and then outside the castle walls. Although Johann Georg had a shawm band by at least 1664, he seems to have added their auroral piping to the protocol at a later date, for it does not appear in the descriptions of feast days found in various diaries compiled between 1659 and 1668; the first mention of it appears in a diary entry for 1672.[53]

After the bells had rung at 6:30, 7:00, and 7:30 a.m. on Christmas morning, the elector and his entourage entered the chapel, where courtiers and perhaps some townspeople were gathered. In the words of a court secretary describing a similar festal occasion, the *Hauptgottesdienst* was then celebrated "with music-making, singing, and preaching."[54] The aptness of the diarist's description is revealed by the orders of worship for Christmas Day in 1665.[55] The morning order of worship well illustrates the establishment of the rank of a high feast by means of music: here four

51. Sächs HStA OHMA N I Nr. 8 [unfoliated], entry for 25 December 1677; the German text appears in Appendix I (no. 22).
52. See in particular the discussions of worship on the elector's birthday and nameday below.
53. SLUB K 117, fol. 4r.
54. "wurd in der Schloß-Kirchen mit *Musici*ren, Singen, und Predigen der ordentliche Gottes=Dienst verrichtet" (Sächs HStA OHMA O IV Nr. 23, entry for 2 July 1668).
55. SLUB Q 243, entry for 25 December 1665.

trumpets and timpani accompany the vocalists and other instrumentalists in the movements of the mass Ordinary, as well as in Peranda's lost "grand concerto," *Gaudete pastores*. As stipulated by the *Kirchen-Ordnung*, every Sunday and festal liturgy involved a twofold rendering of the Gloria—the Latin Gloria was first "*musicirt*" by the *Hofkapelle*, and followed by the congregational singing of the German Gloria hymn *Allein Gott*. Some festal liturgies, however, such as that for Christmas Day, included a twofold Credo as well, which followed the minister's musical recitation of the Gospel. The scale of the mass settings used on these occasions is suggested by both surviving works and those listed in inventories. The few extant mass settings by the two Italians are fully scored works with five to eight voices and a complement of five or six instruments and continuo; some of these may correspond to the works listed by Albrici in the 1681 "Instrument Chamber Catalog."[56] The length of the individual movements in these masses suggests that the performance of the Latin Kyrie, Gloria, and Credo alone required twenty to twenty-five minutes. Other lost settings of the Ordinary listed in various inventories attest to the size of the musical force that was regularly amassed for the musical rendering of the Ordinary in Dresden on feast days. Two lost Kyrie settings by Peranda appear in the Lüneburg inventory, both of which include twenty parts: five vocal soloists, five vocal parts *in ripieno*, as well as four strings, a bassoon, two cornetti, three trombones, and continuo.[57] The Weißenfels inventory of J. P. Krieger lists six masses of Peranda, the majority of which are scored for 10 to 18 parts, as well as one by Albrici, scored for 14 parts.[58] The Leipzig inventory contains no masses by Albrici, but does list four by Peranda, three "à 12" and another "à 14. ò 18."[59]

Following the conclusion of the sermon, which typically lasted about an hour, the *Hofkapelle* made its last appearance in the morning service, on this occasion with a performance of Peranda's *Gaudete pastores* ("Rejoice, Shepherds"). The *Kirchen-Ordnung* prescribes that "ein Groß Concert" was to be presented after the sermon on Christmas Day. Though Peranda's composition does not survive, the diarist's inclusion of the scoring helps to gauge just what constituted a "grand concerto" in the eyes of the elector.[60] The ensemble for *Gaudete* included as many as twenty-six or twenty-seven performers—or fully half of the *Hofkapelle*—depending upon the number of timpanists (one or two) and continuo players (one to three). The scorings given in SLUB Q 243 suggest that the diarist counted the number of performers he saw before him, excluding the continuo group; thus here the ten singers prob-

56. See Appendix II; excerpts from a mass setting by Albrici appear below.
57. Seiffert 1907–08:611.
58. Gundlach 2001:252–53, 306–307.
59. Schering 1918–19:287; the inventory does not include the disposition of parts.
60. The scoring is given by the diarist as "4. Tromb: et Timp: 4 Schallmeÿen, 5 Istr: 4. Soprani. 2. Alt. 2. T. 2. B."

ably represented a group of five *favoriti*, SSATB, and a similarly constituted *ripieno* group. The "5 I[n]str" were likely two violins, two violas, and bassoon, or possibly two cornetti and three trombones; the choice of the latter would have increased the volume significantly. Although the shawms (or perhaps deutsche Schallmei) appear in the diaries both in the *alfresco* hymn-playing context discussed above, and as participants in *Tafelmusik*, at times in conjunction with the "French Violinists," this is the only reference in the diaries to the inclusion of shawms in a sacred work by one of the Italian Kapellmeisters. It is unknown how often the shawm players served in the chapel—or if this performance represented their first and only appearance there; on this particular occasion, Peranda's inclusion of the shawm consort added a literal representation of the pipes of the shepherds mentioned in the Gospel for the day, Luke 2:1–14: "And in that region there were shepherds out in the field, keeping watch over their flock by night" (v. 8, RSV). After the *Hofkapelle* had finished its performance of this doubtless very sonorous composition, the service concluded with prayers, both recited and spoken, and a congregational hymn. Altogether the worship service lasted about three and one-half hours, from 7:30 a.m. until about 11:00 a.m, at which point the court trumpeter heralded the midday meal.[61]

After the meal, the castle bells rang out again at 1:00, 1:30, and 2:00, this time to call the court to vespers, which commenced at 2:00.[62] Once again the service music was amplified by four trumpets and timpani. On Christmas Day, as on Easter Sunday, the form of the vesper service differed in several respects from that given in the *Kirchen-Ordnung* for most other occasions, in that it included no sacred concertos *per se*. Instead, the concerto *post* psalm was replaced by a *figuraliter* performance of the Christmas Story, on this occasion that of Schütz, probably his *Historia, der freuden- und gnadenreichen Geburth Gottes und Marien Sohnes, Jesu Christi* published in Dresden in 1664.[63] Later records indicate that Peranda also composed such a work, performances of which can be documented in 1672, 1675, and 1677.[64] The service also included a performance of the *Magnificat* expanded

61. In most entries for Sundays and feast days, the length of the morning service can be gauged from the times of the last signal bell at 7:30 a.m. and the trumpeter's announcement of the midday meal at 11:00 a.m. An entry for the Feast of St. Michael in 1664, however, makes this explicit and indicates that the morning service lasted from 7:30 a.m. until 11:00 a.m. (Sächs HStA OHMA O IV Nr. 14 [unfoliated], entry for 29 September).

62. SLUB Q 243, entry for 25 December 1665.

63. The diarist gives the title and composer as "Die Geburth Unsers Herrn Jesu Christi *figuraliter. H. S.*"

64. This composition, which is lost, is described as a work sung *figuraliter* in orders of worship for Christmas Day: SLUB K 117 (1672), fol. 8r, and Q 260 (1676), entry for 25 December; Sächs HStA Loc. 8682 Nr. 12 (1677–78), fol. 4v.

with three interpolated congregational hymns, a common Lutheran practice of the seventeenth and eighteenth centuries that was also prescribed in the *Kirchen-Ordnung*.[65] This amplification of the *Magnificat* with hymns (and the length of the Christmas History) probably caused the elector to omit the concerto *post Magnificat* on Christmas Day. Unfortunately, none of the *Magnificat* settings of Peranda or Albrici survive, but the lost works listed in the Leipzig, Lüneburg, and Weißenfels inventories again demonstrate that these too were large-scale compositions, generally scored for ten, fifteen, or twenty parts. The most fully scored of these, a work of Peranda's that once formed part of the music collection at the St. Michaelisschule in Lüneburg, required at least twenty-six performers: two five-part ensembles of *favoriti* plus a five-part vocal *ripieno*, each scored SSATB, with four string instruments, two cornetti, three trombones, bassoon, and continuo.[66] The few psalm settings of Albrici and Peranda that do survive, as well as those listed in inventories, suggest that many of these also employed many voices and instruments; a setting of Ps 148 by Peranda, *Laudate Dominum de caelis*, appears in the Leipzig inventory, where the scoring is given as "a 19."[67]

As the 1665 celebration of the Christmas *triduum* progressed through the Feasts of St. Stephen and St. John the Evangelist, the manner of observance was consciously scaled back, particularly with respect to the scoring of sacred works, all of which in 1665 were composed by Peranda.[68] As the feast continued into its second day, the number of trumpets and timpani fell in number to two; on day 3, they disappeared altogether from the morning liturgy, but reappeared to accompany Peranda's *Magnificat* in the afternoon service, and in this manner marked the end of the three-day celebration. The concerted Credo also disappeared from the morning liturgy and was replaced by a sacred concerto, and the vespers liturgies for both days each featured two sacred concertos. Following the Gospel in the morning service on the Feast of St. Stephen, for example, Peranda presented his *Caeli enarrant*, which does not survive, but which presumably opened with Ps 19: 1: "The heavens are telling the

65. See Spagnoli 1990:180; the same three hymns are listed there and described as the "usual" ("gewöhnlich") hymns.

66. Seiffert 1907–08:611. The Weißenfels inventory includes four *Magnificat* settings by Peranda, scored for ten, twelve, nineteen, and twenty parts, respectively (Gundlach 2001:305–6); the five *Magnificat* settings of Peranda included in the Leipzig inventory have ten, fifteen, sixteen, twenty, and twenty-five parts each (Schering 1918–19:287).

67. Schering 1918–19:287.

68. The following observations are drawn from SLUB Q 243, entries for 26 and 27 December 1665. The scorings discussed are those reported by the diarist, and can be found in Appendix II; all should be assumed to include continuo, which is never mentioned in the diaries.

glory of God."[69] According to the diarist, the concerto was performed by four tenors and four basses—a rather curious scoring for a composition celebrating the firmament. Although not taken from the Gospel, Luke 2:15–20, the Psalm text related to it directly, for the Gospel tells of the shepherds' journey to Bethlehem and their visit to the Christ Child, after which they returned, "glorifying and praising God for all they had heard and seen." After the sermon, however, Peranda presented his *Spirate suaves*, a setting of an encomiastic text that lacks a reference to any specific occasion in the liturgical year. Also likely general in nature was the composition he presented after the psalm at vespers that afternoon, recorded only as "*Florete*" by the diarist. The title probably refers to his lost composition, *Florete flores*; given its use on both Easter Monday and Pentecost Tuesday in various years, the text was likely of a generally festive nature. The title incipit of the concerto performed after the *Magnificat*, however, Peranda's *Audite pastores*, suggests that this work was directly related to the Gospel for the previous day, Luke 2:1–14, in which the angel announces the news of Christ's birth (Luke 2:10–11), and a "multitude of the heavenly host" suddenly appear and praise God (2:13–14). The title—"Listen, shepherds"—suggests that Peranda presented a setting of a paraphrase of the Lukan text, whose message was delivered by three "angels"—soprano castrati.

After having been held in abeyance throughout the season of Advent and the first two days of Christmas, sacred concertos with devotional texts reappeared in the liturgies on the Feast of St. John. In the morning service, Peranda programmed his *O Jesu mi dulcissime* to follow the Gospel. While not explicitly a Christmas text, the devotional relationship of the speaker to the Christ Child can easily be discerned here, as can an allusion to the Gospel for Christmas Day in the line "Jesus, glory of the angels" ("Jesu, decus angelicum"). After the sermon, Peranda presented a "*Motetto*," his *Verbum caro factum est*, the scoring of which was not recorded by the diarist. The text, however, is drawn directly from the final verse of the Gospel for the day, John 1:1–14, "and the Word became flesh and dwelt among us, full of grace and truth" (v. 14, RSV), an interpretation of which the court preacher had just delivered in the sermon.[70] At vespers that afternoon, after his setting of a psalm, *Laudate Dominum*, Peranda presented another Christocentric devotional work, his *Jesu dulcis, Jesu pie*. As the musical conclusion of the feast, a quintet of soloists (SSATB) from the *Hofkapelle* performed Peranda's concerto *Attendite fideles* fol-

---

69. Appears as the second psalm in Lossius's abbreviated Matins for Christmas Day (Lossius 1561/1996, fol. 15b); Lossius includes just the first Nocturn. *Caeli enarrant* appears as the second psalm in the first Nocturn of Matins for Christmas Day in *LU*, 372.

70. *Verbum caro* is also the Responsory in Lossius's abbreviated Matins for Christmas Day (Lossius 1561/1996, fol. 16a) and forms the eighth Responsory for Matins (in the third Nocturn) on Christmas Day in *LU*, 390–91. The chant also appears in Keuchenthal 1573 (fol. 31a–b) as the Responsory for the Vigil of Christmas.

lowing the *Magnificat*; the text of this lost work may also have been related to the themes of the Nativity.

Following these three days of musical magnificence, the court adopted a much more subdued mode of worship for the Sunday after Christmas. In the morning worship service on this day, the *Hofkapelle* once again presented three movements of the Latin Ordinary and an extra-liturgical composition, but performed all *a cappella*, as established in the *Kirchen-Ordnung*.[71] Normally, compositions of Palestrina formed the musical backbone of the *a cappella* services, but the order of worship for 31 December 1665 reveals that Peranda also composed at least one set of *a cappella* mass movements for use on such occasions.[72] For the musical interpolation following the sermon, however, Peranda fell back on Palestrina and selected his "concerto" (as described by the diarist) *O admirabile commercium*, doubtless for the association of the text with the Feast of the Circumcision, which was traditionally celebrated on January 1.[73] That afternoon, concerted music returned for the eve of the feast of New Year's Day, when Peranda presented a concerted psalm by Kerll, two of his own sacred concertos, and his own concerted setting of the *Magnificat*. The sacred concertos, *Quis dabit capiti meo aquas* and *Quo tendimus mortales*, are two of his most powerful compositions. In the latter, which was performed at vespers on New Year's Eve in both 1664 and 1665, the exploration of the *vanitas* theme seems to have held some association with the idea of self-examination at the passing of the old year.

The relative quiet experienced during worship on the Sunday after Christmas, however, was soon shattered by the elaborate celebrations of two feasts that fell during the first week of January, New Year's Day and the Epiphany (January 6). At the Dresden court, January 1 was designated simply New Year's Day; neither the *Kirchen-Ordnung* nor the diaries refer to either of the traditional titles of the feast, the Circumcision and the Name of Jesus. Of the two dates in the liturgical calendar, the Epiphany enjoyed a higher rank, and thus the liturgy included both a Latin Introit and the Latin Credo. The afternoon services, however, seem to reverse the ranking, for vespers on New Year's Day included a sermon, while the service on the Epiphany was designated a "musical vespers."[74] The diaries reveal that the contributions of the *Hofkapelle* to the *Hauptgottesdienst* on both feasts were enhanced with trumpets and timpani, as on the three-day feasts, but the pre-service protocols dif-

71. See Spagnoli 1990:178.

72. SLUB Q 243, entry for 31 December 1665.

73. *O admirabile commercium* appears as the antiphon for the vigil of the Feast of the Circumcision in Lossius 1561/1996, fol. 31b; in the pre-Vatican II Catholic liturgy, it served as the antiphon at Prime, and as the first antiphon at second vespers on the same feast (*LU* 440, 442–43).

74. See the orders of worship for New Year's Day in chapter 7 and the order of worship for Epiphany in Spagnoli 1990:182.

fered. On New Year's Day, the guards were instructed to parade and to give three different types of military salutes, including the firing of three half cannons royal, musket shots from the entire company of guards, and three sixty-four-pound mortars, plus three *Feuerkugeln* with *Schlägen* and *Mordtschlag*, but they were to parade without firing on the Feast of the Epiphany.[75]

New Year's Day in 1665 signaled not only the beginning of a new year, but also the changing of the clerical guard in the chapel, for it marked the first time that Martin Geier, the new Senior Court Preacher, delivered the sermon in the court chapel. In accepting the elector's call, the former Superintendent in Leipzig had exchanged choirboys for castrati, and the music of Sebastian Knüpfer, *Thomaskantor* in Leipzig, for that of Peranda; seven years later, the frustrated cleric would use his funeral sermon for Schütz to condemn publicly both Italian musical style and its purveyors.[76] In the morning service, Peranda presented his own settings of movements of the mass, as well as a setting of the German *Te Deum*.[77] The latter work was heard immediately upon the conclusion of Geier's first sermon, in which the minister first heaped the obligatory praises on the electoral family, and then expressed his own trepidation at the prospect of assuming this new and very prestigious post, before finally engaging in some scriptural exegesis.[78] In the afternoon, Peranda's setting of Ps 121, *Laetatus sum*, was followed by his concerto *Spirate suaves*, and his setting of the *Magnificat* was followed by a seasonal composition, a German concerto on *Daß alte Jahr vergangen ist*, the scoring of which likely included two sopranos and an alto, two violins, bassoon, and continuo.[79] While the vast majority of Peranda's compositions for the court were settings of Latin texts, the diaries reveal that he also set a number of German texts.

75. The instructions appear in OHMA N I Nr. 8, fols. 12r–v and 13r. The last three salutes likely involved fireworks, as they were fired from the *Feuerwergks Platz*, and included fireballs (*Feuerkugeln*), charges fired from small iron tubes (*Schlägen*), and round, hollow balls of iron that exploded when fired (*Mordtschlag*). These instructions differ from those given in the *Kirchen-Ordnung*, which states that the guards are to parade but hold their fire on New Year's Day; see Spagnoli 1990:182.

76. See chapter 2. Geier served as Superintendent in Leipzig from 1661–64; see Gleich 1730:338–43 and Hahn 1990:25.

77. In the entry in SLUB K 80, fol. 2v, the diarist indicated that all of the compositions heard at vespers on 31 December 1664, as well as on 1 January, were those of Peranda.

78. Geier, "Eingang zum neuen Amt am H. Neuen Jahrstage" ("Entry into a new office on Holy New Year's Day") in Geier 1713:960–88.

79. The *Kirchen-Ordnung* specifies a concerto on this hymn as an option for the composition to be performed after the Gospel in the morning service on New Year's Day; the entry for 1 January 1666 in SLUB Q 243 includes the same title and gives the scoring as reported here.

The liturgies for the Feast of the Epiphany were also elevated in status through the inclusion of the Latin Credo after the Gospel, and the accompaniment of trumpets and timpani. They also display a similar degree of intertextuality between the extra-liturgical compositions and the readings appointed for the entire twelve-day Christmas observance, which came to a close on this day. After the sermon in 1667, for example, Peranda presented his *Laetentur coeli*, a large-scale concerto with aria for five *favoriti* (SSATB), a similarly constituted vocal *ripieno* group, and instruments, including trumpets and timpani, with a text that resonates with the Gospel for the day, Matthew 2:1–12, the story of the Three Kings.[80] The extended text begins with an exhortation, "Let the heavens be glad, let the earth rejoice," drawn from I Chronicles 16:31, and continues first with stanzas of poetry that praise the "birth of the powerful infant," the "repeller of darkness"; these are followed by four stanzas from *Jesu dulcis memoria* that introduce devotional themes, here clearly linked to the Infant Christ. In 1673, Geier's Epiphany sermon was followed by Albrici's *Laeti properemus* ("Let us hasten with gladness"), which does not survive; the incipit, however, suggests that the voices raised there were those of the Three Kings. During the "musical vespers" celebrated that afternoon, Albrici followed his setting of *Dixit Dominus* with one of his early concertos with aria, *Venite cantemus*, a setting of devotional poetry scored for three sopranos, three violins, and continuo.[81] After the *Magnificat*, however, Albrici returned to more seasonal subject matter with a concerto entitled *Currite pastores* ("Hasten, Shepherds").[82]

The first apostle's day celebrated after the Christmas season was that of the Conversion of St. Paul, which fell on January 25. Although the *Kirchen-Ordnung* includes the date in the list of apostles' days, without further remark, the court marshal's *Ordnung* elevates the occasion to the status of a "Gedächtnis Tag" (Day of Commemoration), together with Reformation Day and St. Martin [Luther's] Day (November 10 or 11).[83] Despite the special designation, however, the liturgical form of the service celebrated on the Conversion of St. Paul was identical to that of the other apostles' days; it was essentially a "low" service that opened with one of the *Becker Psalms* of Schütz, and continued with hymnic elements of the *deutsche Messe*, but did include sacred concertos in their usual positions following the Gospel and sermon. When the latter were compositions of Peranda or Albrici, they represented the sole examples of the modern Italian musical idiom in the service.[84] For the commemoration

---

80. SLUB Q 245, entry for 6 January 1667.

81. See Appendix II for documented performances.

82. SLUB K 117, fols. 15r–16r. *Currite Pastores* does not survive.

83. Sächs HStA OHMA N I Nr. 8, fol. 11r; see also Spagnoli 1990:190–92.

84. In the diaries compiled between 1660 and 1680, very few orders of worship for apostles' days appear. The diary for 1675–76, however, includes orders of worship for all

in January 1665, Peranda programmed two concertos, neither of which survives.[85] The first of these, however, bore a direct relationship to the commemorated event, for the the incipit, *Saulus adhuc spirans*, corresponds to the opening of the Epistle for the day, Acts 9:1–22: "Saul, still breathing threats and murder against the disciples of the Lord . . ." (v. 1, RSV). Peranda's concerto may have taken the form of a dialogue, with a soloist *cum* narrator relating these first words. Schütz, by constrast, set only the words of Christ in his famous composition, *Saul, Saul, was verfolgst du mich?* (SWV 415, 1650), which was likely composed for the same date in the calendar. The incipit of Peranda's second concerto, *Bone Jesu*, indicates that it was a setting of a devotional text; the full title may have been *Bone Jesu, dulcissime Jesu*.[86] The paucity of orders of worship for the apostles' days, however, hampers any attempt to trace the use of particular pieces. After Peranda's death, his *Si Dominus mecum*, based on Romans 8:31, was performed after the Gospel on the Conversion of St. Paul in 1676; in this concerto with aria, the words of the church's first great proselyte form the text of the opening concerto.[87]

Like the *Hauptgottesdienst* on the Feast of the Epiphany, that on the Feast of the Purification (February 2), which occurred barely a month later, was also elevated in rank above services on ordinary Sundays. The elector's liturgical formulary stipulated the performance of the Latin Credo on this feast day, while the diaries also reveal that the concerted portions of the liturgy were always amplified with trumpets and timpani. The liturgy was also distinguished from all others during the year by a performance of a concerted setting of the Canticle of Simeon, either in German or in Latin, following the sermon, as mandated in the *Kirchen-Ordnung*.[88] The canticle appeared as the concluding passage of the Gospel for the day, Luke 2:22–32 (here vv. 29–32); in the service, the performance took place directly after the preacher's exegesis of the same passage in the sermon. As was the case for all feasts of lesser rank, the full vesper service for Purification did not appear in the

---

but two of these days; these records also reveal that German members of the *Hofkapelle* supplied the sacred concertos on these occasions, in contrast to earlier years, when the concertos were works of the Italians.

85. Orders of worship for 25 January 1665 appear in both SLUB K 80, fol. 12r, and SLUB Q 241.

86. The short form of the title also appears in SLUB Q 243, in the order of worship for *Septuagesima* Sunday; the longer form appears in the same diary on Trinity 1 and Trinity 15, where the diarist has supplied the designation "Motetto."

87. SLUB Q 260, entry for 25 January 1676. The text of the brief opening concerto comprises just the words "If God be for me, who is against me? ("Si Dominus mecum, quis contra me?"); the text continues with poetic stanzas that trope the opening dictum (st. 1: "Infernal horrors, savage furies do not overcome me; troubles do not impede me, hostile things are powerless, nothing makes me despair").

88. Spagnoli 1990:182–83.

Kirchen-Ordnung. Instead, the *Kirchen-Ordnung* provides a rubric instructing that the afternoon service was to conform to the order of worship for vespers on the third day of Christmas; thus it was a "musical vespers" without a sermon. Although the order of worship for Purification 1673 does not specify that Albrici directed the music during the service, it is likely that he did, in that all of the music save the Introit came from his own pen.[89]

Once again, the liturgical record for a feast day documents the performance of mass movements, in this case by Albrici, enhanced with trumpets and timpani. Albrici's sole surviving mass setting, SLUB 1821-D-1, comprises settings of the three elements of the Ordinary performed during this service, the Kyrie, Gloria, and Credo; it is doubly significant in that it includes parts for four trumpets ("Trombe") and timpani ("Timpano"). Albrici's mass is scored for five-part vocal and instrumental ensembles, plus continuo, trumpets, and timpani. Although the parts are not labeled, the vocal cleffing indicates a scoring for two sopranos, alto, tenor and bass, while the instrumental ensemble likely involved two violins, two violas, and bassoon, based again upon the cleffing. Rubrics beneath the continuo part in the score indicate "solo" and "tutti" passages, which suggests that both vocal and instrumental ripienists were involved as well; these rubrics may well stem from Albrici, for other of his surviving large-scale works indicate that such doublings were typical.[90] The opening of Albrici's Kyrie provides a sense of the grandeur with which these festal mass settings were conceived (Ex. 8.2), while the opening of the Christe reveals the more intimate, reduced scorings also employed by Albrici for contrast (Ex. 8.3).

Throughout the mass movements, Albrici varies the texture and scoring to reflect the text, as had been the tradition for several centuries by this time. He opens the Credo with a powerful, declamatory tutti (Ex. 8.4), but then reduces the scoring of a number of sections to a few soloists; he scores the "Crucifixus" for just two sopranos, bass, and continuo. Albrici colors this central portion of the statement of belief with considerable chromaticism and slow suspensions. Not content to conclude with the three sequential statements of "passus et sepultus est," however, he then creates the quiet of the tomb in the final bars, in preparation for the jubilant return of the full ensemble at "Et resurrexit" (Ex. 8.5).

The onset of Lent in the weeks following the Feast of the Purification ushered in the lengthiest penitential period of the church year, which the Dresden court marked with sacred music sung *a cappella*. Prescriptive orders of worship for the Sundays in Lent do not appear in the elector's *Kirchen-Ordnung*, which simply stipulates that the first four are to be sung *a cappella*, and the last two, *Judica* and *Palmarum* (Palm

---

89. SLUB K 117, fol. 26r–v.

90. The five-part instrumental ripieno group normally constituted two cornetti and three trombones.

EXAMPLE 8.2 Albrici, *Missa*, Kyrie, mm. 1–9

EXAMPLE 8.2 (*continued*)

EXAMPLE 8.3 Albrici, *Missa*, Christe, mm. 61–72

Sunday), are to include the singing of the Passion.[91] On these Sundays in Lent, the stylistic gulf between the figural music and the congregational song was not quite as great as on those Sundays and feast days when the music of Albrici and Peranda filled the chapel. On *Reminiscere* Sunday (Lent 2) in 1662, for example, Albrici pre-

91. Spagnoli 1990:178.

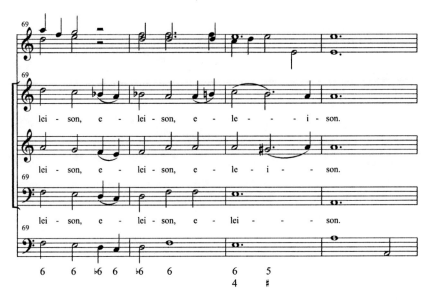

EXAMPLE 8.3 *(continued)*

sented mass movements of Palestrina and a motet by a composer associated with the King of Portugal (the order of worship appears below). In contrast with modern liturgical practice, the Gloria was not suppressed until *Judica* Sunday (Lent 5); the diaries reveal that the liturgies on the first four Sundays of Lent included the twofold Gloria in the form of a movement from a mass by Palestrina followed by the congregational Gloria hymn.[92] But unlike today, the German Gloria hymn reappeared in the liturgy for Holy Thursday.[93]

AM SONTAG *REMINISCERE* WAR DER 23. FEBRUARŸ.[94]	*REMINISCERE* SUNDAY, 23 FEBRUARY 1662
1. O Lamb Gottes unschuldig.	Hymn as Introit
2. *Missa Praenestini da Cappella.*	Kyrie and Gloria, Palestrina
3. Allein Gott in der Höh.	German Gloria hymn
4. *Collecta* und die Epistel.	Collect and Epistle
5. Christus der uns seelig . [macht]	Hymn
6. Evangelium.	Gospel

92. SLUB Q 240, Q 241, Q 243.

93. In 1665, 1666, and 1673, one or the other of the common German Gloria hymns followed the Kyrie hymn (SLUB Q 241, Q 243, K 117).

94. SLUB Q 240, entry for 23 February 1662.

7. *Patrem omnipotentem.*	Credo (from "Patrem" on),
Praenest.	Palestrina
8. Der Glaube.	German creedal hymn
9. Die Predig.	Sermon
10. *Mot: Vivo ego dicit*	Six-part motet by Manuel
Dominus. â 6. Emmanuelis.	Mendes,
Regis Lusitan.	"composer to the King of
	Portugal"
11. Christe der du bist Tag und	Hymn
Liecht.	
12. *Collecta* und Segen.	Collect and Blessing
13. Christe du Lamb Gottes,	Hymn, German *Agnus Dei*,
der du [trägst die Sünd der Welt]	Luther 1528

The Lenten orders of worship found in the diaries reveal that the liturgical form observed on the first four Sundays of Lent conformed to that of festal Sundays, in that it included the Latin Credo, but that the mid-seventeenth-century Italianate musical idiom was replaced by music in *stile antico*. On the final two Sundays (*Judica* and *Palmarum*), however, all Latin elements were dropped, as was the Gloria. These two services were celebrated as *deutsche Messen*, and opened with a German hymn as the Introit, followed by the German Kyrie hymn; the creed was also omitted, and the German members of the *Hofkapelle* presented a musical rendering of the Passion immediately after the reading of the Gospel.[95] The complete silence of the *Kirchen-Ordnung* with respect to the liturgical forms to be used on the last two Sundays of the Lenten period suggests that these remained unchanged under Johann Georg II, and that these services represented a continuation of longstanding traditions in the court chapel.

The sober observance on *Palmarum*, however, often had to yield place to the Feast of the Annunciation (March 25), which was transferred to Lent 6 in those years when it fell during Holy Week.[96] In contrast with contemporary Lutheran

95. Examples survive in SLUB Q 240, entry for 16 March (*Judica*) 1662; SLUB Q 241, entry for 12 March (*Judica*) 1665; and SLUB Q 243, entries for 1 and 8 April (*Judica* and *Palmarum*) 1666. A diary for 1666 explicitly states that the German singers sang the Passion (Sächs HStA OHMA O IV Nr. 19, entry for 13 April 1666). A diary for 1667 indicates that the Germans also sang the Passion on *Judica* Sunday; OHMA O IV Nr. 21, entry for 24 March 1667.

96. So rubricated in the *Kirchen-Ordnung* (Spagnoli 1990:183). If the feast fell in the weeks before Holy Week, it was celebrated on the weekday on which it occurred; in 1679, for example, March 25 fell on the Tuesday after *Oculi*, and the feast was celebrated on that day (Sächs HStA Loc. 8682 Nr. 13, fol. 77v.)

EXAMPLE 8.4 Albrici, *Missa*, Credo, mm. 1–7

EXAMPLE 8.4 (*continued*)

EXAMPLE 8.5 Albrici, *Missa*, Credo, "Crucifixus" and "Et resurrexit," mm. 95–118

EXAMPLE 8.5 *(continued)*

practice, during this era the celebration of the Angel Gabriel's revelation to Mary was regarded as a legitimate reason to break the quiet of the Lenten observance with an elaborate liturgy dominated by concerted music accompanied by instruments. In apparent recognition of the fact that the occasion also marked the beginning of Holy Week, however, the trumpets and timpani remained silent. In 1673, when the feast supplanted the observance of Palm Sunday, Carlo Pallavicino directed the service music in the *Hauptgottesdienst* and presented his own settings of the mass Ordinary, as well as a martial concerto, *Accipite arma*, now lost, the style of which may have resembled that of his two surviving dialogues, *Non tremiscite* and *Ad arma*

EXAMPLE 8.5 (*continued*)

daemones. Pallavicino's co-Kapellmeister Albrici directed in the afternoon, and used the occasion to present a composition on an unabashedly Marian text, *Sancta et immaculata virginitas.*[97] Orders of worship for earlier Annunciation vespers liturgies, however, reveal that in 1665 and 1666, Peranda stayed within the bounds of Lutheran tradition, and presented his Annunciation dialogue, *Missus est Angelus,* the text of which is drawn from the Gospel for the day, Luke 1:26–38a, and concludes with John 1:14.[98] Throughout the recitative portion of the dialogue, Peranda enhances the utterances of the Angel and Mary with a "halo" of strings (Ex. 8.6). At the conclusion of Mary's acceptance of God's plan for her ("behold, I am the handmaid of the Lord; let it be to me according to your word"), the three soloists and strings are joined by cornetti, trombones, and a five-part vocal ensemble, and the entire ensemble concludes the work with St. John's affirmation, "the Word became flesh and dwelt among us" ("verbum caro factum est et habitavit in nobis").

Regardless of the nature of the liturgical observance on Palm Sunday, the observance of Holy Week commenced the following day. Now the normal daily activities of the watchman, signal trumpeter, and guards were suspended, and the court was shrouded in silence.[99] Throughout the week, all of the visual and musical enhancements of the worship space and liturgies celebrated therein reflected the solemnity of these days. After vespers on the Feast of the Annunciation, the "light blue and yellow-gold" paraments used on that occasion were removed from the altar and pulpit and replaced with those of black velvet, "fringed with gold and silver, which hung there till Friday."[100] The morning liturgies were sung and spoken entirely in German and included a bare minimum of figural music; the services on Monday through Thursday opened with one of Schütz's settings from the *Becker Psalter,* and the Good Friday liturgy (below)[101] included the singing of Schütz's "new" St. John Passion by the German choristers.[102]

---

97. SLUB K 117, fols. 35v–36v.

98. SLUB Q 241, entry for 19 March 1665; Q 243, entry for 25 March 1666.

99. SLUB K 80, fol. 47v, entry for 24 March 1665.

100. "Montagk den 20. Martÿ, ware den Predigt Stuhl und Altar mit einem Schwarz Sammeten ümbhang, mit Goldt und Silbern Frantzen, so bis Freÿtags hengen bliebe, bekleidet" (SLUB K 80, fol. 46r). The diary entry for Holy Monday in 1673 indicates that the electoral balcony was also covered in black velvet (SLUB K 117, fol. 37r, entry for Monday, 24 March 1673).

101. SLUB K 80, fol. 47v, entry for 24 March 1665.

102. The services on Monday, Tuesday, and Wednesday mornings took the form of the *Wochenpredigt,* while that on Holy Thursday represented a full *Gottesdienst* (minus the figural music), complete with the singing of the German Gloria hymn (SLUB K 80, fols. 46r–47r).

EXAMPLE 8.6 Peranda, *Missus est Angelus*, mm. 1–24

AM CHAR FREŸTAGE DEN 24. MARTŸ [1665]	ON GOOD FRIDAY, 24 MARCH 1665
1. Der 22. Psalm, Mein Gott, mein Gott	Ps 22, sung *choraliter*[103]
2. Da Jesus an dem Creütze stundt	Hymn
3. *Collecta* und ablesung der 53. Cap: Esaia	Collect and reading of Isaiah 53
4. Ward die Paßion aus dem Evangelisten Johanne nach	The Passion according to St. John, in a new setting

103. The mode of performance is indicated in the entry for Good Friday in 1673 (SLUB K 117, fol. 39r).

EXAMPLE 8.6 (*continued*)

der neuen *Composit:*	by Schütz,
Cappellm: Heinrich	SWV 481a[104]
Schützens, abgesungen	
5. Predigt, so der dritte	Sermon by the third court
Hoffprediger verrichtete,	preacher
6. O Lamb Gottes unschuldig,	Hymn
7. *Collecta* und Seegen,	Collect and Blessing
8. O hilff Christe Gottes Sohn	Hymn

Those at court responsible for the decoration of the chapel doubtless worked assiduously in the morning hours of Holy Saturday, for when the assembly entered the chapel at 3:00 that afternoon for vespers, they encountered a worship space

104. *Das Leiden unsers Herren Jesu Christi, wie uns das beschreibet der heilige Evangeliste Johannes.*

be - ne - di - cta tu, be - ne - di - cta   tu   in mu-li - e - - - ri - bus.

EXAMPLE 8.6 (*continued*)

transformed with an array of elaborate paraments and tapestries, and an altar once again graced with the crucifix and candlesticks. As it had been at Christmas, the chapel was again decorated with a series of ornate tapestries; the content of these ten, however, pictorially related only the events of the *Triduum* and Easter Sunday, and in this respect, recalled the Catholic tradition of Stations of the Cross:

> Saturday the 25th of March, on Holy Easter Eve, the church was decorated in the following manner: the pulpit, altar, and choir as they were on the Feast of the Annunciation of Mary.[105] On the altar stood the usual silver crucifix and candlesticks, and the church was arrayed with silk tapestries richly embroi-

105. The diary entry for the eve of the Feast of the Annunciation in 1665 says only that "the church, as well as the choir and pulpit, was decorated as on the previous New Year's Feast, but the altar [was decorated] with a light-brown velvet parament, richly adorned with gold and pearls" ("Ward die Kirche, wie auch den Chor und Predigt Stuhl, gleich am vergangenen Neuen Jahres Fest, den Altar aber, mit einem viol braun Sammet, mit Goldt und Perlen reich gestückten ümbhang, bekleidet"; SLUB K 80, fol. 44v). The

dered with gold, depicting the following Biblical scenes: on the electoral box, "The Mount of Olives," beneath the arch of the electress's ladies-in-waiting, "Christ as He was taken Prisoner in the Garden," under the adjoining arch, "Christ as He was Led before Caiaphas," next to this to the right of the pulpit, "The Scourging," over the sacristy, "The Crowning [with Thorns]," over the church door, the "*Ecce Homo*," next to this, "The Judgement and Handwashing of Pilate," then underneath the arch of the privy council, "The Procession to Calvary," next to it "The Crucifixion," and beneath the electoral box, "The Easter Lamb."[106]

The Lutheran liturgical tradition of the sixteenth and seventeenth centuries did not include an Easter Vigil analogous to the elaborate service celebrated between None and Vespers on Holy Saturday in Roman Catholic churches. Instead, just as on all other Saturday afternoons in court and city churches, the day was marked with a vesper service. But like the Roman Vigil, the Lutheran vespers on Easter Eve introduced the feast and marked the end of the *Triduum*: the organ, instruments, and elaborate concerted music were reintroduced, and the texts of the hymns and the free musical interpolations now looked ahead to the Resurrection. The service also seems to have marked the return of the Italians to the chapel, for the same 1666 diary indicates that both Italian and German musicians performed during Easter Eve vespers.[107] In Dresden, the festal vespers included all four of the concerted items performed by the *Hofkapelle* on feast days; in 1665, these included a psalm setting by Kerll, as well as two concertos by Peranda.[108] Although both works are lost, the incipits suggest that both were settings of texts traditionally associated with the Easter feast in both the Roman and Lutheran traditions, for both incipits appear in Lossius's *Psalmodia*. Lossius includes *Vespere autem Sabbathi* as the antiphon for the *Magnificat* at the Easter Eve vespers, and includes *Angelus Domini descendit*, which is based on Matt 28:2, as the Alleluia verse on *Quasimodogeniti*.[109] In Dresden, it became traditional to perform these two particular concertos on Easter Eve, for the diaries reveal that they were also presented on this occasion in 1666, 1667, 1668, and 1676.[110]

---

entry for New Year's Day 1665 only mentions the crucifix and candlesticks on the altar for communion and does not include information about the decorations of the church itself (SLUB K 80, fol. 3r).

106. SLUB K 80, fols. 47v–48r; the German text appears in Appendix I (no. 23).
107. OHMA O IV Nr. 19, entry for 14 April 1666.
108. SLUB K 80, fol. 48r–v.
109. Lossius 1561/1996, fols. 93b, 121b–122a.
110. SLUB Q 243, entry for 14 April 1666; SLUB Q 245, entry for 6 April 1667; Sächs HStA Loc. 12026, fol. 245v, entry for 21 March 1668; SLUB Q 260, entry for 25 March 1676.

Like the other major feast days in the calendar, the three-day celebration of Easter was set apart from ordinary Sundays by the use of trumpets and timpani with the mass Ordinary and some of the sacred concertos, as well as through an intermingling of worship and representational elements. With respect to the latter, in his *Kirchen-Ordnung*, Johann Georg ordained that on Easter Sunday, the "shooting, bell ringing, and parading" would be observed "just as on Holy Christmas Day."[111] Descriptions of the morning protocol on Easter Sunday in various years confirm that his wishes were carried out; in 1665, for example, the various guard companies paraded in formation, fired the obligatory salutes, and retreated again, just before the *Hauptgottesdienst* commenced at 7:30 a.m.[112] While the military portion of the pre-service protocol would normally conclude before the service began, on Easter Sunday it continued into the performance of the Introit motet, *Salve festa dies.*[113] The description in the diary indicates that the motet was performed in *alternatim* fashion, with interpolations of the hymn *Also heilig ist der Tag* at three points.[114] But the court marshal's *Ordnung* makes clear that each of these hymnic interpolations was articulated by three blasts from three half cannons royal on the High Wall.[115]

On the initial day of the feast, the entire corpus of texts *de tempore* sung and read during the service commemorated the Resurrection event. After the morning sermon, Peranda presented a concerto entitled simply "*Victoria,*" which does not survive, but which was likely a large-scale work that celebrated Christ's triumph over

111. Spagnoli 1990:202.

112. SLUB K 80, fols. 48v–49r; the liturgies for the three days of Easter appear on fols. 49r–52v, and in SLUB Q 241, entries for 26–28 March 1665.

113. Lossius gives *Salve festa dies* as the hymn to be sung before the Introit on Easter Sunday (Lossius 1561/1996, fols. 99b–101b). Although not so indicated in the 1665 diary, Bernhard's setting of *Salve festa dies* was likely performed here, as it had been on Easter Sunday in 1662, and was again 1673; SLUB Q 240, entry for 20 March 1662; K 117, fol. 40v, entry for 30 March 1673.

114. The German hymn *Also heilig ist der Tag* had long been associated with the Latin hymn *Salve festa dies.* Spangenberg gives *Das Salve festa dies Deudsch* as one of the hymns and sequences that may follow the Epistle on Easter Sunday, and follows the hymn with the rubric "Also heilig ist der tag etc." (1573, fols. xcvia–xcviib). Keuchenthal gives the Latin hymn, as well as a German version, *Sey gegrüst du heiliger Tag,* as the hymn that precedes the Introit (*Resurrexi*) on Easter Sunday, and indicates that *Also heilig* is to be interpolated after the first verse of the German version of the sequence, but does not indicate any other spots at which the second hymn is to be sung. The hymn *Also heilig* follows *Sey gegrüst* in Keuchenthal's collection, and is prefaced by the rubric "Darauff wird gesungen der folgende alte/ Christliche Lobgesang" ("Whereupon will be sung the following old, Christian song of praise"; Keuchenthal 1573, fols. 265b–267a).

115. OHMA N I Nr. 8, fol. 12v. This *alternatim* performance, together with the use of military hardware, was stipulated in the order of worship for Easter in the *Kirchen-Ordnung*; see Spagnoli 1990:184.

death. At vespers that afternoon, the Latin concerted psalm that normally stood in second position in the liturgy was replaced, as per the *Kirchen-Ordnung*, with the German-texted Ps 114, "Als Israel aus Ägypten zog," which was rendered *choraliter* at the lectern. This particular text allegorizes Christ's liberation from the tomb and the realm of the dead in its celebration of Israel's emancipation from bondage and departure from Egypt. After the psalm, the German singers in the *Hofkapelle* performed one of Schütz's *Historien, Die Auferstehung unsres Herren Jesu Christi* (SWV 50), published in 1623.[116] According to the court diaries, Schütz's *Auferstehung* enjoyed a strong performance tradition during the reign of Johann Georg II and was presented at Easter by both Albrici and Peranda; it was finally supplanted in the later 1670s by Resurrection histories by court musicians Johann Müller and Johann Wilhelm Forchheim.[117] In the latter half of the service, Peranda's *Magnificat*, performed with trumpets and timpani, followed the sermon, and was itself followed by his concerto *Surrexit pastor bonus*, for two sopranos and two cornetti.[118] The incipit of this lost work once again suggests that the Dresden Kapellmeisters often reached for Lossius's *Psalmodia* as a source of concerto texts that would pass muster with the senior court preacher, for Lossius includes "Surrexit pastor bonus" (John 10:11) as the Alleluia verse on the second Sunday after Easter.[119]

On Easter Monday, the service again featured trumpets and timpani in the movements of the mass Ordinary as well as in the motet that followed the sermon. After the Gospel, in which two disciples encounter Christ on the road to Emmaus (Luke 24:13–35), Peranda presented his concerto *O vos omnes*, mentioned above in the context of Advent 1, 1666. *O vos omnes* provides an example of a text that is essentially *per ogni tempo*, but which can be contextualized in a number of ways; the content includes references that can be construed as relevant to either Advent or Easter (see the italicized text below), but the text is also general enough to be performed on many other occasions, such as on the elector's birthday:[120]

> O vos omnes ambulantes in tenebris, et umbra mortis, Surgite, properate, venite ad lucem: et si fuistis aliquando tenebrae, eritis Lux in Domino. Eia agite, surgite, properate, venite ad lucem. *Ecce Salvator noster, accedite ad illum, et illuminamini, et facie vestre non confundentur. Hic est enim Deus*

116. A diary entry for Easter 1667 indicates that on that occasion, the *Auferstehung* was sung by the German choristers; Sächs HStA OHMA O IV Nr. 21, entry for 7 April 1667.

117. See Steude 2001/2:170–71.

118. The concerto does not survive; an entry in SLUB Q 243 for Easter (15 April) in 1666 includes the scoring.

119. Lossius 1561/1996, fols.124b–125a.

120. The concerto was also performed on Johann Georg's birthday (31 May) in 1665; that entry preserves the text (SLUB K 80 fols. 77v–78r).

Largitor bonorum, omnium salvans animas, perducens illa ad caelestem Patriam. Curramus ergo properemus, festinemus, et cantemus. O quam suavis es homine, O quam suavis es, omnibus invocantibus te.

After the sermon, the *Hofkapelle* performed Peranda's lost "motet," *Tulerunt Dominum meum,* with trumpets and timpani; the text was likely the traditional antiphon for the *Magnificat* at vespers on Thursday of Easter Week.[121] The antiphon text is based on Mary Magdalene's anxious statement to Simon Peter on Easter morning, found in John 20:13, "They have taken the Lord out of the tomb, and we do not know where to find him." But while the motet text is directly related to the Gospel for Easter Sunday (Mark 16:1–8), it also expands upon the Easter Monday Gospel read earlier in the service, for during the walk to Emmaus, one of the disciples reports a version of these events to Christ, whom he does not recognize: "they were at the tomb early in the morning and did not find his body" (Luke 24:22–23).

At vespers that afternoon, following the singing of the opening versicle, the service continued with two lost compositions by Peranda, his setting of Ps 121, *Laetatus sum,* and a small-scale sacred concerto, *Ad coelestem Jerusalem,* for two sopranos and alto.[122] If the diarist's report of the service is accurate, only the *Magnificat* was accompanied by trumpets and timpani at vespers that afternoon. After the *Magnificat,* Peranda presented his concerto *Dic nobis Maria* ("Tell us, Mary"), scored for two sopranos and bass, two violins, bassoon, and continuo.[123] The text is drawn from the medieval sequence *Victimae paschali laudes,* which appears in Lossius in its traditional position on Easter Sunday:[124]

Dic nobis Maria, quid vidisti in via?	Tell us, Mary, what did you see in the road?
Sepulchrum Christi viventis, ex gloriam vidi resurgentis.	I saw the tomb of the living Christ, and the glory of his rising.
Surrexit Christus spes mea: praecedit vos in Galilaeam.	Christ my hope is risen: he will go before his own into Galilee.
Scimus Christum surrexisse	We know that Christ has truly risen

121. *LU* 800; the antiphon does not appear in Lossius.

122. The scoring appears in the 1681 Dresden Instrument Chamber Catalog; see Spagnoli 1990:225.

123. See Appendix II; modern edition in Frandsen 1997-3:550–65. Musical example prepared from SLUB 1738-E-502a.

124. Lossius 1561/1996, fols. 104b–105b.

a mortuis vere:	from the dead:
tu nobis, victor Rex, miserere.	have mercy on us, you conqueror king.
Alleluia.	Hallelujah.

Peranda also presented *Dic nobis* on Easter Monday in the two subsequent years, but moved it to the morning service, where it followed the Gospel.[125] In the sequence, the author creates a dramatic exchange between the disciples and Mary Magdalene concerning her observations at the tomb, and draws upon the accounts found in all four gospels.[126] Thus, like *Tulerunt Dominum*, the text was related to the Gospels for both Easter Sunday and Easter Monday and helped to draw both together thematically. In his setting of these verses from the sequence, Peranda not only captures the urgency inherent in the apostles' question, but further enhances the dialogic character of the text by using the brief opening concerto, a setting of the crucial question found in v. 4 of the sequence, as a vocal refrain that recurs before each of the three subsequent verses is sung by a soloist (Ex. 8.7). This recontextualizes each of the following lines as additional responses to the question, "what did you see in the road"? The first two of these responses are sung by the soprano castrati (as Mary Magdalene), and the third by the bass; following these solo-tutti exchanges, all three vocalists join forces in an extended Alleluia.

Given the dependence upon traditional liturgical texts with close ties to the Easter Gospels, the textual repertoire presented musically during the first two days of the Feast of the Resurrection represents a unified whole. On Easter Tuesday, however, free texts replaced these liturgical texts; as a result, the musical compositions contributed reactions and allusions to the Resurrection, rather than scripturally based accounts of the event itself. For example, after the Gospel (Luke 24:36–47), in which Christ appears to his eleven disciples and displays the wounds in his hands and feet, members of the *Hofkapelle* presented Peranda's concerto *Ad cantus ad sonos*, for three sopranos, three violins, and continuo. The text survives in two versions, both of which begin with two stanzas of poetry expressive of general rejoicing. The version preserved in the Grimma collection, however, continues with a portion of the traditional Antiphon at the *Magnificat* at second vespers on the Feast of Pentecost, while that preserved in the Bokemeyer collection substitutes Ps 8:2a in this position.

---

125. SLUB Q 243, entry for 16 April 1666; Q 245, entry for 8 April 1667.
126. Matthew 28:7–10, Mark 16:7–8, Luke 24:22–24, and John 20:17–18.

EXAMPLE 8.7 Peranda, *Dic nobis Maria*, mm. 1–10

EXAMPLE 8.7 (*continued*)

Grimma source:
Hodie Spiritus Sanctus
in igne discipulis apparuit,
tribuens eis charismatum
dona.[127]

Today the Holy Spirit
appeared to the disciples in fire,
granting to them charismatic
gifts.

Bokemeyer source:
Domine Dominus noster,
quam admirabile est nomen
tuum
in universa terra.[128]

Lord, our God,
how marvelous is your name

in all the earth.

127. *LU*, 886–87: "Hodie Spiritus Sanctus in igne discipulus apparuit, tribuens eis charismatum dona."

128. Ps 8:2a, "Domine Dominus noster quam admirabile est nomen tuum in universa terra."

All of the documented performances in Dresden took place either at Easter or at Pentecost. But as the textual substitution would appear to make the text more appropriate to ordinary Sundays than to Easter, either the Psalm text served for Easter, or a more feast-specific line of text that does not survive in the musical sources was substituted for the Easter performances. That same morning, Peranda followed the sermon with another concerto, *Plaudite Cÿtharis*, which does not survive. As discussed in chapter 4, Peranda may have borrowed the text from a solo motet by Gratiani and, if so, likely programmed the work for its clear Easter references: "Plaudite vocibus, ludite cytharis filiae Sion ad Domino . . . Dum Christus victor surgit ab inferis, Alleluia. . . . Ecce Salvator noster, ecce humani generis reparator, ad nos venit gloriosus triumphator. . . Alleluia."[129] In the vesper service that afternoon that closed the three-day feast, Peranda followed his setting of Ps 111, *Beatus vir* (lost), with his concerto *Accurrite gentes*. In contrast to *Ad cantus*, this text is strongly Christological in its content, but only its culminating lines make explicit reference to the Resurrection:

Ergo, laeti, decantemus,	Therefore, fortunate ones, let us sing repeatedly,
et triumphos celebremus,	and let us celebrate triumph
resurgenti Domino.	to the risen Lord.
Ut cum eo in aeternum	So that we might triumph
triumphemus.	with him into eternity.
Alleluja.	Hallelujah.

Following the *Magnificat*, a trio of singers (two sopranos and tenor) presented their final musical offering of the three-day festal period, Peranda's concerto *Florete flores*, which does not survive. As mentioned above, this text served for various occasions, including the Feast of St. Stephen (see above) and Pentecost Tuesday; perhaps in this context, Peranda sought to analogize the Resurrection with references to the blooming of flowers in spring.[130]

The liturgies on the first Sunday after Easter, *Quasimodogeniti*, concluded the octave of Easter in a festal manner.[131] As on other lesser feast days, the guards paraded in the early morning hours, but did not salute the elector (and the surrounding community) with musket shots and cannon blasts. Both the activity of the

129. Gratiani, *Plaudite vocibus* (*Motetti a voce sola, Op. 3*), in Schnoebelen 1988:69–78.

130. The performance at vespers on Pentecost Tuesday 1664, which was also the birthday of Johann Georg II, is recorded in Sächs HStA Loc. 12026, fol. 401v.

131. Entry for *Quasimodogeniti* 1665 in SLUB K 80, fol. 53r: "Sontagk *Quasimodogeniti* den 2. *Aprilis* ward daß heilige Oster Fest beschloßen."

guard units and the inclusion of a *Vesperpredigt* in the afternoon, however, elevated *Quasimodogeniti* above the subsequent five Sundays *post* Easter, on which the Italians were only responsible for the morning service; presumably the German choristers sang vespers in the afternoon on those Sundays, but these liturgies do not appear in the diaries.

A survey of the surviving liturgies for the following five Sundays after Easter reveals that Albrici and Peranda took different approaches to the selection of texts for this period of the church year. During the extended Paschal season in the year 1662, members of the *Hofkapelle* performed Carissimi's *Surgamus, eamus*, as well as nine of Albrici's own compositions, none of which survive. The incipits of these compositions, however, suggest that he selected at least one psalm text for musical performance in each liturgy and sometimes drew both texts from the psalms.[132] Under Peranda's watch in 1665 and 1666, however, compositions with mystical-devotional texts, particularly in the position *post*-Gospel, formed the core repertoire in these services.[133] Unfortunately, orders of worship for these five Sundays survive only from the years 1662, 1665, and 1666, making it impossible to track the textual repertoire on these Sundays into the 1670s. Clearly, however, a shift in emphasis took place when Peranda assumed the post of Kapellmeister after Albrici's 1663 departure. But whether the impetus for this shift in emphasis came from the Kapellmeister, the new court preacher, or the elector himself, remains impossible to determine.

Ten days after the celebration of the Feast of the Ascension, the *Hofkapelle* presided musically at the vigil vespers for the Eve of Pentecost, in a court chapel that had again been readied for the celebration of one of the three high feasts of the church year, but in a somewhat different manner than at Christmas and Easter: "On the Holy Eve of Pentecost, Saturday, the 17th of May [1673], the altar and pulpit were decorated with green velvet paraments, while the electoral balcony was bedecked with hangings of green damask, and the church was decorated with greenery, and remained so until the Monday after Trinity."[134] In contrast to Christmas and Easter, the textual repertoire of the third high feast of the church year remains more difficult to characterize, for it includes thematically oriented texts as well as those of a devotional or encomiastic nature, and the presentation of the latter two types

132. See SLUB Q 240, entries for 13, 20, and 27 April, and 4 and 11 May 1662.

133. See SLUB Q 241 and Q 243.

134. SLUB K 117, fol. 50v: "Am Heiligen Pfingst=Abend. Sonnabend, den 17. Maÿ, wardt der Altar und Predigt Stuhl, mit grün Sammeten Umbhang, die Churfürstliche Empohr Kirche aber, mit grün damastenen Umbhängen, und die Kirche mit Meÿen besteckt, So verbliebe biß Montag nach Trinitatis." Graff indicates that the term *Maien* (*Meÿen*) generally indicates oak and birch foliage, and that the practice of decorating the sanctuary in this manner, which can be traced back to the Reformation period, was traditionally associated with Pentecost (Graff 1937: 105).

was not limited to the second or third day of the feast. But Peranda and Albrici did integrate some of their concertos into the thematic fabric of the Pentecost services through texts that expanded on one or two verses from the Gospel in the manner of a gloss or trope. One of the most successful of such works was Peranda's *Repleti sunt omnes*, a concerto for alto, tenor, two violins, two cornetti, and continuo that enjoyed at least five performances between 1664 and 1676.[135] The text opens with a concise verse from the Epistle for Pentecost Sunday, "all were filled with the Holy Spirit and began to speak" (Acts 2:2a). With this simple statement the author of the text summarizes the phenomenon that occurred on the fiftieth day after the Resurrection: the Holy Spirit descended upon the apostles, who began to speak in many different tongues. Peranda sets this text, together with the appended Alleluia, in traditional *concertato* style and may have conceived the long, florid melismas at "alleluia" as the musical metaphor for the glossolalia of the apostles. In the following four sections of the text, the author-compiler adopts a more personal tone and invites the Holy Spirit to come and "fill the hearts of the faithful." He then elaborates on the opening verse with references to the Paraclete as teacher and protector and hearkens back to the Epistle with a reference to the appearance of the Holy Spirit in fire: "you who appeared to the disciples in fire, foster, protect, and teach us the way of truth." From these alternating passages of prose and poetry Peranda fashions a declamatory passage and brief aria for each singer. The text of *Repleti sunt omnes* succeeds in recalling and expanding on the images of the Epistle lesson, while at the same time allowing the listener to participate on a personal level in the appeals to and praise of the Spirit. In his musical response to these texts, Peranda again captures the passion of the speaker, particularly in the emotive and sublimely virtuosic setting of "Veni, Sancte Spiritus," which was probably composed for the alto castrato Francesco Santi (Ex. 8.8).

Johann Georg's birthday fell on May 31, and the occasion was marked each year with a *Hauptgottesdienst* and a *Vesperpredigt*, rather than with a court festival.[136] An order of worship for the birthdays of the members of the electoral family does not appear in the *Kirchen-Ordnung*, however, which simply instructs that the celebrations from previous years should be consulted as models.[137] The orders of worship in the court diaries reveal, however, that the tradition of two services developed early in Johann Georg's reign, and that the *Te Deum*, accompanied by cannon salutes, was deemed liturgically "proper" to this "feast." On Saturday, 31 May 1673, Johann Georg turned sixty years old and celebrated the occasion with services that he likely

135. See Appendix II; modern edition in Frandsen 1997-3:721–37.

136. When the elector's birthday fell on Pentecost Monday or Tuesday, it supplanted the feast and the morning *Gottesdienst* was transformed into a celebration of this local event.

137. Spagnoli 1990:189.

EXAMPLE 8.8 Peranda, *Repleti sunt omnes*, mm. 34–45

designed himself, not only to commemorate this milestone in his life, but also to proclaim once again his commitment to sacred music and to its principal purveyors, past and present, at the seventeenth-century Saxon court. The resulting service represents a combination of the elements "proper" to his birthday with the liturgy for the *Hauptgottesdienst* with communion.

Just as on the other feast days of the church year, the chapel was decorated with embroidered hangings, and, as was the practice on those occasions when the elector received communion, the choir area of the church was prepared to receive him:

His Electoral Highness of Saxony's 61st Birthday, Saturday, the 31st of May [1673]. The bells were rung at 4:30 a.m. for the first time, at 5:00 a.m. for the second time, and at 5:30 a.m. for the third time. The church was decorated in the following manner: the altar and pulpit with the crimson paraments, richly embroidered in gold and with pearls; the choir and balconies with red velvet hangings, and the electoral balcony with a hanging on which the electoral coat of arms was embroidered. The floor of the choir was covered entirely in red cloth. On the altar stood the ivory crucifix, and the two large, solid-gold enameled candlesticks; the small gold chalice was used, together with the paten and all of the other vessels. The houseling cloths were of gold and silver cloth. The rite was celebrated by the middle court preacher, whose chasuble was of crimson velvet, richly embroidered with gold and pearls. After 4:30 a.m. Your Electoral Highness made your confession, at 5:30 a.m. you went down into the church, where there was preluding on the organ until you were in your chair, upon which the worship service was celebrated in the following manner:[138]

1. *Introitus: Laudate Dominum omnes gentes*, der 116. Psalm mit Trompeten und Paucken, Churf. Durchl. eigene *Composition.*	Introit: *Laudate Dominum omnes gentes,* Ps 116, with trumpets and timpani, His Electoral Highness's own composition.
2. *Kÿrie* mit Trompeten und Paucken. *Vinc. Albrici,* ingleichen die folgende *Composition.*	Kyrie, Christe, Kyrie, in a setting by Albrici, with trumpets and timpani; each petition followed by a verse of the Kyrie hymn *Gott der Vater wohn uns bei.*
3. Gott der Vater wohn uns beÿ.	
4. *Christe.*	
5. Jesus Christus wohn uns beÿ.	
6. *Kÿrie.*	
7. Der Heilige Geist der wohn uns beÿ.	
8. *Intonir*te der Mittlere Hoff Prediger fürm Altar das *Gloria*	Intonation of the Gloria before the altar by the middle court preacher.
9. *Missa*, mit Trompeten und Paucken. *V. A.*	Gloria, with trumpets and timpani, Albrici.

138. SLUB K 117, fols. 57r–59r (description and both orders of worship); the German text of the chapel description appears in Appendix I (no. 24). Although Johann Georg turned sixty years old on 31 May 1673, it was literally his sixty-first birthday.

10. Allein Gott in der Höh seÿ Ehr.	German Gloria hymn.
11. *Collecta*, und lase der Priester die ersten 12. *Versicul.* Jesaia c. 26.	Collect and reading of Isaiah 26:1–12 (in the place of the Epistle.)
12. *Litania, musicaliter* teütsch. V. A.	German litany, in a musical setting by Albrici.
13. Lase der Priester den 71. Psalm ab, fürm Altar.	Ps 71 read before the altar (in the place of the Gospel).
14. *Intonir*te darauff das *Credo.*	Intonation of the Credo.
15. *Credo*, mit Trompeten. V. A.	Credo, with trumpets, Albrici.
16. Glaube.	German creedal hymn.
17. Predigt, so der Ober Hoff Prediger, Herr *Doctor* Geÿer, außm 71. Psalm, von 5. biß an den 10. *Versicul* verrichtete, und für dem Vater Unser, den 121. Psalm, Ich hebe meine Augen sehnlich auff, nach der Capellmeister Schützens *composition.*[139]	Sermon, delivered by Senior Court Preacher Martin Geier on Psalm 71, verses 5–10; before the Lord's prayer, Ps 121, "I lift mine eyes to the hills," in the setting by Kapellmeister Schütz.
18. Allein zu dir Herr Jesu Christ.	Communion hymn.
19. *Consecration*, und *communicir*ten Sr. Churf. Durchl., wobeÿ gesungen wurde: Jesus Christus unser Heÿland.	Consecration and communion of Johann Georg II, during which was sung, *Jesus Christus unser Heiland.*
20. *Collecta* und Segen.	Collect and Blessing.
21. *Intonir*te der Priester fürm Altar: Herr Gott dich loben wir, welches vollends vom Chor abgesungen wurde, mit Trompeten und Paucken.	Before the altar, the priest intoned the German *Te Deum*, which was sung in its entirety by the choir, with trumpets and timpani.

139. The psalm number and the attribution to Schütz appear in another record of the service, Sächs HStA OHMA N I Nr. 7, fol. 60v. SLUB K 117, fol. 58r reads: "und für dem Vater Unser: Ich hebe meine Augen sehnlich auff." Most likely this refers to the setting in the *Becker Psalter*.

On Johann Georg's sixtieth birthday, once he and his entourage had been seated, all those in attendance were treated to a performance of one of the elector's own compositions, his *Laudate Dominum omnes gentes*,[140] which was offered as the Introit (Ex. 8.9). As the composition makes its first appearance in these entries, it may have been composed by the elector specifically to mark the occasion.

But for its conclusion, the order of worship conforms with that given in the *Kirchen-Ordnung* for services with communion. While the Ordinary in the Sunday and feast-day services featured twofold presentations of the Gloria and Credo, in German and Latin, this service also includes a twofold Kyrie, and features an *alternatim* style of performance of the ancient plea for mercy in which a verse of the German hymn *Gott der Vater wohn uns bei*, sung by the congregation, follows each of the three petitions as set by Albrici and sung by the *Hofkapelle*. Albrici also contributed the Latin mass movements, which were performed in a festal manner with trumpets and timpani, as well as a concerted version of the Lutheran Litany, which followed the Epistle; in this respect, the communion service represents the only occasion on which figural music was interpolated after the Epistle in worship under Johann Georg. In place of the Epistle and Gospel appointed for this day, the Saturday after Trinity Sunday, passages of scripture were read that were likely chosen by the elector himself. For the sermon text he selected Ps 71:5–10, perhaps for its ninth verse: "Do not cast me off in the time of old age; forsake me not when my strength is spent."

During the Pentecost season, the *Kirchen-Ordnung* stipulated that the hymn *Komm heiliger Geist* was to be sung before the Lord's Prayer, which was prayed both before and after the sermon.[141] For his birthday observance, however, Johann Georg substituted Schütz's setting of Ps 121, "Ich hebe meine Augen sehnlich auf," from the *Becker Psalter* (SWV 226); perhaps the congregation joined in on the melody of this four-part setting. As this was a communion service, the Latin concerto or motet that normally followed the sermon was omitted, and the penitential hymn *Allein zu dir Herr Jesu Christ* accompanied the minister's departure from the pulpit and return to the altar, at which point the communion rite ensued. After the rite, the service normally concluded with a short prayer, a blessing, and a "short hymn or versicle."[142] In honor of the elector's birthday, however, the hymn was always replaced by a performance of the German *Te Deum*, "Herr Gott dich loben wir," accompanied by trumpets and timpani. To bring this special service to a resounding close, the guard

140. D-B Mus. msc. 30210 no. 15. (Attribution: "Comp: del S. A. E:le Giovanno Georgio 2.do Elettor di Sassonia.")

141. See Spagnoli 1990:187 and Schmidt 1961:133.

142. Spagnoli 1990:178.

EXAMPLE 8.9 Johann Georg II, *Laudate Dominum omnes gentes*, mm. 1–25

units then proceeded to enumerate the years of Johann Georg's life with sixty cannon salutes.[143]

Johann Georg's birthday celebration continued in the afternoon with a vesper service that was virtually identical in musical content (including some of the hymns) with the vesper service celebrated one year earlier at the dedication of the new chapel in Moritzburg in June 1672.[144] On that occasion, one of Schütz's settings of Ps 136, "Dancket dem Herren, denn er ist freundlich," performed with trumpets and timpani, replaced the concerted Latin psalm that would normally have followed the opening versicle, and one of his settings of Ps 150, also performed with trumpets and timpani, followed Albrici's *Magnificat*. The latter composition is likely the lost work that Schütz composed to celebrate the return to Dresden of Prince Johann Georg III and his new Danish bride, which received its first performance on 1 January 1667.[145] The inclusion of these two expansive works by Schütz in this service is even more striking when the orders of worship for vespers on the elector's birthday in previous years are examined, for none features any music by Schütz.[146] Perhaps Johann Georg intended this service to serve in part as a musical tribute to the elder Saxon *Oberhofkapellmeister*, who had died some five months after the Moritzburg chapel dedication. Johann Georg seems to have seen a day that marked such a significant turning point in his own life as an appropriate occasion on which to pay tribute to the man who had brought such musical renown to the Saxon court, and with whom he had first "walked through the fields of music" as a young prince.

Whereas the morning service had opened with music of the elector himself, the afternoon celebration featured a sacred concerto intimately associated with the potentate in another manner. At the conclusion of Schütz's setting of Ps 136, members of the *Hofkapelle* performed Albrici's *Sursum deorsum* ("As above, so below"), which does not survive. The incipit itself is Johann Georg's own *symbolum* or motto, and the subsequent text likely troped the motto, as did the text set by Peranda in 1664[147]; Albrici may even have set the same text, which appears

---

143. SLUB K 117, fol. 58v: "So bald Sr. Chf. Durchl. aus der Kirche gingen, Wurden umb die Vestung 60. Stücken gelöset, alß: [an enumeration of the charges follows].

144. Sächs HStA OHMA N I Nr. 6, fol. 37r–v, entry for 22 June 1672.

145. SLUB Q 245, entry for 1 January 1667; see also Rifkin and Timms 1985:130. Schütz's setting seems to have been performed again on the elector's birthday in 1679 (Sächs HStA Loc. 8682 Nr. 13, fol. 109r).

146. Entries for May 31 in SLUB Q 240 (1662), Sächs HStA Loc. 12026, fol. 401v (1664), SLUB K 80 (1665), fol. 78r; and Sächs HStA OHMA N I Nr. 7, fol. 58r (1668).

147. In 1664, Peranda composed *Sursum deorsum* for the elector's birthday, which fell on Pentecost Tuesday. It was performed after the Gospel by three soprano castrati and three violinists (Sächs HStA Loc. 12026, fol. 400r–v). A modern edition of the concerto appears in Frandsen 1997-3:811–32.

below.[148] As a devotional text with mystical overtones, *Sursum deorsum* is a bit unusual in that it is composed in the first person plural. But given the referential nature of the text, which is entirely bound up with the elector's persona, the mode of delivery is not surprising, for through it the text becomes as much a paean to Johann Georg as to the ostensible addressee. The text raises an interesting question about the contextuality of sacred works composed at courts: just how often were seemingly straightforward sacred texts actually charged with extra-religious or secular associations that have been lost through the centuries? Such associations would have significantly added to the complexity of the listening experience of those in the chapel in ways that can never be recovered.

Sursum deorsum.[149]	As above, so below.
Sursum corda, sursum vota,	Hearts upward, prayers upward,
sic deorsum vi permota,	thus below, moved by your power,
tota mens sit fixa sursum,	let the entire mind be intent on what is above,
Jesu praesto sis deorsum.	Jesus, be at hand here below.
Sursum deorsum.	As above, so below.
Jesu, coeli stillans rore,	Jesus, glistening with the dew of heaven,
tuo reple nos odore,	replenish us with your perfume,
corda sursum eleva;	raise our hearts upward;
multa spondes bona sursum,	you promise many good things above,
et nos protegis deorsum.	and you protect us here below.
Sursum deorsum.	As above, so below.
Salve, Jesu, dux sanctorum,	Hail, Jesus, ruler of the saints,
mundi lux, rex angelorum,	light of the world, king of the angels,
nobile solatium;	renowned comfort;

148. As mentioned above, the title (with an attribution to Albrici) appears in the order of worship for 23 June 1672; Albrici also programmed it on 26 January 1673 (SLUB K 117, fol. 24r). During his final tenure in Dresden, Albrici seems to have set another text based on the motto, *Moveantur cuncta sursum deorsum*, which was performed in 1678 and 1679 (Tzschimmer 1680:58 and Sächs HStA Loc. 8682 Nr. 13, fol. 109r).

149. Source of text: Sächs HStA Loc. 12026, fol. 400r–v.

blande nos invitas sursum,	coaxingly you invite us upward,
dum nos respicis deorsum.	while you look back upon us here below.
Sursum deorsum.	As above, so below.
Eia Jesu, bone Deus,	O Jesus, good God,
summum bonum, amor meus,	highest good, my love,
charitatis flammula;	little flame of love;
trahe corda nostra sursum,	draw our hearts on high,
et illabere deorsum.	and flow down [to us] below.
Sursum deorsum.	As above, so below.

SUNDAYS AND FEAST DAYS AFTER TRINITY

As mentioned above, Johann Georg's *Kirchen-Ordnung* only provided individual orders of worship for the feast days in the church calendar and indicated the liturgical form to be observed on ordinary Sundays through rubrics in the composite order of worship given for the first Sunday in Advent. For example, item no. 1 in that liturgy stipulates that *Rorate coeli de super*, the Latin Introit for Advent 1, was to be sung on that occasion, but that "On other Sundays, however, throughout the entire year, a German hymn [shall be sung] instead of the Introit."[150] A similar directive appears in the entry for the concerted Credo (no. 8) and indicates that the musical setting of the Latin Credo will be replaced by "a short concerto or motet on other Sundays."[151] This order of worship also includes rubrics for the celebration of communion during the *Hauptgottesdienst*.[152] The resulting order of worship for an ordinary, i.e. non-feast Sunday was identical to that for many of the lesser feast days, such as that for New Year's Day (given in chapter 7), and included a concerted version of the Kyrie and Gloria and two sacred concertos performed by the *Hofkapelle*, as well as six hymns (including the German Gloria and Credo) sung by the assembly. In this manner, Johann Georg assured that performances by his virtuoso musicians would continue throughout the church year.

In contrast with the liturgical calendar of the first half of the church year, the Trinity season is not dominated by major feasts. As a result, in the selection of Gospel readings for this season in the contemporary lectionary, one sees a move away

150. Spagnoli 1990:195.
151. Ibid.
152. As seen above in the morning liturgy for 31 May.

from texts focused on the three central events of Christ's time on earth to those that relate his acts on earth—his parables, miracles, and teachings. With respect to the musical repertoire performed during the Trinity liturgies in Dresden, this necessitated abandoning the largely festal or seasonally oriented texts that dominated the services during the first half of the year. But the diaries reveal that this change in focus in the lectionary was accompanied not by the introduction of settings of the Trinity Gospels, but by a shift to settings of intimate texts expressive of personal devotion. The introduction of these expressions of personal piety introduced a new quality of intimacy into the worship experience, one in which the "speaker" of the text now represented the individual member of the traditional Lutheran community of believers in his or her quest for a personal relationship with Christ. The mystical world of love and desire in which many of the speakers of these devotional texts dwelled, however, would seem far removed from the physical world of disease, pain, despair, and death inhabited by many of the figures who populate the Trinity Gospels. But when the expressions of mystical devotion set by Albrici and Peranda are considered alongside the Gospels that were recited just before their performance, they often offer up powerful allusions to those central texts and draw out their lessons far more subtly than did the traditional *Spruchmotette*.

The first example of such a relationship, which derives from the morning liturgy celebrated on the first Sunday after Trinity in 1665,[153] demonstrates Peranda's keen sense of the types of connections that might be forged between his concertos and the Gospel readings. The Gospel for this day, Luke 16:19–31, relates Christ's parable of the rich man and Lazarus:

> There was a rich man, who was clothed in purple and fine linen and who feasted sumptuously every day. And at his gate lay a poor man named Lazarus, full of sores, who desired to be fed with what fell from the rich man's table; moreover the dogs came and licked his sores. The poor man died and was carried by the angels to Abraham's bosom. The rich man also died and was buried; and in Hades, being in torment, he lifted up his eyes, and saw Abraham far off and Lazarus in his bosom. And he called out, "Father Abraham, have mercy upon me, and send Lazarus to dip the end of his finger in water and cool my tongue; for I am in anguish in this flame." (vv. 19–24, RSV)

On this occasion, immediately after those assembled in the chapel heard the court preacher recite the rich man's desperate plea, they then heard the rich man cry out again, this time in Peranda's plaintive setting of the words of the prophet Jeremiah, *Quis dabit capiti meo aquas?* ("Who will give waters to my head?"). Peranda's penetrating setting of the speaker's opening phrases instantly plunges the listener into the rich man's agony and seems to embody his desolation. He sets the opening

153. SLUB Q 241, entry for 28 May 1665.

alto-tenor duet in an E minor that is heavily indebted to the Phrygian mode, and employs chromatic colorings and harmonic shifts reminiscent of the Schütz generation. Although the vocal material is presented by two intertwining solo voices, in the manner of the traditional sacred concerto, the effect of a single speaker is not lost. Instead, the textual reiterations only serve to intensify the speaker's disconsolation.

Performed in the context of this particular Gospel, the text of Peranda's *Quis dabit* becomes rife with allusions—the listener might first hear the speaker in the musical work as the personification of the rich man of the parable, who, as the text continues, begs for mercy and forgiveness, and for Christ's intercession. But the listener might also associate himself, a "poor, miserable sinner," with this same speaker, and thus might find himself pleading with Abraham. And some listeners in the chapel, those familiar with the *Sacred Meditations* of Johann Gerhard, may well have recalled a passage from the opening meditation, "True Confession of Sin," upon hearing Peranda's text, particularly the two (nonconsecutive) sections given below:

Peranda:

Ad quem recurram,	To whom shall I return,
ad quem confugiam,	to whom shall I flee
nisi ad te,	except to you,
o benignissime Fili Mariae?	O most kind son of Mary?
	(Ps 139:7)

Quoniam tu es spes mea,	Because you are my hope,
auxiliatio mea,	my help,
et refugium meum,	and my refuge,
o clemens, o pie,	O merciful, O compassionate,
o dulcis Fili Mariae.	O sweet son of Mary.

Gerhard:

And God, the inflexible Judge, the almighty executor of His own external law, accuses me; Him I cannot deceive, for He is wisdom itself; from Him I cannot flee, for everywhere his power reigneth. Whither, then, shall I flee (Ps cxxxix. 7)? To Thee, O blessed Christ, my only Redeemer and Saviour, do I fly for refuge.[154]

The first of the four feasts observed by most Lutherans to fall during the Trinity season was that of St. John the Baptist, which in Dresden was also the elector's name

154. Gerhard 1896:14.

day. As a result, the feast took on political implications and was elevated above those of similar rank; in the words of one court secretary, it was "celebrated with great solemnity" ("Hoch Feÿerlich *celebriret*").[155] Like other feast days, the observance on June 24 began with the parading of the guards, and the service music was again enhanced with trumpets and timpani.[156] Unique to the day, however, was the special musico-military performance of both the German *Te Deum* following the sermon and the final blessing:

> The *Te Deum Laudamus* was sung, with the participation of the trumpets and timpani (which were also used in the Kyrie, Gloria, and Credo), and salvos of three half cannons-royal were fired by the guards, the first at the words "Holy, Holy, Holy," the second at "Daily, Lord God, we praise Thee," and the third as the second court preacher spoke the blessing.[157]

This entry, which derives from a diary for 1665, does not indicate whether the hymn of thanksgiving was sung by the *Hofkapelle* or the congregation, and does not indicate a composer. The Italian Kapellmeisters did provide settings of the *Te Deum*, however; on the Feast of St. John the Baptist in 1674, Peranda's setting of the German *Te Deum* was performed with twenty trumpets and three pair of timpani and was accompanied by cannon salutes.[158] This coordination of a cannonade with particular passages in a sung text must have necessitated some sort of signal system, which is neither described in the diaries nor the senior court marshal's *Ordnung*; the precise location of the cannons also remains unknown. As seen above, the elector's *Kirchen-Ordnung* also stipulates a performance of the *Te Deum* on Trinity Sunday and specifies that it is to be sung in Latin on that occasion. The different modes of performance, however, reveal that while God might well rate trumpets and timpani, cannons were reserved for the elector.

---

155. SLUB K 80, fol. 83v.

156. According to the *Kirchen-Ordnung*, the German choristers were given musical charge of vespers on the name days of the elector and electress (the Feast of Mary Magdalene); Spagnoli 1990:176. These services, however, do not appear in the diaries; in the record from 1665, from which the following quotation derives, no mention is made of a vesper service in the description of the elector's activities after the midday meal.

157. "10. Ward das *Te Deum Laudamus*, mit einstimmung der Trompeten und Paucken (welche auch zur der Meße und Patrem gebrauchet worden) gesungen, und von den *Guardien*, wie auch aus 3. halben Carttaunen, unter den wortten Heÿlig, Heÿlig, Heÿlig, die erste, die andere Täglich Herr Gott wir loben Dich, und die dritte als den andere Hoffprediger den Seegen gesprochen, *Salve* gegeben" (SLUB K 80, fol. 84r). This represents the tenth item in the order of worship. Similarly worded instructions for the performance of the *Te Deum* appear in order of worship in the *Kirchen-Ordnung*; Spagnoli 1990:188.

158. Sächs HStA Loc. 8682 Nr. 9, fol. 36v (entry for 24 June 1674).

Approximately one month later, the court celebrated the name day of Electress Magdalena Sibylla on the Feast of Mary Magdalene, which fell on July 22. Like her husband, the electress was also feted with a celebratory *Gottesdienst* enhanced by brass and percussion; in 1667, Peranda's Kyrie and Gloria were accompanied by two trumpets and timpani, and his motet, *Flavit auster*, sung after the sermon, featured four trumpets along with the kettledrums.[159] On this same occasion, Peranda selected his *O Jesu mi dulcissime* to follow the Gospel, Luke 7:36–50, a passage that relates Christ's visit to the home of a Pharisee. During the course of the visit,

> a woman of the city, who was a sinner, when she learned that he was sitting at table in the Pharisee's house, brought an alabaster flask of ointment, and standing behind him at his feet, weeping, she began to wet his feet with her tears, and wiped them with the hair of her head, and kissed his feet, and anointed them with the ointment. Now when the Pharisee who had invited him saw it, he said to himself, "If this man were a prophet, he would have known who and what sort of woman this is who is touching him, for she is a sinner." (vv. 37–39, RSV)[160]

Peranda's concerto with aria is a setting of four nonsequential strophes from *Jesu dulcis memoria*, throughout which the speaker expresses an intensely personal love for a sweet and merciful Christ. The court diaries reveal numerous performances of this work, which was programmed on various occasions throughout the church year. When performed on the Feast of Mary Magdalene, however, the composition functioned as a sort of trope on the Gospel that encouraged the listener to contemplate the text heard just minutes before.[161]

One of the more striking associations between the two texts resides in the invocation of tears in both. As a result, a listener might easily understand the "pious tears" introduced in the first strophe as those of the woman as she wept over Christ's feet:

O Jesu mi dulcissime,	O Jesus, so sweet to me,
spes suspirandis animae,	hope of my sighing soul,
te quaerunt piae lacrimae,	my pious tears
et clamor mentis intimae.	and the cry of my innermost soul
	seek thee.

159. SLUB Q 245, entry for 22 July 1667.

160. A number of Christian traditions identify this woman with Mary Magdalene.

161. Given both its strong resonance with the Gospel for the Feast of Mary Magdalene and the enhancement of the aria with a string accompaniment, the concerto could have been composed for this particular feast day in 1663 or 1664, years for which either no or few orders of worship have survived.

Such an association between the two texts immediately recontextualizes each of the subsequent strophes, which become the expressions of this same woman. The third strophe, for example, with its references to the speaker's desire to find and hold Christ, recalls her loving care for Christ's feet:

> Quod cunque loco fuero,   Wherever I may find myself,
> mecum Jesu desidero: I desire Jesus with me:
> quod laetus cum invenero,   what joy will be when I find him,
> quam felix, cum tenuero.   what happiness when I hold him.

The speaker's desire to find Christ—to experience Christ's presence in his innermost soul—recalls the anonymous woman's literal search for Christ; according to St. Luke, she "learned that [Christ] was sitting at table in the Pharisee's house," undoubtedly by looking for him and asking after him until she finally found herself in his presence. The speaker's desire to hold Christ—to sense his physical presence—resonates with the inherent sensuality of this particular Gospel, in which a woman kisses and caresses the feet of Christ. Yet another link between the two texts exists in the overarching theme of Christ's ineffable sweetness in the *Jubilus* text and the presumably aromatic oil or ointment with which the woman massaged his feet.[162] Such associations can only have deepened the listening experience of an individual sitting in the court chapel that morning.

In the sermon that followed the concerto (after the congregational singing of the creedal hymn), the court preacher would draw out the lessons of the Gospel text for those assembled in the chapel. Unfortunately, the 1667 sermons of court preacher Martin Geier do not survive. However, a fascinating exegetical exploration of this particular lectionary text appears in Heinrich Müller's *Thränen- und Trost-Quellen*, a set of twenty extended "Betrachtungen" or meditations upon this very Gospel, published less than a decade after the 1667 performance discussed above. Although sermonlike in tone, Müller's rhetorically conceived examinations of this text were intended for the lay person's private meditation in the home; his direct and straightforward language would have been quite accessible to any literate parishioner. In its entirety, Müller's exhaustive phrase-by-phrase exploration of these verses from Luke 7 runs to over 900 pages. Each of the twenty meditations actually comprises numerous shorter meditations, all of which are linked thematically through their focus on the same brief segment of the text. Thus one could read and contemplate a single brief meditation, or a series of several. In the seventh meditation, Müller treats the first part of verse 38, "she wept, and began to wet his feet with her tears":

---

162. Some translations have "fragrant oil" for "ointment."

This woman wept, while the others sat at the table. At mealtime she served up her course of tears with [the other courses]. However much she must have burned with pain, she was not ashamed to weep at the meal. Peter also wept, because he had denied his master, but he went out, and sought to hide his tears. This woman wept publicly, that is, when the guests sat at the table. Who can hold back the sea, when it has overflowed? In her a sea of tears overflowed, which neither shame nor anything else could hold back. She saw that a meal was prepared for the others, so she thought to prepare a meal for herself, a meal of the bread of tears and the drink of tears. As others refreshed themselves with the food, she sought her refreshment in tears. The rain refreshes the dry soil, and tears refresh the thirsty soul of the righteous. Thus spoke David, "Tears are my food day and night." He received his refreshment from tears, the others received theirs from food, and although the others ate their fill, he could not weep his fill; while the others ate only during the day, he wept day and night. So must those who love God do everything to the utmost. Tears alone must be their food, suffering their joy, and sorrow their comfort.[163]

In a number of ways, Müller's meditation approximates the style of sermon that Geier preached during his tenure in the Dresden court chapel and thus provides a sense of what the congregation may have heard from the pulpit upon the conclusion of the concerto. Meditative literature such as this, which underscores the multiple layers of meaning that reside in any scriptural text, likely influenced the ways in which audiences heard and understood compositions of sacred art music.

Among those texts that amplified the themes of the Gospel read prior to their performances are those that develop the theme of *vanitas*. The performance records of Albrici's *Omnis caro foenum*, for example, suggest that his decision to program the work on particular occasions derived from the resonance of its text with the Gospels appointed for those days. The scriptural passage that opens the text of this concerto with aria, Isaiah 40:6 (alt), forms part of the Epistle for the Feast of St. John the Baptist (Isaiah 40:1–8), but the diaries record no performances of the concerto on that occasion. Both of the documented performances occurred in 1662, when Albrici selected the concerto for performance on two Sundays during the long Trinity season, Trinity 11 and 16.[164] On the first of these occasions, the performance of *Omnis caro foenum* followed immediately upon the reading of Luke 18:9–14, the parable of the Pharisee and the tax collector:

---

163. Müller 1675/1724:218–19 (excerpt from Betrachtung VII: "Die Thränen-Quil-lende Sünderin"). The German text appears in Appendix I (no. 25).

164. SLUB Q 240, entries for 10 August and 14 September 1662.

Two men went up into the temple to pray, one a Pharisee and the other a tax collector. The Pharisee stood and prayed thus with himself, "God, I thank thee that I am not like other men, extortioners, unjust, adulterers, or even like this tax collector. I fast twice a week, I give tithes of all that I get." But the tax collector, standing far off, would not even lift up his eyes to heaven, but beat his breast, saying, "God, be merciful to me a sinner!" I tell you, this man went down to his house justified rather than the other; for every one who exalts himself will be humbled, but he who humbles himself will be exalted. (vv. 10–14, RSV)

This particular Gospel is shot through with the age-old notion of "pride goeth before destruction," and the bleak *vanitas* text of *Omnis caro foenum* expands upon this theme. When performed in conjunction with this reading, the speaker in Albrici's concerto text can be heard chiding the Pharisee for his arrogance and vanity and warning him of the potential danger of his lack of humility. Christ's closing admonition reverberates throughout the concerto text, but there takes on a much more ominous tone, for the "humbling" he cautions against is there equated with death, which will arrive when least expected:

O esca vermium, o massa pulveris,	O food of worms, o mass of dust,
o nox, o vanitas, cur sic extolleris?	O ignorance, O vanity, why are you thus exalted?
Ignoras penitus utrum cras vixeris.	You are wholly ignorant if you will be alive tomorrow.
Fac bonum sedulo quam diu poteris.	Do good zealously as long as you are able.

A few weeks later, on Trinity 16, Albrici's *Omnis caro foenum* was heard again, this time in the context of a different Gospel, Luke 7:11–17, the story of the son of the widow of Nain:

Soon afterward he went to a city called Nain, and his disciples and a great crowd went with him. As he drew near to the gate of the city, behold, a man who had died was being carried out, the only son of his mother, and she was a widow; and a large crowd from the city was with her. And when the Lord saw her, he had compassion on her and said to her, "Do not weep." And he came and touched the bier, and the bearers stood still. And he said, "Young man, I say to you, arise." And the dead man sat up, and began to speak. And he gave him to his mother. (vv. 11–15, RSV)

In programming *Omnis caro foenum* to follow this particular Gospel, Albrici emphasized the centrality of the theme of death in both texts. But his selection of this concerto remains curious, for the dark text contains only the most oblique of references to the salvation topos that is foregrounded in the Lukan account. On this occasion, those present in the chapel must have heard the concerto text quite differently than they had back in August, for the theme of *vanitas*, which resonated so strongly with the Gospel on Trinity 11, could not so easily be associated with this Gospel. An examination of the order of worship, however, suggests that Albrici himself may have been uncomfortable with the fact that the concerto text did not affirm the message of hope contained in the Gospel. To follow the sermon that day, he programmed Peranda's *Bone Jesu*, perhaps in an effort to strike a balance, and to lend emphasis to the more apparent theme of the story of the widow's son, that of the compassionate, "good Jesus," who healed the sick and raised the dead.

As demonstrated in several of the liturgies discussed above, the coordination of a musical composition with a passage of scripture could bring to life a nameless and faceless character in a biblical account for the listeners in the chapel. Such was the case on the fourteenth Sunday after Trinity in 1662, when Albrici's *Tu es cor meum* followed the Gospel, Luke 17:11–19:[165]

> On the way to Jerusalem he was passing along between Samaria and Galilee. And as he entered a village, he was met by ten lepers, who stood at a distance and lifted up their voices and said, "Jesus, Master, have mercy on us." When he saw them he said to them, "Go and show yourselves to the priests." And as they went they were cleansed. Then one of them, when he saw that he was healed, turned back, praising God with a loud voice; and he fell on his face at Jesus' feet, giving him thanks. Now he was a Samaritan. Then said Jesus, "Were not ten cleansed? Where are the nine? Was no one found to return and give praise to God except this foreigner?" And he said to him, "Rise and go your way; your faith has made you well." (vv. 11–19)

Through the simple juxtapositioning of this concerto with this particular Gospel, the entire text of *Tu es cor meum* was immediately recontextualized as the fervent soliloquy of the lone leper who, as a result of his healing, came to recognize Christ as a source of love and hope ("tu es cor meum, tu es spes mea, mi chare Jesu") and help for the "lowly," particularly individuals such as himself, members of a marginalized community who were ostracized by society. Thus he expressed his gratitude to Christ with words borrowed from psalmists, evangelists, and prophets:

Quis sicut tu, Domine Jesu Christe?	Who is like you, Lord Jesus Christ?
Excelsus es, immensus, terribilis,	You are exalted, immeasurable, terrible,
et humilia respicis	and you provide for the humble

165. SLUB Q 240, entry for 31 August 1662.

in coelo et in terra.	in heaven and on earth. (Ps 112:5–6)

[...]

Quantus es tu, Rex Regum	How great you are, King of Kings
et Dominus Dominantium,	and Lord of Lords, (I Tim 6:15)
qui imperas astris	you who rule the stars
et apponis erga hominem cor tuum,	and set your heart upon man, (Job 7:17)
o Jesu, Deus, salutare meum.	O Jesus, God, my salvation.

Although predominantly penitential in nature, the text of *Tu es cor meum* also functions as exegesis, for in it, physical deformity and illness are developed as metaphors for sin, which only an act of cleansing—Christ's ultimate sacrifice—can expunge. As the text progresses, the theme of the need for purification gradually rises to the surface, until, at the conclusion of the text, the leper (as speaker) appeals to Christ directly for purification:

Ah, cor meum sana,	Ah, cleanse my heart,
o Jesu amate,	O beloved Jesus,
plus millies grate	a thousand times dear to me,
restaura complana.	restore it and make it smooth.

Given their textual versatility, concertos with devotional texts were often heard on both feast days and regular Sundays, with differing effects. During the 1665 church year, for example, Peranda presented his *Te solum aestuat* on two occasions—at vespers on the Feast of the Ascension, and during the *Hauptgottesdienst* on Trinity 18.[166] While on the former occasion, the lectionary readings apparently played no role in Peranda's selection of this concerto to follow the *Magnificat*, its inclusion in the latter service provides an example of yet another sort of relationship established by the composer between a mystical-devotional text and a particular Gospel. In the text appointed for Trinity 18, Matthew 22:34–46, a Pharisee lawyer challenges Christ with the question, "Which is the great commandment in the law?" In his response, Christ lays down one of the most fundamental of Christian teachings:

You shall love the Lord your God with all your heart and with all your soul and with all your mind. This is the first and great commandment. And the second is like it: you shall love your neighbor as yourself. On these two commandments depend all the law and the prophets. (vv. 36–40, RSV)

166. SLUB K 80, fol. 54r, entry for 4 May 1665, and Q 241, entry for 24 September 1665.

Through his selection of *Te solum aestuat* as the concerto to follow this Gospel, Peranda underscored this "first and great" commandment, to the total exclusion of the second. But although the concerto text shares a focus on love with the Gospel, it removes that love from the realm of abstraction and transforms it into a burning passion felt by the individual for Christ. In this scriptural context, the concerto text could not easily function as the speech of a scriptural character, for here the Pharisee, the only speaker besides Christ, is not motivated by love. But Peranda clearly understood the relationship that this text bore to the Gospel, for it resonates throughout with the central words of Christ's command—"love," "heart," "mind," and "soul"—and thus constitutes a broad trope on the central portion of the reading (emphasis added):

My soul desires,
burns with *love* for you alone,
most sweet Lord Jesus Christ.

O Jesus of my *heart*,
singly most beloved,
transfix, I beseech you,
the center and inmost part of my *soul*
by the sweetest and strongest dart of your *love*.

Jesus, wonderful sweetness,
kindness pleasing to the *heart*,
o what happiness enjoys the *mind*
which your *love* binds.

Guest of my *soul*, sweetest Jesus,
most excellent to me,
O God my life.
My *soul loves* you, faints in you alone.

Yours, Jesus, is pleasure
and spiritual refreshment,
the burning desire of a *lover*,
lacking all haughtiness.

O how great is the multitude of your charms, Lord,
what is there for me in heaven beside you,
and what do I desire on earth?
God of my *heart* and my portion,
God into eternity.

Very mighty king, king of glory,
king of greatest victory,
liberal giver of bountiful glory,
honor of the celestial court.

Several weeks after the Feast of St. Michael, on Trinity 20 1662, Kapellmeister Albrici seems to have handed the musical reins over to his vice-Kapellmeister, Peranda, for music of the latter dominated the service; both the *Missa* (Kyrie and Gloria) and the sacred concertos were of his composition.[167] Peranda used the occasion to present works that expanded upon various aspects of the sermon text for the day, Matthew 22:1–14, in which Christ teaches the parable of the marriage banquet that the invited guests would not deign to attend:

> The kingdom of heaven may be compared to a king who gave a marriage feast for his son, and sent his servants to call those who were invited to the marriage feast; but they would not come. Again he sent other servants, saying, "Tell those who are invited, Behold, I have made ready my dinner, my oxen and my fat calves are killed, and everything is ready; come to the marriage feast." But they made light of it and went off, one to his farm, another to his business, while the rest seized his servants, treated them shamefully, and killed them. The king was angry, and he sent his troops and destroyed those murderers and burned their city. Then he said to his servants, "The wedding is ready, but those invited were not worthy. Go therefore to the thoroughfares, and invite to the marriage feast as many as you find." And those servants went out into the streets and gathered all whom they found, both bad and good; so the wedding hall was filled with guests. But when the king came in to look at the guests, he saw there a man who had no wedding garment; and he said to him, "Friend, how did you get in here without a wedding garment?" And he was speechless. Then the king said to the attendants, "Bind him hand and foot, and cast him into the outer darkness; there men will weep and gnash their teeth." For many are called, but few are chosen. (Matt 22:2–11, RSV)

Peranda framed this Gospel and its extended exegetical treatment by the court preacher with concertos on penitential and devotional texts, each of which focused on an aspect of the parable other than its central allegorical message, God's offering of salvation to the Gentiles. Immediately following the initial reading of the text, members of the *Hofkapelle* presented *Quis dabit capiti meo aquas*. When performed in this pericopal context, the opening lines, taken from the prophet Jeremiah, form the words of the banished guest in his desolate anguish. But in the text of Peranda's musical composition, that anonymous outcast has repented of his sins, and speaks from his exile in eternal darkness to ask Christ for mercy. Thus the concerto text not only extends the narrative of events beyond the limits of the parable, but also personalizes the message of the Gospel and lends it a Christological focus.

---

167. SLUB Q 240, entry for 12 October 1662.

For the musical interpolation *post* sermon on this Sunday in October, Peranda selected his *Fasciculus myrrhae*.[168] Here Peranda's choice seems to have been guided by the concerto text's evocation of the bridegroom, whose spurned wedding celebration provided the pretext for the parable. The sung text opens with phrases of endearment uttered by the *Sponsa* of the Song of Songs (1:12); her initial statement serves to contextualize the stanzas of mystical poetry that follow as her own effusive expressions of devotion to her beloved. This beloved is of course Christ, the allegorical bridegroom of the Gospel parable.[169] Thus, after the court preacher elucidated the symbolism of this Gospel for those assembled in the chapel, Peranda offered another symbolic interpretation of the parable, with a musical composition in which the speaker expresses an ardent love and desire for this same Bridegroom.

Fasciculus myrrhae	A little bundle of myrrh
est meus dilectus,	is my beloved,
intra ubera mea	within my breast
commorabitur.	will he tarry. (SS 1:12)
O vulnera vitae	O wounds of the life
coelestis amantis,	of the heavenly lover,
trophea regnantis,	[O] victories of the ruler,
cor mihi aperite.	lay bare my heart for me.
Transfigite latus,	Pierce my side,
transfigite pectus;	pierce my heart;
o mori beatus,	O to die blessed,
dum ferit dilectus.	as my beloved slays me.
O rosa fragrantes	O fragrant roses
in cruce rubentes;	blushing red on the cross;
o stellae mirantes	O wonderful stars
in coelis micantes.	gleaming in the heavens.
Non mihi rosarum	Not for me a wreath of roses
non gemmis refertum,	crowded with jewels,
sed Jesu spinarum	O Jesus, but rather intertwine
connectite sertum.	a wreath of spines.

168. For details of the scoring of *Fasciculus myrrhae*, see Appendix II.

169. In medieval and early modern allegorical interpretations of the Song of Songs, the *Sponsus* or bridegroom symbolized Christ, whose bride (the *Sponsa*) was interpreted variously as the individual soul, the church, the Virgin Mary, or even the state. See Kendrick 1994: 102–4.

Languet anima mea	My soul faints
amore tui,	with love of you,
o bone Jesu, aestuat,	O good Jesus, it seethes,
suspirat,	it sighs,
et in amore deficit.[170]	and it falters in love.

Accende cor meum,	Inflame my heart,
infunde dulcorem,	pour out [your] sweetness,
quo amem te, Deum,	that I may love you, God,
te verum amorem.	you, the true beloved.

Fasciculus myrrhae . . .	A little bundle of myrrh . . .[171]

Near the conclusion of the church year, on October 31, the court commemorated Luther's *Thesenanschlag* of 1517 with a special *Gedächtnistag* that sought to pay tribute to the Reformer in word and song. In contrast to all of the other services codified in Johann Georg's liturgical formulary, that for Reformation Day, when not celebrated on a Sunday, betrayed a distinctly retrospective spirit and admitted only monophonic repertoire of the Reformation era (see below). On this occasion, the concerto that normally followed the Gospel was omitted, and a hymn replaced the concerto (or motet) performed after the sermon. The latter substitution, together with the addition of the German Kyrie, resulted in a service that included eight hymns, including the hymnic paraphrases of the German Ordinary. The Reformation liturgy exhibits some commonalities with the first part of the communion service celebrated in Dresden, but is closest in form and content to that established in the *Kirchen-Ordnung* for apostles' days. Here, however, Luther's famous hymn *Ein feste Burg* (*A Mighty Fortress*) replaces the Schütz-Becker psalm as the Introit, the Gloria hymn *Allein Gott*, sung on most Sundays and feast days, replaces the alternate *All Ehr und Lob soll Gottes sein*, and the two sacred concertos have been omitted entirely. Given the antipapist rhetoric that doubtless spewed forth from the pulpit, particularly in the period of heightened confessional tensions after 1667, Johann Georg rarely required his Catholic musicians to participate in the celebration of this second "great schism" in the history of the church. As stated in the rubrics found in the *Kirchen-Ordnung* for 31 October,[172] *die Musica* was only to be used "as is usual on

170. Includes references to Song of Songs 2:5, "Fulcite me floribus, stipate me malis, quia amore langueo," and 5:8, "Adiuro vos, filiae Hierusalem, si inveneritis dilectum meum ut nuntietis ei, quia amore langueo."

171. Translated by Margaret E. Garnett.

172. "Mittewoche den 31. October. Am Fest des Ersten Anfangs der *Reformation*, so durch den Theuren Mann Gottes *Lutherum* geschehen" (SLUB Q 243, entry for 31 October 1666). The order of worship conforms to that found in the *Kirchen-Ordnung*.

other Sundays" when the date fell on a Sunday; on these occasions, the order of worship was to be expanded to include the figural Kyrie, Gloria, and Credo. No mention is made, however, of the inclusion of sacred concertos or motets.[173]

Wednesday, the 31st of October [1666].
On the feast of the very beginning of the Reformation,
as brought about by Luther, the inestimable man of God.

1. Eine Veste Burg ist unser Gott
   [Introit:] *A Mighty Fortress Is Our God*, hymn, text (based on Ps 46) and melody by Luther, 1528[174]
2. *Kÿrie*, Gott Vater in Ewigkeit.
   Kyrie, God, Father into Eternity, troped Kyrie hymn, based on *Kyrie fons bonitatis*; Naumburg 1537
3. Allein Gott in der Höh seÿ Ehr.
   German Gloria hymn by Nicolaus Decius, 1522
4. *Collect*, und wird verlesen 2. *Reg:* 23, 1. bis 20.
   Collect and reading of 2 Kings 23:1–20 [in place of the Epistle][175]
5. O Herre Gott dein Göttlich wortt
   O Lord God, your Divine Word, hymn, 15th-c. melody, text by Anarg zu Wildenfels, 1526
6. an statt des *Evangelÿ*, das 14. *Cap:* der Offenbahrung *St: Johannis*.
   "instead of the Gospel, the fourteenth chapter of the Revelation to St. John"

173. Spagnoli 1990:191. During the reign of Johann Georg II, the date fell on a Sunday only in 1658, 1669, and 1675. A diary entry for the Sunday celebration in 1669 does not include the order of worship but states that "because of the church reformation of the blessed Mr. Luther, a feast of recollection, praise, and thanksgiving was held"; the entry also indicates that a *Vesperpredigt* was celebrated in the afternoon, as on other feast days (Sächs HStA OHMA O IV Nr. 24, entry for 31 October 1669). The diaries for 1658 and 1675, SLUB Q 238 and Sächs HStA Loc. 8682 Nr. 9, include no information concerning services on this date.

174. This hymn of Luther is still traditionally sung on Reformation Sunday in Lutheran churches. The information on the hymns sung during this service derives from the *Evangelisches Kirchengesangbuch* [*EKG*].

175. The readings on Reformation Day were left to the discretion of the senior court preacher and changed from year to year (Spagnoli 1990:191). In 1662, for example, Weller selected Revelation 18 as the Epistle and Ps 115 in place of the Gospel (SLUB Q 240, entry for 31 October 1662). In 1667, Martin Geier drew his sermon text from Isaiah 60:23 (Sächs HStA OHMA O IV Nr. 21, entry for 31 October 1667). Today in churches of the ELCA, the Epistle is drawn from Romans 3:19–28, and the Gospel from John 8:31–36.

7. Nun lob mein Seel den Herrn.
   Now Praise the Lord, my Soul, paraphrase of Ps 103, melody from a 15th-c. secular song, hymn version by Hans Kugelmann and Johann Gramann, 1530
8. Wihr Gläuben all an einen Gott.
   We All Believe in One True God, Luther's creedal hymn, 1524
9. Predigt, so Hl: *Magist:* Valentin verrichtete.
   "Sermon, delivered by Herr Magister Valentin [Heerbrandt]" (the second court preacher)
10. Erhalt uns Herr beÿ deinem Wortt.
    Lord, Preserve Us in Your Word, hymn by Luther, 1542/43 (based on the melody of the medieval hymn *Veni redemptor gentium*)
11. *Collect* und der Seegen.
    Collect and Blessing
12. Ach bleib beÿ unß, Herr Jesu Christ.
    Ah, Remain with Us, Lord Jesus Christ, sung to the melody of *Erhalt uns Herr*; v. 1 Philipp Melancthon (after *Vespera iam venit*), vv. 2–9 Nikolaus Selnecker, 1572

CONCLUSION

The court diaries and *Kirchen-Ordnung* of Johann Georg II offer an important glimpse into a lost culture and permit a more detailed look at musico-liturgical life at the court of Dresden than is possible for any other seventeenth-century court or city. The rich musical and liturgical tradition recorded for posterity by Johann Georg II, through his diarists, greatly enhances our understanding of the role of sacred music at a Lutheran court in the later seventeenth century. This corpus of chronicles, when used in conjunction with some important ancillary materials, documents the liturgical forms in use at the time and their codification; the musical repertoires of the *Hofkapelle* and the congregation; the fusion of courtly representation with religious ritual; the framing of worship services with extra-musical, military protocols; the creation of a multidimensional worship ambiance through visual and aural media; the use of music to articulate the high points of the liturgical calendar, and many other important facets of the worship experience in Dresden. And a comparison of the texts of the extra-liturgical works that enhanced the services with those in use in other Lutheran venues helps to establish Dresden as a court well within in the mainstream of trends in Lutheran spirituality, rather than at the periphery, despite the hegemony of Latin and the confession of those in musical authority.

But the diaries and the *Kirchen-Ordnung* do leave a number of musical and liturgical questions unanswered. The level of detail does not extend, for example, to information on clerical processions and the movements of clergy between altar and pulpit, or to the clerical vestments worn during the *Hauptgottesdienst* without communion. The detailed descriptions of the altar and surrounding area during the communion service contrast starkly with the records of the communion liturgies themselves, which radically telescope the details of the rite itself. As a result, no information survives regarding whether the court preachers ever prefaced the Words of Institution with the Paraphrase of the Lord's Prayer, or if the Latin Great Thanksgiving, Proper Preface, and Sanctus were ever used on feast days. One is also left to wonder about other aspects of the communion rite in Dresden, such as the practice of elevating the sacraments, which continued in some Lutheran churches into the seventeenth century.[176] Although the diaries are silent on the issue, the *Hofkapelle* may have performed during the Distribution on those occasions when the celebration of communion occurred during the *Hauptgottesdienst*, as was common in Lutheran churches. Liturgies such as those from the court of Liegnitz indicate that *Hofkapellen* regularly participated in the singing of polyphonic responses to the versicles sung by the priest before the Epistle, the Gospel, and at other points during the services, and although these items do not appear in the court diaries, they probably formed part of the Dresden liturgies as well.[177] And the diaries are particularly silent with respect to the use of the organ. They provide no information whatsoever concerning the organ repertoire heard in the chapel, whether the services regularly began with an organ prelude, outside of the "preluding" required during the elector's procession into the communion service, or the points during the services at which the organ was used. But the practice of introducing the congregational hymns with the organ was so ubiquitous by this time that it can be assumed to have been the rule in Dresden as well.[178] Neither do the diaries indicate the purposes for which the various chapel organs were used; presumably the organists did their "preluding" on the Fritzsche organ in the high balcony and played continuo on the positives in the musicians' balconies.

While not insignificant, these lacunae can never diminish the contribution that Johann Georg's diaries make to the history of religious rites and rituals. The remarkable amount of detailed information preserved in these rare documents allows the reconstruction of the court chapel liturgy and its repertoire on many Sundays and feast days. The diaries demonstrate that the music of the court Kapellmeisters domi-

---

176. The practice continued in the Upper Lusatian city of Görlitz until 1689; see Graff 1937:191–92.

177. See Liliencron 1893/1970:121–31.

178. Much of this information may have been included in the organists' contracts, which do not survive from the reign of Johann Georg II.

nated the repertoire, as is to be expected, but that, depending upon which Kapell-meister was in charge at the moment, those in attendance might also hear the compositions of other contemporary Italian and German composers. The diaries also reveal, however, that this audience heard comparatively little contemporary concerted German repertoire on Sundays and feast days. In addition, these materials demonstrate that the music of the late Renaissance retained a curiously prominent role in the musical life of a court whose sovereign strove to gather exponents of the most modern musical idiom for his court ensemble. But despite its apparent completeness, the repertorial picture contains some lacunae as well, due to the almost total absence of weekday liturgies in the court diaries. These could shed much light on the musical repertoire performed by the German choristers during the daily services, and could reveal to what extent the music of Schütz remained in the choristers' repertoire after 1656.

Perhaps the most surprising fact revealed by the diaries, given the confessional affiliation of the Kapellmeisters, is the extent to which these Catholics strove to forge thematic links through allusion and allegory between their extra-liturgical compositions and the various Gospels. The number of liturgies in which such relationships can be identified leaves little doubt that both Albrici and Peranda shared a keen awareness of the intertextual possibilities afforded by the liturgical structure of the Lutheran *Hauptgottesdienst,* and that they exploited them with fruitful results. Although many of the auditors in the chapel likely understood little or nothing of these Latin texts, certainly those well-schooled aristocrats that populated Johann Georg's *Hofordnung* could boast of a high level of comprehension and must have found their worship experience enriched through the exegetical contributions of the Kapellmeisters. As a result of their efforts, the individual Lutheran who worshiped in the court chapel had access to a multitude of "readings" of familiar scriptural texts, many of the most powerful of which emanated not from the pulpit, but from the musicians' galleries.

Finally, in their revelations of the importance that mystical-devotional texts assumed in the sacred repertoire performed in Dresden during this era, the diaries raise important questions about the elector himself as the ultimate progenitor of that repertoire. Was Johann Georg II a product of the "new spirituality" of the age? Did he enjoy enough familiarity with Italian music ca. 1650 to know that there he would find the type of texts that responded to the individual's quest for a personal relationship with Christ, and did he thus seek out Italian musicians for spiritual as well as musical reasons? Or was it by happy accident that Albrici and Peranda arrived in Dresden just at a time when the type of textual material with which they were accustomed to engage (and the musical style with which they engaged it) was uniquely suited to the new spirit of personal devotion that had developed in seventeenth-century Lutheranism? Perhaps the extent to which Johann Georg's partiality toward Catholic musicians was a consequence of his own spiritual and confessional inclinations will never be known. Whatever its origins, however, the curious confessional alliance that resulted ushered in an era during which the seemingly irreconcilable worlds of courtly representation, corporate worship, and personal devotion not only coexisted peacefully, but interacted in ways that created a dynamic, fascinating synergy.

Epilogue

Johann Georg II Remembered

WHEN JOHANN GEORG II died in August 1680 in Schloß Freudenstein, his residence in Freiberg, the Italianate musical atmosphere that he had cultivated for three decades suddenly changed dramatically. Seemingly overnight the period of Italian hegemony in the court chapel came to a close; most of the Italians departed Dresden in accordance with the wishes of the new elector, Johann Georg III (r. 1680–91), and Christoph Bernhard was finally elevated to the rank of Kapellmeister, in which capacity he now oversaw a much more modest ensemble of German musicians.[1] All but two of the Italian members of the *Hofkapelle* seem to have returned to their native land. Albrici, however, remained in the north, and on 27 May 1681 began a brief tenure as organist at the Thomaskirche in Leipzig, where he converted to Lutheranism.[2] A year later he departed for Prague, where he converted back to Catholicism; he spent his remaining years in service at an Augustinian church, and died in the Bohemian capital in 1690.[3] Melani, on the other hand, remained in service to his late patron's widow, son, and daughter-in-law until ca. 1690, even though he resided primarily in Florence from 1685, where he founded an *ospizio*.[4] He died in Florence in 1693. But already by 1685, Italian musicians began to reappear at the Dresden court, this time primarily as composers and performers of opera. Apparently Johann Georg III did not share his father's partiality toward sacred music in the Italian style; instead, he directed his energies and financial support toward Italian opera. In 1685, he brought Pallavicino back to Dresden as Kapellmeister and

---

1. Fürstenau 1861/1971:262–63.

2. Münnich 1901–02:524; see also Schering 1926-2:246–48.

3. Fürstenau 1861/1971:262. Albrici's death date is often reported as 1696, but Jan Enberg discovered an *epitaph* in Sebastian Labe, *Salium millenarij secundi* (Prague 1691, 71) that suggests that Albrici died six years earlier; Fürstenau also gives 1690 as his death date (ibid.). The author thanks Jan Enberg for sharing the results of his research on Albrici's time in Prague.

4. Fürstenau 1861/1971:260–61, 280. On Melani's activities in Florence ca. 1685–93, see Hill 1986:138–40.

opera composer and also hired the first *prima donna* in Dresden, Margherita Sali-
cola.[5] Following the premature death of Johann Georg III in 1691, his son Johann
Georg IV (r. 1691–94) continued to support Italian opera at court during his brief
reign, and thus with his father laid the groundwork for the most celebrated period
in Dresden operatic life, which began during the reign of his brother, Friedrich
August I (August the Strong, r. 1694–1733).[6]

Through his consistent patronage of Italian musicians and his demonstrable pre-
dilection for the musical idiom of modern Italy, Johann Georg II effectively opened
a new musical age in Dresden, and permanently altered the soundscape in the
electoral court chapel, once dominated by the music of Heinrich Schütz. In order
to accomplish the sweeping changes that he had already begun to envision in the
1640s, he reached beyond the boundaries of his own land, language, and confession,
and augmented his *Hofkapelle* with foreign virtuoso singers and composers. Like
the Catholic sovereigns in Munich and Vienna, he demonstrated a distinct preference for Italian musicians, particularly castrati, and developed relatively successful (if at times rather unorthodox) recruitment strategies to populate his ensemble.
But his penchant for Italian Catholics stood out as curiously anomalous among his
Lutheran peers, most of whom could neither afford nor tolerate the idea of such
cross-confessionalism in their houses of worship. Johann Georg's Italianate musical
predilections proved costly from the start, however, and only added to his financial difficulties, which resulted in large part from his determination to display the
essential trappings of courtly image creation—extensive apparatuses for music, the
festival, and the hunt—despite the crippling debt left behind by his father. Although
at the beginning of his reign Johann Georg attempted to deal structurally with the
financial requirements of his representational agenda, in which music played a
prominent role, the personal indebtedness of musicians such as Albrici demonstrate
that he never truly succeeded in this effort. Given the sorry state of the elector's
finances, the fact that he successfully maintained an ensemble of around fifty musicians for so many years is remarkable.

In one respect, however, a sense of mystery still shrouds the person of Johann
Georg II. Although the court records compiled under his supervision testify to his
musical preferences, his personal confessional leanings remain less scrutable today.
For while he publicly asserted his fidelity to the *reine Lehre* embraced by his ancestors, he privately flirted with the same confession that those forebears had repudi-
ated as heresy and, through it all, managed never quite to reveal his true intentions.
Perhaps, given his apparent interest in Catholicism, his open declarations of allegiance to Lutheran doctrine should be regarded as mere *Schau*, cynically intended

5. Fürstenau 1861/1971:277–87.
6. See Fürstenau 1862/1971:1–179.

only to ensure his own political and economic survival. But his failure to abandon the church of his fathers may also reveal a genuine reluctance on his part, one rooted in deep doctrinal convictions that he could not shake, despite the allure that Catholicism may have held for him. Indeed, his establishment of an annual commemoration of the Reformation, first in his private chapel and then throughout Saxony, suggests that the shadow of the Reformer loomed large in his spiritual consciousness. As a result, the extent to which his fixation on Italian music resulted from his own confessional inclinations—such as they may have been—remains unclear; in one respect, his importation of these musicians and his approval (if tacit) of their settings of mystical-devotional texts might be seen as evidence of Catholic leanings, but the place of such devotion within contemporary Lutheran spirituality, and the importance of this repertoire in other Lutheran centers, makes it problematic to associate his textual preferences with any confessional convictions he may have held privately.

Whatever their origins, Johann Georg II's Italian proclivities had far-reaching consequences for the music at court, and for sacred music in particular. Under Albrici and Peranda, the textual and musical styles of mid-century Rome came to dominate the repertoire of the *Hofkapelle*. By melding the various traditions of the Roman motet with one of the salient features of the German sacred concerto, the active interchange between voices and instruments, Albrici and Peranda developed new, hybrid works that looked forward to the sacred cantata. In their sacred concertos, the prominence of the solo voice helped to underscore the individualistic, devotional nature of so many of the texts. And while they are not unusual in their focus on the creation of intense musical affect in settings of such texts, their compositions for Dresden demonstrate just how closely keyed to the text a musical realization might be. But in addition to their stylistic impact, these hybrid works also had formal implications for the German sacred repertoire; by the end of the century, Albrici's new concerto with aria, firmly rooted in Roman models, had been adopted by German composers as a favorite organizational strategy for sacred compositions. Through these composers and the dissemination of their works, Johann Georg exercised an influence on Lutheran church music that extended beyond the Dresden castle walls.

But perhaps the most unusual role filled by Johann Georg during his reign as elector was that of liturgist. Rather than concede all liturgical responsibility to his court preacher, he demonstrated a keen personal interest in the manner in which worship was celebrated at court and took a firm hand in developing the liturgical forms to be used in the chapel. As a result, virtually all of these were graced by the compositions of his Italian Kapellmeisters. Significantly, however, despite his flirtations with Catholicism, Johann Georg seems to have shied away from any attempt to "Romanize" the chapel liturgies; throughout his reign, they remained reflective of Lutheran worship practices of the later seventeenth century. The steps he took to preserve these liturgies underscore his perceived role as court liturgist, and the result must stand as one of the most important aspects of his legacy, for the descriptive liturgies preserved in his court diaries record details of worship that normally remain inaccessible to scholars. Not only do these documents reveal the liturgical forms employed and the hymns sung during several hundred services, they also speak to the repertorial choices made weekly by church musicians throughout the ecclesiastical year. But perhaps most important, when examined in conjunction with the musical compositions recorded within them, these liturgies also allow an examination of the ways in which contemporary church musicians of this era—Catholic as well as Lutheran—seized upon the opportunities for scriptural commentary and exegesis offered by the Lutheran liturgy through its juxtaposition of the Gospel with a composition of sacred music. The trenchant Gospel commentary offered by many of the compositions of Albrici and Peranda demonstrates the remarkable degree to which musical works, while falling outside the bounds of the liturgy *per se*, contributed to the thematic nexus of individual services during this era.

Thus it is from the perspective of aesthetic achievement, rather than that of political accomplishment, that the legacy of Johann Georg II is best assessed, for in this realm his contributions are significant and can be counted alongside those of his aspirational peers in Bavaria and Austria. His intense interest in the cultivation of the arts, particularly music, more than compensated for his apparent lack of ambition in the political arena, which might well be regarded as a generational aberration in a dynasty long populated by strong leaders. With respect to music, his adoption of a distinctly modernist stance set him apart from his father and had broad and long-lasting musical implications. For nearly thirty years, from his hiring of Bontempi in 1651 until his death in 1680, he maintained a consistent policy devoted to the cultivation of Italian music. Throughout this period, although he did not totally neglect the strong German Lutheran musical traditions that had long been associated with the Dresden court, he did allow their place largely to be usurped by the many Masses, Magnificats, sacred concertos, and other liturgical pieces composed for the court chapel by Albrici, Peranda, Cherici, Pallavicino, and others. His costly cultivation of Italian music not only influenced the development of Lutheran sacred music in Germany during his lifetime, particularly through Albrici's concerto with aria, it also laid the groundwork locally for the Italianate musical brilliance of the eighteenth-century courts of his grandson and great-grandson, Friedrich August I and II. Thus if faced with criticism of his spending priorities, given his pride in his Italianate musical enterprise and the brilliant patina it lent to his court, Johann Georg II might simply have responded with the famous motto of the English Order of the Garter, into which he was invested in 1669: "Shamed be he who thinks ill of it."[7]

7. *Hony soit qui mal y pense.*

Appendix I: Source Documents

1. Sächs HStA Loc. 8562/1, fols. 44v–45r; Henrich Hermann von Oeÿnhausen to Johann Georg II, Venice, 21 September 1649.

Sonsten *florirt* die Music alhir sehr wohl, des Herzogs Kapell besteht in 40 sehr guten *Musicanten*. Und *excellirt* der Capellmeister dergestalt, daß S: Kaÿserl: Maÿ: demselben dinste vndt 4000 Rthr bestallung anbieten laßen, wiewohl der beÿ der Capell befindtliche *organist* dem Capellmeister nach vor gezogen vndt vor gar *singular* gehalten wird; In *summa* der *Parnassus* ist in Italien zu suchen, vndt hat seines gleichen nicht; es seindt nicht allein die *Discantisten* besondern auch die *Altisten* beÿ hisiger *capel* alle *castraten*, vndt die behalten eine bestendige unwandelbahre stimme. Die können wihr nun in teütschland nicht leichtlich haben, besondern müßen vns mit denen verenderlichen stimmen behelffen. Es ist ein Kloster alhir *la Pietà* genant, in welches die findling von mägdlein gethan werden; diese bringen eine solche *Music* zusamen daß nichts druber ist, inmaßen sie sowohl in *vocal* alß *instrumental musicen excelliren*, vndt singt sonderlich eine den alten in solcher vollkommenheit, daß sie mit verwunderung angehört wird, hab offt gewünscht daß selbige *Music* bis in die Churfürstl: Hof Capell nach Dresden erschallen möchte.

2. Sächs HStA Loc. 8563/2, fol. 191r; Johann Georg II to Johann Georg I, 28 April 1651.

Durchlauchtigster, Hochgeborner Churfürst, Allergndigster Herr und Vatter,

E. Gn. berichte ich hirmitt vnttertenigst gehorsambstes, wie das Ich deroselben heute vnrecht berichtet, wegen des [*sic*] *Musicanten*, so habe ich gemeinet E. Gn. meineten dem [*sic*] teutschen so beÿ mir vnd naulicher Tage auch von winkommen, so sindt die letzteren zweÿ, so von winkommen vorgesteren, zweÿ *Italianer*, namens *Bandino Bandini Contro Altiste* vnd *Gioseppi Amaddei Tenoriste*, welche der vorstorbene Cappelmeister in Dennemarck *Augustino Fontani*, so erstlich hirbleiben wolte, vor itzigen Könige in Dennemarck vorschrieben, wohin sie auch ziehen.

3. Sächs HStA Loc. 8560/5, fol. 59r; Roster of Prince Johann Georg's musicians, in his hand, undated (January–February 1652).

1. *Gio: Andrea Bontempi*. von *Perugia. Director, Componist* vnd *Discantist.*
2. *Heinerich* Groh. *Discantist.*
3. *Friederich* Werner. *Altiste* vnd *Cornediste.*
4. Franziscus Ferdinant Francke *Tenoriste.* aus Beueren,
5. *Philip Stoll Tenoriste* vnd *Teorbiste.*
6. *Stephani Sauli* von Rohm *Bassiste.*
7. *Christian* Kittel *Bassiste* vnd *violdicamponiste.*
8. *Michael* Schmitt *Bassiste* vnd *Violiste.* aus Böhmen
9. *Gio: Severo Violiste* von *Verona.*
10. *Baltasar* Sedenük *Violiste* von *Rabe* aus *Ungeren*
11. Der naue so in *Polen* ein Münch gewesen, von Berlin aus der marck *Violiste.*
12. Johan Friederich Volprecht *Violist* vnd Laudeniste,
13. Friederich Westhoff Laudeniste,
14. Gottfriede Basche Laudeniste, ist noch ein Junge.
15. Nauman der *posauniste*, so von Brissel kommen.
16. Matteus Weckman *organiste*,
17.⎫ Zweÿ trompeter jungen so auch zu gleich auff der
18.⎭ posaune vnd viol können.
19. noch ein Cappel knabe so auff der geigen vnd posaun lernet
20. noch ein Cappel knabe so auff der orgel lernet vnd
    zum ab Coppiren gebraucht wirdt.

4. Sächs HStA Loc. 8298/7, fol. 45r; Travel Pass for Domenico Melani and Niccolo Milani, 1 September 1654 (issued by Johann Georg II), draft.

Literae Passus ut vocant pro Dominico Melani et Nicolao Milani

Nos Dei gratia Johannes Georgius, Saxoniae, Juliae, Cliviae et Montium Dux, Electoratus Successor, Landgravius Thuringiae, Marchio Misniae, nec non Superioris et Inferioris Lusatiae, Comes Marchiae et Ravensbergae, Dominus in Ravenstein, Universis et singulis has literas nostras patentes inspecturis, lecturis, aut legere audituris, pro uniuscuiusque dignitate et status conditione, officia, studiaque nostra in omni humanitatis et benevolentiae genere deferimus promptissima, nec non salutem, benignitatem et gratiam nostram, notumque facimus, jussu nostro in Italiam ad expedienda quaedam se conferre, praesentes Musicos nostros Dominicum Melani et Nicolaum Milani. Cuam obrem rogamus amanter et hortamur benigné ac gratiose pro sua quemque dignitate tostatus conditione ut praenominatis Nostris Musicis per quascunque jurisdictionum oras terra inrique proficiscentibus libere ac securé sine ommi molestia eundi et redeundi liberam dent ac tribuant facultatem, eosque pro conditione voluntatis testudij erga Nos, clementer benigné et humaniter juvent, quo facilius, tutius ac celerius hoc iter conficere possint. Factum rem per se aequitati haud inconvenientem, atque officij studÿque Nostri promptitudine, amicitiâ benevolentiâ et benignitate compensandam.

Dabantur sub sigillo nostro majore manusque nostrae subscriptione, ex arce Dresdensi die 1. Septembris Anno Domini Millesimo Sexcentesimo Quinquagesimo quarto.

5. Sächs HStA Loc. 8687/6, fol. 9r–v; German Translation of Domenico Melani's Italian Contract (copy made by Christian Kittel in 1680).

*Sigr. Domenico de Melani Italiani*sche ins Deützsche *Vertirt*e Bestallung
WIR Johann Georg Von Gottes Gnaden Hertzog zu Sachßen, Jülich, Cleve und Berg, Chur Printz, Landgraf in Thüringen, Marggraf zu Meissen, auch Ober: und Nieder: Lausitz, Graf von der Marck und Ravensburg, Herr zu Ravenstein, [etc.], Bekennen, Daß WIR angenommen haben, zu unserm getreüen und geliebten Diener *Sigr: Domenico Melani,* und erklären ihn für unsern *Musicum* der Cammer, in Craft dieses *Patent*s, Das er alß ein getreüer Diener schuldig seÿ, zuverschaffen daß auffnehmen unserer *reputation,* und hoheit, und zu verhindern alles das jenige, so unsern Ehren zu wieder gereichen könte, Über das soll er verbunden seÿn, auff alles unser erfordern beÿ unß zu seÿn, unsere Befehle zuempfangen, und nirgends hin zu verreisen, ohne Unser Uhrlaub, und soll sich in allen und ieden erweisen, alß einen getreüen und fleißigen Diener, Welches er also mit einem Eÿde zugesaget hatt. Zu seiner Besoldung veror[d]nen WIR ihme Tausend Thaler, Und zu Uhrkund dieses, haben WIR gegenwärttiges *Patent* mit eigener Hand unterschrieben, und mit unserm Herzogl: Siegel bedrukket, Zu Dreßden, am 1. *Januarÿ* 1654.

Johann Georg Hertzog zu Sachßen
L.S.

6. Sergio Monaldini, *L'Orto dell'Esperidi: Musici, attori e artisti nel patrocinio della famiglia Bentivoglio (1646-1685)* (Lucca: LIM, 2000), 193. Filippo Melani da Firenze to Ippolito Bentivoglio, 10 June 1664 (excerpt).

Ci sarà occasione di haver un buon tenore, il quale si chiama Vin[cen]zo Leoni che si ritrova in Orvieto, virtuoso che riesce in tutto, tanto in chiesa che camera, e teatro; questo al presente si ritrova senza impiego, e per qualche persecutione non puol' uscir del stato ecclesiastico, essendo qualche tempo fà, referito al Papa che q[ues]to andava à servir l'Elettor di Sassonia, fù da S[ua] S[anti]tà relegato in Orvieto, e per gr[azi]a dopo, concessoli poter stare nel stato ecclesiastico; siche io lo propongo à V. Ecc.ª e quando ella lo voglia me lo avvisi per gr[azi]a subito, acciò non si portasse in altra parte, e per quello mi significa mio fr[ate]llo Aless[andr]o, questo virtuoso, si accomoderà à quello vorrà V.E. Si chè attenderò suoi ordini tanto per il negotio di mio fr[at]ello, quanto per quello del Leoni. [. . .]

7. Sächs HStA OHMA K IV Nr. 3, fol. 110r; Contract for Antonio Fidi, 23 July 1674.

Von Gottes Gnaden WIR, Johann Georg der Ander, . . . thun hiermit kund und bekennen, daß Wir Unsern lieben getreuen *Antonio Fidi* zu Unserm Cammer

Musico angenommen, . . . Insonderheit aber soll er schuldig seÿn, sich wesentlich beÿ Unserer Residentz aufzuhalten, ohne Unsern, oder Unsers würcklichen Capellmeisters bewilligung und Erlaub nicht zu verreisen, so wohl auch Unß, nach verordnung Unsers Capellmeisters (an welchen er hiermit gewiesen wird) beÿdes in der Kirchen und für der Tafel, oder wohin ihm sonsten solches befohlen würde, iederzeit unterthänigstes auffzuwartten, dem *Exercitio* aller-maßen Wir es befehlen allermahls gebührend bey zu wohnen, in *Summa* sich der maßen zu erweißen, was einem getreuen fleißigen Diener, gegen seinem Churfürsten und Herr eignet und gebühret. Welches er dann auch zu halten, durch einen Handschlag an Eÿdesstatt angelobet, und seinen schriflichen Revers darüber ausgehändiget hat. Hingegen und damit er solches seines Dien-stes desto beßer abwartten möge, so wollen wir ihm Jährlich Sieben hundert Vier und Virtzig Thaler zu Besoldung für alles und iedes richtig reichen und fol-gen laßen, Sonder gefährde. Zu Uhrkund haben Wir dieses eigen händig unter-schrieben, und Unser Chur *Secret* hierunter zu drucken befohlen; So geschehen zu Dresden den 23. Junÿ des 1674.sten Jahres.

Johann Georg Churfürst

L. S.

8. Sächs HStA OHMA K IV, 3, fol. 114r; Contract for Johann Jacob Lindner, 30 Sep-tember 1677.

Von Gottes Gnaden, Wir Johann Georg der Ander . . . Thun hiermit Kund und bekennen, daß wir Unsern lieben getreuen Johann Jacob Lindner, zu unserm Hoff *Musico* und Notisten bestellet und angenommen, . . . Insonderheit aber soll er schuldig seÿn, . . . Uns, nach Verordnung Unserer Capellmeistere (an welche er hiermit gewiesen wird) beÿdes in der Kirchen, sowohl des Sonn und Fest Tages als auch wenn sonsten in der Wochen geprediget wird, ingl. beÿ allen Vespern und Bethstunden[,] früh *Communion* und für der Taffel, oder wo ihme sonst solches befohlen würde, iederzeit unterthänigstes fleißes aufzu-warten, dem *Exercitio* allermaßen, wir es anordnen wurden, allemahl gebüh-rend beÿzuwohnen, auch was von Unserm Capellmeister, und *Vice* Capell-meister, ihme von einem und dem andern in Kirchen, und Tafel *Music*, auch Theatralischen sachen, ins reine zu bringen.

9. Sächs HStA Loc. 8687/6, fol. 16r-v; List of Albrici's debts, undated, probably March 1681.

Hr. *Vincenz Albrici* Capellmeistern.

244 thl. 8 gr. 1 d.	Hannß Thomas Friedeln und *Consorten* Handelsmann, vor empfan-gene Wahren, *inclusive* 30 thl. welche Er bahr bekommen,
214 thl. –. –.	Ephraim Bienern, Cramern, *Musico* vor geliefert und empfangenen Wein, laut *Oblig:*
18 thl. 18 gr. –.	George Schmeltzeln, Schustern vor gefertigte und gelieferte Arbeit,
10 thl. 5 gr. –.	Mitreüthern, Schustern vor gelieferte Arbeit,
30 thl. –. –.	Johann Tammen Schneidern, rückstendigen Hauß Zinß,
<u>40 thl</u>	Johann Firscheln Hoff *Musico* Bahr geliehenes Geldt laut *Oblig:*
537 thl. 7 gr. 1 d.	

10. Sächs HStA Loc. 10331/8, fols. 1–2, Saxon Estates ("Anwesende Landschafft von Ritterschafft vnd Städten") to Johann Georg II, 4 April 1661.

Den höchstrühmlichen Eyfer, welchen E. Churf. Dht. wieder die in *Privat* Häusern kurz verruckter Zeit gehaltenen Papistischen Meßen, die leider soviel vns wißend, ohne einziges vorhero erhörtes *exempel* in E. Churf. Dht. *Residenz* bey deroselbst vnd der getreuen Landschafft gesambten Anwesenheit alhier sich vnterstanden worden, erwiesen, haben billich wir mit unterthänigstem Danck zu erkennen vrsach . . . .Vnd ob wir zwar wol gnugsam versichert, daß E. Churf. Durchl. alle dergleichen vernehmen, so wieder die ware Christliche vnverfälsche Religion, wie sie Keyser *Carolo V.* in der *Confession* zu Augspurg übergeben, vnd in Schmalkaldischen Articuln auch der *Formula Concordiae* enthalten, darinnen E. Churf. Dht. geboren vnd erzogen, vnd satsam gegründet, lauffen, vnnd demselben entgegen schon, eyferigst haßen, vnd diesen zu wieder nichts einführen laßen werden, So ist doch nicht zu leugnen, daß die bestellung vieler frembder Ausländischer, auch wiederiger *Religion* zugethaner diener, in wolbestelten Regimentern, vnd also nicht alleine in *Politica* oftmahls große verenderung, Sondern auch in Religions sachen (ungeachtet aller genauen Aufsicht, welche die ienigen, denen die sorgfalt des gemeinen wesens obgelegen, dießfalls erwiesen) dennoch allgemachsam ein vnd ander ärgernis verursachet, das hernach wiederumb aus dem wege zu reumen sch[w]er fallen wollen. . . . Wir tragen keinen Zweifel, E. Churf. Dht. werden in dero ansehnlichen Landen wormit Sie der Allerhöchste begnadet, noch wol dergleichen *qualificir*te *subiecta* finden.

11. *Consilia theologica Witebergensia, das ist, Wittenbergische geistliche Rathschläge dess theuren Mannes Gottes, D. Martini Lutheri, seiner Collegen, und treuen Nachfolger, von dem heiligen Reformations-Anfang, biss auff jetzige Zeit, in dem Namen der gesampten Theologischen Facultät aussgestellete Urtheil, Bedencken, und offentliche Schrifften, in vier Theilen . . . auff vielfältiges Begehren abgefertiget* (Frankfurt am Main: Balthasar Christoph Wust, 1664), pt. 4, 60–61.

Von Moral und Policey=Sachen

1. Ob ein Christlicher Fürst päbstische Musicanten halten dürffe?
2. Ob sie der Pfarrer *facti species* solle in der Kirchen leiden?

[. . .]

Antwort.
Auff angebrachte zwo Fragen/ welche deß Inhalts/ wie folgen wird/ ist unser Theologischen Facultät zu Wittenberg verordneten Professoren auß Gottes Wort bedencken und Erklärung/ wir kürtzlich nach Einführung der Fragen soll gemeldet werden.
[. . .]
Auff diese Frage geben wir nach Anleitung Göttlicher heyliger Schrifft mit Unterscheid kürtzlich zur Antwort/ daß zweyerley Leute seyn welche etwa in Irrthumb stecken. Etliche sind ganz und gar verblendet/ verhärtet und boßhafftig/ welcherley die Phariseer wahren blind und Blinden leiter *Matth. 15.* und die verstockten Juden *Act 13.*

Neben diesem aber finden sich auch viel arme und unbeständige welche von falschen Lehren zum meisten verleitet/ und mit Irrthum sind eingenommen worden/ wie es zu deß Herrn Christi Zeiten mit dem Judischen Pöbel mehrentheils beschaffen war/ welche er selber verirrte Schaffe nennet/ die keinen Hirten haben *Matth. 9.10.15.*

So demnach deß hochgedachten Fürsten Diener; welche hiebevor mit Päbstischem Irrthum eingenommen worden/ sich der Warheit nicht muthwillig wiedersetzen/ dieselbe nicht lästern/ auch andern kein Aergernuß geben/ und bey ihnen Hoffnung/ daß sie mit der Zeit sich weisen lassen möchten/ ist gemeldeter Hoffprediger vermöge seines Amptes schuldig/ mit ihnen als mit schwachen in Christlicher Gedult zustehen/ und die *gradus admonitionum* in aller Sanfftmut und Freundlichkeit/ nach dem klaren und ernsten Befehl deß H. Christi *Matth. 18.* zu halten/ und dahin sich zu bearbeiten/ damit sie auß der Finsternuß zum hellen Licht deß Evangelii vermittelst Göttlicher Hülffe mögen gebracht werden/ allermassen wie der Herr Christus allhie das glimminde Dacht nicht außlöschet/ und das zerbrochene Rohr nicht zerstosset *Esa 42.* und als ein treuer Hirte den verirrten Schäflein in die Wüsten nachgehet *Luc. 15.*

Jedoch soll dieses/ was von irrenden jetzo vermeldet/ ferner nicht gezogen werden/ als so lange und alldieweil sich gedachter *Cantor* und die andere Päbstischen Hoffdiener *dociles* erzeigen/ und zu verhoffen/ daß sie sich zu seiner Zeit werden weisen lassen/ immittelst die Warheit nicht lästern/ und nicht andere neben sich verführen/ welches sich denn äussern wird/ so der Hoffprediger sie insonderheit zu sich bescheidet/ ihnen ihren Irrthum durch Zeugnuß der Schrifft gründlich wiederleget/ und sie mit Gelindigkeit und Bescheidenheit eines Bessern berichtet.

Wann aber alle diese zu unterschiedlichen Zeiten angewendete Mühe und Arbeit nichts helffen wolte/ und sie in ihrem gefaßeten Irrthumb vorsetzlich verharreten/ als denn und auff solchem Fall stehet Christlicher Obrigkeit ihres hohen Ampts halben zu/ solche wiederspenstige Leuthen bey welchen keine Hoffnung/ daß sie der Himlischen Warheit staat geben werden/ bey sich nicht zu gedulden/ damit sie sich ihrer Sünden nicht theilhafftig machen/ den Zorn Gottes sich und die ihren häuffen/ den Schwachen aber einen Anstoß und Aergernüß hiedurch setzen mögen. . . . Das für Eins.

12. Sächs HStA OHMA O IV Nr. 21, entry for 31 October 1667; Celebration of the Reformation in October 1667.

Donnerstags den 31. [October]. Wurd früh und in gegenwart der sämmtlichen Anwesenden Chur= und Fürstl. Gnädigsten Herrschafft, auff Chur=Fürstl. Sächßl. Gnädigste Anordnung, Eine Jährliche Danck= und Gedächtnüß Predigt, auß dem Propheten Jesaia am 60. cap: v. 23. genommen, durch den Herrn Ober=Hof=Predigern Dr. Geÿern abgeleget und gehalten, und darinnen die grosse Wolthat und Güte Gottes, welche Er in diesen Landen Ao. 1517 eben an Diesem Tage, so mit Anschlagung der *Theses* an der Schloß=Kirchen zu Wittenberg, wieder den Päpstischen Ablaß=Crämern Tätzeln, durch den Seel. Herrn D. Mart: Lutherum den Anfang genommen, hat herführ leüchten lassen, hiedurch das Christliche Reformation=Werck angerichtet worden, in einem Zierlichen und außführlichen Bericht und Sermon gedacht und *referi*ret: und ward zum Beschluß das *Te Deum Laudamus* Teützsch abgesungen.

13. Sächs HStA Loc. 30115 [unfoliated], Dresden High Consistory (Carl von Friesen, Christopher Buleus, Martin Geier, Gottfried Berniger, and Johann Fridrich Heigius) to Johann Georg II, 8 March 1668, on the celebration of Mass at the homes of the French and Imperial ambassadors.

Also haben Vermöge unserer schwehren Pflichten auch Wir, deren von E. Churfürstl. Durchl. die aufsicht über die reinigkeit der *Religion* aufgetragen ist, da das Päbstische Meßhalten alhier anfänglich einreißen wollen, keines weges darbeÿ säumig seÿn konnen noch sollen, Sondern albereit fürn Jahre *Mense Februario* unterthänigste anregung gethan, Daß doch denen damahls aufgehenden funcken in des Frantzösischen *Residen*ten Behausung in zeiten gesteuret werden möchte. Allein es hat baldt hernach dergleichen sich auch in des Keÿserlichen *Residen*ten Wohnung ereignet, und ob zwar E. Churfürstl. Durchl. eine und andere abmahnung rühmlichst ergehen laßen, dennoch so hefftig über hand genommen, Daß nunmehr man ungescheuet dahin alß zu einer Wallfarth mit hauffen fähret, reitet, gehet, und noch täglichen der raum von fremden und einheimischen ohne unterschied also angefüllet wird, daß dem Verlaut nach manche wegen des gedrängs darvon bleiben müßen, welche doch gerne hinein wären.

14. Sächs HStA Loc. 10299/1 [unfoliated], "Der Rath zu Dreßden" to Johann Georg II, 13 May 1668.

Alß E. Churf. Durchl. den 9. *huius* Unß gnädigst befohlen:

Weil denen Keÿserl: und Königl: *Residen*ten die gnädigste meinung wegen des Meßopffers, so alhier bißhero gehalten werden wollen, hinterbracht, So solten Wir wenn erwehnter *Cultus* beÿ denen *Residen*ten ferner *celebri*ret werden möchte, darauff ein wachsames auge haben, und nach befindung unterthänigsten Bericht hievon erstatten, Haben solchen gnädigsten befehl zu pflichtschuldigster folge, Wir durch ein paar geschworne Viertelsmeister diese *feri*en über uffsehen laßen, ob das Meßopffer beÿ den Keÿserl. *Residen*ten wie zuvor als auch nuhnmehro *celebri*ret würde, und ob sich einzige frembde Persohnen dabeÿ eingefunden, Welche dann heutiges tages berichtet, daß das Meßopffer beÿ ernanten *Residen*ten in güldenen Adler alhier diese *feri*en über alle 3. tage wie hiebevor geschehen, *celebri*ret worden, es wehren die thüren auch zwischen 8. und 9. Uhren, wie sonsten, uffgewesen, Sie hetten gesehen, Daß des Croaten Rittmeisters Ehefrau dahin kommen und der Herr *Gen*: Kepliers, so wehren auch die Italiänischen Hoff *Musican*ten und andere Italiäner als Citronen händler und dergleichen unterschiedene *Croaten*, etzliche weibes Persohnen und Handtwercks bursche so Sie nicht gekennet diese Feÿertage über in den Meße gewesen.

15. Sächs HStA Loc. 10331/8, fol. 16; Excerpt from Johann Georg's Published Decree Prohibiting Attendance at Mass, 10 February 1676.

Im übrigen aber nicht alleine Unserm OberAmbtManne und dem Rathe allhier/ iedesmahl genaue Auffsicht und fleißige Nachforschung darauf zu legen/ und/ da sie etwas in Erfahrung bracht/ Unß solches ungesäumt zu berichten/ sondern auch dem *Commendant*en absonderlich hiermit befohlen haben wollen/ daß er an behörigen Orten zu denen bekanten Stunden/ durch einen *Officier* und zugeordnete Mannschafft gewisse Anstalt machen solle/ wordurch die zu solcher Meße ankommende/ sie seyn zu Fuße/ Kutschen oder Pferde/ davon abgehalten/ die aber/ so im herauß gehen sich betreten lassen / oder/ wenn sie zurücke getrieben werden/ sich zu widersetzen unterstehen/ nach Gelegenheit der Person in *Arrest* genommen/ oder Unserer Landes=Regierung zu nachdrücklicher *animadversion* alsobald nahmhaft gemacht/ ingleichen die in *arrest* genommene/ wann sie in Hoff= und Kriegs=Diensten/ oder unter das Ambt gehörig/ Unserm OberAmbtManne/ die übrigen aber dem Rathe allhier zu fernerer *Inqvisition* und Bestraffung ungesäumt abgefolget werden.

16. Heinrich Müller, *Geistliche Erquickstunden* (1666), in Winfried Zeller, ed., *Der Protestantismus des 17. Jahrhunderts* (Bremen: Schünemann, 1962), 296–97.

Der Glaube ist das Auge, damit wir Jesum ansehen. Ein blödes Auge ist auch ein Auge, ein weinendes Auge ist auch ein Auge. . . . Der Glaube ist die Hand, damit wir Jesum ergreifen. Eine bebende Hand ist auch eine Hand. Ach, der glaubt, dem das Herz im Leibe bebt, wenn er zugreifen und Jesum fassen soll. . . . Der Glaube ist der Zunge, damit wir schmecken, wie freundlich der Herr ist. Eine am Geschmack geschwächte Zunge ist auch eine Zunge. Auch dann glauben wir, wenn wir kein Tröpflein Trostes schmecken. . . . Der Glaube ist der Fuß, der uns zu Jesus trägt. Ein kranker Fuß ist auch ein Fuß; wer langsam kommt, kommt auch.

17. Andreas Hirsch, *Kircherus Jesuita Germanus Germania redonatus: . . . Das ist/ Philosophischer Extract und Auszug . . . Musurgia Universali; Liber IV. Diacriticus, Pars I. Erotematica, Die 6. Frag:* "Ob/ warum/ und wie die Music eine Kraft hab/ die Gemüter der Menschen zu bewegen/ und obs wahr sei was von den Wunder=würckungen der alten Music geschriben wird," 135–37 (cf. Kircher, *Musurgia Universalis* I, Lib. VII, 549–50).

Ist also zu wissen/ daß ein solche heftige Bewegung auf vilerlei weis bei den Menschen entstehen kan: 1. Uber= und Widernatürlich/ durch die Kraft deß leidigen Teufels/ dann derselbe kan *ad sonum cytharae*, als ein Zeichen deß gemachten Bunds/ die *humores* deß Menschlichen Leibs also mächtig conturbiren und beunruhigen/ daß Tollheit/ Unsinnigkeit/ Wüterey/ und andere dergleichen *impetus* entstehen müssen. Wie man von einem Cytharisten deß Königs in Dänemarck lieset/ daß er den König zu solchem *furore* erreget/ daß derselbe in seiner *rabie* 2. von den Seinigen umgebracht/ welches nicht anderster/ als mit deß Teuffels Hülf/ wie aus den Umständen zu sehen/ hat geschehen können. Der 2. *modus* ist vermischt/ halb Natürlich/ halb über= und wider=natürlich/ dann die Besessene vom Teufel/ wie Saul gewesen/ und andere/ wann durch die Music der Dampf der schwartzen aufgeschwollenen Gallen/ welchen die Teufel/

wann sie die Hertzen perturbiren wollen/ gar gern einzunehmen pflegen/ vertriben wird/ so können sie darvon erlöset werden. Der 3. ist blos Natürlich/ geschicht durch den harmonischen *sonum*, darzu gehören notwendig 4. *conditiones*, mangelt eine/ so hat sie ihre Würckung nicht. Die 1. ist die Harmony selbsten. Die 2. ist die Zahl und die *proportio*. Die 3. die Red selbsten/ oder der Wörter/ so da müssen ausgesprochen werden/ Kraft und Würckung. Die 4. die Beschaffenheit und Fähigkeit deß Zuhörers; und zwar/ die Harmony hat solche Kraft in das Menschliche Gemüt/ so viel sie nach dem harmonischen *motu* deß Lufts den innerlichen eingepflantzten Luft oder lebendigen Geist gleichmässig moviret und beweget/ daher die Lust und Süssigkeit der Music. Komt nun hinzu der *determinirt* und *proportionirte numerus*, so hat die Harmony doppelte Würckung/ bewegt das Gemüt nicht nur zu innerlichen Affecten/ sondern auch zu äusserlichen Leibs=Bewegungen/ wie in dem Tantzen/ . . . . Komt ferner die Kraft der Red hinzu/ sonderlich wann sie pathetisch beweglich ist/ ein schöne Histori/ oder traurigen Fall in sich hält/ so hat die Harmony überaus grosse Kraft allerhand *affectus* zu erregen/ doch muß *animus dispositus, capacitas audientis* vorher gehen/ sonsten würde man eher einen Stein/ als einen Menschen bewegen können.

18. Andreas Hirsch, *Kircherus Jesuita Germanus Germania redonatus: . . . Das ist/ Philosophischer Extract und Auszug . . . Musurgia Universali; Liber IV. Diacriticus, Pars II. Pragmatica, Caput 3.* "*Von der Pathetischen Music/ wann und wo sie anzurichten?*," 153 (cf. Kircher, *Musurgia Universalis* I, Lib. VII, 578).

Musica pathetica ist nichts anderster/ als eine harmonische *melothesi* oder Composition/ von einem erfahrnen *musurgo* der Kunst nach also zugerichtet/ daß sie den Zuhörer bald zu disem/ bald zu einem andern *affectu* bewegen kan; darzu gehören diese 4. *conditiones*: 1. soll der Componist ein solch *thema* erwehlen/ das den Affect zu erwägen dienlich ist. 2. daß er das vorgenommene *thema* in einen bequemen Ton bringe. 3. daß er den *rythmum* oder die Mensur der Wörter nach dem harmonischen *rythmo* einrichte. 4. daß er die Composition von erfahrnen Sängern/ zu bequemer Zeit/ und an bequemen Ort pronunciren und singen lasse.

19. Andreas Hirsch, *Kircherus Jesuita Germanus Germania redonatus: . . . Das ist/ Philosophischer Extract und Auszug . . . Musurgia Universalis; Liber IV. Diacriticus, Pars II. Pragmatica, Caput 4.* "*Von der Pathetischen Music selbsten/ wie sie soll ins Werck gesetzet werden*," 156–57 (cf. Kircher, *Musurgia Universalis* I, Lib. VII, 580).

Underschiedliche Affecten finden sich bei den Menschen/ und einerlei *objecta* können nicht einerlei *subjecta* zu gleichen Affecten bewegen; die Ursach diser Discrepantz zu ergründen/ hat der *author* etwas sonderbares understanden/ hat 8. vornehmste *affectus* erwehlet/ als Lieb/ Leid/ Freud/ Zorn/ Klagen/ Traurigkeit/ Stoltz/ Verzweiflung/ etc. vor dieselbe hat er aus der Heil. Schrift so viel Text oder *themata*, so sich auf diese Affecten ziehen/ ausgezogen/ hats 8. der allervortreflichsten Componisten in gantz Europa überschickt/ und gebeten/ ieder solte diese 8. *themata* setzen nach allen Kunst=Regeln/ und darinnen die gedachte Affecten wohl in acht nehmen/ und sie bester massen exprimiren; dardurch hat er erfahren wollen/ zu welchen Affecten eines ieden Geist/ erstlich die

Componisten selbsten/ darnach ihre Zuhörer/ incliniren würden/ ob alle *Natio-nes, Italia, Germania, Anglia, Gallia,* in dergleichen Affecten überein stimmen/ oder wider einander seyn würden/ und worinnen solche Discrepantz bestehe/ und dardurch hat er zur völligen *restauration* der Pathetischen Music kommen wollen: aber weil die Componisten gar lang verzogen/ ist sein Music=Werck ohn ihre Composition heraus gangen/ sollen doch in einem absonderlichen Buch hernacher folgen.

20. Sächs HStA Loc. 12026, fol. 233r–v; Johann Georg's Proto-*Kirchen-Ordnung*, Fall 1657.

Was S.r Churfurstl: Durchl: ungefehrliche gnedigste meinung wie es ins künfftige mit denen Fest tagen, durchs ganze Jaar zuhalten, und bevorstehende *Advent* Zeit anzufahen, wehre.

1. Würden alle hohe= auch andere fest abente lateinische *Vesper* gehalten.
2. Den ersten *Advent* Sontag, als anfangs des kirchen newen Jaares, würde Vor- und nachmittage geprediget.
3. An den Heil. Christ= Oster= und Pfingst fest würde den ersten tag nach lößung 3.er Stücken auff dem kreüz Thurm, umb 4. uhr, biß halbweg 5. uhr daß fest eingelauttet, und diese tage vor und nach mittage geprediget.
4. Den St: Stephans tag, ingleichen den Oster= und Pfingst Montag, würde vor= und nachmittage geprediget.
5. Den St: Johannis Evangelisten=, Oster= und Pfingst Dienstag würde vormittags Predigt, mittags aber nur *Vesper* gehalten.
6. In der Charwochen, würde von Sontag *Palmarum* biß auff dem Charfreÿtag die ganze Woche geprediget, den Grünen Donnerstag, der *Communion* wegen aber, Vor= und Nachmittage. NB. Wann aber das fest der empfängnüß Christi in der Char Woche, oder Oster tag gefiele, würde es an dem Sontag *Palmarum celebri*ret.
7. Den newen Jaars tag, tag der empfängnüß Christi, Himmel Farts tag, *Trinitatis,* und *Michaelis,* würde vor= und nachmittage geprediget.
8. Der Heil. Dreÿ König Tag, Lichtmeß, *Johannis Baptist:*[,] *Visitationis Mariae,* und Mariae Magdalenae, würde vormittage Predigt, und nachmittags *Vesper* gehalten.

21. Sächs HStA OHMA N I Nr. 8 [unfoliated]; Description of the Chapel on the Eve of Advent 4, 1677.

Wie geliebts GOTT künfftiges M.DC.LXXVIII. Jahr das heylige Christ Fest zu halten. Sonnabend den 22. December / 1. Januarÿ würde die Kirche folgender gestalt bekleidet. Der Umbhang des Predigtstuhls wehre von Weißem Atlas, mit Seidenen Blumen durchnehet, worinnen wie Christus im Tempel denen hohrern zuhöret. Der Altar mit einem Roth Sammeten mit Gold gebremten und gestickten Marien-Bilde, so den Herrn Christum, wie er vom Creüz abgenommen, auff der Schoß hält. Auff dem Altar stünde das Elffenbeinerne Crucifix, und Silbere vergüldete *embellir*te Leüchter mit weißen Wachskerzen. Der Chor würde mit Tapeten, worein die Churf. *Provinz*-Wappen gewircket, ingleichen der Fußboden mit geblümten Tapeten bekleidet, sambt Roth Sammeten Stühlen und Küßen zubereitet. Die Kirche würde mit Gold und Seidenreichen gewirckten Tapeten bekleidet, in welchen nach benandte *Historien.* Zur Rechten Hand des Altars das Abendmahl, und zur linken deßelben die Auffarth Christi. Über der Kirch-Thür das *Ecce Homo*. Daneben unter dem Schwibbogen, wo die Räthe stehen, die Verurtheilung und Handwaschung *Pilati*. Unter dem Churf. Kirch-stüblein, die Himmelfarth, Über der *Sacristeÿ* die Außführung. Zur Rechten Hand des Predigtstuhls, wie Christus am Creÿz, Unter dem Frauenzimmer Schwibbogen die Abnehmung, Aufferstehung und Höllenfarth Christi. An der Churf. Empor-Kirche, die Geburth Christi und Heyl. Dreÿ Könige. Am Kirch-stüblein ein Roth Sammetter Umbhang, woran das Dänische, Chur-Sächsische, und Brandenburgische gestickte Wappen. Und verbliebe diese Bekleydung biß Freytags, da sie wiederumb abgenommen würde.

22. OHMA N I Nr. 8 [unfoliated], entry for 25 December 1677; Description of the pre-service protocol on Christmas Day 1677.

Dienstag den 25. *December*. Am Heÿl: Christ Tage[.] Bläset der Haußmann frühe umb 3 Uhr aufm Schloß Thurm, worauff das Glocken Spiel eine gute halbe Stunde gebraucht wird, und dann umb 4 Uhr aufm Creuzthurm dreÿ halbe 3 lb: Schlangen scharff gelöhst werden, folgends aufm Schloß, Inn und außerhalb der Festung, so wohl auch zu Alten Dreßden, mit allen Glocken, das Fest biß halbweg 5 Uhr eingelautet, darauff aufm Schloßhoff und vor dem Schloß in Zwinger, die Schallmeÿ Pfeiffer Geistliche Lieder blasen, Nachdem halbweg 7. Uhr zum ersten mahl gelautet ziehen die *Guardien* auff, und stellen sich die Trabanten von dem fördern Schloß Thore durch den fordern Hoff, biß durch das innere Schloß Thor, Darauf ziehet die *Compag:* Schweitzer Trabanten in das Schloß, und stellet sich zwischen dem Grünen Thor und Keller. Worauff die 3. *Compag:* von der Unter *Guardie* durch *march*iren, und stellen sich im Zwinger vor das Schloß, beÿm Gold Hause, welchen das Fähnlein Büchßenmeister folget, beÿm Münzberge aufm Hohen Wall zeücht, und aufm feuerwercks Platz sich stellt, denen folgt das Freÿ Fähnel, so sich neben die Unter *Guardie* stellet, Alß denn werden 3. *Salven* gegeben, iedes mahl 3. halbe Carthaunen aufm hohen Wahl, und von den 4 *Compag*nien, So dann ziehet der *Compag:* Schweitzer Trabanten durch das Grüne Thor und Stall wieder ab, denen die 3 *Compag*nien von der Unter *Guardie* und das Freÿ Fähnel folgen. Das Büchßenmeister Fähnel aber zeücht den Münzberg hinauff über die Festung ins Zeughauß, Die Hochteützschen Trabanten biß unter das fördere Thor, und besetzen die Wachen. Nach dem halbweg 8 Uhr zum dritten mahl gelautet, würde der Gottesdienst folgendergestallt gehalten, und *dirig*irte die *Music*, sowohl in der *Vesper*, wie auch folgendes Tages der Capellmeister *Vincenzo Albrici*.

23. SLUB K 80, fols. 47v–48r; Description of the Easter Tapestries, 1665.

Sonnabend den 25. *Martÿ*, am Heÿligen Oster Abende, ward die Kirche folgender gestalt bekleidet, Der Predigt Stuhl, Altar und Chor, gleich wie am Fest *Annunciationis Mariae*, auff dem Altar stunde das gewöhnliche Silberne *Crucifix* und Leüchter, die Kirche wahre mit Goldt und Seÿdenreich gewürckten Tapeten bekleidet, worinnen nachbenente Historien, An der Churf. Empor Kirche der Öhlbergk, unter den Frauenzimmer Schwiebbogen, wie Christus in gartten gefangen wirdt, unter den Schwiebbogen darneben, wie Er vor Caipha geführet worden, darbeÿ zur rechten Handt des Predigt Stuhls die Geißlung, Über der Sacresteÿ die Crönung, über der Kirchthür das *Ecce Homo*, darneben die Verurtheilung undt Handtwaschung Pilati, dann unter der Räthe Schwiebbogen die Ausführung, darnebenst die Creützigung, undt unter den Churf. Kirch Stüblein, das Osterlamb.

24. SLUB K 117 fols. 57r–59r; Description of the Chapel on Johann Georg's Birthday in 1673.

Sr: Churfl: Durchl: zu Sachsen, 61. Geburts Tag. Sonnabend, den 31. *Maÿ*, wurde früh halbweg 5. Uhr zum Ersten, umb 5. Uhr zum Andern, und halbweg 6. Uhr zum Dritten mahl gelautet: Die Kirche war folgender gestalt bekleidet: der Altar und Predigt Stuhl mit den Carmosin-roht sammeten, reich mit Gold und Perlen gestickten Umbhängen: Der Chor und Empor Kirchen, mit rothen sammeten Umbhängen, an welchen an der Churfürstlichen Empor Kirche gestickte Wapen, der Fußboden im Chor, ganz mit rothen Tuch bekleidet. Auff dem Altar stunde das Elfenbeinern *Crucifix*, und die 2. ganz vergoldeten *amÿli*rten großen Leüchter, Und wardt der kleine goldene Kelch, sambt der Paten, und aller zubehör gebrauchet. Die Unterhalt Tüchlein waren von Gold und Silbern Stück. Das Ambt hielt der Mittlere Hoff Prediger, das Meßgewandt war Carmosin roth Sammet, reich mit Gold und Perlen gestickt. Nach halbweg 5. Uhr *confit*irten Sr. Churf. Durch., Umb halbweg 6. Uhr gingen Sie hinunter in die Kirche, allwo mit der Orgel so lange *praeambul*irt wardt, bis Sie in dero Stuhl, darauff ginge der Gottes Dienst folgender Gestalt an:

25. Heinrich Müller, *Thränen- und Trost-Quelle, bey Erklärung der Geschichte, von der Grossen Sünderin* (Hanover, 1724). Excerpt from Betrachtung VII: "Die Thränenquillende Sünderin," 218–19.

Diß Weib weinete, da die andern zu Tische sassen. Bey der Mahlzeit trägt sie ihr Thränen-Gericht mit auf. Wie muß sie für Schmertzen gebrandt haben, die sich nicht geschämet, bey der Mahlzeit zu weinen. Petrus weinete auch, da er seinen Meister verleugnet hatte, aber er gieng hinaus, und suchte seine Thränen zu verbergen. Diß Weib weinet öffentlich, und zwar, da die Gäste zu Tische sitzen. Wer kan den See aufhalten, wann er sich ergossen hat? in ihr hatte sich ein Thränen-See ergossen, den kein Scham, noch sonst etwas aufhalten konte. Sie sahe, daß den andern ein Mahl zubereitet war, so gedachte sie ihr selbst auch ein Mahl anzurichten, ein Mahl von Thränen-Brodt und Thränen-Tranck. Da sich andere erquickten an der Speise, suchte sie ihre Erquickung in den Thränen.* Der Regen erquicket das dürre Erdreich, und die Thränen die durstige Seele der Gerechten. Daher spricht David: Die Thränen sind meine Speise Tag und Nacht. Er hat die Erquickung an den Thränen, die andere haben an der Speise, und da sich andre satt essen, kan er sich doch nicht satt weinen, da andere nur des Tags essen, da weinet er Tag und Nacht. So muß denen, die GOtt lieben, alles zum besten dienen. Die Thränen selbst müssen ihre Speise, das Leyd ihre Freude, die Trübsal ihr Labsal seyn.

---

*Bonæ lacrymæ, spricht Ambrosius, in quibus refectio est justorum. Justi enim vox est: fuerunt mihi lacrymæ meæ panes die ac nocte.

Appendix II: Sacred Vocal Works of the Principal Dresden Court Composers

Extant Collections

A-Wn	Vienna, Österreichische Nationalbibliothek, Musiksammlung
CZ-KRa	Kroměříž, Arcibiskupský zámek, hudební sbírka (Liechtenstein Collection)
CZ-Pkřiž	Prague, Rytířský řád křižovníků s červenou hvůzdou, hudební sbírka (Order of Knights of the Cross with the Red Star, Music Collection)
D-B	Berlin, Staatsbibliothek zu Berlin – Preußischer Kulturbesitz, Musikabteilung mit Mendelssohn-Archiv (sources found predominantly in the Bokemeyer Collection)
D-BNms	Bonn, Musikwissenschaftliches Seminar der Rheinischen Friedrich-Wil-helm- Universität
D-F	Frankfurt, Stadt- und Universitätsbibliothek, Musik- und Theaterabteilung
D-TRb	Trier, Bistumsarchiv
GB-Och	Oxford, Christ Church Library
RUS-Mk	Moscow, Naucnaja muzykaľnaja biblioteka im. S. I. Taneeva Moskovskoj gosudarstvennoj konservatorii im. P. I.
SLUB	Dresden, Sächsische Landesbibliothek – Staats- und Universitätsbibliothek Dresden (D-Dl), Grimma Collection
S-Uu	Uppsala, University Library, Düben Collection
	VMHS: Vokal musik i handskrift
	IMHS: Instrumental musik i handskrift

Inventories of Lost Works:

Ansbach (Schaal 1966)
Dresden Instrument Chamber Catalog (Sächs HStA Loc. 7207; in Spagnoli 1990:223–38)
Leipzig (Schering 1918–19)
Lüneburg (Seiffert 1907–08)
Rudolstadt (Baselt 1963)
Weißenfels (Gundlach 2001)

For a list of lost works, see Frandsen 1997-2:25–32.

Scoring Abbreviations:

S	Soprano (labeled "Cantus" in the sources)
A	Alto
T	Tenor
B	Bass
Rip	Ripieno
Vl	Violin
Va	Viola (da braccio)
Vdg	Viola da gamba
Vta	Violetta
Vc	Violoncello
Vle	Violone
Cor	Cornetto
Cnto	Cornettino
Clr	Clarino (natural trumpet)
Trb	Trombone
Bsn	Bassoon
Th	Theorbo
Tmp	Timpani
Org	Organ
Sp	Spinetta
Bc	Basso continuo
Inst	Instrument(s)
pts	parts
sco	score
tab	tablature
/	indicates "or"
d.	dated

Notes

Scorings in the Düben Collection (S-Uu)

In both the part sets and the tablature sources in the Düben collection, one often encounters the abbreviation "Viol:" or "Viol" as an indicator of string parts. This abbreviation has been resolved in the catalog below in the following manner: when the string parts are labeled specifically as violin or viola in a concordant source in S-Uu, "Viol" is taken to mean violin or viola and is indicated as such in the list of instruments. If the meaning of the copyist's use of "Viol:" cannot be resolved, as is the case with works such as Peranda's *O Jesu mi dulcissime* (VMHS 84:51), "Viol" has been allowed to stand. If the tablature is a unique source and refers to the strings as "Viol," the range of the relevant parts has been considered in the list of instruments (see Albrici's *Dixit Dominus*).

Performance Dates

1. All dates refer to Dresden performances.

2. Performance dates are not given for psalm settings, as the absence of scorings renders it impossible to determine which setting was performed on a particular day.

3. The three days of the high feasts of Christmas, Easter, and Pentecost are indicated with Roman numerals, e.g. Christmas I, II, III.

4. Ordinary Sundays during the seasons of the church year are indicated with Arabic numbers, e.g. Trinity 1, 2, 3, etc. Morning services are indicated as "AM," vesper services as "Vespers."

5. Sundays that are known by their Latin names are given as such (*Septuagesima, Sexagesima*, etc.).

6. Most of the diary entries follow the title of the work with the name or initials of the composer; these are not reproduced here.

Vocal Ensembles in the Dresden Repertoire

A number of works by Peranda and Albrici are scored for two vocal ensembles. In each case, the first group listed represents the parts for soloists, or *favoriti* as they are often designated in the manuscript sources, and the second group represents the parts for ripienists—those singers who double the soloists in certain sections of the composition. None of these are polychoral works in the traditional sense (i.e., works with two equal choirs).

Works of Albrici in Prague

Jan Enberg recently discovered that a number of additional compositions by Albrici may also have survived in several libraries in Prague (private correspondence with the author, July 2002), but the author has been unable to ascertain whether or not this is the case. In this works list, only those pieces listed in the RISM A/II catalog as surviving in CZ-Pkřiž have been included.

WORKS LISTS

VINCENZO ALBRICI

Amo te, laudo te

| S-Uu | VMHS 47:4 (pts) | SS, 2 Cnto, Bsn, Vle, Sp, Org |
| | VMHS 82:2 (tab) | SS, 2 Cnto, Bsn, Sp |

PERFORMANCES

1662: Advent 1, Vespers (SLUB Q 240)

Aurora lucis emicat

| D-B | Mus. ms. 501, no. 18 | SATB, SATB, 2 Vl, 2Vla, Bsn, 2 Cnto, 2 Trb, Bc |

Ave regina

| D-TRb | 104/004 01 (Nr. 4) | STB, Bc |

Ave Jesu Christe, rex benedicte

D-B	Mus. ms. 501, no. 6	SSB, 2 Vl, Bsn, Bc
S-Uu	VMHS 1:3 (pts, d. 1685)	SSB, 2 Vl, Bsn/Va, Org; 2 Va *ad lib.*
	VMHS 81:49 (tab)	SSB, 2 Vl, Bsn, Bc; 2 Va

PERFORMANCES

1662: Trinity Sunday, Vespers; Trinity 19, AM (SLUB Q 240)

Benedicte Domine Jesu Christe

| S-Uu | VMHS 1:4 (pts) | SSB, 2 Cnto/2 Vl, Bsn/Vdg, Bc |
| | VMHS 81:54 (tab) | SSB, 2 Cnto, Bsn, Bc |

PERFORMANCES

1660: Christmas III, Vespers (Sächs HStA Loc. 12026, fol. 60r)
1662: Purification (Feb. 2), Vespers; Visitation (July 2), AM (SLUB Q 240)

Modern edition in Frandsen 1997-3:2–25.

Christus resurgens

| D-TRb | 104/004 01 (Nr. 3) | STB, Bc |

Cogita o homo

D-B	Mus. ms. 501, no. 16	SATB, 2 Vl, Bc
SLUB*	1738-E-515 (pts)	SATB, 2 Vl, Bc
S-Uu	VMHS 1:5 (pts, d. 1663)	SATB, 2 Vl, Bsn/Va, Bc; Rip: S, 2 Va *ad lib.*
	VMHS 77:89 (tab)	SATB, 2 Vl, Bsn, Bc
	VMHS 79:6 (tab)	SATB, 2 Vl, Bsn, Bc; 2 Inst

PERFORMANCES

1662: Purification (Feb. 2), Vespers; Pentecost III, Vespers (SLUB Q 240)
1673: Epiphany 2, AM (SLUB K 117, fol. 21v)
1676: Feast of St. Matthew (Sept. 21), AM (SLUB Q 260)

Modern edition in Frandsen 1997-3:27–58.

---

*SLUB 1738-E-515 bears an attribution to Peranda, which is refuted by references to the work as a composition of Albrici in court diaries from 1662, 1673, and 1676 (SLUB Q 240, entries for 2 February and 20 May 1662; SLUB K 117, fol. 21v, entry for 19 January 1673; SLUB Q 260, entry for 21 September 1676), as well as the existence of concordant sources attributed to Albrici.

Dixit Dominus

S-Uu   VMHS 82:3 (tab)   SSATB, 2 Vl, Bc

Dixit Dominus

D-B   Mus. ms. 501, no. 14   SATB, 2 Vl, 2 Va, Bsn, Bc

Domine Deus exercituum rex

D-B   Mus. ms. 501, no. 17   SATB, SATB, 2 Vl, 2 Va, Bsn, 2 Cor, 3 Trb, Bc

Ecce plangendo

S-Uu   VMHS 86:25 (tab)   ATB, 2 Vl, Bc

Modern edition in Frandsen 1997-3:60–69.

Ego sum resurrectio

D-TRb   104/004 01 (Nr. 2)   STB, Bc
D-TRb   104/121 11   STB, Bc

Factum est praelium

CZ-Pkřiž   XXXV A 55   SSATB, SSATB, 2 Vl, 2 Va, Vle, 2 Cor, 2 Trb, Bsn, 4 Clr, Tmp, Bc

PERFORMANCES

1662: St. Michael (Sept. 29) (SLUB Q 240)
1677: St. Michael (Sept. 29): "Motett: Factum est proelium, mit Trompeten und Paucken" (Sächs HStA Loc. 8682 Nr. 11, fol. 120r)

Fader wår

S-Uu   VMHS 1:6 (pts)   SSATB, 2 Vl, Bc; Rip: SSA, Vl, 2 Va

Haec quae ter triplici

D-Trb   104/004 01 (Nr. 1)   STB, Bc

Hymnum jucunditatis

D-B   Mus. ms. 501, no. 3   SS, 2 Vl, Bsn, Bc
S-Uu**   VMHS 83:65a   SS, Bc
SLUB**   1738-E-532   SS, Bc

**Both the S-Uu and SLUB sources attribute the work to Peranda and lack the violin parts. However, the morning worship service held in conjunction with the 1660 "Friedens-Fest" included a performance of *Hymnum jucunditatis*, and the list of music performed in the service attributes all of the compositions to Albrici (Sächs HStA OHMA N IV Nr. 1, fols. 13r, 16r). The Weißenfels and Rudolstadt inventories also attribute the work to Albrici; neither entry includes violin parts (Gundlach 2001:252; Baselt 1963:115).

1660: *Friedens-Fest/Jubilate*, AM: "Motettino. a. 2. Soprani, 2. Violini, un fagotto con un Spinettino." (Sächs HStA OHMA N IV Nr. 1, fols. 13r, 16r)
1662: Pentecost I, Vespers (SLUB Q 240)

Modern edition in Frandsen 1997-3:71–92.

In convertendo Dominus

| S-Uu | VMHS 1:10 (pts) | SSATB, SATB, 2 Vl, Bc |

In convertendo Dominus

S-Uu	VMHS 47:6 (pts)	SSATB, SSATB, 2 Vl, 2 Va, Bsn, 2 Cor, 3 Trb, Bc
SLUB	1821-E-503 (sco)	SSATB, SATB, 2 Vl, 2 Va, Bsn, Bc
	1821-E-503a (pts)	SSATB, SSATB, 2 Vl, 2 Va, Bsn, 2 Cnto, 2 Trb, Bc

In te Domine speravi

S-Uu	VMHS 1:8 (pts)	A, 2 Vl, Bsn, Org
	VMHS 79:82 (tab)	A, 2 Vl, Bc
	VMHS 81:67 (tab)	A, 2 Vl, Bsn, Bc

Modern edition in Frandsen 1997-3:94–114

Jesu dulcis memoria

| S-Uu | VMHS 1:9 (pts) | SAB, 3 Va, Bc |
| | VMHS 82:4 (tab) | SAB, 3 Va, Bc |

1661: New Year's Day, AM (Sächs HStA Loc. 12026, fol. 64r); Advent 4, Vespers (SLUB Q 240)
1662: Birthday of Johann Georg II (May 31), Vespers; Advent 1, Vespers (SLUB Q 240)

Modern edition in Frandsen 1997-3:116–31.

Jesu nostra redemptio

S-Uu	VMSH 42:6 (pts)	SATB, 2 Vl, Bsn, Vle, Th; Va, 2 Va
	VMHS 47:5 (pts)	SATB, 2 Vl, Bsn, Org
	VMHS 86:28 (tab)	SATB, 2 Vl, Bc

Laboravi clamans

| S-Uu | VMHS 1:11 (pts) | SSATB, 2 Vl, Org |
| | VMHS 80:167 (tab) | 5 vocal pts, 2 Vl, Bc |

Modern edition in Frandsen 1997-3:133–55.

Laetatus sum in his

| S-Uu | VMHS 47:8 (pts) | SATTB, 2 Vl, 2 Va, Bsn, Org |
| | VMHS 84:101 (tab) | SATTB, 5 inst, Bc |

Laudate pueri Dominum

| D-B | Mus. ms. 501, no. 19 | SATB, SATB, 2 Vl, 2 Va, Bsn, 2 Vl, 3 Trb, Bc |

Laudate pueri Dominum

| S-Uu | VMHS 1:13 (pts) | SSB, Org |
| GB-Och | Mus. 1034B (sco)† | SSB, Org |

Laudate pueri Dominum

| S-Uu | VMHS 47:7 (pts) | SSATB, SATB, 2 Vl, 3 Va, Org |
| | VMHS 82:5 (tab, d. 1666) | 9 vocal pts, 2/5 Va, Bc |

*Manifeste est pietatis sacramentum**

| SLUB | 1471-E-500 | SS, Bc |

Mihi autem bonum est

S-Uu	VMHS 1:15 (pts)	S/T, 2 Vl, Vdg/Bsn, Bc
	VMHS 77:131 (tab, d. 1664)	T, 2 Vl, Bsn, Bc
	VMHS 81:58 (tab)	T, 2 Vl, Bsn, Bc

Modern edition in Frandsen 1997-3:157–69.

Misericordias Domini

S-Uu	VMHS 1:14a (pts)	ATB, 2 Vl, Org
	VMHS 1:14 (pts)	ATB, 2 Vl, Vle, Org, Th (lacks final Alleluia)
	VMHS 81:56 (tab)	ATB, 2 Vl, Trb, Bsn, Bc (Trb in Sinfonia only)

†Formerly attributed to Peranda; see the catalog in preparation by John Milsom. (The author thanks Dr. Milsom for a fruitful exchange concerning this manuscript.)

*The manuscript, to which Peter Wollny first called attention, attributes the work to "Signor Vincens"; Wollny suggests that the work is an early composition by Albrici (Wollny 2001:13, 18–19). The scoring and key are identical to a work attributed to Albrici in the Ansbach inventory, where it is listed under "Musicalia Vom Alborizi" as "Manifeste. â 2. Canto. ex D x. stehet in der Partitur. bey des Gratiani Stücken" (Schaal 1966:44). The attribution, however, is not unproblematic, as the same title (with the same scoring) also appears in the same inventory among works of Gratiani and among those by "unknown authors" (ibid., 41, 67). Susanne Shigihara suggested that *Manifeste* might be a work of Gratiani, given its inclusion in the same inventory with works of that composer (Shigihara 1984:128). A number of stylistic and harmonic features cause this author to remain unconvinced of its attribution to Albrici.

PERFORMANCES

1662: *Septuagesima*, AM; Trinity 4, AM (SLUB Q 240)

Modern edition in Frandsen 1997-3:171–83.

Missa (Kyrie, Gloria, Credo)

SLUB	1821-D-1 (sco)	5 vocal pts (cleffing: C1, C1, C3, C4, F4), 5 insts. (cleffing: G2, G2, C3, C4, F4), 4 Tpt, Tmp, Bc; Rip pts indicated by rubrics in the score

Mortales audite

D-B	Mus. ms. 501, no. 5	SS, 2 Vl, Bc
S-Uu	VMHS 47:10 (pts)	SS, 2 Vl, Org, Th
	VMHS 85:52 (tab)	SS, 2 Vl, Org, Th

O admirabile commercium

D-B	Mus. ms. 501, no. 15	SATB, 2 Vl, Bsn, Bc

O amantissime sponse

D-B	Mus. ms. 501, no. 11	SSB, 2 Vl, Bc

O bone Jesu charitas

S-Uu	VMHS 77:136 (tab)	SA, 3 Vl, Bc

PERFORMANCES**

1662: Easter II, Vespers; Feast of St. Michael (Sept. 29), Vespers (SLUB Q 240)
1673: Pentecost Eve, Vespers (SLUB K 117, fol. 50v)

Modern edition in Frandsen 1997-3:185–94.

O cor meum (earlier version, tablature d. 2 February 1664)

S-Uu	VMHS 1:16 (pts)	SS, 2/5 Va, Org
	VMHS 77:114 (tab)	SS, 2/5 Va, Bc

**All entries give the title as "O bone Jesu," and thus may refer instead to Albrici's *O bone Jesu, verbum Patris*, now lost. However, the latter title does not appear in a diary entry until 1673 (SLUB K 117), and Grusnick suggested a copying date of ca. 1663 for VMHS 77:136 (Grusnick 1966:81). Thus the 1662 references to the title *O bone Jesu* quite likely refer to Albrici's extant composition.

PERFORMANCES

1660: Sunday after Christmas (Dec. 30), AM (Sächs HStA Loc. 12026, fol. 60v); as this diary does not include scoring of works performed during the services, the version heard on this date cannot be determined with certainty.

~~Modern edition in Frandsen 1997-3:196–222.~~

O cor meum (later version, tablature d. 1671)

S-Uu	VMHS 47:11 (pts)	SS, 2 Vl, Org
	VMHS 84:26 (tab)	SS, 2 Vl, Bc

PERFORMANCES

1660: (see previous entry)

Modern edition in Frandsen 1997-3:224–45.

O Jesu Alpha et Omega

D-B	Mus. ms. 501, no. 7	SAB, 2 Vl, Bc

O quam terribilis est domus tua†

S-Uu	VMHS 29:8a	SS, Bc

Omnia quae fecit Deus

D-B	Mus. ms. 501, no. 1	S, 2 Vl, Bsn, Bc
S-Uu	VMHS 1:17 (pts)	S/T, 2 Vl, Trb/Va, Bc
	VMHS 1:47 (tab)	T, 2 Vl, Bsn, Bc

Omnis caro foenum

D-B	Mus. ms. 501, no. 13	SATB, 2 Vl, Vta, Bc
SLUB	1821-E-501 (pts)	SATB, Cnto, Vl, Trb, Bsn, Org
	1821-E-502 (pts)	SATB, Cnto, Vl, Trb, Bsn, Bc
S-Uu	VMHS 81:51 (tab)	SATB, 2 Vl, Trb, Bsn, Bc
Continuatio Theatri Musici		SATB, 4 Vl or Vdg, Bc

(Würzburg: Bencard, 1669, attributed to Samuel Capricornus)

†Rejected as a work of Albrici on stylistic grounds. This same composition appears in S-Uu as VMHS 11:16 (pts), attributed to Carissimi, where the Bc part bears the rubric "di Vincenzo Albrici." In his study of the motets of Carissimi, Andrew Jones also rejects this work as a composition of Carissimi on stylistic grounds (Jones 1982-2:78). However, it is much closer in style to the works of the elder Roman composer than to the compositions of Albrici.

PERFORMANCES

1662: Trinity 11, AM; Trinity 16, AM (SLUB Q 240)

Modern editions in Frandsen 1997-3:245–63, and Newton 2004, App. C:367–80.

Quam suave est adorare

| S-Uu | VMHS 86:26 (tab) | SATB, 2 Vl, Bc |

Quantus amor Jesu

| D-B | Mus. ms. 501, no. 2 | B, 2 Vl, Bc |

Quid est mundus

| D-B | Mus. ms. 501, no. 4 | ATB, 2 Vl, Bc |

PERFORMANCES

1678: June 21 (birthday of Prince Johann Georg III, June 20), AM (Sächs HStA Loc. 8682 Nr. 12, fol. 59r)

Modern edition in Frandsen 1997-3:265–304.

Reges Tharsis et insulae

| CZ-Pkřiž | XXXV C 295 | SSATB, SSATB, 2 Vl, 2 Va, Bsn; 4 Tpt, 3 Trb, Timp, Bc |

Regina caeli

| D-TRb | 104/004 00 | SATB, 2 Vl, 3 trb, Bc |

Si bona suscepimus

| CZ-Pkřiž | XXXV A 59 | SSAATTBB, 2Vl, 2Va, Bsn, 2 Cor, 3 Trb, Bc |

Sive vivimus, sive morimur

D-B*	Mus. ms. 17081, no. 7	SAB, 2 Vl, Bc
SLUB	1821-E-500 (sco)	SAB, 2 Vl, Bsn, Bc
	1821-E-500 (pts)	SAB, 2 Vl, Bsn, Org
S-Uu	VMHS 2:2 (pts)	SAB, 2 Vl, Bsn, Org
	VMHS 2:2a (pts)	SAB, 2 Vl, Va, Bsn, Org
	VMHS 78:68 (tab)	SAB, 2 Vl, Bsn, Org

*The Bokemeyer source attributes the work to Peranda, an attribution that is refuted by references to the concerto as a work of Albrici in the court calendar for 1662 (SLUB Q 240, entries for 15 June, 27 July, 7 September, 26 October, and 24 December), as well as by the existence of concordant sources attributed to Albrici.

PERFORMANCES

1662: Trinity 3, AM; Trinity 9, AM; Trinity 15, AM; Trinity 22, AM; Christmas Eve, Vespers (SLUB Q 240)

Modern edition in Frandsen 1997 3:306–316.

Spargite flores

| D-B | Mus. ms. 501, no. 8 | SAT, 2 Vl, Vle, Bc |

PERFORMANCES

1662: *Quasimodogeniti*, Vespers (SLUB Q 240); Birthday of Johann Georg III (June 20), AM (Sächs HStA OHMA N I Nr. 7, fol. 2r); Christmas Eve, Vespers (SLUB Q 240)

Modern edition in Frandsen 1997-3:318–66.

Sperate in Deo

| S-Uu | VMHS 2:4 (pts) | SSB, 2 Vl, Trb, Org |
| | VMHS 82:6 (tab) | SSB, 2 Vl, Trb, Bc |

PERFORMANCES

1661: Advent 4, Vespers (SLUB Q 240)
1662: Pentecost II, Vespers (Q 240)

Te Deum laudamus

A-Wn	SA.67.B.9 (Fond Kiesewetter)	SSATB, SSATB, 2 Vl, 2 Va, Vc, 4 Clr, Tmp, Bc
D-B	Mus. ms. 500	SSATB, SSATB; 2 Vl, 2 Va, 4 Tpt, Tmp, Bc
D-B	Mus. ms. 500/2	SSATB, SSATB; 2 Vl, 2 Va, 4 Tpt, Tmp, Bc

Tu es cor meum

D-B**	Mus. ms. 17081, no. 17	SSB, 2 Vl, Bsn, Bc
S-Uu	VMHS 2:6 (pts)	SSB, 2 Vl, Bsn, Bc
	VMHS 2:6a (pts)	SSB, 2 Vl, Bsn/Vle, Th (missing B and Vl 1 pts)
	VMHS 78:91 (tab)	SSB, 2 Vl, Bsn, Bc

PERFORMANCES

1660: Advent 4, Vespers (Sächs HStA Loc. 12026, fol. 56v)
1662: Pentecost III, Vespers; Trinity 14, AM (SLUB Q 240)

**Attributed to Peranda in the Bokemeyer collection and the Ansbach inventory (Schaal 1966:43). Service orders in court diaries from 1660 and 1662 include references to this work as a composition of Albrici (Sächs HStA Loc. 12026, fol. 56v, entry for 23 December 1660; SLUB Q 240, entries for 20 May and 31 August 1662).

Modern edition in Frandsen 1997-3:368–99

Ubi est charitas

D-B   Mus. ms. 501, no. 9   SAB, 2 Vl, Bc

Venite cantemus

S-Uu   VMHS 81:53 (tab)   SSS, 3 Vl, Bc

  PERFORMANCES

  1661: New Year's Day, Vespers (Sächs HStA Loc. 12026, fol. 65r)
  1662: New Year's Day, Vespers; *Quasimodogeniti*, AM; Trinity 21, AM (SLUB
  Q 240)
  1673: Epiphany (Jan. 6), Vespers (SLUB K 117, fol. 16r); Ascension, Vespers
  (K 117, fol. 49v); Pentecost Eve, Vespers (K 117, fol. 50v); Pentecost III, Vespers
  (K 117, fol. 54v)

Venite filii audite me

D-B   Mus. ms. 501, no. 10   ATB, 2 Vl, Bsn, Bc

Venite omnes gentes

D-B   Mus. ms. 501, no. 12   SSB, 2 Vl, Bc
S-Uu   VMHS 2:7 (pts)   SSB, 2 Vl, Vdg/Bsn, Vle, Org

Modern edition in Frandsen 1997-3:401–24

SEBASTIANO CHERICI   (pieces cited in court diaries only)

All four works appear in *Harmonia di devoti concerti* (Bologna: Monti, 1681)

Deplorandus et amarus

SSB, 2 Vl, Bassetto viola, Org

  PERFORMANCES:

  1675: Christmas Eve, Vespers (SLUB Q 260, entry for 24 December 1675)
  1676: Purification, Vespers (SLUB Q 260, entry for 2 February 1676)

Heu infelix peccata

ATB, Org

  PERFORMANCES:

  1675: Christmas II, Vespers (SLUB Q 260, entry for 26 December 1675)
  1676: *Quasimodogeniti*, AM (SLUB Q 260, entry for 2 April 1676)

O dilectissimi populi

SSB, 2 Vl, Bassetto viola, Org

PERFORMANCES:

1676: New Year's Day, Vespers; Annunciation, Vespers; *Quasimodogeniti*, AM
(SLUB Q 260, entries for 1 January, 19 March, and 2 April 1676)

Venite gentes

SAB, 2 Vl, Bassetto viola, Org

PERFORMANCES:

1676: New Year's Day, AM; Easter Tuesday, Vespers (SLUB Q 260, entries for
1 January, 28 March 1676)

CARLO PALLAVICINO

Ad arma, daemones

SLUB	1813-E-501	SB, 4 Vl, 4 Clr, Lira, Bc

Confitebor tibi Domini

SLUB	1813-D-4	SATB, 2 Vl, 2 Ba, Bsn, Bc

Dixit Dominus

SLUB	1813-D-3	SSAA, 2 Vl, Va, Bc; Rip pts indicated in score

Laetatus sum in his

S-Uu	IMHS 57:2	B, 2 Vl, 2 Va, Bsn, Bc
S-Uu†	VMHS 47:9	B, 2 Vl, 2 Va, Org
D-B	Mus. ms. 30257, no. 1	B, 2 Vl, 2 Va, Bc
SLUB	1813-E-500	B, 2 Vl, 2 Viole, Bsn, Bc

Missa (Kyrie, Gloria, Credo)

SLUB	1813-D-1	SATTB, 2 Vl, Bc

[Missa brevis] Kyrie and Gloria

SLUB	1813-D-2	SSATB, 2 Vl, 2 Va, 3 Cor, Bc

Non tremiscite

SLUB	1813-E-501	SATB, 4 Clr, Bc

†Attributed to Albrici, refuted by concordances and musical style.

GIUSEPPE PERANDA

Abite dolores

SLUB   1738-E-528 (pts)   SS, 2 Vl, Org

> PERFORMANCES
>
> 1676: Easter III, AM (SLUB Q 260)

Modern edition in Frandsen 1997-3:426–51

Accurrite gentes

SLUB   1738-E-510   ATB, 2 Cor, 1 Bsn, Org
S-Uu   VMHS 30:3 (pts, d. 1666)   ATB, 2 Cor/Vl, Bsn, Org
             VMHS 85:26b (tab)   ATB, 2 Vl, Bsn, Bc

> PERFORMANCES
>
> 1665: Easter III, Vespers (SLUB K 80, fol. 52v)
> 1666: Epiphany 5, AM: "3 voci, Alto, Ten. e Basso e 3 Istr: 2 Cornetti e Fagotto"
>   (SLUB Q 243)
> 1667: *Quasimodogeniti*, Vespers (SLUB Q 245)
> 1676: Easter II, AM (SLUB Q 260)

Modern edition in Frandsen 1997-3:453–75

Ad cantus ad sonos

D-B   Mus. ms. 17081, no. 9   SST, 3 Vl, Bsn, Bc
D-F   Ms. Ff. Mus. 448   SST, 3 Vl, Bc
SLUB   1738-E-517 (pts)   SST, 3 Vl, Org

> PERFORMANCES
>
> 1664: Pentecost I, Vespers (Sächs HStA Loc. 12026, fol. 398v)
> 1665: Easter III, AM (SLUB K 80, fol. 51v)
> 1666: New Year's Day, Vespers: "à 6. 3 Violini 2 Sop: et 1 Ten:";
>   Pentecost II, Vespers: "à 3. 2 Sopran: et Tenore" (SLUB Q 243)
> 1667: Easter II, Vespers (SLUB Q 245)
> 1676: Pentecost III, AM (SLUB Q 260)

Modern edition in Frandsen 1997-3:477–99

*Ad dulces amores**

D-B   Mus. ms. 17081, no. 13   SS, Bc

Audite peccatores

D-B   Mus. ms. 17081, no. 11   SB, 2 Vl, Bc

*Misattributed to Peranda in the Bokemeyer collection; appears in Bonifatio Gratiani's Op. 7 collection of motets for 2–5 voices and continuo, *Motetti, libro terzo* (Rome, 1656).

Cantemus Domino

D-B	Mus. ms. 17081, no. 2	SSS, Bc
SLUB	1738-E-511 (pts)	SSS, Org
RUS-Mk	C-42	SSS, Bc

PERFORMANCES

1666: *Quasimodogeniti*, Vespers: "à 3 Soprani" (SLUB Q 243)
1667: Easter III, AM (SLUB Q 245)
1676: Easter III, Vespers (SLUB Q 260)

Cor mundum crea in me

| S-Uu | VMHS 61:15 (pts) | B, 2 Vl, Bsn, Bc |

Modern edition in Frandsen 1997-3:501–18

Credidi propter quod locutus sum

| SLUB | 1738-E-506 (pts) | STB, SATB, 2 Vl, 2 Va, Bsn, Bc |
| | 1857-E-511 (sco) | STB, SATB, 2 Vl, 2 Va, Bsn, Bc |

Da pacem Domine

| D-B | Mus. ms. 17081, no. 10 | SSB, 2 Vl, Va, Bc |

Dedit abyssus vocem suam

SLUB	1738-E-527 (pts)	SSBB, Bc
S-Uu	VMHS 30:4 (pts)	SSBB, Org
	VMHS 78:51 (tab, d. 1667)	SSBB, Bc

PERFORMANCES

1665: *Quasimodogeniti*, Vespers (SLUB K 80, fol. 54r)
1666: Epiphany 1, AM: "à 4. 2 Soprani. 2 Bassi."; Trinity 12, AM: "à 4. 2 Sop: 2 Baß." (SLUB Q 243)
1676: Pentecost III, Vespers (SLUB Q 260)

Modern edition in Frandsen 1997-3:520–548

Dic nobis Maria

| D-B | Mus. ms. 17081, no. 3 | SSB, 2 Vl, Bsn, Bc |
| RUS-Mk | C-43 | SSB, 2 Vl, Bsn, Bc |

PERFORMANCES

1665: Easter II, Vespers (SLUB K 80, fol. 51v)
1666: Easter II, AM: "à 6. 2 Sopr: e Basso 2 Viol: e Fagott" (SLUB Q 243)
1676: Easter I, Vespers (SLUB Q 260)

Modern edition in Frandsen 1997-3:550–65

Dies sanctificatus

| SLUB | 1738-E-513 (pts) | T, 2 Vl, Bsn, Org |

Diligam te Domine

SLUB	1-E-770 (sco)	SSB, 2 Vl, Bsn, Bc
	1738-E-503 (pts)	SSB, 2 Vl, Bsn, Bc

Dum proeliaretur

D-B	Mus. ms. 17081, no. 14	SB, 2 Vl, Bsn, Bc

Modern edition in Frandsen 1997-3:567–80

Ecce ego mittam piscatores

S-Uu	VMHS 30:4 (pts)	SSB, 2 Vl, Bsn, Vle, Org
	VMHS 78:47 (tab)	SSB, 2 Vl, Bsn, Bc

Factum est proelium magnum

D-B	Mus. ms. 17081, no. 1	SSATTB, 2 Vl, 2 Va, 2 Cnto, 2 Trb, Bc
S-Uu	VMHS 61:14 (pts)	SSATTB, SSATB, 2 Vl, 2 Cnto, 2 Trb/Va, Bsn, Bc
	VMHS 61:16 (pts)	SSATTB, 2 Vl, 2 Va, 2 Cnto, Vle, Th (a much abbreviated version of VMHS 61:14)

PERFORMANCES

1666: Feast of St. Michael (Sept. 29), AM (SLUB Q 243)

Fasciculus myrrhae

SLUB	1738-E-509 (pts)	SSATB, SSATB, 2 Vl, 2 Va, Bsn, 2 Cor, 3 Trb, Bc
	1738-E-509a (sco)	SSATB, SSATB, 2 Vl, 2 Va, Bsn, 2 Cor,3 Trb, Bc

PERFORMANCES

1662: Trinity 20, AM (SLUB Q 240)
1665: Trinity 2, AM (SLUB Q 241)
1666: Epiphany 5, AM; Visitation (July 2), AM; Trinity 14, AM (SLUB Q 243)

Florete fragrantibus liliis

SLUB	1738-E-525 (pts)	SST, 2 Vl, Vdg/Bombardo, Org

PERFORMANCES

1665: Christmas II, Vespers: "â 3. 2. Sopra: e Tenore" (SLUB Q 243); entry gives title as "Florete," which may refer to Peranda's *Florete flores*, now lost.

Gaudete, cantate

SLUB	1738-E-523 (pts)	SSB, 2 Vl, Org

Hac luce cunctos assere

SLUB	1738-E-514 (pts)	ATB, 2 Vl, 2 Va, Bsn, Org

Herr, wenn ich nur dich habe

D-B   Mus. ms. 17081, no. 19   ATB, 2 Vl, Bsn, Bc

Historia des Leidens und Sterbens unsers Herrn und Heÿlandes Iesu Christi nach dem Evangelisten St. Marcum

Musikbibliothek der Stadt Leipzig Ms. II 2, 15
Scoring:
    Jesus: Bass
    Evangelista: Tenor
    Youth (Jünge): Tenor
    Petrus: Tenor
    Judas: Alto
    High Priest (Hohe-Priest): Bass
    Maidservant (Ancilla): Soprano
    Pilatus: Bass
    Soldier (Miles): Tenor
    Centurion: Tenor
    Chorus: SATB (Hohepriester, Schrifftgelehrten, Die Jünger Jesu, Falsche Zeugen, Der gantze Hauffe, Die Jüden)

PERFORMANCES**

    1668: Good Friday
    1677: *Judica*
    1679: *Judica*

Jesu dulcis, Jesu pie

SLUB   1738-E-522 (pts)   SAT, 2 Va, Bsn, Org

PERFORMANCES

    1664: Pentecost I, Vespers (Sächs HStA Loc. 12026, fol. 398v)
    1665: Purification (Feb. 2), Vespers (SLUB K 80, fol. 20v); *Misericordias Domini*, AM; Trinity 8, AM (SLUB Q 241); Christmas III, Vespers (SLUB Q 243)
    1666: Trinity 13, AM: "â 6. 1 Sop: 1 Alto 1 Tenore 2 Viole. et 1 Violtagamba" (SLUB Q 243)
    1667: Purification, Vespers; Pentecost III, Vespers (SLUB Q 245)

Modern edition in Frandsen 1997-3:582–98.

**See Steude 2001/2:170–71; Peranda's Passion was likely performed in other years as well; some diary entries do not indicate the composer, and records have not survived for some years. Edition: Heinrich Schütz and Marco Giuseppe Peranda, *Passionsmusiken nach den Evangelisten Matthäus, Lukas, Johannes und Markus. Faksimile nach der Partiturhandschrift der Musikbibliothek der Stadt Leipzig*. Introductory essay by Wolfram Steude. Leipzig: Zentralantiquariat der deutschen demokratischen Republik, 1981.

Kyrie

D-B   Mus. ms. 17079, no. 10   SSATB, 2 Vl, 2 Va, 2 Clr, Vle, Bc

Title page in the hand of Johann Sebastian Bach, parts in the hand of "Anon. BNB 2," copied ca. 1709; see Beißwenger 1992:306. Modern edition: Marco Gioseppe [*sic*] Peranda, *Kyrie in C*, ed. Peter Wollny (Stuttgart: Carus Verlag, 2000).

Laetentur coeli

SLUB   1738-E-531 (pts)   SSATB, SSATB, 2 Vl, 2 Clr, 3 Trb, Bc

PERFORMANCES

1666: New Year's Day, AM: "â 10 voc: et 10 inst: 2 Tromb et Timpagni" (SLUB Q 243)
1667: Epiphany, AM (SLUB Q 245)

Languet cor meum

SLUB   1738-E-508 (pts)   SAT, 2 Vl, Bsn, Org
S-Uu†   VMHS 1:12 (pts)   SAT, 3/5 Va, Bc
           VMHS 81:96 (tab)   SAT, 2 Vl, Bsn, Bc; 3 Inst

PERFORMANCES

1664: Pentecost II, Vespers (Sächs HStA Loc. 12026, fol. 399v); New Year's Eve, Vespers (SLUB Msc. Dresd. K 80, fol. 2v)
1666: Epiphany, Vespers: "â 6. 2 Violini. 1 Fagotto. 1 Sop: 1 Alto et 1 Ten:"; *Misericordias Domini*, AM: "1 Sop: 1 Alto e Ten: 2 Violini et Fagot"; Trinity 21, AM (SLUB Q 243)
1667: Easter III, Vespers (SLUB Q 245)

Modern edition in Frandsen 1997-3:600–618.

Laudate Dominum omnes gentes

S-Uu   VMHS 61:17 (pts + tab)   SSSATB, 2 Vl, 2 Va, Bsn, Org

†The sources for this composition in Uppsala attribute the work to Albrici, an attribution that is refuted by documented performances of the work in Dresden in 1664, 1666, and 1667, all of which attribute the work to Peranda (Sächs HStA Loc. 12026, fol. 399v, entry for 30 May 1664; SLUB Msc. Dresd. K 80, fol. 2v, entry for 31 December 1664; SLUB Msc. Dresd. Q 243, entries for 6 January and 4 November 1666; SLUB Q 245, entry for 9 April 1667). In addition, the inventories from Ansbach, Leipzig, Lüneburg, and Weißenfels all include *Languet cor meum* among the works of Peranda (Schaal 1966:42; Schering 1918–19:287; Seiffert 1907–08:611; Gundlach 2001:305), and Albrici lists it among the works of Peranda in the "Dresden Instrument Chamber Catalog" of 1681 (Spagnoli 1990:225).

Laudate pueri Dominum

| SLUB | 1-E-770 (sco) | SSSB, Bc |

Miserere mei Deus

D-B	Mus. ms. 17081, no. 5	SSSATB, 2 Vl, 3 Va, Bsn, 2 Clr, Tmp, Bc
D-B	Mus. ms. 17080	(same as above; copy ca. 1825)
SLUB	1738-E-512a (pts)	SSSATB, SSSATB, 2 Vl, 3 Va, Bsn, 2 Clr (muted), 3 Trb, Tmp, Bc
	1857-E-512 (sco)	SSSATB, SSSATB, 2 Vl, 3 Va, Bsn, 2 Clr, 3 Trb, Tmp, Bc
S-Uu	VMHS 61:18 (pts)	SSSATB, 2 Vl, 4 Va, 2 Clr (muted), 3 Trb *ad lib*, Tmp, Bc

PERFORMANCES

1670: Palm Sunday, afternoon memorial service for King Frederick III of Denmark: "mit gedämpfften Trompeten, Paucken, Instrumenten" (Sächs HStA Loc. 8681 Nr. 7, fol. 162r)

1677: Sept. 25, afternoon funeral for Oberhofmarschall von Kanne: "mit Trompeten durchs Sordin und die Paucken bedeckt" (Sächs. HStA Loc. 8682 Nr. 11, fol. 117r)

Missa

| D-B | Mus. ms. 17079 | SATB, SATB, 2 Vl, 2 Va, Bsn, Bc |

Missa (copied 1672)

| CZ-KRa | A 34 | SSATB, SSATB, 2 Vl, 2 Va, 2 Cor, 2 Clr, 3 Trb, Vlne, Bc |

Missa B. Agnetis (copied 1671)

| CZ-Kra | A 35 | SSATTB, SSATB, 2 Vl, 2 Va, 2 Cor, 3 Trb, Vle, Bc |
| CZ-Pkřiž (as *Missa St. Josephi*) | XXXV C 73 | SSATTB, SSATB, 2 Vl, 2 Va, 2 Cor, 3 Trb, Vle, Bc |

The Kyrie and Gloria of this complete Mass represent later revisions of these movements as found in the *Missa (brevis)* below (D-B 17079, no. 11); see Wollny, ed., Peranda, *Missa in a*, iii.

Missa St. Josephi (See Missa B. Agnetis.)

| D-B | Mus. ms. 30088, no. 14 | SATB, 2 Vl, 2 Va, Bc |

Missa (brevis)

D-B	Mus. ms. 17019, no. 11 (sco) (*Kyrie* only)	SSATTB, 2 Vl, 3 Va, Bsn, Bc
	Mus. ms. 17019, no. 12 (pts)	SSATTB, 2 Vl, Va, Vc, Vlne, 3 Trb
D-B	Mus. ms. 30098, no. 6	SSATTB, 2 Vl, 3 Va, Bc

D-BNms   Sammlung Klein, Ec 141.1.   SSATTB, 2 Vl, 3 Va, Bsn, Bc

Modern edition: Marco Gioseppe [sic] Peranda, *Missa in a*, ed. Peter Wollny (Stuttgart: Carus Verlag, 2000). The parts for the Kyrie in Mus. ms. 17019, no. 11 are in the hand of J. S. Bach, and were copied in Weimar between 1714-17 (ibid., 47).

Missus est Angelus

SLUB   1738-E-502a (pts)   SSB, SSATB, 2 Vta, 3 Vdg, Org

PERFORMANCES

1665: Annunciation (celebrated on March 19, Palm Sunday, as March 25 fell on Holy Saturday), Vespers (SLUB K 80, fol. 46r)
1666: Annunciation (March 25), Vespers: "à 3. Voci 2. Soprani e Basso. con 5. Viol: G:" (SLUB Q 243)
1673: Advent 1, Vespers (Sächs HStA Loc. 8681 Nr. 8, fol. 202v)

O ardor, o flamma

D-B   Mus. ms. 17081, no. 16   SB, 2 Vl, Bc
S-Uu   VMHS 82:35 (tab)   SB, 2 Vl, Bc

O bone Jesu per dulce nomen tuum

S-Uu   VMHS 61:19   T, 2 Vl, Bc

Modern edition in Frandsen 1997-3:620–38.

O fideles modicum

SLUB   1738-E-518a (pts)   SATB, 2 Vl, Bsn, Org
         1738-E-518 (sco)   SATB, 2 Vl, Bsn, Bc

PERFORMANCES

1666: Easter III, AM: "à 7. 1 Sop: 1 Alto. 1 Tenor e Basso. 2 Violini e Fagotto"; Feast of St. Michael (Sept. 29), Vespers: "à 6. 1 Sop: 1. Alt: 1 Ten: 1 Basso et 2 Violini" (SLUB Q 243)

O Jesu mi dulcissime

S-Uu   VMHS 30:6 (pts)   SSA, 2 Vta/Vl, 2 Vdg, Vle, Org, Th
         VMHS 84:51 (tab)   SSA, 5 "Viol", Bc

PERFORMANCES

1665: Trinity 7, AM (SLUB Q 241); Christmas III, AM: "5. Viol: 2 Soprani e 1 Altto" (SLUB Q 243)
1666: Trinity 20, Vespers: "à 6. 2 Sop: 1 Alt: 2 Violini et 1 Viola da gamba" (SLUB Q 243)
1667: Easter III, Vespers; Mary Magdalene (July 22), AM (SLUB Q 245)
1676: Easter II, Vespers (SLUB Q 260)

Modern edition in Frandsen 1997-3:640–54.

Peccavi o Domine

SLUB	1738-E-524a (pts)	SAB, 2 Vl, Bc
	1738-E-524 (sco)	SAB, 2 Vl, Bc

Per rigidos montes

S-Uu	VMHS 30:8 (pts)	A, 2 Vl, Bsn, Th

Plange anima suspira

S-Uu	VMHS 30:7 (pts)	ATB, Org

Propitiare Domine

SLUB	1738-E-500a (pts)	SSATB, SSATB, 2 Vl, 2 Va, Bsn, Bc
	1738-E-500 (sco)	SSATB, SSATB, 2 Vl, 2 Va, Bsn, Bc

PERFORMANCES

1665: *Jubilate*, AM (Sächs HStA Loc. 12026, fol. 32r)
1666: Epiphany 4, AM; *Jubilate*, AM; Trinity 12, AM; Trinity 21, AM (SLUB Q 243)

Modern edition in Frandsen 1997-3:656–85.

Quis dabit capiti meo

D-B	Mus. ms. 17081, no. 18	ATB, 2 Vl, Bc
Uu*	VMHS 1:18 (pts, d. 1663)	ATB, 2 Vl, Bsn/Va, Org
	VMHS 79:28 (tab)	ATB, 2 Vl, Bsn, Bc
	VMHS 79:116 (tab)	ATB, 2 Vl, Bsn, Bc

PERFORMANCES

1662: Palm Sunday/Annunciation (celebrated on March 19 as March 25 fell during Holy Week), Vespers; Trinity 20, AM (SLUB Q 240)
1665: Trinity 1, AM; Sunday after Christmas/New Year's Eve, Vespers: "à 6. 3 Viol. 1 Alto 1 Teno: 1 Basso" (SLUB Q 241)
1666: Trinity 24, AM: "à 5. 1 Alt. 1 Ten: 1 Bass et 2 Violini" (SLUB Q 243)
1667: Pentecost III, Vespers (SLUB Q 245)

*The Uppsala sources and Rudolstadt inventory (Baselt 1963:117) attribute this work to Albrici; court diaries indicate that this work was performed in Dresden on numerous occasions between 1662 and 1667, however, and always attribute it to Peranda (SLUB Msc. Dresd. Q 240, entries for 23 March and 12 October 1662; SLUB Msc. Dresd. Q 241, entries for 28 May and 31 December 1665 (see scoring above); SLUB Q 243, entry for 25 November 1666 (see scoring above); Sächs HStA Loc. 12026, fol. 255v, entry for 27 May 1667). *Quis dabit* is also included among the works of Peranda listed in the inventories of Weißenfels (Gundlach 2001:307) and Ansbach (Schall 1966:43); the latter indicates the key as "ex G b," which suggests that the work was transposed.

Modern edition in Frandsen 1997-3:687–707.

Quo tendimus mortales

SLUB	1738-E-519 (pts)	SSB, Org
S-Uu**	VMHS 1:19 (pts, d. 1665)	SSB, Org, Th
	VMHS 78:11 (tab)	SSB, Bc

PERFORMANCES

1664: New Year's Eve, Vespers (SLUB K 80, fol. 2v; SLUB Q 241)
1665: New Year's Eve, Vespers: "â 3. 2 Sop: e 1 Basso" (SLUB Q 243)

Modern edition in Frandsen 1997-3:709–19.

Repleti sunt omnes

D-B	Mus. ms. 17081, no. 4	AT/TB, 2 Vl, 2 Cnto, Bc
SLUB	1738-E-501a (pts)	AT, 2 Vl, 2 Cnto, Bsn, Sp, Org
	1738-E-501 (sco)	AT, 2 Vl, 2 Cnto, Bsn, Sp, Bc

PERFORMANCES

1664: Pentecost III/Birthday of Johann Georg II, Vespers (Sächs HStA Loc. 12026, fol. 401v)
1666: Pentecost I, Vespers: "â 8. 1 Alto 1 Ten: et 6 instr:" (SLUB Q 243)
1667: Pentecost I, Vespers (SLUB Q 245)
1673: Pentecost II, AM (SLUB K 117, fol. 52v)
1676: Pentecost III, AM (SLUB Q 245 no, 260)

Modern edition in Frandsen 1997-3:721–37.

Rorate cherubim

CZ-KRa	II, 179	SSA, 2 Vl, Bc

Si Dominus mecum

D-B	Mus. ms. 17081, no. 8	SATB, 2 Vl, Bc
SLUB	1738-E-516 (pts)	SATB, 2 Vl, Bsn, Org
S-Uu	VMHS 2:1 (pts)†	SATB, 2 Vl, Org
	VMHS 78:39 (tab)	SATB, 2 Vl, Bc

**Again the Uppsala sources indicate Albrici as the composer, an attribution that is refuted by court diaries from 1664 and 1665 (SLUB K 80, fol. 2v, entry for 31 December 1664; SLUB Q 243, entry for 31 December 1665). *Quo tendimus* is also listed as a work of Peranda in the Ansbach, Lüneburg, Rudolstadt and Weißenfels inventories (Schaal 1966:43; Seiffert 1907–08:611; Baselt 1963:117).

†The part set in Uppsala bears an attribution to Albrici, which is refuted by the existence of three concordant manuscripts, all of which are attributed to Peranda (including the tablature copied by Düben!), as well as numerous entries in court diaries for 1662, 1665, 1666, and 1676 (SLUB Q 240, entries for 31 May and 24 August 1662; K 80, fol. 43r,

PERFORMANCES

1662: Birthday of Johann Georg II (May 31), Vespers; Trinity 13, AM (SLUB
Q 240)
1665: St. Matthias (Feb. 24), AM (SLUB K 80, fol. 43r); Trinity 2, AM (SLUB
Q 243)
1666: Epiphany 3, AM: "â 6. 2 Violini 1 Sop: 1 Alto 1 Ten: et 1 Basso"; Pentecost
II, Vespers: "â 7. 1 Sop: 1 Alt: 1 Ten: 1 Basso et 3 Instr:"; Trinity 16, AM (SLUB
Q 243)
1676: Conversion of St. Paul (Jan. 25), AM (SLUB Q 260)

Modern edition in Frandsen 1997-3:739–50.

Si vivo mi Jesu (see the note concerning the attribution in the next entry)

D-B	Mus. ms. 17081, no. 12	A, 2 Vl, Bc
SLUB	1738-E-505 (pts)	A, 2 Vl, Bc
S-Uu	VMHS 30:10 (pts)	A, 2 Vl, Bc

PERFORMANCES

(See next entry.)

Modern edition in Frandsen 1997-3:725–67.

Si vivo mi Jesu

SLUB	1738-E-504a (pts)	SST, 3 Vl, Bc
	1738-E-504 (sco)	SST, 3 Vl, Bc
S-Uu*	VMHS 2:3 (pts, d. 1665)	SST/B, 3 Vl, Org; Va (=Bc)
	VMHS 79:7 (tab)	SST, 3 Vl, Bc; 1 Inst (=Bc)

entry for 24 February 1665; Q 241, entry for 4 June 1665; Q 243, entries for 21 January, 4 June, and 30 September 1666; SLUB Q 260, entry for 25 January 1676). Albrici includes *Si Dominus mecum* among the works of Peranda that he lists in the 1681 "Dresden Instrument Chamber Catalog" (see Spagnoli 1990:225), where the scoring includes Bsn. The composition also appears among the list of Peranda's works in the Weißenfels inventory; the entry includes the rubric "a 6 o 7" (Gundlach 2001:307). The Rudolstadt inventory attributes the work to Albrici, and gives the scoring as "à 6, 2 Violini, 4 Voci" (Baselt 1963:117).

*Both the manuscript parts as well as the tablature in Uppsala bear an attribution to Albrici. The resolution of this conflicting attribution presents more difficulties than most of the others, due in large part to the existence of two works with the same title incipit and (largely) the same text. Thus without the scoring, entries in court diaries can shed little light here (this title was performed as a work of Peranda's in 1666, 1667, and 1676; see entries in SLUB Q 243 for 16 April, 27 May, and 21 October 1666; Sächs HStA Loc. 12026, fol. 254v for 27 May 1667; and SLUB Q 260 for 13 May 1676). However, the entry for 27 May 1666 does record the scoring of the work performed during that

PERFORMANCES

1666: Easter II, Vespers: "à 7. 1 Sopra: 1 Alto e Basso 2 Violini 1 Viola da Gamba e Fagotto"; *Exaudi*, AM, "à. 7. 2 Sop. Basso. 2 Violini. 1 Viol. et Fagotto"; Trinity 19, AM (SLUB Q 243)

1667: Easter II, Vespers (SLUB Q 245); Pentecost II, AM (Sächs. HStA Loc. 12026, fol. 254v)

1676: Palm Sunday/Annunciation (celebrated on March 19), Vespers; Pentecost Eve, Vespers (SLUB Q 260)

Modern edition in Frandsen 1997-3:769–80.

Spirate suaves

D-B	Mus. ms. 17081, no. 15	SS, 2 Vl, Bc
S-Uu	VMHS 30:11 (pts)	SS, 2 Vl, Bsn, Bc: Vne, Org
	VMHS 81:157	SS, 2 Vl, Bsn, Bc
	(tab, d. 20.2.1666)	

PERFORMANCES

1665: New Year's Day, Vespers; Purification (Feb. 2), Vespers; *Quasimodogeniti*, AM (SLUB K 80, fols. 5r, 20v, 53r); Christmas II, AM: "à 4. 2. Cornet: 2 Soprani" (SLUB Q 243).

1667: *Quasimodogeniti*, AM (SLUB Q 245)

Modern edition in Frandsen 1997-3:782–809.

Sursum deorsum

| SLUB | 1738-E-530 (pts) | SSS, 3 Vl, Bc |

"Sursum deorsum" ("as above, here below") was the motto (*symbolum* or *Devise*) of Johann Georg II throughout his lifetime; see, for example, David Peck's encomium entitled *Sursum, deorsum principe vere dignum symbolum, quod . . . Johannes Georgius* (Leipzig: Wittigau, 1654), and Martin Geier's funeral sermon for Johann Georg II, *Sursum deorsum! oder die alleredelste Sorgfalt . . . Johann Georgen des Andern . . . .* (Dresden: Bergen, 1680). Peranda's *Sursum deorsum* represents the only work in this repertoire for which a date of composition can be fixed; according to a court

---

particular service as "à. 7. 2 Sop. Basso. 2 Violini. 1 Viol. et Fagotto." In the 1681 "Dresden Instrument Chamber Catalog" Albrici includes a composition entitled *Si vivo mi Jesu* among the works of Peranda, with the following scoring: SAB, 2 Vl, Bsn (Spagnoli 1990:225). The confusion extends to the contemporary inventories: the Weißenfels inventory includes the composition for alto, attributed to Peranda (Gundlach 2001:307), but the Leipzig inventory includes both works as compositions of Albrici (Schering 1918–19:285). The Ansbach inventory lists both under Peranda's name, but also lists the composition for three voices as a work of Albrici (Schaal 1966:42, 66). The Rudolstadt inventory attributes the title to Albrici, but does not give the scoring (Baselt 1963:117). Here the attribution is assigned to Peranda, albeit somewhat tentatively.

diary entry for 31 May 1664, Peranda composed the work expressly for the elector's birthday celebration that year (Sächs. HStA Loc. 12026, fol. 400r: "*Concert. Sursum Deorsum*, welches der Cappellmeister *Peranda* ganz von neuem *componiret*, und der Text nach folgends zu ersehen" [the entire text follows in the diary]).

PERFORMANCES

1664: Pentecost III/Birthday of Johann Georg II (May 31), AM (Sächs HStA Loc. 12026, fol. 400r)

1665: Birthday of Johann Georg II, Vespers (SLUB Q 241)

1668: Trinity Sunday/Birthday of Johann Georg II, Vespers (Sächs HStA OHMA N I Nr. 7, fol. 58r)

1676: Birthday of Johann Georg II, Vespers (Sächs HStA Loc. 8682 Nr. 10, fol. 53r)

Modern edition in Frandsen 1997-3:811–32.

Te solum aestuat

D-B	Mus. ms. 17081, no. 6	SSB, 2 Vl, Bsn, Bc
SLUB	1738-E-521 (pts)	SSB, 2 Vl, Bc
S-Uu	VMHS 30:12 (pts)	SSB, 2 Vl, Bsn, Org
	VMHS 78:73 (tab)	SSB, 2 Vl, Bsn, Bc

PERFORMANCES

1664: Pentecost II, Vespers (Sächs HStA Loc. 12026, fol. 398r)

1665: Ascension, Vespers; Trinity 18, AM (SLUB Q 241)

1666: *Jubilate*, AM: "â 6. 2 Sop: 1 Basso 2 Violi: et 1 Fagot" (SLUB Q 243)

Modern edition in Frandsen 1997-3:839–51.

Timor et tremor

SLUB	1738-E-520a (pts)	SATB, 2 Vl, Org
	1738-E-520 (sco)	SATB, 2 Vl, Bc

Modern edition in Frandsen 1997-3:854–90.

*Valete risus***

SLUB	1738-E-529 (pts)	SS, Bc

Veni Sancte Spiritus

SLUB	1738-E-526 (pts)	SATB, SATB, 2 Vl, 2 Va, Bsn, 2 Cor, 3 Trb, Org

**Possibly a work of Carissimi; Jones lists the title, but indicates that there are "no known musical sources"; he gives the scoring as SS/TT, Bc (Jones 1992-2:114). A similarly titled and scored work appears in the Lüneburg inventory as a work of Carissimi (Seiffert 1907–08:602).

PERFORMANCES

1664: Pentecost II, AM (Sächs HStA Loc. 12026, fol. 399r)
1667: Pentecost Eve, Vespers; Pentecost I, Vespers (SLUB Q 245)
1676: Pentecost I, Vespers (SLUB Q 260)

Modern edition in Frandsen 1997-3:893–929.

Verleih uns Frieden gnädiglich

D-B   Mus. ms. 17081, no. 20   SSB, 2 Vl, Bc

PERFORMANCE

1670: *Exaudi* (15 May) 1670, Baptism of Friedrich August I (OHMA A Nr. 12, fol. 19r)

Vocibus resonent

S-Uu   VMHS 30:13 (pts)   SAB, 2 Vl, Vdg, Vne, Org
             VMHS 78:43 (tab, d. 1667)   SAB, 2 Vl, Va, Bc

Bibliography of Primary Sources

ALGEMEEN RIJKSARCHIEF/ARCHIVES GÉNÉRALES
DU ROYAUME (AGR)

MD 1374

ARCHIVIO DI STATO VENETO (ASV)

Notarile atti, busta 1085 (Bianconi Gregorio)
Notarile atti, busta 3471 Paulini
Notarile atti, busta 6058, Federici 1655
Notarile atti, busta 11050, Piccini 1652, no. 1
Notarile atti, busta 11060, Piccini 1656, no. 1
Notarile atti, Piccini 11092
SGSM, busta 188, fol. 168 [Faustini documents]

ARCHIVUM ROMANUM SOCIETATIS IESU (ARSI)

Chiesa del Gesù 2009, Libro dell'entrata e uscita per la Sagrestia della Chiesa del Gesù
(anni 1637–1654)

HAUPTSTAATSARCHIV STUTTGART

A282, Ba 1391, *Kirchen Castens Verwalltung Jahr Rechnung 1655–56*

SÄCHSISCHE LANDESBIBLIOTHEK — STAATS- UND
UNIVERSITÄTSBIBLIOTHEK DRESDEN (SLUB)

(Each siglum is preceded by the abbreviation "Msc. Dresd.")
K 80, *Diarium Anno Christi M.DC.LXV.*
K 89, *Ordnung / Wie der Durchlauchtigste Hochgeborne Fürst und Herr, Herr Johann
Georg der Ander, . . . es in Dero Hoff=Capella, mit der Musica, an denen Fest= und
Sontagen, auch in der Wochen, hinführo wolle gehalten haben.*

K 113, *Diarium, Was von der Zeit an als der Durchleuchtigste Fürst und Herr, Herr Johann Georg, Herzog und ChurPrintz zu Sachsen, . . . zum Ersten mahl in den Geheimen und Justitien Rath Ihre Session angetreten.*
K 117, *Diarium was sich in Dresden bei Hofe zugetragen.*
Q 230, *Calendar Herzog Johann Georgen des Andern als ChurPrintz 1643. angefangen von 1630.*
Q 231, *Calendar Herzog Johann Georgen des Andern als ChurPrinz die Jahre 1644. 45. 46. 47. 48.*
Q 234, *Alter und Newer Schreib=Calender Auff das Jahr Jesu Messiae M.DC.LI.*
Q 235, *Alter und Neuer Schreib=Calender . . . Auff das Schallt=Jahr . . . M.DC.LII.*
Q 238, *Calender Churfürst Johann Georgens des Andern. Die Jahre 1657. 58. 59. 60. und 61.*
Q 239, *Alter und Neuer Haubt=Calender . . . Auff das Schalt=Jahr . . . M.DC.LX.*
Q 240, *Newer und Alter Schreibkalender auff das Jahr ... M.DC.LXII.*
Q 241, *Alter und Neuer Schreib Calender auff das Jahr . . . M.DC.LXV.*
Q 243, *Alter und Neuer Schreib Calender auff das Jahr . . . M.DC.LXVI.*
Q 245, *Alter und Neuer Schreib Calender auff das Jahr . . . M.DC.LXVII.*
Q 255, *Alter und Neuer Schreib=Calender auf das Schalt-Jahr . . . M.DC.LXII.*
Q 260, *DIARIUM MDCLXXVI.*

SÄCHSISCHES HAUPTSTAATSARCHIV DRESDEN (SÄCHS HSTA)

Geheimer Rat (Geheimes Archiv)

Loc. 910, *Acta Das ChurFürstl. Orchestre . . . 1764. 65. 66. 67. 68. Vol. I.*
Loc. 4452/2, *Die Renovirung der Schloß-Capellen zu Dreßden bet. 1628–1661.*
Loc. 4520/2, *Acta Bestallungen, Expectanz-Schiene, Besoldungen und Reverse belangende ao. 1651. 70 Vol. III.*
Loc. 4452/1, *Unterschiedliche Reparatur auf dem Schlosse zu Dreßden, . . . 1485–1651.*
Loc. 4452/2, *Die Renovirung der Schloß-Capellen zu Dreßden bet. 1628–1661.*
Loc. 7166/4, *Teutsch und Lateinische Kundschafften und Abschieds Päße. 1658–75.*
Loc. 7168 Nr. 1, *Die Bestellung derer Cammer Herren und Cammer Juncker betreffende de ao. 1641–1697.*
Loc. 7287/3, *Einzelne Schriften, Kammersachen, insonderheit Besoldungs-rückstände . . . 1592–1677.*
Loc. 7330/4, *Cammer-Sachen de Anno 1658–74.*
Loc. 8297/2, *Allerhand Päße und Abschiedt Brieffe ao. 1635–56.*
Loc. 8297/3, *Päße von reisende Personen 1634–93.*
Loc. 8298/1, *Allerhand Päße von Ao. 1638. bis Ao. 1656.*
Loc. 8298/7, *Lateinische und Teutsche Päße zur Perigrination . . . 1617–1670.*
Loc. 8298/8, *Paß Brieffe Anno 1655. 56. 57. 58. 59. biß 1669.*
Loc. 8299/1, *Päße No. 2. 1656–76.*
Loc. 8299/3, *Päße und Abschiede, it. Salvaguardien 1660–1680.*
Loc. 8299/5, *Paßbrieffe Anno 1670. 71. 72. 73. 74. 75. 76. 77. 78. 79.*
Loc. 8560/5, no. 21: *Schreiben von und an Chur-Beyern mit Churfürst Joh. Georg I zu Sachßen gewechselt. Anno: 1638. 56. Ingleichen den Chur-Beÿerische Fr. Witwe 1652.*

Loc. 8561/1, *Herzog Johann Georgens und Gebrüdere zu Sachssen, Schreiben u. Antwort. Anno 1633–56.*

Loc. 8561/5, *Correspondenz Churf. Johann Georg II. A-E.*

Nr. 15, *Correspondenz mit Maria Anna, Churfürstin von Bayern, Tochter Kaiser Ferdinand II.*

Nr. 38, *Correspondenz mit August, Herzog von Braunschweig-Wolfenbüttel.*

Nr. 64, *Correspondenz mit P. Athanasius Kircherus. 1665 u. 1671.*

Loc. 8562/1, *Correspondenz Churf. Johann Georg II. K-Q.*

Loc. 8563/1, *Correspondenz Churf. Johann Georg II. [R-Z]*

Loc. 8563/2, *Des Kurprinzen z. S. Johann Georg II. Handschreiben an seinem Vater, den Kurfürsten, 1634–1656. Vol. I.*

Loc. 8681/2, *Des Chur-Printzens Herzog Johann Georgens des Andern . . . Hoffhaltung bet: 1620–56.*

Loc. 8681/3, *Ihrer Fürstl: Durchl: Herrn Johanns Georgen, Hertzogen zu Sachssen, absonderlich allhier in Dressden im Schloß angeordneten Fürstl. Staat und Hoffhalt belangende A° 1639.*

Loc. 8681 Nr. 6, *ChurFürstl: Sächß: Hoff Diaria Von Anno 1662. 63. 64. 65. 66. et 67.*

Loc. 8681 Nr. 7, *ChurFürstl: Sächß: Hoff-Diaria de Anno 1667 usq. 1671.*

Loc. 8681 Nr. 8, *ChurFürstl: Sächß: communicirtes Diarium, de Annis 1672. 1673.*

Loc. 8682 Nr. 9, *ChurFürstl: Sächß: communicirtes Diarium, de Annis 1674. 1675.*

Loc. 8682 Nr. 10, *ChurFürstl: Sächß: DIARIA, de Anno 1676.*

Loc. 8682 Nr. 11, *ChurFürstl: Sächß: Hoff DIARIA, de Anno 1677.*

Loc. 8682 Nr. 12, *ChurFürstl: Sächß: Hoff Diaria, de Anno 1678.*

Loc. 8682 Nr. 13, *Chur-Fürstl: Sächß: Hoff Diarium de Anno 1679 biß in Majum 1680.*

Loc. 8687/1, *Cantoreÿ-Ordnung.*

Loc. 8687/6, *Abrechnungen Etlicher Dienere, nach Chur Fürst Joh: Georg: II. Tod.*

Loc. 8753/6, *Verwendungen für Musiker, Maler, Gelehrte . . . 1651 fl.*

Loc. 8792/5, *Hand-schreiben Italienischer Fürsten an die Chur- und Fürsten zu Sachssen, de Anno 1600–1692.*

Loc. 10293/1, *Reisen verschiedener Privat Personen ao. 1577–1690.*

Loc. 10299/1, *Unterschiedene Religions-Sachen und Gravamina wieder die Catholiquen bel. 1647–84.*

Loc. 10331/8, *Den Päbstl: Gottes-Dienst in Dreßden u. die deshalb getanen Vorstellungen bet. ao. 1661–1691.*

Loc. 12026, *Hofdiarium 1655 fol.*

Loc. 12030, *Hoff-Reformations-Acta. 1656. 1657. 1658.*

Loc. 30115, *Der Catholischen Gesandten Religions-Exercitium am ChurSächß: Hofe betreffent.*

Loc. 32751, *Kammerkollegium. Rep. LII. Gen. no. 849, fols. 145r–148v, Verzeichnüs Der Italienischen und Teutzschen Musicorum so wohl die Vocalisten als Instrumentisten so beÿ Dero Churfürstl. Durchl. Johann Georg des Andern, Glorwürdigsten andenckens in Diensten gestanden.*

Finanzarchiv

Finanzarchiv 10036, Loc. 32967, Nr. 1918w

Oberhofmarschallamt (OHMA)

OHMA A Nr. 12, *Tauffe Printz Friedrich Augustens zu Sachßen auch Kirchgang der Chur=Printzeßin Anno 1670 und anders mehr.*

OHMA B Nr. 13/b, *Beylager Marggrafens zu Brandenburg, Herrn Christian Ernsts mit Churfürstens zu Sachsen Herrn Johann Georgens des Andern Fräulein Tochter, Fräul. Erdmuth Sophien, in Dreßden 1662 und anders mehr. Vol. II.*

OHMA C Nr. 8, *Begräbnüs des Churfürstens zu Sachsen Herrn Johann Georgens des Ersten. 1657.*

OHMA I Nr. 8, *Des Churfürstens zu Sachsen . . . Reisen nach Halla . . . und Anderer Orte in Annis 1638. 1641. 1651. und 1654.*

OHMA I Nr. 10a, *Reise Churfürstens zu Sachßen Herrn Johann Georgens des Andern auf den Wahl- und Crönungs-Tag zu Franckfurth am Maÿn 1658. und anders mehr, Vols. I & II.*

OHMA K IV Nr. 3, *Befehle und Bestallungen einiger Hoff=Officiers und Bedienten, betr: . . . Anno 1611. biß 1705. Vol. 3.*

OHMA N I Nr. 1, *Investitur Sr. ChurFürstl. Durchl.t zu Sachssen Herrn Johannis Georgii. 1669. St. Georgen Feste in Dresden 1671. und 1678.*

OHMA N I Nr. 6, *Ceremoniel beÿ Legung des Grundsteins zur Capelle in Moritzburg 1661 und beÿ Einweihung der Churfürstl. Hoff- und Capelle zu Moritzburg, 1662 und 1672.*

OHMA N I Nr. 7, *Celebrirte Geburths-Täge. 1662. 1665. 1668. 1721.*

OHMA N I Nr. 8, *Ordnung Wie es an hohen Fest- und Sonntägen, auch in der Wochen in der Residenz Dreßden, gehalten werden solte . . . . von Anno 1657. biß mit Anno 1721.*

OHMA N IV Nr. 1, *Friedens- Denck- und Danck-Feste. 1650. 1660. 1676. 1702. und 1721.*

OHMA O IV Nr. 5, *Hof-Journal 1641–1650.*

OHMA O IV Nr. 9, *Alter und Newer Schreibkalender aufs Schaltjahr . . . M.DC.LX.*

OHMA O IV Nr. 14, *Alter und Neuer Schreib Calender auff das Schalt-Jahr . . . M.DC.LXIV.*

OHMA O IV Nr. 16, *Hof-Journal 1665.*

OHMA O IV Nr. 19, *Hof-Journal 1666.*

OHMA O IV Nr. 20, *Alter und Neuer Sonderbahrer Schreibe-Calender Auff das Jahr . . . M.DC.LXVII.*

OHMA O IV Nr. 21, *Alter und Neuer Schreib-Kalender . . . M.DC.LXVII.*

OHMA O IV Nr. 23, *Hof-Journal 1668.*

OHMA O IV Nr. 24, *Hofjournal 1669.*

Rentkammer-Rechnungen

Nr. 9, *Rechnung Über Einnahme Beÿ Des Durchleüchtigsten Fürsten und Herrn, Herrn Johann Georgen des Andern, . . . Renth=Cammer Vom Quartal Reminiscere biß Luciae 1660.* [Includes both credits and debits (*Außgaben*)]

Nr. 191, *Rechnung über Außgabe Geldt, Beÿ Churfürstl: Sächß: Renth=Cammer, Die Quartale Reminiscere undt Trinitatis Anno 1661.*

Nr. 191/1, *Jahres-Rechnung über Außgabe Geldt Beÿ Churfürstl: Sächß: Renth=Cammer Von Crucis Anno 1661 biß dahin 1662.*

Nr. 191/2, *Jahres-Rechnung, über Außgabe Geldt, Beÿ der Churfl: Renth=Cammer von Crucis Anno 1670 biß wiederumb dahin 1671.*

Nr. 410, *Geheimbter Renth Cammer Rechnung vom Ersten Novembris Anno 1660 biß letzten Januarÿ Anno 1662.*

Nr. 411, *Geheimbter Renth Cammer Rechnung vom Ersten Februarÿ 1622 biß letzten
Januarÿ Ao 1663.*

Nr. 412, *Geheimbter Renth Cammer Rechnung vom Ersten Februarÿ Anno 1663 bis letzten
Januarÿ 1664.*

Bibliography of Secondary Sources

PRINTED SOURCES TO 1799
(INCLUDES MODERN FACSIMILE EDITIONS)

Agenda – Das ist/ Kyrchenordnung/ wie sich die Pfarrherrn vnd Seelsorger in jren Ampten vnd diensten halten sollen/ Fur die Diener der Kyrchen in Hertzog Heinrichen zu Sachssen V. G. H. Fürstenthum gestellet. Leipzig: Wolrab, 1540.

Arndt, Johann. *Paradieß-Gärtlein.* Magdeburg: Franck, 1615.

Balde, Jacob, S. J. *Opera Poetica Omnia,* 8 vols. Reprint of the Munich Edition of 1729. Edited and introduced by Wilhelm Kühlmann and Hermann Wiegand. Frankfurt am Main: Keip Verlag, 1990.

Christoph Bernhard, ed. *Geistreiches gesang-buch/ an d. Cornelij Beckers Psalmen und lutherischen kirchen-liedern/ mit ihren melodeyen . . . sammt einem kirchen-gebethbuche.* Dresden: Baumann, 1676.

Bontempi, Giovanni Andrea Angelini. *Historia dell Ribellione d'Ungheria.* Dresden: Seyffert, 1672.

Consilia theologica Witebergensia, das ist, Wittenbergische geistliche Rathschläge dess theuren Mannes Gottes, D. Martini Lutheri, seiner Collegen, und treuen Nachfolger, von dem heiligen Reformations-Anfang, biss auff jetzige Zeit, in dem Namen der gesampten Theologischen Facultät aussgestellte Urtheil, Bedencken, und offentliche Schrifften, in vier Theilen . . . auff vielfältiges Begehren abgefertiget. Frankfurt am Main: Balthasar Christoph Wust, 1664.

Dreßdenisch Gesangbuch . . . wie sie in der Churfürstl. Sächß. Schloß-Kirchen zu Dresden gesungen worden. Dresden: Bergen, 1656.

Geier, Martin. *D. Martin Geiers Weyland Churf. Sächs. Ober=Hof=Predigers und Kirchen=Raths Volumen Concionum miscellanearum, das ist unterschiedliche und denckwurdige Predigten, von sonderbaren nützlichen Materien gewissen Zeiten und Orten gehalten; hiebevor absonderlich anitzo aber mit Fleiß auf vielfältiges Begehren alle zusammen gedruckt, mit einem vierfachen Register.* Leipzig: Gleditsch and Weidmann, 1713.

Gerber, Christian. *Historie der Kirchen-Ceremonien in Sachsen.* Dresden & Leipzig: Sauereßig, 1732.

Gleich, Johann Andreas. *Annales ecclesiastici, oder, Gründliche Nachrichten der Reformations-Historie, Chur-Sächß. Albertinischer Linie.* Dresden and Leipzig: Sauereßig, 1730.

Graduale de tempore iuxta ritum sacrosanctae romanae ecclesiae, Editio Princeps (1614). Edited by Giacomo Baroffio and Manlio Sodi. Monumenta studia instrumenta liturgica, 10. Vatican City: Libreria Editrice Vaticana, 2001.

Graduale de sanctis iuxta ritum sacrosanctae romanae ecclesiae, Editio Princeps (1614–1615). Edited by Giacomo Baroffio and Eun Ju Kim. Monumenta studia instrumenta liturgica, 11. Vatican City: Libreria Editrice Vaticana, 2001.

Hirsch, Andreas. *Kircherus Jesuita Germanus Germania redonatus: sive Artis Magnae de Consono & Dissono, Ars Minor; Das ist/ Philosophischer Extract und Auszug/ aus deß Welt=berühmten Teutschen Jesuitens Athanasii Kircheri von Fulda Musurgia Universali, in Sechs Bücher verfasset.* Schwäbisch Hall: Laidigen, 1662. Facsimile reprint, with afterword by Wolfgang Goldhan. Bibliotheca musica-therapeutica, 1. Leipzig: Zentralantiquariat der DDR, 1988.

Keuchenthal, Johannes. *Kirchen-Gesenge Latinisch und Deudsch.* Wittenberg: Seelfisch/ Schwenck, 1573.

Kircher, Athanasius. *Musurgia universalis.* 2 vols. Rome: Corbelletti [vol. 1]; Grignani [vol. 2], 1650.

Leipziger Kirchen=Staat, Das ist Deutlicher Unterricht vom Gottes=Dienst in Leipzig/ wie es bey solchem so wohl an hohen und andern Festen/ als auch an denen Sonntagen ingleichen die gantze Wocher über gehalten wird. Leipzig: Groschuff, 1710.

Lossius, Lucas. *Psalmodia, hoc est, Cantica sacra veteris ecclesiae selecta.* Wittenberg: Rhau, 1561; facs. rpt., Stuttgart: Cornetto-Verlag, 1996.

Mattheson, Johann. *Grundlage einer Ehren-Pforte.* Hamburg: The Author, 1740. Reprint, edited by Max Schneider. Berlin: Leo Liepmannssohn, 1910; rpt. Kassel: Bärenreiter; Graz: Akademische Druck- u. Verlagsanstalt, 1994.

Merlo Horstius, Jacob. *Paradisus animae Christianae.* Cologne: Egmont, 1716.

Moller, Martin. *MEDITATIONES sanctorum Patrum. Schöne/ andächtige Gebet/ tröstliche Sprüche/ Gottselige Gedancken/ Trewe Bußvermanungen/ Hertzliche Dancksagungen / vnd allerley nützliche vbungen des Glaubens. Aus den heyligen Altvätern Augustino, Bernhardo, Taulero vnd andern. . . .* Görlitz: Fritsch, 1584.

———. *ALTERA PARS Meditationum ex sanctis Patribus. Ander Theyl Andechtiger schöner Gebet/ tröstlicher Gedancken/ trewer Bußvermanungen/ vnd allerley nützlicher vbungen des Glaubens Aus den heyligen Altvätern Cypriano, Hieronymo, Augustino, Bernhardo, Anshelmo, vnd andern. . . .* Görlitz: Fritsch, 1591.

Müller, Heinrich. *Thränen- und Trost-Quellen, Bey Erklärung der Geschichte von der Grossen Sünderin.* Rostock [?] 1675; rpt., with preparatory prayers, etc. by Michael Heinrich Reinhard. Hanover: Förster und Sohn, 1724.

Musculus, Andreas. *Precationes ex veteribus orthodoxis doctoribus: Ex ecclesiae hymnis et canticis: Ex psalmis deniq[ue] Davidis collectae: Et nunc recens recognitae & auctae.* Leipzig: Schneider, 1575.

Printz, Wolfgang Caspar. *Historische Beschreibung der Edelen Sing= und Kling=Kunst.* Dresden: Mieth, 1690; facsimile reprint, ed. Othmar Wessely. Graz: Akademische Druck- u. Verlagsanstalt, 1964.

Rossi, Agostino. *Notitie Historiche di Mont'Alboddo.* Senigallia: Vescouale, 1694; rpt., Bologna: Forni, 1980.

Spangenberg, Johann. *Cantiones ecclesiasticae latinae / Kirchengesenge Deudtsch auff die Sontage . . .* Magdeburg: Lotther, 1545.

Tzschimmer, Gabriel. *Die Durchlauchtigste Zusammenkunft.* Nuremberg: Hoffmann, 1680.

Weck, Anton. *Der Chur=Fürstlichen Sächsischen weitberuffenen Residentz= und Haupt= Vestung Dresden Beschreib und Vorstellung.* Nuremberg: Hoffmann, 1680.

PRINTED SOURCES FROM 1800

Althaus, Paul. *Forschungen zur evangelischen Gebetsliteratur.* Gütersloh: Mohn, 1927; rpt. Hildesheim: Olms, 1966.

Arndt, Johann. *True Christianity.* Translated and introduced by Peter Erb. Preface by Heiko A. Oberman. New York: Paulist Press, 1979.

Auerbach, Bertrand. *La Diplomatie française et la cour de Saxe (1648–1680).* Paris: Hachette, 1887.

Austern, Linda Phyllis. "'All Things in this World is but the Musick of Inconstancie': Music, Sensuality and the Sublime in Seventeenth-Century Vanitas Imagery." In *Art and Music in the Early Modern Period. Essays in Honor of Franca Trinchieri Camiz,* 287–332. Edited by Katherine A. McIver. Aldershot, Hants, England; Burlington, Vt: Ashgate, 2003.

Axmacher, Elke. *Johann Arndt und Paul Gerhardt.* Tübingen; Basel; Francke, 2001.

———. *Praxis Evangelicorum: Theologie und Frömmigkeit bei Martin Moller (1547–1606).* Göttingen: Vandenhoeck & Ruprecht, 1989. [=1989/1]

———. "Die Rezeption mittelalterlicher Mystik durch Martin Moller." *Jahrbuch für Schlesische Kirchengeschichte* 68 (1989/2): 7–26. [=1989/2]

Bach-Dokumente, I: Schriftstücke von der Hand Johann Sebastian Bachs. Edited by Werner Neumann and Hans-Joachim Schulze. Kassel: Bärenreiter; Leipzig: VEB Deutscher Verlag für Musik, 1963.

Baldauf-Berdes, Jane. *Women Musicians of Venice: Musical Foundations 1525–1855.* Oxford: Oxford University Press, 1993.

Barthel, Dietrich. *Musica Poetica: Musical-Rhetorical Figures in German Baroque Music.* Lincoln and London: University of Nebraska Press, 1997.

Baselt, Bernd. "Die Musikaliensammlung der Schwarzburg-Rudolstädtischen Hofkapelle unter Philipp Heinrich Erlebach (1657–1714)." In *Traditionen und Aufgaben der Hallischen Musikwissenschaft,* 105–34. Edited by Walther Siegmund-Schultze. Halle: Wissenschaftliche Zeitschrift der Martin-Luther-Universität Halle-Wittenberg, 1963.

Baufeld, Christa. *Kleines frühneuhochdeutsches Wörterbuch.* Tübingen: Niemeyer, 1996.

Beißwenger, Kirsten. *Johann Sebastian Bachs Notenbibliothek.* Kassel: Bärenreiter, 1992.

Berglund, Lars. *Studier i Christian Geists vokalmusik.* Ph.D. dissertation. Acta Universalis Upsaliensis, *Studia Musicologica Upsaliensia,* nova series, 21. Uppsala: University of Uppsala, 2002.

Bjurström, Per. *Feast and Theatre in Queen Christina's Rome.* Stockholm: Bengtson, 1966.

Blaschke, Karlheinz. "Johann Georg II." In *Neue Deutsche Biographie,* 10: 526–27. Berlin: Duncker & Humblot, 1974.

Blume, Clemens, and Guido Maria Dreves, eds. *Analecta hymnica medii aevi.* 55 vols. Leipzig: Reisland, 1886–1922.

Böttiger, Carl Wilhelm. *Geschichte des Kurstaats und Königreiches Sachsen.* Hamburg: Perthes, 1831.

Bontempi, Giovanni Andrea, and Marco Gioseppe Peranda. *Drama oder Musicalisches Schauspiel von der Dafne.* Edited by Susanne Wilsdorf. Denkmäler Mitteldeutscher Barockmusik, 2. Leipzig: Hofmeister, 1998.

The Book of Concord: The Confessions of the Evangelical Lutheran Church. Translated and edited by Theodore G. Tappert et al. Philadelphia: Muhlenberg, 1959.

Braun, Werner. *Die Musik des 17. Jahrhunderts.* Wiesbaden: Akademische Verlagsgesellschaft Athenaion, 1981.

Brecht, Martin. "Das Aufkommen der neuen Frömmigkeitsbewegung in Deutschland. 2. Johann Arndt und das Wahre Christentum." In *Geschichte des Pietismus I. Der Pietismus vom siebzehnten bis zum frühen achtzehnten Jahrhundert,* 130–51. Edited by Martin Brecht. Göttingen: Vandenhoeck & Ruprecht, 1993.

Bremme, W. *Der Hymnus Jesu dulcis memoria in seinen lateinischen Handschriften und Nachahmungen, sowie deutschen Übersetzungen.* Mainz: Kirchheim, 1899.

Breuer, Dieter, ed. *Frömmigkeit in der frühen Neuzeit: Studien zur religiösen Literatur des 17. Jahrhunderts in Deutschland.* Chloe: Beihefte zum Daphnis, 2. Rodopi: Amsterdam, 1984.

Breviarium Romanum ex decreto sacrosancti Concilii Tridentini restitutum. 4 vols. New York: Benzinger, 1945–46.

Briganti, Francesco. *Gio. Andrea Angelini-Bontempi (1624–1705): Musicista-Letterato-Architetto Perugia-Dresda.* Florence: Olschki, 1956.

Brück, Anton. "Friedrich, Landgraf von Hessen-Darmstadt." In *Neue Deutsche Biographie,* vol. 5. Berlin: Duncker & Humblot, 1960.

Cappelli, Adriano. *Cronologia, Cronografia e Calendario Perpetuo dal Principio dell'èra cristiana ai nostri giorni.* Milan: Hoepli, 1969.

Capricornus, Samuel. *Geistliche Harmonien III.* Edited by Paul Walker. Collegium Musicum: Yale University; 2d Series, 13. Madison: A-R Editions, 1997.

Chemnitz, Martin. *Examination of the Council of Trent.* Part 1. Translated by Fred Kramer. St. Louis: Concordia, 1971.

Culley, SJ, Thomas D. *Jesuits and Music: I. A Study of the Musicians Connected with the German College in Rome during the 17th Century and of their Activities in Northern Europe.* Rome: Jesuit Historical Institute; St. Louis: St. Louis University, 1970.

Dahlhaus, Carl. *Studies on the Origin of Harmonic Tonality.* Translated by Robert Gjerdingen. Princeton: Princeton University Press, 1990.

Distel, Theodor. "Mitteilungen." *Monatshefte für Musik-Geschichte* 28 (1896): 54–55.

Dixon, Graham. *Carissimi.* Oxford; New York: Oxford University Press, 1986.

———. "Liturgical Music in Rome (1605–45)." 2 vols. Ph.D. dissertation, University of Durham (Faculty of Music), St. John's College, Durham, 1981.

Doering, Oscar. *Des Augsburger Patriciers Philipp Hainhofer Reisen nach Innsbruck und Dresden.* Vienna: Graeser, 1901.

Donnini, Mauro. "Le prose e gli inni in latino attribuiti a Iacopone da Todi." In *Iacopone da Todi: Atti del XXXVII Convegno storico internazionale, Todi, 8–11 ottobre 2000,* 299–322. Spoleto: Centro italiano di studi sull'alto medioevo, 2001.

Einstein, Alfred. "Italienische Musiker am Hofe der Neuburger Wittelsbacher, 1614–1716." *Sammelbände der Internationalen Musikgesellschaft* 9 (1907–08): 336–424.

Eitner, Robert, ed. *Biographisch-bibliographisches Quellen-Lexikon der Musiker und Musikgelehrten der christlichen Zeitrechnung bis zur Mitte der 19. Jahrhunderts.* Leipzig: Breitkopf & Härtel, 1898–1904; 2d ed. 1959–60.

Emans, Reinmar. "Die Musiker des Markusdoms in Venedig 1650-1708," I. *Kirchenmusikalisches Jahrbuch* 65 (1981): 45–81.

Evangelisches Kirchengesangbuch, Ausgabe für die Landeskirchen Rheinland, Westfalen und Lippe. Gütersloh: Gütersloher Verlagshaus Gerd Mohn, [1970].

Fellerer, Karl Gustav, ed. *Geschichte der katholischen Kirchenmusik.* 2 vols. Kassel: Bärenreiter, 1976.

Fiebig, Folkert. *Christoph Bernhard und der stile moderno: Untersuchungen zu Leben und Werk.* Hamburg: Wagner, 1980.

Frandsen, Mary E. "Albrici, Peranda, und die Ursprünge der Concerto-Aria-Kantate in Dresden." *Schütz-Jahrbuch* 18 (1996): 123–39.

———. "Allies in the Cause of Italian Music: Schütz, Prince Johann Georg II, and Musical Politics in Dresden." *Journal of the Royal Musical Association* 125 (2000): 1–40.

———. "Eunuchi conjugium: The Marriage of a Castrato in Early Modern Germany." *Early Music History* 24 (2005): 53–124.

———. "The Sacred Concerto in Dresden, ca. 1680–1680." Ph.D. dissertation, University of Rochester/ Eastman School of Music, 1997. 3 vols. [=1997-1, 1997-2, 1997-3]

Fürstenau, Moritz. *Beiträge zur Geschichte der Königlich Sächsischen musikalischen Kapelle.* Dresden: Meser, 1849.

———. "Fürstlicher Gottesdienst im 17. Jahrhundert." *Monatshefte für Musik-Geschichte* 3 (1871): 58–61.

———. *Zur Geschichte der Musik und des Theaters am Hofe zu Dresden.* 2 vols. Vol. 1, *Zur Geschichte der Musik und des Theaters am Hofe der Kurfürsten von Sachsen, Johann Georg II., Johann Georg III., und Johann Georg IV.*; vol. 2, *Zur Geschichte der Musik und des Theaters am Hofe der Kurfürsten von Sachsen und Könige von Polen Friedrich August I. (August II.) und Friedrich August II. (August III.).* Dresden: Kuntze, 1861–62; rpt., 2 vols. in 1, Leipzig: Edition Peters, 1971 [=1861/1971; 1862/1971].

Gerhard, Johann. *Gerhard's Sacred Meditations.* Translated by C. W. Heisler. Philadelphia: Lutheran Publication Society, 1896.

Gianturco, Carolyn. "The Italian Seventeenth-Century Cantata: A Textual Approach." In *The Well Enchanting Skill: Music, Poetry, and Drama in the Culture of the Renaissance. Essays in Honour of F. W. Sternfeld,* 41–51. Edited by John Caldwell, Edward Olleson, and Susan Wollenberg. Oxford: Clarendon Press, 1990.

Gille, Gottfried. "Der Schützschüler David Pohle (1624–1695)—seine Bedeutung für die deutsche Musikgeschichte des 17. Jahrhunderts." Ph.D. dissertation, University of Halle/Saale, 1973.

Glixon, Beth L., and Jonathan E. Glixon, *Inventing the Business of Opera: The Impresario and His World in Seventeenth-Century Venice.* AMS Studies in Music. New York: Oxford University Press, 2006.

Graff, Paul. *Geschichte der Auflösung der alten gottesdienstlichen Formen in der evangelischen Kirche Deutschlands.* Vol. 1. Göttingen: Vandenhoeck & Ruprecht, 1937.

Gritsch, Eric C. "The Views of Luther and Lutheranism on the Veneration of Mary." In *The One Mediator, the Saints, and Mary: Lutherans and Catholics in Dialogue VIII,* 235–48. Edited by H. George Anderson, J. Francis Staffort, and Joseph A. Burgess. Minneapolis: Augsburg-Fortress, 1992.

Grusnick, Bruno. "Die Dübensammlung: Ein Versuch ihrer chronologischen Ordnung." *Svensk Tidskrift för Musikforskning* 46 (1964): 27–82; 48 (1966): 63–186.

Gundlach, Klaus-Jürgen, ed. and annot. *Das Weissenfelser Aufführungsverzeichnis Johann Philipp Kriegers und seines Sohnes Johann Gotthilf Krieger (1684–1732)*. Sinzig: Studio Verlag Schewe, 2001.

Hahn, Joachim. "Zeitgeschehen im Spiegel der lutherisch-orthodoxen Predigt nach dem Dreißigjährigen Krieg – dargestellt am Beispiel des kursächsischen Oberhofpredigers Martin Geier." Ph.D. dissertation, [Karl Marx] University of Leipzig, Faculty for Theology, 1990.

Hammerich, Angul. *Musiken ved Christian den Fjerdes Hof*. Copenhagen: Hansen, 1892.

Hassel, Paul. "Zur Politik Sachsens in der Zeit vom westfälischen Frieden bis zum Tode Johann Georg II." *Neues Archiv für Sächsische Geschichte und Altertumskunde* 11 (1890): 117–44.

Heidrich, Jürgen. "Italienische Einflüsse in Dresdner Messkompositionen zwischen Schütz und Bach." *Schütz-Jahrbuch* 23 (2001): 33–42.

Helbig, Karl Gustav. "Johann Philipp von Mainz und Johann Georg II. von Sachsen während der Erfurter Wirren 1650–1667." *Archiv für die Sächsische Geschichte* 3 (1865): 391–442.

Herl, Joseph. *Worship Wars in Early Lutheranism: Choir, Congregation, and Three Centuries of Conflict*. New York: Oxford University Press, 2004.

Hill, John Walter. "Oratory Music in Florence, III: The Confraternities from 1655 to 1785." *Acta Musicologica* 58 (1986): 129–79.

Hilse, Walter. "The Treatises of Christoph Bernhard." In *The Music Forum* 3, 1–196. Edited by William J. Mitchell and Felix Salzer. New York and London: Columbia University Press, 1973.

Holborn, Hajo. *A History of Modern Germany: The Reformation*. Princeton: Princeton University Press, 1982.

Honecker, Martin. *Cura religionis Magistratus Christiani: Studien zum Kirchenrecht im Luthertum des 17. Jahrhunderts, insbesondere bei Johann Gerhard*. Jus Ecclesiasticum, 7. Munich: Claudius, 1968.

Ilgner, Gerhard. *Matthias Weckmann ca. 1619–1674, Sein Leben und seine Werke*. Wolfenbüttel & Berlin: Kallmeyer, 1939.

Institutio generalis de liturgia horarum. Rome: Typis Polyglottis Vaticanis, 1971.

Irwin, Joyce. *Neither Voice nor Heart Alone: German Lutheran Theology of Music in the Age of the Baroque*. New York: Peter Lang, 1993.

Jones, Andrew V. *The Motets of Carissimi*. 2 vols. Ann Arbor: UMI Research Press, 1982 [=1982-1, 1982-2].

Jung, Hans Rudolf. "Zwei unbekannte Briefe von Heinrich Schütz aus den Jahren 1653/54." *Beiträge zur Musikwissenschaft* 14 (1972): 231–37.

Karant-Nunn, Susan. *The Reformation of Ritual: An Interpretation of Early Modern Germany*. London and New York: Routledge, 1997.

Kast, Paul. "Unbekannte Dokumente zur Oper 'Chi soffre speri' von 1637." In *Helmuth Osthoff zu seinem Siebzigsten Geburtstag*, 129–34. Edited by Wilhelm Stauder, Ursula Aarburg, and Peter Cahn. Tutzing: Schneider, 1969.

Kellenbenz, Hermann. "Königin Christine und ihre Beziehungen zu Hamburg." In *Queen Christina of Sweden: Documents and Studies*, 187–98. Edited by Magnus von

Platen. Analecta Reginensia, 1. Stockholm: Kungl. Boktryckeriet P. A. Norstedt & Söner, 1966.

Keller, Katrin. "Kriegsende und Friedensfest in Kursachsen." *Dresdner Hefte* 56 (1998): 86–93.

Kendrick, Robert L. *Celestial Sirens: Nuns and their Music in Early Modern Milan.* Oxford: Oxford University Press, 1996.

———. "'Sonet vox tua in auribus meis': Song of Songs Exegesis and the Seventeenth-Century Motet." *Schütz-Jahrbuch* 16 (1994): 99–118.

Kirwan-Mott, Anne. *The Small-Scale Sacred Concertato in the Early Seventeenth Century.* 2 vols. Ann Arbor: UMI Research Press, 1981.

Klein, Thomas. *Der Kampf um die zweite Reformation in Kursachsen, 1586–91.* Cologne and Graz: Böhlau, 1962.

Knaus, Herwig. *Die Musiker im Archivbestand des kaiserlichen Obersthofmeisteramtes (1637–1705).* Vol. 1. Vienna: Hermann Böhlaus Nachf., 1967.

Knüpfer, Sebastian, Johann Schelle, and Johann Kuhnau. *Ausgewählte Kirchenkantaten.* Edited by Arnold Schering; new ed. critically revised by Hans Joachim Moser. Denkmäler Deutscher Tonkunst, 1st series, vols. 58–59. Wiesbaden: Breitkopf & Härtel; Graz: Akademische Druck- u. Verlagsanstalt, 1957.

Köchel, Ludwig Ritter von. *Die kaiserliche Hof-Musikkapelle in Wien von 1543–1867.* Vienna: Beck'sche Universitäts-Buchhandlung, 1869; rpt. Hildesheim and New York: Georg Olms Verlag, 1976.

Kolb, Robert. "The Fathers in the Service of Lutheran Teaching: Andreas Musculus' Use of Patristic Sources." In *Auctoritas Patrum II: Neue Beiträge zur Rezeption der Kirchenväter im 15. und 16. Jahrhundert*, 105–23. Mainz: Philipp von Zabern, 1998.

Kretzschmar, Hellmut. "Zur Geschichte der sächsischen Sekundogeniturfürstentümer." 2 pts. *Sachsen und Anhalt* 1 (1925): 312–43, and *Sachsen und Anhalt* 3 (1927): 284–315.

Krüger, Liselotte. "Johann Kortkamps Organistenchronik, eine Quelle zur hamburgischen Musikgeschichte des 17. Jahrhunderts." *Zeitschrift des Vereins für hamburgische Geschichte* 33 (1933): 188–213.

Krummacher, Friedhelm. *Die Überlieferung der Choralbearbeitungen in der frühen evangelischen Kantate.* Berlin: Merseburger, 1965.

———. "Zur Sammlung Jacobi der ehemaligen Fürstenschule Grimma." *Die Musikforschung* 16 (1963): 324–47.

Kümmerling, Harald. *Katalog der Sammlung Bokemeyer.* Kassel: Bärenreiter, 1970.

Landmann, Ortrun. "Zur italienische Komponente in der Geschichte der Dresdner Hofkapelle." In *Dresdner Hefte* 40 (1994): 50–57.

Lausberg, Heinrich. *Der Hymnus Jesu dulcis memoria.* Munich: Huber, 1967.

Lausberg, Heinrich. "Zum Hymnus 'Jesu dulcis memoria'." In *Martyria, Leiturgia, Diakona*, 361–69. Edited by Otto Semmelroth, with Rudolf Haubst and Karl Rahner. Mainz: Matthias-Grünewald Verlag, 1968.

Leaver, Robin A. "Lutheran Vespers as a Context for Music." In *Church, Stage, and Studio: Music and its Contexts in Seventeenth-Century Germany*, 143–61. Edited by Paul Walker. Ann Arbor and London: UMI Research Press, 1990.

———, ed. *Music in the Service of the Church. The Funeral Sermon for Heinrich Schütz.* St. Louis: Concordia, 1984.

Lenz, Rudolf, ed. *Katalog der Leichenpredigten und sonstiger Trauerschriften in der Universitätsbibliothek Gießen.* Marburg/Lahn: Schwarz, 1985.

Lester, Joel. *Between Modes and Keys: German Theory 1592–1802.* Stuyvesant, N.Y.: Pendragon Press, 1989.

The Liber Usualis with Introduction and Rubrics in English. Edited by the Benedictines of Solesmes. Tournai: Desclée, 1953; rpt., Great Falls, Mont.: St. Bonaventure Publications, 1997.

Liliencron, Rochus von. *Liturgisch-musikalische Geschichte der evangelischen Gottesdienste von 1523 bis 1700.* Schleswig: Bergas, 1893; rpt., Hildesheim: Olms, 1970.

Lindau, Martin Bernhard. *Geschichte der königliche Haupt- und Residenzstadt Dresden.* 2d ed. Dresden: Grumbkow, 1885.

Linfield, Eva. "Modal and Tonal Aspects in Two Compositions by Heinrich Schütz." *Journal of the Royal Musical Association* 117 (1992): 86–122.

———. "Toni und Modi und ihre Bedeutung für Schütz' Harmonik." *Schütz-Jahrbuch* 12 (1990): 150–70.

Lundqvist, Karl Gustaf. "Sveriges Förbund med Kur-Sachsen år 1666." *Historiska Studier tillägnade Professor Harald Hjärne*, 353–82. Uppsala and Stockholm: Almqvist & Wiksell, 1908.

Lütolf, Max, ed. *Analecta hymnica Medii Aevi: Register.* 2 vols. Bern: Francke, 1978.

Märker, Michael. "David Pohles Weihnachtskantate 'Nascitur Immanuel' und die Frühgeschichte der Concerto-Aria-Kantate." *Schütz-Jahrbuch* 17 (1995): 81–96.

Mass and Vespers with Gregorian Chant for Sundays and Holy Days. Latin and English Text. Edited by the Benedictines of the Solesmes Congregation. Paris: Desclée: 1957.

Matthias Weckman (1619–1674): Die X Sonaten und Lieder. Deutsche Barock Kammermusik VI. La Fenice and Ricercar Consort. CD recording, Ricercar, RIC 140152, 1995. Booklet notes by Jérôme Lejeune.

May, Walter. "Klengel, Wolf Caspar von." In *Neue Deutsche Biographie*, 12: 40–42. Berlin: Duncker & Humblot, 1980.

Meine-Schawe, Monika. *Die Grablege der Wettiner im Dom zu Freiberg: die Umgestaltung des Domchores durch Giovanni Maria Nosseni, 1585–1594.* Munich: Tuduv, 1992.

Meyers, Herbert W. "Woodwinds." In Stewart Carter, ed., *A Performer's Guide to Seventeenth-Century Music*, 69–97. New York: Schirmer Books, 1997.

Moberg, Carl-Allan. "Vincenzo Albrici und das Kirchenkonzert." In *Natalicia Musicologica Knud Jeppesen Septuagenario collegis oblata*, 199–216. Edited by Bjørn Hjelmborg and Søren Sørensen. Copenhagen: Hansen, 1962.

Möller, Eberhard. "Schütziana in Chemnitz, Freiberg und Schneeberg." *Schütz-Jahrbuch* 13 (1991), 56–90.

Monaldini, Sergio. *L'Orto dell'Esperidi: Musici, attori e artisti nel patrocinio della famiglia Bentivoglio (1646–1685).* Lucca: LIM, 2000.

Morelli, Arnaldo. *Il tempio armonico: Musica nell'oratorio dei Filippini in Roma (1575–1705).* Analecta Musicologica, 27. Laaber: Laaber-Verlag, 1991.

Moser, Hans Joachim. *Heinrich Schütz: His Life and Work.* Translated by Carl. F. Pfatteicher. St. Louis: Concordia, 1959.

Müller, Karl August. *Kurfürst Johann Georg der Erste, seine Familie und sein Hof.* Dresden & Leipzig: Fleischer, 1838.

Münnich, Richard. "Kuhnau's Leben." *Sammelbände der Internationalen Musikgesellschaft* 3 (1901–02), 473–527.

Naumann, Gunter. *Sächsische Geschichte in Daten.* Berlin: Koehler & Amelang, 1991.

New Oxford History of Music, vol. 5: *Opera and Church Music, 1630–1750*. Edited by Anthony Lewis and Nigel Fortune. London: Oxford University Press, 1975.

Newton, Timothy D. "A Study and Critical Edition of Samuel Capricornus's *Theatrum musicum* (1669, 1670) and *Continuatio theatri musici* (1669)." D.M.A. dissertation, University of Illinois at Urbana-Champaign, 2004.

Nickel, Sieglinde. "Zur Wirtschaft, Sozialstruktur, Verfassung und Verwaltung in der Stadt Dresden von der Mitte des 17. Jahrhunderts bis in die dreißiger Jahre des 18. Jahrhunderts." Ph.D. dissertation, [Karl Marx] University of Leipzig, 1986.

Nieden, Hans-Jörg, and Marcel Nieden, eds. *Praxis Pietatis: Beiträge zu Theologie und Frömmigkeit in der Frühen Neuzeit. Wolfgang Sommer zum 60. Geburtstag*, Stuttgart: Kohlhammer, 1999.

Nischan, Bodo. "The Elevation of the Host in the Age of Confessionalism: Adiaphoron or Ritual Demarcation?" In *Lutherans and Calvinists in the Age of Confessionalism*, essay V. Aldershot, Hampshire; Brookfield, Vermont: Ashgate, 1999.

Noack, Friedrich. "Kardinal Friedrich von Hessen, Grossprior in Heitersheim." *Zeitschrift für die Geschichte des Oberrheins*, Neue Folge 41 (1928): 341–86.

Ortgies, Ibo. "Neue Erkenntnisse zur Biographie Matthias Weckmans: Biographische Skizze und Zeittafel." In *Proceedings of the Weckmann Symposium, Göteborg, 30 August–3 September 1991*, 1–24. Edited by Sverker Jullander. Göteborg: Department of Musicology, Göteborg University, 1993.

Palisca, Claude. "Marco Scacchi's Defense of Modern Music (1649)." In *Words and Music: The Scholar's View. A Medley of Problems and Solutions Compiled in Honor of A. Tillman Merritt by Sundry Hands*, 189–235. Edited by Laurence Berman. Cambridge, Mass.: Department of Music, Harvard University, 1972.

Paquette-Abt, Mary. "A Professional Musician in Early Modern Rome: The Life and Print Program of Fabio Costantini, c.1579–c.1644." Ph.D. dissertation, University of Chicago, 2003.

Parker, Geoffrey. *The Thirty Years' War*. New York: Military Heritage Press, 1988.

Pirro, André. *Dietrich Buxtehude*. Paris: Fischbacher, 1913; rpt., Geneva: Minkoff, 1976.

Pörnbacher, Karl. *Jeremias Drexel: Leben und Werk eines Barockpredigers*. Beiträge zur altbayerischen Kirchengeschichte, 24/2. Munich: Seitz, 1965.

Poulain, Augustin, SJ. *The Graces of Interior Prayer: A Treatise on Mystical Theology*. Translated from the 6th ed. by Leonora L. Yorke Smith; corrected to accord with the 10th French ed. with an introduction by J. V. Bainvel. St. Louis: Herder, 1950.

Praetorius, Michael. *Musae Sioniae, Teil V (1607)*. Edited by Friedrich Blume and Hans Költzsch. Gesamtausgabe der musikalischen Werke von Michael Praetorius, 5. Wölfenbüttel: Kallmeyer, 1937; rpt., Wolfenbüttel: Möseler Verlag, 1971.

———. *Polyhymnia Caduceatrix et Panegyrica*. 2 vols. Edited by Wilibald Gurlitt. Gesamtausgabe der musikalischen Werke von Michael Praetorius, 17. Wolfenbüttel: Kallmeyer, 1930–33; Wolfenbüttel: Möseler Verlag, 1971.

Preus, Robert D. *The Theology of Post-Reformation Lutheranism*. 2 vols. St. Louis: Concordia Publishing House, 1970.

"The Problem in the Sixteenth Century." In *The One Mediator, the Saints, and Mary: Lutherans and Catholics in Dialogue VIII*, 23–33. Edited by H. George Anderson, J. Francis Staffort, and Joseph A. Burgess. Minneapolis: Augsburg-Fortress, 1992.

Rautenstrauch, Johann. *Luther und die Pflege der kirchlichen Musik in Sachsen*. Leipzig: Breifkopf & Härtel, 1907; rpt., Hildesheim: Olms, 1970.

Rifkin, Joshua. "Towards a New Image of Henrich Schütz." Part 1. *Musical Times* 126 (1985): 651–58.

Rifkin, Joshua, and Colin Timms, "Heinrich Schütz." In *The New Grove Northern European Baroque Masters*, 1–150. New York and London: Norton, 1985.

Roche, Jerome. *North Italian Church Music in the Age of Monteverdi*. Oxford: Clarendon Press, 1984.

Rosand, Ellen. *Opera in Seventeenth-Century Venice: The Creation of a Genre*. Berkeley: University of California Press, 1991.

Rose, Gloria. "The Cantatas of Giacomo Carissimi." *Musical Quarterly* 43 (1962): 204–15.

Rostirolla, Giancarlo. "La Musica nelle istituzioni religiose romane al tempo di Stradella." *Chigiana* 39 [new series no. 19], part 2 (1982): 575–831.

Roth, Erich. *Die Privatbeichte und Schlüsselgewalt in der Theologie der Reformatoren*. Gütersloh: Bertelsmann, 1952.

Rudén, Jan Olof. "Vattenmärken och Musikforskning: Presentation och Tillämpning ov en Dateringsmetod på musikalier i handskrift i Uppsala Universitetsbibliotekets Dübensamling." 2 vols. Ph.D. dissertation, Uppsala University, 1968.

Rudhart, Franz Michael. *Geschichte der Oper am Hofe zu München*. Freising: Datterer, 1865.

Sadie, Julie Ann, comp. and ed. *Companion to Baroque Music*. New York: Schirmer, 1990.

Sandberger, Adolf, ed. *Ausgewählte Werke des Kurfürstlich Bayerischen Hofkapellmeisters Johann Kaspar Kerll (1627–1693)*. Part I. Denkmäler der Tonkunst in Bayern, Zweiter Jahrgang, 2. Leipzig: Breitkopf & Härtel, 1901.

Sartori, Claudio. *I libretti italiani a stampa dalle origini al 1800*. 5 vols. Cuneo: Bertola & Locatelli, 1990.

Saunders, Steven. *Cross, Sword, and Lyre: Sacred Music at the Imperial Court of Ferdinand II of Habsburg (1619–1637)*. Oxford: Oxford University Press, 1995.

Schaal, Richard. *Die Musikhandschriften des Ansbacher Inventars von 1686*. Wilhelmshaven: Heinrichshofen, 1966.

Schedensack, Elisabeth. *Die Solomotetten Isabella Leonardas (1620–1704): Analysen sämtlicher Solomotetten und ausgewählte Transkriptionen*. 2 vols. Neuhausen: American Institute of Musicology/Hänssler-Verlag, 1998.

Schering, Arnold. "Die alte Chorbibliothek der Thomasschule in Leipzig." *Archiv für Musikwissenschaft* 1 (1918–19): 275–88.

———. *Musikgeschichte Leipzigs in drei Bänden*. Vol. 2 (1650–1723). Leipzig: Kistner & Siegel, 1926.

Schmidt, Eberhard. *Der Gottesdienst am Kurfürstlichen Hofe zu Dresden. Ein Beitrag zur liturgischen Traditionsgeschichte von Johann Walter bis zu Heinrich Schütz*. Veröffentlichungen der Evangelischen Gesellschaft für Liturgie Forschung, 12. Göttingen: Vandenhoeck & Ruprecht, 1961.

Schnoebelen, Anne, ed. *Solo Motets from the Seventeenth Century*. Vol. 9: *Rome II*. New York & London: Garland, 1988.

Schüssler, Hermann. "Calov, Abraham." In *Neue Deutsche Biographie*, vol. 3. Berlin: Duncker & Humblot, 1957.

Schütz, Heinrich. *Symphoniae Sacrae I*. Edited by Siegfried Schmalzriedt. Stuttgarter Schütz-Ausgabe, 7. Stuttgart, Carus Verlag, 1997.

Sehling, Emil. *Die evangelischen Kirchenordnungen des XVI. Jahrhunderts*. 15 vols. Leipzig: Reisland, 1902–13; rpt., Aalen: Scientia Verlag, 1955–79.

Seifert, Herbert. "Die Musiker der beiden Kaiserinnen Eleonora Gonzaga." In *Festschrift Othmar Wessely zum 60. Geburtstag*, 527–54. Edited by Manfred Angerer, Eva Diettrich, et al. Tutzing: Schneider, 1982.

——. *Die Opera am Wiener Kaiserhof im 17. Jahrhundert*. Tutzing: Schneider, 1985.

Seifert, Siegfried. "Jesuiten in Dresden." *Dresdner Hefte* 40 (1994): 75–86.

——. *Niedergang und Wiederaufstieg der katholischen Kirche in Sachsen 1517–1773*. Leipzig: St. Benno-Verlag, 1964.

Seiffert, Max. "Die Chorbibliothek der St. Michaelisschule in Lüneburg zu Seb. Bach's Zeit." *Sammelbände der Internationalen Musikgesellschaft* 9 (1907–08): 593–621.

Senn, Frank C. *Christian Liturgy: Catholic and Evangelical*. Minneapolis: Fortress Press, 1997.

Senn, Walter. *Musik und Theater am Hof zu Innsbruck. Geschichte der Hofkapelle vom 15. Jahrhundert bis zu deren Auflösung im Jahre 1748*. Innsbruck: Österreichische Verlagsanstalt, 1954.

Shigihara, Susanne. "Bonifazio Graziani (1604/05–1664): Biographie, Werkverzeichnis und Untersuchungen zu den Solomotetten." Ph.D. dissertation, Rheinische Friedrich-Wilhelms-Universität in Bonn, 1984.

Sittard, Josef. *Zur Geschichte der Musik und des Theaters am Württembergischen Hofe*. Stuttgart: Kohlhammer, 1890; rpt., Hildesheim: Olms, 1970.

Snyder, Kerala J. *Dieterich Buxtehude: Organist in Lübeck*. New York: Schirmer, 1987.

——. "Johann Rosenmüller's Music for Solo Voice." Ph.D. dissertation, Yale University, 1970.

Sommer, Wolfgang. *Politik, Theologie und Frömmigkeit im Luthertum in der Frühen Neuzeit*. Göttingen: Vandenhoeck & Ruprecht, 1999.

Spagnoli, Gina. *Letters and Documents of Heinrich Schütz, 1656–1672: An Annotated Translation*. Ann Arbor and London: UMI Research Press, 1990.

——. "'Nunc dimittis': The Royal Court Musicians in Dresden and the Funeral of Johann Georg I." *Schütz-Jahrbuch* 10 (1988): 50–61.

Spitzmuller, Henry, ed. *Poésie latine chrétienne du moyen age*. Carmina sacra medii aevi. Bruges: Desclée de Brouwer, 1971.

Sponheim, Kristin. "The Anthologies of Ambrosius Profe (1589–1661) and the Transmission of Italian Music in Germany." Ph.D. dissertation, Yale University, 1995.

Steude, Wolfram. "Die Dresdner Hofkapelle zwischen Antonio Scandello und Heinrich Schütz (1580–1615)." In *Der Klang der Sächsischen Staatskapelle Dresden: Kontinuität und Wandelbarkeit eines Phänomens*, 23–45. Edited by Hans-Günter Ottenberg and Eberhard Steindorf. Hildesheim: Olms, 2001. [=2001/1]

——. "Die Markuspassion in der Leipziger Passionen-Handschrift des Johann Zacharias Grundig." In *Annäherung durch Distanz: Texte zur älteren mitteldeutschen Musik und Musikgeschichte*, 166–83. Edited by Matthias Herrmann. Altenburg: Kamprad, 2001. [=2001/2]

——. "'vndt ohngeschickt werde, in die junge Welt vnd Neueste Manir der Music mich einzurichten': Heinrich Schütz und die jungen Italiener am Dresdner Hof." *Schütz-Jahrbuch* 21 (1999): 63–76.

——. "Das wiedergefundene Opus ultimum von Heinrich Schütz." *Schütz-Jahrbuch* 4/5 (1982–83): 9–18.

Strasser, Ernst. "Der lutherische Abendmahlsgottesdienst im 16. und 17. Jahrhundert." In *Vom Sakrament des Altars: Lutherische Beiträge zur Frage des heiligen Abendmahls*, 194–223. Edited by Hermann Sasse. Leipzig: Dörffling & Franke, 1941.

Sträter, Udo. *Meditation und Kirchenreform in der lutherischen Kirche des 17. Jahrhunderts*. Tübingen: Mohr (Siebeck), 1995.

Sundström, Einar. "Notiser om drottning Kristinas italienska musiker." *Svensk Tidskrift för Musikforskning* 43 (1961): 297–309.

Termini, Olga. "Singers at San Marco in Venice: the Competition between Church and Theatre (c1675–c1725)." *R.M.A. Research Chronicle* 17 (1981): 65–96.

Thill, Andrée, ed. *La Lyre Jesuite: Anthologie de poèmes latins (1620–1730)*. Geneva: Droz, 1999.

Thomas, Ralf. "Kursächsische Religionspolitik gegenüber den Lausitzen." In *Der Westfälischen Frieden 1648 und der Deutsche Protestantismus*, 81–98. Edited by Bernd Hey. Bielefeld: Verlag für Regionalgeschichte, 1998.

Trolda, Emil. "Vincenzo Albrici." *Cyril* 64 (1938), no. 1–2.

Uhsadel, Walter. *Evanglische Beichte in Vergangenheit und Gegenwart*. Gütersloh: Mohn, 1961.

Vehse, Eduard. *Geschichte der Höfe des Hauses Sachsen*. Vol. 4. Geschichte der deutschen Höfe seit der Reformation, Fünfte Abtheilung: Sachsen (vol. 31 in series). Hamburg: Hoffmann and Campe, 1854.

Vercruysse, Jos E., SJ. "Schlüsselgewalt und Beichte bei Luther." In *Leben und Werk Martin Luthers von 1525 bis 1546. Festgabe zu seinem 500. Geburtstag*, 153–69. Edited by Helmar Junghans. Göttingen: Vandenhoeck & Ruprecht, 1983.

Wackernagel, Philipp. *Das deutsche Kirchenlied*. Vol. 1. Leipzig: Teubner, 1864; rpt., Hildesheim: Olms, 1964.

Walker, Paul. "Zur Geschichte des Kontrasubjekts und zu seinem Gebrauch in den frühesten Klavier- und Orgelfugen Johann Sebastian Bachs." In *Das Frühwerk Johann Sebastian Bachs. Kolloquium veranstaltet vom Institut für Musikwissenschaft der Universität Rostock 11.–13. September 1990*, 48–69. Edited by Karl Heller and Hans-Joachim Schulze. Cologne: Studio, 1995.

———. *Theories of Fugue from the Age of Josquin to the Age of Bach*. Eastman Studies in Music, 13. Rochester: University of Rochester Press, 2000.

Walker, Paul, and Diane Parr Walker. *German Sacred Polyphonic Vocal Music Between Schütz and Bach: Sources and Critical Editions*. Warren, Mich.: Harmonie Park Press, 1992.

Walker, Thomas, and Lorenzo Bianconi. "Production, Consumption, and Political Function of Seventeenth-Century Opera." *Early Music History* 4 (1984): 209–96.

Wallmann, Johannes. "Johann Arndt und die protestantische Frömmigkeit." In *Theologie und Frömmigkeit im Zeitalter des Barock. Gesammelte Aufsätze*, 1–19. Tübingen: Mohr (Siebeck), 1995.

Watanabe-O'Kelly, Helen. *Court Culture in Dresden: From Renaissance to Baroque*. Houndmills, Basingstoke, Hampshire and New York: Palgrave, 2002.

Webber, Geoffrey. *North German Church Music in the Age of Buxtehude*. Oxford: Clarendon Press, 1996.

Weckmann, Matthias. *Matthias Weckmann (1619–1674): Gesammelte Werke*. Edited by Gerhard Ilgner. Das Erbe Deutscher Musik, 2d Series: Landschaftsdenkmale Schleswig-Holstein und Hansestädte, 4. Leipzig: Litolff: 1942.

Weiss, Piero, and Richard Taruskin. *Music in the Western World: A History in Docu-ments*. New York: Schirmer, 1984.

Westendorf, Craig. "The Textual and Musical Repertoire of the Spruchmotette." D.M.A. dissertation, University of Illinois at Urbana-Champaign, 1987.

Wilmart, Dom André, OSB. *Auteurs spirituels et textes devots du moyen age latin*. Paris: Librairie Bloud et Gay, 1932.

———. *Le 'Jubilus' dit de Saint Bernard*. Rome: Edizioni di 'Storia e letteratura', 1944.

Wollny, Peter. "Zur stilistischen Entwicklung des geistlichen Konzerts in der Nachfolge von Heinrich Schütz." *Schütz-Jahrbuch* 23 (2001): 7–32.

———. "Zwischen Hamburg, Gottorf, und Wolfenbüttel: Neue Ermittlungen zur Entste-hung der 'Sammlung Bokemeyer.'" *Schütz-Jahrbuch* 20 (1998): 59–76.

Zeller, Winfried, ed. *Der Protestantismus des 17. Jahrhunderts*. Bremen: Schünemann, 1962.

———. *Theologie und Frömmigkeit: Gesammelte Aufsätze*. 2 vols. Edited by B. Jaspert. Marburg: Elwert, 1971, 1978.

ELECTRONIC RESOURCES

Biographisch-Bibliographisches Kirchenlexikon. Edited by Friedrich Wilhelm Bautz. 18 vols. Hamm (Westf.): Verlag Traugott Bautz, 1975. www.bautz.de/bbkl.

Bautz, Friedrich Wilhelm. "Gerhard, Johann." 2:215–16.

Lohmann, Hartmut. "Musculus, Andreas." 6:380–81.

Enberg, Jan. "Vincenzo Albrici's Last Time in Prague, 1682–1690." http://www.enberg .nu/Prague_time/Albrici_in_Prague.htm.

Migne, Jacques-Paul, ed. *Patrologiae cursus completus. Serie Latina. (Patrologia Latina.)* Paris: J.-P. Migne, 1844–1864. http://pld.chadwyck.com.

Grove Music Online. Edited by Laura Macy. http://www.grovemusic.com.

Brumana, Biancamaria, and Colin Timms. "Bontempi, Giovanni Andrea." Accessed 2 November 2001.

Budden, Julian, with Tim Carter, Marita P. McClymonds, Margaret Murata, and Jack Westrup. "Arioso." Accessed 24 March 2002.

Miller, Stephen. "Gratiani, Bonifatio." Accessed 2 February 2002.

Rifkin, Joshua, and Eva Linfield, with Derek McCullough (work list) and Stephen Baron (bibliography). "Schütz, Heinrich." Accessed 21 October 2002.

Saunders, Harris S. "Pallavicino, Carlo." Accessed 19 July 2001.

Silbiger, Alexander. "Weckmann, Matthias." Accessed 4 August 2001.

Smith, Peter, and Marc Vanscheeuvijck. "Colonna, Giovanni Paolo." Accessed 15 August 2001.

Smither, Howard E. "Bicilli, Giovanni." Accessed 31 January 2002.

Surian, Elvidio. "Cherici, Sebastiano." Accessed 20 July 2001.

Weaver, Robert Lamar. "Melani." Accessed 19 July 2001.

Westrup, Jack, and Thomas Walker. "Aria. 2. 17th-Century Vocal Music." Accessed 3 April 2002.

Index

Affect
  Kircher on, 245–51
  in music, 245–51, 440
  and religious devotion, 249–50
  See also Works of Albrici; Works of Cherici;
    Works of Peranda
Agazzari, Agostino, 173
Agenda, Saxon. *See* Heinrich "the Pious," Duke
  of Saxony, 1540 *Agenda* (*Kirchen-Ordnunge*)
Ahle, Johann Rudolph, 243
Albrici, Bartolomeo, 26, 29, 33, 35, 51, 53, 56,
  57, 191
Albrici, Domenico, 25 n.95, 26
Albrici, Vincenzo, 5, 22, 30, 42, 51, 57, 60, 66, 83
  n.27, 98 n.85, 110, 113, 142, 151, 166, 167,
  171, 210, 297, 365, 404, 411, 441
  1681 "Instrument Chamber Catalog" of, 379,
    405 n.122
  and affect in music, 248, 251
  aria style of, 192, 195, 199, 234, 244, 288–89,
    291, 293–96, 312, 313–15
  and arioso style, 199–200, 204–8
  as author-compiler of texts, 111
  birthplace and early biography of, 25–26
  and the Chiesa del Gesù (Rome), 26
  and *concertato* style, 198, 211–14, 233, 239,
    241, 244, 281, 291–92, 299, 313, 319
  and the concerto with aria, 184, 229–43,
    244, 280–90, 312–19, 385, 425, 440,
    441
  and counterpoint, 281–88, 339
  debts of, 73–74
  and declamatory style, 198, 199–208, 241, 274
  and devotional texts, 117, 124–25, 249, 420
  directs music in the castle chapel, 36–37, 43,
    68, 190, 387, 390, 398, 410

  and fugal procedures, 281–88, 292, 312,
    315–19
  and Gratiani, 26, 103, 105–6, 109, 184, 236
  harmonic language of, 191, 197–98, 244,
    251, 270, 289, 292, 299–301, 313, 315,
    339–40
  as Kapellmeister to Elector Johann Georg
    II, 33, 36, 53, 61, 71, 191, 291
  as Kapellmeister to Prince Johann Georg
    II, 26, 28
  in Leipzig, 438
  and the motet principle, 319
  as organist, 26, 438
  in Prague, 438
  return to Dresden of, 58–59, 70, 97, 239
  Roman activity of, 25–26, 69, 103
  and Roman musical style, 26, 172–4, 182,
    188, 190–91, 192, 194, 198–99, 211, 233,
    239, 241, 243–44, 291, 312, 440
  in Stockholm, 26, 192
  travel in Germany of, 59, 287
  travel to England of, 56, 239
  travel to Italy of, 49, 68–69, 95
  writing for virtuoso bass of, 288–90, 293–96
Albrici, Vincenzo, works of, 102
  Ad te levavi (lost), 366
  Amo te, laudo te, 240, 241, 367
  Aurora lucis emicat, 160
  Ave Jesu Christe, 240, 241, 291 n.63
  Beati omnes (Ps 127, lost), 52 n.88
  Benedicte Domine, 234–38, 240, 242, 312
  Cogita o homo, 143, 239, 240, 289–96
  Diligam te Domine (lost), 354
  Dixit Dominus (Ps 109), 374, 375–76
  Domine Deus, 319 n.90
  Dum praeliaretur (lost), 161
  Ecce plangendo, 219